State Responsibility and International Refugee Law

Immigration and Asylum Law and Policy in Europe

Edited by

Elspeth Guild
Valsamis Mitsilegas

VOLUME 55

The titles published in this series are listed at *brill.com/ialp*

State Responsibility and International Refugee Law

History, Theory, and Application

By

Sophie Capicchiano Young

BRILL | NIJHOFF

LEIDEN | BOSTON

The Library of Congress Cataloging-in-Publication Data is available online at https://catalog.loc.gov

Library of Congress Cataloging-in-Publication Data

Names: Young, Sophie Capicchiano editor
Title: State responsibility and international refugee law : history, theory, and application / edited by Sophie Capicchiano Young.
Description: Leiden ; Boston : Brill Academic Publishers, Inc, 2025. | Series: Immigration and Asylum Law and Policy in Europe ; volume 55 | Includes bibliographical references and index.
Identifiers: LCCN 2025031950 | ISBN 9789004722828 hardback | ISBN 9789004722835 epub
Subjects: LCSH: Refugees–Legal status, laws, etc. | Refugees–Legal status, laws, etc.–Europe | Convention Relating to the Status of Refugees (1951 July 28) | Responsibility to protect (International law) | Refugees–Government policy
Classification: LCC KZ6530 .S73 2025 | DDC 341.4/86–dc23/eng/20250722
LC record available at https://lccn.loc.gov/2025031950

Typeface for the Latin, Greek, and Cyrillic scripts: “Brill”. See and download: brill.com/brill-typeface.

ISSN 1568-2749
ISBN 978-90-04-72282-8 (hardback)
ISBN 978-90-04-72283-5 (e-book)
DOI 10.1163/9789004722835

Contents

PART 2
Theory

PART 3
Application

Acknowledgements

This book is an adaptation of my doctoral thesis, undertaken at School of Advanced Study, University of London. In the four years it took to write it, I had two babies, the second born the week after I submitted the final draft to my supervisors. The only challenge that was greater than writing my thesis, was becoming a mother, twice, in quick succession. Each of those challenges was made all the more manageable by the support of my husband, Daniel, to whom this book is dedicated. I cannot count the ways that his presence impacted this project, but it is likely equal to the number of coffees that magically appeared on my desk and by my bedside during that time.

My sincere gratitude is owed to my supervisors, Professor Susan Breau and Associate Professor Reuven (Ruvi) Ziegler, whose relentless encouragement carried me through to the end. I could not have finished this project without them, and I am eternally grateful that I had the chance to benefit from their guidance and tutelage. I would also like to thank Professor David Cantor and Professor Sarah Singer who each provided invaluable feedback and generously gave of their time.

Professor Elspeth Guild and Professor Lawrence Hill-Cawthorne served as my doctoral examiners and the final book has benefited immeasurably from their shared expertise.

Associate Professor Ruvi Ziegler and Professor Violeta Moreno-Lax provided guidance on the first three chapters in their roles as upgrade examiners and I thank them for their insightful comments and the discussion that ensued.

Finally, I wish to extend my sincere gratitude to the editors of the *Immigration and Asylum Law and Policy in Europe* series, Professor Elspeth Guild and Professor Valsamis Mitsilegas, and Lauren Danahy and Akiko Hakuno from Brill.

Abbreviations

AJIL	American Journal of International Law
ASIL	American Society of International Law
ASILPROC	American Society of International Law Proceedings
AnnIDI	Annuaire de l'Institut de Droit International
ARSIWA	Articles on the Responsibility of States for Internationally Wrongful Acts
Asia-Pac JHRL	Asia-Pacific Journal on Human Rights and the Law
BYIL	British Yearbook of International Law
ColumLRev	Columbia Law Review
EcomHR	European Commission on Human Rights
ECHR	European Convention on Human Rights
ECtHR	European Court of Human Rights
HarvHumRtsJ	Harvard Human Rights Journal
HarvIntlLJ	Harvard International Law Journal
INA	Immigration and Nationality Act (USA)
ICLQ	International and Comparative Law Quarterly
ICRC	International Committee of the Red Cross
ICLR	International Community Law Review
ICJ	International Court of Justice
IHRL	International Human Rights Law
IHL	International Humanitarian Law
IJRL	International Journal of Refugee Law
ILO	International Labor Organization
IL	International Law
ILC	International Law Commission
IRL	International Refugee Law
ItYBIL	Italian Yearbook of International Law
JRS	Journal of Refugee Studies
LNOJ	League of Nations Official Journal
LNTS	League of Nations Treaty Series
MelbULRev	Melbourne University Law Review
MichYBIntLS	Michigan Yearbook of International Legal Studies
MichJIntlL	Michigan Journal of International Law
MichLRev	Michigan Law Review
NYUJIntlL&Pol	New York University Journal of International Law and Politics
ActScandJurisGent	Nordic Journal of International Law
PAU	Pan American Union

PCIJ	Permanent Court of International Justice
RdC	Recueil de cours de l'académie de droit international
RIAA	Reports of International Arbitral Awards
RDILC	Revue de droit international et de législation comparée
RGDIP	Revue générale de droit international public
SR	State Responsibility
AALCC	Asian-African Legal Consultative Committee
UNECOSOC	United Nations Economic and Social Council
UNGA	United Nations General Assembly
UNYBILC	Yearbook of the International Law Commission
ZaöRV	Zeitschrift für ausländisches öffentliches Recht und Völkerrecht

Cases

Al-Saadoon and Mufdhi v UK [30 June 2009] ECtHR (App No 61498/08)
Al-Skeini and Others v the United Kingdom [7 July 2011] ECtHR (App No 55721/07)
Alabama Claims Arbitration (*United States of America v United Kingdom*) [1872] II RIAA 713
Amuur v France [25 June 1996] ECtHR (App No 17/1995/523/609)
Anglo-Iranian Oil Co Case (*United Kingdom v Iran*) [1952] ICJ Rep 93
Armed Activities on the Territory of the Congo (*Democratic Republic of the Congo v Uganda*) [2015] ICJ Rep 23
Banković and Others v Belgium and Others [12 December 2001] ECtHR (App No 52207/99)
Boumediene v Bush [2008] 553 US 723
Brief of Amicus Curiae Council 119 In Support Of Plaintiffs' Motion for Summary Judgment And Permanent Injunction, U.T. v Barr [30 June 2020] 1:20-cv-00116
Calvin's Case [1608] 77 ER 377, Co Rep 1a
Cargill, Incorporated v United Mexican States [2009] NAFTA (ICSID)
Case Concerning Application of the Convention on the Prevention and Punishment of the Crime of Genocide (*Bosnia and Herzegovina v Serbia and Montenegro*) [2007] ICJ Rep 47
Case Concerning the Factory at Chorzów (*Germany v Poland*) (Merits) [1928] PCIJ Series A No 17
Case of Salvador Prats v the United States of America [1868] 29 RIAA 187
Case of Vilvarajah and Others v The United Kingdom [30 October 1991] ECtHR (Application No 13163/87; 13164/87; 13165/87; 13447/87; 13448/87)
Certain Activities Carried Out by Nicaragua in the Border Area (*Separate opinion of Judge Donoghue*) [2015] ICJ Rep
Certain Activities Carried Out by Nicaragua in the Border Area (*Separate opinion of Judge Dugard*) [2015] ICJ Rep 842
Chris Sale, Acting Commissioner, Immigration and Naturalization Service, et al. v Haitian Centers Council, Inc., et al. [21 June 1993] 509 US 155
Corfu Channel (*United Kingdom of Great Britain and Northern Ireland v Albania*) [1949] ICJ Rep 244
CPCF v Minister for Immigration and Border Protection & Anor [2015] HCA 1
Cruz Varas and Others v Sweden [20 March 1991] ECtHR (App No 46/1990/237/307)
Cyprus v Turkey [10 July 1978] EComHR (App No 8007/77) DR 13, p 85
Cyprus v Turkey [26 May 1975] EComHR (App Nos 6780/74 and 6950/75) DR 2, p 125
Darweesh v Trump [16 February 2017] 17-CV-480 (CBA)
Elettronica Sicula S.p.A. (*ELSI*) (*USA v Italy*) [1989] ICJ Rep 15

European Roma Rights Centre and Others v the Immigration Officer at Prague Airport and the Secretary of State for the Home Department [20 May 2003] EWCA Civ 666
Execution of German-Portuguese Arbitral Award of June 30th, 1930 (Germany, Portugal) [16 February 1933] III RIAA 1371
Frederick Wipperman Arbitration (United States of America v Venezuela) [1890] III RIAA 3041
Gabčíkovo-Nagymaros Project (Hungary v Slovakia) [1997] ICJ Rep 120
George W. Hopkins (USA) v United Mexican States [1926] IV RIAA 16
Glamis Gold, Ltd. v The United States of America [2009] NAFTA (UNCITRAL)
Haitian Centers Council, Inc. v McNary [29 July 1992] 969 F2d 1350
Haitian Refugee Center v Civiletti [2 July 1980] 503 F Supp 442
Haitian Refugee Center v Smith [14 May 1982] 676 F2d 1023
Haitian Refugee Center, Inc. v Baker [24 February 1992] 953 F2d 1498
Harry Roberts (USA) v United Mexican States [1926] IV RIAA 80
Hess v the United Kingdom [28 May 1975] EComHR (App No 6231/73)
Hirsi Jamaa and Others v Italy [23 February 2012] ECtHR (App No 27765/09)
Horvath v Secretary of State for the Home Department [2000] Imm AR 205
Huisha-Huisha v Mayorkas [4 March 2022] No 21-5200
Ilaşcu and Others v Moldova and Russia [8 July 2004] ECtHR (App No 48787/99)
Island of Palmas (or Miangas) (The Netherlands v The United States of America) [4 April 1928] II RIAA 829
Kamasee v Commonwealth of Australia & Ors (Approval of Settlement) [2017] VSC 537
Kamasee v Commonwealth of Australia & Ors (No 8) (Class closure ruling) [2017] VSC 167
Khlaifia and Others v Italy [15 December 2016] ECtHR (App No 16483/12)
L.F.H. Neer and Pauline Neer [1926] 4 RIAA 73
Lillie S. Kling (U.S.A.) v United Mexican States [8 October 1930] IV RIAA 575
Loizidou v Turkey [23 February 1995] ECtHR (App No 40/1993/435/514)
M v Denmark [14 October 1992] EComHR (App No 17392/90)
M.S.S. v Belgium and Greece [21 January 2011] ECtHR (App No 30696/09)
McNary v Haitian Refugee Ctr., Inc. [20 February 1991] 498 US 479
Medvedyev and Others v France [29 March 2010] ECtHR (App No 3394/03)
Merrill and Ring v Canada [2010] NAFTA (ICSID)
Minister for Immigration and Multicultural Affairs v. Khawar [2002] 210 CLR 1
N.D. and N.T. v Spain [13 February 2020] ECtHR (App Nos 8675/15 and 8697/15)
Naulilaa Arbitration (Portugal v Germany) [1928] II UNRIAA 1011
Plaintiff M70/2011 v Minister for Immigration and Citizenship; Plaintiff M106 of 2011 v Minister for Immigration and Citizenship [2011] HCA 32; 244 CLR 144
Plaintiff S99/2016 v Minister for Immigration and Border Protection [2016] FCA 483
Pulp Mills on the River Uruguay (Argentina v Uruguay) [2010] ICJ Rep 58

Sambiaggio case [1 January 1903] X UNRIAA 499
Sentence arbitrale sur la réclamation numéro 20, présentée pardon Jacinto Gadino [1901] XV RIAA 414
Sentence arbitrale sur la réclamation numéro 71, présentée par Doña Carolina Soria Galvarro, veuve de Don José Cresceri [1901] XV RIAA 449
Sentence arbitrale sur la réclamation número 63, présentée par Don Luis Piola [1901] XV RIAA 444
Spanish Zone of Morocco Claims (*Spain v United Kingdom*) [1925] 2 RIAA 615
SS 'Lotus' (*France v Turkey*) [7 September 1927] PCIJ Series A No 10
Stocké v Germany [12 October 1989] EComHR (App No 11755/85)
T.I. v UK [7 March 2000] ECtHR (App No 43844/98)
Texas v Biden [13 August 2021] No 2:21-cv-067, 2 2021 WL 3603341
Thomas H. Youmans (*USA*) *v United States of Mexico* [23 November 1926] IV UNRIAA 110
Trail Smelter Case (*USA v Canada*) [1938 and 1941] RIAA 3
Trump v. Hawaii [26 June 2018] 17-965
U.T. et al. v Barr et al., Complaint for Declarative and Injunctive Relief [15 January 2020] 1:20-cv-00116
United Phosphorus, Ltd v Angus Chemical Co. [2003] 322 F 3d 942, 948 (7th Cir)
Vearncombe v UK and Germany [18 January 1989] EComHR (App No 12816/87)
Walter A. Noyes (*United States*) *v Panama* [1933] 6 RIAA 253
William E. Chapman Arbitration (*United States of America v United Mexican States*) [1930] IV RIAA 632
Windstream Energy LLC v Government of Canada [2016] NAFTA (UNCITRAL)
X v Federal Republic of Germany [25 September 1965] EComHR (App No 1611/62)
X v UK [15 December 1977] EComHR (App No 7547/76)
X. and Y. v Switzerland [3 October 1978] EComHR (App No 8166/78) DR 13, p 241

Authorities

Argentina, Brasil, Chile, Colombia, Costa Rica, Ecuador, … Uruguay, *Declaración de Quito* (4 Septiembre 2018)

Argentina and Brazil, *Tratado de Amistad, Comercio y Navegación* (Paraná, 7 March 1856)

Argentina and Chile, *Tratado de Amistad, Comercio y Navegación* (Santiago, 30 August 1855)

Argentina and Paraguay, *Tratado de Amistad, Comercio y Navegación* (Asunción, 29 July 1856)

Argentina and Sardinia, *Tratado de Amistad, Comercio y Navegación* (Paraná, 21 September 1855)

Argentina and USA, *Treaty of Friendship, Commerce, and Navigation* (San Jose, 27 July 1853)

Asian-African Legal Consultative Organization, *Bangkok Principles on the Status and Treatment of Refugees* (31 December 1966)

Australia, *Migration Act* (1958)

Australia, *Migration Amendment (Excision from Migration Zone) Act* (2001)

Australia, *The Migration and Maritime Powers Legislation Amendment (Resolving the Asylum Caseload Legacy) Act* (2014)

Australia, *Migration Legislation Amendment Act* (1989)

Australia and Nauru, *Memorandum of Understanding between the Republic of Nauru and the Commonwealth of Australia for Cooperation in the Administration of Asylum Seekers and Related Issues* (11 December 2001)

Belgium, *Loi du 15 décembre 1980 sur l'accès au territoire, le séjour, l'établissement et l'éloignement des étrangers* (5 December 1980)

Belgium and Venezuela, *Protocol between Belgium and Venezuela for the Arbitration of Claims* (Washington, 7 March 1903)

Belize, Costa Rica, El Salvador, Guatemala, Honduras, Mexico and Panama, *Marco Integral Regional para la Protección y Soluciones* (2017)

Brazil, *Law No. 6,815: The Foreigner's Statute (Estatuto do Estrangeiro)* (19 August 1980)

The British Empire, France, Italy, Japan, Greece, Roumania, … Turkey, *Treaty of Lausanne* (Lausanne, 24 July 1923)

The British Empire, France, Italy, Japan, Greece and Turkey, *Protocol Relating to the Karagatch Territory and the Islands of Imbros and Tenedos* (Lausanne, 24 July 1923)

Canada, *Canada-Québec Accord Relating to Immigration and Temporary Admission of Aliens* (1991)

Canada, *Immigration Act* (1976)

Canada, *Immigration and Refugee Protection Act* (2001)

Cartagena Declaration on Refugees, Colloquium on the International Protection of Refugees in Central America, Mexico and Panama (19–22 November 1984)

Colombia and Germany, *Tratado de Amistad, Comercio y Navegación* (Bogotá, 23 July 1892)

Colombia and Italy, *Tratado de Amistad, Comercio y Navegación* (Bogotá, 27 October 1892)

Colombia and Spain, *Tratado adicional al de Paz y Amistad* (Bogotá, 30 January 1881)

'Convention for the Supervision of Trade in Arms and War Munitions' (1926) 20(1) AJIL 151

Convention Implementing the Schengen Agreement of 14 June 1985 between the Governments of the States of the Benelux Economic Union, the Federal Republic of Germany and the French Republic, on the Gradual Abolition of Checks at Their Common Borders (19 June 1990)

Convention Relative to the Slave Trade and Importation into Africa of Firearms, Ammunition, and Spirituous Liquors (Brussels, 2 July 1890)

Convention (XIII) Concerning the Rights and Duties of Neutral Powers in Naval War (1907)

Council of Europe, *European Convention for the Protection of Human Rights and Fundamental Freedoms, as Amended by Protocols Nos. 11 and 14* (4 November 1950) ETS 5

Council of Europe: Committee of Ministers, *Declaration on Territorial Asylum* (18 November 1977)

Council of Europe: Committee of Ministers, *Resolution (67)14: Asylum to Persons in Danger of Persecution* (29 June 1967)

Council of the European Union, *Council Directive 2001/51/EC of 28 June 2001 Supplementing the Provisions of Article 26 of the Convention Implementing the Schengen Agreement of 14 June 1985* (2001)

Denmark, *Aliens Act* (*Udlændingeloven*) (9 June 1983)

European Union, *Convention Determining the State Responsible for Examining Applications for Asylum Lodged in One of the Member States of the European Communities – Dublin Convention* (1997) C 254

European Union, *Regulation (EU) 2016/399 of the European Parliament and of the Council of 9 March 2016 on a Union Code on the Rules Governing the Movement of Persons across Borders* (*Schengen Borders Code*) (2016) L 77/1

European Union: Council of the European Union, *Convention Determining the State Responsible for Examining Applications for Asylum Lodged in One of the Member States of the European Communities* (*Dublin Convention*) (15 June 1990)

European Union: Council of the European Union, *Regulation (EU) No 604/2013 of the European Parliament and of the Council of 26 June 2013 Establishing the Criteria and Mechanisms for Determining the Member State Responsible for Examining an Ap-*

plication for International Protection Lodged in One of the Member States by a Third-Country National or a Stateless Person (Recast) (29 June 2013)

Executive Committee of the High Commissioner's Programme, *Conclusion No. 15 (XXX) on Refugees without an Asylum Country* (16 October 1979)

Executive Committee of the High Commissioner's Programme, *Conclusion No. 19 (XXXI): Temporary Refuge* (16 October 1980)

Executive Committee of the High Commissioner's Programme, *Conclusion No. 22 (XXXII): Protection of Asylum-Seekers in Situations of Large-Scale Influx* (21 October 1981)

France and Venezuela, *Protocol between France and Venezuela for the Arbitration of Claims* (Washington, 27 February 1903)

Germany, *Aliens Act (Ausländergesetz)* (1965)

Germany, *German Ordinance on the Treatment of Enemy Properties* (15 January 1940)

Germany, *Kontingentflüchtlingsgesetz* (1980)

Germany and Venezuela, *Protocol between Germany and Venezuela for the Arbitration of German Claims* (Washington, 7 May 1903)

Greece and Bulgaria, *Convention between Greece and Bulgaria Respecting Reciprocal Emigration* (Neuilly-sur-Seine, 27 November 1919)

Greece and Turkey, *Lausanne Peace Treaty VI: Convention Concerning the Exchange of Greek and Turkish Populations* (Lausanne, 30 January 1923)

Honduras, *Constitución de 1894* (14 October 1894)

ICRC, *Geneva Convention Relative to the Protection of Civilian Persons in Time of War (Fourth Geneva Convention)* (12 August 1949) 75 UNTS 287

Implementing Bilateral and Multilateral Asylum Cooperative Agreements under the Immigration and Nationality Act (19 November 2019) 84 FR 64,008

Inter-American Conference, *Principles of International Law Governing the Responsibility of the State, Tenth Inter-American Conference* (Caracas, 1954)

International Law Commission, *Draft Articles on Diplomatic Protection with Commentaries* (2006)

Italy and Libya, *Treaty on Friendship, Partnership and Cooperation* (30 August 2008)

Italy and USA, *Treaty of Commerce and Navigation* (Florence, 26 February 1871)

Italy and Venezuela, *Protocol between Italy and Venezuela for the Settlement of Italian Claims* (Washington, 13 February 1903)

League of Nations, *Additional Act to the Protocol of September 29, 1923, Relating to the Settlement of Greek Refugees* (19 September 1924) LNTS Vol. XXX, No. 776

League of Nations, *Additional Protocol to the Provisional Arrangement and to the Convention, Signed at Geneva on July 4th, 1936, and February 10th, 1938, Respectively, Concerning the Status of Refugees Coming from Germany* (14 September 1939) LNTS Vol. CXCVIII, No. 4634

League of Nations, *Agreement between the Latvian Democratic Republic and the Ukrainian Socialist Soviet Republic Regarding the Repatriation of Latvian Refugees Who Are at Present in the Territory of the Latter* (Moscow, 3 August 1921) LNTS Vol. XVII, No. 441

League of Nations, *Arrangement Concerning the Extension to other Categories of Refugees of Certain Measures Taken in Favour of Russian and Armenian Refugees* (30 June 1928) LNTS Vol. LXXXIX, No. 63

League of Nations, *Arrangement Relating to the Issue of Identity Certificates to Russian and Armenian Refugees, supplementing and Amending the Previous Arrangements Dated July 5, 1922, and May 31, 1924* (12 May 1926) LNTS Vol. LXXXIX, No. 2004

League of Nations, *Arrangement Relating to the Legal Status of Russian and Armenian Refugees* (30 June 1928) LNTS Vol. LXXXIX, No. 2005

League of Nations, *Arrangement with Respect to the Issue of Certificates of Identity to Russian Refugees* (5 July 1922) LNTS Vol. XIII, No. 355

League of Nations, *Convention Concerning the Status of Refugees Coming from Germany, with Annex* (10 February 1938) LNTS Vol. CXCII, No. 4461

League of Nations, *Convention for the Control of the Trade in Arms and Munition and Protocol Signed at St-Germain-en-Laye* (10 September 1919) LNTS Vol. VII, No. 200

League of Nations, *Convention Relating to the International Status of Refugees* (28 October 1933) LNTS Vol. CLIX, No. 3663

League of Nations, *Protocol Relating to the Settlement of Refugees in Greece and the Creation for This Purpose of a Refugee Settlement Commission* (29 September 1923) LNTS Vol. 20, No. 503

League of Nations, *Provisional Arrangement Concerning the Status of Refugees Coming from Germany* (4 July 1936) LNTS Vol. CLXXI, No. 3952

Mexico and Chile, *Tratado de Amistad, Comercio, y Navegación* (Mexico City, 7 March 1831)

Mexico and Colombia, *Treaty of Commerce Between Colombia and Mexico* (Mexico City, 31 December 1823)

Mexico and USA, *Treaty of Amity, Commerce and Navigation* (Mexico City, 5 April 1831)

Mexico and USA, *Treaty Of Peace, Friendship, Limits, And Settlement* (Guadalupe Hidalgo, 2 February 1848)

Mexico and Venezuela, *Protocol between Mexico and Venezuela for the Arbitration of Claims* (Washington, 26 February 1903)

Netherlands and Venezuela, *Protocol between the Netherlands and Venezuela for the Arbitration of Claims* (Washington, 28 February 1903)

New Zealand, *Immigration Act* (1987)

Nicaragua, *La Constitución de 1893* (10 December 1893)

Organization of African Unity, *Convention Governing the Specific Aspects of Refugee Problems in Africa* (10 September 1969)

Organization of African Unity, *Report of the Administrative Secretary-General on the Conference on Legal, Economic and Social Aspects of African Refugee Problems. Addis Ababa: 9–18 October 1967* (1968) CM/198

Organization of American States, *American Treaty of Pacific Settlement* (Bogotá, 30 April 1948)

Organization of American States, *Convention on the Status of Aliens* (Havana, 20 February 1928)

Organization of American States, *Resolution LXXIV: International Responsibility of the State* (Montevideo, 24 December 1933)

Pan-American Union, *Inter-American Conference on Problems of War and Peace, Mexico City, 21 February 1945, Report Submitted to the Governing Board of the Pan American Union by the Director-General* (1945)

Pan-American Union, *Convention on Asylum* (Havana, 20 February 1928)

Pan-American Union, *Convention on the Duties and Rights of States in the Event of Civil Strife* (Havana, 20 February 1928)

Pan-American Union, *Convention on the Status of Aliens* (Havana, 20 February 1928)

Pan-American Union, *Convention Relative to the Rights of Aliens* (Mexico, 29 January 1902)

Paraguay and USA, *Convention Relating to Claims of United States and Paraguay Navigation Company against the Government of Paraguay* (Asunción, 4 February 1859)

Peru and Argentina, *Tratado de Amistad, Comercio y Navegación* (Buenos Aires, 9 March 1874)

Peru and Austria, *Tratado de Amistad, Comercio y Navegación* (Lima, 2 May 1870)

Peru and Belgium, *Tratado de Amistad, Comercio y Navegación* (London, 16 May 1850)

Peru and Germany, *Tratado de Comercio y Navegación* (Lima, 20 January 1877)

Spain and Cape Verde, *Agreement between the Kingdom of Spain and the Republic of Cape Verde on Monitoring Joint Maritime Areas Under the Sovereignty and Jurisdiction of Cape Verde* (21 February 2008)

Spain and Venezuela, *Protocol between Spain and Venezuela for the Arbitration of Claims* (Washington, 2 April 1903)

Sweden, Norway and Venezuela, *Protocol Respecting the Arbitration of Claims between Sweden and Norway and Venezuela* (Washington, 10 March 1903)

UK and Venezuela, *Protocol between Great Britain and Venezuela for the Settlement of British Claims etc.* (Washington, 13 February 1903)

UN, *Agreement for United Nations Relief and Rehabilitation Administration* (Washington 9 November 1943)

UN, *Agreement 1 between Belgium and the United States of America Concerning the Status and Admission into Belgium of Displaced Persons at Present in the American Zone of Germany (Brussels 23 January 1947)* (1950)

UN, *Constitution of the International Refugee Organization and Agreement on Interim Measures to Be Taken in Respect of Refugees and Displaced Persons* (15 December 1946) UNTS Vol. 18, No. 283

UN, *Convention on the Status of Refugees* (28 July 1951)

UN, *Final Act of the Intergovernmental Conference on the Adoption of a Travel Document for Refugees and Agreement Relating to the Issue of a Travel Document to Refugees Who Are the Concern of the Intergovernmental Committee on Refugees* (15 October 1946)

UN, *Final Act of the International Conference on Human Rights. Resolution XIII: Co-operation with the United Nations High Commissioner for Refugees* (12 May 1968) A/CoNF.3 2/41

UN General Assembly, *Refugees from Algeria in Morocco and Tunisia* (18 December 1961) A/RES/1672(XVI)

UN General Assembly, *Resolution 832(IX): International Assistance to Refugees within the Mandate of the United Nations High Commissioner for Refugees* (21 October 1954) A/RES/832(IX)

UN General Assembly, *Statute of the Office fo the United Nations High Commissioner for Refugees* (14 December 1950) A/RES/428(V)

UN, *The Global Compact for Safe, Orderly and Regular Migration* (11 July 2018)

UN, *Protocol Relating to the Status of Refugees* (31 January 1967)

UN, *Statement by the Representative of the US in the Ad Hoc Committee on Statelessness and Related Problems, Summary Record of the Third Meeting* (26 January 1950) E/AC.32/ SR.3

UN Ad Hoc Committee on Statelessness and Related Problems, *First Session: Summary Record of the Twenty-Sixth Meeting Held at Lake Success, New York, on Friday, 10 February 1950, at 2.15 p.m.* (17 February 1950) E/AC.32/SR.25

UN Ad Hoc Committee on Statelessness and Related Problems, *Report of the Ad Hoc Committee on Statelessness and Related Problems, Lake Success, New York, 16 January to 16 February 1950* (17 February 1950) E/1618, E/AC.32/5

UN Conference of Plenipotentiaries on the Status of Refugees and Stateless Persons: International Confederation of Free Trade Unions, *Proposals Concerning the Draft Convention Relating to the Status Of Refugees* (6 July 1951) A/CONF.2/NGO/5

UN Economic and Social Council, *Resolution 248(IX)(A): Study of Statelessness* (6 and 8 August 1949) E/RES/248(IX)(A)

UN Economic and Social Council, *Resolution 393(XIII): Refugees and Stateless Persons* (10 September 1951) E/RES/393(XIII)

UN Economic and Social Council, *Resolution 565(XIX): International Assistance to Refugees within the Mandate of the United Nations High Commissioner for Refugees* (31 March 1955) E/RES/565(XIX)

UN Economic and Social Council, Resolution 672(xxv): *Establishment of an Executive Committee of the Programme of the United Nations High Commissioner for Refugees* (30 April 1958) E/RES/672(xxv)

UN General Assembly, *Assistance to Refugees and Displaced Persons in Malawi* (7 December 1987) A/RES/42/132

UN General Assembly, *Assistance to Student Refugees in Southern Africa* (7 December 1987) A/RES/42/138

UN General Assembly, *Charter of Economic Rights and Duties of States* (6 November 1974) UN Doc A/RES/3281

UN General Assembly, *Chinese Refugees in Hong Kong* (26 November 1957) A/RES/1167(XII)

UN General Assembly, *Convention Relating to the Status of Refugees* (28 July 1951)

UN General Assembly, *Convention Relating to the Status of Stateless Persons* (28 September 1954)

UN General Assembly, *Declaration and Comprehensive Plan of Action of the International Conference on Indo-Chinese Refugees, Report of the Secretary-General* (22 September 1989) A/44/523

UN General Assembly, *Declaration on Territorial Asylum* (14 December 1967) A/RES/2312(XXII)

UN General Assembly, *Draft Declaration on Territorial Asylum: Report of the 6th Committee* (30 November 1967) A/6912

UN General Assembly, *International Co-operation to Avert New Flows of Refugees: Note by the Secretary-General* (13 May 1986) A/41/324

UN General Assembly, *International Conference on Assistance to Refugees in Africa* (14 December 1981) A/RES/36/124

UN General Assembly, *International Conference on Assistance to Refugees in Africa (ICARA I): Report of the Secretary-General* (11 June 1981) A/36/316

UN General Assembly, *International Covenant on Civil and Political Rights* (16 December 1966) UNTS Vol. 999, p. 171

UN General Assembly, *Measures to Eliminate International Terrorism* (14 January 2013) A/RES/67/99

UN General Assembly, *Meeting on Refugees and Displaced Persons in South-East Asia, Convened by the Secretary-General of the United Nations at Geneva, on 20 and 21 July 1979, and Subsequent Developments: Report of the Secretary-General* (7 November 1979) A/34/627

UN General Assembly, *The Problem of Chinese Refugees in Hong Kong* (7 December 1962) A/RES/1784

UN General Assembly, *Protection of Human Rights and Fundamental Freedoms while Countering Terrorism* (5 April 2011) A/RES/65/221

UN General Assembly, *Refugees and Displaced Persons* (15 December 1946) A/RES/62

UN General Assembly, *Refugees from Algeria in Morocco and Tunisia* (20 November 1959) A/RES/1389(XIV)

UN General Assembly, *Report of the Group of Governmental Experts on International Co-operation to Avert New Flows of Refugees* (13 May 1986) A/41/324

UN General Assembly, *Report of the Secretary-General on the Meeting on Refugees and Displaced Persons in South-East Asia* (29 November 1979) A/RES/34/62

UN General Assembly, *Report of the United Nations High Commissioner for Refugees* (25 October 1955) A/res/925(X)

UN General Assembly, *Report of the United Nations High Commissioner for Refugees* (23 January 1957) A/res/1039(XI)

UN General Assembly, *Report of the United Nations High Commissioner for Refugees* (5 December 1958) 1284(XIII)

UN General Assembly, *Report of the United Nations High Commissioner for Refugees* (20 November 1959) A/res/1388

UN General Assembly, *Report of the United Nations High Commissioner for Refugees* (5 December 1960) A/res/1499(XV)

UN General Assembly, *Report of the United Nations High Commissioner for Refugees* (18 December 1961) 1673(XVI)

UN General Assembly, *Report of the United Nations High Commissioner for Refugees* (12 December 1963) 1959(XVID)

UN General Assembly, *Report of the United Nations High Commissioner for Refugees* (1 January 1965) A/6011/rev.1(SUPP)

UN General Assembly, *Report of the United Nations High Commissioner for Refugees* (8 December 1977) A/res/32/67

UN General Assembly, *Report of the United Nations High Commissioner for Refugees* (29 November 1978) A/res/33/26

UN General Assembly, *Report of the United Nations High Commissioner for Refugees* (29 November 1979) A/res/34/60

UN General Assembly, *Resolution 56/83: Responsibility of States for Internationally Wrongful Acts* (28 January 2002) A/RES/56/83

UN General Assembly, *Resolution 319(IV): Refugees and Stateless Persons* (3 December 1949) A/RES/319(IV)

UN General Assembly, *Resolution 428(V): Statute of the Office of the United Nations High Commissioner for Refugees* (14 December 1950) A/RES/428(V)

UN General Assembly, *Resolution 799(VIII): Request for the Codification of the Principles of International Law Governing State Responsibility* (7 December 1953) A/RES/799(VIII)

UN General Assembly, *Resolution 832(IX): International Assistance to Refugees within the Mandate of the United Nations High Commissioner for Refugees* (21 December 1954) A/RES/832(IX)
UN General Assembly, *Resolution 1006(ES-II)* (9 November 1956) A/RES/1006(ES-II)
UN General Assembly, *Resolution 1129(XI)* (21 November 1956) A/RES/1129(XI)
UN General Assembly, *Resolution 1166(XII): International Assistance to Refugees within the Mandate of the United Nations High Commissioner for Refugees* (26 November 1957) A/RES/1166(XII)
UN General Assembly, *Resolution on Assistance to Refugees in Somalia* (13 December 1985) A/RES/40/132
UN General Assembly, *Resolution on Assistance to Refugees in Somalia* (4 December 1986) A/RES/41/138
UN General Assembly, *Resolution on Assistance to Student Refugees in Southern Africa* (13 December 1985) A/RES/40/138
UN General Assembly, *Resolution on Assistance to Student Refugees in Southern Africa* (4 December 1986) A/RES/41/136
UN General Assembly, *Second International Conference on Assistance to Refugees in Africa* (14 December 1984) A/RES/39/139
UN General Assembly, *Situation of African Refugees* (29 November 1979) A/RES/34/61
UN General Assembly, *Transfer to the United Nations of the Residual Assets and Activities of UNRRA (United Nations Relief and Rehabilitation Administration)* (18 November 1948) A/RES/241
UN General Assembly, *The United Nations Global Counter-Terrorism Strategy* (20 September 2006)
UN General Assembly, *The United Nations Global Counter-Terrorism Strategy Review* (12 July 2012) A/RES/66/282
UN General Assembly, *Universal Declaration of Human Rights* (10 December 1948) A/RES/217(III)
UN High Commissioner for Refugees, *Addendum to the Report of the United Nations High Commissioner for Refugees* (6 November 1979) A/34/12/Add.1
UN Security Council, *Resolution 307(1971): The India/Pakistan Subcontinent* (21 December 1971) S/RES/307
UN Security Council, *Resolution 1624 (2005)* (14 September 2005) S/RES/1624
United Kingdom, *Immigration (Carriers' Liability) Act* (1987)
USA, *Administrative Procedure Act* 5 U.S.C.
USA, *Afghan Allies Protection Act* (2008) 8 U.S.C.
USA, *Cuban Adjustment Act* (1966) 80 Stat. 1161
USA, *Executive Order 12324: Interdiction of Illegal Aliens* (29 September 1981) 46 FR 48109
USA, *Executive Order 12807: Interdiction of Illegal Aliens* (24 May 1992) 57 FR 23133

USA, *Executive Order 13276: Delegation of Responsibilities Concerning Undocumented Aliens Interdicted or Intercepted in the Caribbean Region* (15 November 2002) 67 FR 69983

USA, *Executive Order 13303: Protecting the Development Fund for Iraq and Certain Other Property in which Iraq Has an Interest* (22 May 2003) 68 FR 31929

USA, *Executive Order 13405: Blocking Property of Certain Persons Undermining Democratic Processes or Institutions in Belarus* (16 June 2006) 71 FR 35485

USA, *Executive Order 13441: Blocking Property of Persons Undermining the Sovereignty of Lebanon or Its Democratic Processes and Institutions* (1 August 2007) 72 FR 43499

USA, *Executive Order 13566: Blocking Property and Prohibiting Certain Transactions Related to Libya* (25 February 2011) 76 FR 11315

USA, *Executive Order 13611: Blocking Property of Persons Threatening the Peace, Security, or Stability of Yemen* (16 May 2012) 77 FR 29533

USA, *Executive Order 13692: Blocking Property and Suspending Entry of Certain Persons Contributing to the Situation in Venezuela* (8 March 2015) 80 FR 12747

USA, *Executive Order 13726: Blocking Property and Suspending Entry into the United States of Persons Contributing to the Situation in Libya* (19 April 2016) 81 FR 23559

USA, *Executive Order 13769: Protecting the Nation From Foreign Terrorist Entry into the United States* (27 January 2017) 82 FR 8977

USA, *Executive Order 13780: Protecting the Nation from Foreign Terrorist Entry into the United States* (6 March 2017) 82 FR 13209

USA, *Executive Order 13882: Blocking Property and Suspending Entry of Certain Persons Contributing to the Situation in Mali* (26 July 2019) 84 FR 37055

USA, *Executive Order 13936: The President's Executive Order on Hong Kong Normalization* (14 July 2020) 85 FR 43413

USA, *Executive Order 14010: Creating a Comprehensive Regional Framework to Address the Causes of Migration to Manage Migration Throughout North and Central America, and to Provide Safe and Orderly Processing of Asylum Seekers at the United States Border* (2 February 2021) 86 FR 8267

USA, *Immigration and Nationality Act* 8 U.S.C.

USA, *Immigration Reform and Control Act* (1986)

USA, *Presidential Proclamation 4865: High seas interdiction of illegal aliens* (29 September 1981) 46 FR 48107

USA, *Presidential Proclamation 5517: Suspension of Cuban immigration* (22 August 1986) 51 FR 30470

USA, *Presidential Proclamation 6958: Suspension of Entry as Immigrants and Nonimmigrants of Persons Who Are Members or Officials of the Sudanese Government or Armed Forces* (22 November 1996) 85 FR 84092

USA, *Presidential Proclamation 9983: Improving Enhanced Vetting Capabilities and Processes for Detecting Attempted Entry Into the United States by Terrorists or Other Public-Safety Threats* (31 January 2020) 85 FR 6699

USA, *Proclamation 4865: High Seas Interdiction of Illegal Aliens* (29 September 1981) 46 FR 48107

USA, *Proclamation 7359: Suspension of Entry as Immigrants and Nonimmigrants of Persons Impeding the Peace Process in Sierra Leone* (10 October 2000) 65 FR 60831

USA, *Proclamation 9645: Enhancing Vetting Capabilities and Processes for Detecting Attempted Entry Into the United States by Terrorists or Other Public-Safety Threats* (24 September 2017) 82 FR 45161

USA, *Public Health Service Act* (1944)

USA, *Refugee Crisis in Iraq Act* (2007) 8 U.S.C.

USA and Austria, *A Treaty Between the United States and Austria, Signed on August 24, 1921, to Establish Securely Friendly Relations Between The Two Nations, The United States of America and Austria* (Vienna, 24 August 1921) Vol. VII, No. 184

USA and Brazil, *Treaty of Amity, Commerce, and Navigation* (Rio de Janeiro, 12 December 1828)

USA and Chile, *Convention of Peace, Amity, Commerce, and Navigation* (Santiago, 16 May 1832)

USA and Ecuador, *Settlement of Case of Brig "Morris"* (Quito, 9 February 1850)

USA and Ecuador, *Settlement of Case of Brig "Native"* (Guayaquil, 5 February 1853)

USA and Ecuador, *Settlement of Cases of Brig "Josephine" and Schooner "Ranger"* (Quito, 15 June 1849)

USA and El Salvador, *Agreement between the Government of the United States and the Government of the Republic of El Salvador for Cooperation in the Examination of Protection Claims* (20 September 2019)

USA and Germany, *A Treaty Between the United States and Germany, Signed on August 25, 1921, to Restore Friendly Relations Existing between the Two Nations Prior to the Outbreak of War Germany and the United States of America* (Berlin, 25 August 1921) Vol. XII, No. 310

USA and Guatemala, *Agreement between the Government of the United States and the Government of the Republic of Guatemala on Cooperation in the Examination of Protection Claims* (26 July 2019)

USA and Guatemala, *Agreement between the United States of America and the Republic of Guatemala concerning a Temporary Agricultural Workers Program* (30 June 2019)

USA and Haiti, *Agreement of 23 September 1981* (23 September 1981) 33 UST 3559, TIAS 10241

USA and Honduras, *Agreement between the Government of the United States and the Government of the Republic of Honduras for Cooperation in the Examination of Protection Claims* (25 September 2019)

USA and Honduras, *Agreement Concerning the Temporary Agricultural and non-Agricultural Workers Programs* (27 September 2019)

USA and Hungary, *A Treaty Between the United States and Hungary, Signed August 29, 1921, to Establish Securely Friendly Relations Between the Two Nations the United States of America and Hungary* (Budapest, 29 August 1921)

USA and Spain, *Treaty of Peace Between the United States and Spain* (Paris, 10 December 1898)

USA and Venezuela, *Arrangement for the Settlement of the Case of the Brig "Morris"* (Caracas, 26 February 1844)

USA and Venezuela, *Convention for the Final Settlement of the Case of the Brig "Josephine"* (Caracas, 16 November 1846)

USA and Venezuela, *Convention for the Settlement of the Case of the Brig "Native"* (Caracas, 16 November 1846)

USA and Venezuela, *Convention for the Settlement of the Case of the Brig "Sarah Wilson"* (Caracas, 12 April 1848)

USA and Venezuela, *Convention for the Settlement of the Claim Arising Out of the Seizure and Detention of the Brig "Mount Vernon"* (Caracas, 7 July 1849)

USA and Venezuela, *Protocol between the United States and Venezuela for the Arbitration of Claims* (Washington, 17 February 1903)

USA: Citizenship and Immigration Services, *The Cuban Family Reunification Parole Program* (1 September 2022)

USA: Citizenship and Immigration Services, *Haitian Family Reunification Parole (HFRP) Program* (22 June 2022)

USA: Citizenship and Immigration Services, *Processes for Cubans, Haitians, Nicaraguans, and Venezuelans* (18 May 2023)

USA: Department of Health and Human Services, *Control of Communicable Diseases; Foreign Quarantine: Suspension of the Right to Introduce and Prohibition of Introduction of Persons into United States from Designated Foreign Countries or Places for Public Health Purposes* (11 September 2020) 85 FR 56424

USA: Department of Health and Human Services, *Order Suspending Introduction of Persons from a Country Where a Communicable Disease Exists* (26 March 2020) 85 FR 17060

USA: Department of Homeland Security, *Implementation of a Parole Process for Venezuelans* (19 October 2022) 87 FR 63507

USA: Department of Homeland Security, *Los Angeles Declaration on Migration and Protection* (10 June 2022)

USA: Department of Homeland Security and Department of Justice, *Final Rule: Circumvention of Lawful Pathways* (16 May 2023) 8 CFR Part 208/8 CFR Parts 1003 and 1208

USA: Department of Homeland Security and Department of Justice, *Proposed Rule: Circumvention of Lawful Pathways* (23 February 2023) 8 CFR Part 208/8 CFR Part 1208

Introduction

As a system of public international law, International Refugee Law (IRL) diverges from those that evolved concurrently in certain distinct ways. Though internationally recognised, with a widely ratified Convention,[1] comprising principles broadly considered to have attained the status of customary international law, and with complementary regional instruments and municipal legal regimes that require adherence to its fundamental tenets, the absence of clear instances of the attribution of international State responsibility (SR) is conspicuous. Apart from the obvious lack of direct inter-State litigation, there are no instances of international disputes having arisen from the alleged violation of the primary instruments of IRL.[2] This deficiency makes IRL quite exceptional among systems of public international law.

The recognition of international law (IL) as imposing obligations on States has, as a logical consequence, the acceptance of SR where a violation of these

1 UN General Assembly, *Convention Relating to the Status of Refugees* (28 July 1951) UNTS 189.

2 IRL is defined in this book as all international legal instruments that concern international refugee law. It does not include regional legal instruments or municipal law relating to refugees, with limited adherence among States. See: League of Nations, *Arrangement with respect to the issue of certificates of identity to Russian Refugees* (5 July 1922) LNTS Vol. XIII, No. 355; League of Nations, 'Plan for the Issue of a Certificate of Identity to Armenian Refugees, 31st May 1924. Submitted for the consideration of interested governments by Dr. Nansen, High Commissioner for Russian Refugees in execution of the Resolution of the Council of the League' (1924) 5(7) LNOJ; League of Nations, *Arrangement relating to the Issue of Identity Certificates to Russian and Armenian Refugees, supplementing and amending the previous Arrangements dated July 5, 1922, and May 31, 1924* (12 May 1926) LNTS Vol. LXXXIX, No. 2004; League of Nations, *Arrangement concerning the Extension to other Categories of Refugees of certain Measures taken in favour of Russian and Armenian Refugees* (30 June 1928) LNTS Vol. LXXXIX, No. 63; League of Nations, *Convention relating to the International Status of Refugees* (28 October 1933) LNTS Vol. CLIX, No. 3663; League of Nations, *Convention concerning the Status of Refugees coming from Germany, with Annex* (10 February 1938) LNTS Vol. CXCII, No. 4461; League of Nations, *Additional Protocol to the Provisional Arrangement and to the Convention, signed at Geneva on July 4th, 1936, and February 10th, 1938, respectively, concerning the Status of Refugees coming from Germany* (14 September 1939) LNTS Vol. CXCVIII, No. 4634; UN, *Final Act of the Intergovernmental Conference on the adoption of a travel document for Refugees and Agreement relating to the issue of a travel document to refugees who are the concern of the Intergovernmental Committee on Refugees* (15 October 1946) UNTS Vol. XI, No. 150; UN, *Convention on the Status of Refugees* (28 July 1951) UNTS Vol. 189, No. 2545; UN, *Protocol Relating to the Status of Refugees* (31 January 1967) UNTS Vol. 606, No. 8791.

 | DOI:10.1163/9789004722835_002

obligations is established,[3] and yet, the clear and distinct international obligations imposed by IRL on States appear not to correspond with demonstrable examples of those consequences that flow from the attribution of SR, namely the duty of reparation[4] or alternatively, recourse to countermeasures.[5] As Eagleton wrote in his seminal work on the international responsibility of States:

> The members of the community of nations have, in practice, agreed to respect certain principles for their mutual guidance; and, in so doing, it has been understood that they were thereby accepting obligations to observe the conduct prescribed.[6]

Unlike most other international conventions, the principal legal instrument of IRL – the 1951 *Convention Relating to the Status or Refugees* (1951 Convention)[7] – does not designate an authority to make pronouncements on matters of interpretation. In *Resolution 319 (IV)* of 3 December 1949, the UN General Assembly established a High Commissioner's Office for Refugees to commence work on 1 January 1951.[8] The *Statute of the Office of the United Nations High Commissioner for Refugees*, adopted by the General Assembly on 14 December 1950, endowed the High Commissioner with the competence to supervise the provision of international protection to refugees and to seek permanent solutions for the problem of refugees.[9] To that end, the Statute established that:

---

3 J.P.A. François, 'Régles générales du droit de la paix' (1938–IV) 66 RCADI 275; Charles de Visscher, *La responsabilité des États* (Bibliotheca Visseriana 1924) 90: "state responsibility is the 'necessary corollary' of the equality of States"; see also, Alain Pellet, 'The Definition of Responsibility in International Law' in James Crawford and others (eds), *The Law of International Responsibility* (OUP 2010) 3: "[R]esponsibility is the corollary of international law." Robert Kolb, *The International Law of State Responsibility* (Edward Elgar 2018).

4 International Law Commission, *Responsibility of States for Internationally Wrongful Acts* (2001) II (Part II) Yearbook of the International Law Commission, Articles 31, 34–39.

5 *Id.*, Articles 49–54.

6 Clyde Eagleton, *The Responsibility of States in International Law* (New York University Press 1928) 3.

7 UN General Assembly, *Convention Relating to the Status of Refugees* (28 July 1951) UNTS 189.

8 UN General Assembly, *Resolution 319(IV): Refugees and Stateless Persons* (3 December 1949) A/RES/319(IV).

9 UN General Assembly, *Resolution 428(V): Statute of the Office of the United Nations High Commissioner for Refugees* (14 December 1950) A/RES/428(V). Later, the 1951 Convention charged the High Commissioner for Refugees only with "the task of supervising international conventions providing for the protection of refugees." See: UN General Assembly, *Convention Relating to the Status of Refugees* (28 July 1951) UNTS 189, preambular para.

> The work of the High Commissioner shall be of an entirely non-political character; it shall be humanitarian and social and shall relate, as a rule, to groups and categories of refugees.[10]

Pursuant to paragraph 4 of the Statute, an Advisory Committee on Refugees was established by the UN Economic and Social Council to "advise the High Commissioner at his request in the exercise of his functions."[11] This was later reconstituted as the United Nations Refugee Fund (UNREF) Executive Committee,[12] replaced in 1958 by the *Executive Committee of the High Commissioner's Programme* (ExCom) to serve as the advisory committee foreseen in the UNHCR Statute.[13] The ExCom essentially retained the terms of reference of the Advisory Committee.[14]

Though Article 38 of the 1951 Convention provides that "[A]ny dispute between parties to this Convention relating to its interpretation or application, which cannot be settled by other means, shall be referred to the International Court of Justice at the request of any one of the parties to the dispute", the International Court of Justice (ICJ) is yet to be called upon to preside over any such dispute.[15] As an alternative to an international judicial entity, the ExCom and the UNHCR provide some interpretative authority on the application of IRL through conclusions and guidance notes, respectively, but neither can adequately fill the juridical void, and their pronouncements are, in any case, treated by States as subordinate to municipal law and jurisprudence.

---

10 *Id.*, 2.

11 UN Economic and Social Council, *Resolution 393(XIII): Refugees and Stateless Persons* (10 September 1951) E/RES/393(XIII).

12 UN Economic and Social Council, *Resolution 565(XIX): International Assistance to Refugees within the Mandate of the United Nations High Commissioner for Refugees* (31 March 1955) E/RES/565(XIX) adopted pursuant to UN General Assembly, *Resolution 832(IX): International Assistance to Refugees within the Mandate of the United Nations High Commissioner for Refugees* (21 December 1954) A/RES/832(IX).

13 UN General Assembly, *Resolution 1166(XII): International Assistance to Refugees within the Mandate of the United Nations High Commissioner for Refugees* (26 November 1957) A/RES/1166(XII); UN Economic and Social Council, *Resolution 672(XXV): Establishment of an Executive Committee of the Programme of the United Nations High Commissioner for Refugees* (30 April 1958) E/RES/672(XXV).

14 *Id.*

15 See: Nehemiah Robinson, *Convention Relating to the Status of Refugees: Its History, Significance and Contents* (Institute of Jewish Affairs 1952) 36: "The Convention leaves it to the parties to settle their disputes by whatever peaceful means they desire, such as by mediation or arbitration. If the dispute cannot be settled in another way, any party to the dispute may appeal to the International Court of Justice for a decision; the consent of the other party is not required."

The absence of an enforcement mechanism in IRL has frequently been lamented by scholars as its implicit frailty; a *lacuna* from which a wealth of legal complications have arisen.[16] It has led some to quite overstate the role of International Human Rights Law (IHRL) as a kind of remedial system of IL that substitutes these implicit failures and all but renders IRL defunct.[17] Whether or not the absence of a judicial authority on IRL is quite the problem some scholars believe it to be, the deficiency itself is worthy of some attention, as those consequences that ordinarily arise in general IL from the attribution of SR do not arise in IRL. This is particularly significant where States have not only failed collectively to respect the most fundamental tenets of IRL, but have made concerted, collective efforts to contravene them, and to reinforce the legitimacy of those contraventions through the adoption of municipal and regional law and policy. Furthermore, there remains the obvious complication that, as IRL is primarily implemented at IL through IHRL, general rules of SR have limited effect; IHRL being one of those 'self-contained regimes of international law'[18] that does not derive rules of attribution from general IL. The relevance of SR to IRL is therefore derived from sources outside those inferred in relation to systems of IL that do not rely on complementary implementation.

That said, the collective effort of certain States to pursue an international consensus on the modification of certain critical precepts of IRL is not sufficiently explained by the lack of an interpretative or judicial authority, neither of which are preconditions for the attribution of SR. Instead, the absence of SR

16 James C. Hathaway, Hugo Storey, 'What Is the Meaning of State Protection in Refugee Law – A Debate' (2016) 28(3) International Journal of Refugee Law 480, 482; James C. Hathaway, 'The Architecture of the UN Refugee Convention and Protocol' in Cathryn Costello, Michelle Foster and Jane McAdam (eds), *The Oxford Handbook of International Refugee Law* (OUP 2021) 171, 172; Ruvi Ziegler, 'International Humanitarian Law and Refugee Protection' in Cathryn Costello, Michelle Foster and Jane McAdam (eds), *The Oxford Handbook of International Refugee Law* (OUP 2021) 221, 222.

17 See in particular, Vincent Chetail, 'Are Refugee Rights Human Rights? An Unorthodox Questioning of the Relations between Refugee Law and Human Rights Law' in Ruth Rubio-Marín (ed), *Human Rights and Immigration* (OUP 2014) 19; Vincent Chetail, 'Moving Towards an Integrated Approach of Refugee Law and Human Rights Law' in Cathryn Costello, Michelle Foster and Jane McAdam (eds), *The Oxford Handbook of International Refugee Law* (OUP 2021) 202, 212–213; See also, James C. Hathaway, Michelle Foster, *The Law of Refugee Status* (2 edn, CUP 2014) 1: Refugee law is an "international human rights mechanism." A more nuanced position is advanced by Guy S. Goodwin-Gill, 'The Language of Protection' (1989) 1(1) IJRL 6, 16.

18 Bruno Simma, Dirk Pulkowski, 'Of Planets and the Universe: Self-Contained Regimes in International Law' (2006) 17(3) Eur J Int'l L 483.

in IRL is the product of a long, complex, and varied history, integrating political and economic considerations. This is not an accident of history, nor is it only a consequence of contemporary State conduct. Rather, as this book demonstrates, since the inception of IRL it has been the clear objective of Western States – constituted primarily by the United States, the United Kingdom, Western and Northern States of the European Union, and Australia – to minimise the scope and content of their international obligations and thus of circumstances capable of engaging questions of SR, reinforced at certain critical junctures, where large-scale refugee crises have permitted a rapid development of IL and policy. These critical junctures align with Haddad's broader categorisation of the "three main phases in dealing with the issue of refugees in the twentieth century – the inter-war, the Cold War and the post-Cold War."[19] More specifically, they correspond with the forced displacement of Russian, Armenian, Greek, and Turkish populations during the inter-war period, the refugee crises that unfolded across the African continent in the 1960s and 1970s, the Indo-Chinese refugee crisis of the 1970s, the mass displacement following the break-up of the former Yugoslavia in the 1990s, the rapid influx of refugees to Europe in 2014–2015, and most recently, the massive northward mixed migration from Latin America and the Caribbean to the US. More than any other, these events have guided and framed the theorisation and application of SR in IRL.

1 The Alien and the Refugee in the Law of State Responsibility

In all respects and at all stages, the development of SR – both as a concept and as law – has been concerned with the alien; first with his protection, then with his exclusion. Where a State of origin was unable to fulfil certain obligations to its subjects residing abroad, it effectively delegated its sovereign authority to protect such persons to the host State, who in turn became legally responsible for the alien. The nationality of the individual, and his foreign residence, served as the nexus between State of origin and host State that in turn formed the substantive basis of SR. As such, this system of PIL was, from its infancy, inextricably linked to the protection of non-nationals.[20]

Early international doctrine relative to the law of aliens was in essence supported by two principles: the so-called 'international standard of justice,'

19 Emma Haddad, *The Refugee in International Society: Between Sovereigns* (CUP 2008) 5.

20 Louis B. Sohn, R.R. Baxter, 'Responsibility of States for Injuries to the Economic Interests of Aliens: I. Introduction' (1961) 55(3) AJIL 545.

and the principle of equality between nationals and aliens. Where an alien had suffered an injury by a host State, the State of origin invoked the international standard of justice in order to exercise its sovereign authority to protect its national abroad. In response, the host State asserted its ability to provide the alien with judicial recourse, equal to that of nationals. Each competing principle was at the disposal of one State party to the dispute; each was employed to neutralise the other; each was concerned with the protection of the alien; and each was reliably successful according to the power of the State exercising it.

Over the course of the 19th and 20th centuries, the power dynamics between States exercising rights under the law of aliens developed to exclude the alien entirely and quite deliberately from its scope; States often going to great lengths to legally and logically strain fundamental precepts of IL to minimise SR in respect of injuries to aliens, so that even in the event of an injury inflicted by a host State, the international standard of justice could not be triggered. Once a legal doctrine primarily concerned with the alien, SR was reconceived as a series of generalised secondary rules, repeatedly appraised and revised by legal actors, and articulated finally in the International Law Commission's (ILC) *Articles on the Responsibility of States for Internationally Wrongful Acts* (ARSIWA).[21] In contemporary IL, the underlying principles of 'traditional' SR – being the diplomatic protection of the alien – are now generally considered to have been subsumed by IHRL, and replaced with the secondary rules of general responsibility as conceived by Roberto Ago during his tenure as the ILC's second Special Rapporteur for the responsibility of States for internationally wrongful acts.

The eventual position of the alien as a peripheral figure in SR in turn effected the position of the refugee in modern IRL, as the latter was not constructed from a void of doctrinal principles, but from existing legal precepts, namely the law of aliens. In that sense, the impetus for the development of SR, and its trajectory in respect of injuries to aliens, are necessary preconditions to any thorough analysis of the application and theorisation of SR in respect of IRL. As a derivative of the law of aliens, early IRL was preoccupied with the question of citizenship in a way that contemporary IRL is not. Questions of citizenship and the absence of State protection deriving from it, have since been delineated and are addressed as the separate and distinct phenomenon

---

21 International Law Commission, *Responsibility of States for Internationally Wrongful Acts* 2001) II (Part II) Yearbook of the International Law Commission; UN General Assembly, *Resolution 56/83: Responsibility of States for Internationally Wrongful Acts* (28 January 2002) A/RES/56/83.

of statelessness (though one can certainly be both a refugee and stateless), but in the first half of the 20th century, these statuses did not enjoy a clear legal demarcation. Rather, the existence of the individual in IL – and consequently, his protection – relied on the bond of nationality. Without it, he remained an 'unprotected alien,' and as an unprotected alien, no State could legally assume international obligations for his diplomatic protection. Jessup summarised in the following terms the importance of citizenship to SR:

> The concepts of alienage and citizenship are based on the notion that the individual has no legal significance from the standpoint of international law save as he is related to one state through the bond of citizenship or nationality and thus stands in relation to other states in the role of alien. The responsibility of states for injuries to an individual is owed under international law to another state and not to the individual. Thus there is no responsibility if the injured individual is stateless, that is has no nationality.[22]

The question arises, whether a system of IL relative to the refugee exists in the absence of SR, or whether that absence has permitted the devolution of IRL to a multitude of fractured municipal and regional regimes that are ever more restrictive of the rights they afford to beneficiaries of international protection. As Kolb notes, "[i]f the legal rule could be infringed without legal consequences, this would be tantamount to saying that the law does not contain binding prescriptions."[23] As with any other system of PIL, the obligations of IRL require some mode of expression through the consequences and sanctions of SR if they are indeed to be considered rules of IL.[24] In the absence of demonstrable legal consequences flowing from the attribution of a wrongful act, IRL remains exceptional, and the rationale for this exception-

---

22 Philip C. Jessup, *A Modern Law of Nations* (Archon Books 1968) 9, cited in Antonio Fortín, 'The Meaning of Protection in the Refugee Definition' (2000) 12(4) International Journal of Refugee Law 548, 556. Emphasis added.

23 Robert Kolb, *The International Law of State Responsibility* (Edward Elgar 2018) 1, citing, *inter alia*, Alain Pellet, 'The Definition of Responsibility in International Law' in Crawford and others (eds), *The Law of International Responsibility* (OUP 2010); J.P.A. François, 'Régles générales du droit de la paix' (1938–IV) 66 RCADI; Hermann Mosler, 'The International Society as a Legal Community' (1974–IV) 140 RCADI 172.

24 Again, this refers to international obligations arising between States, requiring actions *inter se*, as opposed to international obligations as they relate to the individual as a subject of IL.

alism merits inquiry. A thorough analysis of traditional SR as it concerned the alien is consequential not only to the theorisation and application of SR in IRL, but to the ongoing effectiveness of IRL as a system of PIL.

2 On Responsibility and Obligation

Any discussion of SR within legal scholarship must first clarify whether it is in fact speaking of responsibility or obligation. Though the terms are often conflated colloquially, they are not synonymous in law. Responsibility, in the legal sense, does not denote a requirement, but an ability to respond where a requirement is unfulfilled. In her treatise *The Need for Roots*, Simone Weil distinguished between 'obligation' and 'rights' in the following terms that are equally applicable to the legal relationship between 'obligation' and 'responsibility':

> The notion of obligations comes before that of rights, which is subordinate and relative to the former. A right is not effectual by itself, but only in relation to the obligation to which it corresponds, the effective exercise of a right springing not from the individual who possesses it, but from other men who consider themselves as being under a certain obligation towards him. Recognition of an obligation makes it effectual.[25]

Just as obligation comes before rights, so too is obligation a precondition for responsibility, which is equally subordinate and relative to the former. Just as a right is not effectual by itself, so too must responsibility correspond with an existing obligation. Just as a right requires that others consider themselves bound by it, legal responsibility may only result from an obligation that is recognised as such by a State that is required to fulfil it. This is the essence of the legal relationship between primary and secondary rules, or between treaty and SR: "[t]he law of treaties is the start of the story, i.e. the place where the rules are created; and the law of State responsibility is the end of the story, where, at the other extreme of the spectrum, the fate of the rules created through the sources is decided once they are breached."[26] Weil's rationale for the consequential relationship between obligations and rights is much

25 Simone Weil, *The Need for Roots: Prelude to a Declaration of Duties towards Mankind* (Routledge 1952) (*L'Enracinement* was first published 1949 by Editions Gallimard, Paris).
26 Robert Kolb, *The International Law of State Responsibility* (Edward Elgar 2018) vii.

the same as the legal rationale advanced by Eagleton and Kolb in relation to international obligation and SR.[27] The dependency of an international legal order on SR requires more than abstract concepts of a moral duty of States. It must entail instances of the attribution of SR for violations of IL, and in the absence of such, the question may legitimately be asked, 'is this international obligation indeed a requirement of IL?'

Within legal literature and discourse, there is often a conflation of the terms 'State responsibility' and 'State obligation,' with the former used more often than not to describe what is in fact the latter. In a similar vein, there is a frequent lack of clarity in the distinction between the domestic and international contexts, and the operation of both State obligation and SR within either realm. Within the international context, the term SR is often employed to refer synonymously to what is essentially a State's moral duty; the actions that a State *ought* to take in light of what is generally considered just. Similarly, the international obligations of States – often characterised improperly as 'international SR' – frequently refer to the actions of a State within its own jurisdiction and subject to its own municipal laws, where responsibility derives not from an explicit international obligation, but from a perceived 'internationalised' moral duty, though it is well-established in IL that "[c]ompliance with municipal law and compliance with the provisions of a treaty are different questions," and that "[W]hat is a breach of treaty may be lawful in the municipal law and what is unlawful in the municipal law may be wholly innocent of violation of a treaty provision."[28] Eagleton summarised this distinction in the following terms:

> [W]hile the responsibility of a state is fundamentally based upon the control which it exercises within its borders, it does not follow that the state may be held responsible for any injury occurring therein. The law of nations does not make the state a guarantor of life and property. It is

27 These are in turn based on the legal theories of Vattel and much later, Kelsen. See generally: Emer de Vattel, *Droit des gens ou principes de la loi naturelle appliqués à la conduite & aux affaires des Nations et des Souverains, Tome II* (London 1758); Hans Kelsen, 'Theorie Generale du Droit International' (1932) 42 RCADI 121.

28 *Elettronica Sicula S.p.A.* (*ELSI*) (*USA v Italy*) [1989] ICJ Rep 1573. Article 3 of the Articles on the Responsibility of States for Internationally Wrongful Acts (ARSIWA) state: "The characterization of an act of a State as internationally wrongful is governed by international law. Such characterization is not affected by the characterization of the same act as lawful by internal law." See: UN General Assembly, *Resolution 56/83: Responsibility of States for Internationally Wrongful Acts* (28 January 2002) A/RES/56/83.

> answerable, under international law, only for those injuries which are internationally illegal in character, and which can be fastened upon the state itself.[29]

This book is wholly concerned with responsibility in the legal sense. It does not seek to exhaustively catalogue those primary obligations that constitute IRL, nor does it analyse the scope and content of those obligations, beyond what is appropriate to substantiate the analysis of SR in IRL. It encompasses only those secondary consequences that arise between States for violations of the primary obligations of IRL. As a consequence, it is concerned only with the horizontal relationship between States, and necessarily excludes any consideration of SR as it relates to the vertical relationship between State and individual. It addresses SR from its two contrapositions: its doctrinal principles and theoretical foundations, and its implementation as a responsibility regime applicable to IRL. Despite the lack of clear instances of attribution of SR in IRL, a prodigious number of measures have been taken to nullify, exclude, or otherwise frustrate its practical application. This is worthy of exploration. As responsibility regimes in practice must be "tested against the framework of functionality in order to analyse how well the regime and its rules correspond to the changing international social and legal settings,"[30] the functionality of SR in IRL should be tested against those rules that have coalesced around a consensus in social and legal settings. Just as obligation and responsibility are complementary, so too are the theoretical and the practical elements of SR, and a thorough comprehension of one necessarily requires the other. Together, they inform the consequences of wrongfulness, situating it 'between illegality and liability.'[31] Furthermore, the theoretical and practical elements of SR in IRL are essential to those broader political, economic, and social elements that have informed it. As Creutz notes:

---

29 Clyde Eagleton, *The Responsibility of States in International Law* (New York University Press 1928), 8.

30 Katja Creutz, *State Responsibility in the International Legal Order: A Critical Appraisal* (CUP 2020).

31 Philip Allott, 'State Responsibility and the Unmaking of International Law' (1988) 29(1) Harv Int'l LJ 6 (fn 18), cited in Christian J. Tams, 'Law-Making in Complex Processes: The World Court and the Modern Law of State Responsibility' in Christine Chinkin and Freya Baetens (eds), *Sovereignty, Statehood and State Responsibility* (CUP 2015) 289.

> [T]here are some issues of international law to which state responsibility appears unconnected. Such issues concern, for example, 'allocation of powers and relationships'.[32]

A truer statement could not be written of the complications that have arisen and continue to arise between States in relation to IRL, which, perhaps more than any other system of IL, is rooted in the practice and evolving doctrine of States, and on power and relationships. The continued relevance of SR in IRL is that its "theoretical significance must be accompanied by meeting the demands of international social reality."[33] That 'international social reality' of power and relationships has created an international responsibility regime in IRL that is mutually reinforced through the theory and practice of those States that define the scope and content of international obligations.

In both its exploration of the theoretical and the practical, this book is based on the same fundamental premise that informs both the development of international legal theory and doctrine, and the practice of States: that the attribution of SR is a primary consideration that guides the decisions of States to be bound by IL. Both theoretical and practical conceptions of SR flow from the same basic premise: that SR is 'the general condition under international law for the State to be considered responsible for wrongful actions or omissions, and the legal consequences which flow therefrom.'[34] Contemporary challenges to SR as it relates to IRL are no different to those encountered in other systems of IL: they are both theoretical and practical, and as practice is founded on theory, and theory reinforced by practice, both SR as it has been conceptualised in law, and SR as it manifests in practice, must both form part of a broader understanding of its meaning and relevance. As this book is a study of an absence rather than a presence, both conceptions of SR are fundamental to provide an account for that absence. The three parts of this book broadly reflect those theoretical and practical explorations.

---

32 Katja Creutz, *State Responsibility in the International Legal Order: A Critical Appraisal* (CUP 2020) 16, citing Ian Brownlie, 'State Responsibility and the International Court of Justice' in Malgosia Fitzmaurice and Dan Sarooshi (eds), *Issues of State Responsibility before International Judicial Institutions* (Bloomsbury 2004) 13. See generally: B.S. Chimni, *International Law and World Order: A Critique of Contemporary Approaches* (CUP 2017), in particular, 56–72.

33 Katja Creutz, *State Responsibility in the International Legal Order: A Critical Appraisal* (CUP 2020) 15.

34 International Law Commission, *Draft articles on Responsibility of States for Internationally Wrongful Acts, with Commentaries* (2001) II (Part II) Yearbook of the International Law Commission, para 1.

3 On Responsibility and Morality

The legal scholarship on SR and IRL is limited, and for that reason, it is closely interconnected and self-referential. As a consequence, much of it derives from the same sources, and relies on specific conceptions of the legal bases of SR and its application to IRL. A significant limitation in the relevant literature and discourse on SR in IRL is the over-reliance on the ARSIWA.[35] It is at times presumed that the ARSIWA provide such a comprehensive enumeration of the principles of SR that nothing beyond its ambit may be properly characterised as such. Additionally, the ARSIWA are often referenced as if they were imbued with the same legal qualities as other binding international instruments, capable of establishing *per se* the existence of an internationally wrongful act in the absence of clear primary rules of IL. There is a temptation – particularly in IRL, where the moral and ethical treatment of refugees motivates a degree of academic activism – to begin with one of the numerous constructions of SR provided by the ARSIWA, and adapt a given scenario or variation of refugeehood to the chosen construction in order to demonstrate the proscribed nature of the conduct. Such arguments not only present a broad reliance on the ARSIWA as the sole arbiter of SR, but regard it as if it were an instrument of IL; as binding as a treaty, without the requirement of a corresponding international obligation. This presumes the attribution of wrongfulness in the absence of a clear primary rule. It is worth mentioning also that many such arguments concern the responsibility of the State of origin, to whom no primary rules of IRL attach.

These lines of inquiry often tangentially derive SR from sources of law external to either IRL, or the broader doctrine of SR that exists outside the scope of the ARSIWA, typically attributing wrongfulness with reference to municipal laws or moral precepts. None attempts to resolve the question of how these two systems of IL interact; neither the doctrine of SR in IRL, nor the historical significance of the refugee to SR.

Collectively, the literature reflects the same errors identified by former ILC Special Rapporteur on the Responsibility of States for Internationally Wrongful Acts, Gaetano Arangio-Ruiz, who attributes certain conceptual errors in the relevant scholarship to an uncritical reliance on the normative theory of

35 International Law Commission, *Report of the International Law Commission on the work of its fifty-third session, 23 April – 1 June and 2 July – 10 August 2001, Official Records of the General Assembly, Fifty-sixth session, Supplement No. 10* (2001) (A/56/10).

attribution, and its reduction to mere doctrine, rather than "a provision of general import applying to all the ILC Articles on State Responsibility [...]."[36] In the opinion of Arangio-Ruiz, the normative theory of attribution fails on two crucial accounts: First, it relies on an erroneous reading of arbitral and judicial decisions as endorsing a normative theory of attribution by the mere recognition of a link of factual causality, rather than the attribution of conduct to the State as a subject of IL based on criteria determined by IL.[37] Second, it rests on a fundamental error regarding the theoretical foundation that underpins SR, based on certain deductive premises, specifically, the concept of international and national law as parts of one and the same legal system. This is in turn based on the presumption that the latter forms the basis of a set of customary international rules on attribution.[38]

These same conceptual errors appear to underpin the aforementioned deficiencies in the relevant literature. The attribution of SR in IRL seems to rely on the recognition of factual causality, based on rules of attribution taken from municipal law, and the proscribed nature of certain conduct within domestic contexts. The conflation of obligation and responsibility, the lack of distinction between domestic and international contexts, and the mischaracterisation of the ARSIWA as a comprehensive legal instrument, account only for attribution as a normative, rather than a factual exercise. As attribution of SR relies on the existence of an international obligation, and must be strictly

36 Gaetano Arangio-Ruiz, 'State Responsibility Revisited. The Factual Nature of the Attribution of Conduct to the State' (2017) C Quaderni della rivista di diritto internazionale 1–2.

37 *Id.*, 1, citing para 4 of the International Law Commission, *Draft articles on Responsibility of States for Internationally Wrongful Acts, with Commentaries* 2001) II (Part II) Yearbook of the International Law Commission: "As a normative operation, attribution must be clearly distinguished from the characterization of the conduct as internationally wrongful. Its concern is to establish that there is an act of the State for the purposes of responsibility. To show that conduct is attributable says nothing, as such, about the legality or otherwise of that conduct, and rules of attribution should not be formulated in terms which imply otherwise. But the different rules of attribution stated in Chapter II have a cumulative effect, such that a State may be responsible for the effects of the conduct of private parties, if it failed to take necessary measures to prevent those effects. For example a receiving State is not responsible, as such, for the acts of private individuals in seizing an embassy, but it will be responsible if it fails to take all necessary steps to protect the embassy from seizure, or to regain control over it. In this respect there is often a close link between the basis of attribution and the particular obligation said to have been breached, even though the two elements are analytically distinct."

38 Arangio-Ruiz, *id.*, 8.

determined pursuant to IL (as is specified in the ARSIWA and its accompanying commentary),[39] the body of relevant literature suffers from the same general deficiency that Arangio-Ruiz identified in SR scholarship more broadly, premised on the simple fact that "failing ascription to a State, no internationally wrongful act (and consequent responsibility) would even be conceivable."[40] Such misconceptions of SR have not only produced a disjointed body of scholarship, but have allowed the discourse to stray into the realm of morality and ethics, and away from the strictly legal precepts of violation, attribution, and reparation.

> When a certain prescription gives rise to the consequences of responsibility, this prescription will be called legal; conversely, if it does not produce such consequences, the prescription will remain outside the bounds of strict law, in the confines of soft law, or political or moral obligations. Its breach may well then provoke an array of other consequences, such as political reprimand, but it will not give rise to legal responsibility.[41]

Article 3 of the ARSIWA addresses a slightly different, but nonetheless related construction of the municipal–international relationship. The characterisation of an act of a State as internationally wrongful is governed by IL alone. It is not affected by the characterisation of the same act as lawful or otherwise in municipal law. This is true even where the conduct in question violates a provision of the State's own law.

The origins of these conceptual errors are likely attributable to the fact that, as previously mentioned, IRL it has no international arbiter; neither an international judicial body, nor a treaty body that makes pronouncements on its interpretation and application. It remains the remit of domestic and certain regional judicial bodies to interpret and apply principles of IRL in line with corresponding municipal and regional laws relative to asylum seekers and refugees as the beneficiaries of the 1951 Convention and subjects of IL. These

---

39 International Law Commission, *Responsibility of States for Internationally Wrongful Acts* (2001) II (Part II) Yearbook of the International Law Commission Article 1; International Law Commission, *Draft Articles on Responsibility of States for Internationally Wrongful Acts, with Commentaries* (2001) II (Part II) Yearbook of the International Law Commission, commentary to Article 1, pg 32.

40 Simple though it is, Arangio-Ruiz has noted that "that error is a very common one." See: Gaetano Arangio-Ruiz, 'State Responsibility Revisited. The Factual Nature of the Attribution of Conduct to the State' (2017) C Quaderni della rivista di diritto internazionale 12.

41 Robert Kolb, *The International Law of State Responsibility* (Edward Elgar 2018) 2.

are invariably adjudicated under IHRL in the international sphere, or immigration law in the municipal. This is not in itself an irregularity when it comes to SR as "many issues of responsibility involving individuals or other subjects of IL are ultimately settled in municipal law under municipal law statutes."[42] But the conclusion that an internationally wrongful act may be inferred from a judicial decision at the municipal level appears to rest primarily on the premise that such decisions correspond with either of the two primary pillars of IRL: refugee status (Article 1A), and *non-refoulement* (Article 33). The litigation of these international norms within domestic or regional contexts has been taken at times as evidence of a functioning system that attributes SR. This is not the case. Normative developments at municipal and regional levels do not necessarily represent parallel developments at IL, or otherwise form the basis of an international normative framework. The lack of a clear distinction between municipal and international law is cited once again by Arangio-Ruiz as a general deficiency in the relevant scholarship.

Similarly, as Eagleton wrote, "the study of the responsibility of states in international law involves an examination of the theory upon which reparation may be demanded by one state of another, and of the processes by which it may be obtained."[43] SR is not attributable to a State simply by the determination that there is a duty owed, but in claiming the *performance* of that duty.[44] This construction of SR may be considered excessively narrow by some, but it has the advantage of excluding those arguments that are based predominantly on assertions that an obligation violated is akin to SR attributed. The fact remains that SR requires the attribution of conduct in order to fulfil the 'law of international obligations,' which requires both international obligation and international responsibility.[45] This is the minimum level at which the law should be regarded as being 'effective', that is, "binding and by that fact legal rather than moral."[46]

Since the inception of the 1951 Convention, there has been a litany of State-led initiatives that have consolidated certain policies relative to the interpretation and application of IRL, many of which have resulted in claiming the performance of duties alluded to as being part of IRL. Yet each of these initia-

42 *Id.*, 16.

43 Clyde Eagleton, *The Responsibility of States in International Law* (New York University Press 1928), 3.

44 *Id.*

45 Robert Kolb, *The International Law of State Responsibility* (Edward Elgar 2018), vii, though Kolb considers that it is possible to speak abstractly of responsibility where there is an internationally wrongful act but no attribution. See 34.

46 *Id.*, 1.

tives has, in one way or another, facilitated the legitimisation of restrictive practices primarily relating to the reception of refugees, and now increasingly, to their 'safe, orderly, and lawful' arrival,[47] making the implied duty of performance an abuse of SR. Herein lies the most consequential limitation presented by the absence of an oversight mechanism in IRL. The absence of a global oversight mechanism has permitted IRL to develop for the benefit of particular States,[48] in particular, Western States; increasingly shielded from becoming 'States of arrival' and instead permitted to designate themselves almost exclusively as 'States of resettlement,' while the vast majority of refugees remain in those States geographically proximate to the State of origin. This inevitably leads to a "lack of 'clear parameters [to] describe how states should help one another with hosting refugees' and the crisis in the global economic order that fosters even more restrictive policies on the part of countries of prospective asylum."[49]

As SR is not constituted simply by the determination of a duty owed, but in claiming the performance of that duty, the attribution of wrongfulness alone does not aid in the determination of prescribed or proscribed conduct for the purposes of establishing SR. To amalgamate the theses of Weil and Arangio-Ruiz, obligation comes before responsibility, which is subordinate and relative to the former, and the realisation of responsibility is affected not by the mere recognition of a factual context, but by States who consider themselves bound by such obligations. All this ultimately relies on a clear articulation of attribution as a legal measure, rather than merely a doctrinal exercise. If one accepts this construction as 'the law of international obligations,' then one must also accept that IRL has remained an outlier in PIL since its inception. This book is concerned ultimately with this fact, and the rationale for it.

47 See Chapter 6.

48 As Hathaway has noted: "[t]he modern apparatus of international refugee law is more closely tied to the safeguarding of developed states than to the vindication of claims to protection." See: James C. Hathaway, 'A Reconsideration of the Underlying Premise of Refugee Law' (1990) 31(1) Harv Int'l LJ 129, 175, citing Guy S. Goodwin-Gill, 'Refugees: The Functions and Limits of the Existing Protection System' in Alan E. Nash (ed), *Human Rights and the Protection of Refugees Under International Law* (Canadian Human Rights Foundation 1988) 142, 168–169.

49 Peter Gatrell, *The Making of the Modern Refugee* (OUP 2013) 200, citing UN High Commissioner for Refugees, *The State of the World's Refugees: In Search of Solidarity* (UNHCR 2012) chapter 8.

4 State Responsibility and the State of Origin

Where it pertains to IRL, much of contemporary legal scholarship on SR is premised on the obligations of the State of origin; both those obligations considered to be moral and just, and those that are affected by its municipal laws, and characterised as the State's 'duty to protect' its subjects. This is commonly predicated on the assumption of a moral obligation, attributable to the State of origin, principally for wrongful conduct related to causation. That is, that the State ought to bear responsibility for the failure to protect persons that later become refugees, and the subsequent creation of conditions affecting refugee movement. This is not an academic innovation. The attribution of SR to States of origin was, for many years, a preoccupation of the League of Nations (LoN) and later the UN, though as a legal question it found no resolution.[50] But, the assertion is invariably predicated on the attribution of SR for injuries purportedly sustained by States of reception, which requires reparation for the 'injury' caused by the heavy burden imposed by hosting a refugee population. Such arguments are, in reality, far more concerned with broad questions of human rights and international relations than with IRL or SR, though as a precedent, it would be no less hazardous under any other system of IL.

The vast majority of these assertions can be traced back to a single source – R.Y. Jennings' 1939 article, 'Some International Law Aspects of the Refugee Question', in which he posited that "[I]f the conduct of the state of origin be in the first place illegal, it seems to follow that it is under a duty to assist settlement states in the solution of the problem to which it has given rise.'[51] But while Jennings devoted only a few pages to the question of SR and the State of origin, and concluded only that there "seem[ed] to be good ground for stating that the wilful flooding of other states with refugees constitutes not merely an inequitable act, but an actual illegality," the question raised in his article inspired further scholarship on the subject, much of which unduly attributes a degree of certainty and insistence to Jennings' article, concluding that State of origin responsibility is a well-founded principle of PIL.

To that end, commentators appear to have formed a consensus that there could be, or should be, an international legal injury attached to the creation or exacerbation of refugee movement, though there remains a distinct lack of clarity as to the precise content of the legal obligation that would establish

---

50 The attribution of SR to States of origin is discussed in Chapters 2 and 5.

51 R. Yewdall Jennings, 'Some International Law Aspects of the Refugee Question' (1939) 20 BYIL 98, 113.

such a responsibility, and the mechanism through which it would be enforced. This appears to be based largely on a moral imperative rather than a legal obligation. Some assert that such an obligation is inherent and may be derived from the moral offence of having caused displacement,[52] or rely on legal derivatives taken from broad norms of municipal immigration law. Akhavan and Bergsmo, for example, argue that the principle that States may not create international displacement is supported "by the unequivocal duty of states to re-admit nationals."[53]

Also drawn from Jennings' 1939 article, several scholars have treated the question of SR and the State of origin as subject to the same principles as certain international injuries, decided before the ICJ, specifically, the legal maxim, *sic utere tuo ut alienum non laedas* (use your own property in such a manner as not to injure that of another). The maxim itself is derived from Roman law, and was applied over centuries to civil proceedings concerning injuries arising from the use of property causing damage to the property of another, particularly in the US and the UK.[54] In IL, the principle has been applied in environmental cases concerning transboundary harm, where the use of property by one State (or authorised private use) has been to the detriment or injury of another, most notably in the *Trail Smelter* arbitration,[55] in which the US was awarded compensation for the transboundary air pollution emanating from a smelter in Trail, British Columbia.[56] Proponents of the application of this maxim to IRL assert that a State of reception may "resort to objective liability in the sense that a state of origin, whatever its human rights record, is duty-bound to repair the damage caused to other states by

52 Gervase J.L. Coles, *State Responsibility in Relation to the Refugee Problem, with Particular Reference to the State of Origin: A Study* (1993) 11; Paul Sieghart, *The International Law of Human Rights* (Clarendon Press 1983).

53 Payam Akhavan, Morten Bergsmo, 'The Application of the Doctrine of State Responsibility of Refugee Creating States' (1989) 58(3–4) Nordic J Int L 243, 247.

54 G.A.I. 'Sic Utere Tuo Ut Alienum Non Laedas' (1907) 5 MichLRev 673.

55 Jennifer Peavey Joanis, 'A Pyrrhic Victory: Applying the Trail Smelter Principle to State Creation of Refugees' in Rebecca M. Bratspies and Russell A. Miller (ed), *Transboundary Harm in International Law: Lessons from the Trail Smelter Arbitration* (CUP 2006) 254, 265; Gervase J.L. Coles, *State Responsibility in Relation to the Refugee Problem, with Particular Reference to the State of Origin: A Study* (1993), 146; Luke T. Lee, 'The Right to Compensation: Refugees and Countries of Asylum' (1986) 80(3) AJIL 532, 555; Rainer Hofmann, 'Refugee-Generating Policies and the Law of State Responsibility' (1985) 45 ZaöRV 694; Payam Akhavan, Morten Bergsmo, 'The Application of the Doctrine of State Responsibility of Refugee Creating States' (1989) 58(3–4) Nordic J Int L 243, 245.

56 *Trail Smelter Case* (*USA v Canada*) [1938 and 1941] RIAA 3.

the massive influx of its nationals into the territory of other states."[57] Coles and Hofmann both argued that there was a growing body of jurisprudence to support the notion that in IL, there had developed a "general rule limiting the sovereignty of states in as far as they may not allow activities on their territory which will cause damage on the territory of other states."[58] In his 1983 monograph, Goodwin-Gill expressed discomfort with the association of refugees with transboundary harm, but claimed that, unpleasant as the comparison may appear, "the basic issue [...] is the responsibility which derives from the fact of control over territory."[59]

Irrespective of the distasteful comparison between refugees and noxious fumes, there is no legal precedent for the application of the *sic utere* maxim where the property that has been used injuriously is not legal property.[60] The subjects of a State are not regarded as its legal property, and have not been regarded as such for a considerable time. For obvious reasons, IL reviles the treatment of persons as legal property. While the maxim captures, at least in part, some of the more tortious aspects of the regime Jennings imagined; namely, that intent is superfluous to injury, and that a violation of an established right will in general, *per se*, constitute an injury for which damages are recoverable,[61] there remains the invalid legal characterisation of a State's subjects as its *de jure* property, capable of causing international injury akin to transboundary harm.

---

57 Nafees Ahmad, 'Refugees: State Responsibility, Country of Origin and Human Rights' (2009) 10(2) Asia-Pac JHRL 1; see also: Payam Akhavan, Morten Bergsmo, 'The Application of the Doctrine of State Responsibility of Refugee Creating States' (1989) 58(3–4) Nordic J Int L 243, 246.

58 Rainer Hofmann, 'Refugee-Generating Policies and the Law of State Responsibility' (1985) 45 ZaöRV 694; Gervase J.L. Coles, *State Responsibility in Relation to the Refugee Problem, with Particular Reference to the State of Origin: A Study* (1993) 146, citing R. Yewdall Jennings, 'Some International Law Aspects of the Refugee Question' (1939) 20 BYIL 98; see also: Luke T. Lee, 'The Right to Compensation: Refugees and Countries of Asylum' (1986) 80(3) AJIL 532; Jack I. Garvey, 'Toward a Reformulation of International Refugee Law' (1985) 26(2) Harv Int'l LJ 483; John Fischer Williams, *Chapters on Current International Law and the League of Nations* (Longmans, Green and Co. 1929).

59 Guy S. Goodwin-Gill, *The Refugee in International Law* (Clarendon Press 1983), though in the 2007 edition, the references to *Trail Smelter* and transboundary harm for the creation of refugees are removed; see also: Jennifer Peavey Joanis, 'A Pyrrhic Victory: Applying the Trail Smelter Principle to State Creation of Refugees' in Miller (ed), *Transboundary Harm in International Law: Lessons from the Trail Smelter Arbitration* (CUP 2006) 254, 265.

60 Sophie Capicchiano Young, 'State Responsibility for COVID-19: Does International Contagion Constitute Transboundary Harm?' (2021) 11(2) Asian JIL 372.

61 G.A.I. 'Sic Utere Tuo Ut Alienum Non Laedas' (1907) 5 MichLRev 673.

This may be overcome, at least in Goodwin-Gill's construction, by the 'fact of control over territory;' the injury then arising from the wrongful use of a State's sovereign territory resulting in displacement. In a similar vein, it has also been argued that the 'creation' of refugees by the State of origin may be regarded as a violation of the State of reception's sovereignty,[62] an injury for which compensation may be due for "the costs of caring for refugees it generated not only directly, but also indirectly; for example, through actual or threatened military intervention in the internal affairs of a state resulting in the flight of the latter's citizens for fear of persecution."[63] Both proposals are morally questionable and legally unsound. First, it is not made clear to which international legal obligation the alleged violation attaches. It is not a requirement of IRL that a State of origin refrain from causing refugee movement. The 1951 Convention does not attach any international obligations to the State of origin in this regard or in any other. Second, this construction relies on the existence of an 'injury' – in this case, it is presumably a financial one – and yet damage is *not* a requirement for the attribution of SR. It is sufficient that a breach of an international obligation has occurred. Third, as an event characterised as transboundary harm specifically, it is not the use of the injurious State's sovereign territory that is the source of the State of reception's purported 'injury,' but the 'burden' placed on it by the presence of refugees. The causal nexus between injurious act and injury sustained then becomes far too abstract and tenuous to establish transboundary harm. Most importantly, alternative arguments concerning sovereignty are overcome by the simple fact of consent. States parties to the 1951 Convention and the 1967 *Protocol Relating to the Status of Refugees*[64] have given their consent to be bound by IRL in the knowledge that it requires certain conduct vis-à-vis refugees. In any case, States continue to retain legislative and administrative sovereignty in matters of municipal immigration law, and are, in many instances, provided with a margin of appreciation in extending certain benefits to refugees.[65]

A separate argument considers the ARSIWA construction of collective responsibility and applies it to situations of chain *refoulement* to argue that a

62 Luke T. Lee, 'The Right to Compensation: Refugees and Countries of Asylum' (1986) 80(3) AJIL 532, 532; Nafees Ahmad, 'Refugees: State Responsibility, Country of Origin and Human Rights' (2009) 10(2) Asia-Pac JHRL 1, 14.

63 Lee, *id.*, 558.

64 UN, *Protocol Relating to the Status of Refugees* (31 January 1967) UNTS Vol. 606, No. 8791.

65 In relation to numerous contingent rights, the 1951 Convention provides that States shall accord to refugees the same treatment as is accorded to aliens generally, and requires only 'sympathetic consideration' in relation to the conferral of other benefits.

plurality of States may be internationally responsible for the wrongful act of *refoulement*.[66] Others have made various assertions that the responsibility of States of origin for the creation of refugees may be established under the *Universal Declaration of Human Rights* (UDHR),[67] the *International Covenant on Civil and Political Rights* (ICCPR),[68] or even under the *Declaration on Principles of International Law concerning Friendly Relations and Co-operation among States*.[69] Tomuschat considers that State of origin responsibility may be derived from the ICCPR, as the right of everyone not to be deprived of the right to enter his own country under Article 12 "implicitly recognizes a right of abode."[70] According to Tomuschat, such a breach of an international engagement necessarily involves the obligation to make reparation per the principle established by the Permanent Court of International Justice in *Germany v Poland* (*Factory at Chorzów* case).[71]

The 'right of abode' also forms the basis of Ahmad's argument that, although the relevant human rights treaties remain largely silent on the issue of consequences deriving from non-compliance, the premise is always that a State must fulfil what it has formally pledged to do. Thus, to the extent that one may assume the existence of an individual entitlement under IL,

---

66 Maarten Den Heijer, 'Refoulement' in André Nollkaemper and Ilias Plakokefalos (ed), *The Practice of Shared Responsibility in International Law* (CUP 2017) 481, 482; Niels Frenzen, 'Extraterritorial Refugee Protection' in Nollkaemper and Plakokefalos' in André Nollkaemper and Ilias Plakokefalos (eds) (CUP 2017) 506, 510–513.

67 Luke T. Lee, 'The Right to Compensation: Refugees and Countries of Asylum' (1986) 80(3) AJIL 532, 539.

68 Nafees Ahmad, 'Refugees: State Responsibility, Country of Origin and Human Rights' (2009) 10(2) Asia-Pac JHRL 1 3–4; Christian Tomuschat, 'State Responsibility and the Country of Origin' in Vera Gowlland-Debbas (ed), *The Problem of Refugees in the Light of Contemporary International Law Issues* (Brill Nijhoff 1995) 42–43.

69 Payam Akhavan, Morten Bergsmo, 'The Application of the Doctrine of State Responsibility of Refugee Creating States' (1989) 58(3–4) Nordic J Int L 243, 248.

70 Christian Tomuschat, 'State Responsibility and the Country of Origin' in Gowlland-Debbas (ed), *The Problem of Refugees in the Light of Contemporary International Law Issues* (Brill Nijhoff 1995) 42–43.

71 *Id.*, 44, 46. In *Factory at Chorzów*, the Permanent Court of International Justice provided that:

"It is a principle of international law that the breach of an engagement involves an obligation to make reparation in an adequate form. Reparation therefore is the indispensable complement of a failure to apply a convention and there is no necessity for this to be stated in the convention itself."

See: *Case Concerning the Factory at Chorzów* (*Germany v Poland*) (Merits) [1928] PCIJ Series A No 17.

there exists a right to specific performance.[72] The "most pertinent right," Ahmad suggests, is that of every person to "live without disturbance" in his or her country, as derived from the ICCPR and the right of everyone not to be deprived of the right to enter their country of nationality, which implicitly recognises a right of abode.[73] A similar claim is made by Lee, that "[w]hen a state forces its citizens into becoming refugees either directly or indirectly, it is violating such movement-related provisions of the *Universal Declaration of Human Rights*.[74] In a somewhat extensive application of the UDHR, Lee claims that the creation of displacement constitutes a violation of all other Articles of the Declaration as the full and effective enjoyment of all Articles hinges on the ability of a person to live in his own country, which possibly even qualifies it as an international crime.[75] It is by this standard that Lee concludes "the country that turns its own citizens into refugees is in violation of *all* the articles of the Universal Declaration of Human Rights."[76]

This question of enforcement of SR *vis-à-vis* the State of origin commonly relies on the third pillar of the so-called 'responsibility to protect' (R2P); the collective obligation of States to protect a population whose State of origin manifestly fails to do so. Certain scholars have seemingly abandoned questions of legality and legitimate enforcement in favour of the moral imperative of the 'international community' to respond to displacement by means of intervention.[77] Those who propose such measures assert that the gravity of displacement may be such as to warrant international intervention by virtue of the doctrine of R2P. Cohen advocates for the application of R2P to situations of internal displacement but warns that the relationship between humanitarian issues and R2P raises a series of complicated questions that essentially concern the limits of such a response, the consistency of its application, and its susceptibility to realpolitik.[78] Cohen provides the example of

72 Nafees Ahmad, 'Refugees: State Responsibility, Country of Origin and Human Rights' (2009) 10(2) Asia-Pac JHRL 1, 7; Menno T. Kamminga, *Inter-State Accountability for Violations of Human Rights* (University of Pennsylvania Press 1992) 133–134.

73 *Id.*, 3–4.

74 Luke T. Lee, 'The Right to Compensation: Refugees and Countries of Asylum' (1986) 80(3) AJIL 532, 539.

75 *Id.*

76 *Id.*

77 Lindsey N. Kingston, Saheli Datta, 'Strengthening the Norms of Global Responsibility: Structural Violence in Relation to Internal Displacement and Statelessness' (2012) 4(4) Global Responsibility to Protect 475; Gareth Evans, *The Responsibility to Protect: Ending Mass Atrocity Crimes Once and For All* (Brookings Institution Press 2008) 4.

78 Roberta Cohen, *The Responsibility to Protect: Human Rights and Humanitarian Dimensions* (Brookings Institute 2009).

the Carter administration that did not act against the Khmer Rouge in Cambodia or institute economic sanctions against South Africa on account of its own political and economic interests, and of the failure of the permanent members of the UN Security Council to apply R2P to atrocities in Sudan, Somalia or the Democratic Republic of the Congo "in part because of the political and economic interests of members."[79]

Kingston, Datta, and Stahn summarise the realpolitik in such scenarios, warning that R2P should be understood partly as a political catchword that gained quick acceptance because it could be interpreted by different actors in different ways.[80] Kingston, Datta, and Bass warn that humanitarian intervention has the innate potential to become a means of neo-imperialism, and that there is a danger that the protracted imposition of R2P measures may escalate into a state of 'permanent emergency.'[81] Similarly, Bellamy cautions that strict limitations on the application of R2P are necessary to avoid abuse and manipulation of the norm where proponents of intervention are able to manipulate principles to support their agenda.[82] Cohen considers a principle issue in resolving the question of R2P and displacement to be the temporal scope of intervention measures, specifically, whether actions should extend beyond the initial violence that risks the displacement of a population in the name of effective protection, or whether any intervention should be limited in scope to preventing displacement.[83] However, this would presumably require the 'international community' to mobilise at the time that displacement was still internal, and prior to it becoming a matter of IRL in order to avoid the result of an international injury; the principal issue with that being that the 'international community' invariably refers to Western States who

79 *Id.*

80 Lindsey N. Kingston, Saheli Datta, 'Strengthening the Norms of Global Responsibility: Structural Violence in Relation to Internal Displacement and Statelessness' (2012) 4(4) Global Responsibility to Protect 475; Carsten Stahn, 'Responsibility to Protect: Political Rhetoric or Emerging Legal Norm?' (2007) 101(1) AJIL 99, 102.

81 Lindsey N. Kingston, Saheli Datta, 'Strengthening the Norms of Global Responsibility: Structural Violence in Relation to Internal Displacement and Statelessness' (2012) 4(4) Global Responsibility to Protect 482 citing Gary J. Bass, *Freedom's Battle: The Origins of Humanitarian Intervention* (Vintage Books 2008) 356, 365.

82 Alex J. Bellamy, 'Whither the Responsibility to Protect? Humanitarian Intervention and the 2005 World Summit' (2006) 20(2) Ethics & International Affairs 143, 169.

83 Roberta Cohen, *The Responsibility to Protect: Human Rights and Humanitarian Dimensions* (Brookings Institute 2009).

are historically the most egregious offenders in the exercise of realpolitik and neo-imperialism.

A further substantive argument considers offences of causation attributable to States of reception, particularly in relation to occupation and invasion, though it is a minority view. Souter has suggested that under certain conditions, asylum can serve as a remedy provided by States that are causally responsible for harm leading to displacement, though he contends that discerning causation and attribution in SR require a scalar approach in which an Iraqi refugee claiming asylum in the US since its invasion would have a stronger claim than a Rwandan seeking asylum in Belgium in account of past colonial rule. Nevertheless, he posits that reparative justice should be one amongst several considerations in prioritising claims for refugee status.[84] This proposal seemingly overlooks the unlikelihood in which a refugee would consider his situation remedied by the provision of refugee status by the same State that invaded his country and made his presence untenable in the first place.

With the exception of the first proposal regarding transboundary harm, which at least attempts to rationalise SR in respect of the international obligation to refrain from causing injury, each of these constructions considers the attribution of SR on the basis of general failures of States' implicit or moral duties in the absence of a clearly defined international obligation; far less one that is identifiable as forming part of IRL. In their determination to attribute SR as a means of coercing States into compliance with perceived internal duties, such proposals are predominantly based on the characterisation of refugees as capable of constituting an international injury. Furthermore, they rest on the purported obligation of the loosely defined 'international community' to take collective action, despite not having identified what egregious violations of IL would justify what are essentially countermeasures. This does not account for the realities of contemporary IRL and the political and economic considerations that continue to drive its development. They are in that sense, purely theoretical exercises that do not account for their own validity.

84 James Souter, 'Towards a Theory of Asylum as Reparation for Past Injustice' (2014) 62(2) Political Studies 326, 340, cited in Selya Benhabib, Nishin Nathwani, 'The Ethics of International Refugee Protection' in Cathryn Costello, Michelle Foster and Jane McAdam (eds), *The Oxford Handbook of International Refugee Law* (OUP 2021) 114, 121.

5 Race and the Development of IRL

Though it does not grapple directly with the question of SR in IRL, there is a particularly prevalent and interrelated theory in IRL scholarship that merits a brief, pre-emptive response: That is, that the scope and content of international obligations in IRL developed in response to changes in the ethnic origins of refugee populations – being that, at a certain point, they were no longer predominantly white or European.[85] Hathaway and Foster have asserted that due to "increasing numbers of refugees from countries that were politically, racially, and culturally 'different' from Western asylum countries, the historical openness of the developed world to refugee flows was replaced by a new commitment to exploit legal and other means to avoid the legal duty to admit refugees."[86]

This theory presupposes a number of factors. First, that the general global approach to refugee policies during the 1960s, 1970s and 1980s (being broadly the exchange of international humanitarian aid for local encampment, sometimes followed by swift repatriation), which coincided with these demographic changes, were born of some level of racial hostility that did not exist in previous decades in respect of other refugee populations, and did not play a role in the development of earlier responses to refugee crises, which were presumably, by comparison, far less influenced by questions of race. As a premise, this is demonstrably false. Indirectly, it ascribes a general 'whiteness' or 'European-ness' to previous refugee populations that does not account for conceptions of race and its conflation of nationality and religion at those material times, during which refugee populations were certainly not considered to be white or European. Most notably, it indirectly deems Jewish refugees – the most consequential refugees to contemporary IRL – as somehow considered homogenous or compatible with populations of Western States, rather than the objects of highly restrictive and exclusive immigration regimes, on the basis of 'race.'

Second, it does not consider the numerous political and economic factors that were integral to the theorisation and application of SR in IRL, to which

85 Rosemary Byrne, Andrew Shacknove, 'The Safe Country Notion in European Asylum Law' (1996) 9 Harv Hum Rts J 185, 213; Guy S. Goodwin-Gill, 'Asylum: The Law and Politics of Change' (1995) 7(1) IJRL 1, 5.

86 James C. Hathaway, Michelle Foster, 'Internal Protection/Relocation/Flight Alternative as an Aspect of Refugee Status Determination' in Erika Feller, Volker Türk and Frances Nicholson (eds), *Refugee Protection in International Law: UNHCR's Global Consultations on International Protection* (CUP 2003) 357, 359–360; James C. Hathaway, 'The Emerging Politics of Non-Entrée' (1992) 91 Refugees 40.

questions of race were irrelevant. As this book demonstrates, the scope and content of those obligations that constitute IRL are inextricably a reflection of States' priorities and apprehensions in forming and limiting the circumstances in which SR could be attributed. A sober examination of those factors is necessarily excluded by generalised pronouncements on matters of race.

Third, the argument seems to be regarded by its proponents as self-evident. Very little evidence is presented in support of this notion, though it is in reality a very serious charge that should require extensive substantiation. It appears to rest solely on the rise of the aid and development era of refugee protection and its correlation with massive refugee crises across Africa and Asia. Without discounting the role that race played in the trajectory of refugee policy in that era, correlation is not causation, and other pertinent events and considerations that discernibly contributed to the development of IRL should form part of any such evaluation.

6 The Scope and Content of This Book

The development of IL is not always linear but must account for a multitude of factors. Koskenniemi has noted that IL develops in shifts of emphasis between periods of confidence and confusion, routine and innovation, construction and critique.[87]

Haddad has made a similar observation in respect of IRL specifically: "[T]he fact that the way an issue is understood cannot be divorced from history or the political environment is frequently overlooked."[88] Both the history and the political environment in which SR and IRL developed are critical to any discussion about their contemporary interconnectedness. For that reason, "it makes most sense to approach this from the standpoint of *lex posterior derogat priori* because a chronological approach reveals the evolution of these obligations and provides the proper context."[89] This book comprehensively analyses the history, theory, and application of norms of SR in IRL, and those events, considerations, and external factors that shaped the development of

87 Martti Koskenniemi, *International Legal Theory and Doctrine* (Max Planck Encyclopedia of Public International Law, Max Planck Institute and OUP 2012) 1, 2.

88 Emma Haddad, *The Refugee in International Society: Between Sovereigns* (CUP 2008) 4.

89 Robert Barnidge, 'The Due Diligence Principle under International Law' (2006) 8(1) ICLR 81, 92.

those norms in relation to the latter. In particular, it is concerned with the limitation of the scope and content of international obligations where that limitation was demonstrably the result of concern regarding the attribution of SR. Its conclusions consider not only how SR has been theorised and applied to IRL, but what discernibly remains of SR in IRL and what the implications of that may be for IRL as a system of PIL.

It argues that the bases from which both SR and IRL evolved were not only interconnected but that SR was theorised and applied with a view to the minimisation of circumstances engaging SR relative to the treatment of non-nationals, and that this established the basis for its application to IRL. It demonstrates that persistent concerns about future legal questions regarding alienage, nationality, and immigration status played a significant role in the development of both SR, and later, IRL. The implications of this are significant, as they raise questions about the effectiveness of IRL as a system of PIL, and the ongoing role of IRL as capable of imposing international obligations on States vis-à-vis refugee protection.

The scope of what constitutes IRL is limited in this book to its primary international legal instruments, namely, the Arrangements of 5 July 1922,[90] 31 May 1924,[91] 12 May 1926,[92] 30 June 1928,[93] the Conventions of 28 October 1933,[94] and 10 February 1938,[95] the Protocol of 14 September 1939,[96] the Agree-

90 League of Nations, *Arrangement with respect to the issue of certificates of identity to Russian Refugees* (5 July 1922) LNTS Vol. XIII, No. 355.

91 League of Nations, 'Plan for the Issue of a Certificate of Identity to Armenian Refugees, 31st May 1924. Submitted for the consideration of interested governments by Dr. Nansen, High Commissioner for Russian Refugees in execution of the Resolution of the Council of the League' (1924) 5(7) LNOJ969.

92 League of Nations, *Arrangement relating to the Issue of Identity Certificates to Russian and Armenian Refugees, supplementing and amending the previous Arrangements dated July 5, 1922, and May 31, 1924* (12 May 1926) LNTS Vol. LXXXIX, No. 2004.

93 League of Nations, *Arrangement concerning the Extension to other Categories of Refugees of certain Measures taken in favour of Russian and Armenian Refugees* (30 June 1928) LNTS Vol. LXXXIX, No. 63.

94 League of Nations, *Convention relating to the International Status of Refugees* (28 October 1933) LNTS Vol. CLIX, No. 3663.

95 League of Nations, *Convention concerning the Status of Refugees coming from Germany, with Annex* (10 February 1938) LNTS Vol. CXCII, No. 4461.

96 League of Nations, *Additional Protocol to the Provisional Arrangement and to the Convention, signed at Geneva on July 4th, 1936, and February 10th, 1938, respectively, concerning the Status of Refugees coming from Germany* (14 September 1939) LNTS Vol. CXCVIII, No. 4634.

ment of 15 October 1946,[97] the Convention of 28 July 1951,[98] and the Protocol of 1967.[99] Collectively, these are the only international instruments of IRL adopted under the auspices of the LoN or the UN. Though those instruments preceding the 1951 Convention are well and truly obsolete, they each in turn formed the legal basis of subsequent instruments, and as such, a clear genealogy exists between them, relevant not only to the legal bases of their provisions, but to the prevailing legal doctrine of the time, relative to the specific circumstances of those refugee crises they addressed.

Having stated what is within the scope of this book, it is perhaps important to state what is not. This book is *not* concerned with individual rights. Though rights also flow from obligations (rights and responsibility being its two legal consequences), it is beyond the scope of this book to analyse the relationship between State obligations and individual rights. As such, it does not address the refugee as an individual or as a subject of IL. It also excludes those provisions of the International Law of Armed Conflict and International Criminal Law that relate to the treatment of refugees and other displaced persons as subjects of IL. It is concerned only with the legal relationship that arises between States in respect of IRL.

This book is presented in three parts. Part 1 comprises Chapters 1 to 3, and examines the inter-related histories of SR and IRL. Part 2 comprises Chapters 4 and 5, and analyses the theorisation of SR as it applies to IRL. Part 3 comprises Chapters 6 and 7, and considers the contemporary application of SR in IRL.

Chapter 1 thoroughly analyses the doctrine of SR; its origins and its relevance to the law of aliens as the basis for both traditional SR and IRL. There are several reasons for this. First, like all systems of law, IRL did not spring forth from a void, but was constructed of pre-existing laws, policies, doctrines, and principles. This is also true of SR, the history of which lends itself particularly well to misinterpretations.[100] The representation of SR as a body of secondary rules codified in the ARSIWA omits a critical history, notably in relation to IRL and the theorisation and application of SR therein. Chapter 1 considers the conception of SR and the legal status of the alien at its foundations. It analyses how, when, and why SR as it related to the alien became a

---

97 UN, *Final Act of the Intergovernmental Conference on the adoption of a travel document for Refugees and Agreement relating to the issue of a travel document to refugees who are the concern of the Intergovernmental Committee on Refugees* (15 October 1946) UNTS Vol. XI, No. 150.

98 UN, *Convention on the Status of Refugees* (28 July 1951) UNTS Vol. 189, No. 2545.

99 UN, *Protocol Relating to the Status of Refugees* (31 January 1967) UNTS Vol. 606, No. 8791.

100 Jan Arno Hessbruegge, 'The Historical Development of the Doctrines of Attribution and Due Diligence in International Law' (2004) 36 NYUJIntlL&Pol 265, 267.

source of concern for both States of origin and States of reception. It proposes that the relationship between Western States and Latin American States, and the threat posed by the alien to the interests of the former, were central considerations in the development of SR, and that the alien was excluded from the doctrine of SR through State practice and the manipulation of certain legal concepts, aided in part by the exploitation of political instability across Latin America. It concludes that by the time SR was on the cusp of codification, the non-national had already been excised from the doctrine through the consistent practice of Western States in the service of economic interests.

Chapter 2 provides an analysis of the theorisation and application of SR in the earliest international responses to refugee crises following the formation of the LoN. It considers the Russian, Greco-Turkish, and Armenian refugee crises of the 1920s, and proposes that IRL in the inter-war period was developed and implemented with a view to divide and assign legal obligations based on the limitation of circumstances engaging questions of SR, and the protection of Western States from long-term financial or legal obligations, imposing such obligations instead onto developing States and refugees themselves. It posits that as crises unfolded, international agreements to address 'the refugee question' were developed reactively, taking account of various priorities of Western States, among them, swift access to employment and the corresponding need for free movement. It proposes that such States controlled the scope and content of SR in respect of early IRL, assigning financial and legal obligations to developing States, while controlling the administration of policy. It concludes that while early IRL differed in many ways to its modern iterations, its underlying purpose was the same: to affect the repatriation or containment of refugees, and to retain control over the division and assignment of obligations for their maintenance. Chapter 2 argues that under the auspices of the LoN, Western States developed, implemented, and refined a number of international laws, policies, and mechanisms that were critical to the theorisation and application of SR in respect of IRL, and which formed its conceptual basis. It evaluates the unique conditions that made the refugee an anomaly in IL, which required a new conceptualisation of SR, and argues that these conditions led to concern among both States and the LoN that the assumption of certain international obligations would result in enduring responsibility for refugee populations. It demonstrates that these concerns led to a conservative approach to the development of international obligations requiring their division into elements that could be assigned to various actors, including refugees themselves.

Chapter 3 addresses SR in the context of the refugee crises of WWII and the development of the 1951 Refugee Conventions, and the 1967 Protocol, with respect to SR. It considers the mandates of the United Nations High Commissioner for Refugees (UNHCR) and its now-defunct predecessors, the United Nations Relief and Rehabilitation Administration (UNRRA), the Intergovernmental Committee on Refugees (IGCR), and the International Refugee Organisation (IRO), as they pertain to the division of obligations between States and organisations, and considers the principles and policies that developed under these organisations and during this era with respect to SR, for example, the prioritisation by the IRO of 'early return,'[101] and the implications of this policy on the responsibility of both the State of origin and the returning State. Chapter 3 argues that the resolution by the LoN of the 'Jewish refugee problem' – both during and after WWII – was treated in similar terms to the refugee crises of the previous decades, insofar as the economic viability of refugee resettlement was prioritised over notions of humanitarianism and informed the scope and content of international obligation and the further limitation of circumstances in which SR might be attributed for violations of IRL. It argues that, compared with those international legal instruments that preceded it, the innovations of the 1951 Convention were relatively few, and those few innovations were themselves not great departures from the preceding framework of IRL. It concludes that persistent concerns regarding the scope and content of international obligations arising in IRL were further exacerbated by the apprehension that nascent IHRL and IRL would eventually amalgamate into one expansive system of international obligations, threatening State sovereignty.

Chapter 4 considers the 1951 Convention in light of the meaning of refugee protection. It posits that the primary theoretical difference between the 1951 Convention and its predecessors was the rejection of 'the presumption of severance' – the definitive rupture in the relationship between the individual and the State – in favour of 'the presumption of enduring nationality' – the recognition of the partial continuation of that relationship in IL. Chapter 4 examines this theoretical shift in the meaning of protection, and its legal and practical consequences, both short- and long-term. Chapter 4 argues that the

101 The Constitution of the International Refugee Organization provided that, "as regards displaced persons, the main task to be performed is to encourage and assist in every way possible their early return to their country of origin" (preamble; Annex I); and that the functions of the IRO would be exercised with a view "to encouraging and assisting in every way possible the early return to their country of nationality, or former habitual residence, of those persons who are the concern of the Organization [...]" (Article 2(1)(a); Annex III). See UN, *Constitution of the International Refugee Organization and Agreement on interim measures to be taken in respect of refugees and displaced persons* (15 December 1946) UNTS Vol. 18, No. 283.

central legal innovation of the 1951 Convention, and the expression of that innovation in certain provisions incorporating norms of SR, permitted the inclusion of refugees in the legitimate exercise of countermeasures (albeit in a limited and regulated capacity) specifically on account of their enduring nationality. In practice, countermeasures have indeed repeatedly included recognised refugees, but have not satisfied the requirements of legitimacy, instead commonly taken against States of origin for the purported failure to comply with the foreign policy objectives of Western States, in the absence of an identifiable international obligation and its violation by the former. It presents extensive evidence of contemporary examples of countermeasures, and the manner in which refugees have been subject to their effect, through the presumption of enduring nationality. Drawing on the legal innovations of the 1951 Convention, and those provisions incorporating norms of SR, Chapter 4 challenges certain common theories of the meaning of refugee protection, arguing that the ongoing relevance of diplomatic protection as the legal basis of protection in IRL is supported by a wealth of evidence that is frequently overlooked.

Chapter 5 examines the evolution of IRL in the 'aid and development' era, and the rapid shift in multilateral approaches to refugee crises in the 1960s and 1970s, in particular, with the destabilisation of Africa. It considers the implications of the shifts in the conceptualisation of protection and the scope and content of those international obligations required by the 1951 Convention. It argues that this 'aid and development' era institutionalised a global bartering system, requiring States of reception to contain refugee populations in exchange for the provision of aid and development funding. It contends that the era was representative of a global retreat from multilateralism to date, and its rapid reinvention through regional international refugee policy, justified by the phenomenon of 'mass influx.' The chapter explores the invention of quasi-legal principles that imposed novel obligations principally on States of reception, while permitting donor States to limit their role to that of benefactor. Chapter 5 concludes that the aid and development era fundamentally redefined the scope and content of refugee protection, substituting legal rights for humanitarian aid and enabling the attribution of SR through countermeasures in the form of financial penalisation. This period, it argues, should be seen as a constructive withdrawal from the 1951 Convention, marking a significant and lasting transformation in the international response to refugee crises.

Chapter 6 analyses the conceptualisation of jurisdiction as a means to evade the attribution of SR. It considers the limitation and qualification of international obligations and the general reliance on interpretations of jurisdiction to affect such developments. It argues that the obfuscation of jurisdiction through the exclusion of refugees and asylum seekers has never been more pervasive than during the past four decades, during which time the reconceptualisation of jurisdiction has been arguably the central focus of States in the interpretation and application of IRL. Chapter 6 argues that globally, a receding line of jurisdiction has developed in response to judicial decisions concerning the scope and content of refugee protection, which has had a profound effect on certain fundamental conceptions of SR, particularly that of attribution. Such measures have been actively pursued by the US in its foreign relations with Latin American and Caribbean States (in particular with Central American States), by the European Union (both within the EU itself between Central and Southern European States, and with North African States), and by Australia in its foreign relations with South-East Asian and Pacific Island States. It presents numerous examples of the interaction between judiciaries and legislatures in conceiving of novel interpretations of jurisdiction as they pertain to IRL.

Chapter 7 argues that in the absence of an international framework for SR in the context of IRL, the strongest and most reliable mechanisms for the attribution of SR lie in the due diligence standards that have developed within and across national and regional jurisdictions. It argues that the consistent application of certain standards of conduct have had a harmonising effect on IRL and exact a common standard in the application and interpretation of its fundamental precepts. Chapter 7 argues that several overarching assumptions underpin the current conception of due diligence in general IL and IRL. It posits that the due diligence standards that apply to IRL are conditioned by a number of distinct factors that in large part turn on the perception of risk. Furthermore, it argues that due diligence standards are contained within the primary instruments of IRL, comprising both obligations of result and obligations of conduct, conditioned by different levels of risk, and requiring different regimes of proof. It concludes that, with reference to the assessment of risk, the conception of fault, and the rules of attribution, judicial opinion, and State practice favour the conception of due diligence in IRL as indivisible from the primary obligation itself, thereby requiring international standards of conduct by virtue of the 1951 Convention.

Finally, this book reconsiders the questions raised in the introduction regarding the force of international obligations in IRL in the absence of clear attribution of SR, and concludes that SR continues to play a vital, though peripheral role. It argues that in contemporary IRL, the primary question is not necessarily modifications to the definition of 'refugee,' but rather the incremental creeping ground that brings refugees as a class of person further within the ambit of regular immigration law, and regards them less as a special class with a distinct legal category. The effect of this is also the incremental shift away from IL towards domestic legal frameworks. It concludes that the protection and reinforcement of SR in IRL is becoming an increasingly urgent matter as the interest in 'root causes' of displacement in general, and the shift towards addressing 'refugees and migrants' under one unified legal platform in the context of mixed migration is fuelling a growing international push towards weakened refugee protection, specifically, under the guise of creating 'safe, orderly, and lawful' pathways.

7 Sources and Methodology

This book employs qualitative legal methods, relying primarily on doctrinal methodology, as it is defined by Hutchinson and Duncan as legal concepts and principles of all types – cases, statutes, and rules, comprising a synthesis of various rules, principles, norms, interpretive guidelines and values, to explain, make coherent, or justify a segment of the law as part of a larger system.[102] This is consistent with the predominant methodologies applied in IL. As Koskenniemi notes, more than in other fields of law, "international law's centre of gravity has been with theoretical abstraction and doctrinal construction. Its links with philosophy and political theory have been close and persistent."[103] Koskenniemi defines the line between 'theory' and 'doctrine' in the following terms (though he acknowledges that it is not always an obvious distinction):

> In general terms, it may be said that where the former asks questions about international law as a whole – as a 'system' or an 'instrument' of policy – doctrine deals with particular, substantive aspects of the law, such as, for example, the rules on the use of force, [or] the principles of State responsibility.[104]

One focuses on rules and legal sources and seeks to create a reliable conception of binding law; another works with processes and objectives in order to

102 Terry Hutchinson, Nigel Duncan, 'Defining and Describing what we do: Doctrinal Legal Methods' (2012) 17(1) Deakin Law Review 83, 84, citing Trischa Mann (ed), *Australian Law Dictionary* (OUP 2010) 197.

103 Martti Koskenniemi, *International Legal Theory and Doctrine* (Max Planck Encyclopedia of Public International Law, Max Planck Institute and OUP 2012) 1.

104 *Id.*

link the law firmly to its social 'context.'[105] Both theory and doctrine are critical to the research question raised by this book, and are considered and incorporated in equal measure. In that regard, this book makes extensive use of primary sources of international, regional, and domestic law as the basis for its analysis and primary arguments, with strong emphasis on the chronology of legal developments within and between the relative systems of IL. It is supported in its analysis by secondary sources, which form the basis of its central arguments, and as such, its rationalisation as an original contribution to the literature.

105 *Id.*

PART 1

History

CHAPTER 1

The Law of State Responsibility, Diplomatic Protection, and the 'Alien'

1 Introduction: Sovereignty and Imperialism in the Law of State Responsibility

As the structure and composition of European power slowly devolved from absolute monarchies to sovereign nation States, so too did States become responsible to their subjects, albeit gradually and in a limited capacity.[1] With the devolution of power to elected representatives, the subjugated populace – once the chattel of the crown – obtained a degree of personal liberty and legal autonomy. With that liberty and autonomy came the enjoyment of certain rights, enforceable against the State, and by extension, a duty to respond – a responsibility – owed by the State to its subject where the State had failed to fulfil a sovereign obligation in respect of an individual right. As sovereign obligations extended only to the State's own subjects, the enjoyment of rights and the capacity to enforce them depended on the subject's nationality. The protection of the person and property of aliens was considered essential to a State's reputation in the comity of nations. Early theses on the law of nations insisted that the maintenance of good international relations and the retention of political allies depended in part on the State's treatment of its foreign residents.[2]

The protection of the alien was, however, not an obligation owed to the alien himself, nor did the alien have an individual right to enforce his protection. As the individual was not a subject of IL, but rather an object of it, the obligation of a host State to provide for his protection was an obligation owed to his State of origin. Any failure to perform those obligations resulted in the

1 See generally: Jan Arno Hessbruegge, 'The Historical Development of the Doctrines of Attribution and Due Diligence in International Law' (2004) 36 NYUJIntlL&Pol 265.

2 D.J. Bederman, *International Law in Antiquity* (CUP 2004) 85; Francisco de Vitoria, *De Indis et De Iure Belli, Relectiones* (first published 1557, Carnegie Institution of Washington 1917) 144–145; Hugo Grotius, *De iure belli et pacis* (first published 1625, Thomas Basset 1682) 79–82; Emer de Vattel, *Droit des gens ou principes de la loi naturelle appliqués à la conduite & aux affaires des Nations et des Souverains, Tome II* (London 1758), paras 324–325; Emanuelle Jouannet, *Emer de Vattel et l'émergence doctrinale du droit international classique* (Pedone 1998) 406–407.

 | DOI:10.1163/9789004722835_003

responsibility of the host State to the State of origin. As IL was concerned solely with relations between States, traditional SR – being the system of primary rules of IL concerned with the diplomatic protection of the alien – dictated that an injury inflicted on an alien by a host State was an offence against the State of origin, requiring remedy. This was recognised in law as in legal theory.[3] In the *Calvin* case of 1608, Justice Coke declared that there was a "mutual bond and obligation between the King and his subjects, whereby subjects are called his liege subjects, because they are bound to obey and serve him, and he is called their liege Lord, because he should maintain and defend them."[4] By virtue of that bond, the protection of the King applied "without the realm, as within" and carried with it a guarantee "that his Subjects in all places may be protected from violence, and that justice may equally be administered to all his Subjects."[5]

Over a century later, reflecting on the relationship between the State and its subjects, Vattel wrote: "[A]nyone who mistreats a citizen directly offends the State. The sovereign of that State must avenge its injury, and if it can, force the aggressor to make full reparation or punish him, since otherwise the citizen would simply not obtain the main goal of civil association, namely, security."[6] But that 'security' and the 'civil association' by which the subject was restored, foreshadowed – as the ILC Special Rapporteur for Diplomatic Protection put it – "one of the main criticisms of the institution, namely, that it is in essence discriminatory because only powerful States are able to use it against weaker States [...] Moreover, diplomatic protection has served as a pretext for intervention in the affairs of certain countries."[7]

This is precisely what transpired in the theorisation and application of SR as it pertained to the alien. Throughout the 19th century, the concept that a State was internationally responsible for the protection of aliens was widely accepted and practiced. It served as a basis for the protection of the life, liberty, and economic security of those conducting business abroad.[8] But con-

3 Dallal Stevens, 'What Do We Mean by Protection?' (2013) 20(2) International Journal on Minority and Group Rights 233, 236.

4 *Calvin's Case* [1608] 77 ER 377, Co Rep 1a, cited in Dallal Stevens, 'What Do We Mean by Protection?' (2013) 20(2) International Journal on Minority and Group Rights 233, 236.

5 *Id.*

6 Emer de Vattel, *Droit des gens ou principes de la loi naturelle appliqués à la conduite & aux affaires des Nations et des Souverains, Tome II* (London 1758), chapter VI.

7 Mohamed Bennouna, *Preliminary report on diplomatic protection, by Mr. Mohamed Bennouna, Special Rapporteur* (4 February 1998) (A/CN.4/484), 311.

8 *Id.*; Edwin M. Borchard, *The Diplomatic Protection of Citizens Abroad* (The Banks Law Pub. Co. 1915); F.S. Dunn, *The Protection of Nationals: A Study in The Application of International*

sensus began to waver where international free trade increased between Latin America and the West. The exploitation of Latin American resources was facilitated by an international labour force of Western nationals, residing in Central and South America, but the instability of those host States, and the real or perceived inequalities between local and foreign labourers, frequently resulted in injuries to the person or property of aliens. States became locked in indemnification disputes, often with a chilling effect on diplomacy, which in turn threatened to destabilise relations between States allied in the lucrative exploitation of natural resources. The doctrine of SR became a great inconvenience to the advancement of free trade, and it soon became a common interest of States to limit the circumstances capable of engaging questions of SR, and to exclude the alien from the purview of a State's international obligations.

Since WWII, the 'essential rights of man' are generally considered to have subsumed the principles that underpinned traditional SR. Many scholars consider that the objectives of the doctrine are now achieved by the universal application of IHRL, and the invalidity of a legal distinction between nationals and aliens.[9] Not only is traditional SR nullified by post-war developments in

Law (The Johns Hopkins Press 1932); Clyde Eagleton, *The Responsibility of States in International Law* (New York University Press 1928); A.V. Freeman, *The International Responsibility of States for Denial of Justice* (Longmans, Green and Company 1938).

9 Vincent Chetail, 'Are Refugee Rights Human Rights? An Unorthodox Questioning of the Relations between Refugee Law and Human Rights Law' in Rubio-Marín (ed), *Human Rights and Immigration* (OUP 2014) 19, but note that Chetail has revisited this question in Vincent Chetail, 'Moving Towards an Integrated Approach of Refugee Law and Human Rights Law' in Costello, Foster and McAdam (eds), *The Oxford Handbook of International Refugee Law* (OUP 2021) 202; F.V. García Amador, Louis Bruno Sohn, Richard R. Baxter, *Recent Codification of the Law of State Responsibility for Injuries to Aliens* (Oceana Publications Inc. 1974) 1, 5; F.V. García Amador, 'First Report on State Responsibility' (1956) 2 UNYBILC 173, 192, 199–201; See also: Pan American Union, *Inter-American Conference on Problems of War and Peace, Mexico City, 21 February 1945, Report Submitted to the Governing Board of the Pan American Union by the Director-General* (1945) PAU 69; F.V. García Amador, 'State Responsibility in the Light of the New Trends of International Law' (1955) 49(3) AJIL 339, 344; Stephen D. Ramsey, 'State Responsibility Under the Restatement' (1989) 83 ASILPROC 232, 233; American Law Institute, *Restatement (Third) of the Foreign Relations Law of the United States* (American Law Institute Publishers 1987). The introductory note to Part VII entitled 'Protection of Persons (Natural and Juridical)' explains that "[t]he difference in history and in jurisprudential origins between the old law of responsibility for injury to aliens and the new law of human rights should not conceal their essential affinity and their increasing convergence." See contra: Richard B. Lillich, 'The Current Status of the Law of State Responsibility for Injuries to Aliens' (1979) 73 ASILPROC 244, 246.

IL – the recognition of the individual as a subject, and not merely an object of IL, and the advent of IHRL – it has been superseded by 'equivalent' international legal provisions, and is therefore irrelevant to the modern conception of SR.[10] This theory is supported in part by the broad acceptance of the ARSIWA as the final word on SR. By extension, all that preceded the ARSIWA is regarded as either tangential, extraneous, or simply a historical remnant with little correlative value to contemporary IL.[11] As a consequence, and where the substance of traditional SR *is* considered relevant, the decision of the ILC to formally abandon the primary rules that underpinned it, and to proceed instead with the codification of general secondary rules of responsibility, is accepted as having been the only practical way forward.[12] This echoes the sentiments of the ILC itself as well as several ILC Special Rapporteurs on the topic, that to attempt a codification of primary rules concerning the treatment of aliens would have been entirely impractical.[13]

---

10 UN General Assembly, *Charter of Economic Rights and Duties of States* (6 November 1974) UN Doc A/RES/3281; Article 2(2)(c) adopts both the national treatment standard and the Calvo Doctrine, which affirmed that rules governing the jurisdiction of a State over aliens and the collection of indemnities should apply equally to all States, irrespective of size, and that aliens who held property in Latin American States and who had claims against the governments of such States should apply to the courts within those States for redress instead of seeking diplomatic intervention. See also: Richard B. Lillich, 'The Current Status of the Law of State Responsibility for Injuries to Aliens' (1979) 73 ASILPROC 244, 247.

11 Giovanni Distefano, *Fundamentals of Public International Law: A Sketch of the International Legal Order* (Brill 2019); James Crawford, *State Responsibility: The General Part* (CUP 2013); James Crawford, *Brownlie's Principles of Public International Law* (9 edn, OUP 2012); Helmut Philipp Aust, *Complicity and the Law of State Responsibility* (CUP 2011); Ian Brownlie, *Principles of Public International Law* (7th edn, OUP 2008); Ian Brownlie, *System of the Law of Nations: State Responsibility, Part I* (1 edn, OUP 1983); L. F.E. Goldie, 'State Responsibility and the Expropriation of Property' (1978) 12(1) The International Lawyer 63; see generally, Christine Chinkin, Freya Baetens (eds), *Sovereignty, Statehood and State Responsibility: Essays in Honour of James Crawford* (CUP 2015).

12 Robert Rosenstock, 'The ILC and State Responsibility' (2002) 96(4) AJIL 792; James Crawford, 'On Re-Reading the Draft Articles on State Responsibility' (1998) 92 ASILPROC 295, 296; Richard B. Lillich, 'The Current Status of the Law of State Responsibility for Injuries to Aliens' (1979) 73 ASILPROC 244; Mahnoush H. Arsanjani, Thomas E. Carbonneau, 'The Codification of the Law of State Responsibility' (1989) 83 ASILPROC 227.

13 'Second Session of the Committee of Experts for the Progressive Codification of International Law' (1926) 20 AJIL Supplement 18, 187; David Caron, 'The ILC Articles on State Responsibility: The Paradoxical Relationship between Form and Authority' (2002) 96(4) AJIL 857, 861.

This theory is somewhat retrospective. It attributes human rights characteristics to IL at a time when there was little evidence to suggest that human rights existed as a legal concept. The identification of a clear intention to create individual rights at any point during the drafting or administration of these historic antecedents is seldom forthcoming. Instead, there is a great deal of generalised attribution to the preservation of human dignity,[14] and of justice for the individual,[15] which helps to frame the genealogy of IRL as simply a continuation of pre-existing legal concepts, and the development of PIL as a linear progression of emerging ideas of individualism.

Chapter 1 challenges these theories. It argues that the neutralising effect that IHRL purportedly had on traditional SR has been quite overstated, and that by the time SR was addressed in a post-war context, the exclusion of those traditional principles that underpinned it was in fact already a *fait accompli*. The development of SR from primary rules of obligation concerning the protection of aliens, to general, secondary rules of SR, had begun over a century prior to WWII, motivated (as opposed to affected) by the commercial interests of Western States in the exploitation of Latin America. During this period, sustained and concerted efforts were made by Western States to cultivate an 'international' legal doctrine of SR, concerned primarily with the preservation of significant financial interests in the region, and corresponding unregulated markets, which in turn required the minimisation of the scope and content of traditional SR that provided protection to the alien under IL.

Chapter 1 traces the origins of SR and the status of the alien within it. Part 2 provides a detailed account of the impact that Latin American independence had on the theorisation and application of SR, including certain related incidents of diplomatic protection, and the legal distinctions that emerged between the treatment of injuries to individuals, and injuries to property. Part 3 provides an analysis of the vast legal scholarship that emerged in response to the recalibration of SR. Part 4 posits that the broader historical context for the theorisation and application of SR has been significantly overlooked, and that the preservation of particular commercial interests was central to the development of the contemporary doctrine of SR, and the status of the alien in IL. Part 5 considers the many attempts to codify SR, from the earliest regional procedures, to the codification of the *Articles on the Responsibility of States for Internationally Wrongful Acts* and the work of the ILC Special Rapporteurs on the subject. It analyses the central concerns of States in codifying SR, in particular, the competing theories of responsibility origi-

14 James C. Hathaway, *The Rights of Refugees under International Law* (CUP 2010) 5.

15 C.F. Amerasinghe, *State Responsibility for Injuries to Aliens* (Clarendon Press 1967) 285.

nating in European and American doctrine, and the urgency to assert one over the other.

Chapter 1 concludes that the financial and political interests (in that order) of Western States determined the trajectory of SR, in turn affecting its scope and content as it pertained to IRL as a derivative of the law of aliens, and that the international obligations that were constructed among States principally served those economic objectives. It argues that the principle of equality of all persons, and shared concern about the effect of decolonisation on SR were primary drivers in its codification, and that the codification of the ARSIWA shifted accordingly away from primary rule to general secondary rules of IL.

2 The Exploitation of Latin America and Traditional State Responsibility

The aftermath of the Spanish American Wars of Independence saw a proliferation of Free Trade Agreements (FTAs), which were concluded between Latin American States and Western States, invariably incorporating provisions that guaranteed the mutual protection of aliens. Overwhelmingly, it was European and US subjects that resided abroad in Latin America; engaged in commercial activities in the host State, and enriching the economy of the State of origin. It was thus the protection of Western States with which protective provisions were concerned.

Given the era of their conclusion, FTAs were not concerned with the conferral of individual rights. Treaties of 'Friendship, Commerce, and Navigation' – as FTAs were commonly called – served mutual economic interests. Latin America had vast natural resources and agricultural potential, and newly established States required powerful economic allies. The host State traded assurances for the protection of aliens for competitive advantage in the economic exploits of crude oil, mineral deposits, and precious metals. Aliens engaged in commercial activities were guaranteed reciprocity of certain rights and freedoms, including the freedom to engage in commercial activities without distinction from nationals;[16] the right to taxation at the

16 Mexico, USA, *Treaty of Amity, Commerce and Navigation* (Mexico City, 5 April 1831) Article III; USA, Chile, *Convention of Peace, Amity, Commerce, and Navigation* (Santiago, 16 May 1832) Article II; USA, Brazil, *Treaty of Amity, Commerce, and Navigation* (Rio de Janeiro, 12 December 1828) Article III.

common rate,[17] and the entitlement to protection before the law, equal to that of nationals.[18]

But while most of the region achieved political independence, lasting internal peace rarely prevailed. As post-independence insurrections and revolutions ensued, internal disturbances precipitated numerous claims for reparation for injuries to aliens. It was at this juncture that States became reticent to the inclusion of aliens among their international legal obligations. Consensus formed instead around the rejection of circumstances capable of engaging SR and in that regard, capable of triggering the 'international standard of justice.' In the aftermath of reparation claims, and once order was restored, new FTAs were frequently concluded, but with the inclusion of provisions specifying that States could *not* be held responsible for any injury to an alien arising from an internal disturbance.[19] Latter FTAs shielded States against indemnification claims arising from riots, insurrections, and armed conflicts that preceded a change of government. Several Latin American Constitutions, redrafted after civil wars, included such provisions that shielded the State against indemnification of aliens in the event that civil war broke out again.[20]

---

17 Mexico, Colombia, *Treaty of Commerce Between Colombia and Mexico* (Mexico City, 31 December 1823) Article XIII; Mexico, Chile, *Tratado de Amistad, Comercio, y Navegación* (Mexico City, 7 March 1831) Article III; Mexico, USA, *Treaty of Amity, Commerce and Navigation* (Mexico City, 5 April 1831) Article III; Argentina, USA, *Treaty of Friendship, Commerce, and Navigation* (San Jose, 27 July 1853) Article X; Argentina, Chile, *Tratado de Amistad, Comercio y Navegación* (Santiago, 30 August 1855); Argentina, Sardinia, *Tratado de Amistad, Comercio y Navegación* (Paraná, 21 September 1855); Argentina, Brazil, *Tratado de Amistad, Comercio y Navegación* (Paraná, 7 March 1856); Argentina, Paraguay, *Tratado de Amistad, Comercio y Navegación* (Asunción, 29 July 1856).

18 Peru, Belgium, *Tratado de Amistad, Comercio y Navegación* (London, 16 May 1850) Article IV; Peru, Argentina, *Tratado de Amistad, Comercio y Navegación* (Buenos Aires, 9 March 1874) Article III; Peru, Austria, *Tratado de Amistad, Comercio y Navegación* (Lima, 2 May 1870) Article IV; Peru, Germany, *Tratado de Comercio y Navegación* (Lima, 20 January 1877) Article III.

19 Colombia, Italy, *Tratado de Amistad, Comercio y Navegación* (Bogotá, 27 October 1892) Article 21; Colombia, Germany, *Tratado de Amistad, Comercio y Navegación* (Bogotá, 23 July 1892). See also: Colombia, Spain, *Tratado adicional al de Paz y Amistad* (Bogotá, 30 January 1881) Article 4.

20 Both the Nicaraguan Constitution of 1893 and the Honduran Constitution of 1894 provided that foreigner residents who made claims or demands for compensation from the State, and whose applications did not end 'amicably,' would lose their right to reside in the State. See: Nicaragua, *La Constitución de 1893* (10 December 1893) Article 13; Honduras, *Constitución de 1894* (14 October 1894) Article 14, Article 15.

Alternative measures of international dispute resolution were developed with the specific objective of limiting the circumstances capable of engaging the 'international standard of justice' for injuries to aliens through the widespread and consistent use of diplomatic negotiations,[21] the conclusion of new treaties apportioning general compensation,[22] and the establishment of independent claims commissions to determine questions of SR and reparation.[23] Not only did States choose to address questions of SR for injuries to aliens informally rather than as recompense legally due for the violation of a treaty, but also legislated such legal revisions. The law of aliens consequently lost much of its relevance as the basis for the law of SR. The relationship between the State of origin and its subject no longer demanded appeals to be made on behalf of the injured State whose subject had sustained injury.

Though principally the product of Western interests, these alternative measures of international dispute resolution were advantageous also to Latin American States, as a means to reinforce the principle of non-intervention. The insertion into FTAs of such clauses limited the circumstances engaging SR were limited to the denial of justice only. At the same time, Latin American States responded to Western aggression by expanding the scope of the Calvo Doctrine (named for the Argentine jurist Carlos Calvo), which provided that diplomatic protection could not be extended to national corporations, or natural persons, unless and until there had been an exhaustion of domestic legal remedies. Though traditionally applied to commercial disputes, the Calvo Doctrine was critical to Latin American efforts to redefine the doctrine of SR on the continent. Not only did it preclude States from invoking the international standard of justice until all domestic remedies had been exhausted, it had the added advantage of reinforcing the principle of non-intervention that had plagued the region in past decades. Latin American States had often been subjected to extreme uses of force by foreign powers for the purported failure to provide compensation for injuries to aliens. Echoed later by the ILC Special Rapporteur for diplomatic protection,[24] one jurist noted at the time, "powerful states have at times exacted from weak states a

---

21 See Section 3.

22 See for example: Paraguay, USA, *Convention Relating to Claims of United States and Paraguay Navigation Company against the Government of Paraguay* (Asunción, 4 February 1859); Mexico, USA, *Treaty Of Peace, Friendship, Limits, And Settlement* (Guadalupe Hidalgo, 2 February 1848).

23 Spanish Treaty Claims Commission, *Final Report of the Spanish Treaty Claims Commission* (Government Printing Office 1910).

24 Mohamed Bennouna, *Preliminary report on diplomatic protection, by Mr. Mohamed Bennouna, Special Rapporteur*4 February 1998) (A/CN.4/484).

greater degree of responsibility than from states of their own strength."[25] Great Britain had blockaded the Port of Rio de Janeiro in 1863, and detained Brazilian merchant ships, demanding apology and indemnification for the sinking of a British vessel.[26] Italy had threatened to blockade the ports of Colombia in 1898 after Colombia failed to pay compensation for injuries to an Italian national in accordance with an arbitral award.[27] Germany had anchored two warships at Port-Au Prince, Haiti in 1897 and demanded compensation for purported injuries to a German subject, apologies to the German Government, a salute to the German flag, and the reception by the Haitian President of the German Chargé d'Affaires.[28] Each of these events would later be cited in reports on legal materials by the Department of Legal Affairs at the Organization of American States (OAS), entitled *Contributions of the American Continent to the Principles of International Law that Govern the Responsibility of the State*,[29] and presented during the codification of SR.

This disproportionate use of force by Western States in purportedly enforcing SR was both an infringement on the principle of equality between nationals and aliens, and on the principle of equality among nations. It created both a privileged class among aliens, who were in effect entitled to a higher level of protection than nationals, and subjected comparatively weaker States to aggression and humiliation.[30] As one commentator noted, Western States practically abandoned military intervention as a strategy, instead favouring "efforts by their jurists toward the restriction of the domain

25 Edwin M. Borchard, *The Diplomatic Protection of Citizens Abroad* (The Banks Law Pub. Co. 1915) 178.

26 Richard Graham, *Britain and the Onset of Modernization in Brazil 1850–1914* (CUP 1968) 167–171; Robert Conrad, *The Destruction of Brazilian Slavery 1850–1888* (University of California Press 1972) 43; 'Christie Affair' in Jay Kinsbruner (ed) *Encyclopedia of Latin American History and Culture* (2 edn) (Gale Cengage, 2008). Though Brazil eventually yielded to British demands, the Brazilian Minister maintained that the payment was "made solely in consequence of the illegal and violent proceedings committed upon Brazilian ships in the territorial waters of the Empire, and is the simple result of force [...]." See: 'The Brazil correspondence in the cases of the "Prince of Wales" and officers of the "Forte" (Reprinted from the Papers laid before Parliament)' (1863) *W. Ridgeway* 324.

27 'The Cerruti Arbitrations' (1912) 6(4) AJIL 965, 966, 970; Segismundo Moret, 'Italy V. Colombia (The Cerruti Case)' (1912) 6(4) AJIL 1003, 1005–1006, 1010.

28 Jacques Nicolas Léger, *Haiti, her History and her Detractors* (The Neale Publishing Company 1907) 250; See also: Solon Ménos, *L'Affaire Lüders* (Imprimerie J. Verrollot 1898).

29 Pan American Union, *Contributions of the American Continent to the Principles Governing the Responsibility of the State* (1961).

30 F.V. García Amador, Louis Bruno Sohn, Richard R. Baxter, *Recent Codification of the Law of State Responsibility for Injuries to Aliens* (Oceana Publications Inc. 1974) 5.

of international responsibility,"[31] which had at its core, the exclusion of the alien. Accordingly, it was principally Western States that drove the revisionism of SR, both through the pursuit of economic interests, and the threat of aggression towards Latin America.

2.1 *Force Majeure, Incapacity, and "Spontaneous" Compensation*

A number of legal justifications were advanced in reconceptualising SR in a way that excluded the indemnification of States for injuries to aliens, some of which were inferred from other systems of law, and some of which were very much innovations. The irregular practices that had emerged contributed to the systematic degradation of the international obligations of the State and the position of the alien as a third-party beneficiary of PIL. In turn, this contributed to the formation of a conceptual basis from which SR in IRL would later be theorised and applied. Several of these concepts would later enjoy some revival in academia, particularly where questions pertain to compensation.

Generally speaking, irregular practices emerged from the increase in the number of violent incidents between national and foreign labour forces. These incidents exacerbated concerns that the doctrine of traditional SR interfered impermissibly with what were essentially matters of State. As with latter FTAs, in resolving such incidents, States favoured informal and non-judicial practices over a strict application of IL principles. The entitlement of an injured State to compensation pursuant to IL was substituted by informal offers of 'spontaneous' payments, often made with 'a thought of humanity,' which wholly circumvented any requirement to examine a State's alleged violations of its international obligations. This was aided in part by the grossly expansive definition of *force majeure*, which sought to include voluntary, individual acts in a legal term that referred only to natural phenomena such as floods, fires, and high winds. This expanded definition was employed by numerous States in defence of their purported failures to quell riots, insurrections, and other various classifications of conflict and civil disturbance. Each of these scenarios was incapable of engaging SR by definition where there was reduced capacity or foreseeability. States accused of failing to quell internal disturbances and prevent injuries to aliens frequently sought to invoke a liberal interpretation of the term as a legitimate defence to their unwillingness or incapacity to prevent resultant harm.

---

31 Louis Pons, *La responsabilité de l'état à raison de dommages causés sur son territoire aux étrangers* (Imprimerie F. Boisseau 1936) 15.

Common to several such diplomatic incidents was the assertion by the injurious State that the alleged injuries to aliens arose from the actions of civilians, and that it was therefore outside the scope of their international obligations and therefore did not engage questions of SR. Either the State could not be internationally responsible for the acts of non-State actors or it lacked the power to repress the acts of "lawless individuals" who had overpowered the State's authorities, where it had otherwise "put forth every legitimate effort" to quell the violence and protect foreign nationals.[32] Beyond the scope of legitimate effort, these events were considered to be a result of *force majeure*, a classification that precluded the international standard of justice for injuries arising from it.

One such argument was put forward by the US in response to a compensation claim from China, arising from injuries to Chinese subjects in Denver, Colorado, in late 1880.[33] The US dismissed the damage as having resulted from 'the conduct of a lawless mob' that had overpowered local authorities. As the State had taken all legitimate measures to supress the violence, but lacked the capacity to quell it before injuries were sustained,[34] SR could not properly be attributed to it, and there was "no principle of national obligation [...] which renders it incumbent on the Government of the United States to make indemnity to the Chinese residents of Denver [...]."[35] The US contended that in any case, the claim was illegitimate, as the incident was a matter for the state of Colorado, and that the powers of direct intervention on the part of the US government were limited by the Constitution.[36]

32 'Mr. Evarts to Chen Dan Pin' (Washington, 30 December 1880) Papers Relating to the Foreign Relations of the United States, Transmitted to Congress, with the Annual Message of The President (Department of State, 5 December 1881); See generally: John Bassett Moore, A Digest of International Law, Volume VI (Government Printing Office 1906) 821.

33 'Chen Lan Pin to Mr. Evarts' (Washington, 10 November 1880) *Papers Relating to the Foreign Relations of the United States, Transmitted to Congress, with the Annual Message of The President* (Department of State, 5 December 1881).

34 'Mr. Evarts to Chen Dan Pin' (Washington, 30 December 1880) Papers Relating to the Foreign Relations of the United States, Transmitted to Congress, with the Annual Message of The President (Department of State, 5 December 1881); 'Mr. Evarts to Chen Dan Pin' (Washington, 30 December 1880) Papers Relating to the Foreign Relations of the United States, Transmitted to Congress, with the Annual Message of The President (Department of State, 5 December 1881); See generally: John Bassett Moore, A Digest of International Law, Volume VI (Government Printing Office 1906) 821.

35 'Mr. Evarts to Chen Dan Pin' (Washington, 30 December 1880) Papers Relating to the Foreign Relations of the United States, Transmitted to Congress, with the Annual Message of The President (Department of State, 5 December 1881).

36 *Id.*

Several years later, the US made the same argument in favour of the obligations of individual states of the Union, when a diplomatic incident erupted between the US and Italy. A vigilante group had taken possession of a jail and murdered eleven Italian subjects being held for the murder of the New Orleans Chief of Police.[37] Relying on a bilateral *Treaty of Commerce and Navigation*, providing for the mutual protection of aliens,[38] Italy requested indemnification for the "unjustifiable conduct of the local authorities."[39] The US claimed that it "did not by the treaty with Italy become the insurer of the lives or property of Italian subjects resident within [its] territory."[40] In a bizarre exchange of cables, it asserted that, far from denying the right to indemnity, the Federal Government recognised the right of indemnity to the murdered Italian subjects,[41] then later claimed that in the previous note, it had not "recognised that an indemnity is due to the families of the victims" but had instead "recognised *the principle* of indemnity" which was distinct.[42] It

37 'Consul Corte to Baron Fava (New Orleans, 14 March 1891)' (9 December 1891) *United States Government Printing Office* 'Consul Corte to Baron Fava' (New Orleans, 14 March 1891) *Papers Relating to the Foreign Relations of the United States, Transmitted to Congress, with the Annual Message of The President* (Department of State, 9 December 1891)'Consul Corte to Baron Fava' (New Orleans, 14 March 1891) *Papers Relating to the Foreign Relations of the United States, Transmitted to Congress, with the Annual Message of The President* (Department of State, 9 December 1891); 'Baron Fava to Mr. Blaine' (Washington, 15 March 1891) *Papers Relating to the Foreign Relations of The United States, Transmitted to Congress, with the Annual Message of the President* (United States Government Printing Office, 9 December 1891). See also: 'Marquis Rudini to Baron Fava' (Rome, 14 March 1891) *Papers Relating to the Foreign Relations of The United States, Transmitted to Congress, with the Annual Message of the President* (United States Government Printing Office, 9 December 1891); 'Marquis Rudini to Baron Fava' (Rome, 15 March 1891) *Papers Relating to the Foreign Relations of The United States, Transmitted to Congress, with the Annual Message of the President* (United States Government Printing Office, 9 December 1891).

38 Italy, USA, *Treaty of Commerce and Navigation* (Florence, 26 February 1871) Article III.

39 'Consul Corte to Baron Fava (New Orleans, 14 March 1891)' (9 December 1891) *United States Government Printing Office*'Consul Corte to Baron Fava' (New Orleans, 14 March 1891) *Papers Relating to the Foreign Relations of the United States, Transmitted to Congress, with the Annual Message of The President* (Department of State, 9 December 1891)'Consul Corte to Baron Fava' (New Orleans, 14 March 1891) *Papers Relating to the Foreign Relations of the United States, Transmitted to Congress, with the Annual Message of The President* (Department of State, 9 December 1891).

40 'Mr. Blaine to Marquis Imperiali' (Washington, 14 April 1891) *Papers Relating to the Foreign Relations of the United States, Transmitted to Congress, with the Annual Message of The President* (Department of State, 9 December 1891).

41 *Id.*

42 *Id.* Emphasis added.

then settled finally on the position that it was not the Federal Government that was responsible, but the state of Louisiana. It maintained this position until the end, claiming eventually that while the injury was not inflicted directly by the US, "the President nevertheless feels that it is the solemn duty, as well as the great pleasure, of the National Government to pay a satisfactory indemnity."[43]

The defence of incapacity in the face of *force majeure* was also advanced several times by France. The first occasion was in response to a Spanish claim for indemnification following the significant loss of life and damage to property sustained during an incursion in the town of Saïda, French Algeria, in June 1881.[44] France rejected the claim, advancing the defence of incapacity, as "the events at Saïda fell into the category of inevitable facts" and were therefore the result of *force majeure*. France also utilised its own past claims for indemnification by Spain as leverage in an attempt to coerce Spain into indemnifying its own subjects, proposing to 'exchange views' on "the means to grant equitable compensation to the *respective* nationals who have suffered in the last years of civil strife";[45] an allusion to the claim it had made for injuries to its subjects sustained during the Cuban war of independence and the Carlist wars of Spain. Spain had previously denied this claim on the basis of *force majeure*. France reminded Spain that it had quite recently "availed itself of this universally consecrated theory of declining the obligation to repair the damage resulting from civil strife or civil war" and that it should be "not surprising, therefore, that the French Government wishes to recall, according to the same rules of international law, that it is not obliged to compensate the victims of Algeria."[46] The impasse was broken when the Spanish government claimed

43 'Mr. Blaine to Marquis Imperiali' (Washington, 12 April 1892) *Papers Relating to the Foreign Relations of the United States, Transmitted to Congress, with the Annual Message of The President* (Department of State, 9 December 1891). In 2019, the mayor of New Orleans offered an apology to Italian-Americans and issued a proclamation in recognition of the lynching. See: Associated Press, 'New Orleans to apologise for worst mass lynching in America's history' (1 April 2019) The Guardian.

44 'S. Exe. M. le Duc De Fernan-Nunez, Ambassadeur d'Espagne, à M. Barthélemy-Saint-Hilaire, Ministre des Affaires étrangères, à Paris' (Paris, 30 June 1881) *Ministère des affaires étrangères, Documents Diplomatique: Affaires de Saïda: 1881–1882 ("Affaires de Saïda")* (imprimerie nationale, 1882).

45 'M. Barthélemy-Saint-Hilaire, Ministre des Affaires étrangères, à S. Exe. M. le Duc De Fernan-Nunez, Ambassadeur d'Espagne à Paris' (Paris, 23 July 1881) *Ministère des affaires étrangères, Documents Diplomatique: Affaires de Saïda: 1881–1882 ("Affaires de Saïda")* (imprimerie nationale, 1882). Emphasis added.

46 *Id.*

that it had "never intended to claim compensation in the strict and legal sense of this term" but that compensation may be understood, in a customary sense, as being "spontaneously and freely granted by a State."[47] In that regard, and "without prescribing a precedent" it was happy to reply to French indemnity of Spanish subjects with the indemnification of French subjects in Cuba and Spain.[48] France agreed that in strict law, there was no legal obligation for either State to compensate the other.[49]

France also used its own indemnification as leverage after violence broke out between French and Italian labourers in the French town of Aigues-Mortes.[50] While many Italian subjects were killed and injured in France, violent counter-protests in Rome, Naples and Genova damaged several French government buildings, and became the subject of counter-claims by France against Italy.[51] France ordered an immediate inquiry into the events at Aigues-Mortes, but concluded only that the Italian government was responsible for the destruction of French property in Rome.[52] Notwithstanding, France was prepared to provide a subsidy to the Italian victims of the events at Aigues-Mortes "*dans une pensée d'humanité*"[53] on the condition that Italy also recog-

47 'S. Exe. M. le Duc De Fernan Nunez, Ambassadeur d'Espagne, à M. Barthélemy-Saint-Hilaire, Ministre des Affaires étrangères, à Paris' (Paris, 19 September 1881) *Ministère des affaires étrangères, Documents Diplomatique: Affaires de Saïda: 1881–1882* (*"Affaires de Saïda"*) (imprimerie nationale, 1882).

48 *Id.*

49 'M. Barthélemy-Saint-Hilaire, Ministre des Affaires étrangères, à Paris à S. Exe. M. le Duc De Fernan Nunez, Ambassadeur d'Espagne' (Paris, 19 September 1881) *Ministère des affaires étrangères, Documents Diplomatique: Affaires de Saïda: 1881–1882* (*"Affaires de Saïda"*) (imprimerie nationale, 1882).

50 'Chronique des faits internationales' (1894) RGDIP 172.

51 'Le Vicomte de Lavaur de Sainte-Fortunade, Chargé d'affaires de France près le Gouvernement italien à M. Develle, Ministre des Affaires étrangères' (Rome, 21 August 1893) *Ministère des affaires étrangères, Documents Diplomatique: Indemnités franco-italiennes* (*"Indemnités franco-italiennes"*) (imprimerie national, 1894); 'Le Vicomte de Mouy, gérant le Consulat général de France à Naples, à M. Develle, Ministre des Affaires étrangères' (Naples, 21 August 1893) *Ministère des affaires étrangères, Documents Diplomatique: Indemnités franco-italiennes* (*"Indemnités franco-italiennes"*) (imprimerie national, 1894); 'M. Meyer, Consul général de France à Gênes, à M. Develle, Ministre des Affaires étrangères' (Genoa, 21 August 1893) *Ministère des affaires étrangères, Documents Diplomatique: Indemnités franco-italiennes* (*"Indemnités franco-italiennes"*) (imprimerie national, 1894).

52 'Le Vicomte de Lavaur de Sainte-Fortunade, Chargé d'affaires de France près le Gouvernement italien, à M. Develle, Ministre des Affaires étrangères' (Rome, 30 August 1893) *Ministère des affaires étrangères, Documents Diplomatique: Indemnités franco-italiennes* (*"Indemnités franco-italiennes"*) (imprimerie national, 1894).

53 'Chronique des faits internationales' (1894) RGDIP 174.

nised that compensation was due to the French who suffered damage during the counter-protests.[54]

This informal, diplomatic settlement of what was previously a well-accepted precept of IL degraded the international standard of justice by asserting that a variety of circumstances in which an alien could sustain injury fell outside the scope of international obligations. By extension, it reduced the State's international obligation to protect the alien to simple acts of diplomatic goodwill, and minimised the position of the alien as an object of IL, entitled to indemnification through the enforcement of SR by his State of origin. This was not just a simple development of law, but a rejection of the Calvo Doctrine, and consequently, of Latin American doctrine of PIL. This created a legal environment in which alienage alone excluded a potential claimant from making a legitimate claim through his State of nationality against a State for an injury to his person or property.

The deliberate exclusion of the alien from the doctrine of SR not only permitted the eventual rejection of alienage as a critical substantive matter at the point of codification of SR, but importantly, implied later that the refugee (initially defined by his lack of nationality) did not benefit from any justiciable rights against the State of reception. Later, when the 1951 Convention revised the status of the refugee and deemed him to continue to enjoy enduring nationality, it allowed the limits of those international obligations to be minutely defined. The international legal framework that would have otherwise supported IRL as incorporating precepts of SR was so thoroughly undermined during this period as to exclude the attribution of SR for injuries to aliens almost entirely.

2.2 *The Practice of 'State Substitution'*

Perhaps the most irregular practice to emerge from this period was what might be called 'State substitution,' in which an injured State would stand in the place of its injurious counterpart and adjudicate the claims made by its own nationals against the latter. The former would then apportion compensation to its own nationals using its own public funds, creating the paradoxical situation in which the taxpayer contributed to his own indemnification. Though not a popular practice, State substitution reveals the depths of States'

54 'M. Casimir-Périer, Président du Conseil, Ministre des Affaires étrangères, à S. Exe. M. Ressman, Ambassadeur d'Italie à Paris' (Paris, 9 December 1893) *Ministère des affaires étrangères, Documents Diplomatique: Indemnités franco-italiennes ("Indemnités franco-italiennes")* (imprimerie national, 1894).

concerns regarding the expanding scope and content of the circumstances in which SR could be attributed to a State. That such a highly irregular practice would emerge as a means to admit the principle of compensation only in the narrowest of terms, further excluding the individual as a tertiary benefactor of PIL, even where the individual was the State's own subject, is testament to the desire to retain control over the trajectory of the law of aliens and of developing norms of SR alike.

An early example of State substitution arose in France, which had considered such a scheme in respect of French subjects for injuries suffered on French territory during the Franco-German war. In 1871, the National Assembly of France took the unusual step of voting to recognise the existence of a law of compensation that would be applied to zones that had suffered from the German invasion.[55] Until this point, no State had recognised itself as owing compensation to its own subjects for damages caused by another.[56] At the time of the vote, two correlative ideas were put forward: First, that the responsibility for indemnification of injured French subjects was that of the State that had waged the war. As it was France that had waged war on Germany, this would have effectively placed the financial burden of indemnification of French subjects on French subjects themselves. The alternative was to declare that a duty to indemnify did not infer strict liability, and that the State should only admit a duty of equity accomplished by relief, in so far as resources were available,[57] but even this alternative proved to be too costly. The law finally adopted on 6 September 1871 did not promise full compensation. Instead, despite the fact that the scheme for compensation was intended to address injuries sustained in wartime, the obligation to indemnify was treated as unfounded for damages resulting from military operations.[58]

55 Ludwig von Bar, 'De la responsabilité des États à raison des dommages soufferts par des étrangers en cas de troubles, d'émeute ou de guerre civil' (1899) Revue de droit international et de législation comparée 464, 469. See generally: Achille Morin, *Les Lois Relatives a la Guerre Selon le Droit des Gens Moderne, le Droit Public et le Droit Criminel des Pays Civilisés (Tome II)* (Imprimerie et Libraire Générale de Jurisprudence Cosse, Marchal et Billard 1872) chap XIII; Emilio Brusa, 'Responsabilité des États à raison des dommages soufferts par des étrangers en cas d'émeute ou de guerre civile' (1898) 17 AnnIDI 96, 111.

56 Emilio Brusa, 'Responsabilité des États à raison des dommages soufferts par des étrangers en cas d'émeute ou de guerre civile' (1898) 17 AnnIDI 96, 110.

57 *Id.*, 110–111.

58 Guillaume Nahon, 'Bombardements, dommages de guerre et réquisitions' (March 2019) Archives de Paris; Emilio Brusa, Ludwig von Bar, 'Responsibilité des États à raison des dommages soufferts par des étrangers en cas d'émeute ou de guerre civile' (1900) 18 AnnIDI 47.

Another clear example of State substitution – both its substance and its underlying purpose – may be found in the Treaty of Paris and the activities of the Spanish Treaty Claims Commission that the treaty established. At the close of the Spanish–American war, the two powers ratified the *Treaty of Peace Between the United States and Spain*, also known as the Treaty of Paris, providing in part that both Contracting Parties relinquished all claims for indemnity of every kind against the other party arising since the beginning of the Cuban insurrection and prior to the exchange of the treaty's ratifications, including all claims for indemnity for the cost of the war.[59] The treaty also provided that the claims made specifically by US nationals against Spain for injuries sustained during the conflict, and since relinquished under the treaty, would be adjudicated and settled by the US itself.[60]

This arrangement effectively required the US to stand in the place of Spain, and defend the foreign State against claims made against it by US citizens. It would then adjudicate the claims and award compensation to injured US citizens on behalf of Spain using US taxpayer dollars. This radical arrangement became the basis of a mandate for the Spanish Treaty Claims Commission, established in 1901, which in turn established its own bizarre practice to affect the exclusion of as many claimants as possible, in order to minimise the cost of indemnification. Confronted with the prospect of indemnifying thousands of US citizens, the Commission devised a way to exclude a great number of claimants from its process by claiming that it would be prudent to first establish 'cardinal principles of admissibility,' based on a sample of claims, which would allow it "to determine in advance of the taking of testimony the cardinal principles of law which should govern in the allowance or disallowance of claims."[61] Unsurprisingly, after reviewing a number of statements, the Commission concluded that:

> [B]elligerent rights were never granted to the insurgents by Spain or the United States so as to create a state of war in the international sense, which exempted the parent governments from liability to foreigners for the acts of the insurgents.

59 USA, Spain, *Treaty of Peace Between the United States and Spain* (Paris, 10 December 1898) Article VII.

60 *Id.*

61 Spanish Treaty Claims Commission, *Final Report of the Spanish Treaty Claims Commission* (Government Printing Office 1910) 5.

> [W]here an armed insurrection has gone beyond the control of the parent government, the general rule is that such government is not responsible for damages done to foreigners by the insurgents.[62]

Based on its conclusions, the Commission excluded the vast majority of claims for property losses and personal injuries, awarding a total of less than $1.5 million out of a total $65 million claimed by its own injured nationals.[63]

While the scope and content of SR in PIL was on a steady path to the minimisation of individual claims for injuries, it is critical to note the comparative trajectory of commercial claims in private international law. While the material differences between injured individuals and injured enterprises were relatively few, their legal treatment could not have been more distinct. While bilateral treaties, national constitutions, and State practice excluded individuals from the purview of SR, injuries of a commercial nature, *sustained in precisely the same contexts*, were treated as akin to war reparations; not just capable of being attributed to the State, but inherently requiring remedy.

Commercial disputes were not characterised as arising from the acts of unruly private citizens, as was the case in relation to injured aliens, but were readily considered public acts and therefore capable of properly engaging SR. Cases of damage to property owned by the State or by private enterprise were commonly submitted to arbitration, as was the customary practice in respect of war reparations. Conversely, States did not submit claims for injuries to their subjects to arbitration, preferring to settle such disputes privately through diplomatic channels. This was partly practiced so as to avoid the indemnification of aliens becoming part of the *ratione materiae* of arbitral commissions.

There are a number of striking examples of this disparity. One concerns the case of Venezuela and Ecuador who, in the midst of their separation from Greater Colombia, detained and sold five US brigs and their cargo. Over the course of two decades, the US concluded individual treaties for each of the five sequestered brigs with both Ecuador and Venezuela; effectively settling some of the same claims twice.[64] The treaties included provisions "for the

---

62 *Id.*, 6(2)–(3).

63 *Id.*, 20.

64 USA, Venezuela, *Arrangement for the Settlement of the Case of the Brig "Morris"* (Caracas, 26 February 1844); USA, Venezuela, *Convention for the Settlement of the Case of the Brig "Native"* (Caracas, 16 November 1846); USA, Venezuela, *Convention for the Final Settlement of the Case of the Brig "Josephine"* (Caracas, 16 November 1846); USA, Venezuela, *Convention for the Settlement of the Case of the Brig "Sarah Wilson"* (Caracas, 12 April 1848); USA, Venezuela, *Convention for the Settlement of the Claim Arising Out of the*

absolute indemnification of the principal of the losses and injuries which the persons interested [...] have claimed" as well as the interest arising from the sequestrations of the vessels and the sale of cargo.[65]

Similarly, at the close of the Venezuelan civil war, a vast number of mixed claims commissions were established to adjudicate claims arising between Venezuela and Germany, Great Britain, Italy, France, the United States, Belgium, Spain, Mexico, Sweden-Norway, and the Netherlands, respectively. Venezuela was given an ultimatum by Britain and Germany to pay the series of claims or face a blockade of its ports.[66] The two States, soon joined by Italy, eventually blockaded a number of Venezuelan ports and seized several of its vessels. Venezuela eventually relented and the mixed claims commissions were established through a series of individual protocols with each Claimant State.[67]

In one other particularly stark example, a fatal incident between French and US seamen in the US state of Georgia in 1811 resulted in the pre-emptive offering of indemnity by the US to the French government, though the indemnity was not for the killing of two French seamen by US sailors, but for the extensive damage caused to the two French vessels, then stationed in the port of Georgia.[68]

Seizure and Detention of the Brig "Mount Vernon" (Caracas, 7 July 1849); USA, Ecuador, *Settlement of Cases of Brig "Josephine" and Schooner "Ranger"* (Quito, 15 June 1849); USA, Ecuador, *Settlement of Case of Brig "Morris"* (Quito, 9 February 1850); USA, Ecuador, *Settlement of Case of Brig "Native"* (Guayaquil, 5 February 1853).

65 USA, Ecuador, *Settlement of Case of Brig "Morris"* (Quito, 9 February 1850) Article 1.

66 Heather Bray, 'Venezuelan Claims Commissions' in *Max Planck Encyclopedias of International Law* (OUP, 2018).

67 UK, Venezuela, *Protocol between Great Britain and Venezuela for the Settlement of British Claims etc.* (Washington, 13 February 1903); Italy, Venezuela, *Protocol between Italy and Venezuela for the Settlement of Italian Claims* (Washington, 13 February 1903); USA, Venezuela, *Protocol between the United States and Venezuela for the Arbitration of Claims* (Washington, 17 February 1903); Mexico, Venezuela, *Protocol between Mexico and Venezuela for the Arbitration of Claims* (Washington, 26 February 1903); France, Venezuela, *Protocol between France and Venezuela for the Arbitration of Claims* (Washington, 27 February 1903); Netherlands, Venezuela, *Protocol between the Netherlands and Venezuela for the Arbitration of Claims* (Washington, 28 February 1903); Belgium, Venezuela, *Protocol between Belgium and Venezuela for the Arbitration of Claims* (Washington, 7 March 1903); Sweden and Norway, Venezuela, *Protocol respecting the Arbitration of Claims between Sweden and Norway and Venezuela* (Washington, 10 March 1903); Spain, Venezuela, *Protocol between Spain and Venezuela for the Arbitration of Claims* (Washington, 2 April 1903); Germany, Venezuela, *Protocol between Germany and Venezuela for the Arbitration of German Claims* (Washington, 7 May 1903).

68 John Bassett Moore, *A Digest of International Law, Volume VI* (Government Printing Office 1906) 809–810.

The disparity between the treatment of injuries to aliens and injuries to property illustrates the integral nature of State interests to the doctrine of SR. Its trajectory was motivated and proactively affected by the prioritisation of international commerce. The law was accordingly adapted to facilitate the economy, and once again, the greatest loss was born by the alien.

3 Legal Conceptions of State Responsibility

Over the following decades, the subject of SR for injuries to aliens and the events of the late 19th century became an almost obsessive focus of international legal scholarship. A vast number of legal theses were penned by scholars of international law who sought to restore what they perceived to be the foundational principles of the legal doctrine, namely the position of the alien as a passive subject of SR.[69] Competing theories emerged as to how this should be achieved. Central to this academic inquiry were the competing theories of fault (subjective responsibility) and risk (objective responsibility). Though at the time the debate had little effect on the trajectory of SR, the central questions raised by scholars would re-emerge multiple times at later stages, both in relation to the development of SR, and in the application of its norms to IRL.

3.1 *Sovereignty, Capacity, and the Competing Theories of Fault and Risk*

Much of the relevant scholarship turned on the question of a State's capacity. While proponents of risk considered capacity to be superfluous to sovereign authority and international obligation, proponents of fault considered it to be at the core of the divergences in the doctrine of SR, that without resolution would misinform all other elements. They accused proponents of risk of ignoring the question of capacity altogether, as an inquiry into capacity would

69 See, for example: Emilio Brusa, Ludwig von Bar, 'Responsibilité des États à raison des dommages soufferts par des étrangers en cas d'émeute ou de guerre civile' (1900) 18 AnnIDI 47; Emilio Brusa, 'Responsabilité des États à raison des dommages soufferts par des étrangers en cas d'émeute ou de guerre civile' (1898) 17 AnnIDI 96; Ludwig von Bar, 'De la responsibilité des États à raison des dommages soufferts par des étrangers en cas de troubles, d'émeute ou de guerre civil' (1899) Revue de droit international et de législation comparée; Heinrich Triepel, 'Les Rapport entre le Droit International et le Droite Interne' (1923) 1 RdC; Heinrich Triepel, *Droit International et Droit Interne* (OUP 1920) ('Völkerrecht und Landesrecht' originally published in German, 1899); Charles de Visscher, 'Notes sur la responsabilité internationale des états et la protection diplomatique d'après quelques documents récents' (1927) RDILC 253; Louis Delbez, 'Responsabilité internationale d'un Etat pour des crimes commis sur le territoire d'un Etat' (1930) RGDIP 470.

reveal fundamental flaws in the theory of risk. No State, however well organised, could claim that it was so thoroughly clairvoyant that foreseeability should not be considered, nor so omnipotent that at all times it exercised the 'power to prevent,' nor so perfectly organised that civil unrest could not threaten the peace.[70] A State that lacked capacity therefore could not be responsible for the violation of an international obligation.

In previous decades, it had been common practice for arbitral commissions to find that SR could not be properly attributed to a State where it had concluded that the State lacked the competent means to prevent the occurrence of those acts imputed to it.[71] In making such a determination, arbitral commissions often employed a test of 'manifest negligence,' which in turn comprised a test of capacity known as the 'power to prevent.'[72] A State lacked the power to prevent injury where the actions that occasioned the injury were not foreseeable. Where the injurious acts lacked foreseeability, the State was not obliged to implement repressive countermeasures.[73] This included the acts of individuals.

By contrast, across the Americas, it had become established State practice that 'indirect responsibility' (deriving from civilian action occasioning injury) was imputable to a State if it involved some action or omission on the part of the authorities. The imputability of such an act or omission depended on the scope of the duties required of a State in preventing or repressing the injurious acts of individuals.[74] In the case of injuries inflicted on aliens by civilians, the distinction between the State's obligation to prevent, and its obligation to repress was an important one: the discharge of preventative obligations necessarily required foreseeability.[75] Indeed, foreseeability was the primary element taken into consideration by numerous Claims Commis-

70 Emilio Brusa, 'Responsabilité des États à raison des dommages soufferts par des étrangers en cas d'émeute ou de guerre civile' (1898) 17 AnnIDI 96, 100.

71 See generally: John Bassett Moore, *A Digest of International Law, Volume III* (Government Printing Office 1906).

72 John Bassett Moore, *A Digest of International Law, Volume III* (Government Printing Office 1906) 2990.

73 *L.F.H. Neer and Pauline Neer* [1926] 4 RIAA 73; *Walter A. Noyes (United States) v Panama* [1933] 6 RIAA 253; Hersch Lauterpacht, *Annual Digest and Reports of Public International Law Cases: 1933–1934* (Butterworth & Company 1933).

74 See: *Case of Salvador Prats v the United States of America* [1868] 29 RIAA 187; John Bassett Moore, *A Digest of International Law, Volume III* (Government Printing Office 1906), 2893. See also: Pan American Union, *Contributions of the American Continent to the Principles Governing the Responsibility of the State*1961) 15.

75 Pan American Union, *Contributions of the American Continent to the Principles Governing the Responsibility of the State*1961) 17.

sions in determining the 'indirect responsibility' of the State for the failure to repress injury to aliens.[76] The question of a link between sovereignty and capacity was therefore especially relevant to the question of fault and the defence of necessity in Latin American doctrine, as the legitimacy of the latter relied first on a common understanding the former. Accordingly, the State was responsible for the positive acts it committed that were contrary to law, as it was with gross negligence committed by its delegates and functionaries, and for its omissions to prevent the commission of injurious acts by civilians.[77] By extension, a State that knew of an injurious act and did not intervene, itself became complicit in the act and derived its own liability through either the tacit approval of the unlawful conduct,[78] or negligence[79] as in the case of Aigue-Mortes.[80]

The Latin American doctrine of 'indirect responsibility' provided that the responsibility of the State was not derived from the positive acts of every individual that was subject to its sovereign power, but from the obligation to prevent the commission of wrongful acts. Accordingly, small acts of civil disobedience were excluded from the scope of international obligations, as the injured State could not reasonably expect to receive satisfaction for the small acts of 'irresponsible civilians.'[81] A State's international obligations could only be viewed as a responsibility to reduce and restrain, and comprised only an obligation to use all measures of prevention or repression that the authority had at its disposal.[82] If the State in which the act was committed had not, for

76 See: John Bassett Moore, *A Digest of International Law, Volume III* (Government Printing Office 1906).

77 Ludwig von Bar, 'De la responsibilité des États à raison des dommages soufferts par des étrangers en cas de troubles, d'émeute ou de guerre civil' (1899) Revue de droit international et de législation comparée 471.

78 Dionisio Anzilotti, *Teoria generale della responsibilità dello Stato nel diritto internazionale* (F. Lumachi Libraio-Editore 1902) 15; Louis Delbez, 'Responsabilité internationale d'un Etat pour des crimes commis sur le territoire d'un Etat' (1930) RGDIP 470.

79 Emilio Brusa, 'Responsabilité des États à raison des dommages soufferts par des étrangers en cas d'émeute ou de guerre civile' (1898) 17 AnnIDI 96, 97; Charles de Visscher, 'Notes sur la responsabilité internationale des états et la protection diplomatique d'après quelques documents récents' (1927) RDILC 253, citing G. Baudry-Lacantinerie, *Précis de Droit Civil Contenant des Principes et dans Une Deuxième les Questions de Détail et les Controverses (Tome II)* (Libraires de la Société du Recueil Sirey 1913) 835.

80 See Section 2(ii).

81 *Id.*

82 Charles de Visscher, 'Notes sur la responsabilité internationale des états et la protection diplomatique d'après quelques documents récents' (1927) RDILC 251–252.

example, provided necessary security against an eventual injury, it may be rendered negligently responsible for the fault of abstention.[83]

The practical limitations of the State's authority were a primary consideration for proponents of fault. They contended that the legitimacy of 'manifest negligence' and the 'power to prevent' turned first on the question of the State's sovereign powers to 'command, prohibit and repress' threats to nationals and aliens, and to 'maintain order and social peace on its territory and to protect the rights of all.'[84] The objective capacity of a State itself was the determinant of the State's sovereign powers to prevent injury. In that regard, States that were not regularly organised, or who were in an embryonic phase of development, lacked the 'mature existence' required to carry the weight of international relations. They could not therefore be subject to the law of nations, and accordingly could not bear responsibility for lack of capacity.[85]

It was suggested that States may consider the individual circumstances of aliens in allocating relief, such as their poverty, but others argued that this would create a privileged class among aliens and create tension between immigrants and the national population.[86] Additionally, it would violate the principle of distinction between nationals and aliens and would amount to differential treatment on an arbitrary basis; tantamount to a declaration that an injury suffered by an alien was more severe that an injury suffered by a national.[87] It was also suggested that any claim of indemnity by foreign residents should be subject to the absolute condition that they have not been guilty of violating the laws of neutrality and public order, either by participation in or supply of civil disturbances. Similarly, an alien should lose the right

83 Heinrich Triepel, *Droit International et Droit Interne* (OUP 1920) 335; Dionisio Anzilotti, *Teoria generale della responsibilità dello Stato nel diritto internazionale* (F. Lumachi Libraio-Editore 1902) 172.

84 Emilio Brusa, 'Responsabilité des États à raison des dommages soufferts par des étrangers en cas d'émeute ou de guerre civile' (1898) 17 AnnIDI 96, 98, 107; Heinrich Triepel, 'Les Rapport entre le Droit International et le Droite Interne' (1923) 1 RdC 116.

85 Ludwig von Bar, 'De la responsibilité des États à raison des dommages soufferts par des étrangers en cas de troubles, d'émeute ou de guerre civil' (1899) Revue de droit international et de législation comparée 468; Emilio Brusa, 'Responsabilité des États à raison des dommages soufferts par des étrangers en cas d'émeute ou de guerre civile' (1898) 17 AnnIDI 96, 105.

86 Emilio Brusa, 'Responsabilité des États à raison des dommages soufferts par des étrangers en cas d'émeute ou de guerre civile' (1898) 17 AnnIDI 96, 98.

87 Heinrich Triepel, 'Les Rapport entre le Droit International et le Droite Interne' (1923) 1 RdC 116.

to request diplomatic protection if they have moved to the country against the advice of their government.[88]

Proponents of risk considered the import of fault to muddy the waters of SR and permit subjective assessment of each individual case. If the theory of a 'mature existence' extended to States not in a state of development, but nevertheless lacking capacity to fulfil international obligations, then not only was the obligation to protect aliens not absolute, and liability not strict, but it was subject to a wide and variable set of criteria. Scholars of objective responsibility sought to apply a threshold of absolute liability, according to which it was an international obligation to compensate an injured alien irrespective of the circumstances that occasioned the injury. It was therefore gratuitous to examine whether the government or the authorities had committed a negligent act.[89]

This theory was based on the presumption that the relationship that existed between a State and an alien implied a veritable guarantee of security, from which the State could not be exonerated under any circumstances, including reduced capacity, and including where it was demonstrated that the State had exercised the full extent of vigilance permissible under law, and with all the material power at its disposal. This was not a particularly popular theory. As previously stated, proponents of absolute liability frequently omitted an examination of capacity from their theses as to do so would reveal that the all-seeing, all-powerful State did not exist even among the most sophisticated and wealthy nations.

Scholars of subjective responsibility observed that the maintenance of public order often required the State to *cause* damage to personal property and persons in cases of civil war or insurrection, and that any damage caused in the maintenance of that public order was *necessary* to accomplish the State's primary functions.[90] The defence of necessity was however still subject to the condition that damaged property was returned to its proprietor in the form of pecuniary indemnity, as it was in the case of expropriated property,[91] but nonetheless, this was evidence that liability was more nuanced than presented under the theory of risk. Notably, Anzilotti rejected the the-

88 *Id.*, 117.

89 Ludwig von Bar, 'De la responsibilité des États à raison des dommages soufferts par des étrangers en cas de troubles, d'émeute ou de guerre civil' (1899) Revue de droit international et de législation comparée 471.

90 Emilio Brusa, 'Responsabilité des États à raison des dommages soufferts par des étrangers en cas d'émeute ou de guerre civile' (1898) 17 AnnIDI 96, 108.

91 *Id.*

ory of fault altogether, asserting instead that the State was responsible where it had not fulfilled the obligation imposed upon it by international law. It did not require a direct or indirect connection between its will and the action of the individual, nor for a possible culpable or malicious intention. In that regard, it was the lack of diligence in itself, in the prevention of the act of the individual or in its punishment, and not the fault, that constituted the violation of international law.[92] Similarly, De Visscher rejected both fault and risk as constituent elements of SR, arguing that the theory of fault was laden with psychological elements that must necessarily exclude it from PIL, and that the theory of risk goes too far if it tends to provide the individual with an absolute guarantee of security.[93] Such a system is essentially the one followed in all the codification procedures described in Chapter 1, which was consistent with practice at the time. As García Amador noted (somewhat prophetically as it applies to due diligence standards):

> [B]oth the notion of 'fault' and the notion of 'risk' involve conditions which play, at the most, a secondary role as constituent elements of international responsibility. What really matters in all the cases and situations is the objective existence of an injury and that this injury has been caused by an unjustified breach of a well-established obligation or, if such were the case, by an abuse of rights, either one legally imputable to a subject of international law.[94]

The question of a State's capacity to fulfil international obligations would reemerge multiple times over the decades, including in the 1920s in response to the Russian refugee crisis, in opposition to repatriation on the basis that the State lacked the capacity to exercise its sovereign powers of protection over its nationals, and during various codification procedures, when States considered the application of fault and risk to SR.[95]

---

92 Dionisio Anzilotti, *Teoria generale della responsibilità dello Stato nel diritto internazionale* (F. Lumachi Libraio-Editore 1902) 172–173.

93 Charles de Visscher, 'Responsabilité Internationale des États à raison des dommages causes sur leur Territoire a la Personne ou aux biens des Étrangers' (1927) 33 III(III) AnnIDI 81, 106.

94 F.V. García Amador, 'State Responsibility: Some New Problems' (1958) 94 RDCADI 367, 391–392.

95 See Section 5(i)–(ii) of this chapter.

3.2 *The Definition of 'Force Majeure'*

Proponents of absolute liability posited that not even the necessity of maintaining public order exempted the State from the obligation to repair damages. The only acts that could disturb the correlative nature of rights and obligations in the case of SR for injuries to aliens were acts of *force majeure*.[96] But *force majeure* and necessity were so closely linked that quite often, the declaration of one preceded the other, and strict distinctions between the two concepts were at times difficult to articulate. This was primarily on account of the fact that civil disturbances were regularly described as acts of *force majeure* and could therefore quite easily extend to include the actions of the State taken in response to civil disturbances, particularly those actions classified as 'necessary,' so that necessary acts of State would become acts of *force majeure* and would therefore fall outside the scope of international liability.

States relied on an expansive interpretation of *force majeure* to preclude the element of will. Though some scholars contended that this was easily refutable as every act of war, riot, or insurrection required will, and could not reasonably constitute *force majeure*,[97] this addressed only half the question. States had characterised not only acts of civil disobedience as *force majeure*, but also the acts of the State in repressing such action. The question of a State's will was particularly relevant to the defence of necessity, as the State's exercise of authority in response to civil disturbances were often classified as necessary and therefore *force majeure*. This theory found some (albeit limited) scholarly support, as some posited that *force majeure* was indicative of an event that could not be avoided by any reasonable measure, even where careful measures of precaution were taken, and that accordingly the expression was applicable to disturbances of the peace.[98] Such an interpretation would however require an examination of every individual case for the same reasons suggested by those opposed to the inclusion of civil disturbances in the definition: for an event to be properly classified as *force majeure*, it must be proven that the event lacked foreseeability and that the State lacked capacity to mount a defence.[99]

---

96 *Id.*

97 Emilio Brusa, 'Responsabilité des États à raison des dommages soufferts par des étrangers en cas d'émeute ou de guerre civile' (1898) 17 AnnIDI 96, 97.

98 Ludwig von Bar, 'De la responsibilité des États à raison des dommages soufferts par des étrangers en cas de troubles, d'émeute ou de guerre civil' (1899) Revue de droit international et de législation comparée 466.

99 *Id.*

As discussed in Section 2, in previous decades, numerous States had relied on a particularly expansive interpretation of what constituted *force majeure*, in an effort to evade SR for injuries to aliens. The term was applied regularly to riots, insurrections, and other disturbances of the peace and disagreements between injured and injurious States concerning the definition of the term frequently contributed to the final decision to settle claims informally by diplomatic means. While some rejected the application of *force majeure* to anything that was not strictly an 'act of God,' others accepted that it could apply to civil disturbances in rare cases, subject to a number of conditions. A State could not, for example, invoke *force majeure* where it could be proven that it had received warning of an impending danger and possessed the necessary measures of defence to suppress it,[100] as in the case of New Orleans.[101] Others were of the view that the classification of any act of riot, insurrection, or war – whether civil or international – as *force majeure* was utterly inappropriate, as a disturbance of the peace and an earthquake or a flood were entirely incomparable. Advocates of such an interpretation did acknowledge however that the theory was in contradiction with the principle that States must be held responsible for acts of violence committed against aliens.[102] Yet, as a State could not reasonably be expected to defend aliens against acts of *force majeure*, any injury sustained as a result could not be compensated. There was no duty to repair, and the State had no obligation to indemnify.[103] If the State took the decision to provide resources to injured parties, it could only be considered an "act of benevolence," as had been practiced in previous decades.

These precise arguments have since been advanced numerous times in respect of SR in IRL. The notion that a State that lacks capacity to intervene to provide refugee protection has been repeatedly used as a defence in judicial proceedings.[104] The argument has been made repeatedly by States that the

100 Ludwig von Bar, 'De la responsibilité des États à raison des dommages soufferts par des étrangers en cas de troubles, d'émeute ou de guerre civil' (1899) Revue de droit international et de législation comparée 466–467.

101 See Section 2(ii).

102 Ludwig von Bar, 'De la responsibilité des États à raison des dommages soufferts par des étrangers en cas de troubles, d'émeute ou de guerre civil' (1899) Revue de droit international et de législation comparée 467; Emilio Brusa, 'Responsabilité des États à raison des dommages soufferts par des étrangers en cas d'émeute ou de guerre civile' (1898) 17 AnnIDI 96, 96.

103 *Id.*

104 See Chapter 5.

lack of foreseeability should exclude the attribution of SR for wrongful acts in respect of IRL, most notably, in respect of search and rescue operations, and in respect of inquiries made during such operations in regard to the status of those aboard intercepted vessels.[105] These events are discussed in detail in Chapter 5, but it is worth noting here that the genealogy of such legal arguments has clear roots in the diverging doctrine of SR at this critical juncture in history, when States exerted substantial effort to reinforce certain concepts of SR that, in reality, had little legal foundation in law or practice.

3.3 *The 'Privatisation' of Public Law*

While much scholarship evaluated the relationship between municipal law – referred to then as 'internal' law – and IL, the subject that attracted near uniform condemnation was the informality and inconsistency of the rules of attribution of SR that had become a distinctive feature in the settlement of indemnification matters; what might be called the 'privatisation' of PIL. Correlations between public and private international law received much academic scrutiny as States continued to apply substantive and procedural concepts of private law to matters previously accepted as having a distinctively public character. Certain commentators considered contemporary State practice to be reflective of an attempt to shift the principles of obligation, responsibility, attribution, and indemnification away from public law and toward private law, as exemplified by the widespread application of private law principles in the settlement of claims involving Latin American States.

Many observed that the resolution of international indemnity cases, pursuant either to principles of private law or to diplomatic intervention, had not been permitted by any nation of Europe or Latin America in the preceding years.[106] This led some to conclude that governments of powerful nations were exercising or imposing an 'invented law' against relatively weaker States, and by doing so, had themselves committed an abuse of power that could not be justified under IL or political convention.[107] Scholars rejected attempts by

105 *Id.*

106 Emilio Brusa, 'Responsabilité des États à raison des dommages soufferts par des étrangers en cas d'émeute ou de guerre civile' (1898) 17 AnnIDI 96; Carlos Calvo, *Le droit international théorique et pratique, Volume 2* (4 edn, Guillaumin 1888) paras 1280, 1297; P. Pradier-Fodére, *Traité de droit international public Européen et Américain suivant les progrès de la science et de la pratique contemporaine* (G. Pedone-Lauriel 1885) para 205.

107 *Id.*

States to characterise compensation as "a simple duty of charitable benevolence."[108]

Proponents of traditional SR dismissed the characterisation of State acts and omissions as akin to personal injury under civil law as an unnecessary complication of what was essentially a simple matter of public law.[109] Those in favour of a public law interpretation of SR believed that where the injurious act was committed within a State's territory, it fell within the scope of the State's power to prevent, "the state [was] responsible for the acts that international law obliges it to prevent, and for the omission of acts that international law obliges it to execute."[110] This argument was bolstered by the fact that States had not tolerated their conduct being subjected to diplomatic intervention, and therefore it could not be true that the principle of indemnification of injured aliens as subject to private law. This was a matter of logic. Principles of substantive public law could not be subjected to principles of procedural private law.[111]

The 'privatisation of public law,' including those measures describes in Section 2 of this chapter, minimised the number of instances in which the conduct of a State could be attributed to it as wrongful, as the actions and omissions of its agents were no longer the subject of strict liability, let alone absolute liability. Instead, the requirement for proof of fault meant that the doctrine of SR would incorporate a presumption of refutability. This left the door ajar for the repudiation of fault, which in turn led to the creative and liberal interpretation of *force majeure*, and the further exclusion of the individual from the ambit of SR.

108 Emilio Brusa, 'Responsabilité des États à raison des dommages soufferts par des étrangers en cas d'émeute ou de guerre civile' (1898) 17 AnnIDI 96, 97, 99, 102, 109; see also: Heinrich Triepel, *Droit International et Droit Interne* (OUP 1920), 334.

109 Dionisio Anzilotti, *Teoria generale della responsibilità dello Stato nel diritto internazionale* (F. Lumachi Libraio-Editore 1902), 161, 172.

110 Heinrich Triepel, *Droit International et Droit Interne* (OUP 1920) 335; Jacque Dumas, 'Du déni de justice considéré comme condition de la responsabilité internationale des États en matière criminelle' (1929) RDILC 279–280; Dionisio Anzilotti, 'La Responsibilité Internationale des États à raison des dommages soufferts par des étrangers' (1906) 13 RGDIP 28.

111 *Id.*; Heinrich Triepel, *Droit International et Droit Interne* (OUP 1920) 334.

4 The Missing Link: Guns, States, and Aliens

As is frequently the case in legal and political commentary, the scrutiny of SR as an element of PIL does not account for broader, peripheral factors relevant to its development.[112] Mounting concern over the regulation of international trade and commerce, and the imposition of international regulations in respect of such, served as the principle impetus for the actions of States in respect of the limitation of circumstances capable of engaging SR. The indemnification of injured aliens was of concern to States insofar as the expanding scope of international obligations threatened to impact the viability of certain commercial interests that may implicate the responsibility of the State for injurious acts to aliens, particularly injurious acts caused by negligence. In that respect, the most significant factor to influence the pursuit of informalisation and privatisation of SR was the increased regulation of the international arms trade.

The global economy in weapons was (and remains) an extremely lucrative enterprise, and States leading production and export were naturally concerned with any increased regulation of it. That included regulation that threatened to attribute SR to the exporter State for the use of merchandise occasioning injury. Regulation of the arms trade, together with as-yet uncodified norms of SR, and international support for the theory of subjective responsibility (which admitted the theory of negligence), created an imminent risk that arms regulation may encompass a negative obligation of supplier States to refrain from exporting weapons to third States where they may be used to inflict injury during civil disturbances. By extension, such an obligation might apply in private law to enterprises engaged in the fabrication and supply of arms and munitions.

The US, Great Britain, and France in particular had benefitted immensely from the provision of material support during the Latin American Wars of Independence. To admit the theory of fault in respect of injuries to aliens sustained during civil disturbances would have had significant ramifications for exporter States. As such, a consensus on SR for injuries to aliens was formed between weapons-producing States that was utilised to steer the broader international regulation of the arms trade. This was achieved in several ways. Arms-producing States established a consensus that the sale and

112 An exception to this is Alan Nissel, who contends that the contemporary doctrine of SR resulted from two 20th-century events: the U.S. protection of foreign investments and the German doctrinalisation of public law. See: Alan Nissel, 'The Duality of State Responsibility' (2013) 44 Colum Hum Rts L Rev 793.

export of weapons could occur freely where the exporting State took no official position on the conflict in the importing State. Weapons-producing States frequently adopted a position of neutrality, permitting the sale and export of arms and munitions to all parties to a conflict, as a declaration of support for one side would have prohibited the supply of material assistance to others.

Those same States created international instruments to ensure that once weapons were outside their jurisdiction, their use (or misuse) could not engage questions of SR. Multilateral instruments concluded among arms-producing States comprised two overarching elements: the liberalisation of circumstances in which weapons could be sold and exported, and the restriction of SR of exporter States for subsequent use. Arms-producing States would go on to exercise significant influence over the international regulation of the arms trade, further reinforcing a doctrine of SR that reflected the interests of global powers. Their intervention was a pre-emptive and complementary measure, not only intended to solidify a permissive international environment for the sale and export of weapons, but also to ensure the minimisation of any future exposure to the attribution of SR. The concerted efforts to direct the evolving doctrine of SR were so effective, that both the international regulation of weapons and the responsibility of States for injuries to aliens never recovered. Central to the pursuit of this consensus was the use of neutrality. The absence of a declaration by a State in support of a party to a conflict left it free to maximise exportation of weapons by supplying arms to all sides. In order to avoid the imposition of an arms embargo against a party to a conflict, and to maximise economic opportunities, arms-producing States frequently adopted a position of neutrality.

During the Chilean revolution of 1891, Britain and France refused to forbid national companies from selling arms, either to the Chilean government or revolutionary forces, though representatives of both the Revolutionary Junta, and Chilean State Agents appealed to both States to halt all sales to the opposing party.[113] The British government went so far as to published a decree by the Chilean government in the London Gazette prohibiting the importation into Chile of "arms, ammunition, and war material of every description" in support of revolutionaries.[114] But the publication was not accompanied by any declaration by the British government on its position on the conflict, which under-

113 Harold Blakemore, 'Chilean Revolutionary Agents in Europe, 1891' (1964) 33(4) Pacific Historical Review 425.

114 (No title) (24 February 1891) The London Gazette 1004.

standably created confusion among weapons manufacturers and exporters.[115] The British Consul-General at Hamburg sought the position of the British government in respect of the conflict, as he had been informed that agents of the Chilean revolutionaries had purchased arms and would likely ship them from Antwerp to Chile. The British government directly instructed the Consul-General at Antwerp to take no action unless approached by individual British ship-owners hoping to transport the goods. That same month, the British shipping firm Walford & Co., aware of the Chilean decree, sought clarification from the Consul-General regarding the British position on the supply to Chilean revolutionary forces of what was vaguely described as "coal or other merchandise."[116] Having raised no objection to the transaction, Walford & Co. chartered a British steamer to carry cargo to the Falkland Islands comprising 500 tons of coal, 5,000 rifles, 4,000,000 cartridges, 6 cannons, and 2,700 grenades.[117]

Private citizens with substantial interests in the nitrate mines of Northern Chile also made overtures to the British government, as did the legal representative of the Nitrate Railways Company,[118] as the conflict seriously threatened the private ownership of the mines and risked falling into the hands of revolutionary forces. The former implored the British government to prohibit the company Armstrongs from supplying arms to the ship *Pinto*; one of two warships under construction in France.[119] France itself had inquired as to the British attitude to the possibility of Chilean government ships, then under construction in France, seeking arms in Great Britain, to which the British Foreign Office responded that "no sufficient ground existed for any action by Her Majesty's government."[120] In response to those private citizens concerned with the armament of the *Pinto*, the British Foreign Office responded that it had no power to interfere in commercial matters unless there was a "general

115 Harold Blakemore, 'Chilean Revolutionary Agents in Europe, 1891' (1964) 33(4) Pacific Historical Review 425.

116 *Id.*

117 *Id.*, 443–444.

118 *Id.*, 425; John R. Brown, 'The Chilean Nitrate Railways Controversy' (1958) 43 The Hispanic American Historical Review 465–448.

119 Harold Blakemore, 'Chilean Revolutionary Agents in Europe, 1891' (1964) 33(4) Pacific Historical Review 432.

120 Augusto Matte, Agustín Ross, *Memoria presentada a la excelentísima junta del gobierno* (Imprimerie et Libraire Administrative et Classique, Paul Dupont 1892) 125–127.

prohibition as a measure for the defence of Great Britain."[121] As Britain had maintained a position of neutrality throughout the conflict, the defence of Great Britain was not at issue, and the State and national companies were free to sell and export weapons to both sides of the Chilean conflict.

The US also adopted a position of neutrality during the Cuban War of Independence, in an explicit attempt to maximise sales of weapons to the Caribbean State. The US Government refused to subscribe to reclamations made by Spain after Cuban nationals exiled in the US provided weapons to insurgents.[122] Congress repeatedly tried to move both the Cleveland (1893–1897)[123] and McKinley (1897–1901) administrations to classify Cuban rebels as belligerents, which would legalise their attempts to buy and receive arms from the US,[124] but the government refused to recognise the insurgent as having belligerent status, as to do so would, in the words of Cleveland: "[be] clearly perilous and injurious to our own interests."[125] Instead, the administration adopted a policy of strict neutrality.[126] In defence of the liberal position on weapons regulation, Cleveland himself wrote:

> Many Cubans reside in this country and indirectly promote the insurrection through [...] the purchase and shipment of arms [...] which the spirit of our institutions and the tenor of our laws do not permit to be made the subject of criminal prosecutions.[127]

Neutrality was only one practice employed by States to maximise the sale and export of weapons. More important for the protection of the industry was to

---

121 Harold Blakemore, 'Chilean Revolutionary Agents in Europe, 1891' (1964) 33(4) Pacific Historical Review 432.

122 Louis Delbez, 'Responsabilité internationale d'un Etat pour des crimes commis sur le territoire d'un Etat' (1930) RGDIP 467.

123 Cleveland in fact served two terms as President of the United States, the first between 1885 and 1889.

124 Christopher Harris, 'Edwin F. Atkins and the Evolution of United States Cuba Policy, 1894–1902' (2005) 78(2) The New England Quarterly 202.

125 Grover Cleveland, 'American Interests in the Cuban Revolution' in *United States Department of State, Papers Relating to Foreign Affairs* (United States Department of State, 1896) 27.

126 Christopher Harris, 'Edwin F. Atkins and the Evolution of United States Cuba Policy, 1894–1902' (2005) 78(2) The New England Quarterly 213.

127 Grover Cleveland, 'Message from the President' in *Papers Relating to the Foreign Relations of the United States, with The Annual Message of the President Transmitted to Congress December 7, 1896, and the Annual Report of the Secretary of State* (United States Government Printing Office, 1897).

exercise control over the burgeoning regulation of the arms trade, which posed a great threat to the industry, not only by reducing opportunities to sell and export, but by virtue of its treatment under IL, it would prescribe certain international obligations and therefore defined the circumstances in which SR could be attributed to an exporter State. Like much of the activities of economic powers in the previous decades, the conduct of arms-producing States in the regulation of the international arms trade focused on the question of SR. As in other international settings, a common position was cultivated among Western States in relation to the scope and content of this burgeoning field of IL. This was motivated by the exclusion of circumstances capable of engaging SR for injuries to individuals.

The *Convention Relative to the Slave Trade and Importation into Africa of Firearms, Ammunition, and Spirituous Liquors* of 1890, also known as *The General Act of Brussels*, was a collection of anti-slavery measures signed by a vast number of European powers, Persia, the Ottoman Empire, the Independent State of Congo, and Zanzibar.[128] It prohibited the importation of arms and munitions to certain territories except in prescribed circumstances. Unsurprisingly, those prescribed circumstances were exceptionally broad and the responsibility of the exporting State for subsequent use of merchandise was excluded completely by one specific provision. While most of its provisions regulated the movement of arms and munitions once inside Africa, it provided that all imported firearms "shall be deposited, at the cost, risk and peril of the importers, in a public warehouse under the supervision of the State government."[129] No withdrawal of firearms or imported munitions from warehouses was permitted without the previous authorisation of the said government,[130] ensuring that any injury suffered by individuals, resulting from the unlawful use of merchandise remained the sole responsibility of the importing State.

Further regulation of the arms trade came at the close of WWI when the Allied Powers and the Republic of German-Austria signed *The Convention for the Control of the Trade in Arms and Ammunition*, also known as the *Treaty of Saint-Germain-en-Laye*.[131] The Treaty was intended to "prevent the importation of arms, except under the strictest possible control, to certain defined areas inhabited by backward peoples" specifically into African States and

128 *Convention Relative to the Slave Trade and Importation into Africa of Firearms, Ammunition, and Spirituous Liquors* (Brussels, 2 July 1890).

129 *Id.*, Article IX.

130 *Id.*

131 League of Nations, *Convention for the Control of the Trade in Arms and Munition and Protocol signed at St-Germain-en-Laye* (10 September 1919) LNTS Vol. VII, No. 200.

States bordering the Red Sea.[132] But the treaty posed a significant threat to the burgeoning positive framework that supported the limitation of international obligations for exporting States and as such, concerted efforts were made to prevent its entering into force. The provisions of the treaty were extremely far-reaching and would have prohibited the export of artillery of all kinds; whether complete or in parts, apparatuses for the discharge of all kinds of projectiles, machine-guns and rifled weapons of all kinds, as well as munitions for use with such arms.[133] It would have also required that data relating to the quantities and destinations of arms, munitions, and implements, exported by the signatory States, be published by a central office at the LoN.[134]

The Treaty never entered into force. The US Senate refused to consent to its ratification on the basis that it contained the Covenant of the LoN, to which the US did not wish to become a Member State.[135] Instead, it concluded separate bilateral Peace Treaties with Austria, Hungary, and Germany, each of which stipulated that while the US would fully enjoy all the rights and advantages for its benefit in the 1919 *Treaty of St. Germain-en-Laye*, notwithstanding the fact that it had not been ratified by the US, it would not be bound by certain provisions of the treaty, and would assume no obligations in relation to others.[136] But accession to the Covenant of the LoN was not the only reason that the US did not wish to become a signatory to the treaty. It viewed the treaty as an extension of the 1925 *Convention for the Supervision of Trade in Arms and War Munitions,* and an imposition of further restriction on the sale

132 League of Nations, 'Conference for the Control of the International Trade in Arms, Munitions and Implements of War' (Geneva 1925), 10.

133 *Id.*, Article 1.

134 *Id.*, Article 5.

135 *The Commission to Negotiate Peace to the Secretary of State* (*Paris, 9 October 1919*) (1935) Papers Relating to the Foreign Relations of the United States, 1920, Volume I: United States Government Printing Office.

136 USA, Austria, *A Treaty Between the United States and Austria, Signed on August 24, 1921, to Establish Securely Friendly Relations Between The Two Nations, The United States of America and Austria* (Vienna, 24 August 1921) LNTS Vol. VII, No. 184, Article 1; USA, Germany, *A Treaty Between the United States and Germany, Signed on August 25, 1921, to Restore Friendly Relations Existing Between the Two Nations Prior to the Outbreak of War Germany and the United States of America* (Berlin, 25 August 1921) LNTS Vol. XII, No. 310, Article 1; USA, Hungary, *A Treaty Between the United States and Hungary, Signed August 29, 1921, to Establish Securely Friendly Relations Between the Two Nations the United States of America and Hungary* (Budapest, 29 August 1921) Article 1 (not registered with the LoN).

and exportation of weapons.[137] This was particularly troublesome to the US at that particular time, as imminent sales of weapons to Latin America would have been threatened if it were to sign the Treaty. As a direct result of the US abstention, the treaty was not ratified by many of the principal arms-producing powers, and did not receive sufficient signatures.[138]

But it was not sufficient to abstain from becoming a signatory to the Treaty. Even without the signature of the US, the treaty would have posed a threat to the global arms trade and to the principle of non-responsibility of States in relation to the sale and export of weapons; an impermissible intrusion on the economic interests of the State. Accordingly, the US sought to undermine the overall process; ultimately leading to the failure of the treaty, and significant US control over the terms of a new, more favourable international agreement. Two days prior to it signing, the US received information from the British Embassy that Venezuela wished to purchase airplanes, bombs, and munitions from the US. The British Embassy considered that in view of the approaching signature of the treaty, the His Majesty's Government presumed the US would "not be disposed to permit the exportation of armaments to Venezuela."[139] In a latter exchange between the British and US governments, the two States agreed that it would *not* be a violation of the treaty if they were to fulfil orders for arms and munitions to non-signatory States, *if* their governments secured from the purchasing government certain vague undertakings. The British Ambassador suggested to the US Secretary of State that:

> [i]n some of these cases there can be no objection to the transaction, other than the difficulty arising from the delay in the ratification of the Convention. His Majesty's Government are of opinion that this difficulty might properly be surmounted by the signatory power obtaining from the purchasing Government an undertaking to sign the Convention *when an opportunity occurs*, and it is proposed to be guided by

137 'Convention for the Supervision of Trade in Arms and War Munitions' (1926) 20(1) AJIL 151, 152.

138 *Id.*

139 'The Acting Secretary of State to the Commission to Negotiate Peace' (Washington, 8 September 1919) *Papers Relating to the Foreign Relations of the United States, Volume I*1920) The Acting Secretary of State to the Commission to Negotiate Peace, *Papers Relating to the Foreign Relations of the United States, 1920, Volume I* (Washington, 8 September 1919).

> these principles in any future negotiations for the sale of arms under the conditions stated.[140]

The British Ambassador inquired as to whether the US Government "concur[red] in this interpretation of the obligations of the signatory powers to the Convention and Protocol,"[141] following which the British government proceeded unilaterally to secure such assurances from non-signatory States including the Argentine Republic, Chile, Venezuela, Colombia, Denmark, Norway, Sweden, Switzerland and The Netherlands. The British Ambassador then wrote again to the Secretary of State informing him that such assurances had been offered by those States; at least one of which wished to imminently procure arms from the US.[142]

The following month, the British Ambassador wrote again to the Secretary of State that His Majesty's Government had been informed by a private company that it had been unable to export "various articles of naval armament" to Brazil, and that it was "becoming seriously hampered by the very large stocks which this disability obliges them to retain on the premises." The British government had requested the Brazilian authorities to offer an undertaking on the treaty, to which they refused "stat[ing] that they had no intention of signing it, at all events in the near future." Such a categorical refusal could not be said to satisfy even the lenient conditions of the British and US governments. The British government, considering itself obliged to withhold export licenses to Brazil, requested the views of the US on the export of weapons to a State so unwilling to consider becoming a signatory to the treaty.[143]

The US replied that it would "decline to sell arms to non-signatory States except under a guarantee that the non-signatory power in question [would] adhere to the Arms Traffic Convention *when an opportunity is offered*."[144] Under such a strict application, this would include Brazil, but the Secretary of State hastened to add that "it may be found necessary in certain cases to make exceptions to this course of action."[145] It was added that with few excep-

140 'The British Appointed Ambassador on Special Mission (Grey) to the Secretary of State' (Washington, 13 November 1919) *Papers Relating to the Foreign Relations of the United States, Volume I*1920).

141 *Id.*

142 *Id.*

143 *Id.*

144 'The Secretary of State to the British Chargé (Lindsay)' (Washington, 6 January 1920) *Papers Relating to the Foreign Relations of the United States, Volume I*1920). Emphasis added.

145 *Id.*

tions, the US government itself was not controlling the exportation of arms and munitions by private companies to any government, signatory or non-signatory, and that the British government might overcome its current difficulties by adopting a similar policy of deregulation.[146]

In a communication to the President of the Council of the LoN, outlining the reasons that the ratification of the Treaty was defeated in the Senate, the US Secretary of State wrote that:

> There is particular objection to the provision by which the contracting parties would be prohibited from selling arms and munitions to states not parties to the convention. By such provisions, this government would be required to prevent shipments of military supplies to such Latin American countries as have not signed or adhered to the convention, however desirable it might be to permit such shipments, merely because they are not signatory powers and might not desire to adhere to the convention [...].[147]

Upon receipt of the communication, the Council of the LoN inquired whether the US would be disposed to cooperate in efforts to revise the Treaty. The US responded affirmatively, and preliminary meetings were held at Geneva and Paris in 1924. From the preliminary meetings, a Draft Convention was prepared, and the points of objection raised by the US to the *Treaty of St. Germain-en-Laye* of 1919 were eliminated from what would become *The Protocol for the Prohibition of the Use in War of Asphyxiating, Poisonous or other Gases, and of Bacteriological Methods of Warfare,* also known as the Geneva Protocol of 1925.[148] As it was noted the following year in the *American Journal of International Law,* with specific reference to Latin America "[t]he proposed Geneva [Protocol] lays down certain general requirements that would be applicable to the arms trade with all countries, but does not attempt to restrict the actual volume of such trade."[149] Conspicuously, the Geneva Protocol of 1925 did not provide for the supervision by the LoN of the international arm trade. Rather, States would undertake self-supervision as a sovereign matter, without external interference. Furthermore, they were not prevented from permitting the shipment of arms to any other State merely on account of the fact that State

146 *Id.* Emphasis added.

147 'Convention for the Supervision of Trade in Arms and War Munitions' (1926) 20(1) AJIL 151, 152.

148 *Id.*, 152, 154.

149 *Id.*, 154.

had not adhered to the Protocol. Accordingly, the Protocol did not provide for the lawful use of arms and munitions by third States.

These events reveal the economic ambitions of those States most disposed to influence the trajectory of IL, and the efforts expounded to ensure that those interests were protected under IL. The consequence of those actions was the deliberate exclusion of the protection of foreign nationals from the ambit of the State's international obligations.

5 The Codification of State Responsibility

Between 1899 and 1957, nine separate attempts were initiated to codify norms of SR, and with the exception of the latter stages of the ILC's codification of what would become the ARSIWA, none of them were able to achieve anything close to international consensus.[150] There are several reasons for this categorical failure, principal among which was the discord between States concerning the extent to which injuries to aliens would be included – or for that matter, excluded – from the codification process. Competing theories of SR and the urgency to ensure the supremacy of one over the other impelled certain actors to undertake codification procedures in anticipation of efforts by others. This was particularly true of procedures initiated in Europe and the Americas. In this respect, the chronology of codification procedures is not insignificant. Though the LoN was the first to announce its intention to codify SR for injuries to aliens, it was the Pan-American Union (PAU), led by the US, that first proceeded to codification. The haste with which the PAU commenced and con-

150 In 1925, the American Institute of Law conducted a project on 'diplomatic protection'; in 1926, a Draft Code of International Law was adopted by the Japanese branch of the International Law Association and the Kokusaiho Gakkwai (International Law Association of Japan); in 1927, the Institute of International Law prepared a Resolution on 'international responsibility of States for injuries on their territory to the person or property of foreigners'; also in 1927, a 'Draft Treaty concerning the responsibility of a State for internationally illegal acts' was prepared by Professor Strupp; Draft Conventions on 'responsibility of States for damage done in their territory to the person or property of foreigners' were prepared by Harvard Law School in 1929, and 1961; in 1930, a 'Draft Convention on the responsibility of States for injuries caused in their territory to the person or property of aliens' was prepared by the Deutsche Gesellschaft fur Volkerrecht (German International Law Association); in 1932, Professor Roth prepared a 'Draft Convention on the responsibility of States for international wrongful acts'; in 1957, Mr. F. V. García Amador, Special Rapporteur of the International Law Commission on State responsibility prepared the 'Draft on international responsibility of the State for injuries caused in its territory to the person or property of aliens.'

cluded codification created strong consensus among its Member States prior to the procedure of the LoN, and allowed the PAU to wield considerable power at the Hague Conference, where the LoN's draft articles on SR were to be adopted. The pre-emptive actions of the PAU were particularly important in respect of the alien and of injuries sustained during riots, insurrections, and other forms of civil unrest.

Yet despite the appearance of differences, all codification procedures attempted to affect the restriction of the scope and content of international obligations that correlated with traditional SR, so that the 'international aspect' of SR (being the elements that deemed it permissible for one State to invoke the responsibility of another) was either engaged in few contexts or not engaged at all. This was particular to cases involving injuries to aliens. By contrast (as it was in previous decades), the treatment of commercial injuries was distinct.

Several contentious issues persistently plagued the multiple procedures, each of which represented the competing interests of regional doctrine and theories of SR. Legal scholarship typically delineates regionality in respect of theories of SR along Anglo-American and European lines (Anglo-American doctrine being primarily concerned with State liability,[151] and European doctrine with the codification of secondary norms).[152] This incorrectly designates the US interpretation of IL as forming part of the Anglo-American tradition. The doctrine of the US was in fact far more complex and non-compliant than popularly categorised. The underlying motivations for the development of theories of SR are both broader, and more aptly divided down Anglo-European and Latin American traditions. Where Latin America was intent

151 L.F.E. Goldie, 'State Responsibility and the Expropriation of Property' (1978) 12(1) The International Lawyer 63; C.F. Amerasinghe, *State Responsibility for Injuries to Aliens* (Clarendon Press 1967), pg?; F.G. Dawson, I.L. Head, P.E. Herzog, *International Law, National Tribunals and the Rights of Aliens* (Syracuse University Press 1971); F.S. Dunn, *The Protection of Nationals: A Study in The Application of International Law* (The Johns Hopkins Press 1932); Clyde Eagleton, *The Responsibility of States in International Law* (New York University Press 1928); F.V. García Amador, Louis Bruno Sohn, Richard R. Baxter, *Recent Codification of the Law of State Responsibility for Injuries to Aliens* (Oceana Publications Inc. 1974); A.V. Freeman, *The International Responsibility of States for Denial of Justice* (Longmans, Green and Company 1938); E. Root, 'The Basis of Protection to Citizens Residing Abroad, Proceedings' (1910) 4 ASIL 20.

152 Goldie, *id.*, 66; Gregory Tunkin, *Theory of International Law* (Harvard University Press 1974); Georg Schwartzenberger, *A Manual of International Law* (Stevens and Sons 1967); Freeman, *id.*

on pursuing traditional SR, and European States pushed for the codification of "responsibility *stricto sensu*" (as one ILC member put it),[153] the US attempted multiple times either to undermine the codification process altogether, or to control its development in order to minimise the circumstances capable of engaging SR.

The origins of the European theory of responsibility are equally unaccounted for in legal scholarship. The eventual decision to recalibrate the substance of the ILC's work away from primary rules and towards secondary rules was governed by several considerations that lay outside the mandate of the ILC, and were motivated in large part by concerns about attribution of SR in the context of impending decolonisation. Though the competing interests of global regions during codification procedures were frequently categorised as a 'lack of consensus,'[154] much like the 'impracticality' of primary rules, the lack of consensus did not take account of the reasons for such.

The decolonisation of Africa and the treatment of nationalised property were of great concern to Western States. In the same way that international obligations for the alien was of consequence to SR, the rights and entitlements of a decolonised populace against the colonising State were as yet undefined. To create a law of liability before defining the position of the possible source of liability was considered to be imprudent.

Accordingly, there was persistent concern among Latin American States regarding the exclusion of Latin American doctrine, which would admit diplomatic protection, and the supremacy of European doctrine, which strongly preferred the codification of general secondary rules of SR. This was evident from the first multilateral attempts to codify SR, to the extensive and comprehensive work on the subject by the ILC, culminating in the adoption by the UN General Assembly of the ARSIWA. As Pisillo Mazzeschi has noted:

> [T]he issue of the international responsibility of the State toward the individual should have been given greater attention in the [ILC] Draft, because it constitutes an important element of contemporary international law on State responsibility. In fact, the ILC Draft Articles […] remain almost completely organized around traditional international law, with its focus on "interstate" relations.[155]

---

153 *Mr. Tsuroaka's "Working Document" for the International Law Commission* (1963) 2, 24.

154 David Caron, 'The ILC Articles on State Responsibility: The Paradoxical Relationship between Form and Authority' (2002) 96(4) AJIL 857, 861.

155 Riccardo Pisillo Mazzeschi, 'The Marginal Role of the Individual in the ILC's Articles on State Responsibility' (2004) 14 ItYBIL 39; See also: Edith Brown Weiss, 'Invoking State

Similarly, Jessup had observed that "[t]he international law governing the responsibility of states for injuries to aliens is one of the most highly developed branches of that law."[156] Yet the topic was suddenly and broadly considered to be too controversial and even too embryonic to merit codification.[157]

5.1 *Competing Regional Doctrines of State Responsibility*

As early as 1889, the International Conference of American States addressed the principle of civil equality between aliens and nationals, and the principle of non-intervention. The Conference ultimately recommended that aliens were entitled to enjoy all the civil rights enjoyed by nationals, including legal procedures and remedies, but that the "international standard of justice" did not apply in their favour.[158] Accordingly, Member States of the PAU were able to present regional resolutions during the Hague Conference, and to exercise a degree of control over the LoN's codification procedure, particularly where discussion turned to riots, insurrections, and civil disturbances. Questions related to public violence and injuries to aliens were later excluded from discussion at the Hague Conference due to the pressure exerted by PAU States over the course of consultations, and the theory of fault would be admitted only in the most limited of circumstances.

In 1924, the LoN commenced the study of various questions of IL, with a view to their eventual codification,[159] among them, whether a State may be liable for injuries caused on its territory to the person or property of foreigners.[160] Input was sought from States prior to the finalisation of a report on

---

Responsibility in the Twenty-First Century' (2002) 96(4) AJIL 798, 798; Christian J. Tams, 'All's Well That Ends Well: Comments on the ILCs Articles on State Responsibility' (2002) 62 ZaöRV 759, 762–763.

156 Phillip Jessup, 'Responsibility of States for Injuries to Individuals' (1946) 46(6) Colum L Rev 903, 904.

157 Comments by Mr Bartos, International Law Commission, *Summary record of the 415th meeting* (1957) (A/CN.4/SR.415), 167; Comments by Mr Amado, International Law Commission, *Summary record of the 415th meeting* (1957) (A/CN.4/SR.415), 168; Comments by Mr Spiropoulos, International Law Commission, *Summary record of the 415th meeting* (1957) (A/CN.4/SR.415), 168; Comments by Mr Fitzmaurice, International Law Commission, *Summary record of the 415th meeting* (1957) (A/CN.4/SR.415), 163.

158 Pan American Union, *Contributions of the American Continent to the Principles Governing the Responsibility of the State*1961) 1; Inter-American Juridical Committee, *Contributions of the American Continent to the Principles of International Law that Govern the Responsibility of the State* (Organization of American States 1962) 13.

159 'Appointment of Committees and Distribution of Work' (1924) 21 LNOJ Special Supplement 7.

160 *Id.*; 'Second Session of the Committee of Experts for the Progressive Codification of International Law' (1926) 20 AJIL Supplement 18.

the subject – named the Guerrero report after its primary author – but States expressed serious doubt as to the viability of achieving international consensus on the subject.[161] In particular, the "wide divergence of views on the fundamental legal principles at stake,"[162] specifically, the "wide divergence which exists between the Latin American and Anglo-Saxon systems"[163] would likely render any attempt to establish a uniform system of world law "impractical and quite unlikely to succeed."[164] Latin American States intent on asserting the primacy of the PAU's activities on the subject, were concerned that the encroachment of codification on the 'international aspect' of SR "too-closely affect[ed] the internal or the external policy of states" to be internationally codified,[165] and suggested that the finalisation of the Guerrero report await the upcoming Pan-American Conference, at which Member States would address conciliation procedures for the settlement of international relations.[166]

Eventually, draft articles were produced from the Guerrero report for a 'Convention on the Responsibility of States,'[167] though by many accounts, it stood little chance of achieving the required majority. For one, the preparatory material for the conference was considered flawed to such an extent as to handicap the entire procedure from its commencement. In drafting the Convention, the relevant committee did not consider a number of the bases of discussion prepared by the relevant committee, among them, SR arising from insurrections, riots or other disturbances, and the questions of illegal acts against foreigners during war. In that respect, the Guerrero report "departed materially, in some of its fundamental postulates and premises (representing minority views) from the subsequent Bases of Discussion, which reflected the views of the majority of the replying governments"[168]

161 'Appointment of Committees and Distribution of Work' (1924) 21 LNOJ Special Supplement 7. It is interesting to note that Questionnaire No. 4 originally inquired whether it was 'possible to establish by way of a general convention provisions as to the legal position and the functions of consuls. No explanation for the change in subject matter was provided by the report.

162 'Appointment of Committees and Distribution of Work' (1924) 21 LNOJ Special Supplement 7, 181.

163 *Id.*, 201.

164 *Id.*, 187.

165 *Id.*, 165.

166 *Id.*, 146, 148.

167 'Special Supplement No. 53; reproduced in AJIL Special Supplement 22 (1928)' (October 1927) LNOJ 231.

168 Edwin M. Borchard, '"Responsibility of States" at the Hague Codification Conference' (1930) 24(4) AJIL 517.

and accordingly, "the theoretical foundations of the topic were not prepared carefully enough."[169]

The preparatory materials also cited very few resources. In her report following the events of the Hague Conference, adviser to the US Secretaries of State on IL, Marjorie Whiteman, noted the lack of a broad review of relevant jurisprudence by the delegates. A total of only twelve cases decided in IL were cited during the sessions of the main Committee, and of those, only eight were mentioned by name. During the first five sessions reference was made to only one single case, and this was made 'indirectly.' She noted however that the US presented 47 precedents in defence of its position that the denial of justice was the only 'international aspect' of SR.[170]

As predicted, the Draft Convention failed to achieve the required two-thirds majority at final reading,[171] due in part to the competing theories of fault and risk, representative of the European and Pan-American doctrinal traditions, respectively. As the codification procedure continued, PAU States would utilise the prior work of the PAU to exercise power over the admission of the theory of fault, with a degree of success.

For their part, European States pushed for the admission of fault to the Draft Convention presented at the Hague Conference. The minimisation of SR was among their primary strategic interests, and quite apparently so. As Whiteman noted at the closing of the Hague conference:

> Certain delegates seemed to feel that [the codification of IL] could be accomplished not only by achieving definiteness of responsibility by states, but also by decreasing the number of situations in which such responsibility could arise.[172]

The French delegate proposed the text, based on the French Civil Code, which was intended to incorporate the theory of fault as the basis of responsibility, as distinct from the theory of risk.[173] It provided that a State was responsible for any failure on the part of its organs, where the failure to perform international

169 Ian Brownlie, *System of the Law of Nations: State Responsibility, Part I* (1 edn, OUP 1983) 13.

170 Marjorie M. Whiteman, 'The Codification of the Responsibility of States' (1930) 8(2) New York University Law Quarterly Review 185, 205.

171 *Id.*, 192. Article XX of the Rules of Procedure adopted in Plenary Session of the Conference required a two-thirds majority for the text to be adopted.

172 *Id.*, 191.

173 Edwin M. Borchard, '"Responsibility of States" at the Hague Codification Conference' (1930) 24(4) AJIL 517, 519.

obligations caused damage to the person or property of an alien. Article 8 provided that a State was not internationally responsible if an official's lack of authority was so apparent that the foreigner should have been aware of it and could in consequence have avoided the damage. In this way, "[t]he last paragraph contemplate[d] two operative facts – the manifest *ultra vires* of the officer, and the power of the foreigner to have escaped injury."[174]

Article 8 reflected the recommendations of the Guerrero Report, which had admitted liability for unauthorised acts within the narrowest limits, and at the Hague Conference, only 20 States voted for broader liability of State agents. At this point, however, the conference reached a deadlock, and it was reported later that some States contemplated withdrawing from the conference altogether. When proposals for a compromise on Article 8 were submitted by the minority, all reference to the responsibility of State agents for unauthorised acts was omitted.[175]

European States also sought to clarify certain terminology, while insisting on the increased 'elasticity' of others. Specifically, there was discussion on the need to further clarify what precisely was meant by the term 'international obligations,'[176] and whether it related only to treaty law or extended to include international custom. As Latin American legal tradition had firmly established a regional custom in relation to SR for public violence, it was essential for European States that the limits of 'international obligations' were clear.[177] Similarly, the vagueness of certain terminology was critical to the advancement of the European doctrine, and some delegates voiced support for vagueness and ambiguity in favour of sovereign interpretation. The delegate for Spain noted, with reference to the omission of the text "reparation for damage caused to a foreigner" from the Basis of Discussion on the exhaustion of local remedies:

> [E]ven if the formula were to lose in exactitude as a result of this deletion, I believe it would gain in elasticity. It would be vaguer, perhaps, but in that way it would be like a good many other formulae which we have

174 *Id.*, 531.

175 *Id.*, 530–531.

176 Concerns were raised by Doctor Guerrero of Salvador; Professor Sipsom of Rumania; His Excellency M. Dinichert of Switzerland; His Excellency M. Miguel Cruchaga-Tocornal of Chile.

177 See: Marjorie M. Whiteman, 'The Codification of the Responsibility of States' (1930) 8(2) New York University Law Quarterly Review 185, 208.

> accepted. They have been accepted because they are vague and will cover more than one interpretation.[178]

The Chairman of the Committee agreed with the 'reduction of exactitude,' stating that while precision must be sought, "we must also try to maintain elasticity."[179] This so-called 'elasticity' was, for Latin American delegates, a cause for concern. Uruguay opposed imprecise terminology for the very same reason that others supported it; to do so would be to permit States to apply variations of interpretation at will, undoubtedly in furtherance of evading SR by narrowly admitting those circumstances capable of engaging it.[180] The delegate from India noted that:

> [...] Surely in this year 1930 we ought not to think of whittling down the rights of the individual as against the state, but rather to aim at making the state less and less the sovereign of mediaeval theory and more and more a public servant and a benefactor [...].[181]

In the wake of the Hague Conference, the LoN continued to promote the progressive codification of IL but took no further action in relation to the question of SR.[182] It was noted later by the Inter-American Juridical Committee that the reason for the lack of success of the Hague Conference "was the collective resistance of the Latin American nations to support theories of the so-called international common law which were contrary to American doctrine."[183] Others concurred that "the complete failure of [the Hague Conference] was due in large measure to the resistance put up by certain American States [...]."[184]

This did not however, signal the end of Latin American efforts to assert the primacy of regional doctrine. In 1953, the UN General Assembly requested the

178 *Id.*, 198.

179 *Id.*

180 *Id.*, 199.

181 *Id.*, 192.

182 International Law Commission, *First report on State responsibility by Mr. Roberto Ago, Special Rapporteur – Review of previous work on codification of the topic of the international responsibility of States* (1969) (A/CN.4/217 and Corr.1 and Add.1), 132.

183 Organization of American States: Inter-American Juridical Committee, *Contributions of the American Continent to the Principles of International Law that Govern the Responsibility of the State* (1962) 16.

184 Jean L'Huillier, *Elements de Droit International Public* (Editions Rousseau et Cie. 1950) 354.

ILC to undertake the codification of the principles of IL governing SR.[185] In light of that development and with a view to 'encouraging closer relations and cooperation' between the ILC and the inter-American organs, the Tenth Inter-American Conference recommended the preparation of a report on the contributions of the American Continent to the development and the codification of the principles of IL that govern SR.[186]

The Department of Legal Affairs at the OAS prepared two reports on legal materials, both entitled *Contributions of the American Continent to the Principles of International Law that Govern the Responsibility of the State.*[187] The reports made clear that the role of the American Continent was in opposing the theory that the European interpretation of IL was in fact a proxy for IL in itself. It stressed:

> [U]nder the pretext of effectively charging a state with responsibility, many cases of intervention have taken place on the continent, thus creating a situation which, if it persisted, would have terminated the very existence of the Latin American nations as free, autonomous international entities. [...] the precise American contribution has been in modifying precepts of international law and opposing, to some extent, the theories set forth by eminent European internationals.[188]

The report cited the very many examples of intervention in Latin America by the US and European powers, not only as violations of sovereignty, but as justification for the critical importance of the Latin American doctrine of SR. It provided:

185 UN General Assembly, *Resolution 799(VIII): Request for the codification of the principles of international law governing State responsibility* (7 December 1953) A/RES/799(VIII).

186 Inter-American Conference, *Principles of International Law Governing the Responsibility of the State, Tenth Inter-American Conference* (Caracas, 1954) Appendix I, Resolution CIV.

187 Pan American Union, *Contributions of the American Continent to the Principles Governing the Responsibility of the State*1961) (1961); Organization of American States: Inter-American Juridical Committee, *Contributions of the American Continent to the Principles of International Law that Govern the Responsibility of the State*1962) (1962); See also: Organization of American States: Inter-American Juridical Committee, *Contributions of the American Continent to the Principles of International Law that Govern the Responsibility of the State* (1965).

188 Organization of American States: Inter-American Juridical Committee, *Contributions of the American Continent to the Principles of International Law that Govern the Responsibility of the State* (1962) 3.

> [t]he hemisphere, while recognizing and giving effect to the right of a state to present by diplomatic representation a claim for reparation, responded to the unfortunate abuses of this right by developing the limiting principle that states must submit a dispute to impartial third-party decision or other pacific means rather than unilaterally intervening into the affairs of another state.

It is unsurprising therefore that the report reasserted the theory of risk, by concluding "[T]he state responsible for an aggressive war is responsible for damages that may arise therefrom."[189] But like other codification procedures, little came of the PAU reports, and, like other regional outputs on the subject of SR, they would receive little attention in the efforts to codify the subject, led by European States and the US.

5.2 *The 'International Aspect' of State Responsibility and the Minimisation of Circumstances Engaging It*

Certain codification procedures placed clear emphasis on the internal settlement of claims, and maintained that the 'international aspect' of SR was limited to the denial of justice. The 'international aspect' of SR had already been restricted through State practice, to cases where there had been either a denial of justice or an exhaustion of internal remedies but a number of codification procedures sought to either minimise it further, or to exclude it altogether, allowing injuries to aliens to remain strictly within the realm of municipal law. This was aided in part by the limitation of instances in which a State could be responsible not only for the violent acts of private persons, but also for the acts of State agents in quelling violence. In this way, the competing theories of risk and fault were reintroduced as central and contentious themes in the numerous attempts to codify SR, again, between Pan-American and European doctrines, which both regions were keen to assert.[190]

---

189 Organization of American States: Inter-American Juridical Committee, *Contributions of the American Continent to the Principles of International Law that Govern the Responsibility of the State* (1962) 7.

190 In addition to official and unofficial codification procedures, two private procedures of codification were undertaken by preeminent legal scholars, however neither final draft garnered much support, nor were referenced or relied upon in subsequent procedures, either official or unofficial, other than a mention in passing by Roberto Ago in his first report as Special Rapporteur on State Responsibility. See: International Law Commission, *First report on State responsibility by Mr. Roberto Ago, Special Rapporteur – Review of previous work on codification of the topic of the international responsibility of States*1969) (A/CN.4/217 and Corr.1 and Add.1) 125, citing K. Strupp, *Die völkerrechtliche Haftung des*

The consensus created during the procedures of the PAU and the LoN conspicuously precluded injuries to aliens sustained during insurrections, riots and armed conflicts from the scope of the 'international aspect.' This was a relative innovation of the codification era, as the history of SR and its application clearly incorporated the acts of State agents occasioning injury to the person or property of aliens, albeit in a limited range of circumstances. The material produced by the Americas consistently minimised the scope of what constituted circumstances engaging the international aspect relative to acts of war (both civil and international) and other forms of civil unrest. The *Convention Relative to the Rights of Aliens*, adopted in 1902 at the Second International Conference of American States (not to be confused with the *Convention on the Status of Aliens* of 1928),[191] reiterated that the principles of civil equality and non-intervention were complementary, and precluded the engagement of the international aspect where aliens suffered injury through "acts of rebels or individuals, and in general, for damages originating from fortuitous causes of any kind" including during domestic and international war. It provided exception however, for the failure of authorities to comply with their duties.[192] In that sense, the international aspect was only engaged where the State failed to provide legal remedy and thus committed a denial of justice.[193]

By comparison, the treatment of injuries to corporations was an entirely different matter. Prior to the Sixth International Conference of American States, held in Cuba in 1928, the American Institute of International Law presented a series of projects on conventions that would form the basis of a code of public international law, among them, Project No. 15 on the Responsibility of Governments.[194] It endorsed the view that injuries to individuals and injuries to corporations were to be regarded as legally distinct under the doctrine of SR. Injuries to individuals were to be treated as private domestic matters;

Staates insbesondere bei Hanshagen Privater, Abhandlung zur fortschreitenden Kodification des internationalen Rechts, Heft 1 (Kiel 1927); A. Roth, *Das völkerrechtliche Delikt vor und in der Verhandlungen auf der Haager Kodifications Konferenz 1930* (Universitatsverlag von Robert Noske 1932) 177.

191 Organization of American States, *Convention on the Status of Aliens* (Havana, 20 February 1928).

192 Pan-American Union, *Convention Relative to the Rights of Aliens* (Mexico, 29 January 1902).

193 At the Sixth Conference, States approved the *Convention on the Status of Aliens*. See: Pan-American Union, *Convention on the Status of Aliens* (Havana, 20 February 1928); see also: Pan-American Union, *Convention on Asylum* (Havana, 20 February 1928); Pan-American Union, *Convention on the Duties and Rights of States in the Event of Civil Strife* (Havana, 20 February 1928).

194 'American Institute of International Law: Texts of Projects' (1926) 20(4) AJIL 328.

only capable of engaging SR where the 'international aspect' was present. Conversely, injuries to corporations were to be regarded as capable of engaging SR *prima facie* and did not require the presence of any 'international aspect.' Project No. 15 reiterated the principles of the *Convention Relative to the Rights of Aliens*, that the American Republics did not recognise obligations or responsibilities in favour of foreigners, other than those established for their own nationals. Matters of individuals - national or alien - were strictly domestic.[195]

American States (including the US) would continue to reinforce minimal engagement of the international aspect at the Seventh International Conference of American States in 1933, where Member States adopted a resolution on the *International Responsibility of the State*,[196] reaffirming certain principles that had been laid down at previous conferences, including those of Project 15.[197] This would be further reinforced a decade later by the *American Treaty of Pacific Settlement*, also known as the Pact of Bogotá, which bound the High Contracting Parties to refrain from making diplomatic representations on behalf of their nationals.[198]

But the reinforcement of regional doctrine was not sufficient. It was critical that the Americas exercise a degree of control over the 'international' efforts to codify questions of SR, being those involving Europe. At the Seventh International Conference of the OAS, Member States resolved that the study of the whole problem should be undertaken in coordination with the codification work by the LoN.[199] Although this collaboration never came to fruition, the PAU would go on to wield considerable influence over the LoN codification process, particularly with respect to the subject matter of Project 15.

Procedures undertaken in an unofficial capacity by non-governmental institutions were also preoccupied with the exclusion of the international aspect of SR. The *Institut de Droit International* produced a resolution on SR, requiring equality in the protective measures accorded to nationals and aliens, but civil equality also ensured the exclusion of international involvement. It afforded aliens the same rights to obtain compensation as nationals, and there could be no denial of justice where justice was metered out to all persons, irrespective of status. In such circumstances, the international aspect of

195 *Id.*

196 Organization of American States, *Resolution LXXIV: International Responsibility of the State* (Montevideo, 24 December 1933).

197 *Id.*

198 Organization of American States, *American Treaty of Pacific Settlement* (Bogotá, 30 April 1948) Article VII.

199 *Id.*

SR could not be engaged, as there could be no denial of justice where there was equality of treatment.[200] Several decades later, the *Institut* produced two more resolutions, further minimising the international aspect of SR: one on 'The Rule of the Exhaustion of Local Remedies,' adopted in 1956,[201] and one on 'The National Character of an International Claim Presented by a State for Injury Suffered by an Individual,' adopted in 1965.[202] Unsurprisingly, both resolutions sought to reinforce the domestic resolution of claims involving foreign nationals.

The 1929 Draft Convention on 'Responsibility of States for Damage Done in their Territory to the Person or Property of Foreigners,' produced by Harvard Law School's 'Harvard Research in International Law Group,' also provided that injuries to individuals were matters of private domestic law.[203] Specifically, aliens should enjoy domestic judicial recourse in cases of 'tort and contract as well as in the event of damages suffered during times of war or insurrection.'[204] The conflation of tort and wartime injury further supported the notion that injuries sustained in the course of conflict lacked the international aspect necessary to engage SR and were in any case 'private' law.

Certain other procedures attempted to introduce novel qualifications and exceptions that in effect minimised or excluded the international aspect. In 1926, the Japanese branch of the International Law Association adopted a draft code of international law, which included a chapter on the 'Rules Concerning Responsibility of a State in Relation to the Life, Person and Property

200 'Résolutions votes par l'institut au cours de sa XXXIVème session: Responsabilité internationale des états a raison des dommages causés sur leur territoire a la personne et aux biens des étrangers' (1927) 33(3) AnnIDI 330; M.L. Strisower, 'Responsabilité internationale des États à raison des dommages causés sur leur territoire à la personne ou aux biens des étrangers' (1927) 33(1) AnnIDI 455.

201 Institut de Droit International, *The Rule of the Exhaustion of Local Remedies* (1956).

202 Institut de Droit International, *The National Character of an International Claim Presented by a State for Injury Suffered by an Individual* (1965).

203 Harvard Research in International Law Group, *Draft Convention on 'Responsibility of States for Damage Done in their Territory to the Person or Property of Foreigners'* (1929) 23.

204 James T. Kenny, 'Manley O. Hudson and the Harvard Research in International Law 1927–1940' (1977) 11(2) The International Lawyer 319, 324, citing Edwin M. Borchard, *Draft Convention on the Law of Responsibility of States* (February 1929). This was an unpublished, confidential draft, prepared under the direction of Edwin M. Borchard for submission to members of the Advisory Committee of the Research in International Law.

of Aliens.'[205] It provided that a State could not *disclaim* responsibility for an injury sustained by an alien during an insurrection or mob violence, if the alien had been made the object of injury *for the reason that he was an alien or was of a particular nationality*.[206] This introduced a special intent criterion that was unique among codification procedures and lacked any substantive basis in State practice.

The following year, in anticipation of the forthcoming Hague Conference, the Institute of International Law adopted a Resolution on 'International responsibility of states for injuries on their territory to the person or property of foreigners.'[207] As with the process by the Japanese International Law Association, the resolution simultaneously promoted the concept of fault and the minimisation of circumstances capable of engaging it. While a State was responsible for damages caused to aliens by the acts or omissions of any State authorities, it precluded responsibility where the failure to observe the obligation was not the consequence of fault, thereby excluding the injurious acts of private persons, except where the State omitted to take proper measures of prevention. Accordingly, the Resolution provided exculpatory clauses that were intended to cover incidents of civil unrest, and at the same time, designate such incidents as *force majeure*, over which the State could not exercise control, even with measures of prevention. By definition, such events could not be the consequence of fault on the part of the State and could not therefore engage SR.

5.3 *Compensation and the Responsibility of the State of Origin*

In all but one of the codification procedures, the topic of refugees was conspicuously absent. Even while the LoN (and later the UN) confronted numerous European refugee crises, the codification of SR and the position of aliens within its rules entirely failed to acknowledge refugees as a legal class. The first time that any codification procedure considered the question of SR in the same context as asylum was in 1958, during the codification procedure by the Asian-African Legal Consultative Committee (AALCC). The committee, constituted by the governments of Burma, Ceylon, India, Indonesia, Iran, Japan, and Syria, was established to serve as an "Advisory Body of Legal

205 Sanford D. Cole, 'Draft Code of International Law Adopted by the Japanese Branch of the International Law Association, and the Kokusaiho Gakkwai (International Law Association of Japan)' (1926) 34 International Law Association Reports of Conferences 378.

206 Emphasis added.

207 'Resolutions of the Institute of International Law Adopted at Lausanne' (1928) 22(1) AJIL 330–333.

Experts to help deal with problems that may be referred to it, and to help in exchange of views and information on matters of common concern between the participating countries."[208] At its second session, the committee considered the question of the 'Status of Aliens' but did not confine itself to an analysis of the question in terms of the 'responsibility of states for the treatment of foreign nationals.' Rather, the question of the treatment of aliens was considered "in all its aspects," which included the right of asylum.[209]

At its third session, the Secretariat delivered its report in the form of Draft Articles, which the Committee itself noted contained "certain new concepts on the law on the subject."[210] The Draft Articles rejected the 19th-century theory of 'minimum standards of treatment' for aliens as being "outmoded" in favour of 'equality of treatment' between nationals and aliens.[211] The Committee was particularly interested in the Universal Declaration of Human Rights (UDHR) in this regard, but while the principles of equality and individual rights formed the basis of its conclusions on the treatment of aliens, the Committee stopped short of embracing the UDHR as it applied to asylum. In reference to the right of asylum, the Committee declared that Article 14(1) of the UDHR, which provided that "Everyone has the right to seek and enjoy in other countries asylum from persecution" was "not acceptable to the states of the Committee."[212] This reflected the notion that the right of asylum referred to the right of States to offer asylum, not the right of individuals to be granted asylum. The Draft Articles provided that in the absence of a treaty to the contrary, a State had the right to offer or provide in its territory asylum to political refugees or to political offenders on such conditions that the State may stipulate appropriate in the circumstances.[213] The final report of the Committee on the Status of Aliens, though it did not relate specifically to political asylees, provided that such persons were a class of alien, and as such the scope of the Draft Articles should extend to apply to them. The definition of 'alien' in the

208 Asian-African Legal Consultative Committee, *Report: First Session, New Delhi: India, April 18 to 27, 1957* (1957) 1.

209 Asian-African Legal Consultative Committee, *Report of the Second Session, Cairo: 1 – 13 October 1958* (1958) 83.

210 Asian-African Legal Consultative Committee, *Report of the Third Session, Colombo: 1960* (1960) 83.

211 Asian-African Legal Consultative Committee, *Report of the Second Session, Cairo: 1 – 13 October 1958*1958).

212 Asian-African Legal Consultative Committee, *Report of the Third Session, Colombo: 1960*1960), 95.

213 Asian-African Legal Consultative Committee, *Report of the Fourth Session, Tokyo: 1961* (1961) 47.

Draft Articles reflected that, broadly encompassing persons "who [were] not a citizen or national of the State concerned."[214]

At its sixth session in 1964, the subject of asylum was taken up for consideration once again, and the Committee directed its secretariat to collect further material relating to minimum standards of treatment in the State of asylum, and the possibility of resorting to international tribunals for determination of compensation that could be claimed by a refugee. The following year, the Committee adopted certain general principles on the rights of the refugee, including that a refugee shall have the right to receive compensation from the State that he left or to which he was unable to return. The commentary to the article provided that compensation "shall be for such loss as bodily injury, deprivation of personal liberty in denial of human rights, death of dependents of the refugee or of the person whose dependent the refugee was, and the destruction of or damage to property and assets, caused by the authorities of the state, public officials or mob violence."[215] The question of compensation for the inability to return was introduced by Pakistan, which expressed the desire that the relevant provision should be extended to provide compensation for refugees "who are desirous of returning to their country,"[216] but the question was again rejected by a number of delegates. No further substantive work was ever done by the committee on the subject.

Although this was the first time that the question of compensation by the State of origin was discussed in a codification procedure, it was certainly not the first time it was addressed in an international or multilateral forum. This question had already been introduced numerous times in international fora and would be considered many more times since.[217] But where the interest for establishing such a principle was almost always high, States inevitably stumbled over questions of the legal foundations for such a notion, and the means for its enforcement. The drive to revisit the question of State of origin responsibility, even in the absence of clear legal foundation, is demonstrative of the legal ambitions of States of reception. The financial burden presented by a refugee population was such a concern that it motivated the repeated reintroduction of this same question, despite it never finding anything approaching a resolution.

---

214 *Id.*, 46.

215 Asian-African Legal Consultative Committee, *Report of the 7th Annual Session, Baghdad: 1965* (1965) 30.

216 Asian-African Legal Consultative Committee, *Report of the Tenth Session, Karachi, 1969* (1969) 43.

217 This is discussed in detail in Chapter 2, and later in Chapter 5.

5.4 *The International Law Commission and the Special Rapporteur on State Responsibility*

Several years after its establishment, the ILC was entrusted with the codification of the principles of IL governing SR.[218] Many decades later, its work would culminate in the ARSIWA. Though the ILC procedure would too suffer from interventions and obstructions, this particular attempt to affect the trajectory of SR would prove to be successful. As "one of the [ILC's] longest running and most controversial studies,"[219] the work of the Commission on SR was considered by some to represent "the long-term destructive effect of a government-dominated commission on the development of international law"[220] and its output to be "at such a high level of abstraction as to be of almost no practical value."[221] In 1989, Meron advised somewhat prophetically that it would be inappropriate to approach the Draft Articles – later the ARSIWA – as if they were a source of law;[222] a warning that would be repeated by others following the adoption of the final ARSIWA.[223] Bodansky and Crook noted:

> [T]heir seductive clarity, seeming concreteness, and treaty-like form, together with the paucity of other sources on some important issues, may tempt decision makers to apply the articles verbatim, rather than treat them only as evidence of the relevant international rule.

The final ARSIWA were considered by some to be "mature and well-balanced"; representative of "a compromise between different approaches, stances and expectations of the members of the international community,"[224] and by

---

218 UN General Assembly, *Resolution 799(VIII): Request for the codification of the principles of international law governing State responsibility* (7 December 1953) A/RES/799(VIII).

219 Daniel Bodansky, John R. Crook, 'Symposium: The ILC's State Responsibility Articles: Introduction and Overview' (2002) 96 AJIL 773.

220 Philip Allott, 'State Responsibility and the Unmaking of International Law' (1988) 29(1) Harv Int'l LJ 2.

221 Richard B. Lillich, 'The Current Status of the Law of State Responsibility for Injuries to Aliens' (1979) 73 ASILPROC 244, 246.

222 Theodor Meron, *Human Rights and Humanitarian Norms as Customary Law* (Clarendon 1989) 137.

223 David Caron, 'The ILC Articles on State Responsibility: The Paradoxical Relationship between Form and Authority' (2002) 96(4) AJIL 857, 858; Daniel Bodansky, John R. Crook, 'Symposium: The ILC's State Responsibility Articles: Introduction and Overview' (2002) 96 AJIL 773, 775.

224 Władyslaw Czapliński, 'UN Codification of Law of State Responsibility' (2003) 41(1) Archiv Des Völkerrechts 62, citing International Law Commission, *Report of the International Law Commission on the work of its fifty-third session, 23 April – 1 June and 2 July –*

others to be "sometimes controversial and even more often unclear."[225] Irrespective of their characterisation as authoritative or otherwise, the codification procedure of the ILC reveals a great deal about both the persistent regional theories of SR, and the continued concern regarding the broader legal environment in which they would operate.

The concerns of Western States at this historical juncture differed significantly to those of previous years, but were no less critical to the ILC's codification procedure, which shifted from the preservation of an unregulated arms trade to the equality of all persons under IHRL, and the impact of principles of equality on various aspects of decolonisation. As IHRL did away with any distinction between nationals and aliens as beneficiaries of rights, and deemed the individual a subject of IL, SR may be attributed for injuries to persons subject to a State's jurisdiction, irrespective of nationality, irrespective of the injury having occurred on the State's sovereign territory, and without the need for a foreign State to act as claimant. Furthermore, the uncertain legal status of a decolonised populace left some doubt as to the rights of such a group to make claims against the colonising State. The declaration that post-war IL admitted the acts of the State and its agents both on its territory and abroad, against all persons, irrespective of status, was considered to be a serious degradation of State sovereignty, and was a particularly precarious admission at the time of decolonisation.

5.4.1 The Equality of Nationals and Aliens in International Human Rights Law

In his first report on the topic, the ILC's Special Rapporteur on State Responsibility, Francisco V. García Amador, concluded that the topic of SR was so broad, and involved such diverse factors, that it would not be possible to proceed immediately with a comprehensive codification, as "it would be difficult to find a topic beset with greater confusion and uncertainty."[226] Rather, the ILC should adopt a gradual approach, codifying first that part of the topic that was most ripe for codification. That part was, in the opinion of García Amador,

---

*10 August 2001, Official Records of the General Assembly, Fifty-sixth session, Supplement No. 10*2001) (A/56/10); James Crawford, Jacqueline Peel, Simon Olleson, 'The ILC s Articles on Responsibility of States for Internationally Wrongful Acts: Completion of the Second Reading' (2001) 12(5) EJIL 963.

225 David Caron, 'The ILC Articles on State Responsibility: The Paradoxical Relationship between Form and Authority' (2002) 96(4) AJIL 857, 858.

226 *F.V. García Amador, 'First Report on State Responsibility'* (1956) 2 UNYBILC 173, 175; F. V. García Amador, 'State Responsibility: Some New Problems' (1958) 94 RDCADI 367, 369.

SR for damage caused to the person or property of aliens.[227] He placed significant emphasis on this,[228] contending that post-war developments in IL had definitively done away with any distinction between groups subject to the same jurisdiction. García Amador identified what he referred to as 'traditional doctrine and practice'[229] which he divided into two categories: the "ill-defined or even undefinable,"[230] and acts or omissions that for which SR was attributable for "damage done in their territories to the person or property of foreigners."[231] It was this category, he determined, that was the principal subject of the literature, private and official codification procedures, and judicial decisions that defined SR.[232] García Amador also insisted that there was no longer any legitimate legal basis upon which to distinguish between the State's obligation to protect aliens, and its obligation to protect all persons within its jurisdiction. He noted that there was a principal difference between 'traditional law and practice' and post-war IL that necessitated "a complete reappraisal of the entire problem,"[233] as the passive subject of SR could now be an individual that had inflicted an injurious act, and the direct subject now included the individual upon whom an injurious act was inflicted.[234] The principle of equality and the prohibition of discrimination were front and centre of "fundamental human rights and freedoms."[235] Needless to say, García Amador's position was controversial. Members of the ILC principally took issue with two elements of his report. First, with the continued conflation of SR with the protection of aliens, and second, with the proposed expansion of traditional SR to include all individuals as subjects of IL.

This shift from traditional law and practice to post-war IL was evident as pre-war codification procedures – with their emphasis on State sovereignty – were now clearly incongruent with modern IL. The Guerrero report, for example, claimed that no subject other than the State could have, or acquire, international rights, as individuals "move on a lower plane, where their lives are regulated in accordance with standards set up by a single will – the will of the

227 International Law Commission, *Report on International Responsibility by Mr. F.V. García Amador, Special Rapporteur* (1956) (A/CN.4/96) 221.

228 *Id.*, Chapter VI.

229 *Id.*, Chapter I.

230 *Id.*, 181.

231 *Id.*

232 *Id.*

233 *Id.*, 185.

234 *Id.*, 185, 192.

235 *Id.*, 193.

State."[236] Harvard University Law School had similarly asserted that "[t]he injury for which a State is responsible is always an injury to another State," arising from "what was originally loss or damage inflicted upon its national."[237] According to García Amador, this was plainly no longer a valid position in the post-war international environment, as clearly evidenced by the Nürnberg principles; a distinction he later referred to as "the traditional concepts and the transformations of international law."[238]

After the publication of García Amador's first report, the ILC considered its contents over a number of sessions, during which time it became clear that members would not accept the principal recommendation.[239] It was suggested that the Special Rapporteur abandon injuries to aliens as a line of inquiry, and that the ILC should instead focus its efforts on codifying secondary rules. García Amador did not heed the advice, and the following year he presented his Second Report as Special Rapporteur, including the first Draft Articles on SR. It was clear that the Draft Articles – entitled '*Draft on international responsibility of the State for injuries caused in its territory to the person or property of aliens*' – were never intended to constitute secondary rules of IL, referring instead to the denial of justice, and civil equality between aliens and nationals, and SR for the violation of recognised "fundamental human rights."[240] Even in relation to the codification of Article 1 defining the term 'international obligation,' García Amador noted:

> The purpose of the present codification, however, as indeed of all its predecessors, is precisely to determine what acts or omissions give rise to the international responsibility of the State, i.e., *to enunciate the rules which govern the State's conduct with respect to aliens.* Clearly, a mere general reference to the sources of international obligations and to the "rules accepted by the community of nations" cannot accomplish the

236 *Id.*, 192.

237 Harvard Law School, *Research in International Law, II. Responsibility of States* (1929) 141; see also: Edwin M.Borchard, *The Diplomatic Protection of Citizens Abroad* (The Banks Law Pub. Co. 1915) 178; Dionisio Anzilotti, *Teoria generale della responsibilità dello Stato nel diritto internazionale* (F. Lumachi Libraio-Editore 1902) 461.

238 F.V. García Amador, 'State Responsibility: Some New Problems' (1958) 94 RDCADI 367, 369.

239 '(1956). Tuesday, 19 June 1956, at 9:30 a.m.' (1956) 1 UNYBILC 226, 232.

240 International Law Commission, *Second report of the Special Rapporteur, Mr. F.V. García Amador* (1957) (A/CN.4/106) 107.

> purpose of this codification *which is, precisely, to enumerate those very obligations and rules and to define their content.*[241]

This "innovation," as it was called by certain ILC members,[242] was considered relatively uncertain and undefined. Unsurprisingly, particular concern was voiced about Chapter V of the Draft Articles, on the 'acts of individuals and internal disturbances.' Per Articles 10 and 11 of the Chapter, the State was responsible for injuries caused to an alien, both by acts of ordinary private individuals, and in consequence of riots, civil strife, or other internal disturbances, if the organs or officials of the State were "manifestly negligent" in taking the measures that were normally taken to prevent or punish such acts. At the same time, per Article 12, the State was responsible for injuries caused to an alien by measures taken by its armed forces or other authorities for the purpose of preventing or suppressing an insurrection or any other internal disturbance, if the measures taken "affected private persons directly and individually."[243] This high threshold for liability of State agents threatened to reintroduce the theory of risk to the doctrine of SR. Members were concerned that the standard of liability may slip back to strict or even absolute. Objective liability, together with the legal standing of the individual as a subject of IL, created a heightened level of risk at the time of decolonisation and State succession, where questions of IL and its application were as yet undefined.

The explanatory notes on the Draft Articles did little to assuage concern about Chapter V. In interpreting arbitral decisions relative to 'the scope of responsibility,' García Amador wrote that is seemed "impossible to deny" SR in respect of all persons subject to a State's jurisdiction, as it was implicit in the functions of the State to ensure conditions on its territory that guarantee the safety of persons and property.[244] At the same time, García Amador insisted on the absence of a distinction between classes of person, on the basis of nationality. The equality of nationals and aliens, which was once the *ratione materiae* of the 'international standard of justice' under the 'traditional law and practice' of SR, was now accomplished by the international recognition

---

241 *Id.* Emphasis added.

242 See comments by Mr Bartos at International Law Commission, *Summary record of the 415th meeting* (1957) (A/CN.4/SR.415); see comments by Mr Spiropoulos, International Law Commission, *Summary record of the 416th meeting* (1957) (A/CN.4/SR.416) at 168.

243 *Id.*

244 International Law Commission, *Second report of the Special Rapporteur, Mr. F.V. García Amador*1957) (A/CN.4/106) 106. Emphasis added.

of the 'essential rights of man.' Accordingly, the 'international standard of justice' appeared to have been "outgrown by contemporary international law."[245] The legal distinction between nationals and aliens no longer had any *raison d'être*,[246] as all persons were now under the direct protection of IL.[247] But the scope of IHRL far exceeded that of the traditional law and practice on SR. The application of human rights principles to the doctrine of SR implied a scope so broad that the State would in effect become internationally responsible for damages caused to all persons subject to its jurisdiction "by reason of the character and consequences of the act" irrespective of territorial considerations, and "whether they be citizens or aliens."[248]

This was far too radical a notion. To admit the 'essential rights of man' to the codification process would constitute an impermissible violation of State sovereignty just at the inflection of decolonisation. Several members raised concerns that the Special Rapporteur had unilaterally exceeded his mandate,[249] asserting that, "some matters were, and should remain, within the domestic jurisdiction of a state."[250] One member noted that in Europe, the subject of the status of aliens was dealt with in treatises on private IL, and the status of aliens as discussed in those treatises was deemed one of the matters essentially within the domestic jurisdiction of States.[251] Another member suggested that "a subject so controversial and still in course of evolution did not lend itself to codification [...]" and that the Special Rapporteur was "ill-advised in presenting relative innovations as constituting existing, recognised law."[252] Another agreed that "[t]he subject was not really worthy of the attempts to enlarge it" and that "[i]nternational responsibility was virtually nothing more than a question of damages, a pecuniary matter."[253] It was agreed that the study should be limited to "rules of a more or less

245 *Id.*, 113. Emphasis added.

246 *Id.*

247 *Id.*, 113–116.

248 *Id.*, 113, 128.

249 International Law Commission, *Summary record of the 415th meeting* (1957) (A/CN.4/SR.415) 162, 163.

250 *Id.*, 165–166. See also comments by Mr Faris Bey El-Khouri, International Law Commission, *Summary record of the 416th meeting* (1957) (A/CN.4/SR.416) 169.

251 See comments by Mr Bartos, International Law Commission, *Summary record of the 415th meeting* (1957) (A/CN.4/SR.415) at 167.

252 *Id.*

253 See comments by Mr Amado, International Law Commission, *Summary record of the 415th meeting* (1957) (A/CN.4/SR.415) at 168.

procedural nature,"[254] as articles 5 and 6 on the subject of respect for fundamental human rights were "not fully relevant to the question of international responsibility."[255] Other members addressed the issue of whether the violation of so-called "fundamental human rights"[256] could form part of SR, pointing out that the UDHR was not a legal instrument, and that the proposed covenants on human rights were still under discussion.[257]

During debate on the Draft Articles, Roberto Ago – then a member of the ILC – suggested three courses of action, of which the third would allow the Commission to:

> [L]eave all the matters concerning the definition of the obligations of the state as to the conditions of aliens, and confine itself to the examination of the questions within the framework of responsibility proper, i.e., of the *consequences* of an international illicit act committed in the field under consideration.[258]

This was, in Ago's opinion, the way forward, as it "would enable the Commission to do a useful job without engaging in a debate on the treatment of aliens."[259] It was broadly agreed among members that the Special Rapporteur should be given "clear instruction" for his future work,[260] and that the continuation of the task might be entrusted to a committee, rather than left to García Amador to continue alone.[261] The Commission could embark on a discussion

254 See comments by Mr Spiropoulos, International Law Commission, *Summary record of the 416th meeting* (1957) (A/CN.4/SR.416) at 168; Comments by Mr Fitzmaurice, International Law Commission, *Summary record of the 415th meeting* (1957) (A/CN.4/SR.415) 163.

255 See comments by Mr Spiropoulos, International Law Commission, *Summary record of the 416th meeting* (1957) (A/CN.4/SR.416) 168.

256 International Law Commission, *Summary record of the 415th meeting* (1957) (A/CN.4/SR.415) 163, 164, 168.

257 *Id.*, 166.

258 International Law Commission, *Second report of the Special Rapporteur, Mr. F.V. García Amador* (1957) (A/CN.4/106) 167. Emphasis added.

259 *Id.*

260 *Id.*; See comments by Mr Tunkin at 165, Mr Ago, Mr Bartos, and Mr Liang at 167, International Law Commission, *Summary record of the 415th meeting* (1957) (A/CN.4/SR.415); See comments by Mr Matine-Daftary, International Law Commission, *Summary record of the 416th meeting* (1957) (A/CN.4/SR.416) 171.

261 See comments by Mr Bartos, International Law Commission, *Summary record of the 415th meeting* (1957) (A/CN.4/SR.415) 167.

of the articles drafted by the Special Rapporteur, setting aside those substantive rules relating more or less to the status and treatment of aliens.[262]

A Sub-Committee on SR was established by the ICL in 1962, with a mandate to work on "general aspects" and to produce memoranda relating to the main aspects of the subject, from which the Chairman would prepare a report.[263] As Chairman of the Sub-Committee, Roberto Ago declared in the report that the ILC should concentrate on "the whole of responsibility and nothing but responsibility."[264] Under his leadership, the Sub-Committee quickly turned its attention to the secondary rules of SR, setting aside the traditional doctrine of SR for injuries to aliens and other primary rules of international law that had been the substance of the Special Rapporteur's work to date. During its general discussions, the Sub-Committee agreed unanimously to recommend that the Commission give priority to the definition of the 'general rules' governing the international responsibility of the State,[265] and agreed that while the material 'already gathered' by García Amador would not be neglected, "careful attention should be paid to the *possible repercussions* which new developments in international law may have had on responsibility."[266]

Certain members of the Sub-Committee rejected the codification of general rules, and advocated instead for priority to be given to the field in which most of State practice had arisen, namely that of the responsibility of the State towards aliens.[267] It was contended that "the problem of injuries to aliens had not become obsolete"[268] but was very much "still alive" and accordingly, "the Commission should not hesitate to draw on the vast experience gained in

---

262 Mr. El-Erian, International Law Commission, *Summary record of the 416th meeting* (1957) (A/CN.4/SR.416) 169.

263 International Law Commission, *Report of the International Law Commission covering the work of its 14th session, 24 April-29 June 1962* (1962) (A/5209) pg 34, para 68.

264 International Law Commission, *Report by Mr. R. Ago, Chairman of the Sub-Committee on State Responsibility* (16 January 1963) (A/CN.4/152) 227, 228.

265 International Law Commission, *Report of the International Law Commission on the work of its Fifteenth Session, 6 July 1963, Official Records of the General Assembly, Eighteenth Session, Supplement* (A/5509) (1963) (A/CN.4/163) 229–230.

266 *Id.*, 228. Emphasis added.

267 See comments by Mr. Jimenez de Aréchaga at 231, Mr Tsuruoka at 231, and Mr Gross at 230, in International Law Commission, *Report of the International Law Commission on the work of its Fifteenth Session, 6 July 1963, Official Records of the General Assembly, Eighteenth Session, Supplement* (A/5509) (1963) (A/CN.4/163).

268 See comments by Mr Gross, International Law Commission, *Report of the International Law Commission on the work of its Fifteenth Session, 6 July 1963, Official Records of the General Assembly, Eighteenth Session, Supplement* (A/5509) (1963) (A/CN.4/163) 230.

the matter of State responsibility for the treatment of aliens."[269] But when Ago was formally appointed Special Rapporteur following the submission of his report, García Amador's work to date was essentially abandoned.

With this changing of the guard, the codification of SR definitively turned away from primary rules toward the codification of secondary rules of IL, and the international protection of the non-national lost relevance. At its 16th Session, the ILC Secretariat presented a Working Paper summarising the discussions in various UN organs on the subject of SR and resulting decisions,[270] and a Digest of relevant decisions of international tribunals.[271] Both documents were exceedingly narrow in scope, and excluded materials on injuries to aliens.[272] The Digest considered only a very limited number of cases related to injuries to the person or property of aliens, several of which were in any case unsuccessful.[273] At its 21st Session, the Secretariat presented Supplements to the Working Paper and to the Digest of the 16th Session.[274] Like the Digest, the Supplement to the Digest did not include SR for injuries to aliens.[275] The Supplement to the Working Paper suffered from many of the same deficiencies. It was also organised by thematic issue, none of which addressed injuries to aliens, and was based on an extremely narrow temporal and material scope. Where the Supplement referred to cases involving the death of an alien, it referred only to cases in which the accidental nature of

269 *Id.*

270 International Law Commission, *State Responsibility – Summary of the discussions in various United Nations organs and resulting decisions – Working paper prepared by the Secretariat* (1964) (A/CN.4/165 and Corr.1).

271 International Law Commission, *Digest of the decisions of international tribunals relating to State responsibility, prepared by the Secretariat* (1964) (A/CN.4/169).

272 International Law Commission, *State Responsibility – Summary of the discussions in various United Nations organs and resulting decisions – Working paper prepared by the Secretariat*1964) (A/CN.4/165 and Corr.1) 131.

273 *Spanish Zone of Morocco Claims (Spain v United Kingdom)* [1925] 2 RIAA 615; *Walter A. Noyes (United States) v Panama* [1933] 6 RIAA 253.

274 International Law Commission, *Supplement, prepared by the Secretariat, to the "Digest of the decisions of international tribunals relating to State responsibility"* (1969) (A/CN.4/208); International Law Commission, *Proposals submitted to, and decisions of, various United Nations organs relating to the question of State Responsibility: supplement prepared by the Secretariat to document A/CN.4/165* (1969) (A/CN.4/209).

275 Instead, it considered "the relevant aspects of the decisions of the International Court of Justice since 1964 and of other international tribunals whose awards are contained in volumes XII–XVI of the Reports of International Arbitral Awards"; of which the relevant volumes only covered the period 1944 to 1966. See International Law Commission, *Supplement, prepared by the Secretariat, to the "Digest of the decisions of international tribunals relating to State responsibility"* 1969) (A/CN.4/208) 102.

the killings *precluded* SR, or where the question of fault remained unresolved.[276] It was only at its 30th session in 1978, that the ILC finally addressed SR for injuries to aliens in the context of civil disturbances, when the Secretariat presented a precluding wrongfulness,[277] but by this time, the decision had firmly been made to pursue the codification of secondary rules of IL and to exclude injuries to aliens from the ambit of discussion.

5.4.2 The 'Complication' of Decolonisation and the 'Maintenance of Peace'

Just as the revision of diplomatic protection of aliens was motivated by matters extraneous to the issue itself, so too was the codification of SR affected by certain peripheral concerns of States. The decision to depart from the codification of primary rules of IL in favour of a 'general approach' to secondary rules of SR, was motivated in large part by serious concerns about the 'possible repercussions' that the codification of primary rules would have on State succession in the context of decolonisation.

It was noted by one proponent of a generalised approach that it was not advisable to begin work by a consideration of the implementation of the principles governing SR in a specific field, for example, that of claims for injuries to aliens as:

> The ending of the era of colonialism left many privileged situations which needed revision in a number of the newly independent states. The changed circumstances called for flexible solutions, and the whole subject of responsibility in relation to those matters did not lend itself readily to codification.[278]

Those "flexible solutions" called for the Sub-Committee to consider the best course of action in the interest of the 'maintenance of peace' and 'good relations' between States. Though decolonisation was not the only factor that

---

276 *Sentence arbitrale sur la réclamation número 63, présentée par Don Luis Piola* [1901] XV RIAA 444; *Sentence arbitrale sur la réclamation numéro 71, présentée par Doña Carolina Soria Galvarro, veuve de Don José Cresceri* [1901] XV RIAA 449; *Sentence arbitrale sur la réclamation numéro 20, présentée pardon Jacinto Gadino* [1901] XV RIAA 414.

277 International Law Commission, *"Force majeure" and "fortuitous event" as circumstances precluding wrongfulness: survey of State practice, international judicial decisions and doctrine – Study prepared by the Secretariat* (1978) (A/CN.4/315).

278 See comments by Mr. Yasseen, International Law Commission, *Report of the International Law Commission on the work of its Fifteenth Session, 6 July 1963, Official Records of the General Assembly, Eighteenth Session, Supplement* (A/5509)1963) (A/CN.4/163) 230.

"complicated the present situation," it was regardless, "an important factor in that respect."[279] The question was also relevant to that of trust territories, of which there were several at the time, and to the indirect or vicarious responsibility of the administering power in respect of acts performed in administered trust territory.[280] Critically, by extension it was also relevant to the question of military occupation – a particularly sensitive question at that time.[281] Ago himself noted:

> If the courts of the occupying Power committed a denial of justice, should responsibility for that denial of justice attach to the occupying or to the occupied State? A similar problem could also arise in other cases where one State exercised certain powers in the territory of another State with the consent of the latter.[282]

Yet of all the complications of State succession, the issue of nationalisation of property was of particular concern. Nationalisation had historically required the compensation of the newly established State by the former colonial power. One member cited the monograph, *The Duty to Compensate for the Nationalization of Foreign Property*, submitted to members of the Sub-Committee,[283] in which the author noted some fifty post-WWII global compensation agreements for the nationalisation of property.[284] France and Great Britain had paid compensation for nationalisation measures of banks, airlines, insurance companies, transportation, and steel and coal industries,[285] and this formula had been accepted by other States including Switzerland, the US and Belgium.[286] In the *Anglo-Iranian Oil Co. case* (United Kingdom v Iran),[287] the UK had itself submitted in its memorial to the ICJ that the payment of com-

279 *Id.*, 231.

280 See comments by Chairman Ago, International Law Commission, *Report by Mr. R. Ago, Chairman of the Sub-Committee on State Responsibility* 16 January 1963) (A/CN.4/152).

281 *Id.*, 234–235.

282 *Id.*, 235–236.

283 Jimenez de Aréchaga, 'The duty to compensate for the nationalization of foreign property' in International Law Commission, *Report of the International Law Commission on the work of its Fifteenth Session, 6 July 1963, Official Records of the General Assembly, Eighteenth Session, Supplement* (A/5509) (1963) (A/CN.4/163).

284 *Id.*, citing Isi Foighel, *Nationalization: A Study in the Protection of Alien Property in International Law* (Stevens & Sons 1957) 132–133.

285 *Id.*, 238.

286 Id., 120–123.

287 *Anglo-Iranian Oil Co Case* (*United Kingdom v Iran*) [1952] ICJ Rep 93.

pensation should be made for nationalisation measures.[288] Though the working paper did not explicitly reference a link between nationalisation and decolonisation, the member that cited the Working Paper contended that the agreements "clearly demonstrated that *nationalisation was a continuing problem and one that constituted a source of state responsibility*."[289]

Indeed, the 'continuing problem' that decolonisation posed to the codification of SR raised numerous concerns that there already existed sufficient State practice for the compensation of nationalisation measures that any codification of primary rules would be remiss not to recognise it, and that this "complicated the present situation."[290] Members of the Sub-Committee addressed this issue under the guise of the discord that would be sewn between States should the compensation of nationalised property be codified as IL, noting that it would create a "very important problem from the point of view of the maintenance of good relations between states,"[291] being that "the consolidation of international peace and the development of friendly relations among states" was in fact the "principle objective" of IL.[292] With that in mind, members were implored to consider "[W]hat particular rules governing state responsibility were most important for the *cause of peace*?"[293]

Ago himself encouraged consideration of the 'maintenance of peace' in deciding whether to codify primary rules, or to take instead a more 'general approach' to the codification of 'responsibility proper.' While recognising that it was "true that there exist numerous precedents in this field" he concluded "they are far from being unanimous."[294] Instead, members proposed the Sub-Committee should consider that:

> In the present period of the liquidation of the colonial regime and the correction of certain privileged situations obtained under that regime, it

288 *Memorial submitted by the Government of the United Kingdom of Great Britain and Northern Ireland* (10 October 1951) pg 104, para 29.

289 See comments by Mr. Gros, International Law Commission, *Report of the International Law Commission on the work of its Fifteenth Session, 6 July 1963, Official Records of the General Assembly, Eighteenth Session, Supplement* (A/5509) (1963) (A/CN.4/163) 230. Emphasis added.

290 *Id.*, 231; See also, comments by Mr. Yasseen, 231.

291 *Id.*

292 See comments by Mr. Tunkin, *Id.*, 233.

293 *Id.* Emphasis added.

294 International Law Commission, *Report by Mr. R. Ago, Chairman of the Sub-Committee on State Responsibility* (1963) (A/CN.4/152).

> is difficult to ensure a calm atmosphere for working out a generally accepted code of law.[295]

Not all members viewed the 'maintenance of good relations between States' and of a 'calm atmosphere' as a legitimate rationale for the abandonment of a detailed study of established primary rules of IL. Efforts to assuage the concerns regarding decolonisation focused on the absence of a connection between the law of aliens and decolonisation, citing the same working paper on compensation agreements for nationalisation measures, none of which concerned decolonisation.[296] Nor was it unanimous among members of the Sub-Committee that it had a mandate to entertain such considerations. As one member contended:

> If the Commission was not to shrink from its task, it certainly should not disregard [...] responsibility for the gravest violations of international law, such as [...] the refusal to grant independence to colonial peoples, and the violation of the sovereign rights of states.[297]

Accordingly, "consideration should be given to the legal problems arising from the disintegration of the colonial system"[298] rather than to the cost of compensation associated with the decolonisation process. But the voices of dissent were few, and the ILC proceeded with the codification of general secondary rules of SR.

After having unanimously approved his report as Chairman of the Sub-Committee on SR, the ILC appointed Roberto Ago as Special Rapporteur for SR at its 15th session in 1963.[299] In his second report as Special Rapporteur – the first being an account of codification procedures to date – Ago "focus[ed] his examination on the subjective and objective conditions for the existence

295 *Id.*, Appendix II: Memoranda submitted by members of the Sub-Committee on State Responsibility, Working Paper prepared by Mr Yasseen 251.

296 Mr. Paredes, citing Working Paper by Mr. Jiménez de Aréchaga, in International Law Commission, *Report of the International Law Commission on the work of its Fifteenth Session, 6 July 1963, Official Records of the General Assembly, Eighteenth Session, Supplement* (A/5509)1963) (A/CN.4/163) 230.

297 See comments by Mr. Tunkin, *Id.*, 233.

298 *Id.*

299 International Law Commission, *Report of the International Law Commission on the work of its Fifteenth Session, 6 July 1963, Official Records of the General Assembly, Eighteenth Session, Supplement* (A/5509)1963) (A/CN.4/163) 224.

of an internationally wrongful act."[300] The general rules contained in the report were to form the basis for the preparation of draft articles, with a view to the eventual conclusion of an international codification convention, and though the final draft articles would not reference injuries to aliens at all, Lillich noted that "[I]ronically, the commentaries accompanying the draft articles are based almost exclusively upon the traditional law of state responsibility for injuries to aliens and thus are a goldmine of state practice. The norms in the articles, however, are stated very generally indeed."[301]

Between 1969 and his election to the ICJ in 1980, Ago would produce seven more reports as Special Rapporteur, proposing several draft articles at a time, relating predominantly to part 1 of the ARSIWA. In the words of Bodansky and Crook, "Ago allowed the ILC to elaborate lawyers' law, which with a few exceptions was not threatening to states."[302] This formula was continued by Special Rapporteurs Riphagen, Arangio-Ruiz, and Crawford who, in 2001, concluded the work of the Special Rapporteur on the topic. After many decades and multiple drafts, Crawford achieved enough of a consensus to see the ILC finally adopt the *Articles on the Responsibility of States for Internationally Wrongful Acts*. Riphagen stressed that particular primary rules may specify the consequences of their breach; an idea conveyed by the articles through the recognition of *lex specialis*. It was his opinion also that the articles should only address SR for wrongful acts, to the exclusion of liability for injuries arising from lawful acts. Only five articles were provisionally adopted during his seven-year tenure, the most important focusing on the definition of the 'injured State,' which was, in any case, largely revised by Crawford. Over the next eight years, the ILC completed its first reading of parts 2 and 3 of the draft articles. Although most of these articles are reflected in the final text of the ARSIWA, the part addressing dispute settlement – perhaps the subject most associated with Arangio Ruiz – did not survive the second reading. On 12 December 2001, the UN General Assembly took note of the ARSIWA, annexed the text to GA Resolution 56/83, and recommended it to all governments without prejudice to their future adoption or other appropriate action.[303]

300 International Law Commission, *Second report on State responsibility, by Mr. Roberto Ago, Special Rapporteur: The origin of international responsibility* (20 April 1970) (A/CN.4/233) 178.

301 Richard B. Lillich, 'The Current Status of the Law of State Responsibility for Injuries to Aliens' (1979) 73 ASILPROC 244, 247.

302 Daniel Bodansky, John R. Crook, 'Symposium: The ILC's State Responsibility Articles: Introduction and Overview' (2002) 96 AJIL 773, 778.

303 UN General Assembly, *Resolution 56/83: Responsibility of States for Internationally Wrongful Acts* (28 January 2002) A/RES/56/83, 3–4.

6 Conclusion

By the end of the 20th century, it was evident that the codification of SR was as much a codification of the exclusion of traditional SR as it was a codification of an international juridical order governing the consequences for the commission of internationally wrongful acts. Following an exceedingly long history of obfuscation, evasion, selection, and exclusion, the alien was no longer a tertiary beneficiary of the norms of SR, as the relationship that previously existed between the State of origin, and the State of reception, by way of the alien, no longer retained its status in IL.

The minimisation of circumstances capable of engaging questions of SR had been a progressive and consistent process, driven by Western States, primarily in service of their economic interests, but also as a countermeasure to the risk posed by an expanding scope of IHRL. The fora for such action have been varied, but nonetheless reveal a high level of international consensus among such States. The result was the successful cultivation of an international legal environment in which the obligations of the State to protect the subjects of foreign States on its territory no longer existed in the clearly defined manner it once did, though this of course would change with the development of IHRL. In its place was a set of secondary rules, codified in the ARSIWA, but also a new conceptualisation of the position of aliens in IL.

It is worth emphasising the distinctive character of this approach to SR. Common law does not admit a general regime of legal responsibility. Instead, substantive rules of responsibility are defined with reference to their relative obligation. This is clear from common law regimes of criminal law, tort, contracts, property, and family law. Each is characterised by its own regime of remedies, rules of attribution, and invocation.[304] In that sense, the ARSIWA represented a codification of the European civil law tradition that delineates obligation and responsibility. It also conspicuously proceeded to codification with full consideration of contemporary political factors. Though it had accused García Amador of a unilateral expansion of his mandate, the ILC's Sub-Committee on SR undertook its own mission creep in pursuing codification with a mind to 'the maintenance of good relations between States' as

304 Daniel Bodansky, John R. Crook, 'Symposium: The ILC's State Responsibility Articles: Introduction and Overview' (2002) 96 AJIL 773, 780, fn 51. One of the few exceptions in the common law is civil procedure, which sets forth a distinctive set of rules that apply across the various substantive areas of law, although the common law still distinguishes civil procedure from criminal and administrative procedure and thus does not treat procedure as a fully homogeneous field.

opposed to the widespread and consistent law and practice of States. Though codification is a matter of consolidation, not of invention, the Sub-Committee ensured the minimisation of SR, first in respect of aliens, then in respect of non-nationals subject to its jurisdiction, despite it having formed the basis for SR. Though some minor differences can be noted between other codification procedures, all were concerned with the minimisation of the substantive scope of SR.

This legal revisionism did not, however, begin with the ILC. Many decades prior, the rules of SR had begun its transition from a doctrine of PIL, expressly theorised and applied to the protection of aliens, to a private law concept that did not require legal response from an offending State, affected in part to facilitate the economic exploitation of Latin America, and aided by the popularisation of the theory of fault, and the broad reading of *force majeure*. It was also critical to the protection of an unregulated arms trade, which threatened to prohibit certain actions taken in respect of the sale and export of weapons, where they were subsequently used unlawfully, including against aliens. In that respect, and as weapons flowed into Latin America, the position of the alien within the rules of SR hindered the advancement and protection of specific interests by exposing certain States to the attribution of SR, through the imposition of additional international obligations.

As well as affecting the international status of the alien in IL, the consensus that formed during the codification era justified the conceptual basis from which SR would be theorised and applied in IRL. It informed the policies that would be employed in response to the international refugee crises that unfolded over the first decades of the 20th century. Historic precedent, reinforced by widespread and consistent practice (at least by those States of consequence to IL), would provide a conceptual blueprint, transposed from the law of aliens to the burgeoning law of refugees, as groups with analogous legal conditions, but for the stateless status of the latter.

CHAPTER 2

Early International Responses to the 'Refugee Question'

1 Introduction: The Division and Delegation of International Obligations

From the beginning of the 1920s, the 'question of the refugee'[1] became an enduring one for the newly formed League of Nations (LoN), though Member States would not recognise it as such until many years later.[2] In the first years of its operation, the institution was confronted with several refugee crises: the Russian, the Greek, and the Armenian, which unfolded in rapid succession, each distinct in character from the previous, but all immense in scale.[3] In response to each crisis, States operating under the auspices of the LoN developed, implemented, and refined a number of international treaties, policies, and mechanisms critical to the theorisation and application of SR in the burgeoning system of IRL.

These earliest international efforts to resolve refugee crises confronted a number of novel legal problems, principally, that the refugee presented an anomaly in IL. The unique legal conditions that distinguished the refugee from the alien required a new conceptualisation of the international obligations that were ordinarily associated with the protection of the alien. Consequently, a number of novel legal questions arose in respect of SR. This led to concern among Western States in particular, that the assumption of certain international obligations and associated functions may result in the attribu-

1 In LoN documentation, refugee matters are referred to consistently as 'refugee questions' with reference also to the state of origin or assigned minority status of the refugee population.

2 League of Nations, *Conference on Russian and Armenian Refugee Questions: Report by the High Commissioner* (5 June 1926) (C.327.1926) 1; Matthew Frank, Jessica Reinisch, 'Introduction: Refugees and the Nation-State in Europe, 1919–1959' (2014) 49(3) JContempHist 477, 481; Robert W. Ditchburn, 'The Refugee Problem' (1939) 28(110) Studies: An Irish Quarterly Review 275, 279–280.

3 Though the classification of the Greek crisis as a 'refugee' crisis is questionable in light of the 1951 *Refugee Convention* definition of the term, the event in question occurred many decades prior to the modern conceptualisation of 'refugee.' More critically, the crisis was treated by the League as a 'refugee' crisis specifically for reasons that are provided in Section 5 of this chapter.

 | DOI:10.1163/9789004722835_004

tion of SR for omissions associated with the maintenance of refugee populations. This led to a conservative approach to the theorisation and application of SR in early IRL, requiring the division of international obligations into categories that could be assigned to various actors, including to refugees themselves. Under the auspices of the LoN, Western States developed, implemented, and refined a number of international laws, policies, and mechanisms that later formed the conceptual basis for the theorisation and application of SR in IRL. Once again, the evolving priorities of States in resolving refugee crises informed the development of international responses, leading to the implementation of 'permanent solutions,' in particular, the facilitation of employment, then repatriation, then colonisation.

The relevance of the interwar period to contemporary IRL cannot be overstated, though it is often overlooked in legal scholarship, which tends to disjoin the early interwar period from the later, and overwhelmingly considers the events of the late 1930s through to the adoption of the 1951 Convention to constitute the most significant innovations in IRL.[4] Despite this, early interwar multilateralism on the 'refugee question' as distinct from, or extraneous to latter developments, discounts the fact that the scope and content of international obligations in IRL were first conceived of during this period. Consequently, the theorisation and application of SR in IRL was also first conceived of during this era. Together, these formed the theoretical basis for the 'international law of obligations'[5] of modern IRL. In that sense, the early international refugee responses are far more critical to contemporary IRL and the role of SR within it than might have previously been considered, as this model of dividing and assigning international obligations for the maintenance refugees has endured in various forms and iterations throughout the decades.

4 Many authoritative sources on the history of refugee law either substantially overlook the work of the LoN, or essentially commence with the work of the UN. Betts writes that the refugee protection regime was "created in the aftermath of the Second World War." See Alexander Betts, *Survival Migration: Failed Governance and the Crisis of Displacement* (Cornell University Press 2013) 173; Dennis Gallagher, 'The Evolution of the International Refugee System' (1989) 23(3) Int Migr Rev 579; Guy S. Goodwin-Gill, Jane McAdam, *The Refugee in International Law* (3rd edn, OUP 2007); Michelle Foster, Hélène Lambert, *International Refugee Law and the Protection of Stateless Persons* (OUP 2019); Jason M. Pobjoy, *The Child in International Refugee Law* (CUP 2017). See also: Jill Goldenziel, 'The Curse of the Nation-State: Refugees, Migration, and Security in International Law' (2016) 48(3) Ariz St LJ 579; Hasan-Askari Rizvi, 'United Nations and the Refugee Problem' (1985) 38(1) Pakistan Horizon 46; Susan F. Martin, 'The Global Refugee Crisis' (2016) 17(1) GJIA 5; UN High Commissioner for Refugees, *Self-Study Module 1: An Introduction to International Protection. Protecting Persons of Concern to UNHCR* (1 August 2005).

5 Robert Kolb, *The International Law of State Responsibility* (Edward Elgar 2018).

This is a particularly critical omission in light of the fact the first priority of the LoN at the time was the immediate and practical need to facilitate pathways to employment and to maintain a degree of geographical containment while actively minimising circumstances capable of engaging questions of SR; priorities that are increasingly notable in the resolution of contemporary refugee and mixed migration crises. This omission has also permitted the propagation of a certain mythology regarding the intentions and motivations of States in assuming international obligations for elements of the refugee question,[6] in particular, that in constructing IRL in the post-war environment, States were seized of a humanitarian imperative.[7] But the characterisation of early international efforts under the auspices of the LoN as being 'humanitarian' in nature, 'concerned with the welfare' of refugee populations, and motivated by an 'international resolve' to provide 'assistance and protection,' is contradicted by the record.[8] As Chapter 2 demonstrates, early iterations of IRL (being the international instruments implemented during the period in question) were crafted with much greater consideration of political and economic objectives, than of humanitarian ideology.

---

6 Ivor C Jackson, 'The 1951 Convention Relating to the Status of Refugees: A Universal Basis for Protection' (1991) 3 IJRL 403–404; Pierre Bertrand, 'An Operational Approach to International Refugee Protection' (1993) 26 Cornell Int'l LJ 495, 497; Alice Edwards, 'Tampering with Refugee Protection: The Case of Australia' (2003) 15 IJRL 192, 210; See also: Walker's discussion of the tension between humanitarian interests and State interests: Kristen Walker, 'Defending the 1951 Convention Definition of Refugee' (2003) 17 GeoImmigrLJ 583, 584–585.

7 Bubb et al. consider that the 1951 Convention "can be understood as an agreement among states to supply the global public good of refugee protection." See: Ryan Bubb, Michael Kremer, David I. Levine, 'The Economics of International Refugee Law' (2011) 40(2) J Leg Stud 367; Lubbers referred to the international community having developed "an international conscience." See: Ruud Lubbers, 'Asylum for All: Refugee Protection in the 21st Century' (2002) 24(1) HarvIntLJ 60. See also: Guy S. Goodwin-Gill, 'The Language of Protection' (1989) 1(1) IJRL 6, 14: "The protection of refugees has its origins in a human rights context. General Assembly resolutions gave early attention to aid for the most needy, to reaffirming the basic principles relating to solutions, and to recommending increased protection activities."

8 James C. Hathaway, 'The Evolution of Refugee Status in International Law: 1920–1950' (1984) 334 Int'l & Comp LQ 348, 351, 361; Eric A. Ormsby, 'The Refugee Crisis as Civil Liberties Crisis' (2017) 117(5) ColumLRev 1191, 1194; Rafiqul Islam, 'The Origin and Evolution of International Refuge Law' in Rafiqul Islam and Jahid Hossain Bhuiyan (eds), *Refugee Law* (Brill 2013) 13–15; Gil Loescher, 'The International Refugee Regime: Stretched to the Limit?' (1994) 47(2) JIntAff 351, 354; Matthew Frank, Jessica Reinisch, 'Introduction: Refugees and the Nation-State in Europe, 1919–1959' (2014) 49(3) JContempHist 477, 481; Martyn Housden, 'White Russians Crossing the Black Sea: Fridtjof Nansen, Constantinople and the First Modern Repatriation of Refugees Displaced by Civil Conflict, 1922–1923' (2010) 88(3) Slavon East Eur Rev 495, 479, 500.

Section 2 considers the unique conditions that made the refugee an anomaly in IL, requiring a new conceptualisation of SR. It argues that in the early 20th century when the world was faced with numerous sequential refugee crises, SR had already developed into a relatively well-defined set of legal principles, though it was adapted to the condition of the alien, not the refugee. In the absence of a coherent international juridical order to address the question of refugee movement – characterised by the rupture in the relationship between State and subject – no legal mechanism existed to attribute SR, as it did in the context of traditional SR. Accordingly, the doctrine of SR was theorised and applied to the treatment of refugees in an entirely different manner than it was to the treatment of aliens. Principally, the obligations of the State of origin were generally presumed to have ceased in the wake of denationalisation, which was considered to indeed constitute a definitive rupture in the State-subject relationship. This gave rise to a 'presumption of severance' of the State of origin's obligation to provide diplomatic protection. Section 2 argues that these conditions led to concern among both States and the LoN that the assumption of certain obligations may result in the attribution of SR for the violation of international agreements pertaining to the maintenance of refugee populations in the absence of a State of origin capable of providing diplomatic protection to its subject.

Section 3 evaluates the shifting priorities of States in the resolution of the 'refugee question' and the relevance of these shifts to the theorisation and application of SR in IRL. It argues that in resolving refugee crises, the first priority of the LoN was the immediate and practical need to facilitate pathways to employment. In the eventual creation of the Nansen passport and the Arrangements relative to refugee populations, LoN Member States were not motivated by political or social imperatives to define refugee status for humanitarian reasons, but were instead seized of the practical requirement to provide a document that permitted movement across international borders for refugee populations that had predominantly been denationalised by their State of origin. In respect of the latter, it argues that not only was the question of a legal status not a priority for the LoN, but that the question was evaded until such time as more pressing questions of SR could be resolved.

Section 3 posits that, at a certain point, the prioritisation of refugee employment shifted to accommodate repatriation as the preferable permanent solution, and that paradoxically, the primacy of employment as a solution to the refugee question did not endure due to the *availability* of employment and its impact on the permanence of refugee populations. The unwillingness of refugees to repatriate resulted in the recalibration of IRL to other 'methods of relief' that prioritised repatriation in its various forms. Section 3 argues that this recalibration reveals a deep preoccupation with the question of SR, ultimately leading to the division of international obligations into broad categories, comprising 'financial and administrative' on the one hand and 'legal' on the other; assigning the former and reserving the latter. It demonstrates that the question of SR in IRL was theorised and applied reactively, taking account of the common priorities of Western States to maintain control over the development of IL, while maintaining distance from the refugee population itself.

Section 4 addresses the policy of agricultural colonisation in the context of financial obligations, and argues that the policy provided a comprehensive solution to the question of SR in IRL. It allowed for the initial assignment of financial obligations to refugees themselves, and later, for the incremental assignment of the totality of international obligations to the State of reception. Section 4 also considers international population exchanges as part of States' irredentist policy (whereby a territory or population is subject to 'restoration' where it was perceived to have been 'lost'). It details how population exchange was conceptualised as 'repatriation' by the LoN and argues that although considered relevant to 'minorities' rather than to refugees, population exchanges provided an essential link in the development of IRL in that they evolved from traditional repatriation and allowed for the development of 'colonisation' as a method of relief. Section 4 argues that as a method of relief, population exchanges provided a theoretical basis for the eventual cessation of State (and institutional) obligations, acting as a model for future refugee repatriation. It concludes that the response of the LoN had dire consequences for the conception of SR in respect of refugees in that it implicitly recognised that the denationalisation of an undesirable population constituted a cessation of the relationship between the refugee and the State of origin.

Section 5 addresses two elements of early IRL that were critical to the conception of SR within it: that of 'enduring nationality,'[9] and of a uniform legal status. It argues that the question of the former was not resolved during this period due to the evolving circumstances in which enduring nationality was addressed, and the differing priorities of the LoN and Member States in responding to those evolving circumstances. In respect of the latter, it argues that not only was the question of a legal status not a priority for the LoN, but

9 This is a term used by the author to describe the common approach of the LoN in the resolution of refugee crises brought about by denationalisation and irredentism. The term is discussed in detail at section 5.

that the question was evaded until such time as more pressing questions of SR could be resolved.

Section 6 analyses the prevailing legal doctrines on 'capacity' and 'compensation' that were so frequently cited at the material time. It argues that both concepts were explored under the guise of State of origin 'duties' – both to its former subjects and to States of resettlement – but that in reality, these proposals supported the desired trajectory of Western States in the development of SR in IRL; that is, exacting compensation and reparation for the damage caused by the imposition of an unwanted refugee population. It argues that the conception of capacity was introduced and reintroduced numerous times during the inter-war period, and that with each iteration, it incrementally decreased in its utility and relevance to the refugee, instead relating primarily to any enduring obligations of the repatriating State that may arise as a result of its actions. While the preoccupation with the security and safety of repatriated refugees was directly related to the question of State of origin capacity to fulfil its 'duties' to its subjects, repatriation was not primarily concerned with the safety and security of the refugee population in terms of an individual human right to such guarantees. Of equal importance to capacity was the question of compensation and the inferred 'duty' of the State of origin to provide it to States of reception where the latter had absorbed a large number of the former's denationalised subjects. Section 6 argues that much like discussions on capacity, the concept of compensation in the context of displacement was revisited time and time again, despite it not having legal precedent, however unlike the attempts to legally implement the question of capacity, States of reception were in fact able to exact compensation from States of origin in several instances, supported in this endeavour by the League of Nations.

Chapter 2 concludes that, much like early SR, the inter-war responses to 'the refugee question' were devised primarily by Western States under the auspices of the LoN, with the view to shift the burden of refugee populations onto economically fragile States, and to ensure that the vast majority of funds required for refugee maintenance remained the obligation of private persons and organisations. In that respect, State (and indeed, institutional) responsibility were theorised and applied in IRL in such a way as to shield Western States from the assumption of financial obligations, while ensuring the retention of control over the determination of law and policy. It concludes that for these reasons, early international refugee responses are far more critical to contemporary IRL and the role of SR within it than might have previously been considered, as this model of dividing and assigning international obligations for refugees has endured throughout the decades.

2 Statelessness and Legal Status: Who Is Responsible for the Refugee?

The refugee crises that unfolded in the first half of the 20th century concerned stateless refugees, lacking in law and in fact the diplomatic protection of a State.[10] Denationalisation decrees issued by the Soviet Union in 1921, and by Turkey in 1924, stripped a vast number of citizens of their nationality,[11] but although SR had, at this point in history, developed into a relatively well-defined set of legal principles, it did not encompass the condition of the refugee, and a coherent international juridical order did not exist to address the question of refugee movement. Rather, as it concerned the individual, SR accommodated the legal condition of the alien. Comparatively, the legal condition of the refugee that distinguished him entirely from the alien was that he no longer enjoyed the protection of his State of origin.[12]

The foundation of traditional SR had been that the alien remained tethered to his State of origin by virtue of his nationality, which in turn formed the basis of the legal relationship between the State of reception and the State of origin, and raised questions of SR where there had been a failure in the protective obligations assumed by the former on behalf of the latter. By contrast, the rupture in the relationship between State and subject in the case of the refugee meant also that a rupture had occurred in the relationship between the two States, so that no legal mechanism existed to attribute SR, as it did in the context of traditional SR. Without the protection of a State of origin, the refugee was stateless, and a novel conception of SR was required to address his condition.

10 UN Economic and Social Council, *Special Committee on Refugees and Displaced Persons: Suggested draft of broad definition, for the purposes of the work of the Committee, of the terms "refugee" and "displaced person". Note by the Director of the Intergovernmental Committee on refugees* (10 April 1946) (E/REF/12).

11 A decade later, denationalisation decrees would be issued by the Russian government to deprive nationality to Russians abroad who failed to obtain recognition of their citizenship and permission to reside outside Russia, and the German government would issue decrees depriving nationality to Jews from Poland and Russia who had become naturalised Germans. See: Robert W. Ditchburn, 'The Refugee Problem' (1939) 28(110) Studies: An Irish Quarterly Review 275, 284.

12 League of Nations, *Arrangement relating to the Issue of Identity Certificates to Russian and Armenian Refugees, supplementing and amending the previous Arrangements dated July 5, 1922, and May 31, 1924* (12 May 1926) LNTS Vol. LXXXIX, No. 2004; Robert W. Ditchburn, 'The Refugee Problem' (1939) 28(110) Studies: An Irish Quarterly Review 275, 276; Paul Weis, 'The International Protection of Refugees' (1954) 48(2) AJIL 193, 199.

Accordingly, the doctrine of SR was theorised and applied to the treatment of refugees in an entirely different manner than it was to the treatment of aliens. Principally, as it related to the treatment of refugees, the obligations of the State of origin were generally presumed to have ceased. Denationalisation had, in that sense, served its purpose with great success; it had been accepted roundly by the comity of nations that denationalisation indeed constituted a definitive rupture in the State–subject relationship, giving rise to a 'presumption of severance' of the State of origin's obligation to provide diplomatic protection, and required only an international response in the form of aid and legal pathways to employment and resettlement for those subject to the relevant decree. Consequently (and in much the same way that SR was intrinsically linked to the law of aliens), from the beginning, IRL was intrinsically linked to SR and the law of aliens, developing from the absence of an appropriate international legal mechanism to organise and attribute various international obligations that would relieve certain conditions brought about by statelessness, though it did not at first attempt to resolve the question of legal status and diplomatic protection.

The LoN first broached the subject of refugees in March 1921, after the International Committee of the Red Cross sent a letter to the Secretary-General regarding 'the question of the Russian refugee.'[13] The letter detailed some 800,000 Russian refugees scattered throughout Europe without legal protection or representation.[14] The ICRC considered the LoN to be "the only supernational political authority capable of solving a problem which [was] beyond the power of exclusively humanitarian organisations"[15] and requested the LoN to intervene in order to find some solution. Specifically, the organisation requested the LoN define the legal position of the refugee, co-ordinate the efforts already undertaken for assistance to refugees, and either assure the right of the refugee to employment in other States, or in the alternative, initiate repatriation to Russia.[16]

From the moment the letter was received, Member States of the LoN were preoccupied with the limitation of both the institutional responsibility of the LoN and the circumstances in which SR may be attributed in the context of new and undefined legal obligations. Member States asserted that the LoN lacked the legal authority to involve itself in the resolution of the refugee

13 League of Nations, 'The Question of the Russian Refugees' (1921) 2(2) LNOJ 225.
14 *Id.*, 227–228.
15 *Id.*
16 *Id.*

crisis, as the Covenant of the LoN did not provide a mandate for the relief of refugees.[17] From its first sessions on the subject, it was suggested that the coordination of assistance and relief efforts were best undertaken by other organisations, specifically the League of Red Cross Societies and the ICRC, as it was "not within the province of the LoN to undertake the practical organisation of relief nor [to] undertake the financial responsibility."[18] At the time, a number of aid programmes were already active, and a significant amount of aid was already being provided by private charitable organisations. Member States were keen to maintain this *status quo* as it provided a simple solution to a complex question, and eliminated any risk of SR. The novel and uncertain position of the refugee in IL meant that the scope, limits, and division of State and institutional obligations were undefined. In particular, both the LoN and individual Member States were hesitant to assume financial obligations for any element of the refugee question in case it unwittingly led to the assumption of enduring legal obligations.

Though the LoN was steadfast in resisting its own involvement in the refugee crises that unfolded during its tenure; safeguarded by its oft-cited lack of protective mandate, it conceived of a necessity to divide obligations into 'financial and administrative' on the one hand, and 'legal' on the other, assigning the former and reserving the latter. In that way, it retained control over the development of IRL, and simultaneously asserted its own institutional incapacity to provide legal solutions. Financial and administrative obligations were considered to be complementary, though they were in practice divided, while legal obligations were a category apart, and were treated as wholly distinct. While financial obligations would be borne by the State of reception (and in some cases, by refugees themselves), the LoN would retain administrative obligations through a separate authority, appointed for the purpose of administering relief programmes. The question of legal obligations would remain suspended until the dissolution of the administrative authority, at which point the State of reception would assume the totality of obligations for the refugee population it now hosted. This was achieved in part through the appointment of a High Commissioner for Refugees, with a mandate separate and distinct from the LoN, but nonetheless responsible to it. The LoN reinforced the absence of its own mandate for refugees by

17 Louise W. Holborn, 'The League of Nations and the Refugee Problem' (1939) 203 Annals Am Acad Pol & Soc Sci 124.

18 League of Nations, 'The Question of the Russian Refugees' (1921) 2(2) LNOJ 225, 226.

concluding a resolution providing that it lacked any authorisation to render assistance to refugees.[19]

In addressing each crisis, the LoN was required to speak to the question of State (and indeed, institutional) responsibility in IRL, as relief could only be provided where international obligations had been assigned, attributed, or assumed. Perhaps unsurprisingly, the question of SR in IRL was addressed only indirectly and with seemingly little interest beyond its limitation; a fact that at times has been attributed to the unwillingness of Member States to divest themselves of national funds,[20] but is more likely attributable to the general unwillingness to delineate the precise terms of SR in a new and uncertain international legal environment where the limits and constraints on sovereignty were as yet unclear. The general aversion to the definitive resolution of legal questions affecting the refugee, for example, was the consequence of a deep preoccupation with enduring obligations and the attribution of SR, as demonstrated by the deliberate avoidance of critical questions such as the legal status of refugees. It is also attributable to the fact that for many years, and even as crisis followed crisis, the refugee question was considered to be a transient one, and was treated accordingly.[21]

3 'Methods of Relief' and Freedom of Movement

As the refugee crises of the 1920s and 1930s were perceived as temporary emergencies, the earliest international attempts to resolve them were dictated by the perceived impermanence of the refugee in IL, both as a class of person and as an individual. As a result, early refugee policy was developed according to the presumption that the refugee was an anomaly in IL. This is evident not only from the written records, but is reflected in the policies that were devised in response to the refugee crises that ensued during the brief existence of the LoN. As late as June 1926, the High Commissioner

19 'Resolution on the Russian Refugee Problem' adopted by the Council of the League of Nations on 27 June 1921. See: League of Nations, 'Relief Work in Russia and the Question of the Russian Refugee' (1922) 3(4) LNOJ 338.

20 Matthew Frank, Jessica Reinisch, 'Introduction: Refugees and the Nation-State in Europe, 1919–59' (2014) 49(3) JContempHist 477, 481; Robert W. Ditchburn, 'The Refugee Problem' (1939) 28(110) Studies: An Irish Quarterly Review 275, 279–280.

21 Robert W. Ditchburn, 'The Refugee Problem' (1939) 28(110) Studies: An Irish Quarterly Review 275, 280.

himself still considered the Refugee Service of the ILO to be "an entirely temporary service" as did the LoN.[22]

In providing legal relief, administering maintenance, and ultimately assigning obligations for various aspects of the 'refugee question', the LoN conceived principally of four solutions, or 'methods of relief' as they were commonly called,[23] comprising repatriation, assimilation, colonisation, and population exchange as measures to resolve, at least in part, the refugee crises of the 1920s and 1930s. Some methods of relief have undergone something of an evolution to become permanent fixtures in contemporary policy, and others rapidly lost relevance. From the moment the LoN turned its attention to the question of the Russian refugee, its unwavering first priority, around which all 'methods of relief' were devised, was to relieve States of reception of the financial burden of hosting unemployed refugees. As the earliest attempts to resolve the Russian refugee crisis demonstrate, the need to define a legal status was critical only insofar as it was required to secure pathways to employment. The denationalisation of persons affecting their displacement – being the condition that overwhelmingly brought about refugeehood – was relevant only insofar as it impeded identification and therefore international travel. As Holborn noted, though it became known as the 'Nansen passport,' "[T]he document is not identical with a national passport. It is an identity certificate issued for one year, which can be used as a travel document."[24] International cooperation on the resolution of the refugee question was in essence a continuation of previous cooperation, undertaken by the International Labour Office (ILO) and its Refugee Service, which was solely concerned with the conferral of work permits to refugees. In that sense, the work of the LoN was not intended to provide remedy to denationalisation as such, but to provide documentation to refugees lacking identification as a means to facilitate employment.

In June 1921, the Council of the LoN resolved to appoint a High Commissioner for the LoN to secure intergovernmental action on the refugee question, and provided the objectives for his eventual work. According to the report adopted by the Council, it would not be possible for the High Com-

22 League of Nations, *Conference on Russian and Armenian Refugee Questions: Report by the High Commissioner*5 June 1926) (C.327.1926) 1.

23 Robert W. Ditchburn, 'The Refugee Problem' (1939) 28(110) Studies: An Irish Quarterly Review 275, 287.

24 Louise W. Holborn, 'The League of Nations and the Refugee Problem' (1939) 203 Annals Am Acad Pol & Soc Sci 124, 126.

missioner to make himself responsible in any way for direct relief for the distress of refugees. “His task was rather to be confined to enabling the refugees to support themselves by securing their dispersal in countries where the cost of living was small and where there was a good chance of their obtaining productive employment.”[25] The appointment of a High Commissioner, rather than the creation of a specialised body, paralleled the waning interest of Member States in the question of displaced persons, as well as their growing financial and political disengagement. On 27 June that year, the Council of the LoN approved his mandate for one year (later renewing it on a yearly basis).

Fridtjof Nansen was eventually appointed High Commissioner for Refugees. He was to determine the legal status of Russian refugees, to repatriate them or to allow them to find employment in States of reception, and to coordinate the efforts already undertaken on their behalf by humanitarian organisations. Almost contemporaneously, through an *ad hoc* conference convened by the ICRC in August 1921, Nansen was appointed High Commissioner of the Geneva Conference for the fight against famine in Russia; work for which he was awarded the Nobel Peace Prize in 1922.

Upon the suggestion of the Secretariat of the LoN and non-governmental organisations directly engaged with the relief of refugees, Nansen created the Advisory Committee for Private Organizations in September 1921 and tasked it with consulting the High Commissioner on matters of common interest. He also convened general conferences in August and September 1921, and at a third conference in July 1922, Nansen called an Intergovernmental Conference to consider his proposals for the provision of a Certificate of Identity for Russian refugees. This document would be issued by individual governments to Russian refugees in their territory, and considered valid by all other adhering States. The purpose of the Certificate of Identity was to provide a special status to stateless refugees, and did not primarily recognise nor confer a ‘refugee status’ on beneficiaries. As Watenpaugh noted:

> [The passport] was not an intervention on behalf of political grievance or on the basis of justice claims. The Nansen Passport made no provision for the refugees to have any ability to act politically in any arena. It provided states with *a reservoir of controllable workers deprived of any ability to claim political agency or civil rights*; thus they could expect no

25 League of Nations, ‘Relief Work in Russia and the Question of the Russian Refugee’ (1922) 3(4) LNOJ 338, 341.

legal protection from host countries, and the host countries had no binding obligations to them of any kind.[26]

The Nansen passport was created to provide a special status to stateless refugees. However, the document did not recognise persecution or the right of the individual to a special humanitarian status, and though one of its purposes was to allow international travel, it was not intended to be a travel document *per se*. Rather, the primary function of the Nansen passport was to act as a *de facto* international employment permit, conferring the right to work on stateless refugees through the provision of a special immigration status.[27] As Hyndman notes, "[T]he main thrust of the early conventions was to make provision for the granting of travel and identity documents to the particular group of refugees in question."[28] Holborn wrote of the process to secure the Certificate of Identity:

> Nansen's aim was to turn as quickly as possible from relief and charity to measures which would enable the refugees to become self-supporting. In order to do so it was necessary to get information in regard to the number, age, sex, and profession of the refugees and to secure a legal status for them which would give them standing in the countries of refuge so that they could seek employment, or would enable them to travel in search of opportunities elsewhere.[29]

That legal status was made necessary by the fact that most of the Russian refugees were either without nationality because of the Soviet decree of 15 December 1921 or without valid papers.[30] Accordingly, it was only as a consequence that the Nansen passport recognised a status of 'refugee' and the con-

---

26 Keith David Watenpaugh, 'Between Communal Survival and National Aspiration: Armenian Genocide Refugees, the League of Nations, and the Practices of Interwar Humanitarianism' (2014) 5(2) Humanity: An International Journal of Human Rights, Humanitarianism, and Development 159, 172. Emphasis added.

27 In Weis' construction, the Arrangements were intended "to remove a serious obstacle particularly to the resettlement of refugee." See: Paul Weis, 'The International Protection of Refugees' (1954) 48(2) AJIL 193, 206.

28 Patricia Hyndman, 'The 1951 Convention Definition of Refugee: An Appraisal with Particular Reference to the Case of Sri Lankan Tamil Applicants' (1987) 9 HumRightsQ 49.

29 Louise W. Holborn, 'The League of Nations and the Refugee Problem' (1939) 203 Annals Am Acad Pol & Soc Sci 124, 125.

30 *Id.*, fn 4.

ditions that created it, and it was also only as a consequence of the imperative to transfer refugees to States with employment prospects, that the 'freedoms' of refugees were first discussed. But much like the question of 'capacity,' the subtext of discussions about 'freedoms' did not refer to individual human rights, but to the limited ability of beneficiaries to travel to States of their choice; that is, the regulated freedom of movement that was required to allow for the procurement of employment. The deficiencies of the Nansen passport contributed to what Watenpaugh called "the moral and ethical vacuity (even uselessness) of the interwar refugee regime."[31]

As noted in this chapter, the *de facto* safety and security of the refugee population was not a paramount concern. Rather, the rapid resettlement of refugees in States of reception, and the assumption of legal obligations by the latter was prioritised, in large part to ensure that the LoN and certain Member States were immune from future questions of SR. Where a State assumed the role of State of reception, the international obligations of others to support resettlement efforts ceased to exist. The institutional obligations of the LoN would also no longer apply as the refugee was now the charge of one State and any grievances he might have would be an internal matter. For Member States, the assumption of international obligations was dependent on the avoidance of financial obligations vis-à-vis refugee populations, lest it result in the attribution of SR. This was evident from the first international efforts to resolve the Russian refugee crisis. Member States were urged by the LoN to further the settlement of unemployed Russian (and later Armenian) refugees, in part by issuing visas enabling their departure from the territory in order to seek employment.[32] These visas conferred the 'freedom of movement,' which permitted refugees to enter and exit the territories of other States.[33] Other international instruments enabled freedom of movement between States for the purposes of securing employment based on labour shortages in States of

31 Keith David Watenpaugh, 'Between Communal Survival and National Aspiration: Armenian Genocide Refugees, the League of Nations, and the Practices of Interwar Humanitarianism' (2014) 5(2) Humanity: An International Journal of Human Rights, Humanitarianism, and Development 159, 172.

32 'Questions Concerning Russian and Armenian Refugees' (1926) 7(12) LNOJ 1667.

33 See: League of Nations, *Arrangement relating to the Issue of Identity Certificates to Russian and Armenian Refugees, supplementing and amending the previous Arrangements dated July 5, 1922, and May 31, 1924* (12 May 1926) LNTS Vol. LXXXIX, No. 2004.

reception, yet these suffered from the same deficiencies as the Nansen passport where it came to the assumption of international obligations.

4 Methods of Relief and the Limitation of State Responsibility

In 1922, the first of what would be three Arrangements was signed in Geneva. It permitted States to issue certificates of identity to Russian, and later Armenian, refugees. The certificates would allow Russian refugees to proceed to States where they could procure employment in a regular and lawful manner.[34] A report by the High Commissioner accompanying the first Arrangement detailed similar measures that had already been undertaken. Refugees in Egypt and Cyprus were sent to Bulgaria "where the cost of living is extremely low and where there is work to be found."[35] They would also be subject to labour exchanges in various other States.[36] An arrangement had been made for Austria to receive 200 agriculturists and their wives, as "in the country there is a great shortage of labour"[37] and similar arrangements were being negotiated with Hungary, Australia, and Canada.[38] The High Commissioner requested other Member States to consider whether special categories of workers could not be supplied from among the Russian refugees to remedy similar conditions in their own territory.[39] Arrangements such as these permitted a rapid assumption of obligations by the State of reception by ensuring that the obligations associated with the maintenance of the refugee population remained a domestic, rather than international matter. Even as the Conference for the third Arrangement established a 'working capital fund' (or 'revolving fund') to which Member States would collectively contribute for the transportation and settlement of Russian and Armenian refugees, the contributions entailed no enduring legal obligations, and were treated as donations.[40]

34 League of Nations, *Arrangement with respect to the issue of certificates of identity to Russian Refugees* (5 July 1922) LNTS Vol. XIII, No. 355.
35 League of Nations, 'Russian Refugees in Annexes' (1922) 3(6) LNOJ 556, 614.
36 *Id.*, 614–615.
37 *Id.*
38 *Id.*, 615.
39 *Id.*
40 'Questions Concerning Russian and Armenian Refugees' (1926) 7(12) LNOJ 1667.

In 1924, a second international Arrangement was concluded relative to both Russian and Armenian refugees.[41] The previous year, the president of the Armenian National delegation, Gabriel Noradounghian, addressed two letters to the Council of the LoN, reporting the conditions of post-genocide Armenians and asking for the extension of Nansen's mandate to include this group. Several years after that, a third Arrangement provided that the term 'refugee' related to any Russian or Armenian who did not enjoy, or no longer enjoyed the protection of the USSR or Ottoman Empire respectively, and who had not acquired another nationality.[42] But although the Conference that established the third Arrangement endeavoured to provide a definition of the term 'refugee,' it was not intended to serve as a legal status in recognition of persecution. Rather, it provided only a designation of those groups that were entitled to the provision of identity certificates. As such, even the 3rd Arrangement remained very much concerned with the provision of employment. As the High Commissioner noted at the time:

> It is believed that the application of this Arrangement will confer not only obvious benefits on large numbers of refugees estimated at more than one million but also on the countries for whom the unemployed refugees present a heavy expense, and on the immigration countries anxious to increase their productive populations.[43]

Though initially, States of reception were willing to provide swift pathways to employment in order to avoid refugee populations becoming a public charge, and States that were desirous of a population increase to stimulate certain industries were keen to become States of resettlement, such enthusiasm did not endure, particularly among Western European States. The primacy of employment as a solution to the refugee crisis remained the critical element around which early IRL was constructed, until such time as it became evident that the primary impetus for the *unwillingness* of refugees to repatriate to their

41 League of Nations, 'Plan for the Issue of a Certificate of Identity to Armenian Refugees, 31st May 1924. Submitted for the consideration of interested governments by Dr. Nansen, High Commissioner for Russian Refugees in execution of the Resolution of the Council of the League' (1924) 5(7) LNOJ.

42 League of Nations, *Arrangement relating to the Issue of Identity Certificates to Russian and Armenian Refugees, supplementing and amending the previous Arrangements dated July 5, 1922, and May 31, 1924* (12 May 1926) LNTS Vol. LXXXIX, No. 2004.

43 League of Nations, *Conference on Russian and Armenian Refugee Questions: Report by the High Commissioner*5 June 1926) (C.327.1926) 2.

States of origin was precisely the *availability* of employment. At that point, two significant shifts in the division of international obligations can be noted, both of which coincided with shifts in the perception of the refugee's permanence. First, a clear preference emerged among Member States of the LoN for either rapid self-sufficiency through the method of relief of 'colonisation,' or repatriation as solutions to the refugee question. Second, the preoccupation with the scope and content of IRL shifted from the implications of enduring obligations and SR to the pursuit of a definitive cessation of international obligations.

Following the initial efforts to provide solutions to the refugee question through access to labour markets, the second method of relief devised by the LoN was repatriation.[44] This provided perhaps the most simple and complete solution to the question of both institutional responsibility and SR, by enabling the resumption of the relationship between the State of origin and the refugee. Once it became clear that the availability of employment hindered efforts to repatriate refugees, alternative 'methods of relief' were devised that not only provided a remedy to this problem by ensuring alternative sources of income, but more importantly, ensured that a clear path existed to the cessation of international obligations by the LoN and Member States.

In pursuit of repatriation as a method of relief, a number of States advanced a model pursuant to which refugee populations would either became financially self-sufficient in a short period of time, or otherwise would be repatriated. Both policies were primarily concerned with the minimisation of SR. The presentation of these two alternatives as the only viable solutions to the refugee question would persist through subsequent refugee crises and would drive much of the development of early IRL.

4.1 *Repatriation, Self-Sufficiency, and the Cessation of Responsibility*

The term 'repatriation', as it was used by the LoN, encompassed several methods of relief. This included the exchange of populations, and the colonisation of sparsely populated territories within the State of origin, as well as the voluntary return of refugee populations to their former habitual residence (the latter of which was the most infrequently utilised method of relief during the relevant period). In this sense, 'repatriation' as it applied to IRL in the 1920s and 1930s should not be understood retroactively with reference to contemporary refugee repatriation, as it was neither utilised nor referenced in later decades as a template for modern durable solutions. Instead, the alternatives

44 Louise W. Holborn, 'The League of Nations and the Refugee Problem' (1939) 203 Annals Am Acad Pol & Soc Sci 124, 129.

of self-sufficiency and repatriation were first presented within the broader context of 'capacity.' The policy purported to be based on the incapacity of States of reception to maintain the refugee population. This first arose in 1922, when certain Member States of the LoN expressed mounting concern that Constantinople was unable to support the cost of maintaining its Russian refugee population.[45]

Repatriation as an international policy was not an invention of the LoN. Indeed, most of the methods of relief deployed by the LoN in response to the refugee question had historical precedents in State practice or institutional policies. In 1921, the governments of Latvia and Ukraine had concluded a treaty to the effect that Latvian refugees residing in the territory of Ukraine who had expressed a desire to be repatriated would be returned to Latvia.[46] Though not directly affected by the economic question presented to Constantinople in hosting a refugee population, numerous Member States were concerned with the general question of SR, and requested that the LoN intervene to find a solution.[47] Nansen was invited to organise the repatriation of refugees or in the alternative, to arrange their 'allocation to the various countries which might be able to receive them and to find means of work for them.'[48] Nansen himself had proposed the relocation of Russian refugees from Constantinople to neighbouring Slavic States where the cost of living was lower and where refugees would be able to obtain productive employment,[49] but he now faced pressure to guarantee either total financial self-sufficiency or commit to repatriation.

The LoN initially considered repatriation to be out of the question, as it was unable to enter into any discussions with the Soviet authorities on the subject,[50] but several months later the subject of repatriation was broached again

45 League of Nations, 'Fifth Meeting (Public) Eighteenth Session of the Council' (1922) 3 LNOJ 530.

46 League of Nations, *Agreement Between the Latvian Democratic Republic and the Ukrainian Socialist Soviet Republic Regarding the Repatriation of Latvian Refugees who are at present in the Territory of the Latter* (Moscow, 3 August 1921) LNTS Vol. XVII, No. 441.

47 League of Nations, 'Fifth Meeting (Public) Eighteenth Session of the Council' (1922) 3 LNOJ 530.

48 Peter Gatrell, *The Making of the Modern Refugee* (OUP 2013) 56.

49 League of Nations, 'Second Meeting (Private) Seventeenth Session of the Council' (1922) 3(5) LNOJ 375, 376, 379; League of Nations, 'Report of the High Commissioner for Russian Refugees (Annex 321b)' (17 March 1922) 3(5) LNOJ.

50 League of Nations, 'The Question of the Russian Refugees' (1921) 2(2) LNOJ 225, 226; See also: Peter Gatrell, The Making of the Modern Refugee (OUP 2013) 56.

at the Conference on the Question of the Russian Refugee,[51] and this time, it received greater support. The Conference considered that although it was not desirous to *compel* refugees to return to Russia, it would nonetheless be expedient for the High Commissioner to obtain particulars concerning the number of refugees desirous of repatriation. The High Commissioner was instructed to investigate "the practical possibilities of carrying out repatriations and the guarantees which must be obtained for this purpose."[52] Though the practical aspects of repatriation were discussed extensively, the question of guarantees from States of origin for the safety and security of refugees received very little attention.

In December 1923, the LoN adopted a report it had commissioned on the subject of education and employment of Russian refugees. The report concluded that the ultimate solution to the refugee question was "general repatriation."[53] It stated that "in view of the strong desire of an increasing number of the Russian refugees to return to their homes, the Members of the LoN could further be invited to assist the High Commissioner to assure the return of these refugees to Russia under satisfactory conditions."[54] Several months later, the High Commissioner invited Member States and other interested governments to afford him "every possible facility to give effect to the wishes of the refugees in this direction"[55] and to "indicate the attitude of the refugees towards the question of repatriation."[56] The replies received from Member States revealed that it was in fact the existence of employment opportunities that dictated the willingness of the refugee population to be repatriated. Nansen himself noted that "there seems no desire on the part of the Russian refugees in France to return to Russia. This is probably due to the fact that all the refugees in France desirous and capable of working can find employment."[57] Indeed, when it came to employment, French refugee policy was so permissive that it even allowed Russian refugees to join the armed forces.[58] In con-

51 League of Nations, 'Conference on the Question of the Russian Refugees' (1921) 2(8) LNOJ 899.

52 *Id.*, 901.

53 M. Hanotaux, 'The General and Professional Education and the Employment of Russian Refugees' (1924) 5 LNOJ 373, 382.

54 *Id.*

55 *Id.* See also: League of Nations, 'Russian Refugees: Report by the High Commissioner Submitted to the Council on March 15th, 1924' (1924) 5 LNOJ 551, 731.

56 League of Nations, 'Russian Refugees: Report by Dr. Fridtjof Nansen, High Commissioner for Refugees, presented to the Council on June 12th, 1924' (1924) 5 LNOJ 958, 959.

57 *Id.*, 960.

58 *Id.*, 959.

trast, the High Commissioner noted that in States such as Germany, China, and Poland, where employment prospects were seriously limited, substantial numbers of Russian refugees had expressed the desire to be repatriated.[59] He concluded that with few exceptions, the willingness of Russian refugees to be repatriated depended reliably on the existence of employment prospects in the State of reception.[60]

At this juncture, the apparent international consensus that employment should be the first priority of refugee policy shifted quite dramatically. The importance of employment as a method of relief and the role of the State of reception in providing the legal conditions necessary to facilitate that employment was eclipsed by methods of repatriation and later, colonisation; paradoxically due to its success. This sharp recalibration in international refugee policy was evident from the beginning of the LoN's involvement in the Greek and Armenian refugee crises, which followed closely on the heels of the Russian refugee crisis.

4.2 *From Repatriation to 'Agricultural Colonisation'*

In September 1923, the Council of the LoN approved the Greek government's plan to establish a Refugee Settlement Commission, for the settlement of Ottoman Greek refugees. As part of a Protocol concluded between the LoN and Greece, Greece would assign more than 800,000 hectares of arable land and 65,000 houses abandoned by the evacuated Muslim Turks to the Refugee Settlement Commission.[61] The land and the properties would form a designated settlement for the refugees in Greece, who would be required to reside within the designated zones, or otherwise be engaged in "productive work."[62] This policy was referred to as "agricultural colonisation."[63]

59 *Id.*, 960.

60 *Id.*

61 League of Nations, *Additional Act to the Protocol of September 29, 1923, Relating to the Settlement of Greek Refugees* (19 September 1924) LNTS Vol. XXX, No. 776; Walter Adams, 'Extent and Nature of the World Refugee Problem' (1939) 203 Annals Am Acad Pol & Soc Sci 26, 27.

62 League of Nations, *Protocol Relating to the Settlement of Refugees in Greece and the Creation for this Purpose of a Refugee Settlement Commission* (29 September 1923) LNTS Vol. 20, No. 503; John Hope Simpson, 'The Work of the Greek Refugee Settlement Commission' (1929) 8(6) Journal of the Royal Institute of International Affairs 583, 585.

63 *Id.* It is interesting to note that the Commission hired a great number of Russian refugees to carry out the survey of land and distribution of property to the Ottoman Greek refugees. See: John Hope Simpson, 'The Work of the Greek Refugee Settlement Commission' (1929) 8(6) Journal of the Royal Institute of International Affairs 583, 593.

As a method of relief, agricultural colonisation became an enduring one, employed in several refugee crises as a means to relieve a State of reception of an 'undesirable population,' to provide the refugee with employment, and to afford a burgeoning State with a means to build domestic capital through the exploitation of its agricultural sector. Though the term 'colonisation' was quickly replaced with 'relocation,' in substance the terms described precisely the same method of relief, and in practice, the method was far more aptly described by the former. Just as with repatriation, and later, population transfer (discussed in the following sub-section), colonisation was not an invention of the LoN. The practice had successfully been applied in Paraguay several years earlier, when the ILO and the Paraguayan government had enabled the relocation of Russian refugees and provided them with arable land to increase the State's population and stimulate the agricultural sector. Similarly, thousands of Russian refugees from Germany had previously resettled in Brazil and were also offered land, as a scheme devised by the Brazilian government and the ILO.[64]

As a policy, agricultural colonisation provided a total solution to the question of SR by entailing the eventual assumption of all obligations by the State of reception and the refugee population itself, while the LoN maintained control over the process through the temporary retention of administrative obligations. In exchange, the State of reception received a productive work force and a boost to the national economy. Initially, the State of reception would assume financial obligations for all elements of the transfer of the colonising population, either through the provision of national funds, or by raising international loans. The guarantor of the loan was either the State of reception, or the transferred refugee population itself, who guaranteed the loans against the agricultural yield of the colonised territory and repaid it through the sales of produce. Though financial obligations fell to the State of reception, a LoN-appointed authority would assume administrative obligations and land would be transferred to it to hold as its absolute property. Eventually, when the loans were repaid, the administration of the territory would cease, the appointed authority would be dissolved, and legal obligations for the population would be assumed by the State of reception. The rights, freedoms, and legal status of the individual were relevant only insofar as they enabled his labour to contribute to the repayment of loans raised for his transfer and resettlement.

64 League of Nations, 'Russian Refugees: Report by Dr. Fridtjof Nansen, High Commissioner for Refugees, presented to the Council on June 12th, 1924' (1924) 5 LNOJ 958, 962.

The agricultural colonisation of Greece served as the ideal model for the limitation of SR, as over time, Greece assumed all obligations for the transferred population. Initially, financial obligations for the agricultural colonisation of Greece fell to Greece itself. The Greek government was required not only to raise the £9 million loan required for the operation of the Commission,[65] but also to assign the designated Greek land to the Commission to be held as its absolute property.[66] Several years later, the Greek government and the Commission concluded a convention for the dissolution of the Commission and the assumption by the Greek government of all property, funds, rights and claims previously held by the Commission, so that it would then "stand [...] in the place of the Refugee Settlement Commission"[67] and "assume and undertake to discharge, all the obligations, of every kind whatsoever, binding the Commission."[68]

During the same period, the policy of agricultural colonisation was used as a method to assign all international obligations for Armenian refugees to the newly established Armenian State. Under the 1920 Treaty of Sèvres, the Armenian people had been given a large area of land to consider their homeland, in part due to the unsuccessful efforts to find some States willing to accept a mandate for their protection.[69] For three consecutive years, the LoN Assembly had passed resolutions urging the Council to provide a national home for the Armenians,[70] and the LoN itself had been asked to allocate a homeland, but it declined, insisting that the obligation to protect Armenians must be undertaken by States with the means to do so, though no such State could be found.[71] At the Lausanne Peace Conference of 1922–1923, a proposal to provide a homeland for the Armenian people was met with strong opposition. A more meagre proposal was put forward to provide the Armenian people with an

65 League of Nations, *Additional Act to the Protocol of September 29, 1923, Relating to the Settlement of Greek Refugees* (19 September 1924) LNTS Vol. XXX, No. 776; League of Nations, 'Sixth Meeting (Public, Then Private) Forty-Fifth Session of the Council' (1927) 8 LNOJ 791, 796.

66 John Hope Simpson, 'The Work of the Greek Refugee Settlement Commission' (1929) 8(6) Journal of the Royal Institute of International Affairs 583, 586.

67 League of Nations, 'Convention Concluded at Geneva Between the Hellenic Government and the Refugee Settlement Commission on January 24th, 1930' (1930) 11 LNOJ 555, 730.

68 *Id.*; Walter Adams, 'Extent and Nature of the World Refugee Problem' (1939) 203 Annals Am Acad Pol & Soc Sci 26, 27.

69 League of Nations, 'Fourth Meeting (Public) Forty-Fifth Session of the Council' (1927) 8 LNOJ 773, 774.

70 *Id.*

71 *Id.*, 774.

area of land, but this too was opposed, and no further attempts to resolve the question were made at the Conference.[72]

Initially, when the Armenians were driven out of Turkey, the High Commissioner had asked the Greek government whether the State would open its frontiers to the refugee population. Greece had agreed, but since that time, the Greco-Turkish population exchange (discussed in the following subsection) had required Greece to settle its 'own' refugees, which made it "materially impossible for the country to absorb the Armenians also."[73] The State was not able to raise additional loans for the settlement of Armenians when it could barely afford to settle the Ottoman Greek refugees.[74] As an alternative, the Greek government proposed the relocation of the Armenian refugees to the Russian Caucasus.[75] It provided in support of the proposal, a letter from the Secretary of the Armenian Refugees Fund, stating his awareness that a considerable number of Armenian refugees were willing to go to the Russian Caucasus to become colonists in Armenia. Anxious for the Armenian refugees already in Greece to be transported to Armenia, the Greek government agreed to absorb, in part, financial obligations for the transfer of the population.[76]

In March 1924, the National Armenian Delegation requested LoN Members to issue a public appeal for funds for the establishment of a colony of 50,000 Armenians in Armenia. Two years prior, the Armenian Refugee's Fund had established 7,000 Armenians from Mesopotamia as colonists in Armenia, whom had reportedly become 'self-sufficient' within a period of 12 months.[77] It was the opinion of the Armenian National Delegation that "conditions in the Russian Caucasus [were] sufficiently satisfactory to justify the settlement of their refugees in this area."[78] The government of the USSR was favourably disposed towards the project, as it was believed that the colonisation of Arme-

---

72 *Id.*

73 League of Nations, 'Armenian Refugees in Greece: Memorandum' (1924) 5 LNOJ 933, 971–972.

74 League of Nations, 'Fourth Meeting (Public) Forty-Fifth Session of the Council' (1927) 8 LNOJ 773, 775.

75 League of Nations, 'Armenian Refugees in Greece: Memorandum' (1924) 5 LNOJ 933, 971–972.

76 League of Nations, 'Reply from the Greek Prime Minister to the Settlement Commission' (1924) 5 LNOJ.

77 League of Nations, 'Extract from the Letter from the Secretary of the Armenian Refugees (Lord Mayor's Fund to Mr. Morgenthau)' (1924) 5 LNOJ 973.

78 *Id.* The UK responded that it would issue an appeal for funds with the notable condition that "it was understood and made clear that His Majesty's Government could accept no responsibility whatever for the success of the scheme or for the disposal of any funds which might be subscribed [...]."

nia would "mean the production of cotton [would] be increased."[79] It authorised irrigation works in Armenia in preparation for its colonisation and agreed to issue a loan for this purpose.[80]

In June 1927, the LoN Assembly requested the Council to set up a committee, chaired by the LoN but comprised of private organisations, to investigate funding options.[81]

The LoN considered that the issue of a public loan could not be contemplated due to "legal and other conditions prevailing in the territory" and so concluded (once again) that it could not accept any financial obligation for a loan under the same form as had been adopted in other cases (Austria, Hungary, Greece, and Bulgaria). It recommended that the Council "should not accept *any legal or moral responsibility* with regard to the actual securities of a loan."[82] Instead, the LoN adopted a resolution stating that it was prepared to *supervise* the expenditure of a loan, provided that funds were forthcoming from private organisations or individuals.[83] In this sense, the LoN would maintain a remote supervisory role while ensuring that the institution was removed entirely from the assumption of any binding international obligation. In particular, financial obligations were considered prejudicial to future questions of 'moral responsibility' – a euphemism for SR – which the organisation hoped very much to avoid.

The Committee of Experts that visited Armenia concluded that if a loan of one million pounds could be raised, an area of land could be cultivated to absorb 30,000 Armenian refugees, but this conclusion was not supported by all parties. A report from the Armenian Refugee Settlement Commission stressed the importance of investment to develop the land *prior* to resettlement, as: "without aid for the development of her great latent natural resources, it is impossible for Armenia to receive any considerable number of refugees and to settle them in a satisfactory manner."[84] The proposal was rejected, and Armenian refugees were once again without a resettlement solution.[85] Frustrated with the inaction of the LoN, Nansen proposed to the Armenian government that it might take over the irrigation work and raise the funds

---

79 *Id.*

80 League of Nations, 'Work of the Armenian Refugee Settlement Commission' (1926) 7(7) LNOJ 896, 982.

81 League of Nations, 'Fourth Meeting (Public) Forty-Fifth Session of the Council' (1927) 8 LNOJ 773, 773.

82 *Id.* Emphasis added.

83 *Id.*

84 *Id.*, 975.

85 *Id.*, 773.

itself. He promised the Armenian government that if it were able to raise the funds, he would do his utmost to raise the money at least for the transport of Armenian refugees and to settle them on the irrigated land.[86] But even to fund the transport, appeals to States were unsuccessful.[87]

The fragmented resolution of the Armenian refugee crisis reveals the depth of States' concerns regarding the future implications of financial obligations to the broader question of SR. The general uncertainty regarding the burgeoning field of IRL led to extreme conservatism in the resolution of the crisis, even as a pathway to the assumption of all international obligations was established for Armenia.

4.3 *Population Exchanges and the Cessation of International Obligations*

Though the LoN exhibited great resistance to the assumption of international obligations for refugee matters, it took a leading and active role in the resolution of refugee crises where the refugee population was also deemed a minority. While the protection of refugees did not form part of the LoN's mandate (as it repeatedly asserted) the protection of minorities did. At the close of WWI, the protection of minorities became a question for IL, as the so-called 'Minorities Treaties' were imposed on ten Central and Eastern European States at the Paris Conference, despite bitter resistance,[88] and were placed under the guarantee of the LoN.[89]

Under the guise of repatriation, the LoN facilitated several population exchanges in the 1920s, between so-called racial minorities, which were in fact religious minorities whose minority status had made them the target of ethno-nationalist governments pursuing irredentist policies.[90] Although at the time, national affiliation often relied on the common religious affiliation of the majority,[91] the classification of religious minorities as belonging to a certain State

---

86 League of Nations, 'Fourth Meeting (Public) Forty-Fifth Session of the Council' (1927) 8 LNOJ 773, 775.

87 League of Nations, 'Refugee Questions' (1928) 9(6) LNOJ 838; League of Nations, 'Refugee Questions' (1928) 9(9) LNOJ 1408.

88 Joseph S. Roucek, *The Working of the Minorities System Under the League of Nations* (Orbis Publishing Co. 1929) 25–42.

89 See generally: Carole Fink, 'The League of Nations and the Minorities Question' (1995) 157(4) World Affairs 9.

90 Shacknove refers to the population exchange as "international access to internally displaced persons." See: Andrew Shacknove, 'Who Is a Refugee?' (1985) 95 Ethics 274, 283.

91 See in general: Joseph S. Roucek, 'Minorities - A Basis of the Refugee Problem' (1939) 203 Annals Am Acad Pol & Soc Sci 1, 7.

lent itself to the notion that population exchanges in fact constituted a 'restoration' of peoples, though in reality those subject to population exchanges had never resided in the States of reception, but had instead resided in the transferring State for centuries. As such, population exchanges were considered to be a form of repatriation, 'returning' minorities to their true State of origin, rather than validating their forcible removal from it.

As with repatriation, population exchanges were not an invention of the LoN, but drew from prior bilateral agreements. In November 1919, Greece and Bulgaria had signed the Greco-Bulgarian 'Reciprocal Emigration' Convention, providing for the reciprocal voluntary emigration of the racial, religious, and linguistic minorities in Greece and Bulgaria.[92] The population exchange would strip both emigrant groups of the State of origin's nationality from the moment of their departure, and would confer on them the nationality of the receiving state from the moment of their arrival.[93]

On 30 January 1923, the governments of Greece and Turkey concluded the *Convention Concerning the Exchange of Greek and Turkish Populations*, as part of the peace treaties signed at Lausanne at the end of WWI and the Greco-Turkish war.[94] The Convention provided *inter alia* for the "compulsory exchange of Turkish nationals of the Greek Orthodox religion established in Turkish territory, and of Greek nationals of the Moslem religion established in Greek territory."[95] The population exchange would include the compulsory denationalisation of each population and the compulsory acquisition of the state of reception's nationality.[96] The 1923 *Treaty of Lausanne*, signed several months after the Convention, formalised the population exchange, and placed the fulfilment of Turkey's obligations under the supervision of the LoN.[97] The High Commissioner would be responsible for the health conditions of refugees during the exchange,[98] and a Mixed Commission would be appointed to supervise and facilitate the emigration.[99] The following year,

92 Greece, Bulgaria, *Convention Between Greece and Bulgaria Respecting Reciprocal Emigration* (Neuilly-sur-Seine, 27 November 1919).

93 'Supplement: Official Documents' (1920) 14(4) AJIL 356.

94 Greece, Turkey, *Lausanne Peace Treaty VI: Convention Concerning the Exchange of Greek and Turkish Populations* (Lausanne, 30 January 1923).

95 *Id.*, Article 1.

96 *Id.*, Article 7.

97 The British Empire and others, *Treaty of Lausanne* (Lausanne, 24 July 1923) Article 44.

98 Raoul Blanchard, 'The Exchange of Populations between Greece and Turkey' (1925) 15(3) GeogrRev 449, 451.

99 Greece, Turkey, *Lausanne Peace Treaty VI: Convention Concerning the Exchange of Greek and Turkish Populations* (Lausanne, 30 January 1923) Article 12.

the Mixed Commission for the Exchange of Greek and Turkish Populations was established with a mandate to administer the exchange of the Greek Orthodox minority in Constantinople and the Turkish Muslim minority in Western Thrace.

Though the classification of the Greco-Turkish population exchange as a 'refugee crisis' raises questions by contemporary definitional standards – particularly when one considers the manufactured elements of the crisis – at the time, these minority groups were in every sense, refugees. At the time, there was very little difference between the approach to law and policy engaging questions of SR for the protection of refugees on the one hand, and minorities on the other. No clear delineation of policies existed that distinguished one group from the other, and the term 'refugee' still lacked an international legal definition. Most importantly, the Greco-Turkish population exchange was *not* a voluntary programme in any respect. Both populations were forcibly displaced from their States or origin and stripped of their nationality and property. Though the exchange of populations undoubtedly saved many lives,[100] the use of this "humanitarian-bureaucratic tool"[101] also served to "[relieve] countries like Turkey of their responsibility to their own citizens-made-refugees."[102] The tension between protection of minorities and validation of ethno-nationalist policies was noted at the time by some scholars who considered that the formalisation of the exchange would:

> [P]ut an effective end to propaganda and irredenta, but it breaks up the homes of thousands of inhabitants. Under the guarantee of an enlightened League of Nations, it may be questioned whether such radical leg-

100 The League of Nations first turned its attention to the question of the Greek refugee after the genocide of the Christian Ottoman Greek population in Turkey had already been carried out in furtherance of the ultra-nationalist 'Turkification' of the Ottoman Empire. The exchange also served the ethno-nationalist agenda of both States. The Greek leader Eleftherios Venizelos regarded the transfer as an opportunity to 'Hellenise' the territory that Greece had recently acquired from Bulgaria. See: Sarah Shields, 'The Greek-Turkish Population Exchange: Internationally Administered Ethnic Cleansing' (2013) 267 Middle East Report 2, citing Stephen P. Ladas, Bureau of International Research of Harvard University and Radcliffe College, *The Exchange of Minorities: Bulgaria, Greece and Turkey* (Macmillan Co 1932) 279.

101 Keith David Watenpaugh, 'Between Communal Survival and National Aspiration: Armenian Genocide Refugees, the League of Nations, and the Practices of Interwar Humanitarianism' (2014) 5(2) Humanity: An International Journal of Human Rights, Humanitarianism, and Development 159, 172.

102 *Id.*

islation does not establish a precedent which would be regrettable were other nations to adopt it as a model for dealing with minorities.[103]

Other contemporary scholars agree that the population exchange under the 1923 *Treaty of Lausanne* "legitimised mass displacement as a prophylactic device to promote ethnic homogeneity" and that in taking an active role, the refugee status of the populations was in fact "the product of deliberate international action."[104]

Though it may be true that the LoN facilitated, and indeed legitimised, the denationalisation and displacement of populations, the alternative was quite unthinkable. The eagerness with which the LoN facilitated population exchanges is not only attributable to this preoccupation with the protection of minorities, but also to the knowledge of the imminent danger that those Greek and Armenian populations would have faced had they remained in Turkey.[105]

Though the charge that the LoN legitimised mass displacement through its active role in population transfers might be tempered somewhat by the realities of Turkish irredentist policy, there is another element to this early international refugee response that is infrequently considered but nonetheless critical to the conception of SR in IRL. That is that population exchanges implicitly recognised that the denationalisation of an undesirable population by a State constituted a cessation of the relationship between an expelling State and its former subject. This presumption of severance formed the basis of population exchange as a method of relief, as well as the rationale for the inclusion of the affected population among those designated as refugees. In that sense, perhaps more critically than the actual physical exchange of populations, the LoN facilitated ethnic cleansing.[106]

In practice, the general resistance of the LoN and Member States to the assumption of international obligations was indistinguishable from the resis-

103 Frances Kellor, Antonia Hatvany, *Security Against War* (The MacMillan Co. 1924) 409.

104 Peter Gatrell, *The Making of the Modern Refugee* (OUP 2013) 54; See also, Sarah Shields, 'The Greek-Turkish Population Exchange: Internationally Administered Ethnic Cleansing' (2013) 267 Middle East Report 2.

105 British Foreign Secretary Lord Curzon delicately referred to the Greek-Turkish population exchange as bringing an end to 'old deep-rooted causes of quarrels.' See: Peter Gatrell, *The Making of the Modern Refugee* (OUP 2013) 63–64, citing Matthew Frank, *Expelling the Germans: British Opinion and Post-1945 Population Transfer in Context* (OUP 2008) 22–23; Claudena Skran, *Refugees in Inter-War Europe* (OUP 1995) 158–159.

106 Shields refers to the Greco-Turkish population exchange as "internationally administered ethnic cleansing." See: Sarah Shields, 'The Greek-Turkish Population Exchange: Internationally Administered Ethnic Cleansing' (2013) 267 Middle East Report 2.

tance shown in respect of other groups of refugees. Though the economic conditions in Greece were such that the employment of the refugee population was an impossibility, the LoN took no action in promoting the resettlement of refugees to third States, and despite its supervisory role in the protection of minorities, it would again refuse to assume financial obligations for the administration of its own policies. Initially, there was a concerted international effort to assign financial and legal obligations for all aspects of the crisis to Greece, but as with the early discussions on Russian State of origin responsibility, the concept was soon abandoned. The costs of the population transfer were in the end borne by charitable organisations, by States including Poland, Norway, Belgium, and France, and eventually by refugees themselves.[107]

5 A Legal Status for Refugees

Paradoxically, much of the uncertainty concerning the scope and content of IRL prevailed specifically because States took a deeply conservative approach in responding to refugee crises, and particularly in relation to the definition of refugee status. Initially, the central concern within the broader question of refugee status was that of enduring nationality and the definitive cessation of State of origin obligations. Holzer asserts that:

> There was little need for these arrangements to define refugees because the Russian and Armenian refugees had already been granted *en masse* the protection of the League of Nations.[108]

In fact, the definition of the term refugee was avoided for wholly different reasons. The question of a uniform, international legal status for refugees had been broached on several occasions during early refugee crises, but it was not regarded as an urgent matter until the exodus of Austrian and German Jews was well underway and the LoN began to accept that as a class of person, the refugee was now a permanent fixture in IL. Instead, the LoN considered that the legal status of refugees was "primarily a matter for the Govern-

107 John Hope Simpson, 'The Work of the Greek Refugee Settlement Commission' (1929) 8(6) Journal of the Royal Institute of International Affairs 583, 584.

108 Vanessa Holzer, *Refugees from Armed Conflict: The 1951 Refugee Convention and International Humanitarian Law* (CUP 2015) 29.

ments of the countries in which many of the refugees are living."[109] When the LoN finally turned its attention to the question of an international legal status, it was not primarily motivated by a desire to resolve the international legal status of refugees, but to create some consistency in State practice. Initially, Member States wanted to limit the classes of person that could benefit from the existing system put in place by the Arrangements, but after the LoN became aware of widespread expulsion and denial of re-entry to persons already benefiting from the Arrangements, it became clear that consistent practice could not be achieved if the conferral (and denial) of status were to remain wholly a sovereign matter.

Without a clear international definition of the term 'refugee' and the circumstances in which the status could be conferred, States were able to exercise greater control over the fragmentary approach of the LoN to the designation of various groups as beneficiaries of the Arrangements. States had resisted the creation of a uniform, international definition of 'refugee,' preferring the system of the Arrangements, which permitted to exercise a greater degree of control over the expansion of refugee status, as each revision of the Arrangements was deliberated within the LoN structure.[110] As Sjöberg noted in relation to the Arrangements, "[T]his cooperation did not necessarily result from any more profound humanitarian considerations."[111] Ad hoc arrangements also enabled States to exercise greater control over the scope and content of their obligations to various groups, as the extension of Arrangements considered each group separately; a system that a uniform status would not allow. The fragmentary approach of the LoN to the designation of certain groups as beneficiaries of the Arrangements is further evidence of Member States' unwillingness to define the condition of 'refugee' before the precise nature of the status could be fully accounted for in international law, specifically as that status affected the scope and content of SR.

---

109 League of Nations, 'The Question of the Russian Refugees' (1921) 2(2) LNOJ 225, 226. See also: League of Nations, 'Conference on the Question of the Russian Refugees' (1921) 2(8) LNOJ 899–900.

110 Andrew Shacknove, 'Who Is a Refugee?' (1985) 95 Ethics 274, 275, has noted that even post-1951 Convention "There are in fact dozens of definitions in effect within various jurisdictions." Grahl-Madsen similarly wrote that "The concept of "refugee" has no single, simple meaning. To be sure, it has a core on which most of us should be able to agree, but the fringes may be differently defined for different." See: Atle Grahl-Madsen, 'International Refugee Law Today and Tomorrow' (1982) 20(4) Archiv des Völkerrechts 411, 418; Atle Grahl-Madsen, *The Status of Refugees in International Law, Volume I* (Sijthoff 1966) 73.

111 Tommie Sjöberg, *The Powers and the Persecuted: The Refugee Problem and the Intergovernmental Committee on Refugees (IGCR), 1938–1947* (Lund University Press 1991) 27.

On 10 December 1926, the Council of the LoN adopted a resolution limiting the definition of 'refugee' to those persons whose condition was analogous to that of the Armenian and Russian refugees as a consequence of the war and events directly connected with it.[112] The following year, the High Commissioner recommended the extension of measures to assist Russians and Armenians to other classes of refugees. He included in the report a list of individual cases appealed to him in support of an extension of measures, and requested the LoN Council to instruct him to examine the appeals, and to submit proposals for the extension of the identity certificate system.[113] The LoN obliged, but was very careful to limit the scope of inquiry to appeals made by Assyrians, Assyro-Chaldeans, Montenegrins, and Turks only. It also emphasised that in assessing appeals, "[N]o attempt should be made to frame a definition."[114] Clearly concerned with the apparent scale and frequency of such crises, it was noted:

> [T]he mere fact that certain classes of persons are without the protection of any national Government *is not sufficient to make them refugees*; for on that theory all classes of person without nationality and persons of doubtful nationality would have to be included.[115]

The following year, after reviewing the limited appeals, the High Commissioner submitted a report on the extension of the measures taken to assist Russians and Armenians to other categories of refugees. Though only a few Member States offered observations, the results were somewhat predictable. Those States hosting large refugee populations were opposed to the extension of the identity certificate system to refugee populations within their territory.[116] The year after that, having agreed that it was necessary to define the

---

112 League of Nations, 'Fifth Meeting (Public, Then Private)' (1927) 8(7) LNOJ 152, 155.

113 League of Nations, 'Sixth Meeting (Public, Then Private) Forty-Fifth Session of the Council' (1927) 8 LNOJ 791, 1137.

114 *Id.*, 1137–1138.

115 *Id.* Emphasis added.

116 Austria did not want the identity certificate system extended to the Ruthenian and Hungarian refuges in Austria. Italy saw no objection to the extension of measures to certain other groups on the condition that their status resulted from the war and of events directly connected with it. See: League of Nations, *Arrangement concerning the Extension to other Categories of Refugees of certain Measures taken in favour of Russian and Armenian Refugees* (30 June 1928) LNTS Vol. LXXXIX, No. 63, 1000; League of Nations, 'Refugee Questions' (1928) 9(9) LNOJ 1408; League of Nations, 'Refugee Questions' (1928) 9(5) LNOJ 2008.

class of person more clearly, a limited number of Member States that had taken part in the Conference concerning Russian and Armenian refugees[117] adopted two resolutions concerning the question of a legal status, specifically in relation to Russian and Armenian refugees.[118] The first recommended that it should be the High Commissioner and his appointees that assume the obligation to, *inter alia*, certify the identity and the position of refugees, insofar as such services did not lie within the exclusive competence of the national authorities.[119] States would retain the authority to decide whether such documents would be recognised as having an official character.[120] The second provided that certain measures taken in favour of Russian and Armenian refugees should be extended to Turkish, Assyrian, Assyro-Chaldean, and 'assimilated refugees.'[121] Several months later, the Secretary-General invited other States that had adopted the Arrangements in favour of Russian and Armenian refugees to extend the benefit of those Arrangements to Assyrian, Assyro-Chaldean and Turkish refugees, but even with such a limited scope, only two States approved the proposal.[122]

Designation of refugees by nationality (or former nationality) continued to be the approach of the LoN into the 1930s, when Arrangements were made for German refugees from the Saarland after the 1935 plebiscite. In the 1936 *Provisional Arrangement concerning the Status of Refugees coming from Germany*,[123] the term 'refugee coming from Germany' applied to:

> [A]ny person who was settled in that county, who does not possess any nationality other than German nationality, and in respect of whom it is

117 Louise W. Holborn, 'The League of Nations and the Refugee Problem' (1939) 203 Annals Am Acad Pol & Soc Sci 124, 687.

118 League of Nations, *Arrangement relating to the Legal Status of Russian and Armenian Refugees* (30 June 1928) LNTS Vol. LXXXIX, No. 2005; League of Nations, *Arrangement concerning the Extension to other Categories of Refugees of certain Measures taken in favour of Russian and Armenian Refugees* (30 June 1928) LNTS Vol. LXXXIX, No. 63.

119 League of Nations, *Arrangement relating to the Legal Status of Russian and Armenian Refugees* (30 June 1928) LNTS Vol. LXXXIX, No. 2005.

120 *Id.*, 57.

121 League of Nations, *Arrangement concerning the Extension to other Categories of Refugees of certain Measures taken in favour of Russian and Armenian Refugees* (30 June 1928) LNTS Vol. LXXXIX, No. 63.

122 League of Nations, 'Refugee Questions' (1929) 10(2) LNOJ 323.

123 League of Nations, *Provisional Arrangement concerning the Status of Refugees Coming from Germany* (4 July 1936) LNTS Vol. CLXXI, No. 3952.

established that in law or in fact he or she does not enjoy the protection of the Government of the Reich.[124]

A principal difference between the treatment of the Russian and Greek refugee crises, and the Armenian refugee crisis, was that although the latter group was also rendered stateless through a policy of denationalisation, the LoN was now unwilling to accept Turkish irredentism – which aspired to achieve ethnic and religious homogeny – as having any legitimacy under IL. It rejected the presumption of severance and instead adopted a presumption of enduring nationality, where denationalisation was not accepted as a *fait accompli*, but was instead considered a basis for the inclusion of the affected population among those designated as refugees. Accordingly, the resolution of the Armenian refugee crisis began with the presumption that the Armenian population had *not* been denationalised. By extension, it was presumed that the relationship between the State (Turkey) and the subject (the Armenian) had *not* ruptured. The position of the LoN therefore, was that refugee status may be conferred *without prejudice* to the enduring bond between the State and its subjects. In planning for the adoption of a certificate for Armenian refugees, identical to that accorded to Russian refugees under the Arrangement of July 1922,[125] the High Commissioner noted that in contrast to the Russian Arrangement, the object of the Armenian Arrangement was solely to secure the provision of an *emergency status* and did not in any way "prejudice any question as to national status."[126] In his book *Armenia and the Near East*,[127] Nansen expressed reproach for the Western powers of Europe and the United States that had long and unsuccessfully promised the creation of a 'national home' for the Armenians.

Despite its more assertive public position, the LoN's presumption of enduring nationality had no effect on Turkish irredentism in respect of the Armenian population, nor did it have any effect in the end on the division and delegation of obligations in respect of colonising populations. As time went on, the presumption in favour of enduring State of origin obligations proved to

124 *Id.*, Article 1.

125 League of Nations, 'Russian Refugees: Report by Dr. Fridtjof Nansen, High Commissioner for Refugees, presented to the Council on June 12th, 1924' (1924) 5 LNOJ 958, 968.

126 League of Nations, 'Plan for the Issue of a Certificate of Identity to Armenian Refugees, 31st May 1924. Submitted for the consideration of interested governments by Dr. Nansen, High Commissioner for Russian Refugees in execution of the Resolution of the Council of the League' (1924) 5(7) LNOJ 969.

127 Fridtjof Nansen, *Armenia and the Near East* (George Allen & Unwin Ltd 1928).

be another political tool in the LoN's arsenal, to which it apparently had no ideological attachment. The presumption was not based on the legal protection of refugees, but once again, supported the establishment of financial obligations, and critically, the legal basis for the right to compensation. SR would later be utilised as a means to exact heavy financial penalties from the State of origin for the costs of transferring and housing refugees, under the guise of 'compensation.' Funds were not used for the benefit of refugees themselves, but rather were provided to States of reception as subsidies for the economic burden they had assumed in settling the refugee population. In that sense, the presumption in favour of enduring nationality became a means to establish compensation and thus enforce SR.

Much like those measures taken in respect of Armenian and Greek refugees, the measures taken in respect of Assyrians undoubtedly saved a great many lives, but the historical documentation of this event does not support the narrative of an organisation gripped by humanitarian imperative. Rather, it is a history of a balance sheet that was weighed, precisely considered, and reconciled before any action was taken in respect of acute human suffering.

6 Of Compensation and Capacity: State Responsibility and the State of Origin

During the earliest discussions on the Russian refugee crisis, two important questions were put forward, relative to SR and the enduring obligations of the State of origin: that of compensation, and that of capacity. Both concepts would be reintroduced several times during the development of early international refugee responses under the guise of State of origin 'duties' – both to its former subjects and to States of resettlement. In reality, these proposals supported the objectives of the developing theorisation and application of SR in IRL; exacting compensation and reparation for the damage caused by the imposition of an unwanted refugee population. The justifications proffered at the time for the repatriation of refugee populations rested primarily on the notion of 'capacity,' though it was both loosely defined and legally unprecedented in IL. The term was, of course, euphemistic, and proved to be sufficiently elastic to refer to both the financial ability or willingness of a State of reception to absorb refugees, and to the attribution of SR to the State of origin for the violation of its 'duties' that precipitated the refugee movement in the first place. In the case of the State of reception, capacity referred to the States ability to support colonisation or population exchanges. In the case of the State of origin, capacity referred either to repatriation, compensation, or restitution for having created the conditions that hastened the refugee crisis, inferring that an injury had been sustained by the State of reception.

Of equal importance to the question of capacity was that of compensation. In much the same manner as those discussions on capacity, the concept of compensation in the context of large-scale refugee movement was revisited time and time again, though it also lacked legal precedent in IL. Once again, discussions concerning question of compensation referred to the purported 'duty' of the State of origin to compensate the State of reception. However, unlike capacity, the question of compensation was able to find some legal resolution and was thus implemented several times. States of reception exacted compensation from States of origin in a number of instances, aided by the justification of such measures as forming part of the 'duties' of a State of origin. These measures were implemented under the auspices of the LoN.

6.1 *The Capacity of States of Origin*

One of the many iterations of capacity vis-à-vis the State of origin ostensibly concerned the safety of the refugee population in the context of voluntary repatriation. Long notes in relation to repatriation of Russian refugees from Bulgaria, that far from a debate about the voluntariness of repatriation, "[T]he real debate was over questions of 'safety,' which related directly to understandings of state capacity to protect returnee citizens, and sovereignty."[128] Yet with each iteration, the conception of capacity incrementally decreased in its utility and relevance to the refugee, instead relating primarily to any enduring obligations of the repatriating State that may arise as a result of its actions. While the preoccupation with the security and safety of repatriated refugees was directly related to the question of State of origin capacity to provide protection to its subjects, as a method of relief, repatriation was not primarily concerned with the safety and security of the refugee population in terms of an individual human right to such guarantees. On the contrary, the safety and security of refugee populations was relative to the enduring obligations of States and any SR that may be attributable should the population in question be subjected to physical harm subsequent to their repatriation. In that sense, 'capacity,' or rather the lack thereof, was utilised as a defence against enduring international obligations in the still uncertain legal terrain of early IRL.

Long also acknowledges this, noting that while repatriation was seen as "a deliberate restoration of citizens' rights, which carried with them the legal

128 Katy Long, 'Early Repatriation Policy: Russian Refuge Return 1922–1924' (2009) 22 JRS 133, 134.

guarantees of safety inherent in the concept of state protection,"[129] it was also an execution of State obligations in respect of refugees:

> [T]he preoccupation with the safety and security of repatriation may be better understood as a proper discharge of duty on the part of the states of reception, rather than evidence of early conception of refugee protection as internal protection. The concern with safe return was very much a reflection of the obligations of states of reception to provide external protection, which included as a fundamental principle, the obligation of *non-refoulement*.[130]

Concerns with the discharge of duty are evident from the first efforts to resolve the 'Russian refugee question.' The repatriation of Russians was complicated by a number of factors of which the LoN was fully aware, and which endangered the safety and security of the repatriated refugees. As Sir John Hope Simpson noted, famine and the threat of State violence made the proposal at best 'speculative' and an exercise in 'political prophesy.'[131] At worst, it was inherently dangerous and in Nansen's own estimation, "impossible."[132] Despite clear evidence of insecurity and threats to safety, Russian refugees were eventually repatriated to zones considered suitable by any given authority, with little consistency or structure in the assessment of such determinations. Typically, the substance of the assessment concerned the conditions of the land, rather than the legal, social, or political conditions that might affect the repatriated population. In order to commence repatriation, very little was required beyond the good condition of the land, and the willingness of refugees to repatriate. In that sense, any implication that the LoN had in mind the safety and security of repatriated Russian refugees where it referred to 'capacity' is not supported by evidence.

Instead, much of the justification for repatriation rested on the loosely defined and legally unprecedented notion of 'capacity.' The term was euphemistic and elastic enough to refer to both the financial ability or willingness of a State of reception to absorb refugees, and for the attribution of SR to the State of origin for the conduct that brought about refugee movement. In the case of the State of reception, this took the form of colonisation or population ex-

129 *Id.*, 138.

130 *Id.*

131 John Hope Simpson, *The Refugee Problem: Report of a Survey* (OUP 1939) 529.

132 League of Nations, '17th Session of the Council, Annex 321' (1922) 3 LNOJ; League of Nations, '18th Session of the Council, Annex 344' (1922) 5 LNOJ.

changes, and in the case of the State of origin, capacity referred either to repatriation, compensation, or restitution for having caused the refugee crisis in the first place. As early as June 1921, it was suggested that the State of origin should assume, at least in part, the financial obligations for having created the conditions that created refugees. At the same time that the LoN appointed a High Commissioner to coordinate the actions taken by governments and private organisations on refugee matters, it also unanimously adopted a resolution instructing the LoN Secretariat to undertake a practical study of the political, legal, and financial problems involved in any definite settlement of the refugee question.[133] The final report, submitted by the French delegate, Hanotaux, concluded that the Russian refugee question was "mainly a financial problem"[134] and that:

> [i]t would be of interest to ascertain whether, among the funds belonging to former Russian Governments and at present deposited in various countries, there are any which could be wholly or partially devoted to the use of the Russian refugees.[135]

The report suggested also that a committee of experts could be appointed to undertake a study of the liquidation of Russian assets for the benefit of the 'Russian refugee question.'[136] Though the proposal came to nothing on this occasion, discussion turned very quickly to the question of capacity. It was suggested by the Czecho-Slovak delegate that the only truly effective method of dealing with the famine in Russia was by "an economic restoration of Russia herself" and hence the repatriation of Russian refugees, ostensibly for the benefit of the Russian State.[137] In this construction, capacity was relevant to refugees only insofar as they were apparently required – by virtue of their nationality – to return to their State of origin and rebuild her infrastructure and resources. The High Commissioner rejected this proposal on the basis that the capacity of the Russian State to exercise its sovereign powers of protection over its nationals was seriously depleted, and that despite the fact that "the effective economic reconstruction" of Russia required "the presence of a sound, honest and sufficient supply of labour," this in turn relied upon "an

133 League of Nations, 'The Question of the Russian Refugees' (1921) 2(6) LNOJ 485.
134 *Id.*, 755, 757.
135 *Id.*, 485.
136 *Id.*
137 League of Nations, 'Relief Work in Russia and the Question of the Russian Refugee' (1922) 3(3) LNOJ 274, 324.

internal capacity for action which it [would] take many years and much labour to develop."[138] Yet Nansen was not opposed to repatriation as a solution. On the contrary. He believed it to be "obvious that in the long run there can be no final and satisfactory solution of the problems created by the presence in Europe of 1.5 million refugees except by repatriation to their native lands."[139] But the safety and security of refugees subject to repatriation needed to be guaranteed, not simply entrusted to a State that was likely incapable to offering such assurances.

Questions of capacity were also raised with reference to the willingness and ability of the repatriating State to shoulder the burden of repatriation alone. The Chinese government revealed that it was in negotiations for the repatriation of several thousand Russian refugees, and called on the LoN to provide funds for the repatriation, the cost of which China was neither willing nor able to absorb alone.[140] This was not the first time that the LoN had been implored to assume financial obligations for the Russian refugee question. Concerned with the preservation of its own institutional responsibility, the LoN had refused to provide the 30,000 pounds required for the evacuation of 15,000 refugees from Constantinople several years earlier.[141] In that case, it was instead left to private organisations and States to absorb the cost of evacuation. The British government contributed a third of the required amount for the repatriation of Russian refugees from Constantinople, but pressure on the LoN to provide the remaining 20,000 did not abate. The American Relief Administration offered to sustain the 15,000 refugees for four months at an estimated cost of 100,000 dollars on the condition that the LoN provide the remaining funds necessary to carry out the evacuation,[142] but it continued to resist. Finally, financial support was provided by Brazil, China, Switzerland, and Belgium.[143]

As the Special Investigator for the American Relief Administration wrote in his report on the Russian Famine, referring to the Comité international de secours à la Russie, organised under the auspices of the LoN:

138 *Id.*, 338–339.

139 Katy Long, 'Early Repatriation Policy: Russian Refuge Return 1922–1924' (2009) 22 JRS 133, 137.

140 League of Nations, 'Third Meeting (Public) Twenty-Seventh Session of the Council' (1924) 5(2) LNOJ 330.

141 League of Nations, 'Fifth Meeting (Public) Eighteenth Session of the Council' (1922) 3 LNOJ 530.

142 *Id.*, 530–531.

143 League of Nations, 'Evacuation of the Russian Refugees from Constantinople' (1922) 3(7) LNOJ 725–726.

> An International Commission has been organized. It has held meetings in Geneva and Brussels, but not one cent of money or one pound of food has been provided by this International Commission. [...] The Swedish Red Cross is sending in a Red Cross unit. Norway has given one million kronen. The Save the Children League of England has put in Mr. Nansen's hands money enough to buy food for 250,000 children for six months: that is about the total of European relief.[144]

At each stage, the question of capacity decreased in relevance to the refugee, and increased in relevance to the State and the international obligations it might inadvertently assume in providing financial support to the resolution of the refugee crisis. The LoN claimed that it lacked the institutional capacity required to provide funds in respect of refugees. States of reception claimed that they had no capacity to absorb refugees, and the High Commissioner implored Member States to accept that States of origin had no capacity to exercise their protective functions in respect of their exiled populations. In that respect, the issue may have been perceived superficially to be of concern to refugee 'protection' in the sense that it is understood in contemporary IRL. Instead, 'capacity,' or rather the lack thereof, was utilised as a defence against the assumption of international obligations in the still uncertain legal terrain of early IRL.

6.2 *The Compensation of States of Reception*

Of equal importance to capacity was the question of compensation and the purported duty of the State of origin to provide it to States of reception. Much like discussions on capacity, the concept of compensation in the context of displacement was revisited time and time again, despite it not having legal precedent, but unlike the issue of capacity, States of reception were able to exact compensation from States of origin in several instances, though their methods for doing so were blatant exercises of power and little legal justification was offered in support of them.

As it was with matters of capacity, compensation was framed as a 'duty,' though the precise origin of that duty was never substantiated. In the mid-1930s, the Committee on International Assistance to Refugees reported that in view of the heavy burden placed on States of reception, it considered it "an international duty" for States of origin "at least to alleviate to some extent, the burdens imposed by the presence of refugees in the territory of

144 Vernon Kellogg, 'The Russian Famine Region' (1922) 100 Annals Am Acad Pol & Soc Sci 105, 107.

other states."[145] Statements and suggestions such as this can be noted sporadically throughout the early international refugee responses, but these discussions were short-lived and found no immediate resolution. The fundamental impediments to resolving questions of State of origin responsibility remained the legality of such measures, and more practically, the implementation of an international enforcement mechanism. Despite those clear obstructions, it is interesting to note the repeated and circular discussions regarding the establishment of a law or policy that would permit such a compensation scheme to be implemented. The implications of these conversations to the question of SR are clear: the eagerness to find a financial solution through exacting compensation from the State of origin released other States not only from the financial burden associated with the maintenance of refugees, but also dissipated any question of SR stemming from violation or non-performance of those duties.

These objectives are evident from the response of the LoN to Iraq's measures to rid itself of its Assyrian population. The LoN effectively used the presence of the undesirable population to hold Iraq hostage to its own policy of ethnic cleansing, and to force the State to pay for the cost of expelling the undesired population. It was decided on 19 January 1934 that the Assyrian population would be settled in the French-mandated territories of the Levant, in modern-day Syria and Lebanon. The following year, the Secretary-General appealed for funds to finance the proposed settlement,[146] and in that context, during a mission to the region, senior LoN officials solicited a 'contribution' of £250,000 from the Iraqi government; an amount it considered to be "reasonable" given the circumstances.[147] The Iraqi government offered £125,000 towards what it euphemistically referred to as "the realisation of a scheme of settlement in Syria,"[148] but the mission did not regard the counter-offer as "an adequate basis for carrying out a suitable plan" and claimed that without the requested funds, it would not be possible to "take steps to begin moving the Assyrians forthwith."[149] This tactic proved effective. Threatened with the prospect of an enduring Assyrian presence, the Iraqi government relented and agreed to absorb the cost of sending its own undesirable population into exile.

---

145 League of Nations: Committee on International Assistance to Refugees, *Report by the Committee Submitted to the Council of the League of Nations* (1936).

146 League of Nations, 'Settlement of the Assyrians of Iraq' (1935) 16(9) LNOJ 989.

147 *Id.*, 992.

148 *Id.*

149 *Id.*

The Committee of the Council for the Settlement of the Assyrians of Iraq solicited an advance of £60,000 towards the settlement of Iraqi Assyrians in the Khabur region of Syria, but soon after urged Iraq to substantially increase its contribution.[150] The pressure on Iraq, as the State of origin, to assume financial obligations for the transfer of Assyrian Iraqis did not only come from the LoN. The British government independently urged Iraq to more generously subsidise the work of the LoN in settling Assyrians in Syria. Britain too held Iraq to ransom for the transfer, promising to increase its own contribution to the scheme, should Iraq comply with its request.[151]

The case of the Assyrian refugees reveals once again the deep preoccupation of States with questions of financial and legal obligations and the uncertainty surrounding the implications of assuming such obligation in a relatively undefined field of IL. As a secondary matter, it demonstrates that any commitment to the rights and freedoms of refugees that may be ascribed to the LoN or its Member States during the period in question is not supported in evidence. The events described in this section instead demonstrate that the unwavering priority was at all times the preservation of State sovereignty and the limitation of international obligations.

The notion that a State of origin should bear some kind of international responsibility for the creation of refugee populations has enjoyed a number of revivals over the decades. As early as 1936, the Committee on International Assistance to Refugees presented a report to the Council of the LoN, expressing concern for the accountability of States of origin for effecting forced displacement:

> In view of the heavy burden placed on the countries of refuge, the Committee considers it an international duty for the countries of origin of the refugees at least to alleviate to some extent, the burdens imposed by the presence of refugees in the territory of other states.[152]

Only a few years after the negotiation with Iraq, the LoN (and later the UN) would confront the same proposed system of exchange, when the German government would enter into negotiations with the LoN to permit Jewish-Germans to leave the State in exchange for the transfer of Jewish assets at extremely low rates. As Chapter 3 notes, several prominent historians of the

150 *Id.*, 990.

151 League of Nations, 'Fifth Meeting (Private, Then Public)' (1935) 16(11) LNOJ 1159, 1170–1171.

152 League of Nations: Committee on International Assistance to Refugees, *Report by the Committee Submitted to the Council of the League of Nations*1936).

Holocaust have stated that the failure of the 'international community' to accept the terms of the German government, and its insistence that it could exact more financially favourable terms, led directly to the implementation of the 'final solution.'

As late as 1991, in its Conclusion on UNHCR's Note on Protection, the ExCom took note of the emphasis on "the need for countries of origin to assume a significant responsibility in the search for appropriate solutions, including through addressing root causes and facilitating voluntary repatriation and the return of their nationals who are not refugees" and "more detailed articulation of the concept of State responsibility, particularly as it relates to the responsibilities of the countries of origin."[153] Though a legal basis for State of origin obligations to provide financial assistance in response to a refugee crisis continues to evade States and institutions, these circular discussions persist, revealing the continued fixation with the establishment of such a principle.

7 Conclusion

Though there were several iterations of early international refugee responses, at the most fundamental level, each was based on essentially the same underlying premise: the retention of administrative obligations by the LoN, the conferral of financial obligations on States of reception and on refugees themselves, and the eventual assumption of all international obligations by the State of reception. Though colonisation and population transfer differed in some material aspects, in essence they both achieved the same goal: the minimisation of circumstances engaging SR. In all respects and at all stages, the priority of those States driving the development of refugee law and policy was to extricate themselves from any long-term, onerous financial or legal obligations.

Far from being concerned with the resolution of complicated legal questions of refugee status, the primary interest of the LoN, and indeed the 'international community' (being in this case its Member States) was the immediate resolution of the unemployment crisis on the one hand, and the maintenance of geographical containment on the other. The characterisation of the LoN's work as concerned with the welfare, protection, or human rights of refugees is contradicted by the steadfast resistance of the organisation to the assumption

153 UN High Commissioner for Refugees, *Note on International Protection* (1990) (A/AC.96/750).

of international obligations associated with the affected populations, and the clear disinclination to resolve the question of an international legal status. While it may be true that the first international rights and freedoms that accumulated to the refugee under the Arrangements were that of freedom of movement, and the right to work, the former was intended to facilitate the latter within a system that was intended to complement, if not serve, the needs of States. In that sense, the question of SR in the context of early IRL was addressed reactively, taking into account the varying economic priorities of States as they dealt with large influxes of refugees.

This is evident from the policies devised by the LoN in response to the Russian and Greek crises, both of which influenced subsequent refugee responses, particularly in respect of questions of SR. The transfer of undesirable populations out of expelling States created an opportunity for States of reception wishing to stimulate the agricultural sector in certain regions, absent any concern for the safety and security of the refugee population itself. When it came to colonisation, the assumption of international obligations in respect of refugees did not rely in any part on the methods by which the population had been displaced. It was not material to the objectives of receiving States that the population had been denationalised or transferred. Rather, resettlement depended greatly on the economic needs of the State of reception, and as such, the implementation and administration of methods of relief relied greatly on the financial incentivisation of States of reception, specifically, through the provision of a labour force with no political agency and few legal rights.

As with the development of SR for injuries to aliens, the international response to early refugee crises was led by the economic powers of the West, under the auspices of the LoN, and the 'international' response to the refugee question was, in reality, representative of a limited consensus. It is unsurprising in that sense that the international response to the numerous refugee crises of the 1920s and early 1930s did little to implicate Western States, and instead ensured that international obligations were contained among States designated as States of reception through policies such as agricultural colonisation and population exchanges. This was further reinforced through the promotion of the concept of enduring State of origin responsibility, which then required the State to provide compensation for the imposition of a financial burden on the State of reception.

It is also unsurprising that, against this backdrop, the preference in the resolution of refugee questions was for repatriation or one of its variations, and that where repatriation was not possible due to security concerns, State of origin responsibility was revived once again as a political tool to enforce compensation. To an extent, the same may be said of the prioritisation of employment in early refugee policy. Though the enthusiasm for employment waned, at its core the policy was intended to achieve the same outcome as colonisation, population transfer, and repatriation, in that it contained international obligations within a controlled geographic sphere. On that basis, it is perhaps easy to understand how policies such as the repayment of refugee loans by refugees, and the exchange of Iraqi funds for the removal of Iraq's Assyrians developed. Though variations existed between early international refugee policies, each developed from the prioritisation by certain States of the limitation of circumstances capable of engaging SR.

In that sense, these early international refugee responses were in many ways far more critical to modern multilateralism in IRL and related policy than the treatment of the subject in the 1951 Convention, in that those early iterations of IRL formed the conceptual basis of IRL as a system of IL, and as a consequence, the scope of its international obligations and the limits of SR within it. As the following chapter illustrates, by contrast, the innovations of the 1951 Convention were comparatively few, and its provisions were in large part informed by the legal developments of those preceding instruments.

The question might then turn on the utility of drawing connections between a contemporary framework of IL and its earliest iterations; the resolution of conflicts, the limitation of international obligations, the scope and content of State of origin responsibility, the right to compensation, and the contrast between the urgent need to achieve self-sufficiency in a regime that began one hundred years ago. The answer is that the issues of labour in the resolution of 'refugee questions' that have emerged since the drafting of the 1951 Convention have not ceased to be relevant. On the contrary, the right to work has continued to be of primary importance in the development of SR in respect of refugees. In contrast with the permissive labour conditions utilised in the resolution of refugee crises in the early 20th century, and with a few recent notable exceptions, labour restrictions have since become a primary means of controlling the admission and voluntary repatriation of refugee populations.

CHAPTER 3

State Responsibility and the Jewish Refugee 'Problem'

1 Introduction

When Jewish refugees began to flee Austria and Germany, much was made of the fact that these 'dispersive movements' were incomparable to previous refugee crises, and must therefore be treated in an entirely distinct manner.[1] As largely non-agricultural populations fled to adjacent States with which they had few intimate ties, it was considered that Jewish refugees had been "distributed fortuitously and without planned relationship to the economic, social, or political absorptive capacities of the receiving countries."[2] Comparatively, some argued that previous crises had been organised and politically authorised. What was once a 'refugee question' was now a 'refugee problem,' characterised by the "forced and chaotic dumping of unfortunate peoples in large numbers."[3]

In reality, the movement of Jewish refugees – whether more or less 'dispersive' or 'chaotic' than that of other populations – was treated no differently than previous refugee crises. States continued to promote the advantages of agricultural colonisation, and later prioritised swift repatriation in the aftermath of hostilities. As with previous refugee crises, the resolution of the Jewish refugee 'problem' was understood principally to be one of labour, which would be remedied in the short term by limited freedom of movement and the right to enter and exit the territories of Allied States, and in the long term by the establishment of colonies across South America, Africa, and to a lesser

1 See: 'Confidential Communication from the Director to the Chairman and Vice-Chairman of the Intergovernmental Committee' (July–August 1938) *Myron C. Taylor Papers – Evian Intergovernmental Committee Conference (folder 2) F.D.R. Library*; Walter Adams, 'Extent and Nature of the World Refugee Problem' (1939) 203 Annals Am Acad Pol & Soc Sci 26, 35–36; Intergovernmental Committee, 'Verbatim Report of the First Meeting (Public)' (6 July 1938) *Myron C. Taylor Papers – Evian Intergovernmental Committee Conference, F.D. R. Library* 6.

2 Walter Adams, 'Extent and Nature of the World Refugee Problem' (1939) 203 Annals Am Acad Pol & Soc Sci 26, 35–36.

3 Intergovernmental Committee, 'Verbatim Report of the First Meeting (Public)' (6 July 1938) *Myron C. Taylor Papers – Evian Intergovernmental Committee Conference, F.D.R. Library.*

 | DOI:10.1163/9789004722835_005

extent, Asia, where refugees would rapidly become self-sufficient and eventually acquire the nationality of the State of reception.

While the former was achieved through a number of special measures, the latter was not successfully instituted on the scale that was desired, though extraordinary effort went into the exploration of colonisation in those continents outside Europe and North America.

These efforts represented a continued and unwavering pursuit of the minimisation of circumstances potentially engaging SR on the part of Western States, and a concerted effort to contain international obligations in States of the 'New World' (being Latin America), Colonial Africa, and certain States of South-East Asia. Eventually it would transpire that private charities and refugees would once again bear the financial burden of resettlement and the provision of humanitarian aid.

The failure of extensive colonisation by no means disqualifies this period as integral to the theorisation and application of SR in IRL. On the contrary. The objectives that would otherwise have been achieved through colonisation were accomplished instead through alternative means, spurred on specifically by the *failure* of colonisation. In the background of these efforts was the persistent concern of Western States about the expanding scope of international obligations; further exacerbated by a preoccupation with nascent IHRL, and the apprehension that the burgeoning systems of IRL and IHRL would amalgamate to threaten State sovereignty. It is unsurprising in that sense, that the purpose of inter-governmental cooperation was to ensure that refugee resettlement remained wholly a sovereign matter. This is clear from the first multilateral attempts to resolve the crisis; from the 1936 *Provisional Arrangement concerning the Status of Refugees Coming from Germany*,[4] which provided that freedom of movement was "without prejudice" to the State's sovereign right to determine residency, to the overwhelming failure that was the 1938 Evian Conference, the invitation to which carefully provided that any action in respect of the Jewish refugee would be determined by States in accordance with their own laws and policies. This would be reiterated multiple times throughout proceedings and recorded in the final Decision of the Conference.[5]

As with previous crises, Western interests drove much of the response to the Jewish refugee crisis. Both the UK and the US were able to maintain a degree of control over the development of IRL through the retention of administrative

4 League of Nations, *Provisional Arrangement concerning the Status of Refugees Coming from Germany* (4 July 1936) LNTS Vol. CLXXI, No. 3952.

5 Intergovernmental Committee, 'Verbatim Report of the First Meeting (Public)' (6 July 1938) *Myron C. Taylor Papers – Evian Intergovernmental Committee Conference, F.D.R. Library.*

and legal obligations, and the delegation of financial obligations; overwhelmingly to private charitable organisations and to refugees themselves. At the same time, Western States continued to implement restrictive and inflexible domestic immigration laws, while insisting that Latin American States throw open their doors to large refugee resettlement schemes.

Chapter 3 considers the significance of this period in consolidating a number of fundamental premises in the conceptualisation of SR in IRL. It argues that the treatment of the Jewish refugee crisis turned largely on its characterisation as a problem of labour. It analyses the treatment of the crisis with reference to the international response, and posits that, far from being the genesis of modern IRL, the response demonstrates a continued genealogy from prior multilateral efforts to resolve refugee questions, which provided little innovation and was broadly unconcerned with the protection of the refugee as a persecuted individual. Instead, the refugee was treated as a commodity; capable of filling labour shortages despite any questions of unwillingness or unsuitability on the part of the refugee. The forceful pursuit of solutions through the agricultural colonisation of various regions throughout the world was a response to the preoccupations of States not only with the minimisation of costs, but with the assumption of international obligations concerning the maintenance of refugee populations in an evolving international legal environment in which the violation of those obligations may lead to the attribution of SR.

Section 2 examines the limitation of international obligations and SR at the Evian Conference. It highlights in particular the disparity between the willingness of Western States to assume any significant role in the resolution of the refugee crisis, and the insistence by the same States that the 'New World' should shoulder the burden by becoming States of reception. In particular, the benefits of agricultural colonisation were presented as self-evidently advantageous to the participating States of Latin America. The unwillingness of Western States to commit to refugee resettlement, and their simultaneous insistence that the States of the 'New World' should willingly and disproportionately assume the role of States of resettlement was the fatal misjudgement of the conference organisers. Though the organisers had presumed that the refugee crisis could be coordinated within the framework of existing migration laws and practices of participating States, the great failure of the Evian Conference had in fact been the attempt to resolve a large-scale crisis within the framework of competing regional interests, and the unwillingness of parties to offer concessions.

Section 3 considers the role of the Inter-Governmental Committee on Refugees (IGCR) in the resolution of the Jewish refugee crisis and argues that this State-based system merely continued to protect the interests of those States it represented; prioritising the limitation of international obligations and imposing financial burdens on refugees themselves. Though the mandate of the IGCR was certainly ambitious – vesting the organisation with the authority to negotiate with Germany to improve conditions of emigration; negotiate with governments for permanent resettlement; and coordinate research activities with the ILO – in its short tenure, the IGCR was not able to achieve any resolution remotely approaching these terms. Its inability to deliver any resolution to the refugee crisis was the result of a number of impediments that compromised its ability to undertake its work. Of principle concern was the question of capital transfer from Germany and Austria to States of resettlement. The position of the German Government had been made clear prior to the Evian Conference that it would not cooperate with any State that sought to interfere in the 'German Jewish problem.' Specifically, the Reich refused to permit the transfer of capital. This not only significantly hampering attempts to resolve the crisis, but was the basis upon which Western States engaged with the Reich in negotiations to bring about a solution to this refugee 'problem.' As Section 3 demonstrates, the fixation on capital and its ultimate benefactors was not only that of the Reich, but was shared also by Western States, preoccupied with the financial incentivisation of the New World.

Section 4 considers the role of the United Nations Relief and Rehabilitation Administration (UNRRA), and the continued prioritisation of employment as the basis for resettlement schemes. It analyses both the benefits of this method of relief and its negative consequences in creating a 'hard core' of refugees. Those Agreements established between UNRRA and the occupying powers provided that the military forces of each State were in charge of administering all basic supplies, coordination of movements, transport in connection with repatriation, security and maintenance of law and order, with UNRRA responsible for the administration of the centres that housed refugees, including coordination of the agencies working within them, and cooperation with military authorities in repatriation. Later, in cooperation with the ILO, UNRRA and its successor organisation, the IRO, created an occupational classification system, compiling information on the skills and capabilities of refugees. In resettling Displaced Persons (DPs) and refugees, States were cognizant of the financial advantages gained by the contributions of resettled persons to national economies, and this was in effect weighted against the costs of resettlement, and the likelihood of DPs and refugees becoming a public charge. Such a policy inevitably created a hard core of DPs and refugees, as States predictably gave preferential treatment to single young men. Those that remained could neither be resettled nor repatriated.

Section 5 examines the role of the International Refugee Organisation (IRO) with particular reference to the resolution of the 'hard core' question, and the continuation of employment schemes. In assuming responsibility for the execution of the agreements previously concluded between the IGCR and resettlement States, the IRO found itself with a 'hard core' of over 700,000 mostly women, children, the elderly, and the infirmed,[6] due to the overwhelming preferential treatment of single young men for resettlement programmes. The continued presence of the hard core posed a serious financial problem to the occupying powers, in particularly the US. Though the principle operational service provided by the UNRRA and later the IRO remained that of resettlement, in practice, it remained firmly within the control of the US. This created the conditions necessary for the division of legal, and financial and administrative obligations between States and organisations and critically, marked the beginning of the designation of legal aspects as constituting 'protection,' though the meaning of protection would later evolve to refer to an array of humanitarian provisions.

Chapter 3 concludes that throughout the relevant period, the division of legal, and financial and administrative obligations continued to be a critical consideration in the development of relevant law and policy, as it did in previous crises, forming the basis of those multilateral efforts intended to provide solutions to the Jewish refugee 'problem,' but in reality, reflecting once again the limited international consensus of Western States. As such, the early development of both the scope and content of IRL, and the theorisation and application of SR relative to it, continued to be driven by global powers, to the detriment of those developing States that wielded limited authority in international settings.

2 International Obligation and Refugee Resettlement at the Evian Conference

The Intergovernmental Meeting of principally European and Latin American States, known simply as the Evian Conference, was convened in July 1938 by US President Franklin D. Roosevelt, to consider what steps could be taken to facilitate the international resettlement of political refugees from Germany

6 Intergovernmental Committee, 'Memorandum' (3 June 1947) *Myron C. Taylor Papers – Intergovernmental Committee on Political Refugees Correspondence, 1947–1954*.

and Austria to "other countries."[7] As it was the Western States that had hitherto determined IRL through the financial control of administrative and operational elements of inter-governmental action, those "other countries" referenced in the Conference agenda to which resettlement would be directed, were understood to be the participating States of Latin America. The Evian Conference was intended to address not only those refugees that had left the territory of the Third Reich, but also those who remained within it, and desired to leave,[8] though intergovernmental cooperation would primarily concern the latter. Publicly, the Conference would evaluate and supplement the work concurrently undertaken by the LoN and the former High Commissioner for Refugees Coming from Germany, James McDonald, who served the office between 1933 and 1935, by establishing a dedicated inter-governmental organisation that would "concern itself with all refugees, wherever governmental intolerance shall have created a refugee problem."[9] Privately, the Evian Conference was an expression of the Anglo-American desire to retain a degree of control over the resolution of the refugee problem, through the promotion of agrarian colonisation schemes to Latin American States, and the limitation of international obligations that had been so integral to the refugee agenda of Western States.

The population and development of various regions across the world was viewed (and certainly presented) as self-evidently advantageous, particularly with reference to the success of previous refugee resettlement schemes.[10] Others saw the schemes as inherently problematic, and the treatment of refugees as colonists to boost economic prosperity akin to the export of merchandise.[11] Though anti-Semitic sentiment was certainly spreading within civil societies, questions of race and of social cohesion were either secondary or absent from the public considerations of most participating States, and in some cases proved to be subordinate to the opportunity presented by the

---

7 Intergovernmental Committee, 'Agenda of the Committee, Communicated by the Government of the United States of America to the Governments invited' (5 July 1938) *Myron C. Taylor Papers – Evian Intergovernmental Committee Conference, F.D.R. Library*.

8 *Id.*

9 *Id.*; See speech by Mr. Taylor, Intergovernmental Committee, 'Verbatim Report of the First Meeting (Public)' (6 July 1938) *Myron C. Taylor Papers – Evian Intergovernmental Committee Conference, F.D.R. Library*.

10 J. Steinberg, 'A Jewish Settlement in the Kimberleys' (1940) 12(1) The Australian Quarterly 24–30; Bernard Wolbarst Levmore, 'A Stimulus for American Industry: Nonprofessional Refugees' (1939) 203 Annals Am Acad Pol & Soc Sci 162–167.

11 Vera Micheles Dean, 'European Power Politics and the Refugee Problem' (1939) 203 Annals Am Acad Pol & Soc Sci 18, 24.

settlement of a refugee population in the interests of economic development. This is with the notable exception of Australia, which in pursuit of its 'White Australia' Policy, only permitted British immigration, declaring that "having no real racial problem, we are not desirous of importing one [...],"[12] and of Canada, whose Director of Immigration, Frederick Blair, declared, "none is too many" in response to the question, 'how many of Europe's persecuted Jews should be permitted to emigrate to Canada?'[13]

2.1 *The Colonisation of the 'New World'*

In organising the Evian Conference, it was understood by the US that the question of financial obligations constituted a primary – if not *the* primary – concern of participating States. It was decided in advance of the Evian Conference, and recorded in its final decision, that participating States would not absorb financial obligations for any element of refugee resettlement, but that this task "would be undertaken by private organisations within the respective countries."[14] As a result, the IGCR, which was created by a decision of the Conference, was denied an operational budget. Though its establishment was the only achievement of the Conference, it would function in large part to protect Western interests.

Much like previous refugee questions, the Jewish refugee crisis was understood principally as a labour crisis, and its resolution was treated accordingly. Within domestic frameworks, few States legally distinguished between refugees and immigrants. The prevailing model of immigration law corresponded directly to the economic development of the State. As such, a number of participating States sent ministers of trade, commerce, and labour, ILO delegates, and private industrialists as their delegates to the Evian Conference.[15] The

12 'The Bolivian Option' (2007) 40(4) The Shekel 9.

13 See generally: Irving Abella, Harold Tropper, *None is Too Many: Canada and the Jews of Europe, 1933–1948* (University of Toronto Press 2012).

14 The UK departed from this principle in June 1939, after it became clear that it "may find [itself] within the next few months faced with the problem of having to deal with bankrupt organisations, unable either to maintain the refugees they have brought into this country or to finance their emigration to other countries." See: Tommie Sjöberg, *The Powers and the Persecuted: The Refugee Problem and the Intergovernmental Committee on Refugees (IGCR), 1938–1947* (Lund University Press 1991) 42. See also: 'The Secretary of State to the Ambassador in the United Kingdom (Kennedy)' (23 March 1938) *Foreign Relations Of The United States Diplomatic Papers, 1938, General, Volume I*.

15 Including Australia, Belgium, Bolivia, Chile, Haiti, Ireland, Sweden. See: Intergovernmental Committee, 'Revised List of Delegates' (July 1938) *Myron C. Taylor Papers – Evian Intergovernmental Committee Conference, F.D.R. Library*, 1–7.

LoN itself was jointly represented by the General-Secretary and the president of its Labour Commission.

In order to advance resettlement under domestic immigration systems, participating States were invited to furnish the Preparatory Committee with statements of existing immigration law, practice, and policy, and to provide general statements "of the number and type of immigrants it is now prepared to receive or that it might consider receiving."[16] In their responses, States were very eager to draw attention to the conditions affecting labour markets, which in turn justified the necessity for restrictive immigration policy. State after State declared itself prepared to assist in principle, but unable to do so unless through small-scale agricultural colonisation programmes.[17]

Citing the devastating effects that the Great Depression had had on Western economies, Latin American States (repeatedly referred to collectively as the 'New World') were encouraged, and in some cases incentivised, to shoulder the burden of the refugee 'problem' through the establishment of agrarian colonies; an appeal that was widely derided and rejected by Latin American States as a transparent attempt to direct obligations southward, and a failure to equitably share the burden.[18] The role of Latin America was critical to the early agricultural labour schemes, as Western States promoted, and in some cases successfully established, small resettlement schemes within the region.

By comparison, Western States were not desirous of increased immigration; a prospect that they considered as importing a great economic burden by adding to the existing rates of unemployment. The principle of 'no public charge,' incorporated into the immigration laws of the US, Britain, and Australia, and variously requiring immigrants to land with a designated amount of capital or guaranteed employment, was presented in confidential submissions to the Preparatory Committee as justification for the impracticality of refugee admission.[19] France declared itself to have already reached "the extreme point of

---

16 *Id.*

17 See speeches by Mr. Helio Lobo (Brazil), Mr. de Foy (Belgium), Mr. Hume Wrong (Canada) in Intergovernmental Committee, 'Verbatim Report of the Second Meeting' (7 July 1938) *Myron C. Taylor Papers – Evian Intergovernmental Committee Conference, F.D.R. Library*; Mr. Garola Oldini (Chile), Mr. Gastelu (Ecuador), Mr. Garoia Calderon (Peru), Mr. Cremins (Ireland) in Intergovernmental Committee, 'Verbatim Report of the Third Meeting (Public)' (9 July 1938) *Myron C. Taylor Papers – Evian Intergovernmental Committee Conference, F.D.R. Library*.

18 David S. Wyman, *The Abandonment of the Jews: America and the Holocaust, 1941–1945* (Pantheon Books 1984) 57.

19 Intergovernmental Committee: Technical Sub-Committee, *Statement of Details Regarding the Number and the Type of Immigrants which the Government of the United States in Prepared to Receive Under its Existing Laws and Practices* (8 July 1938) Myron C. Taylor

saturation as regards admission of refugees."[20] Switzerland proposed that it could accept limited numbers of refugees on a non-permanent basis, but that this policy would in any case be implemented as a trial period.[21] Norway and Sweden both simply stated that they had 'never been countries of immigration.'[22] Perhaps cautious of the comments by the British delegate that countries of first refuge should "signify their readiness to absorb [...] the refugees from Germany and Austria who have already been admitted to their territories,"[23] the Netherlands was eager to disclaim any enduring obligations for the refugees it had not legally admitted, but whom were nonetheless present in its territory, declaring that "owing to the density of its population, the part played by the Netherlands in granting assistance to refugees must always be rather that of a country of temporary sojourn."[24]

Instead, appeals were made to "the Republics of the New World" to "throw their doors wide open to political migrants from Europe."[25] The Swedish Government was particularly unequivocal that refugees should be directed to Latin America, declaring, "if tangible and satisfactory results are to be obtained, this emigration must be so arranged that it is directed to countries outside Europe."[26] The benefits of agricultural colonisation were very much

---

Papers – Evian Intergovernmental Committee Conference, F.D.R. Library; Intergovernmental Committee: Technical Sub-Committee, *Statement of the Immigration Laws and Practices of the United States of America Governing the Reception of Immigrants* (8 July 1938) Myron C. Taylor Papers – Evian Intergovernmental Committee Conference, F.D. R. Library; Intergovernmental Committee: Technical Sub-Committee, *Memorandum on Australian Immigration Laws and Practices and the Present Policy of his Majesty's Government in the Commonwealth of Australia* (8 July 1938) Myron C. Taylor Papers – Evian Intergovernmental Committee Conference, F.D.R. Library.

20 Technical Sub-Committee Intergovernmental Committee, *Declaration by the Norwegian Delegation on the Immigration Laws and their Application in Norway* (8 July 1938) Myron C. Taylor Papers – Evian Intergovernmental Committee Conference, F.D.R. Library; Speech by Mr. Engzell (Sweden), Intergovernmental Committee, *Verbatim Report of the Fourth Meeting (Public)* (11 July 1938) Myron C. Taylor Papers – Evian Intergovernmental Committee Conference, F.D.R. Library.

21 *Id.*

22 *Id.*

23 Speech by Lord Winterton, Intergovernmental Committee, 'Verbatim Report of the First Meeting (Public)' (6 July 1938) *Myron C. Taylor Papers – Evian Intergovernmental Committee Conference, F.D.R. Library.*

24 *Id.*, Speech by Mr. Beucker-Andreae (Netherlands).

25 *Id.*, Speech by Mr. Bérenger (France).

26 Speech by Mr. Engzell (Sweden), Intergovernmental Committee, *Verbatim Report of the Fourth Meeting (Public)*11 July 1938) Myron C. Taylor Papers – Evian Intergovernmental Committee Conference, F.D.R. Library.

intended to convince the participating States of Latin America to accept vast numbers of refugees. It was in the end a fatal misjudgement of Western States to presume that the 'New World' would consider extensive immigration as self-evidently advantageous. Indeed, the hypocrisy of the West was not lost on those pressured to assume the disproportionate burden. In response to the Swedish statement, the Colombian delegate declared:

> [T[he appeal which was addressed here to the American Republics should be regarded as applying also to those European nations who still possess colonial territories in America. Indeed, paraphrasing the historic phrase that everyone knows very well, we might repeat here "Messieurs les français, Messieurs les anglais, Messieurs les hollandaise, it is for you to act first; it is to you that this appeal is addressed."[27]

Confronted with the resistance of the 'New World,' and as an apparent substitute for the admission of refugees to their own territories, States of the 'Old World' proposed, as an alternative, modest resettlement schemes within their colonies and dominions. As the great colonial power of the time, the UK declared itself to be "highly industrialised, fully populated and still faced with the problem of unemployment,"[28] but announced that it was in the process of examining the possibility of settlement in certain East African territories for "a limited number of select families."[29] It proposed that a "small-scale settlement of Jewish refugees" might be possible in Kenya; a suggestion that did not arouse much enthusiasm.[30] A committee was later established to examine the possibility of a settlement in Uganda, and later surveys were carried out of various regions of potential resettlement in British Guiana and Northern Rhodesia.[31] As the colonial authority in the Philippines, the US initiated a similar survey of the island of Mindanao.[32] Australia was briefly cited

27 Speech by Mr. Yepes (Colombia) Intergovernmental Committee, 'Verbatim Report of the Third Meeting (Public)' (9 July 1938) *Myron C. Taylor Papers – Evian Intergovernmental Committee Conference, F.D.R. Library* 10.

28 *Id.*, 1.

29 *Id.*, 4.

30 Speech of Lord Winterton, *Verbatim Report of the Sixth Meeting (Public)* (15 July 1938) Myron C. Taylor Papers – Evian Intergovernmental Committee Conference, F.D.R. Library; 'Evian Conference on Political Refugees' (1938) 12(3) Social Service Review 514, 516.

31 Intergovernmental Committee, *The Refugee Problem After the War* ((no date recorded)) Myron C. Taylor Papers – Intergovernmental Committee on Political Refugees Correspondence, 1942–1943.

32 *Id.*

as a possibility for colonisation owing to its geographic isolation, which meant that "settlers would not be competing with the labour market generally,"[33] until the Australian delegate declared unambiguously that the State would not accept Jewish refugees.[34]

The attitude of the British to the colonisation of its dominions was considered particularly critical for another reason. Not only did it have extensive and sparsely populated colonies in Africa, South America, Canada, and Australia, but it held the LoN mandate over Palestine. In that regard, the multiple proposals presented by the British for Jewish settlement in other colonial territories were attempts to assuage the international pressure to permit Jewish immigration to Palestine.

At the close of the Evian Conference, it became painfully obvious that no State was willing to make any concessions for the resolution of the refugee problem, beyond the strictest application of existing agricultural immigration programmes. The Resolution of the Conference was meagre in its recommendations, stating only that the involuntary emigration of large numbers of people was "disturbing to the general economy" since it occurred "at a time when there is serious unemployment," and that the IGCR should continue its work in cooperation with the existing services of the LoN and the ILO.[35]

One of great failure of the Evian Conference had been the assumption by its organisers that the refugee crisis could be coordinated within the framework of existing migration laws and practices of Governments, and thus resolved within the confines of traditional attitudes toward immigration.[36] This coupled with the global economic collapse and the spread of anti-Semitic sentiment is cited as evidence that the Conference was destined to achieve nothing of substance. But this does not account entirely for the inflexibility of domestic immigration regimes in favour of refugees. It was also due in part to the fact that the emigrating population did not present a viable labour resource for the vast majority of participating States, being largely non-agrarian. But primarily, the failure of the Evian Conference was a matter of regional conflicting interests; the self-preservation of Western States against increased immigration and the threat it posed to the already-decimated industrial sector, and the

33 Michael Blakeney, 'Proposals for a Jewish Colony in Australia: 1938–1948' (1984) 46(3/4) Jewish Social Studies 277, 280; Norman Bentwich, 'The Evian Conference and After' (1928) Fortnightly Rev 291.

34 'The Bolivian Option' (2007) 40(4) The Shekel 9.

35 Intergovernmental Committee, *Decision taken at the Evian Conference on Jewish Refugees* (14 July 1938).

36 Michael Blakeney, 'Proposals for a Jewish Colony in Australia: 1938–1948' (1984) 46(3/4) Jewish Social Studies 277, 279.

unwillingness of Latin American States to disproportionately shoulder the burden of refugee resettlement, due either to existing trade relations with Germany, or the fact that such proposals was grossly inequitable.

In the years that followed the Evian Conference, attempts to resolve the Jewish refugee crisis continued to rely on resettlement in States of the New World and Africa, and the imposition of the financial burden on the world Jewish community. The determination of clear and defined international obligations was limited specifically because of ongoing concern regarding the creation of circumstances engaging SR. Specifically, the reticence to the assumption of financial obligations continued to be motivated by concerns about the long-term implications of such.

The US pursued its own investigations and surveys of African and Latin American States for the purposes of refugee resettlement. In 1938, Roosevelt sought to establish a colony in Italian-occupied Ethiopia, corresponding privately with Mussolini on the prospect of such a scheme.[37] Mussolini rejected the proposal and suggested in the alternative, a settlement in Russia or North America.[38] The State Department also pursued a Jewish settlement in Portuguese Angola, which President Salazar dismissed. At the 1943 Anglo-American Conference in Bermuda, delegates revived the possibility of transferring 2000 refugees to Portuguese Angola. In December 1939, undeterred by the failure of his Ethiopia proposal, Roosevelt talked of one or two large settlements, covering one million square miles and supporting millions of people, where refugees might develop a "self-sustaining civilisation" of their own.[39] The following year, he engaged the services of an archaeologist and anthropologist, Henry Field on what was called 'Project "M."' Field was to complete a series of studies of settlement possibilities throughout the world. A total of 666 studies were produced under Project M, almost all of which were utterly useless, not least because Project M was not declassified until 1960. Field revealed in 1962 that one of Roosevelt's plans was to use desalinated water to transform the deserts of North Africa into fertile agrarian zones of refugee resettlement.[40]

---

37 Allen Wells, *Tropical Zion: General Trujillo, FDR, and the Jews of Sosúa* (Duke University Press 2009) 39; David S. Wyman, *The Abandonment of the Jews: America and the Holocaust, 1941–1945* (Pantheon Books 1984) 58.

38 *Id.*, Wyman.

39 Allen Wells, *Tropical Zion: General Trujillo, FDR, and the Jews of Sosúa* (Duke University Press 2009) 39; David S. Wyman, *The Abandonment of the Jews: America and the Holocaust, 1941–1945* (Pantheon Books 1984) 59.

40 *Id.*, Wyman; Henry Field, *"M" Project for F.D.R.: Studies on Migration and Settlement* (Ann Arbor 1962).

At the same time, Roosevelt was fixated on the idea of Venezuela as a location for colonisation by European Jews. The Venezuelan government was receptive to the proposal, provided that colonisers "were trained agriculturists and not simply agriculturists for the purpose of gaining entry," possessing "the necessary good character, in order to develop agricultural activities,"[41] and on the strict proviso that "they would be parcelled and obliged to purchase land, initially granted by the Government even if such purchase required many years for fulfilment."[42] Roosevelt was specifically interested in the Orinoco River valley, and enlisted the services of geographer and president of John Hopkins University, Isaiah Bowman, to survey the area.[43] Bowman subsequently conveyed his serious doubts to the President that the region would be suitable for colonisation, but Roosevelt pressed Bowman to survey other areas of the Orinoco valley.[44] Conditions there were not improved. Four years later and still undeterred, Roosevelt wrote to anthropologist, Aleš Hrdlička, of the Smithsonian Institute on the question of post-war land settlement in the Orinoco basin.[45]

In 1940, former US President Herbert Hoover and financier Bernard Baruch foresaw a State in the Central African highlands for ten million war victims,[46] and appealed to London to gauge British interest. In yet another attempt to engage private actors in the subsidisation of refugee resettlement, the plan was to call on world Jewry to tithe themselves in order to raise the $300-$500 million required for the resettlement.[47]

In some cases, failed attempts to forcibly impose international obligations on States resulted in the deaths of refugees. Despite not having ascertained

41 'Letter from Antonio C. Gonzalez to Franklin D. Roosevelt' (Caracas, 15 September 1938) *Myron C. Taylor Papers.*

42 'Letter from Antonio C. Gonzalez to Secretary of State, 'Interview with General López Contreras, President of Venezuela'' (Caracas, 16 December 1938) *Franklin D. Roosevelt Presidential Library & Museum, series 3, box 53 'Venezuela'* pg 5.

43 See generally: 'President's Personal File 5575 – Bowman, Isaiah, 1938–1939' (undated) *Franklin D. Roosevelt Presidential Library & Museum.*

44 'Letter from Franklin D. Roosevelt to Isaiah Bowman' (2 November 1938) *'President's Personal File 5575 – Bowman, Isaiah, 1938–1939' Franklin D. Roosevelt Presidential Library & Museum.*

45 David S. Wyman, *The Abandonment of the Jews: America and the Holocaust, 1941–1945* (Pantheon Books 1984) 60; David H. Price, Anthropological Intelligence (Duke University Press 2008).

46 Wyman, *id.*, 59.

47 Monty Noam Penkower, *Decision on Palestine Deferred: America, Britain and Wartime Diplomacy, 1939–1945* (Routledge 2013).

resettlement commitments, ships continued to transport vast numbers of refugees, only to be met with firm closed-border policies. In early 1939, German steamship companies sent vessels with refugees aboard to Latin America without the proper documentation required for entry. Despite receiving notice that the Cuban government had nullified all landing permits already issued, officials of Germany's Hamburg-American line permitted the *St. Louis* to set out for Havana in mid-May 1939. On reaching Cuba, 907 refugees aboard were unable to land. In one particularly tragic case, 769 refugees boarded the *Struma* in Romania, bound for Palestine, only to be forbidden to land at Istanbul unless British Palestine officials granted subsequent entry into Palestine. Permission was not forthcoming, and despite the protestations of the vessel's captain that it was not seaworthy, the *Struma* was towed out of the port, shortly after which it exploded and sank killing all but two on board.[48]

3 The IGCR and the Financial Obligations of Refugees

The IGCR was created in 1938 on the initiative of President Roosevelt and was tasked with the administration of intergovernmental efforts to resettle refugees from Nazi Germany, and later from across Europe. In the final decision of the Evian Conference, participating States had expressed their willingness to "cooperate in finding an orderly solution" to the involuntary emigration of refugees still in Germany and Austria, on the condition that the Reich enabled involuntary emigrants to take with them their property and possessions and emigrate in an orderly manner.[49] In that respect, the IGCR had been empowered to negotiate with Germany for orderly emigration. Its work continued until 1947, when it was terminated, and its activities were assumed by the IRO. The official account of the US Government in advocating for the creation of the IGCR was that it was motivated by 'humanitarian concerns' and by an increasing awareness that the LoN's refugee machinery was ill-equipped to manage the emerging refugee problem. It was now recognised that the LoN's policy had been built on the erroneous presumption

48 David S. Wyman, *Paper Walls: America and the Refugee Crisis 1938–1941* (Pantheon Books 1985) 39 (originally published in 1968).

49 Intergovernmental Committee, *Decision taken at the Evian Conference on Jewish Refugees* (14 July 1938); Speech by Mr. Hume Wrong (Canada) in Intergovernmental Committee, 'Verbatim Report of the Second Meeting' (7 July 1938) *Myron C. Taylor Papers – Evian Intergovernmental Committee Conference, F.D.R. Library.*

that the refugee question was a temporary one,[50] and accordingly, a "new imaginative and more generous approach" was required.[51] In practice, the IGCR did not achieve anything remotely fulfilling these ambitions. It was neither imaginative in the development of new policy, nor generous in the resettlement of refugees, and has been regarded as an "ineffectual creation" and "a proven failure."[52] Only three months after the first meeting of the IGCR, Roosevelt himself privately conveyed his concerns about its inactivity to the US delegate, Myron Taylor, writing that the Committee "has not yet produced the concrete results I had hoped" and that "the time has come when a special effort must be made to make the Committee's work really effective. We must produce them soon."[53]

The inability of the IGCR to produce any concrete result was somewhat preordained. Its role had been threefold: It would negotiate with Germany to improve conditions of emigration; negotiate with governments for permanent resettlement; and coordinate research activities with the ILO. In each of these functions, the work of the IGCR had been compromised. In respect of its second and third functions, the Evian Decision required participating States to furnish the IGCR with details regarding "such immigrants as each Government may be prepared to receive under its existing laws and practices," and that in doing so, States of refuge and settlement were "entitled to take into account the economic and social adaptability of immigrants."[54] As the vast majority of participating States had designed immigration policy around agricultural colonisation, intellectuals, merchants, traders, and others of the professional class were excluded from resettlement by definition. The unwillingness of States to permit a degree of flexibility in immigration policy meant that the statements of immigration law provided to the IGCR did not materially assist.

---

50 'Memorandum to Secretary of State' (undated) *box 3, Myron C. Taylor Papers* 'Memorandum to Secretary of State' (undated) box 3, Myron C. Taylor Papers.

51 'Confidential Memorandum for the American Delegate' (undated) *box 3, Myron C. Taylor Papers*; 'Memorandum' (9 August 1938) *'August 1938' folder, Myron C. Taylor Papers*; 'Taylor to Secretary of State' (July 7, 1938) *Myron C. Taylor Papers*; 'Hull to Taylor' (8 July 1938) *Myron C. Taylor Papers*; 'Taylor to Hull' (20 July 1938) *Myron C. Taylor Papers.*

52 David S. Wyman, *Paper Walls: America and the Refugee Crisis 1938–1941* (Pantheon Books 1985) 107.

53 'Letter From President Franklin D. Roosevelt to Myron C. Taylor' (23 November 1938) *Myron C. Taylor Papers.*

54 Intergovernmental Committee, *Decision taken at the Evian Conference on Jewish Refugees*14 July 1938).

In respect of its first function – to negotiate with Germany for an orderly emigration – the great impediment to the IGCR's success had been the question of capital transfer from Germany and Austria to States of resettlement. The German Government had made it clear to its British counterpart prior to the Evian Conference, that it would not cooperate with any government that sought to interfere in the 'German Jewish problem,' and as it was a policy of the Reich that emigrating Jews were not permitted to 'transfer German capital accumulated by them,' there could be no exception for States participating in the Evian Conference.[55] Despite having received this assurance, the final text adopted at the Conference, submitted by the American, British and French delegations, observed that "states of origin should cooperate in finding a solution of the problem created by forced emigrations, by enabling refugees to bring with them their property or possessions."[56]

The successful transfer of capital was hindered also by the inflexibility of participating States in the application of the 'no public charge' principle. Just as the German Government would not permit emigration with capital, States of potential resettlement would not permit Jewish refugees to be admitted without it, and in some cases, without proof of assured employment. In this respect, the IGCR was also hindered by its own policy. It had declared that the entirety of administrative and financial obligations for refugee resettlement fell properly to States of reception, as did the legal obligation to define and confer a legal status. This, it considered, was a sovereign right of States, for the national judicature to decide in accordance with the applicable Arrangements.[57] Accordingly, States very clearly defined the parameters of financial obligations as those imposed by existing immigration law and policy. This hesitation to define international obligations led to the application of a multitude of ineffectual municipal regimes that stymied the ability of the IGCR to fulfil its objectives.

The basis upon which the IGCR proceeded to negotiate with Germany for the transfer of Jewish capital is a particularly remarkable one. The Committee permitted Germany a number of very significant concessions – though admittedly at a time when the German policy was one of expulsion, not extermination – and seemingly did not attempt to gain any latitude in the negotiation process by advancing any real counterproposals. The IGCR in fact considered that the Committee itself could benefit from leveraging taxes on refugees for

55 'Deputy Foreign Minister von Weizsaecker to the British Ambassador in Berlin: Memorandum AA 83/29 8/7' (8 July 1938).

56 'The Evian Conference on Refugees (2)' (1938) 15 Bulletin of International News 8.

57 'Fourth Meeting (Private, Then Public)' (1935) 16(6) LNOJ 628, 633.

the transfer of capital, similar to the rates imposed by the German Government. Though it was never implemented due to the outbreak of war, the IGCR extensively planned to placate States of resettlement and protect Western States from the assumption of international obligations by ensuring that financial obligations for refugee resettlement were born by refugees themselves. The IGCR pursued a policy that would allow it to confiscate Jewish capital to then redistribute it, purportedly for the benefit of the Jewish refugee. In reality, this plan was intended to financially benefit States of resettlement, as the taxes imposed on transferred capital would be directed towards the transfer, resettlement, and retraining of refugees, and would ensure that the State would not be economically disadvantaged by resettlement. In this sense, the financial obligations otherwise assumed by a State of resettlement would be neutralised by the capital of its resettled refugee population. The discussions and negotiations on the transfer of capital are all the more mercenary when one considers the circumstances in which Jewish capital was regarded.

Since the introduction in the summer of 1931 of currency restrictions in Germany, various types of credit accounts - or '*sperrmarks*' - were created, including the 'emigrants' *sperrmark*; capital left behind by German Jews unable to transfer capital from Germany to another State. The German prohibition of 1933 on the foreign transfer of capital by German Jews meant that the sale of these accounts was the only method by which refugees could transfer any capital at all; the procedure being that the refugee would convert his property into cash, pay it into an emigrants' *sperrmark*, then sell it through a foreign bank with substantial losses. The value of emigrants' *sperrmark* was negotiated on the foreign stock exchange, and their buyers were frequently foreign importers of German goods who held a concession from the German authorities that permitted them to make payments using the purchased accounts. This practice continued until June 1938, when the acquisition of emigrants' *sperrmark* was prohibited and all importer concessions were cancelled. The result was that the only buyers on the market for emigrants' *sperrmarks* were the German Reichsbank and its associates. As sole competitor, the Reichsbank dropped the rate of exchange to 8%, resulting in a loss of 92% of the transferred capital. The 1933 and 1938 prohibitions enriched the Reichsbank enormously. In 1938, it was estimated that the annual turnover of emigrants' *sperrmarks* alone constituted a profit of several hundred million marks.[58]

58 'Transfer of Jewish and Non-Aryan Property from Germany Including Austria. Part A.: Jewish Emigration and Transfer of Jewish Property since 1933' (15 August 1938) *Myron C. Taylor Papers – Evian Intergovernmental Committee Conference (folder 2)*.

The only exception to the transfer of Jewish capital permitted by the German Government was for emigration to Palestine under the *Haavara Transfer Agreement*.[59] Negotiated between private actors and the German Government, the *Haavara Transfer Agreement* permitted emigration from Germany to Palestine by breaking the international boycott of German imports and permitting the transfer of some capital. The funds to be transferred were paid by prospective emigrants into the account of a Jewish trust company in Germany, which then used the funds for the purchase of German goods, which the Haavara Transfer Office then sold in Palestine. The profits of sale were then distributed to Jewish refugees in Palestine. Though it was heavily criticised for breaking the international boycott and accused of capitulating to the Reich, in the six years that it was active, the Haavara Transfer Office facilitated the emigration of 60,000 Jews.[60]

Between the prohibition of 1933 on the foreign transfer of capital, and the 1938 prohibition of the use of *sperrmarks* by foreign companies, the vast majority of German-Jewish refugees did not emigrate to Palestine but to other States where they could not transfer capital through the sale of emigrants' *sperrmarks* to the Reichsbank. The result was that "the prohibition of the sale of *sperrmarks* has now brought this method of individual emigration to a complete standstill."[61] As the IGCR itself recognised:

> This prohibition of the transfer through the sale of emigrants' *sperrmarks* constituted the most severe handicap to emigration, the implications of which were not fully realised by the public in the countries receiving refugees.[62]

Though efforts had been made to negotiate capital transfer to other States on the same basis as the Haavara system, none had been successful. When examining the question of whether the IGCR could, with some chances of success, enlist German co-operation on a commercial basis for the transfer of Jewish emigrants' capital, it was advised that "special attention must be paid to the

59 See: Edwin Black, *The Transfer Agreement: The Dramatic Story of the Pact between Nazi Germany and Jewish Palestine* (Carroll & Graf Publishers 2001).

60 *Id.*

61 'Transfer of Jewish and Non-Aryan Property from Germany Including Austria. Part A.: Jewish Emigration and Transfer of Jewish Property since 1933' (15 August 1938) *Myron C. Taylor Papers – Evian Intergovernmental Committee Conference (folder 2)*.

62 *Id.*

complete failure of all previous efforts to introduce a transfer system based on the export of goods to countries other than Palestine."[63]

The IGCR proposed that a permanent contribution of foreign exchange could be made by Germany as a basis of the organised transfer of capital, and that the German State could cancel the tax premium of 100% on the personal assets of Jewish emigrants, and it could cancel any further application of the Goering Decree, which prohibited any Jew from holding the position of manager in an Austrian business. Once again, this plan was spurred by the notion that the cost of resettlement could be borne by private individuals, in this case, by world Jewry. Privately, the IGCR professed that should Germany agree to its terms, the financial obligations of States would be spared, as Jewish organisations would have no trouble in raising the funds required for the transport of refugees:

> Religious and racial fervour, supported by first-class organisation, has achieved a very large measure of success. Finance hitherto has not been a difficulty, since the community as a whole has been willing to provide necessary funds on a very generous scale, and will no doubt be willing to do so in the future.[64]

In furtherance of its proposed solution, the IGCR considered the establishment of its own Special Transfer Office for the liquidation of Jewish property in Germany and Austria, which would finance emigrants without means, but this presented a unique humanitarian question, as the 'Aryanisation' of Jewish businesses in Germany and Austria was carried out through rampant undervaluation, and the IGCR would be acquiring property at a grossly devalued rate. The solution, according to the IGCR, was that the future Special Transfer Office and a corresponding organisation of the German Government would jointly acquire Jewish property, and that the liquidation of that property would occur through the Special Transfer Office. The value of assets would be negotiated between the Special Transfer Office and the German Government and at the time of emigration, and the owner of the capital would receive a designated amount.

It was estimated that the profits would be immense. Based on its proposal, the IGCR projected that the Special Transfer Office would receive between

63 *Id.*

64 Intergovernmental Committee, *The Refugee Problem After the War*(no date recorded)) Myron C. Taylor Papers – Intergovernmental Committee on Political Refugees Correspondence, 1942–1943.

187,300,000 and 295,700,000 reichsmark from liquidated Jewish property, to be used "for the organised emigration of German and Austrian Jews."[65] But of that projected amount, very little would be returned to refugees themselves. Instead, the funds would be directed towards States of resettlement. In a confidential report on the Special Transfer Office, the IGCR declared that:

> As the Transfer Office [...] would be in a position to charge transfer premiums of between 70 and 80%, it is evident that a considerable reichsmark profit would result from the difference between the sum to be paid on the one hand for the purchase of the foreign exchange, and on the other hand charged to the emigrants.[66]

Reflecting on this plan years later, it was recorded in confidential documents of the IGCR, that "it was hoped that the cooperation of the German Government would result in an orderly system of emigration, and that its finance would be largely provided from the assets of the emigrants themselves."[67] Indeed, the eventual administrative and operational budget of the IGCR consisted in part of assets from the liquidation of German property in neutral States amounting to $25,000,000 USD and an "undetermined amount from looted property and heirless funds."[68]

The relentless pursuit of private finance continued in 1939, essentially forming the basis of negotiations between the first director of the IGCR, George Rublee, and the designated representatives of the Reich – first Dr Hjalmar Schacht, President of the Reichsbank, then with Dr Wohlthat of the Economics Ministry.[69] At talks between Rublee and Schacht in January 1939, Schacht presented Rublee and others with a plan to ease restrictions on Jewish emigration in exchange for increased German exports above the "norm." The 'Schacht plan' as it was called, envisaged an international loan being raised with the property left by emigrants as security. The loan – reported to be

65 'Transfer of Jewish and Non-Aryan Property from Germany Including Austria. Part A.: Jewish Emigration and Transfer of Jewish Property since 1933' (15 August 1938) *Myron C. Taylor Papers – Evian Intergovernmental Committee Conference (folder 2).*

66 *Id.*

67 Intergovernmental Committee, *The Refugee Problem After the War* (no date recorded)) Myron C. Taylor Papers – Intergovernmental Committee on Political Refugees Correspondence, 1942–1943.

68 Myron C. Taylor, 'Confidential Memorandum for the President Regarding Refugees 1938–1947' (30 July 1947) *Myron C. Taylor Papers – Intergovernmental Committee on Political Refugees Correspondence, 1947–1954.*

69 *Id.*

between 300 and 375 million dollars – would again be raised by world Jewry, and serviced through increased German exports. In exchange, the Schacht plan permitted emigration over a three-year period of 150,000 German-Jewish men and women of working age, and 250,000 dependent women and children. 200,000 others of the so-called 'hard-core' – the elderly, infirmed, and incapacitated, who were "not suited to the conditions of settlement in other countries,"[70] would stay in Germany and persecution against them would cease.[71] It was reported that Rublee did not come to the London talks with any prepared counter proposal.[72]

The Schacht plan was denounced as refugee barter, extortion, and blackmail,[73] but negotiations continued between Schacht and Rublee, and after Schacht's dismissal, between Wohlthat and Rublee. Rublee was able to negotiate some concessions, though the beneficiaries of those concessions, again, would have been States of resettlement, not refugees themselves. He provisionally secured the establishment of a trust fund of at least 25% of Jewish property in Germany to pay for German exports to be used either to equip emigrants or to develop refugee colonisation projects for the settlement of 150,000 German Jews. The question of increased foreign imports of German goods was avoided. This modified deal was called the Rublee Plan, and was approved by the US State Department.[74]

By February 1939, a provisional arrangement was reached with the German Government to adopt a policy which would facilitate organised emigration, and which would permit *inter alia* emigrants to take with them personal effects free of taxes and levies, and the cancellation of the flight tax, but the details were not finalised before the outbreak of war.[75] There is little doubt

70 'Speech by Myron C. Taylor (USA) Intergovernmental Committee to Continue and Develop the Work of the Evian Meeting' (3 August 1938) *box 3, Myron C. Taylor Papers – Evian Intergovernmental Committee Conference (folder 2), July–August 1938.*

71 David S. Wyman, *The Abandonment of the Jews: America and the Holocaust, 1941–1945* (Pantheon Books 1984) 53; 'Johnson to Rublee to Hull: Telegram' (16 December 1938) *Documents on German Foreign Policy 1918–1945*; Hjalmar Schacht, *Confessions of 'The Old Wizard': The Autobiography of Hjalmar Horace Greeley Schacht* (1956).

72 Jewish Telegraphic Agency, 'Schacht Plan to Form Basis of Rublee Talks, Opening in Berlin Today' (11 January 1939).

73 David S. Wyman, *The Abandonment of the Jews: America and the Holocaust, 1941–1945* (Pantheon Books 1984) 54–55.

74 *Id.*

75 'Strictly Confidential Memorandum: The Emigration of Jews from Germany' (February 1939) *Myron C. Taylor Papers – Confidential memorandum regarding Refugees by Myron C. Taylor, 1938–1947*; Intergovernmental Committee, *The Refugee Problem After*

which States were intended to be incentivised by what would have been the confiscation and redistribution of Jewish capital by the IGCR. In confidential correspondence to the Chair and Vice-Chair of the IGCR, George Rublee wrote:

> Misapprehensions now prevail in certain quarters to the effect that the old world wishes to shove off upon the new the immediate burden, which under prevailing conditions of disorderly exodus, involuntary emigration now brings to the receiving country.
>
> It may be further anticipated, assuming for the moment concrete results from eventual negotiations with the German Government on the transfer problem, that countries of final settlement will also appreciate the fact that the aggregate of tangible wealth, which would accrue to a country willing to receive involuntary immigrants in substantial numbers, would be significant.[76]

Prior to it being succeeded by the IRO, the IGCR entered into resettlement agreements with the governments of nine Latin American States – Argentina, Brazil, Bolivia, Chile, Colombia, Ecuador, Paraguay, Peru, and Venezuela, most of whom had sent 'selection missions' to Europe, to select refugees with a desirable labour profile.[77]

It has been suggested by a number of scholars that the failure of participating States to permit the emigration of German and Austrian Jews without capital in part led to the decision of the Reich to shift its policy from one of expulsion to one of extermination. Wyman has claimed that the original policy of the Reich was clearly to force Jews to emigrate, but that "the shift to

---

the War (no date recorded) Myron C. Taylor Papers – Intergovernmental Committee on Political Refugees Correspondence, 1942–1943.

76 'Confidential Communication from the Director to the Chairman and Vice-Chairman of the Intergovernmental Committee' (July–August 1938) *Myron C. Taylor Papers – Evian Intergovernmental Committee Conference (folder 2) F.D.R. Library.*

77 USA: Congress Committee on Foreign Affairs, *Displaced Persons and the International Refugee Organization. Report of a Special Subcommittee on the Committee on Foreign Affairs* (1947) Government Printing Office, 61–62; Intergovernmental Committee, 'Memorandum by George L. Warren' (4 June 1947) *Myron C. Taylor Papers – Intergovernmental Committee on Political Refugees Correspondence, 1947–1954.* Agreements had also been entered into with Canada, United Kingdom, France, Belgium, Holland, Morocco, and Tunisia.

extermination came only after the emigration methods had failed, a failure in large part due to lack of countries open to refugees."[78]

> When the campaign against the Jews turned to large-scale terror in 1938, the refugee flow out of Germany failed to become a flood only because the dikes and dams of the world's immigration barriers held firm.[79]

Though it is beyond the scope of this book to determine whether 'the final solution' was not contemplated by the Reich until the inaction of Western States hampered the expulsion of German and Austrian Jews, it is possible to say with certainty that Western States immobilised the emigration of Jewish refugees in order to negotiate financially favourable terms that would limit the scope and content of those international obligations that Western States would otherwise assume, and to ensure that States of the New World would be incentivised by the prospect of becoming beneficiaries of Jewish capital.

In addressing the Jewish refugee problem, the IGCR devised a system of classification that permitted a presumption in favour of repatriation. It distinguished between 'short-term refugees' and 'long-term refugees' to describe those that could be repatriated in the immediate aftermath of the war, and those whose position would be protracted, though the objective in respect of both groups was ultimately repatriation. The stated purpose of the system was "to discourage exaggeration of the long-term problem, to be reluctant to accept individuals as permanently displaced from their own countries until it is clear that this in fact is the position [...]."[80] It stipulated that the distinction between long-term and short-term refugees would not be immediately obvious, and accordingly, it should be assumed that refugees were short-term refugees and therefore repatriable "until it is clear from the facts that they will have to be treated as [long-term refugees]."[81] In that respect, all refugees were classified as *prima facie* short-term refugees.

The basis for the presumption in favour of repatriation was never provided, but it was clear that it correlated not to the circumstances of refugees, but to the urgent need of States to repatriate in favour of economic recovery and the

---

78 David S. Wyman, *Paper Walls: America and the Refugee Crisis 1938–1941* (Pantheon Books 1985).

79 *Id.*

80 Intergovernmental Committee, *The Refugee Problem After the War* (no date recorded)) Myron C. Taylor Papers – Intergovernmental Committee on Political Refugees Correspondence, 1942–1943.

81 *Id.*

nationalisation of their own labour markets. States were hesitant to implement naturalisation programmes as such policies "might involve demobilized nationals remaining out of work while foreigners were allowed to compete in the labour market."[82] It would be necessary to await the stabilisation of national economies and the recovery of labour markets before naturalisation could be pursued as a policy, which would in turn require a presumption in favour of repatriation. The US in particular was eager to avoid the perception of forcible repatriation, while at the same time increasingly concerned with its extrication from the European refugee problem.[83] Wyman has argued that the US fell short of its potential as a refugee haven due to the solidity of the national origins quota system, and that the quotas were not widened because the chances of driving liberalised immigration legislation through Congress in the 1930s and early 1940s were virtually non-existent.[84]

Throughout the Jewish refugee crisis, the West remained firmly committed to the limitation of circumstances that may engage questions of SR, in particular, those entailing financial obligations. From its second meeting, the IGCR began to exclude certain categories of refugees to whom obligations would *not* be owed for various reasons, specifically those groups that made up the 'hard core,' including the elderly, who were "not suited to the conditions of settlement in other countries and will evidently be provided for by remittances from those who have emigrated."[85] In a letter to the Chairman of the IGCR, detailing the need to re-establish approximately 660,000 'involuntary emigrants,' those with various disabilities and incapacitations were included in the number of refugees that could be eliminated from immediate concern, and who in any case, "would prefer not to leave the country of origin."[86] It was deduced at a very early stage that "it might, in consequence, be that our

82 *Id.*

83 Tommie Sjöberg, *The Powers and the Persecuted: The Refugee Problem and the Intergovernmental Committee on Refugees (IGCR), 1938–1947* (Lund University Press 1991) 58.

84 David S. Wyman, *The Abandonment of the Jews: America and the Holocaust, 1941–1945* (Pantheon Books 1984) 209.

85 'Speech by Myron C. Taylor (USA) Intergovernmental Committee to Continue and Develop the Work of the Evian Meeting' (3 August 1938) *box 3, Myron C. Taylor Papers – Evian Intergovernmental Committee Conference (folder 2), July–August 1938.*

86 Intergovernmental Committee, 'Intergovernmental Committee to Continue and Develop the Work of the Evian Meeting: Copy of a letter dated 19 August, 1938, to the Chairman of the Committee from the Chairman of the United States of American Delegation' (19 August 1938) *Myron C. Taylor Papers – Evian Intergovernmental Committee Conference (folder 2), July–August 1938.*

immediate problem would consist in the need to resettle approximately 300,000 people in a first period, say of five years."[87]

Resistance to resettlement was consistently reasserted by the West in its attempts to resolve the Jewish refugee crisis. The Bermuda Conference of 1943 was convened by the UK and the US to discuss the question of the Jewish refugee, thought by many to have in fact been organised to placate an agitated public rather than to find solutions to the refugee problem.[88] During proceedings, both States rejected any negotiation with the Reich government for orderly emigration, on the grounds that "many of the potential refugees are empty mouths for which Hitler has no use" and that their release "would be relieving Hitler of an obligation to take care of these useless people."[89] The delegates also rejected the proposal to send shipments of food as a violation of the Allied blockade of Axis Europe, despite having made an exception for German-occupied Greece in 1941.[90] The British delegates briefly considered Jamaica might accept 500 refugees, but like most of the discussions that took place during the Bermuda conference, the proposal found no resolution.[91] At the end of the conference, the Allied powers decided that the report and the recommendations should be kept secret, and released only a one-page bulletin to the press, stating that "military considerations" meant that the recommendations had to remain confidential.[92] Congressman Samuel Dickstein, chairman of the House Immigration Committee, declared: "Not even the pessimists among us expected such sterility."[93]

Much like the early responses to refugee crises, resistance to resettlement eventually gave way to repatriation as the only logical solution. In 1945, the UK informed the US that it was "strongly of the opinion that at least all persons

87 *Id.*

88 Jewish Agency official Arthur Lourie noted that "the whole procedure adopted by the British and American Governments with regard to the refugee question is directed towards quieting public opinion without undertaking anything effective." It was noted by many that the location was likely selected as wartime regulations restricted all access to the Island, and therefore excluded the press and other observers.

89 David S. Wyman, *The Abandonment of the Jews: America and the Holocaust, 1941–1945* (Pantheon Books 1984) 115.

90 USA: The White House, *Memorandum for the Secretary of State Hon. Norman H. Davis for the Necessary Action, F.D. R.* (8 November 1941) Myron C. Taylor Papers, Official File 3865, F.D.R. Library.

91 David S. Wyman, *The Abandonment of the Jews: America and the Holocaust, 1941–1945* (Pantheon Books 1984) 116.

92 *Id.*

93 *Id.*

displaced as a result of the war must be regarded as eventually or politically reparable."[94] Both the British and the Americans eventually closed access to their camps in their mutual zones in Germany and Austria. Britain denied admission to the camps in their zone to all that arrived after 30 June 1946.[95] The US followed suit in April 1947.[96]

4 The UNRRA and the Solution of Employment

Between 1939, when an additional protocol was added to the 1938 *Convention concerning the Status of Refugees coming from Germany*,[97] and 1946, when another agreement on travel documents was adopted at yet another intergovernmental conference,[98] international cooperation on the refugee question was limited to the creation of entities charged with the resolution of the crisis. On 9 November 1943, forty-four States signed the *Agreement Creating the United Nations Relief and Rehabilitation Administration,* pledging to plan, coordinate, administer, or arrange for the administration of measures for the relief of victims of war in any area under the control of any of the UN through the provision of food, fuel, clothing, shelter and other basic necessities, medical and other essential services through the United Nations Relief and Rehabilitation Administration (UNRRA).[99] During its short tenure as the international refugee authority, UNRRA prepared and arranged for the "return of prisoners and exiles to their homes and for assistance in the resumption of urgently needed agricultural and industrial production and the restoration of essential services."[100]

94 Tommie Sjöberg, *The Powers and the Persecuted: The Refugee Problem and the Intergovernmental Committee on Refugees (IGCR), 1938–1947* (Lund University Press 1991) 213.

95 Gil Loescher, John A. Scanlan, *Calculated Kindness: Refugees and America's Half-Open Door, 1945 to the Present* (Free Press 1986).

96 *Id.*

97 League of Nations, *Additional Protocol to the Provisional Arrangement and to the Convention, signed at Geneva on July 4th, 1936, and February 10th, 1938, respectively, concerning the Status of Refugees coming from Germany* (14 September 1939) LNTS Vol. CXCVIII, No. 4634.

98 UN, *Final Act of the Intergovernmental Conference on the adoption of a travel document for Refugees and Agreement relating to the issue of a travel document to refugees who are the concern of the Intergovernmental Committee on Refugees* (15 October 1946) UNTS Vol. XI, No. 150.

99 UN, *Agreement for United Nations Relief and Rehabilitation Administration* (Washington 9 November 1943) Article 1, Section 2.

100 *Id.*, preamble.

At the Third Session of the General Council of UNRRA in August 1945, the organisation assumed obligations for 'displaced persons otherwise eligible for care even though they are unwilling to be repatriated or returned to their homes.' In doing so, the UNRRA widened its authority to assist refugees, even without the consent of the State of origin.[101] In practice however, it was the Supreme Headquarters Allied Expeditionary Force (SHAEF), led by future US President Dwight D. Eisenhower, that assumed the obligations for the maintenance of DPs, and carried out almost all repatriations. It was not until July 1945, when SHAEF was liquidated, that maintenance for DPs was divided between the UNRRA and the occupying authorities of the Allied Governments in Germany, with the exception of the Soviet Union which did not permit UNRRA to carry out any activities in its occupied zone. The remaining Allied Governments each concluded separate agreements with UNRRA. Contrary to UNRRA's mandate, the Agreements it established with occupying powers established that the military forces of each State were in charge of administering all basic supplies, coordination of movements, transport in connection with repatriation, security, and maintenance of law and order. UNRRA was in essence only responsible for the administration of the centres that housed refugees, including coordination of the agencies working within them, and cooperation with military authorities in repatriation.[102]

Prior to the formation of UNRRA, labour resettlement schemes had been undertaken by the IGCR. A number of bilateral and tripartite agreements had been concluded between authorities of the occupied zones, third States, and the IGCR, for small-scale resettlement schemes based on the labour profile of DPs. Private entities were able to offer employment contracts and to negotiate agreements for the resettlement of new recruits through their national government. In those circumstances, the financial obligations associated with the schemes were born by those private entities, and the State of resettlement assumed political and legal obligations associated with the establishment and residence of the DP. After its reorganisation in 1943, the IGCR was prevented from dealing directly with DPs for resettlement without the invitation of a host government. In addition, the authorised activities of the IGCR were limited mainly to stateless Jewish refugees from Germany and

101 Louise W. Holborn, *Refugees, a Problem of Our Time: The Work of the United Nations High Commissioner for Refugees, 1951–1972, Volume 1* (Scarecrow Press 1975) 22.

102 Holborn, *id.*, 21.

Austria to the exclusion of other groups.[103] These limitations raised serious practical questions for the IGCR. Limited as it was in the scope of its activities, the IGCR in essence became an international employment agency, receiving requests from States for DPs with a specific labour profile, and coordinating their transportation with the ILO and the State of resettlement.

Among those settlement schemes, the Belgian and US Governments contracted to transfer 20,000 workers and their families – a total of about 60,000–70,000 people – from the US zone in Germany to Belgium to work for the Belgian Federation of Coal Mines.[104] The Netherlands accepted skilled nurses, and up to 8,500 single men and women artisanal and industrial workers, and France convinced 300 woodworkers and 180 family members to move from the US occupation zone to the French zone to be employed by the French Army.[105] The Canadian Department of Labour would routinely send the IRO quotas for twenty different types of labour, which the IRO would then try to fill.[106] The UK initiated a policy named *Westward Ho!* for the admission of unmarried manual labourers for unmanned industries.[107] Australia admitted 182,000 refugees (which it justified only by their "economic value" in the inner regions of the State).[108] The US *Displaced Persons Act* of 1948 admitted 200,000 DPs over two years,[109] but stipulated that 30% of visas were reserved

103 Tommie Sjöberg, *The Powers and the Persecuted: The Refugee Problem and the Intergovernmental Committee on Refugees (IGCR), 1938–1947* (Lund University Press 1991) 225.

104 UN, *Agreement I between Belgium and the United States of America Concerning the Status and Admission into Belgium of Displaced Persons at Present in the American Zone of Germany (Brussels 23 January 1947)* (1950) UNTS Vol. 23 No. 721.

105 USA: Department of State, 'Statement by Lieutenant-Colonel Jerry M. Sage, United States Army, Headquarters of European Command, Frankfurt, Germany, Before the House Subcommittee on Immigration and Naturalization' (2 July 1947) *Myron C. Taylor Papers – Intergovernmental Committee on Political Refugees.*

106 John Stoessinger, *The Refugee and the World Community* (University of Minnesota Press 1956) 122.

107 USA: Federal Congress, *Committee on Foreign Affairs, Displaced Persons and the International Refugee Organization. Report of a Special Subcommittee on the Committee on Foreign Affairs* (1947) Government Printing Office, 63; *Id.*, Stoessinger, 115.

108 Tommie Sjöberg, *The Powers and the Persecuted: The Refugee Problem and the Intergovernmental Committee on Refugees (IGCR), 1938–1947* (Lund University Press 1991) 225, citing: Michael Blakeney, 'Proposals for a Jewish Colony in Australia: 1938–1948' (1984) 46(3/4) Jewish Social Studies 277, 312.

109 The term 'displaced persons' referred to those that had not been formally denationalised, but whom nonetheless were displaced by the war.

for agriculturists and agricultural labourers; a provision intended to fulfil the needs of the US economy in the Midwest.[110]

UNRRA, and later its successor organisation, the IRO, in turn ran similar operations. In cooperation with the ILO, UNRRA created an occupational classification system in 1946, compiling information on the skills and capabilities of refugees. The first partial survey at the end of 1947 made it clear that the 330,000 refugees registered represented a rich source of labour in a world in which nearly all States were confronted with severe labour shortages.[111] This was common to the responses of all States – labour markets and economic stability were principal considerations in the assumption of obligations for DPs and refugees. The financial advantages gained by the contributions of resettled persons to national economies were weighted against the costs of resettlement, and the likelihood of DPs and refugees becoming a public charge. This led naturally to the preferential treatment of single men, and as a consequence, the creation of a 'hard core' of refugees that could neither be resettled nor repatriated.

5 The IRO and the Question of the 'Hard Core'

Founded in 1946, the International Refugee Organisation (IRO) was established as a temporary specialised UN agency, charged with arranging the care and repatriation or resettlement of European Jews in the wake of WWII. Just as the IGCR before it, "the IRO functioned as an enormous employment agency."[112] From its inception, the IRO considered its employment and vocational training programme to be an essential activity.[113] In assuming the resettlement mandate of the IGCR, one of the first objectives of the IRO was to update the information in the occupational classification system. In conjunction with a representative of the Employment Service from the US Department of Labor, the IRO developed a system of occupational registration and classification, which enabled labour resettlement programmes to proliferate

110 Leonard Dinnerstein, *America and the Survivors of the Holocaust* (Columbia University Press 1982) 116.

111 Louise W. Holborn, 'The League of Nations and the Refugee Problem' (1939) 203 Annals Am Acad Pol & Soc Sci 124, 274.

112 Tommie Sjöberg, *The Powers and the Persecuted: The Refugee Problem and the Intergovernmental Committee on Refugees (IGCR), 1938–1947* (Lund University Press 1991) 225.

113 Louise W. Holborn, 'The League of Nations and the Refugee Problem' (1939) 203 Annals Am Acad Pol & Soc Sci 124, 272.

and for DPs and refugees to have permanent resettlement options.[114] Under the programme, the occupational skills of refugees were classified, registered, tested and then graded on a scale from 'master craftsman' to 'helper,' verified, and pre-selected for resettlement.[115] By the time the IRO had been operational for six months, approximately half the total population of DPs and refugees under its mandate were actively employed or receiving vocational training.[116] Due to the success of the programme, a Division of Employment and Vocational Training was established at the IRO headquarters in Geneva.

In the aftermath of WWII, it became clear that the only truly viable solutions to the 'refugee problem' were resettlement or repatriation, though there was considerable preference for the latter, and a concerted effort was made to ensure that as many DPs and refugees as possible were repatriated.[117] Despite the preference for repatriation, labour resettlement schemes continued apace, and although certain problems arose under resettlement Agreements concluded by IGCR, the resettlement role of UNRRA, and later the IRO, was ultimately successful in resolving the question of the 'hard core'; over 700,000 displaced persons who did not want to be repatriated,[118] the vast majority of whom resided in the US Zone.[119] In concluding resettlement agreements, States placed considerable emphasis on the occupational skills of refugees.[120] The occupational data collected, upgraded, and classified by the IRO formed the basis of labour resettlement schemes,[121] thought the organisation was far more cautious of the circumstances in resettlement States than its predecessors, and used the protective elements of its mandate to assert its authority over living conditions. In taking over the agreements concluded between the

114 *Id.*

115 *Id.*, 272, 275.

116 *Id.*

117 League of Nations, 'Russian, Armenian, Assyrian, Assyro-Chaldean and Turkish Refugees' (1930) 11(11) LNOJ 1324, 1462, Article 2 (1)(a).

118 Intergovernmental Committee, 'Memorandum' (3 June 1947) *Myron C. Taylor Papers – Intergovernmental Committee on Political Refugees Correspondence, 1947–1954*.

119 'Memorandum' (3 June 1947) *Myron C. Taylor Papers – Confidential memorandum regarding Refugees by Myron C. Taylor, 1938–1947*. Official numbers of those under American control vary between 300,000 and 500,000. See: USA: Department of State, 'Statement by Lieutenant-Colonel Jerry M. Sage, United States Army, Headquarters of European Command, Frankfurt, Germany, Before the House Subcommittee on Immigration and Naturalization' (2 July 1947) *Myron C. Taylor Papers – Intergovernmental Committee on Political Refugees*.

120 Louise W. Holborn, 'The League of Nations and the Refugee Problem' (1939) 203 Annals Am Acad Pol & Soc Sci 124, 275.

121 *Id.*, 274.

IGCR and resettlement States, the IRO was dissatisfied with the conditions of labour provided in certain Agreements with Latin American States in particular, and organised special missions to the region for further investigations, later suspending the transfer of refugees to certain States for agricultural resettlement. The mandate of the IRO permitted it to enter into contracts with States or with occupying authorities for the care and maintenance of DPs and refugees "under the supervision of the Organization,"[122] and in concluding resettlement agreements, it would ensure the "protection of [the] legitimate rights and interests" of refugees and displaced persons subject to them.[123]

Under its Constitution, the IRO was responsible for refugees and DPs, whom it would assist "either to return to their countries of nationality or former habitual residence, or to find new homes elsewhere,"[124] but as the US Congress expressed, "[T]he IRO constitution is explicit about the secondary nature of resettlement."[125] Repatriation was the preference. In addition to the administration of material support, the IRO was also responsible for the legal and political protection of refugees and DPs, or as Holborn described it, "safeguarding the most essential rights of human beings."[126] This was something of an overstatement. In reality, the IRO Constitution referred only once to the rights of refugees in the context that they were "protected in their rights and legitimate interests," being their care, assistance, and useful employment.[127] At the time, the US government commented, "[i]t is to the credit of the IRO that it will not resettle displaced persons in doubtful conditions merely to enable a reduction in its load of care and maintenance."[128] A likely explana-

122 UN, *Constitution of the International Refugee Organization and Agreement on interim measures to be taken in respect of refugees and displaced persons* (15 December 1946) UNTS Vol. 18, No. 283, Article 2(2)(d).

123 *Id.*, Article 2(2)(j).

124 *Id.*, preamble, Article 2(1)(a).

125 USA: Congress Committee on Foreign Affairs, *Displaced Persons and the International Refugee Organization. Report of a Special Subcommittee on the Committee on Foreign Affairs* (1947) Government Printing Office, 60.

126 Louise W. Holborn, 'The League of Nations and the Refugee Problem' (1939) 203 Annals Am Acad Pol & Soc Sci 124, 313.

127 UN, *Constitution of the International Refugee Organization and Agreement on interim measures to be taken in respect of refugees and displaced persons* (15 December 1946) UNTS Vol. 18, No. 283 preamble.

128 USA: Congress Committee on Foreign Affairs, *Displaced Persons and the International Refugee Organization. Report of a Special Subcommittee on the Committee on Foreign Affairs*1947) Government Printing Office, 62.

tion for the perceived inadequacies of the agreements was that for some months the only States to have indicated their desire to cooperate with the organisation in admitting refugees for labour resettlement were Latin American States.[129]

In executing agreements for labour agreements, the overwhelming preference of States was for single young males, leaving women, children, the elderly, and the infirmed to make up that group of 'unrepatriables.' In total, they had numbered approximately 8 million – over 7 million of whom had been repatriated in the previous two years, most of them within a few months after liberation – but there remained the 'hard core' of over 700,000.[130] The continued presence of the hard core posed the occupying governments a serious financial problem, particularly the US. Sjöberg argues that the US emphasis on an immediate solution to the refugee problem originated primarily from the War Department's concern to be relieved of the economic burden for the refugees in the US occupation zone.[131] But the question of what to do with over half a million DPs that remained within the US zone was one to which zone personnel themselves lamented "we [have] no answer."[132]

The question was considered by US Congress in 1947, and in presenting the four possible solutions to the House Subcommittee on Immigration and Naturalization, Lieutenant-Colonel Jerry M. Sage warned, "the alternative of repatriation must, at this point, be definitely termed 'forcible repatriation'."[133] He advised strongly against the implementation of repatriation policy, warning that the practical realities of such a strategy would mean that those 'unrepatriable' persons "would have to be rounded up by the U.S. Constabulary or German Police and forced into repatriation trains with gun and bayonet."[134] As the UNGA had concluded a Resolution the year prior, stating that "no refugee or displaced persons [...] shall be compelled to return to their country of origin," the US was naturally cautious of apparent coercion.[135] The second

129 *Id.*, 61.

130 Intergovernmental Committee, 'Memorandum' (3 June 1947) *Myron C. Taylor Papers – Intergovernmental Committee on Political Refugees Correspondence, 1947–1954*.

131 Tommie Sjöberg, *The Powers and the Persecuted: The Refugee Problem and the Intergovernmental Committee on Refugees (IGCR), 1938–1947* (Lund University Press 1991) 211.

132 USA: Department of State, 'Statement by Lieutenant-Colonel Jerry M. Sage, United States Army, Headquarters of European Command, Frankfurt, Germany, Before the House Subcommittee on Immigration and Naturalization' (2 July 1947) *Myron C. Taylor Papers – Intergovernmental Committee on Political Refugees*.

133 *Id.*

134 *Id.*

135 UN General Assembly, *Refugees and Displaced Persons* (15 December 1946) A/RES/62.

alternative was to close the camps and assign the fulfilment of political and social rights to the German people. This was equally unviable as "the Germans have not forgotten the Nazi indoctrination which looked on the non-German as an inferior person to be exploited by the 'Master Race'."[136] Equally unconscionable was the indefinite financial maintenance of refugees, which would create a relationship of dependence, and perpetuate a heavy burden on the US taxpayer. The fourth, and as it was presented, only option, was resettlement. The US War Department considered that the resettlement of refugees should be undertaken by an entirely American civilian agency that would assume obligations for refugees in the US zone. That task eventually became the principle operational service provided by the UNRRA and later the IRO, but in practice, it remained firmly within the control of the US.

The division of legal, and financial and administrative obligations was a critical consideration when it came to the establishment of the IRO, though importantly, legal aspects would now be framed as 'protection.' During initial discussions, a fourth category was introduced; that of 'political aspects,' so that now, Member States spoke of 'political and legal protection' on one hand, and 'administrative and financial aspects' on the other. It was suggested by the Secretary-General not only that legal aspects and administrative and financial aspects were distinct and should be divided between organs, but that political and legal protection may also be treated as distinct. Either a single office could assume obligations for both political and legal protection, or these functions could also be divided between two organs. It was decided finally that these aspects of the refugee problem would be divided and classified under two banners; that of 'protection' and that of 'operation,' so that the Secretary-General was entrusted with the 'political and legal protection' of refugees,[137] and the IRO would assume the 'administrative and financial aspects,' including humanitarian relief.[138] The term 'responsibility' was confined to discussions of State sovereignty. This division of 'protection' and 'aid' as the two essential branches of a burgeoning framework of IRL permitted the relative stability of the meaning of protection for a number of decades that followed. During the period in question, it was unambiguous that the meaning of protection was constituted by the provision of a legal status and a number of

136 *Id.*

137 League of Nations, 'Russian, Armenian, Assyrian, Assyro-Chaldean and Turkish Refugees' (1930) 11(11) LNOJ 1324, 1462.

138 *Id.*, 1462; League of Nations, 'Eighth Meeting (Public, Then Private) Sixty-First Session of the Council' (1930) 11(11) LNOJ 1527, 1532.

limited rights and entitlements to the beneficiary, which he could claim against the State that conferred his 'protection.'

On 30 September 1953, the IRO was finally liquidated. During the four and a half years that it was operational, approximately 90% of all cash, goods, and personnel placed at its disposal were provided by voluntary denominational organisations.[139]

6 Conclusion

Despite efforts to classify the Jewish refugee 'problem' as distinct from previous crises, based on its unplanned and unmanaged nature, in reality it was treated no differently to the Russian, Armenian, and Greco-Turkish refugee crises, and did not represent a significant recalibration in the development of refugee protection nor in the theorisation and application of SR in burgeoning IRL. States continued to advocate for the almost immediate financial independence of the affected population in the context of resettlement, supported and subsidised by private charitable entities, and later prioritised swift repatriation where resettlement was not practicable on the desired scale.

The treatment of the Jewish refugee crisis depended largely on the same understanding as previous refugee crises, being that methods of relief were based in the resolution of a labour crisis. Those methods of relief devised to combat that central issue necessarily required limited freedom of movement and the right to enter and exit the territories of States. This was, however, a short-term solution. As this chapter demonstrated, the long-term objectives of Western States were to establish refugee settlements across those States of the 'New World;' further dividing the 'Global North' and 'Global South' in terms of those international obligations arising from early IRL.

The significant efforts that were expounded in exploring and pursuing these objectives were not matched by their success but must not be disregarded on that basis. Rather, it should be noted that from the very beginning of those international efforts to resolve significant refugee crises, the unwavering priority of Western States was the minimisation of circumstances potentially engaging SR, and the corresponding effort to contain international obligations in States of the 'New World.' Furthermore, it should be noted that much of the conduct of Western States was driven by a preoccupation with nascent IHRL and the concern – real or imagined – that IHRL and IRL

139 Louise W. Holborn, 'The League of Nations and the Refugee Problem' (1939) 203 Annals Am Acad Pol & Soc Sci 124, 146.

together posed a threat to State sovereignty. It is unsurprising therefore that the purpose of inter-governmental action was to ensure that refugee resettlement remained wholly a sovereign matter. This is clear from the proceedings of the Evian Conference and those internal communications that concerned it. Western interests drove the event and the total inflexibility of those States resulted in an entirely ineffectual international meeting, resolving nothing of substance. Instead, the Conference was an expression of a Western desire to exercise control over the resolution of the refugee crisis.

Many of these complications, priorities, and concerns were reflected in the work of the early international organisations established for the resolution of the Jewish (and later, European) refugee crisis. The inability of the IGCR to produce any concrete result was the direct consequence of the restrictive immigration laws and policies of those same States attempting to resolve the crisis through the mechanism of the IGCR. Its work was also significantly hampered by the question of capital transfer. As this chapter demonstrated, the history of capital transfer, and the participation of States in the material exploitation of Jewish refugees in efforts to remedy the 'no public charge' principle of so many immigration systems, has led several prominent historians of the Holocaust to conclude that this contributed in no small part to the murder of millions of people.[140]

The UNRRA and the IRO in turn ran similar operations to the IGCR in respect of prioritising employment as the primary solution to the refugee crisis, but were by comparison less encumbered by the inter-governmental nature of their predecessor. During its short tenure as the international refugee authority, UNRRA prepared and arranged for the "return of prisoners and exiles to their homes and for assistance in the resumption of urgently needed agricultural and industrial production and the restoration of essential services."[141] The IRO similarly considered the employment and vocational training programme to be an essential activity,[142] and was responsible for the labour resettlement of many DPs and refugees under its mandate.

140 See: David S. Wyman, *The Abandonment of the Jews: America and the Holocaust, 1941–1945* (Pantheon Books 1984); David S. Wyman, *Paper Walls: America and the Refugee Crisis 1938–1941* (Pantheon Books 1985); John Stoessinger, *The Refugee and the World Community* (University of Minnesota Press 1956).

141 UN General Assembly, *Transfer to the United Nations of the residual assets and activities of UNRRA (United Nations Relief and Rehabilitation Administration)* (18 November 1948) A/RES/241, preamble.

142 Louise W. Holborn, 'The League of Nations and the Refugee Problem' (1939) 203 Annals Am Acad Pol & Soc Sci 124, 272.

Throughout this period, the division of legal obligations on one hand, and financial and administrative obligations on the other, continued to be a critical consideration in the development of IRL, in particular the evolving scope and content of the term 'protection,' and formed the basis of multilateral efforts to provide solutions to the crisis, but as with previous refugee crises, this was reflective of a limited international consensus, and thus the early development of both the scope and content of refugee protection, and the theorisation and application of SR relative to it, was driven by the West in pursuit of specific interests.

PART 2

Theory

CHAPTER 4

Refugee Protection and State Responsibility in the 1951 Convention

1 Introduction

In the wake of WWII, and faced with the unprecedented scale of the refugee crisis it had created, a new international Convention was required to address the immense displacement. The 1951 *Convention Relating to the Status of Refugees* included several provisions that distinguished it from the Arrangements of 1922, 1924, 1926, and 1928, the Conventions of 1933 and 1938, the Protocol of 1939, and the Agreement of 1946. While previous instruments were substantively identical, the 1951 Convention was not only intended to "revise and consolidate previous international agreements relating to the status of refugees" but also to "extend the scope of and protection accorded by such instruments by means of a new agreement."[1] In doing so, the 1951 Convention achieved some modest, but critical legal innovations.

First, it discontinued the regime of statutory designation of refugees that had plagued the Arrangements and the pre-1951 Conventions that had extended the benefits of recognition to new populations by virtue of their former nationality.[2] The *ad-hoc* approach to the inclusion of certain groups in the Arrangements had been the principal cause of the constant revision of IRL.[3] Second, it drew a distinction between refugees and stateless persons – previously referred to as displaced persons and refugees, respectively – as separate groups with different juridical conditions, but it extend the benefit of the 1951 Convention to both groups, without distinction, where persecution on Convention grounds had affected their displacement, in recognition of the fact that one could be both a refugee and stateless, though neither condition was necessary for the fulfilment of the other. Third, it included as a provision

1 UN General Assembly, *Convention Relating to the Status of Refugees* (28 July 1951) UNTS 189, preambular paragraph 3.

2 Though it retained geographical and temporal limitations that were only removed by article 1(2) of the 1967 Protocol.

3 Though it limited the benefit of refugee status to those affected by "events occurring before 1 January 1951." Contracting States were, however, permitted to specify upon signature, ratification, or accession whether this would be understood to mean "events occurring in Europe *or elsewhere* before 1 January 1951."

 | DOI:10.1163/9789004722835_006

an obligation of the refugee "to the country in which he finds himself";[4] a highly irregular provision in a treaty that otherwise regulated State conduct, and unprecedented in previous instruments.

Finally, and in fulfilment of its preambular objectives, it resolved the persistent question of the scope and content of legal protection by acknowledging that the enduring nationality of the refugee was a separate matter to the conferral by the State of reception of diplomatic protection. It achieved this innovation in a number of ways. First, while previous instruments qualified the conferral of protection on the loss of nationality, the 1951 Convention treated the questions of enduring nationality and of refugee protection as distinct. This in itself made the scope and content of protection in the 1951 Convention exceptional among instruments of IRL, which previously relied on the presumption of severance as the basis for the conferral of refugee protection. Second, it incorporated several provisions that acknowledged the continuity of the relationship between the refugee and the State of origin. That is, that the assumption of obligations by the State of reception as provider of diplomatic protection did not affect the continuity of the State–subject relationship that exists between the State of origin and the refugee. In contrast to previous instruments, the 1951 Convention did not recognise denationalisation as a *fait accompli*. As a consequence, these provisions also linked the State of origin to the State of reception, creating a relationship between the two States in much the same way that the law of aliens linked the State of origin to the host State through the individual's nationality of the former and alienage in the latter. This innovation was fundamental to the development of the contemporary regime of IRL, and to the theorisation and application of SR within it.

Though it might appear that the 1951 Convention incorporated norms of SR only insofar as Article 38 provides for the referral of disputes relating to the interpretation or application of the Convention to the ICJ,[5] fundamental rules of SR may also be noted in two seemingly inconsequential provisions relative to countermeasures, and to circumstances precluding wrongfulness as they relate to the lawful use of such. Article 7 (exemption from reciprocity) and Article 8 (exemption from exceptional measures) implicitly permit the limited inclusion of refugees in the lawful use of countermeasures by States of reception in respect of States of origin, affecting nationals and refugees alike. Both

4 Article 2.

5 The provision provides in full: 'Any dispute between parties to this Convention relating to its interpretation or application, which cannot be settled by other means, shall be referred to the International Court of Justice at the request of any one of the parties to the dispute.'

Articles are unprecedented in previous instruments of IRL, and both rely on the continued nationality of the refugee. They are among the only provisions of the Convention that explicitly link the Contracting State, through the refugee, to the municipal laws of the State of origin.[6] Together, they are evidence of the most significant innovation of the 1951 Convention – its rejection of the presumption that the relationship between State and subject had been definitively severed, in favour of the presumption that the nationality of the refugee endured, irrespective of his status as such.

Articles 7 and 8 not only allowed States to differentiate between nationals on one hand, and refugees and aliens from the same State of origin on the other, but acknowledged the continued (though limited) legal effect of the State of origin's municipal laws on refugees despite their status as such, and obliged the State of reception to observe their effect. By extension, Articles 7 and 8 support a reading of the Convention as extending a modified form of diplomatic protection, in which the State of reception provided legal protection *irrespective* of the enduring nationality of the refugee, but with a number of notable exceptions, which *relied* on the enduring nationality of the refugee.

Chapter 4 considers the implications of Articles 7 and 8, and evaluates their implementation as part of unilateral countermeasures taken by States of reception against States of origin. Section 2 considers the scope and content of 'protection' in the 1951 Convention and challenges some conventions regarding the inherently human rights character of the instrument, and hence the meaning of protection. It argues that the benefit of the 1951 Convention was the provision of legal protection, in turn derived from the absence of diplomatic protection. It considers that in the intervening decades, the meaning of protection has lost its common definition and that as a consequence, it has been expanded and applied to a broad spectrum of activities, in particular, to the provision of humanitarian aid. Specifically, Section 2 engaged with the theory of surrogate protection. It argues that the theory of surrogacy largely evades the complexities of the interaction between States and individuals, and between States *inter-se* in the context of IRL, and legal realities that arise from both the 1951 Convention, and IL generally. It posits that much of the underlying presumptions that support the prevailing theories on protection and its meaning rely on a series of conceptual errors, some of which relate to the litigation of the 1951 Convention, and others that concern the recognition of factual causality of

6 The third provision in this category is Article 12: Personal Status, which provides for the continued effect of certain laws of the State of origin relating to the personal status of the refugee.

events causing refugee movement, based on rules of attribution taken from municipal law.

Section 3 considers the competing doctrines concerning the bonds of nationality, referred to as the 'presumption of severance' and the 'presumption of enduring nationality.' In considering Articles 7 and 8, it advances two arguments: First, and relative to IRL, that the most significant legal innovation of the 1951 Convention was the adoption of the presumption of enduring nationality and its rejection of the presumption of severance as the basis for the provision of protection as an international legal concept. Second, and relative to SR, it argues that these provisions permit the unilateral use of countermeasures by States of reception again States of origin affecting refugees as they affect nationals, based on the presumption of enduring nationality. It argues that while the overarching question of a legal status for refugees was of very minor consequence in early IRL, the question took on significantly more importance following WWII, in particular, where the issue of legal status interacted with questions of SR and the retention of State sovereignty. These preoccupations were exacerbated by the rapid development of IHRL, and the apprehension of many States that the two systems of IL would soon become indistinguishable. Section 3 posits that these concerns in part informed and guided the drafting of the 1951 Convention, which permitted certain dominant States ultimately to retain sovereignty over matters that fell within scope and content of IRL.

Section 4 analyses the scope and content of Article 7. It argues that the provision supports a reading of the 1951 Convention as extending a modified form of diplomatic protection to refugees, as the exemption from reciprocity recognised that as a notion, reciprocity was at the core of the legal status of aliens, and must therefore be applicable in some measure to refugees. In supports of this assertion, it posits that a critical feature of Article 7 is that it does not draw a distinction between refugees that are *de jure* stateless and those that retain the nationality of their State of origin, a feature that by contrast did not form part of the Arrangements nor of the early Conventions. It argues that Article 7 does not extend the protection of exception from legislative reciprocity until three years have lapsed, meaning the refugee is subject to the same legislative reciprocity as other aliens generally during the first three years of residence, during which time a refugee or stateless person maintains their connection with the legal regime of the State of origin, in furtherance of the presumption of enduring nationality. Section 4 argues that in that sense, the innovation of Article 7 is not only that it links the refugee with the laws of the State of origin, but that it links the State of *reception* with the external municipal legal regime of the State of origin.

Section 5 analyses the scope and content of Article 8, which obliges the State of reception to provide legal protection against the exceptional measures it would otherwise take in respect of nationals of the same State of origin, and argues that in that respect, Article 8 requires differential treatment of aliens and refugees of the same nationality. Much like Article 7, Article 8 acknowledges that refugees often formally retain the nationality of the State of origin, and that the link of nationality remains unaffected by the provision of refugee status. By way of examples, it provides evidence that the activities regulated by this provision have been subject to the enforcement of SR through the use of countermeasures and through litigation of those countermeasures under municipal regimes of constitutional law and immigration law, and in international courts and tribunals exercising jurisdiction over IHRL matters. It considers the legitimacy of those countermeasures subject to norms of SR, with particular reference to the defence of necessity.

Chapter 4 concludes that the application of SR norms to precepts of IRL are present in these provisions, which not only speak to the meaning of protection in the 1951 Convention, but to the enforcement of SR in respect of IRL – both the actions taken by States, and their legitimacy, and that in the context of countermeasures taken in respect of Articles 7 and 8 of the 1951 Convention, the requirements to comply with the most basic rules of SR are invariably unfulfilled. Instead such measures are to be viewed only as unlawful exercises of power, taken by Western States against comparatively weaker States.

2 The Scope and Content of Protection in the 1951 Convention

Much of the legal characterisation of the 1951 Convention depends on the distinction it draws between groups subject to the same jurisdiction – between refugees and nationals, and between refugees and aliens generally. This commonly turns on the meaning of the term 'protection' and its import to the object and purpose of the 1951 Convention. But the term does not have a common definition and consequently, has been applied broadly to refer to a whole spectrum of activities, from the minimum standards of treatment applicable prior to the formal recognition of refugee status, to the conferral of refugee status, to the provision of durable solutions, and from the coordination of technical services to the delivery of humanitarian activities, to name but a few.[7] This has created a number of problems for the meaning of protection,

7 Guy S. Goodwin-Gill, 'The Language of Protection' (1989) 1(1) IJRL 6, 7.

as this final category has proved particularly flexible.[8] First, the classification of non-State actors as capable of providing Convention protection, for example, relies in part on a lack of distinction between legal protection and humanitarian assistance. Storey has argued that Article 1D (excluding from the benefit of the Convention persons already receiving protection or assistance from organs or agencies of the UN other than the UNHCR) "stands as a clear testament to the fact that States are not the only entities that can afford protection under the Refugee Convention and indicates that protection under Article 1A (2) is also to be understood in the same functional sense [...]."[9] In this Storey conceives of 'protection and assistance' as referring conjunctively to a comprehensive approach to refugee protection, though the provision of assistance should not be conflated with the provision of legal protection, which was at all times a separate and distinct obligation of Contracting States. This is clear from the text of the Convention itself, which disjunctively provides in full at Article 1D:

> This Convention shall not apply to persons who are at present receiving from organs or agencies of the United Nations other than the United Nations High Commissioner for Refugees protection *or assistance*.
>
> When such protection *or assistance* has ceased for any reason, without the position of such persons being definitively settled in accordance with the relevant resolutions adopted by the General Assembly of the United Nations, these persons shall ipso facto be entitled to the benefits of this Convention.[10]

Second, it relies on imprecise language to obfuscate the need for legal justification. Apart from the 'term of art' that is 'protection' and its scope and content, the language of 'surrogacy' – in particular to describe the legal correlation between State obligations and individual rights – largely avoids rationalising the legal realities of that complex interaction. Some scholars have taken certain provisions of the cessation clause as the basis for the theory that the protection provided by the 1951 Convention is surrogate in nature.[11] Hathaway

8 As Goodwin-Gill notes, protection has become something of a term of art, obscuring the scope of an activity that ought to be fundamentally clear. *Id.*

9 James C. Hathaway, Hugo Storey, 'What Is the Meaning of State Protection in Refugee Law – A Debate' (2016) 28(3) International Journal of Refugee Law 480, 482.

10 Emphasis added.

11 Specifically, provisions (1), (4), (5), and (6).

and Foster have asserted that the purpose of refugee law is twofold: to afford surrogate protection pending the resumption or establishment of meaningful national protection, and to restore at-risk individuals to membership of a national community, the latter of which the authors consider to be "the Refugee Convention's central purpose."[12] The latter is achieved by the former, as "refugee law intervenes to afford surrogate or substitute national protection for the duration of the risk."[13] This infers the right to "enjoy basic rights and humane treatment until the above objective is achieved – that of renewed belonging in a community."[14] But the concept of 'surrogate national protection'[15] is rooted in a number of presumptions that are not borne out by the record.

As the authors refer to "surrogate national protection" it would seem that surrogacy is intended to infer the provision of protection on an equal footing to that of national protection; that is, that the refugee is to be treated as a national.[16] This is not the case. If by 'national protection' Hathaway and Foster refer to the rights and freedoms that accumulate to an individual by virtue of their nationality, then it must be said that their conception of 'surrogate protection' is fundamentally flawed. The benefit of the 1951 Convention is categorically *not* a substitute for national protection in this sense. As its provisions make abundantly clear, refugees are to be treated *as aliens*, and *not* as nationals in respect of the vast majority of the benefits that accumulate to them. The State of reception is not obliged by the 1951 Convention to accord to refugees the rights and freedoms that accumulate to nationals, except in a limited number of very specific circumstances.

Third, certain theories of protection generally consider the term only within the meaning of Article 1A(2) as the basis for the benefits that attach to refugee status, conflating the definition of protection with the definition of a Convention refugee. Storey considers that protection must be understood to have five qualities which operate as necessary but not sufficient requirements in order to satisfy the refugee definition set out in article 1A (2): willingness to protect, ability to protect, effectiveness, accessibility, and

---

12 James C. Hathaway, Michelle Foster, *The Law of Refugee Status* (2 edn, CUP 2014) 462–463. See also: James C. Hathaway, *The Rights of Refugees under International Law* (CUP 2010).

13 Hathaway & Foster, *id.*, 463.

14 UN High Commissioner for Refugees, *Note on International Protection* (1986) (A/AC.96/680) at [4]–[5].

15 James C. Hathaway, Michelle Foster, *The Law of Refugee Status* (2 edn, CUP 2014) 465.

16 *Id.*, 470: "[Article 1C2] [...] is predicated on the view that refugee status comes to an end if a refugee declines the surrogate protection of refugee status in favor of the national protection of her country of origin."

non-temporary durability.[17] However, if the scope of 'protection' is defined by the totality of the provisions of the 1951 Convention, it encompasses not only obligations in terms of State competencies, but also the extent to which States may exercise the sovereign right to limit or qualify the benefit of certain entitlements otherwise provided to nationals and aliens. These elements are integral to the definition of protection by virtue of its limitation.

Fourth, it assumes a level of implicit interconnectedness between IRL and IHRL that seems to require little justification. Goodwin-Gill posits that "[t]he protection of refugees has its origins in a human rights context, in the right of every human being to life, liberty and security, which may be jeopardized by breach of the principle of refuge," and that in the refugee law context, "protection encompasses an unrestricted human rights competence, contingent only on a sufficient connection between rights and solutions."[18] In Storey's view, the most pertinent area of IL for constructing a definition of protection is IHRL. Yet he acknowledges that even when considered as a set of norms governing State protection, IHRL does not yield anything definite, beyond the notion that States have a duty to protect their populations (not only limited to citizens) against violations of peremptory norms of IL.[19] There are a number of fundamental differences in the content and application of IHRL and IRL that mean the language of 'protection' and of 'surrogacy' are not simply a matter of semantics. IHRL does not distinguish between legal classes of persons. Its fundamental principles – universality and non-discrimination – mean that all persons are entitled to equal protection, with few limited exceptions. By contrast, the benefit of the 1951 Convention is the provision of legal protection derived from the absence of diplomatic protection, itself a derivative of the law of aliens. In respect of SR, this is a critical distinction.

Fifth, and in connection to this presumption, the argument that the 1951 Convention is a living instrument and therefore requires incorporation of IHRL developments, relies on the extensive litigation of individual civil disputes subject to IHRL, and the importance attached to the absence of an enforcement mechanism in IRL in favour of the availability of IHRL remedies. This appears to be based on the fact that the vast majority of individual cases concern alleged violations of either the application of Article 1 or Article 33. As

---

17 James C. Hathaway, Hugo Storey, 'What Is the Meaning of State Protection in Refugee Law – A Debate' (2016) 28(3) International Journal of Refugee Law 480, 481.

18 Guy S. Goodwin-Gill, 'The Language of Protection' (1989) 1(1) IJRL 6.

19 James C. Hathaway, Hugo Storey, 'What Is the Meaning of State Protection in Refugee Law – A Debate' (2016) 28(3) International Journal of Refugee Law 480, 482.

discussed in the introduction, points 4 and 5 rely on the perceived frailty of the 1951 Convention in the absence of a specific judicial mechanism.

The imperative to establish some kind of authority for the attribution of SR has long been advanced by refugee law scholars, and its absence is often considered a failure of IRL. Hathaway refers to this as a "tragic failure to establish an effective system for oversight of duties under the Convention,"[20] and notes that "the refugee regime is today the only widely subscribed UN human rights regime that lacks an independent supervisory mechanism capable of defining its terms in an authoritative way."[21]

> The continuing viability of this careful compromise embedded in the architecture of the Convention and Protocol is, however, increasingly threatened by the failure to establish an independent mechanism to supervise compliance with obligations or to ensure the fair distribution of protection burdens and responsibilities arising thereunder.[22]

Ziegler notes that IRL (like IHL) relies on a decentralised scheme of implementation "absent robust international supervisory mechanisms."[23] Chetail relies on this absence to justify the assertion that IHRL has superseded IRL as the provider of protection (though Chetail has since modified this position to describe the relationship as one of 'complementarity'),[24] noting that human rights law addresses the conspicuous lack of a complaint mechanism in the 1951 Convention.[25] Goodwin-Gill has also stated that IHRL has eclipsed IRL as the "primary source of refugee protection."[26] He argues that multilateral instruments or regional arrangements based on IHRL may provide for supervisory, enforcement or reporting mechanisms, and thus expand the range of

20 *Id.*, fn 26.

21 *Id.*, 484.

22 James C. Hathaway, 'The Architecture of the UN Refugee Convention and Protocol' in Costello, Foster and McAdam (eds), *The Oxford Handbook of International Refugee Law* (OUP 2021) 171, 172.

23 Ruvi Ziegler, 'International Humanitarian Law and Refugee Protection' in Costello, Foster and McAdam (eds), *The Oxford Handbook of International Refugee Law* (OUP 2021) 221, 222.

24 See generally: Vincent Chetail, 'Moving Towards an Integrated Approach of Refugee Law and Human Rights Law' in Costello, Foster and McAdam (eds), *The Oxford Handbook of International Refugee Law* (OUP 2021) 202.

25 *Id.*, 213.

26 *Id.*

remedies available to those whose rights may be violated, or who may face danger if expelled or *refouled*.

> The lack of specific legal obligations is a feature of the middle ground, where the functional responsibilities of UNHCR diverge from the legal obligations of States; the absence of specific rules, however, does not imply an absence of principles; the law may be confined to the periphery of action, but a creative use of human rights resources can only enhance the legal status of refugee and asylum-seeker.[27]

In embracing IHRL and its contributions to refugee protection, there appears to be at least some imprecision in the evaluation of SR *vis-á-vis* where the refugee is a subject of IL and where the refugee is a subject of municipal laws derived from IL. As discussed in the introduction to this book, the characterisation of an act of a State as internationally wrongful is governed by IL alone, and is not affected by the characterisation of the same act as lawful or otherwise in municipal law. Much of the attribution of SR in IRL appears to rely on this conceptual error – the recognition of factual causality, based on rules of attribution taken from municipal law, and the proscribed nature of certain conduct within domestic contexts. The rights and obligations that are conferred and imposed by the 1951 Convention might be better served through IHRL and through municipal legal frameworks such as immigration law or constitutional law, than they are through the norms of DP taken from traditional SR, but whether the norms created by these provisions have been subsumed by IHRL, or are better protected by municipal laws, is inconsequential to their validity as international legal obligations of States *inter-se*.

The perceived failure or frailty might be overcome if scholars were to accept the 1951 Convention as an instrument of PIL, governing the horizontal relationship between States, and relinquished the need to reconcile the instrument as one of IHRL, governing the vertical relationship between State and refugee, while lamenting its inability to fit as an inherent failure of the instrument. The notion that in the absence of clear legal obligations, and the notable absence of an enforcement mechanism, IRL is constituted by principles, is in itself a reflection of the limitation implicit in the characterisation of the 1951 Convention as an instrument of IHRL, to the exclusion of municipal legal systems as guarantors of SR in IRL.

27 Guy S. Goodwin-Gill, 'The Language of Protection' (1989) 1(1) IJRL 6, 16.

Leaving aside the practical impediments to establishing such an authority and the obvious challenge in garnering support for it, the necessity of such an authority is perhaps not as apparent as some might believe. It is perhaps more a question of implementation than it is the variation of interpretations. It is also a reflection of the lack of provision for asylum procedures, which are "compensated by the procedural guarantees endorsed in human rights treaties."[28] As these procedures form the basis of litigation in refugee law, the body of jurisprudence relative to IRL is, of course, skewed by IHRL as the common judicial forum.

An explanation for the obscurity of Articles 7 and 8, both in law and in scholarship, may indeed be due to their being superseded in relevance by the remedies provided by domestic and IHRL regimes and other complementary municipal laws. As Kolb notes in relation to diplomatic protection:

> To some extent, modern human rights law [...] with [its] individual remedies, [has] overshadowed the older layer of [diplomatic protection]. The individual now has a series of remedies he can pursue without having to receive the blessings of discretionary [diplomatic protection] by the home State.[29]

Despite this, those provisions remain subject to the norms of SR, which is not made redundant by the availability of municipal remedies.[30] Despite having lost much of their relevance in modern IRL, the importance of these provisions cannot be overlooked simply because they are more effectively litigated under other legal regimes. The primary norms created by these provisions continue to impose international obligations on States, despite any breaches of equivalent municipal laws, which remain internal affairs. The preoccupation with the absence of an IRL enforcement mechanism obscures one further critical and related issue in the theorisation and application of SR in IRL. That is the extent to which States of reception have unilaterally taken countermeasures against States of origin in respect of nationals of the latter, irrespective of refugee status; such measures not being litigated in IHRL courts and tribunals, but limited in most cases to municipal regimes of immigration law.

---

28 Vincent Chetail, 'Moving Towards an Integrated Approach of Refugee Law and Human Rights Law' in Costello, Foster and McAdam (eds), *The Oxford Handbook of International Refugee Law* (OUP 2021) 202, 212.

29 Robert Kolb, *The International Law of State Responsibility* (Edward Elgar 2018) 186.

30 *Id.*, 187.

3 The Presumption of Severance and the Presumption of Enduring Nationality

Of the many varied theories of 'protection,' a number appear to be based on assumptions regarding the concept of nationality in the 1951 Convention. The 1951 Convention and its precedents were each based on certain presumptions regarding nationality, which defined the conditions in which the State of reception could become the provider of legal protection. Prior to 1951, instruments were based on what might be called the presumption of severance; the notion that the legal bond between national and State of origin had been definitively severed through the act of denationalisation. By contrast, the 1951 Convention adopted what might be called the presumption of enduring nationality. Neither the determination of persecution by the State of origin nor the conferral of protection by the State of reception depended on the formal withdrawal of nationality, in contrast to the treatment of Russian, Armenian, Greek, and Turkish populations under previous instruments. The 1951 Convention did not recognise the mass denationalisation of Jews across Europe as having the same legal effect on their enduring nationality as did previous instruments. Contracting States would provide diplomatic protection, but the refugee would remain tied to the State of origin for certain purposes.

Contracting States retained the sovereign right to apply differential treatment to nationals, aliens generally, and refugees in certain circumstances and in a limited, prescribed manner, based on the presumption of enduring nationality, aligning IRL with the law of aliens, rather than with nascent IHRL. This sovereign right of Contracting States to permit differential treatment between classes of persons subject to their jurisdiction was essential to obtaining broad support for the 1951 Convention. It alternately guaranteed the treatment of the refugee at least as favourable or the same as that accorded to nationals,[31] his treatment on the same terms or not less favourable than that accorded to aliens generally,[32] and his treatment akin to the most favourable treatment accorded to nationals of a foreign country in the same circumstances.[33] This in itself was a significant development in the status of refugees. As Robinson noted in his commentary, the treatment accorded to refugees by the 1951 Convention was frequently more favourable than that accorded by any of the previous Agreements. While the Conventions on Russian and German refugees accorded to them no more than the most favourable treatment

---

31 Article 4; Article 14; Article 16; Article 20; Article 22; Article 23; Article 24; Article 29.

32 Article 7; Article 13; Article 18; Article 19; Article 21; Article 26.

33 Article 15; Article 17.

granted to foreigners in respect of the social security and relief provisions, the 1951 Convention "equalize[d] their status with that of nationals of the country of refuge."[34]

The importance of striking this balance between classes of person is clear from the drafting history of the Convention. At the first session of the drafting Committee in Lake Success, the Committee used as the basis for its discussions, a commentary on a draft Convention prepared by the Secretary-General, who wrote:

> Refugees who have been deprived or their nationality or who in fact no longer enjoy the protection and assistance of their country of origin run the risk of not being recognized in every place as persons before the law, owing to the difficulty of submitting the documents issued to them in their country of origin which constitute evidence of their identity and status [...]. In any case, they no longer enjoy the various advantages attaching to the possession of a nationality and they live in the abnormal conditions peculiar to de jure or de facto stateless persons.[35]

Fortín notes that during the discussion of the draft Convention by the Committee, the representative of Israel, Mr Robinson, stated that the terms 'stateless *de facto*' and 'stateless *de jure*' employed in that text were open to question so far as, statelessness being a legal concept, it could *only* be *de jure*, and that what was designated in the draft Convention as stateless *de facto*, 'was in effect merely the lack of diplomatic protection.'[36] This recognition of *de facto* statelessness as the absence of diplomatic protection is enormously important. It recognises that among those that sought refuge, in essence, there was little differences between those that were subject to denationalisation decrees, and those that retained documentation. Both groups were stateless, and any distinction drawn between them on the basis of *de jure* and *de facto* classifications was in fact moot. From a purely legal perspective, the effect of dena-

34 Nehemiah Robinson, *Convention Relating to the Status of Refugees: Its History, Significance and Contents* (Institute of Jewish Affairs 1952) 7.

35 Ad Hoc Committee on Refugees and Stateless Persons, *Ad Hoc Committee on Statelessness and Related Problems, Status of Refugees and Stateless Persons – Memorandum by the Secretary-General* (3 January 1950) (E/AC.32/2) 14, cited in Antonio Fortín, 'The Meaning of Protection in the Refugee Definition' (2000) 12(4) International Journal of Refugee Law 548, 561.

36 Ad Hoc Committee on Statelessness and Related Problems, *Summary Record of the Fourth Meeting* (E/AC.32/SR.4) cited in Fortín, *id.*, 561.

tionalisation was no different to an unwillingness or inability to avail oneself of protection.

Though the overarching question of a legal status for refugees was of very minor consequence in early IRL, preoccupations with the limitation of SR and the retention of State sovereignty persisted where the question became more urgent following WWII. This was exacerbated by preoccupations with nascent IHRL and the apprehension that the two systems of IL would become so-interconnected as to be indistinguishable. These concerns in part informed and guided the drafting of the 1951 Convention, which allowed the overarching framework of international obligations to remain limited to a degree that certain dominant States retained an acceptable level of sovereignty and were assured that the benefits of the Convention would extend only to a limited group of beneficiaries.

Contrary to the belief that "[t]he drafters of the Refugee Convention generally understood the substance of the refugee definition to be broad and applicable to almost all known categories or groups of refugees,"[37] the abandonment of the statutory framework, which defined refugees by reference to State of origin, gave rise to a number of concerns about the 'blank cheque' that would be written in doing so. The International Confederation of Free Trade Unions had argued that the term 'refugee' should be made to include "possible future victims who qualify as refugees if no arbitrary deadline were stipulated,"[38] however, the open-endedness of this proposition was not widely supported. It was considered that "[t]oo vague a definition, which would amount [...] to a blank cheque, would not be sufficient."[39] In place of a statutory regime defined by States of origin, the Drafting Committee instead admitted geographical and temporal limitations that tied the refugee to events occurring before 1 January 1951, either in Europe or in Europe and elsewhere.[40] A

37 Terje Einarsen, 'Part One Background, Drafting History of the 1951 Convention and the 1967 Protocol' in Andreas Zimmermann, Felix Machts and Jonas Dörschner (eds), *The 1951 Convention Relating to the Status of Refugees and its 1967 Protocol: A Commentary* (OUP 2011) 64, 66.

38 UN Conference of Plenipotentiaries on the Status of Refugees and Stateless Persons: International Confederation of Free Trade Unions, *Proposals Concerning The Draft Convention Relating To The Status Of Refugees* (6 July 1951) A/CONF.2/NGO/5.

39 UN, *Statement by the representative of the US in the Ad Hoc Committee on Statelessness and Related Problems, Summary Record of the Third Meeting* (26 January 1950) E/AC.32/SR.3, 37. See also: Paul Weis, 'Legal Aspects of the Convention of 21 July 1951 Relating to the Status of Refugees' (1953) 30 BYBIL 478, 488, 479.

40 See Article 1B(1).

broader definition would make it difficult for States "to sign a blank cheque and undertake obligations toward future refugees, the origin and number of which would be unknown."[41] A limited temporal scope "enable[d] Governments to know at the time they become parties to the Convention the extent of their obligations."[42]

As it was in previous instruments, the concept of protection in the 1951 Convention was intended, at least at draft phase, to refer solely to diplomatic protection, rather than to 'internal national protection.'[43] An amendment submitted by France, the UK, and the US, was designed to exclude 'internal refugees' – those that retained the diplomatic protection of the State of nationality or habitual residence – so that the Convention would "not apply to a person who is recognized by the competent authorities of the country in which he has taken residence as having the rights and obligations which are attached to the possession of the nationality of that country."[44] The exclusion of 'internal refugees' would also have a material impact, as it would minimise "the possible appeals to the High Commissioner for material assistance."[45]

Initially, there had been strong support by Belgium, Canada and the UK for a simple global definition of the term 'refugee,' but the US had opposed this vigorously on the grounds that such a definition would commit the UN to the protection of unknown groups of refugees and "divest the Assembly of its freedom of action to deal with new refugee situations that might arise in the future."[46] The US anticipated the support of Canada, Belgium, and the United Kingdom in giving "strong leadership" to the effort to "amend Article 1 of the Convention by substituting a simple global definition in exchange for the

41 UN Ad Hoc Committee on Statelessness and Related Problems, *Report of the Ad Hoc Committee on Statelessness and Related Problems, Lake Success, New York, 16 January to 16 February 1950* (17 February 1950) E/1618, E/AC.32/5, Annex II: Comments of the Committee on the Draft Convention Relating to the Status of Refugees, 38.

42 *Id.*, 39.

43 Antonio Fortín, 'The Meaning of Protection in the Refugee Definition' (2000) 12(4) International Journal of Refugee Law 548.

44 *Position Paper Prepared in the Department of State* (Washington, 9 September 1950) Foreign Relations of the United States, 1950, The United Nations; The Western Hemisphere, Volume II.

45 *Id.*

46 *Id.* See also: UN Ad Hoc Committee on Statelessness and Related Problems, *Report of the Ad Hoc Committee on Statelessness and Related Problems, Lake Success, New York, 16 January to 16 February 1950* (17 February 1950) E/1618, E/AC.32/5, Annex II: Comments of the Committee on the Draft Convention Relating to the Status of Refugees, 39.

present text which defines refugees by categories."[47] The 'present text' referred to the proposal by ECOSOC in Resolution 248(IX)A to maintain the definition provided in the Constitution of the IRO as persons belonging to certain specified groups, including victims of the Nazi or fascist regimes, Spanish Republicans, and persons who were considered refugees before the outbreak of the Second World War (being persons designated as refugees under the Arrangements and the 1933 Convention).[48] This appealed to the US as "it define[d] the refugees to be protected by the United Nations precisely and cover[d] *all existing categories of refugees* requiring international protection in their civil status."[49] The US considered that it had "given strong leadership in securing the present text which covers all present clearly identified groups of refugees who lack civil status and require international protection."[50] It considered the definition "not narrow but precise,"[51] with any refugees who could be clearly identified in the future to be added later to the competence of the High Commissioner by the General Assembly. Until then, "the General Assembly should retain freedom of action"[52] where new refugee situations arose.

Chief among the concerns of the US was the inclusion of persons that *did not lack citizenship*, and therefore did not require diplomatic protection. In internal State documents, the US was very clear that the diplomatic nature of the 1951 Convention should be explicitly recognised. In a position paper on the Convention, the State Department affirmed that "[T]he convention in effect establishes the civil status of refugees in countries of residence whose national legislation fails to provide such status."[53] The State Department con-

---

47 *Position Paper Prepared in the Department of State* (Washington, 9 September 1950) Foreign Relations of the United States, 1950, The United Nations; The Western Hemisphere, Volume II.

48 The Resolution requested the governments of Members of the UN and other states "to provide, after the termination of the IRO, the necessary legal protection for refugees who have been the concern of the IRO under its mandate." See: UN Economic and Social Council, *Resolution 248(IX)(A): Study of Statelessness* (6 and 8 August 1949) E/RES/248 (IX)(A); UN, *Constitution of the International Refugee Organization and Agreement on interim measures to be taken in respect of refugees and displaced persons* (15 December 1946) UNTS Vol. 18, No. 283, Annex I, Part I. Emphasis added.

49 UN Economic and Social Council, *Resolution 248(IX)(A): Study of Statelessness* (6 and 8 August 1949) E/RES/248(IX)(A).

50 *Id.*

51 *Id.*

52 *Position Paper Prepared in the Department of State* (Washington, 9 September 1950) Foreign Relations of the United States, 1950, The United Nations; The Western Hemisphere, Volume II 542, 546.

53 *Id.*, 545.

sidered it a "great danger" that the adoption of a simple global definition "would involve the United Nations in responsibilities for so-called internal refugees such as those in Germany, Greece, India, Pakistan and in China *who do not require international protection because they enjoy the rights of citizenship* in their present countries of residence but who nevertheless raise serious problems of material assistance."[54]

At the same time, much effort was put into maintaining clear distinctions between future human rights instruments and the 1951 Convention. At the core of the US concern was not necessarily that the 1951 Convention would make reference to economic and social rights, but that the social and economic benefits that might accrue to the refugee under the Convention would then be included in the Covenant on Human Rights,[55] also in draft phase. The US State Department instructed its delegation to the UNGA on the drafting of the Covenant that:

> The prior consideration of the Refugee Convention would very likely prejudice the views of other delegations against the position of the United States with respect to some aspects of the draft Covenant on Human Rights. For example, provisions on certain economic and social rights are set forth in the Refugee Convention, and the prior consideration of this Convention may result in added pressure by other delegations for the inclusion of articles on economic and social rights in the draft Covenant on Human Rights also.[56]

In order to avoid such an event, the US considered that as a procedural matter, it should undertake to secure consideration of the draft Covenant on Human Rights *prior* to the Refugee Convention.[57] Canada shared the concern that the 1951 Convention would result in an expansive system of individual rights. The

54 *Id.*, 546. Emphasis added.

55 The drafting of the covenants on human rights was undertaken in March 1947 by the Drafting Committee, a sub-organ of the Commission on Human Rights composed of eight members. Originally, the drafters intended to create one document covering all rights enumerated in the Universal Declaration of Human Rights of 1948. Eventually, the UNGA would adopt the International Covenant on Economic and Social Rights and the International Covenant on Civil and Political Rights as well as the Optional Protocol.

56 *Department of State Instruction, to the United States Delegation to the Fifth Regular Session of the General Assembly* (Washington, 5 September 1950) Foreign Relations of the United States, 1950, The United Nations; The Western Hemisphere, Volume II.

57 *Id.* Delegates were urged to support the recommendation that the draft Covenant be reconsidered at the 1951 session of the Commission on Human Rights, slated to occur after the GA resolution on the 1951 Convention, and that they should urge that the

Canadian Prime Minister was especially concerned that individual rights would be asserted by political asylees from the USA – specifically, communists escaping McCarthy's Red Scare, seeking asylum in Canada.[58] Writing to the Canadian delegation during the Conference of Plenipotentiaries, the State's Acting Under-Secretary of State expressed concern that, as it was, the Convention would "almost certainly give rise to misunderstanding as to its consequences." In particular:

> [T]he Convention was *between the countries that were parties and did not confer any rights on individuals*. There would, however, almost certainly be a general feeling that it did confer individual rights or, alternatively, that legislation should be passed giving parallel individual rights under domestic law.[59]

For these reasons, the notion that States explicitly expressed concerns regarding the risks of unlimited diplomatic protection in the codification of one international legal regime, but wholeheartedly embraced it in the drafting of another contemporaneous treaty, is not supported by the record. As it related to refugees, diplomatic protection was applied in a number of ways from the inception of the first Arrangements through to the pre-1951 Conventions. These instruments were a kind of real-time experiment in IL as it related to diplomatic protection, and errors were noted and corrected as time went on and new crises appeared. As detailed in Chapter 3, internal communications in several States at the time of the Convention's drafting reveal two principal concerns: first, there was a keen interest among States generally to maintain the legal concept of 'protection' as diplomatic in nature, and second, that a great deal of effort was expended to ensure that the potentially expansive effects of nascent IHRL would be clearly delineated from IRL so that Contracting States might continue to exercise the right to permit differential treatment among classes of persons. As with previous efforts to control the trajectory of IL, the US was instrumental in the attempt to maintain the *status quo* of diplomatic protection, and ensure that refugees were defined specifically with reference to the group that required protection, resisting efforts to incorporate

---

discussion in the General Assembly concerning the draft Covenant "should as far as possible be in general terms only."

58 *Id.*, 2–3.

59 USA: Department of State, *Memorandum: Acting Under-Secretary of State for External Affairs, with attached letter to the Deputy Minister of Citizenship and Immigration and draft telegram* (4 July 1951) Library and Archives Canada (T-2367), 2. Emphasis added.

a global definition of the term into the 1951 Convention. Though this was ultimately unsuccessful, it is critical to note the number of States that endorsed the US position and the impetus for pursuing a limited application of the 1951 Convention.

The fundamental importance of diplomatic protection in IL and the right of States to assert it was stated by the PCIJ in the *Mavrommatis Concessions in Palestine* case:

> It is an elementary principle of international law that a State is entitles to protect its subjects, when injured by acts contrary to international law committed by another State, from whom they have been unable to obtain satisfaction through the ordinary channels. By taking up the case of one of its subjects and by resorting to diplomatic action or international judicial proceedings on his behalf, a State is in reality asserting its own rights – its right to ensure, in the person of its subjects, respect for the rules of international law.[60]

Since the inception of the 1951 Convention, the scope of refugee protection as it encompasses diplomatic protection has been further reinforced by the *Protocol to the European Convention on Consular Functions* of 1967,[61] and the ILC's *Draft Articles on Diplomatic Protection* of 2006.[62] The former provides that signatory States recognise "the right of a Contracting Party to decline to admit a consular officer as being entitled to act on behalf of, or otherwise concern himself with, a national of his State who is a refugee."[63] The consular officer of the State where the refugee has his habitual residence shall be entitled to protect such a refugee and to defend his rights and interests in conformity with the Convention, in consultation with the UNHCR.[64] The latter provides that a State may exercise diplomatic protection in respect of a stateless person or a refugee who, at the date of injury and at the date of the official presentation of the claim, is lawfully and habitually resident in that State,

60 See generally: Robert Kolb, *The International Law of State Responsibility* (Edward Elgar 2018) 12.

61 Council of Europe, *Protocol to the European Convention on Consular Functions concerning the Protection of Refugees* (1967) (ETS 61A).

62 International Law Commission, *Draft Articles on Diplomatic Protection with commentaries* (2006).

63 Article 2(1).

64 Article 2(2).

though this does not apply in respect of an injury caused by an internationally wrongful act of the State of nationality of the refugee.[65]

As much of the discourse on protection is limited in its scope to matters arising from Articles 1 and 33 of the 1951 Convention, to the exclusion of other, seemingly less important provisions, the import of those other Articles to the concept of protection is somewhat obscured. Articles 7 and 8 of the Convention reveal much about the extent of legal protection; what it does and does not entail, its scope and content, and the relevance and application of SR to IRL. Furthermore, these articles do not support a reading of the 1951 Convention as providing surrogate protection, or as being an early iteration of IHRL, but rather that it is, like its predecessors, an instrument of PIL, creating binding obligations between States, with the notable difference that it reconceived of nationality, and in doing so, admitted some fundamental precepts of SR.

4 Article 7: Exemption from Legislative Reciprocity

Of the five provisions in the 1951 Convention that concern the juridical condition of refugees, Article 7 provides that refugees enjoy exemption from legislative reciprocity. Legislative reciprocity allows some aliens to enjoy rights in certain States subject to reciprocal treatment, so that State A grants certain rights and benefits to nationals of State B where State B has granted those same rights and benefits to nationals of State A. The opposite is also true: State B may refuse to grant a right or benefit to nationals of State A where State A refuses to grant that right or benefit to nationals of State B. Article 7 provides in full:

1. Except where this Convention contains more favourable provisions, a Contracting State shall accord to refugees the same treatment as is accorded to aliens generally.
2. After a period of three years' residence, all refugees shall enjoy exemption from legislative reciprocity in the territory of the Contracting States.
3. Each Contracting State shall continue to accord to refugees the rights and benefits to which they were already entitled, in the absence of reciprocity, at the date of entry into force of this Convention for that State.

---

65 Draft Article 8. The ILC's explanatory notes on Draft Article 8 provide that it is "an exercise in progressive development of the law" which "departs from the traditional rule that only nationals may benefit from the exercise of diplomatic protection and allows a State to exercise diplomatic protection in respect of a non-national where that person is either a stateless person or a refugee."

4. The Contracting States shall consider favourably the possibility of according to refugees, in the absence of reciprocity, rights and benefits beyond those to which they are entitled according to paragraphs 2 and 3, and to extending exemption from reciprocity to refugees who do not fulfil the conditions provided for in paragraphs 2 and 3.
5. The provisions of paragraphs 2 and 3 apply both to the rights and benefits referred to in articles 13, 18, 19, 21 and 22 of this Convention and to rights and benefits for which this Convention does not provide.[66]

The purpose of Article 7 was to ensure that the State party placed the refugee in the same position as that in which his own country placed aliens.[67] During the drafting of the 1928 Arrangements it was asked: "Which country or which Government can be reached through the person of a refugee? Can the refugee be held responsible for the legislation of his country of origin? Clearly, the rule of reciprocity, if applied to refugees, is pointless and therefore unjust."[68] Article 7 principally required States to accord refugees the same treatment as accorded generally to aliens, and to ensure exemption from reciprocity after a period of three years' residence. Its purpose was to ensure that the State party placed the national of a foreign country in the same position to that in which his own country placed aliens.[69]

The protection provided by Article 7 applies whether the right or benefit in question is guaranteed by municipal law or by international law; whether customary or treaty-based. Grahl-Madsen noted in his commentary to the 1951 Convention that:

> Provisions to the effect that refugees should be exempted requirement of reciprocity are to be found in all the international instruments dealing with the status of refugees.[70]

66 The rights and benefits referred to in Articles 13, 18, 19, 21 and 22 concern movable and immovable property, self-employment, liberal professions, housing, and public education, respectively.

67 Paul Weis, *The Refugee Convention, 1951: The Travaux Preparatoires Analysed with a Commentary by Dr Paul Weis* (UNHCR 1990) 40.

68 Ad Hoc Committee on Refugees and Stateless Persons, *Ad Hoc Committee on Statelessness and Related Problems, Status of Refugees and Stateless Persons – Memorandum by the Secretary-General* 3 January 1950) (E/AC.32/2), 28–29.

69 Paul Weis, *The Refugee Convention, 1951: The Travaux Preparatoires Analysed with a Commentary by Dr Paul Weis* (UNHCR 1990), 40.

70 Atle Grahl-Madsen, *Commentary on the Refugee Convention 1951* (1963 UNHCR) 56. See: League of Nations, *Arrangement relating to the Legal Status of Russian and Armenian Refugees* (30 June 1928) LNTS Vol. LXXXIX, No. 2005, Article 4; League of Nations, *Convention relating to the International Status of Refugees* (28 October 1933) LNTS Vol.

This is only partially accurate. A critical feature of Article 7 is that it does not draw a distinction between refugees that are *de jure* stateless and those that retain the nationality of their State of origin. But this was not a feature of the Arrangements nor of the early Conventions. Despite containing provisions on legislative reciprocity, refugee instruments preceding the 1951 Convention sought to remedy a presumption of severance of the State–subject relationship through diplomatic protection. The 1923 Protocol of Lausanne, which provided for the exchange of Greek and Turkish populations, mandated the loss of nationality of the State of origin and the acquisition of the nationality of the State of reception.[71] The Arrangement of 1926 defined Russian and Armenian refugees as persons who do not enjoy, or who no longer enjoy, the protection of the government, and who had not acquired another nationality.[72] The 1928 *Arrangement relating to the legal status of Russian and Armenian refugees* sought to remedy the legal effect of denationalisation on legislative reciprocity, recommending that:

> [T]he exercise of certain rights and the benefit of certain privileges granted to foreigners on condition of reciprocity shall not be refused to Russian and Armenian refugees on the ground that reciprocity cannot be obtained in their case.[73]

Although the 1928 Arrangement provided for an exemption from legislative reciprocity, the 1928 *Arrangement concerning extension to other categories* defined all groups subject to the Arrangement as either being one that "does not enjoy or who no longer enjoys the protection of the State to which he previously belonged and who has not acquired or does not possess another

---

CLIX, No. 3663, Article 14; League of Nations, *Convention concerning the Status of Refugees coming from Germany, with Annex* (10 February 1938) LNTS Vol. CXCII, No. 4461, Article 17.

71 The British Empire and others, *Protocol Relating to the Karagatch Territory and the Islands of Imbros and Tenedos* (Lausanne, 24 July 1923) Article III provided that "The Greek inhabitants of Karagatch shall be subject to the exchange of populations for which provision is made in the Convention signer the 30 January 1923, between Greece and Turkey. They shall benefit from the stipulations of the said Convention, but they shall only be compelled to emigrate six months after the re-establishment of a state of peace between Greece and Turkey."

72 League of Nations, *Arrangement relating to the Issue of Identity Certificates to Russian and Armenian Refugees, supplementing and amending the previous Arrangements dated July 5, 1922, and May 31, 1924* (12 May 1926) LNTS Vol. LXXXIX, No. 2004. Emphasis added.

73 League of Nations, *Arrangement relating to the Legal Status of Russian and Armenian Refugees* (30 June 1928) LNTS Vol. LXXXIX, No. 2005.

nationality" (Assyrian, Assyro-Chaldean, and assimilated refugees) or as one who was "previously a subject of the Ottoman Empire, who under the terms of the Protocol of Lausanne, does not enjoy or no longer enjoys the protection of the Turkish Republic and who has not acquired another nationality" (Turkish refugees).[74] The 1933 Convention provided at Article 14: "The enjoyment of certain right and the benefit of certain favours accorded to foreigners subject to reciprocity shall not be refused to refugees in the absence of reciprocity."[75] Article 17 of the 1938 Convention recommended that "the benefit of legal assistance and if possible exemption from the *cautio judicatum solvi* shall be granted to Russian and Armenian refugees irrespective of reciprocity."

By contrast, Article 7 does not extend the protection of exception from legislative reciprocity until three years have lapsed, meaning the refugee is subject to the same legislative reciprocity as other aliens generally during the first three years of residence, during which time a refugee or stateless person *maintains their connection with the legal regime of the State of origin.* In that sense, the innovation of Article 7 is not only that it links the refugee with the laws of the State of origin, but that it links the State of *reception* with the external municipal legal regime of the State of origin.[76] Weis noted in his commentary on the 1951 Convention:

> Paragraph 2 constitutes a step backward compared with the pre-war agreements and conventions in that only legislative reciprocity is referred to […]. The pre-war treaties provided for exemption from reciprocity in general, thus including diplomatic reciprocity.[77]

There are several important elements of Article 7 that should be noted. First, it requires that refugees be accorded the same treatment as aliens generally in respect of legislative reciprocity. Where certain aliens are subject to legislative reciprocity, so too are such measures applicable to refugees. Second, the treat-

74 League of Nations, *Arrangement concerning the Extension to other Categories of Refugees of certain Measures taken in favour of Russian and Armenian Refugees* (30 June 1928) LNTS Vol. LXXXIX, No. 63.

75 However, Belgium, Egypt, and Norway – three of the six States that were a party to the 1933 Convention – made reservations to the Article that rendered it ineffectual.

76 Skordas notes also that Article 7 links the 1951 Convention with external legal regimes. See: Achilles Skordas, 'Article 7: (Exemption from Reciprocity/Dispense de Réciprocité)' in Andreas Zimmermann, Felix Machts and Jonas Dörschner (eds), *The 1951 Convention Relating to the Status of Refugees and its 1967 Protocol: A Commentary* (OUP 2011) 714.

77 Paul Weis, *The Refugee Convention, 1951: The Travaux Preparatoires Analysed with a Commentary by Dr Paul Weis* (UNHCR 1990) 47.

ment of refugees akin to aliens generally ceases to apply after a period of three years, at which point the refugee enjoys the benefit of Article 7. Third, the State of reception is obliged to accord to refugees the rights and benefits to which they were already entitled, *in the absence of reciprocity*, meaning that, where the imposition of legislative reciprocity interferes with the existing rights and entitlements of refugees – for example, affecting other provisions of the 1951 Convention – the State is in violation of Article 7. Fourth, it is suggested that the State consider the possibility of extending exemption from reciprocity to those who have not yet fulfilled the residency requirement of three years.

Where it applies to stateless persons, the Convention does not treat differently those refugees who are *de jure* stateless, and those who formally possess the nationality of their State of origin. As the latter are not protected by their State of habitual residence, they are unable to invoke treaties that might exist between their State of origin and their State of residence.[78] The exemption from reciprocity provision recognised that the idea of reciprocity was at the root of the juridical status of aliens, and must therefore be applicable in some measure to refugees. The purpose of the Article was to cover legislative, *de facto*, and diplomatic reciprocity, but not necessarily special and preferential rights, which were granted to nationals of certain foreign States under treaty provisions.[79] Article 7 made civil rights contingent on extended residence. It deliberately did not place refugees on same footing as nationals and as civil rights were the basis of 'protection,' protection was not synonymous with the enjoyment of full civil rights as a national.

5 Article 8: Exemption from Exceptional Measures

Article 8 of the Convention provides for exemption from exceptional measures. It accords refugees a privileged legal position solely on account of their refugee status, but despite their nationality:

78 Atle Grahl-Madsen, *Commentary on the Refugee Convention 1951* (1963 UNHCR) 17.

79 UN Ad Hoc Committee on Statelessness and Related Problems, *First Session: Summary Record of the Twenty-Sixth Meeting Held at Lake Success, New York, on Friday, 10 February 1950, at 2.15 p.m.* (17 February 1950) E/AC.32/SR.25, 2-3; See also: Paul Weis, *The Refugee Convention, 1951: The Travaux Preparatoires Analysed with a Commentary by Dr Paul Weis* (UNHCR 1990) 41.

> With regard to exceptional measures which may be taken against the person, property or interests of nationals of a foreign State, the Contracting States shall not apply such measures to a refugee who is formally a national of the said State solely on account of such nationality. Contracting States which, under their legislation, are prevented from applying the general principle expressed in this article, shall, in appropriate cases, grant exemptions in favour of such refugees.

Article 8 obliges the State of reception to provide legal protection against the exceptional measures it would otherwise take in respect of nationals of the same State of origin. In that respect, it requires differential treatment of aliens and refugees of the same nationality. Stateless persons enjoy a comparable benefit under the Convention Relating to the Status of Stateless Persons.[80] Article 8 was intended to prevent the recurrence of practices resorted to during WWII when refugees from Germany and its satellites were subjected in certain Allied States to internment and other restrictions as "enemy aliens" on account of their enemy nationality, in spite of their opposition to Nazism and Fascism.[81] Though at the time of drafting, exceptional measures against foreign nationals included internment and restriction of movement, in recent decades it is more likely to include actions against property or interests including freezing or seizures of property, prohibition, or restriction of certain economic activities.

As Zimmermann notes, the assumption of Article 8 is that, under certain circumstances, IL generally permits exceptional measures employed by a State *vis-à-vis* another State or the nationals of another State, particularly in times of conflict or dispute.[82] Like Article 7, Article 8 acknowledges that refugees often formally retain the nationality of the State of origin, and that the link of nationality is not extinguished by the fact of refugee status. Though the refugee's nationality might, in other circumstances, render them subject to exceptional measures, the 1951 Convention imposes a negative obligation on the State of reception to refrain from extending such measures to refugees that might otherwise be treated as 'enemy aliens.' Article 8 assumes that the

---

80 UN General Assembly, *Convention Relating to the Status of Stateless Persons* (28 September 1954) UNTS Vol. 360, p. 117.

81 Paul Weis, 'The Development of Refugee Law' (1982) 3(1) Mich J Int'l L 27, 29.

82 Andreas Zimmermann, 'Article 8: (Exemption from Exceptional Measures/Dispense de Mesures Exceptionnelles)' in Andreas Zimmermann, Felix Machts and Jonas Dörschner (eds), *The 1951 Convention Relating to the Status of Refugees and its 1967 Protocol: A Commentary* (OUP 2011) 755, 757.

bonds of loyalty that exist between State and subject, and are presumed to strengthen during times of conflict, do not extend to refugees.[83]

The model provision for Article 8 is to be found at Article 44 of the *Geneva Convention Relative to the Protection of Civilian Persons in Time of War* (Geneva Convention IV), which protects refugees under the control of belligerent States or occupying powers:[84]

> In applying the measures of control mentioned in the present Convention, the Detaining Power shall not treat as enemy aliens exclusively on the basis of their nationality 'de jure' of an enemy State, refugees who do not, in fact, enjoy the protection of any government.[85]

This recognition that a State might still treat a refugee as an 'enemy alien' despite the lack of protection of the 'enemy State' is distinct from the treatment of exceptional measures in pre-1951 refugee instruments, in that none obliged governments to refrain from the application of exceptional measures at all. Instead, their *raison d'etre* was to remedy the dissolution of the State–subject relationship, which, in its absence, could not justify the inclusion of provisions prohibiting adverse treatment on the basis of nationality. By contrast, the 1951 Convention recognised that such measures were taken against refugees and stateless persons irrespective of denationalisation. In fact, as Grahl-Madsen noted, during and after WWII, many refugees who had been persecuted by the Governments of the Axis countries were subjected to exceptional measures taken in the Allied countries against 'enemy aliens.' This included internment and sequestration of property. Such measures were taken specifically because such persons were still nationals of the Axis States. Article 8 sought to remedy the injustice of such treatment.[86]

The 1952 *Convention on the Settlement of Matters Arising Out of the War and the Occupation* between the US, the UK, France, and Germany restored property rights that had previously been the subject of exceptional measures:

83 *Id.*

84 *Id.*, 758.

85 ICRC, *Geneva Convention Relative to the Protection of Civilian Persons in Time of War (Fourth Geneva Convention)* (12 August 1949) 75 UNTS 287.

86 Atle Grahl-Madsen, *Commentary on the Refugee Convention 1951* (1963 UNHCR) 23–24. See also: UN Ad Hoc Committee on Statelessness and Related Problems, *Report of the Ad Hoc Committee on Statelessness and Related Problems, Lake Success, New York, 16 January to 16 February 1950* (17 February 1950) E/1618, E/AC.32/5, Annex II, Art 5.

> Insofar as this has not already been done, the Federal Republic will take all steps necessary to ensure that the nations, persons and companies referred to in paragraph 3 of this Article shall be able to secure the return of their property in its present condition, and the restoration of their rights and interests in the Federal territory to the extent to which such property, rights or interests suffered discriminatory treatment.

The term "discriminatory treatment" referred to:

> [A]ction of all kinds applied between 1 September 1939 and 8 May 1945 to any property, rights or interests, *as a result of any exceptional measures which were not applicable generally to all non-German property, rights or interests,* and giving rise to prejudice, deprivation or impairment without the free consent of the interested parties and without adequate compensation.[87]

Specifically, the term referred to those exceptional measures taken under the *German Ordinance on the Treatment of Enemy Properties* of 15 January 1940, which governed the treatment of property in Germany owned either directly ("enemy property") or indirectly ("under decisive enemy influence") by enemies of Germany.[88]

The principle of exemption from exceptional measures is effectively represented in IHRL instruments in the form of derogation provisions, which permit the implementation of certain exceptional measures in times of public emergency, including during times of conflict, where such derogations are consistent with existing international obligations.[89] The inclusion of prohibited grounds for discrimination in Article 4(1) of the ICCPR ensures that exceptional measures enacted against persons solely on the basis of nationality or ethnicity are strictly prohibited, reflecting the same international obligation as that of Article 7 of the 1951 Convention and Article 44 of Geneva Convention IV. The General Assembly and the Security Council have reiterated numerous times the importance of observing existing IL obligations, including those of

---

87 Emphasis added.

88 Germany, *German Ordinance on the Treatment of Enemy Properties* (15 January 1940) Chapter 10, Article 1.

89 Council of Europe, *European Convention for the Protection of Human Rights and Fundamental Freedoms, as amended by Protocols Nos. 11 and 14* (4 November 1950) ETS 5, Article 15; UN General Assembly, *International Covenant on Civil and Political Rights* (16 December 1966) UNTS Vol. 999, p. 171, Article 4(1).

IRL, when implementing exceptional measures in the global fight to combat terrorism.[90]

But by contrast to its continued relevance in IHRL, exceptional measures have all but been forgotten in IRL. None of the conclusions of the UNHCR ExCom address Article 8. The UNHCR, despite its role as supervisory entity of the 1951 Convention, continues to use the term in ways devoid of its Convention meaning. In Universal Periodic Reviews, and recently in documents concerning the activities of States during the COVID-19 pandemic, the organisation has repeatedly used the term to refer to something akin to 'unprecedented actions.'[91] This loss of meaning may imply that exceptional measures is an antiquated concept and that Article 8 no longer has any relevance to the protection of refugees, but as the following sections demonstrate, this is far from the case.

5.1 *The Extraterritorial Application of Article 8*

Like Article 7, Article 8 has not been the subject of much inquiry in legal scholarship. The commentaries on the Convention provide little information on the Article. Weis did not include Article 8 in his commentary, and Grahl-Madsen and Robinson referred only briefly to its drafting history. The seminal works on refugee status also omit reference to Article 8. Goodwin-Gill and McAdam only briefly reference the Article, Grahl-Madsen did not provide a substantive analysis of Article 8 in his works on refugee status, and Hathaway included only a brief drafting history. Presumably, these omissions reflect the apparent lack of relevance that Article 8 has to the contemporary treatment of refugees. Only in Zimmerman and Dörschner's commentary on the 1951 Convention does Zimmermann provide a thorough, substantive analysis of Article

90 UN General Assembly, *Measures to Eliminate International Terrorism* (14 January 2013) A/RES/67/99; UN General Assembly, *Protection of Human Rights and Fundamental Freedoms while Countering Terrorism* (5 April 2011) A/RES/65/221; UN General Assembly, *The United Nations Global Counter-Terrorism Strategy* (20 September 2006); UN General Assembly, *The United Nations Global Counter-Terrorism Strategy Review* (12 July 2012) A/RES/66/282; UN Security Council, *Resolution 1624 (2005)* (14 September 2005) S/RES/1624.

91 See for example: UN High Commissioner for Refugees, *UNHCR Submission for the Universal Periodic Review – Bolivia – UPR 34th Session* (2019); UN High Commissioner for Refugees, *UNHCR Submission for the Universal Periodic Review – Colombia – UPR 30th Session* (2018); UN High Commissioner for Refugees, *Note on International Protection* (10 July 2020) (A/AC.96/1200) 6; UN High Commissioner for Refugees, *Practical Recommendations and Good Practice to Address Protection Concerns in the Context of the COVID-19* (9 April 2020) 1, 4.

8. He acknowledges that while Article 8 had some practical relevance at the time of drafting, today's meaning is less clear:

> The extent to which refugees are presently privileged by the article depends on the permissibility of exceptional measures under international law in general. The more human rights law or humanitarian law undermine the legitimacy of exceptional measures, the fewer privileges derive from the provisions of Art. 8.[92]

But the benefit of Article 8 to refugees is not measured solely by the permissibility of exceptional measures under IL generally, though it is a good indicator of the strength of the provision. Nor should the meaning and relevance of exceptional measures be derived from the extent to which refugees are presently privileged by the Article. The permissibility of exceptional measures is more appropriately derived from its implementation subject to municipal law, as Article 8 was intended to prohibit the conduct of Contracting States against those subject to its jurisdiction. Furthermore, it is the extent to which exceptional measures are implemented *to the detriment of refugees*, which must substantiate the contemporary meaning of Article 8.

While it is the case that the use of exceptional measures is limited in IHRL and IHL, far from undermining the privileges that derive therefrom, IHRL has not only provided refugees with a remedy to the conduct which Article 8 prohibits – at least in the European context – but by extension, has provided valuable jurisprudence identifying the contemporary actions taken by States that constitute exceptional measures. Incidentally, the exceptional measures enacted by States under municipal law, and the jurisprudence resulting from its litigation clarifies a secondary and interrelated issue – that of the extraterritorial application of exceptional measures. In his commentary on the Convention, Grahl-Madsen proposed that exceptional measures could apply in certain circumstances:

> There can be no doubt that the Article applies to all Convention refugees, irrespective of whether they are present in the territory of the Contracting State concerned, and irrespective of the duration and char-

92 Andreas Zimmermann, 'Article 8: (Exemption from Exceptional Measures/Dispense de Mesures Exceptionnelles)' in Zimmermann, Machts and Dörschner (eds), *The 1951 Convention Relating to the Status of Refugees and its 1967 Protocol: A Commentary* (OUP 2011) 755, 758.

> acter of their presence (legal or illegal). Consequently country A may not apply exceptional measures (for example sequestration of property) to a refugee from country B who has found asylum and is living in country C.[93]

To Zimmermann, the suggestion that Article 8 has extraterritorial effects is difficult to sustain. As the territory of each Contracting State primarily determines the scope of its jurisdiction *ratione loci,* so too does it determine the territorial limitations of exceptional measures. Where declarations are made under Article 40 of the 1951 Convention (territorial application clause), its applicability might extend further to territories for the international relations of which the contracting State is responsible, including colonies, protectorates, mandated territories, but this does not include 'country C.'[94]

In order for a refugee from country B to claim the protection of Article 8 while residing in country C, country A would need to have implemented exceptional measures against all nationals from country B, irrespective of their location. Presented in these terms, this is not such an implausible scenario, particularly when one considers that Article 8 requires only that a State enact exceptional measures against nationals of a certain State without exception for refugees. In that sense, it is not necessary to consider jurisdiction. In imposing exceptional measures against a refugee from State B residing in State C, State A *is not exercising extraterritorial jurisdiction.* It is not therefore a requirement that an Article 40 declaration apply or that State C have any colonial relationship with State A. The more critical matters are: (a) the extent to which State A is obliged by international law to respect the refugee status granted to persons from State B by State C; and (b) whether the declaratory nature of refugee status provides Article 8 protection to asylum seekers outside the territorial bounds of State A. Extraterritoriality is engaged only insofar as State A implements exceptional measures against nationals of State B not within the bounds of its territorial jurisdiction.

In the *German–Portuguese* arbitration of 1933, it was noted that:

> Only reprisals taken against the provoking State are permissible. Admittedly, it can happen that legitimate reprisals taken against an offending

93 Atle Grahl-Madsen, *Commentary on the Refugee Convention 1951* (1963 UNHCR) 25.

94 Andreas Zimmermann, 'Article 8: (Exemption from Exceptional Measures/Dispense de Mesures Exceptionnelles)' in Zimmermann, Machts and Dörschner (eds), *The 1951 Convention Relating to the Status of Refugees and its 1967 Protocol: A Commentary* (OUP 2011) 755, 769.

> State may affect the nationals of an innocent State. But that would be an indirect and unintentional consequence which, in practice, the injured State will always endeavour to avoid or to limit as far as possible.[95]

In the case of those measures taken affecting Articles 7 and 8, an 'indirect and unintentional consequence' would include the application of those countermeasures to refugees residing in States other than the State of reception. This scenario may appear to be very much hypothetical but for the fact that these precise issues have been engaged time and time again. The extraterritorial application of exceptional measures to 'country C' in Grahl-Madsen's construction, without exception to refugees, is confirmed by the extensive use of such measures – often directly and intentionally affecting refugees – by the United States.

5.2 *The Use of Exceptional Measures in Contemporary International Law*

Though there are few States that implement exceptional measures without provision for refugees in contemporary IL, none appear to do so more often that the US. Numerous US Presidents have invoked the authority of §1182(f) of the *Immigration and Nationality Act* (INA) (Inadmissible aliens; Suspension of entry or imposition of restrictions by President) to suspend or deny the entry of broad classes of aliens from certain States of origin, without exception for refugees, and in several cases, with the clear intention to apply those measures to persons seeking international protection, that is, those that have not yet been declared to be refugees, but who nonetheless are clearly fleeing persecution. §1182(f) of the INA provides for the lawful application of exceptional measures:

> Whenever the President finds that the entry of any aliens or of any class of aliens into the United States would be detrimental to the interests of the United States, he may by proclamation, and for such period as he shall deem necessary, suspend the entry of all aliens or any class of aliens as immigrants or nonimmigrants, or impose on the entry of aliens any restrictions he may deem to be appropriate.

95 *Execution of German-Portuguese Arbitral Award of June 30th, 1930 (Germany, Portugal)* [16 February 1933] III RIAA 1371, 1056–1057.

In 1981, then US President Reagan suspended the entry of undocumented aliens from the high seas, enacting an interdiction programme targeting Haitian nationals.[96] Executive Order 12324 instructed the US Coast Guard vaguely to "make inquiries of those on board, examine documents and take such actions as are necessary to establish the registry, condition and destination of the vessel and the status of those on board the vessel."[97] A week earlier, the US and Haiti had entered into an Interdiction Agreement under whose terms US authorities were authorised to board Haitian flag vessels on the high seas and make certain inquiries regarding the condition and destination of such vessels and the status of those on board.[98] The agreement also provided that it is "understood that the United States, having regard for its international obligations pertaining to refugees, does not intend to return to Haiti any Haitian migrants the United States determines qualify for refugee status."[99] The legality of the Order was upheld by the Supreme Court in the infamous *Sale v. Haitian Centers Council* case, in which the Court held that "[n]either §243(h) nor Article 33 [of the 1951 Convention] limits the President's power to order the Coast Guard to repatriate undocumented aliens intercepted on the high seas."[100] The litigation laid bare the operational extent of the refugee verification process. This decision spurred the pervasive use of such Executive Orders affecting refugees without exemption from the exceptional measures.

President Reagan later suspended the entry of Cuban nationals as immigrants in *Presidential Proclamation 5517*, with few exceptions, none of which applied to refugees.[101] President Bush Snr. issued *Executive Order 12807*, empowering the US Coast Guard to "enforce the suspension of the entry of undocumented aliens by sea and the interdiction of any defined vessel carrying such aliens."[102] The Attorney General was granted unreviewable discretion to decide that a person who is a refugee will not be returned without his consent. President Clinton restricted the entry into the US as immigrants

---

96 USA, *Presidential Proclamation 4865: High seas interdiction of illegal aliens* (29 September 1981) 46 FR 48107.

97 USA, *Executive Order 12324: Interdiction of Illegal Aliens* (29 September 1981) 46 FR 48109.

98 USA, Haiti, *Agreement of 23 September 1981* (23 September 1981) 33 UST 3559, TIAS 10241.

99 Emphasis added.

100 pp. 170–188.

101 USA, *Presidential Proclamation 5517: Suspension of Cuban immigration* (22 August 1986) 51 FR 30470.

102 USA, *Executive Order 12807: Interdiction of Illegal Aliens* (24 May 1992) 57 FR 23133.

and nonimmigrants members of the Government of Sudan, officials of that Government, and members of the Sudanese armed forces in *Presidential Proclamation 6958*.[103] An exception was provided with respect to "any person otherwise covered by section 1 where the entry of such person would not be contrary to the interests of the United States," but did not apply explicitly to refugees. President Clinton later restricted the entry into the US as immigrants and nonimmigrants, "certain foreign nationals who plan, engage in, or benefit from activities that support the Revolutionary United Front or that otherwise impede the peace process in Sierra Leone, and the spouses, children of any age, and parents of such persons" in *Presidential Proclamation 7359*.[104] Exceptions applied again to "any person otherwise covered by section 1 where the entry of such person would not be contrary to the interests of the United States" who would be "identified pursuant to such procedures as the Secretary may establish under section 5 of this proclamation," but with no explicit exemption for refugees.

Executive Order 13276 empowered the Attorney General to maintain custody, at any location deemed appropriate, of any undocumented aliens he had reason to believe were seeking to enter the US and who were interdicted or intercepted in the Caribbean region.[105] The Attorney General had authority to "provide and operate a facility, or facilities, to house and provide for the needs of any such aliens." Such facilities were to be located "at Guantanamo Bay Naval Base or any other appropriate location." The Attorney General could conduct any screening of such aliens that he deemed appropriate, "including screening to determine whether such aliens should be returned to their country of origin or transit, or whether they are persons in need of protection who should not be returned without their consent." But the Order explicitly provided that it should "not be construed to require any procedure to determine whether a person is a refugee or otherwise in need of protection."

Under President George W. Bush *Executive Order 13692* blocked all property and interests in property of a long list of Venezuelan nationals, and suspended entry of those nationals into the US, as immigrants or nonimmigrants, "except where the Secretary of State determines that the person's entry is in the

103 USA, *Presidential Proclamation 6958: Suspension of Entry as Immigrants and Nonimmigrants of Persons Who Are Members or Officials of the Sudanese Government or Armed Forces* (22 November 1996) 85 FR 84092.

104 USA, *Proclamation 7359: Suspension of Entry as Immigrants and Nonimmigrants of Persons Impeding the Peace Process in Sierra Leone* (10 October 2000) 65 FR 60831.

105 USA, *Executive Order 13276: Delegation of Responsibilities Concerning Undocumented Aliens Interdicted or Intercepted in the Caribbean Region* (15 November 2002) 67 FR 69983.

national interest of the United States."[106] Obama enacted *Executive Orders 13566* and *13726* that took the same measures against a long list of Libyan nationals, without exception for refugees.[107]

Finally, in perhaps the most infamous use of executive powers in recent times, President Trump instituted numerous Orders and Proclamations to exclude nationals from certain Muslim-majority States from entering the US. *Executive Order 13769* (known colloquially as 'the Muslim ban') suspended for 90 days the entry of certain aliens from Iran, Iraq, Libya, Somalia, Sudan, Syria, and Yemen.[108] It also suspended the US Refugee Admissions Program (USRAP) for a period of 120 days, and suspended indefinitely the entry of Syrian refugees, proclaiming that their entry as refugees was "detrimental to the interests of the United States." The Executive Order granted a discretionary right to the Secretaries of State and Homeland Security to permit, on a case-by-case basis, the admission of refugees subject to a number of limitations. After 120 days, the Secretary of State was to resume USRAP admissions "only for nationals of countries for which the Secretary of State, the Secretary of Homeland Security, and the Director of National Intelligence have jointly determined that such additional procedures are adequate to ensure the security and welfare of the United States."[109]

Executive Order 13769 was the first time executive powers were used to *explicitly* apply exceptional measures to refugees as an identified group. It applied not only to asylum seekers that had not yet been subject to a refugee status determination, but it explicitly applied to recognised refugees from Syria – refugees from 'country B' in the territories of 'country Cs.' Importantly, the Order applied to those Syrian refugees that had been determined as such *by the US itself* under the USRAP. It did not involve a scenario in which exceptional measures were imposed on refugees declared as such by 'country Cs.'

Later, and in response to a flurry of litigation, *Executive Order 13780*, which revoked and replaced *Executive Order 13769*, excluded from the scope of the previous order any foreign national who had been granted asylum; any refu-

106 USA, *Executive Order 13692: Blocking Property and Suspending Entry of Certain Persons Contributing to the Situation in Venezuela* (8 March 2015) 80 FR 12747.

107 USA, *Executive Order 13566: Blocking Property and Prohibiting Certain Transactions Related to Libya* (25 February 2011) 76 FR 11315; USA, *Executive Order 13726: Blocking Property and Suspending Entry Into the United States of Persons Contributing to the Situation in Libya* (19 April 2016) 81 FR 23559.

108 USA, *Executive Order 13769: Protecting the Nation from Foreign Terrorist Entry into the United States* (27 January 2017) 82 FR 8977.

109 *Id.*

gee who had already been admitted to the US; or any individual who had been granted withholding of removal, advance parole, or protection under the Convention Against Torture. However, the Order suspended the travel of refugees into the US under the USRAP, and suspended decisions on applications for refugee status, for 120 days after the effective date of the Order, thus still applying to both refugees recognised as such by the USRAP and to asylum seekers awaiting a refugee status determination.[110] The critical distinction between those subject to the new Order, and those excluded from it was territorial jurisdiction. In line with the jurisprudence of the Supreme Court, only those within the territory of the US were able to claim the benefit of Article 8 protection. Those not within the US, but nonetheless recognised by the USRAP as refugees, could not claim exemption from exceptional measures.

Later, *Proclamation 9645* extended the scope of immigration restriction to include nationals of Chad, North Korea, and Venezuela.[111] This use of executive power explicitly excluded recognised refugees "who [have] been granted asylum by the United States," to those refugee "who [have] already been admitted to the United States" and to those "granted withholding of removal or protection under the Convention Against Torture." The Proclamation appeared to remedy the application of exceptional measures to refugees, however it did not apply to those seeking asylum outside the US, or those recognised as refugees by other States.

> Nothing in this proclamation shall be construed to limit the ability of an individual to seek asylum, refugee status, withholding of removal, or protection under the Convention Against Torture, consistent with the laws of the United States.

Similarly, *Presidential Proclamation 9983* did not provide exemption from exceptional measures to refugees residing outside the US. It suspended the entry of nationals from Myanmar, Eritrea, Kyrgyzstan, Nigeria, Sudan, and Tanzania subject to the exceptions of *Proclamation 9645*, which excluded any foreign national who had been granted asylum by the US; any refugee who had already been admitted to the country; or any individual who had

110 USA, *Executive Order 13780: Protecting the Nation from Foreign Terrorist Entry into the United States* (6 March 2017) 82 FR 13209.

111 USA, *Proclamation 9645: Enhancing Vetting Capabilities and Processes for Detecting Attempted Entry Into the United States by Terrorists or Other Public-Safety Threats* (24 September 2017) 82 FR 45161.

been granted withholding of removal, advance parole, or protection under the Convention Against Torture.[112] It did not exempt those nationals of 'country Bs' residing in, and recognised as refugees by 'country Cs.'

All of these measures were subject to litigation. The case concerning *Executive Order 13769*, which suspected the USRAP programme and suspended indefinitely the entry of Syrian refugees, included as the first petitioner an individual that held an Iraqi Special Immigrant Visa (SIV).[113] The second petitioner held a Follow to Join (FTJ) Visa.[114] The case was subject to settlement; however, petitioners submitted that:

> 72. The INA forbids discrimination in issuance of visas based on a person's race, nationality, place of birth, or place of residence. 8 U.S.C. § 1152(a)(1)(A).
>
> 73. Respondents' detention and mistreatment of Petitioners and the members of the proposed class pursuant to the January 27 EO, as set forth above, is not authorized by the INA.[115]

§ 1152(a)(1)(A) of the INA provides:

> Except as specifically provided in paragraph (2) and in sections 1101(a)(27), 1151(b)(2)(A)(i), and 1153 of this title, no person shall receive any preference or priority or be discriminated against in the issuance of an immigrant visa because of the person's race, sex, nationality, place of birth, or place of residence.

The litigation of Proclamation No. 9645 went all the way to the Supreme Court. Initially, the District Court granted a nationwide preliminary injunc-

---

112 USA, *Presidential Proclamation 9983: Improving Enhanced Vetting Capabilities and Processes for Detecting Attempted Entry Into the United States by Terrorists or Other Public-Safety Threats* (31 January 2020) 85 FR 6699.

113 US Congress created the Iraqi and Afghan Special Immigrant Visa (SIV) programmes to provide safety and refuge in the United States for Iraqis and Afghans who faced serious threats on account of their service to the United States. The programmes were established pursuant to the USA, *Refugee Crisis in Iraq Act* (2007) 8 U.S.C § 1157 and the USA, *Afghan Allies Protection Act* (2008) 8 U.S.C § 1101.

114 8 U.S.C. § 1157(c)(2)(A); 8 U.S.C. § 207.7(a) (spouse or child of refugee "shall be granted refugee status if accompanying or following-to-join the principal alien").

115 *Darweesh v Trump* [16 February 2017] 17-CV-480 (CBA) 'Petition For Writ of Habeas Corpus and Complaint For Declaratory and Injunctive Relief' (28 January 2017).

tion barring enforcement of the restrictions, following which the Ninth Circuit affirmed the decision, concluding that the Proclamation contravened two provisions of the INA: §1182(f), which authorises the President to "suspend the entry of all aliens or any class of aliens" whenever he "finds" that their entry "would be detrimental to the interests of the United States," and §1152(a)(1)(A), which provides that "no person shall [...] be discriminated against in the issuance of an immigrant visa because of the person's race, sex, nationality, place of birth, or place of residence." The Court held that the President has lawfully exercised the broad discretion granted to him under §1182(f) to suspend the entry of aliens into the United States and that By its terms, "§1182(f) exudes deference to the President in every clause."[116]

The measures described above are only those taken by executive action subject to section 1184(f) of the INA. It does not include those executive actions taken in respect of other provisions of the US Code. As Zimmermann notes, exceptional measures are commonly referred to in the US as 'emergency economic powers,'[117] and the list of sanctions imposed by US presidents under §1701 of the *International Emergency Economic Powers Act* (unusual and extraordinary threat; declaration of national emergency; exercise of Presidential authorities) on nationals of specified State without explicit exception for refugees is equally extensive.[118] But as the following section shows, the implementation of exceptional measures without provision for refugees have been recognised by the US itself as unlawful, albeit implicitly.

116 *Trump v. Hawaii* [26 June 2018] 17–965, 2.

117 Andreas Zimmermann, 'Article 8: (Exemption from Exceptional Measures/Dispense de Mesures Exceptionnelles)' in Zimmermann, Machts and Dörschner (eds), *The 1951 Convention Relating to the Status of Refugees and its 1967 Protocol: A Commentary* (OUP 2011) 755, 772.

118 See: USA, *Executive Order 13441: Blocking Property of Persons Undermining the Sovereignty of Lebanon or Its Democratic Processes and Institutions* (1 August 2007) 72 FR 43499; USA, *Executive Order 13882: Blocking Property and Suspending Entry of Certain Persons Contributing to the Situation in Mali* (26 July 2019) 84 FR 37055; USA, *Executive Order 13405: Blocking Property of Certain Persons Undermining Democratic Processes or Institutions in Belarus* (16 June 2006) 71 FR 35485; USA, *Executive Order 13936: The President's Executive Order on Hong Kong Normalization* (14 July 2020) 85 FR 43413; USA, *Executive Order 13611: Blocking Property of Persons Threatening the Peace, Security, or Stability of Yemen* (16 May 2012) 77 FR 29533; USA, *Executive Order 13303: Protecting the Development Fund for Iraq and Certain Other Property in Which Iraq Has an Interest* (22 May 2003) 68 FR 31929.

6 Exceptional Measures and State Responsibility

The actions historically taken by States against the persons, property, and interests of certain nationalities, have served as unilateral sanctions taken by States against other States during times of conflict. When considered in light of the actions that it was intended to remedy, it is clear that the purpose of Article 8 is to provide protection against reprisals and countermeasures in the context of SR. The use of exceptional measures, including the (albeit limited) litigation of such, provides clarification on several matters.

First, the extraterritorial application of exceptional measures does not necessarily require the exercise of extraterritorial jurisdiction. In addition to those scenarios covered by Article 40 of the 1951 Convention, Zimmermann allows for the possibility that an occupying power may be obliged to provide Article 8 protection where it is the only entity able to do so. "Here, and here only, Grahl-Madsen's suggestion of the extraterritorial effects of Art. 8 bears at least some plausibility."[119] However the use of executive powers in the US targeting refugees abroad – even those that the US itself has determined to be refugees – must surely constitute a prohibited application of exceptional measures in the context of Article 8, having fulfilled all the elements of the provision and being affected through the municipal law of a Contracting State. Though these measures were not subject to inter-State litigation or deemed to constitute countermeasures, internal litigation caused the executive to reverse and otherwise modify the scope of exceptional measures so that certain groups of refugees were excluded from its application. That is, the State itself acknowledged that at least some refugees were entitled to Article 8 protection.

In the case of the so-called 'Muslim-ban' and arguably the case of Haitian and Cuban migrants, exceptional measure were taken in respect of the 'person, property, or interests' of nationals irrespective of refugee status and applied to those in 'country C' specifically to avoid the territorial obligation to refrain from imposing exceptional measures on refugees; the US being soundly of the position that international obligations in respect of refugees do not apply extraterritorially. In *Sale v. Haitian Centers Council* Justice Blackmun, dissenting, insisted that exceptional measures could never apply to refugees where the application of such resulted in *refoulement*:

119 Andreas Zimmermann, 'Article 8: (Exemption from Exceptional Measures/Dispense de Mesures Exceptionnelles)' in Zimmermann, Machts and Dörschner (eds), *The 1951 Convention Relating to the Status of Refugees and its 1967 Protocol: A Commentary* (OUP 2011) 755, 770.

> The terms [of Article 33 of the 1951 Convention] are unambiguous. Vulnerable refugees shall not be returned. The language is clear, and the command is straightforward; that should be the end of the inquiry.[120]

Second, Article 8 protection may extend to persons of certain ethnicities, where that ethnicity is considered to be the basis of a conferral or denial of nationality. Zimmermann argues that "refugees cannot rely on the first sentence of Art. 8 of the 1951 Convention when exceptional measures are not tied to nationality but to different personal characteristics, such as religion or social or ethnic origin."[121] However technical distinctions between nationality and ethnicity are often irrelevant during times of conflict. Consider as an example, the convergence of 'nationality' and 'ethnicity' (and indeed religion) during the break-up of the former Yugoslavia, and the role it played in the extreme violence and repression that ensued. It could not be logically argued that exceptional measures taken in respect of Bosniaks residing in Serbia or ethnic Albanians residing in Kosovo could not be subject to the protection of Article 8 because, technically, neither group was a 'nationality.' Consider also (more pertinent to the 1951 Convention) the numerous declarations that German, Polish, Italian, and Dutch nationals (to name but a few) who were also Jewish, were of the separate Jewish 'race,' and were therefore less entitled to enjoy the benefit of nationality of those States in which they had resided for hundreds of years. It could not be that the 1951 Convention was not intended to provide protection from exceptional measures taken against nationals of a certain State where that purported nationality was in fact an ethnicity.

Third (though less pertinent to SR), in addition to recognised refugees within and outside the territory of State A, Article 8 protection extends to refugees whose status has not been the subject of a formal determination. Robinson asserted that Article 8 only applies to *bona fide* refugees;[122] however, the assessment of a claimant's *bona fides* is only achieved through the RSD process. Furthermore, the determination of refugee status merely affirms the fact of refuge status. It could not be the case, therefore, that Article 8 excludes from its ambit the protection of refugees that have not yet been subject to a

120 *Chris Sale, Acting Commissioner, Immigration and Naturalization Service, et al. v Haitian Centers Council, Inc., et al.* [21 June 1993] 509 US 155, 190.

121 Andreas Zimmermann, 'Article 8: (Exemption from Exceptional Measures/Dispense de Mesures Exceptionnelles)' in Zimmermann, Machts and Dörschner (eds), *The 1951 Convention Relating to the Status of Refugees and its 1967 Protocol: A Commentary* (OUP 2011) 755, 774.

122 Nehemiah Robinson, *Convention Relating to the Status of Refugees: Its History, Significance and Contents* (Institute of Jewish Affairs 1952) 91.

refugee status determination, particularly where the imposition of exceptional measures has at times relied on the fact that certain groups have not been subject to formal conferral of refugee status as a means to include those persons within the scope of exceptional measures.

The defence of necessity has been invoked numerous times in the justification of countermeasures affecting Articles 7 and 8 of the 1951 Convention. The US frequently employed the defence of necessity, claiming that the ongoing threat to national security required that the measures be taken. In the *Gabčíkovo–Nagymaros Project* case, the ICJ stressed that "[A]s soon as the state of necessity ceases to exist, the duty to comply with treaty obligations revives."[123] However, the breadth and subjectivity of what precisely constitutes a threat to national security permits the long-term implementation of countermeasures where the purported threat has not ceased to require the state of necessity.

Article 25 (necessity) of the ARSIWA provides that the defence may not be invoked by a State as a ground for precluding the wrongfulness of an act not in conformity with an international obligation of that State unless the act is the only way for the State to safeguard an essential interest against a grave and imminent peril. While the integrity of State sovereignty and the protection of national security are defensible as among the essential interests of a State, the existence of a 'grave and imminent peril' is less clear in these cases. Additionally, the state of necessity must not seriously impair an essential interest of the State or States towards which the obligation exists, or of the international community as a whole. It may be said that it is within the interests of the international community to protect the principle of *non-refoulement* and to guarantee the benefit of Convention protection.

Article 49 of the ARSIWA (object and limits of countermeasures) required that the injured State only take countermeasures against a State responsible for an internationally wrongful act *in order to induce that State to comply with its obligations*. Furthermore, Article 51 (proportionality) requires that countermeasures be commensurate with the injury suffered, taking into account the gravity of the internationally wrongful act and the rights in question. Article 49 also requires that countermeasures be limited to non-performance of international obligations. The actions taken by President Clinton restricting the entry into the United States as immigrants and nonimmigrants designated persons under *Presidential Proclamations 6958* and *7359* may constitute non-performance. By contrast, *Executive Order 13276*, empowering the Attorney General to maintain custody, of undocumented aliens interdicted or inter-

123 *Gabčíkovo-Nagymaros Project* (*Hungary v Slovakia*) [1997] ICJ Rep 120, p. 63, para. 101; See also: p. 38, para. 47.

cepted in the Caribbean region, and authorising the Attorney General to operate a facility to house such aliens at Guantanamo Bay goes beyond the object and limits of countermeasures provided by Article 49. This is not to say that countermeasures cannot have a coercive character, but as is made clear in Article 49, their function is to induce a wrongdoing State to comply with obligations of cessation and reparation towards the State taking the countermeasures.[124]

Article 50 of the ARSIWA requires that countermeasures shall not affect obligations for the protection of fundamental human rights, nor other obligations under peremptory norms of general IL. The former raises questions of competing norms of IL, being the legitimacy of discrimination on the basis of nationality, and those provisions of the 1951 Convention that allow it. The use of countermeasures that make exception for refugees only after three years' residence does not satisfy the requirements of IHRL to refrain from differential treatment on the basis of nationality. By comparison, the latter obligation to refrain from countermeasures that violate peremptory norms of general international law delegitimise those measures taken that resulted in the *refoulement* of asylum seekers, and in the denial of refugee protection.

7 Conclusion

As noted in Grahl-Madsen's commentary, the 1951 Convention instituted both an upper limit (treatment as favourable as possible) and a lower limit (treatment not less favourable than that accorded to aliens generally in the same circumstances) to the scope of a Contracting State's obligations.[125] Had the lower limit not been established, refugees would be placed in "an unjustifiable position of inferiority."[126] Articles 7 and 8 are exceptions. The lower limit established in both Articles places refugees in a position of inferiority where the three-year-residence requirement has not been fulfilled, and in that sense, allows for the differential treatment of refugees on account of nationality during that period. Paradoxically, this is the product of the Convention's most important legal innovation – the presumption of enduring nationality and

124 International Law Commission, *Draft articles on Responsibility of States for Internationally Wrongful Acts, with Commentaries* 2001) II (Part II) Yearbook of the International Law Commission, 70.

125 Atle Grahl-Madsen, *Commentary on the Refugee Convention 1951* (1963 UNHCR) 22.

126 Paul Weis, 'Legal Aspects of the Convention of 21 July 1951 Relating to the Status of Refugees' (1953) 30 BYBIL 478.

the rejection of the presumption of severance; a conception of protection that extended the benefit of the Convention's modified DP to many millions of refugees, and yet carved out these exceptions that would expose refugees to discrimination.

That said, there are numerous examples of the use of unilateral countermeasures affecting refugees that go well beyond the scope of what is permitted by Articles 7 and 8, and what conforms to norms of SR. Although "it is not the purpose of the Convention to give refugees a position so sheltered that it will interfere with the general legal policy of the State concerned,"[127] if the interpretation or application of municipal law leads to less favourable treatment of refugees than that provided by Articles 7 and 8, the Contracting State is in violation of the 1951 Convention.[128]

While countermeasures meeting certain substantive and procedural conditions may be legitimate,[129] those conditions under which a State may be entitled to respond to a breach of an international obligation by taking countermeasures are necessarily limited. The lawfulness of countermeasures depends on the initial commission of an internationally wrongful act. In addition to fulfilling substantive requirements, the legitimacy of countermeasures depends also on certain procedural conditions. Per Article 22 of the ARSIWA, an injured State may be justified in taking non-forcible countermeasures in order to procure the cessation of wrongful acts and to achieve reparation for the injury, but countermeasures must be intended to ensure the fulfilment of the international obligations of the responsible State. In the absence of these requirements being fulfilled, any countermeasure taken by a State against another will necessarily be an unlawful exercise and will itself incur SR.

In the context of countermeasures taken in contravention of the international obligations of the injured State – such as the non-performance of Articles 7 and 8 of the 1951 Convention – these require compliance with the relative norms of SR. Compliance hinges on the existence of an international obligation in the first instance, and of its violation in contravention of IL. The nature of the 'injury' defines in part the extent of reparation and the propor-

127 Atle Grahl-Madsen, *Commentary on the Refugee Convention 1951* (1963 UNHCR) 21.

128 Achilles Skordas, 'Article 7: (Exemption from Reciprocity/Dispense de Réciprocité)' in Zimmermann, Machts and Dörschner (eds), *The 1951 Convention Relating to the Status of Refugees and its 1967 Protocol: A Commentary* (OUP 2011) 714, 729.

129 *Gabčíkovo-Nagymaros Project (Hungary v Slovakia)* [1997] ICJ Rep 120, para 83; *Naulilaa Arbitration (Portugal v Germany)* [1928] II UNRIAA 1011, 1025–1026; *Execution of German-Portuguese Arbitral Award of June 30th, 1930 (Germany, Portugal)* [16 February 1933] III RIAA 1371, 1052.

tionality of countermeasures taken to exact it. In the case of certain US executive actions, the injury purportedly suffered does not correspond with the existence of an international obligation. The objective of those countermeasures was rather intended to ensure compliance with the State's political objectives, not with IL. Those executive actions taken in 2020 and 2021 were purportedly taken with a view to enforcing the compliance of affected States with international standards of data sharing and information sharing, though this was not identified as an international obligation, as such.

Despite these being clear abuses of executive powers, there remains the question of how to adjudicate their lawfulness under IL. This returns us once again to the question of the implicit 'deficiencies' of the 1951 Convention in not providing a designated authority for the adjudication of IRL. Again, this is not the problem it appears to be. It is less a question of compliance with the relevant provisions of IRL than it is with the lawful use of countermeasures as a means of enforcing SR.

It is clear that the inclusion of refugees in countermeasures affecting reciprocity and exceptional measures are in many cases inconsistent with the requirements of both IRL and SR. In those cases, it is the remit of courts and tribunals with jurisdiction over municipal laws and over IHRL to provide remedy. The litigation of matters involving measures taken under Articles 7 and 8 are not necessarily compromised by the absence of an international legal mechanism for the enforcement of Convention provisions, but by the fact that the provisions of the 1951 Convention are increasingly regarded as IHRL in nature and are decreasingly considered to be an instrument of PIL governing inter-State relations, and subject to the rules of SR governing the legitimate use of countermeasures. As the following chapters demonstrates, this disconnect has broad ramifications, far beyond the use of countermeasures.

CHAPTER 5

'Aid and Development' in International Refugee Policy: The Reinvention of Multilateralism

1 Introduction

As the global number of refugees and displaced persons (as they were then distinguished) fell in the wake of WWII, the harmonisation of IRL and the coordination of responses to refugee questions no longer demanded the same urgent multilateralism as they did prior, and until the latter part of the 1970s, the development of IRL slowed in pace. Between the activities of the League in the 1920s and 1930s, and the last years of the 1970s, the format of international conferences on 'refugee questions' became somewhat obsolete. Many of those instruments and resolutions drafted in the interim were more matters of formal recognition and reiteration than developments of significant consequence, though with some notable exceptions. The 1967 *Protocol relating to the Status of Refugees* removed the limitations on the personal and geographical scope of the 1951 Convention to include persons who became refugees after 1 January 1951, and due to events occurring outside Europe, but this was rather a recognition of existing circumstances than a revision of IRL.[1] UN General Assembly resolutions of the late 1950s and early 1960s already noted that increasing attention was being paid in many countries to the problems of refugees "who do not come within the immediate competence of the United Nations."[2] Furthermore, the first activities of the UNHCR following WWII had been to make arrangements for emergency assistance to Hungarian refugees in Austria following the 1956 Hungarian revolution,[3] to encourage arrangements for contributions and to provide assistance to Chinese refugees

1 UN, *Protocol Relating to the Status of Refugees* (31 January 1967) UNTS Vol. 606, No. 8791.

2 See, for example: UN General Assembly, *Report of the United Nations High Commissioner for Refugees* (5 December 1960) A/RES/1499(XV); UN General Assembly, *Report of the United Nations High Commissioner for Refugees* (20 November 1959) A/RES/1388; UN General Assembly, *Chinese Refugees in Hong Kong* (26 November 1957) A/RES/1167(XII).

3 See: UN General Assembly, *Resolution 1129(XI)* (21 November 1956) A/RES/1129(XI); UN General Assembly, *Resolution 1006(ES-II)* (9 November 1956) A/RES/1006(ES-II).

 | DOI:10.1163/9789004722835_007

in Hong Kong,[4] and to assist in the maintenance, and later the orderly return, of Algerian refugees in Morocco and Tunisia following the Algerian War of Independence.[5]

Similarly, what would become the 1967 *Declaration on Territorial Asylum*,[6] under consideration as early as 1960,[7] constituted an elaboration of Article 14 of the 1948 *Universal Declaration of Human Rights*,[8] and was specifically *not* intended to propound legal norms. It was stated clearly in the draft Declaration that it "would not affect existing international undertakings or national legislation relevant to the subject of asylum and related matters."[9] Instead, it would "lay down broad humanitarian and moral principles upon which States might rely in seeking to unify their practice relating to asylum."[10] The resolution on *Co-operation with the United Nations High Commissioner for Refugees*, adopted as part of the Final Act of the 1968 *Tehran Conference on Human Rights*, called upon Governments "to co-operate with the United Nations High Commissioner for Refugees in the performance of his functions concerning refugees falling under the competence of his Office,"[11] and reiterated the terms of UN General Assembly Resolution 428(V) of 1950, adopting the statute of the office of the High Commissioner for Refugees.[12] Resolutions of the UN

4 UN General Assembly, *The Problem of Chinese Refugees in Hong Kong* (7 December 1962) A/RES/1784; UN General Assembly, *Chinese Refugees in Hong Kong* (26 November 1957) A/RES/1167(XII).

5 See: UN General Assembly, *Refugees from Algeria in Morocco and Tunisia* (18 December 1961) A/RES/1672(XVI); UN General Assembly, *Refugees from Algeria in Morocco and Tunisia* (20 November 1959) A/RES/1389(XIV).

6 UN General Assembly, *Declaration on Territorial Asylum* (14 December 1967) A/RES/2312 (XXII).

7 This was initially a 'Draft Declaration on the Right of Asylum.' See: UN Economic and Social Council, *Report of the Commission on Human Rights* (25 July 1960) (E/RES/772 (XXX)), Part E.

8 Article 14 of the *Universal Declaration of Human Rights* provides: "1. Everyone has the right to seek and to enjoy in other countries asylum from persecution. 2. This right may not be invoked in the case of prosecutions genuinely arising from non-political crimes or from acts contrary to the purpose and principles of the United Nations." See: UN General Assembly, *Universal Declaration of Human Rights* (10 December 1948) A/RES/217(III).

9 UN General Assembly, *Draft Declaration on Territorial Asylum: Report of the 6th Committee* (30 November 1967) A/6912.

10 *Id.*, pg 7.

11 UN, *Final Act of the International Conference on Human Rights. Resolution XIII: Co-operation with the United Nations High Commissioner for Refugees* (12 May 1968) A/CoNF.3 2/41.

12 UN General Assembly, *Statute of the Office of the United Nations High Commissioner for Refugees* (14 December 1950) A/RES/428(V).

General Assembly following the adoption of the 1951 Convention were equally unremarkable. A UN Refugee Fund was first established in 1954,[13] and subsequent resolutions continued to appeal to States to provide contributions and lament the fact that those contributions consistently fell short of yearly targets.[14] The preference for the resolution of refugee crises, as each of these resolutions reiterated, continued to be the three permanent solutions of voluntary repatriation, resettlement, and local integration (or assimilation).

An exception to the relatively inconsequential developments of the period was the elaboration of a regional binding instrument, formulating a new definition of an African refugee, bearing in mind the specific aspects of the refugee situation on the continent. The 1966 *Bangkok Principles on the Status and Treatment of Refugees*, led by the Asian-African Legal Consultative Organization, broadened the terms defining a refugee in the 1951 Convention to include persons compelled to leave their place of habitual residence owing to "external aggression, occupation, foreign domination or events seriously disturbing public order."[15] The 1967 Conference on the Legal, Economic and Social Aspects of African Refugee Problems utilised in part the language of the Bangkok Principles in its recommendations.[16] The Conference led to the eventual adoption of the 1969 *OAU Convention Governing the Specific Aspects of Refugee Problems in Africa*, which defined refugee in the same terms as the Bangkok Principles.[17]

---

13 UN General Assembly, *Resolution 832(IX): International assistance to refugees within the mandate of the United Nations High Commissioner for Refugees* (21 October 1954) A/RES/832(IX).

14 UN General Assembly, *Resolution 832(IX): International Assistance to Refugees within the Mandate of the United Nations High Commissioner for Refugees* (21 December 1954) A/RES/832(IX); UN General Assembly, *Report of the United Nations High Commissioner for Refugees* (25 October 1955) A/RES/925(X); UN General Assembly, *Report of the United Nations High Commissioner for Refugees* (23 January 1957) A/RES/1039(XI); UN General Assembly, *Report of the United Nations High Commissioner for Refugees* (5 December 1958) 1284(XIII); UN General Assembly, *Report of the United Nations High Commissioner for Refugees* (20 November 1959) A/RES/1388; UN General Assembly, *Report of the United Nations High Commissioner for Refugees* (18 December 1961) 1673(XVI); UN General Assembly, *Report of the United Nations High Commissioner for Refugees* (12 December 1963) 1959(XVID).

15 Asian-African Legal Consultative Organization, *Bangkok Principles on the Status and Treatment of Refugees* (31 December 1966).

16 Organization of African Unity, *Report of the Administrative Secretary-General on the Conference on Legal, Economic and Social Aspects of African Refugee Problems. Addis Ababa: 9–18 October 1967* (1968) CM/198.

17 Organization of African Unity, *Convention Governing the Specific Aspects of Refugee Problems in Africa* (10 September 1969) UNTS Vol. 1001, No. 14691.

This exception aside, the stagnation in multilateralism relative to IRL changed rapidly with the destabilisation of Africa. Across the continent, the refugee problem had augmented at such an accelerated rate, that between 1964 and 1967, the number of estimated refugees had risen from 400,000 to 1 million.[18] By May 1979, this number had reached approximately 4 million.[19] By 1980, it had increased to 5 million,[20] and by 1988, Africa was home to more than half the world's estimated 10 million refugees.[21] By the late 1970s, the fragile system of multilateralism that supported IRL to date began to unravel, replaced, in the words of Melander, "by something like the law of the jungle."[22] Though by no means a new sentiment, a perception emerged that multilateralism in IRL to date constituted a threat to State sovereignty in the face of 'mass influxes' of refugees. This sentiment formed the pretext for States to turn defensively inward, toward regionalised refugee law and policy that not only sought to modify, qualify, and limit the scope and content of the 1951 Convention, but reconceptualised 'protection' as distinct from its international obligations, constituted instead by the provision of foreign humanitarian aid.

Within a few short years, the international conference was revived for the coordination of regional consultations on 'refugee questions' and became a conduit for the proliferation of International Refugee Policy (IRP), which at its core was concerned with the modification of IRL. As a response to the "unwanted child of States,"[23] the development of IRP increasingly became a regionalised exercise necessary to address "massive" influxes of refugees,[24]

18 See: Lars-Gunnar Eriksson, Gören Melander, Peter Nobel (eds), *An Analysing Account of the Conference on the African Refugee Problem, Arusha, May 1979* (Scandinavian Institute of African Studies 1981).

19 *Id.*

20 UN General Assembly, *International Conference on Assistance to Refugees in Africa (ICARA I): Report of the Secretary-General* (11 June 1981) A/36/316, 7; UN General Assembly, *International Conference on Assistance to Refugees in Africa* (14 December 1981) A/RES/36/124.

21 Allen Armstrong, 'Aspects of Refugee Wellbeing in Settlement Schemes: An Examination of the Tanzanian Case' (1988) 1(1) Journal of Refugee Studies 57.

22 Göran Melander, 'Basic Differences in Refugee Policy in Western Europe and North America' (1989) In Defense of the Alien 97, 100.

23 Rosemary Byrne, Andrew Shacknove, 'The Safe Country Notion in European Asylum Law' (1996) 9 Harv Hum Rts J 185, 187.

24 See, for example: UN General Assembly, *International Co-operation to Avert New Flows of Refugees: Note by the Secretary-General* (13 May 1986) A/41/324; UN General Assembly,

and to provide regional solutions to refugee questions through the coordination of zonal developments and the delivery of humanitarian aid, the appointment of steering committees and mixed commissions charged with the task of overseeing implementation, and comprehensive plans of action to address emerging refugee crises.

By 1985, 107 of the 112 refugee settlements believed to have been established worldwide, were located in Africa,[25] each established through financial and organisational support from international assistance agencies, and States of reception that had now positioned themselves as 'donor States'; benefactors of the new 'protection' elsewhere. In most cases, this 'aid and development' model that supported the new inter-regional relationship between donor and recipient States created new communities with "rural economies based primarily on agriculture, thus enabling the refugees to attain self-sufficiency and re-establish their lives without continuing to act as a drain on the resources of their hosts."[26] States of reception across Eastern, Central, and Southern Africa were already among the poorest in the world with "precarious national economies and an inability to meet the basic needs of even their own populations,"[27] and concerns about inequitable distribution and availability of resources – real or perceived – plagued many States in the region.

Though regional in nature, this new generation of multilateralism reconceptualised and reinforced certain global concepts of IL relative to the scope and content of protection, and as a result, the circumstances in which SR could be attributable to a State for the violation of IRL. While in previous decades, State of origin responsibility had been conceived of as corresponding with the obligation to financially contribute to the amelioration of displacement of a State's own population, it was now reimagined as corresponding with the obligation to avert and contain 'massive flows' of refugees through

Official Record of the Twentieth Session, 3rd Committee, 1361st Meeting (1 December 1965) (A/C.3/SR.1361) pg 421, para 22; UN General Assembly, *Official Record of the Twenty-First Session, 3rd Committee, 1449th Meeting* (6 December 1966) (A/C.3/SR.1449) pg 437, para 44.

25 Omar Bakhet, 'UNHCR Experience in Implementing Rural Settlements for Refugees' (1985) Conference Box RSC Archives, Refugee Studies Programme, Oxford, cited in Allen Armstrong, 'Aspects of Refugee Wellbeing in Settlement Schemes: An Examination of the Tanzanian Case' (1988) 1(1) Journal of Refugee Studies 57.

26 Armstrong, *id.*, 58.

27 *Id.*, 57.

"improved international co-operation at all levels";[28] what Aleinikoff refers to broadly as 'source-control strategies.'[29]

> With a little ingenuity, a source-control model can be explained as consistent with a state-centered approach premised on the notion of equal and independent states. First, as noted by the Group of Governmental Experts, mass flight "may affect the political and social stability, as well as the economic development, of the receiving States, and also carry adverse consequences for the economies of the countries of origin and entire regions, thus endangering international peace and security."[30] On this account, the creation of refugees may be characterized as an offense against the system of states warranting remedial measures by the international community.[31]

In a similar way, State of reception obligations were suddenly qualified by the invention of 'first States' as actors with distinct international obligations in IRP. In the case of both first States and States of reception, protection was compromised. It required, *inter alia*, the implementation of 'regional' solutions that contained refugee populations in geographically limited 'zones,'[32] and minimised the circumstances in which refugee status could be conferred. By extension, SR was attributed in circumstances where 'source-control' had failed. As the aid and development era was characterised by the bartering of aid in exchange for the restriction of refugee movement, countermeasures took the form of conditionality of aid, both for the maintenance of refugee camps and for military and development assistance. This was the result of a period characterised by the dilution of decipherable international obligation,

28 UN General Assembly, *Report of the Group of Governmental Experts on International Co-operation to Avert New Flows of Refugees* (13 May 1986) A/41/324.

29 T. Alexander Aleinikoff, 'State-Centered Refugee Law: From Resettlement to Containment' (1992) 14(1) Mich J Int'l L 120, 130–133.

30 *Id.*, 120.

31 *Id.*, 131, citing UN General Assembly, *Report of the Group of Governmental Experts on International Co-operation to Avert New Flows of Refugees* (13 May 1986) A/41/324, Prelim. List Item 78, at 16, and Jack I. Garvey, 'Toward a Reformulation of International Refugee Law' (1985) 26(2) Harv Int'l LJ 483; see also: James C. Hathaway, 'Reconceiving Refugee Law as Human Rights Protection' (1991) 4(2) Journal of Refugee Studies 113, 124.

32 Rosemary Byrne, Andrew Shacknove, 'The Safe Country Notion in European Asylum Law' (1996) 9 Harv Hum Rts J 185, 212; Andrew Shacknove, 'From Asylum to Containment' (1993) 5 IJRL 516.

replaced by quasi-legal terms that imparted no binding character, and lacked a clear scope and content.

Like the international conferences of the 1920s and 1930s, those conferences of the 'aid and development' era were utilised to divide and assign international obligations, and to create legal mechanisms that would enable that division and assignment, and were concerned primarily with the 'self-sufficiency' of refugees, the eventual re-establishment of State of origin obligations, and the establishment of what has become one of the most pervasive principles of contemporary IRP; that of first State obligations. Settlements, or 'zones' as they were now called – were maintained through the provision of aid packages, often controlled by international entities, then handed over to host States. Refugees formed agrarian settlements and derived income from the yield of their crops. A limited ability to derive income freely, meant that the means of labour were predetermined as part of the settlement scheme. These schemes differed in no material way from those detailed in Chapter 2. In what could just as easily be a description of the stages of settlement programmes established in the early 20th century, Harrell-Bond wrote of the aid and development era:

> There are three stages to the settlement program. First, refugees are given relief aid and transported to camps, to inhabit houses built for them or which they are expected to build for themselves. During the second stage they are provided with land, tools and seeds, and primary education is organized. During this period refugees are expected to be motivated to work and get on their own feet quickly, by being told that there will be a gradual reduction in their food rations after the first harvest. In the third stage, aid is withdrawn, on the grounds that the refugees should by then be 'self-sufficient' and 'integrated' into the local community.[33]

Numerous studies at the time confirmed that organised settlement was the least favoured option of refugees themselves,[34] with one study in particular finding that between 80% and 90% of refugee settlers in one particular refu-

33 Barbara Harrell-Bond, *Imposing Aid: Emergency Assistance to Refugees* (OUP 1986) 10.

34 E. Lugusha, 'Socio-Economic Survey of Burundi Refugees in Kigoma Region, Economic Research Bureau' (1981) University of Dar es Salaam; B. Ocbru, *Tanzanian Refugee Caseload Survey* (1983) UNHCR, Dar es Salaam, both cited in: Allen Armstrong, 'Aspects of Refugee Wellbeing in Settlement Schemes: An Examination of the Tanzanian Case' (1988) 1(1) Journal of Refugee Studies 57.

gee settlement would opt for repatriation, given the chance.[35] In Gasarasi's 1984 study of refugees transferred to the Mishamo refugee settlement, he noted that the initial mass transfer was "very much against their will" and that "refugees are not only forced migrants but also, in many cases, reluctant settlers."[36] Unsurprisingly, the complications that arose from zonal developments included the degradation of the settlement after handover. Armstrong noted that settlements formed:

> [A]n isolated and vulnerable community (especially after handover), settlers can easily become neglected, exploited and severely disadvantaged. In Tanzania's settlements, the restricted rights of refugees under the 1965 Refugee Control Act together with the vesting of significant power into the hands of the Government's Settlement Commandant have encouraged, in the words of one UNHCR report (1974), "an almost military leadership structure." The authoritarian attitudes of a centralised administration concerned with imposing order have, not infrequently, led to abuses of power and the imposition of restrictions such as the closing of all private shops at Matekwe settlement.[37]

Armstrong recognised the 'recidivistic' tendencies of many refugee settlements established in Africa, which often experienced rapid decline and required renewed assistance at an early stage, noting also that a significant decline and deterioration of services and conditions almost inevitably occurred after handover.[38]

In the rapid development of IRP, a number of features came to distinguish the aid and development era. Principally, and as already noted, the interest of third States in importing a refugee labour force no longer existed, and as a consequence, refugee status, freedom of movement, and labour rights were not as inter-dependent as they were previously. Second, and by extension, the prevailing policies of the era relied significantly on the temporal limitation of protection. The differentiation between temporary and permanent protection allowed a distinct international regime to emerge that effectively con-

---

35 Hanne Christensen, *Refugees and Pioneers, Report 85–84* (1985) UNHCR Research Institute for Social Development.

36 Charles Gasarasi, *The Life of a Refugee Settlement: the Case of Muyenzi in Ngara District* (1976) UNHCR Research Project, Dar es Salaam, cited in Allen Armstrong, 'Aspects of Refugee Wellbeing in Settlement Schemes: An Examination of the Tanzanian Case' (1988) 1(1) Journal of Refugee Studies 57, 71.

37 Armstrong, *id.*, 67.

38 *Id.*

ferred limited refugee protection on a temporary basis. This allowed the scope and content of 'protection' to evolve significantly to infer the provision of humanitarian aid, rather than the international legal obligations to confer civil, social, and economic rights within the terms of the 1951 Convention's contingent rights. Third, it was bolstered by an emphasis on the principles of 'international solidarity' and 'burden-sharing'; quasi-legal obligations that referred to the relationship between 'donor' and 'host' States (or States of reception and 'first' States as they are better understood) under the aid and development model of multilateralism. The imposition of novel international obligations on 'first' States ultimately led to widespread and protracted encampment, the severe restriction of contingent rights through the temporal limitation of protection, and the reconceptualisation of such as constituted by humanitarian aid in lieu of explicitly defined international legal obligations.

The purported objective of such measures was to introduce 'order' to the departure of refugees from States of origin, and to provide humane and safe conditions in what would otherwise be a chaotic dispersal of persons. In reality, it once again permitted Western States to contain refugee populations in States geographically proximate to the State of origin, and to enact selective resettlement schemes that prioritised refugees with certain profiles, in much the same way as the schemes implemented in the interwar period and in the aftermath of WWII. This continued well into the 1980s and 1990s. In the US, the 1989 Lautenberg Amendment prioritised the resettlement of Soviet Jews, Evangelical Christians, Ukrainian Catholics, and members of the Ukrainian Orthodox Church, based on a lower evidentiary threshold than that established by the *Refugee Act* of 1980.[39] In the 1990s, Canada began integrating refugee resettlement with its broader immigration policies, prioritising refugees who could contribute to the national economy, including those with technical or professional skills.[40] In the 1990s, Germany prioritised the resettlement of Jewish refugees from the former Soviet Union,

39 USA: Department of State, *Soviet Refugees: Processing and Admittance to the United States* (1990) (GAO/NSIAD-90-158) 4–5.

40 Canada, *Canada–Québec Accord Relating to Immigration and Temporary Admission of Aliens* (1991) 18; Canada, *Immigration and Refugee Protection Act* (2001) sections 3, 12, and 14.1. The Act provides that a 'foreign national' means "a person who is not a Canadian citizen or a permanent resident, and includes a stateless person." It does not delineate refugees as a legal class subject to the law prescribed for foreign nationals.

extending legislation originally enacted for the resettlement of South-East Asian refugees.[41]

There are a number of explanations for the retreat from IRL and the reinvention of multilateralism in IRP. First, in the decades that followed the ratification of the 1951 Convention, adherence to IHRL had become a primary objective of IL. The rapid production of instruments of IHRL and statutory offices dedicated to their supervision coincided with the eventual ratification of the 1951 Convention, and continued through the 1960s, when the temporal and geographical limitations of the 1951 Convention were removed by the 1967 Protocol. The expanding scope of IHRL, and its application to refugees and asylum seekers obliged States of reception to observe an increasing number of international standards and principles and apply them universally and without discrimination, in contrast to the previous international order, which permitted the vast majority of decisions on the integration of IRL to fall within the ambit of a State's sovereign power to legislate domestically. The universal application of IHRL required a degree of homogeneity in the structure and administration of national asylum frameworks, and as a consequence, refugee status was no longer generally limited in its legislative expression to municipal laws of immigration and labour, but was increasingly relevant to individual rights and complementary concepts of 'minimum standards.'

The inclination to turn inward was also a matter of limited State resources. First States - many of them affected by the related ills of political instability, the global recession, and economic mismanagement - stressed the need for 'international burden sharing,' so that they could cope with the adverse impact of refugees on their economy, environment and infrastructure. At the same time, a number of donor States wished to limit their foreign aid expenditure, and were becoming "increasingly reluctant to devote their resources to open-ended 'care and maintenance' programmes for refugees in low-income countries."[42] As Crisp noted, "the limitations of the international community's established approach to refugee assistance and settlement began to attract renewed attention, particularly in Africa. For instead of

41 Germany, *Kontingentflüchtlingsgesetz* (1980); See generally: Barbara Dietz, Uwe Lebok, Pavel Polian, 'The Jewish Emigration from the Former Soviet Union to Germany' (2002) 40(2) International Migration 29.

42 Jeff Crisp, 'Mind the Gap! UNHCR, Humanitarian Assistance and the Development Process' (2001) 35(1) The International Migration Review 168, 170.

becoming self-sufficient, many refugee camps and their inhabitants continued to rely upon international assistance."[43] According to Crisp, the aim of donors:

> [W]as to reduce the number of refugees on the international community's books. They certainly did not want to invest very large sums of money in refugee camps and settlements which were going to remain dependent on external assistance for an indefinite period of time.[44]

Some scholars considered that the aid and development era achieved very little, due in part to the essentially ambiguous nature of its objectives. As Stein wrote:

> [T]he concept of refugee aid and development remained ill-defined. This problem was directly related to a fundamental split between donor states and host states (and, to a lesser degree, countries of origin) about the nature and purpose of refugee assistance.[45]

As he asked in a paper prepared for UNHCR, was its purpose to promote the settlement and eventual integration of refugee populations in countries of asylum? Or was its aim to ameliorate the situation of refugees, the host community and State, pending the day when those refugees returned to their country of origin?[46] As this chapter explains, the objectives of the era were perhaps not as ambiguous as Stein suggests. Nor were its achievements few. In fact, a great deal was achieved during the aid and development era. Indeed, if one considers the dramatic and permanent effect that this period has had on the scope and content of refugee protection, it should be considered the most important period of IRL. It redefined the scope and content of international obligations relative to IRL through the rapid development of IRP that supported novel definitions of refugee protection, substituting legal rights for humanitarian aid, and it enabled the attribution of SR to States of first reception, permitting the imposition of countermeasures for perceived 'violations' of novel legal concepts. Collectively, this period and the measures that char-

---

43 Jeff Crisp, 'Working Paper No. 43: Mind the gap! UNHCR, humanitarian assistance and the development process' (2001) New Issues in Refugee Research, 2.

44 *Id.*, 4.

45 Barry Stein, *Returnee Aid and Development* (1 May 1994) (EVAL/RAD/15).

46 Stein, *id*, cited in: Jeff Crisp, 'Mind the Gap! UNHCR, Humanitarian Assistance and the Development Process' (2001) 35(1) The International Migration Review 168, 172.

acterised it should be viewed as the beginning of a constructive withdrawal from the 1951 Convention.

Section 2 of this chapter considers the evolution of refugee protection and its meaning in the era of 'aid and development.' It argues that as States began to abandon multilateralism to date, the refugee events of the 1960s, 1970s, and 1980s caused the most significant shift in the conception of international obligations and SR in IRL. In particular, that the protection required by the 1951 Convention was watered down to temporary protection, and that broad acceptance of temporary protection as an alternative to the conferral of refugee status enabled the aid and development agenda. Section 2 contends that this shift was driven by the framing of refugee crises as 'humanitarian emergencies,' permitting the prioritisation of containment and aid over permanent solutions. It posits that the proliferation of zonal developments institutionalised the limitation of critical Convention requirements, including the severe restriction of movement, and of access to labour markets, while fostering dependency on humanitarian assistance. In particular, the section contends that the securitisation of refugee movement justified the implementation of IRP that permitted exceptions to *non-refoulement* on grounds of national security and public order, particularly in cases of mass influx. Section 2 concludes that the period redefined protection as a temporary and conditional measure with serious and lasting consequences for the integrity of IRL.

Section 3 considers the use of countermeasures implemented during the aid and development era, which were not only widespread but deliberately employed as a means to enforce adherence to the bartering system established and reinforced by the multilateral development of IRP. Countermeasures were predominantly financial in nature and were commonly premised on the conditionality of humanitarian aid, material and technical assistance, and military and development aid. The conditionality of aid involved various mechanisms, such as the implementation of containment policies, the restriction of secondary movement, and cooperation with resettlement programmes. Additionally, it often required host States to provide assurances of political alignment and to undertake broader economic reforms. During the refugee crises of the 1960s and 1970s in particular, donor States frequently leveraged the conditionality of aid to exert significant influence over sovereign matters of refugee management under domestic law and policy, often with the support of international organisations.

Section 4 examines the revival of the international conference as a forum for the resolution of refugee crises. It argues that the objectives of conferences during this period did not depart in any material way from those of the interwar period, though the means of realising global policy objectives differed significantly. Western States would once again exert political and economic authority over proceedings, leading to the consolidation of the aid and development era through the IRP intended to address mass-influx situations across Africa and South-East Asia, but they became conduits for the invention of novel international obligations, required by the new multilateralism in IRP, and for operationalising terms such as 'burden-sharing' and 'international solidarity.' Like their predecessors, the international conferences of the aid and development era was concerned primarily with the financial obligations assumed by Western States, the maintenance of geographically proximate States as primary States of reception, and the financial incentivisation of the 'Global South.'

Chapter 5 concludes that the institutionalisation of encampment and the restriction of refugee movement, which defined the aid and development era, have had profound and lasting consequences for IRL and for the broader understanding of protection and its scope and content. By confining refugees to geographically limited zones and severely restricting access to livelihoods, education, and opportunities for integration, the aid and development era not only entrenched cycles of dependency, but has permitted its legacy to advance the incorporation of refugee protection into systems of 'migration management' that prioritises restriction of movement and of access to labour markets over durable solutions, reflecting a significant departure from the international obligations of the 1951 Convention. The result is a system that is increasingly fragmented, regionalised, and conditional, as symptoms of the broader retreat from multilateralism and the erosion of IRL.

2 The Meaning of Protection in the Era of Aid and Development

The resolution of refugee crises in the 1960s and 1970s in particular, was premised on the characterisation of refugee questions as situations of acute humanitarian need, as opposed to matters of States' rights.[47] As such, the period marked a pivotal shift in the conceptualisation of State obligations in IRL. The humanitarian premise permitted a new construction of multilateralism in IRP; a bartering system that enabled States of reception to contain refugees in special zones for protracted periods of time, often under the

47 UN High Commissioner for Refugees, *Addendum to the Report of the United Nations High Commissioner for Refugees* (6 November 1979) A/34/12/Add.1, 43.

guise of awaiting repatriation, while prolonging dependency on humanitarian aid. By the late 1970s, "it had become clear that emergency assistance operations and care and maintenance programmes were placing refugees into a situation of dependency."[48]

The zonal developments of the 1960s were at the core of the aid and develop era.[49] Their establishment permitted a number of other policies to naturally develop that complimented, or were necessary for, their existence. Temporary protection emerged as a widely accepted alternative to the conferral of refugee status, consequently effecting a number of critical contingent rights that would have permitted integration and self-sufficiency. These included the restriction of refugee movement outside zones, which in turn justified the limitation of the right to employment, and perpetuated a system of dependency on humanitarian aid, both of the State of reception and refugees themselves.

This model of 'protection' also permitted humanitarian aid to become something of a bartering system that substituted third State obligations to resettle refugees for material support of host States.

From the mid-1960s, a distinct recalibration in the preference for 'permanent solutions' can also be noted. Where previously solutions to refugee questions were, with few exceptions, either local integration and rapid self-sufficiency, or voluntary repatriation, consensus formed around the conception of protection as the provision of humanitarian aid and the maintenance of refugee populations in physical environments conducive to the continuation of their regular agrarian lifestyle. The rationale for the preference was a sound and logical one. As the High Commissioner for Refugees explained to the General Assembly:

> One of the main common features of the problems of refugees in Africa is that they concern people who are used to live on the land or to breed cattle. Local settlement in agriculture appeared therefore to be the most appropriate solution in most cases, except of course where the refugees had opted for voluntary repatriation. In accordance with the general principles of UNHCR its main object was to help the refugees to become

---

48 Barry Stein, *Returnee Aid and Development*1 May 1994) (EVAL/RAD/15).

49 Robert F. Gorman, 'Beyond ICARA II: Implementing Refugee-Related Development Assistance' (1986) 20(2) The International Migration Review 283, 284; Jeff Crisp, 'Mind the Gap! UNHCR, Humanitarian Assistance and the Development Process' (2001) 35(1) The International Migration Review 168.

> self-supporting as rapidly as possible, and thus to reduce the period of time during which they need emergency aid.[50]

In much the same way that European refugees of professional backgrounds were neither willing nor able to be resettled as agriculturalists, local integration of African refugees through the creation of zonal developments was considered to be "a durable solution to the problems of restoring to refugees their right to earn their own livelihood and of returning them to a normal way of life, perhaps permanently, in their host country."[51] Multiple resolutions of the UN General Assembly commended States encouraging voluntary return, and urged them to continue to co-operate closely with the High Commissioner in efforts to achieve the self-sufficiency and integration of refugees in countries of asylum, and to accept refugees for resettlement, where possible.[52] This required two things: first, the establishment of zones, and second, the commitment of substantial resources. The former required the development of IRP to the detriment of IRL (specifically, the modification of refugee protection within the terms of the 1951 Convention to minimum standards of treatment, and of securitisation in the context of mass influx), and the latter permitted the bifurcation of international obligations into the exercise of physical control over refugee populations, and the provision of humanitarian aid necessary to suspend the population in a state of dependency, with limited civil and economic rights. This modified 'meaning of protection' was reinforced by the new era of multilateralism that permitted consensus to foment around international and regional refugee policy that supported such modifications.

Zonal developments were subject to much criticism, as being "flawed in their conceptualisation and implementation" and consequently "fail[ing] to meet their intended objectives."[53] Those objectives, and indeed the justification for encampment and the limitation of movement, often hinged on the perceived security risks posed by refugees to the States of reception in the context of mass influx. National security and public order were fundamental

---

50 UN General Assembly, *Report of the United Nations High Commissioner for Refugees* (1 January 1965) A/6011/REV.1(SUPP), pg 8, para 79.

51 Allen Armstrong, 'Aspects of Refugee Wellbeing in Settlement Schemes: An Examination of the Tanzanian Case' (1988) 1(1) Journal of Refugee Studies 57–58.

52 UN General Assembly, *Report of the United Nations High Commissioner for Refugees* (29 November 1978) A/RES/33/26; UN General Assembly, *Report of the United Nations High Commissioner for Refugees* (8 December 1977) A/RES/32/67

53 Jeff Crisp, 'Mind the Gap! UNHCR, Humanitarian Assistance and the Development Process' (2001) 35(1) The International Migration Review 168.

considerations in the development of IRP which provided exception to the principles of *non-refoulement*, expulsion, and compulsory return for such overriding reasons; terms that were invoked particularly in the case of mass influx. *The Principles Concerning Treatment of Refugees*, adopted by the Asian-African Legal Consultative Committee (AALCC) in 1966, provided exception to *non-refoulement* for "overriding reasons of national security or public order."[54] Resolution 14 (1967) on *Asylum to Persons in Danger of Persecution*, adopted by the Committee of Ministers of The Council of Europe,[55] contemplated exception to *non-refoulement*, recommending that States should, in such circumstances, "accord to the individual concerned the opportunity of going to a country other than that where he would be in danger of persecution."[56] Article 3(2) of the 1967 *Declaration on Territorial Asylum* explicitly acknowledged that States may derogate from the principle of *non-refoulement* in cases where national security or public order was at risk:

1. No person referred to in article 1, paragraph 1, shall be subjected to measures such as rejection at the frontier or, if he has already entered the territory in which he seeks asylum, expulsion or compulsory return to any State where he may be subjected to persecution.
2. Exception may be made to the foregoing principle only for overriding reasons of national security or in order to safeguard the population, as in the case of a mass influx of persons.[57]

The 1977 United Nations *Conference on Territorial Asylum* attempted to produce draft articles, and though unsuccessful in its endeavour, it is interesting to note that proposed article 9 was provisionally entitled 'right of qualification' and provided that:

> Qualification of the grounds for granting asylum or applying the provisions of this Convention appertains to the Contracting State whose territory the person concerned has entered or seeks to enter and seeks asylum.[58]

54 Asian-African Legal Consultative Committee, *Principles concerning Treatment of Refugees* (1966).

55 Council of Europe: Committee of Ministers, *Resolution (67)14: Asylum to Persons in Danger of Persecution* (29 June 1967).

56 Article III, Paragraph 3.

57 UN General Assembly, *Declaration on Territorial Asylum* (14 December 1967) A/RES/2312 (XXII).

58 UN General Assembly, *Report of the United Nations Conference on Territorial Asylum* (21 April 1977) (A/CONF.78/12) Annex I, pg 63.

With only minor proposed changes, the article was supported, *inter alia*, by both France and the UK. ExCom Conclusion No. 15 (XXX) of 1979 also provided that:

> In cases of large-scale influx, persons seeking asylum should always receive *at least temporary refuge*. States which because of their geographical situation, or otherwise, are faced with a large-scale influx should as necessary and at the request of the State concerned *receive immediate assistance from other States in accordance with the principle of equitable burden-sharing*. Such States should consult with the Office of the United Nations High Commissioner for Refugees as soon as possible to ensure that the persons involved are fully protected, are given emergency assistance, and that durable solutions are sought.[59]

This rapid development in IRP permitted the incremental introduction of temporary protection as an alternative to the conferral of refugee status and allowed the limitation and qualification of protection on the grounds of national security and public order in the case of mass influx as an accepted modification to IRL by IRP. By the late 1970s, temporary refuge had been resoundingly endorsed as a pragmatic response to mass influx. This era thus marked a decisive departure from the clear requirements of protection as provided by the 1951 Convention, recalibrating IRL into a series of conditional humanitarian measures, and aligning it with the priorities of Western States to position themselves as benefactors of 'refugee protection' in the developing world.

2.1 *Temporary Protection and Mass Influx of Refugees*

By stagnating refugee movement through the provision of humanitarian aid, now considered to constitute 'protection,' States were able to legitimise the implementation of an alternative to voluntary repatriation in the case of mass influx – that of temporary protection. Temporary protection was ostensibly implemented to facilitate the observance of *non-refoulement* while evading the provision of permanent solutions, replacing them instead with what was now termed 'durable' solutions. While in 1972, the UN General Assembly continued to recognise voluntary repatriation as a 'permanent solution to the ref-

59 Executive Committee of the High Commissioner's Programme, *Conclusion No. 15 (XXX) on Refugees without an Asylum Country* (16 October 1979).

ugee problem,'[60] the language of 'durable solutions' began to emerge towards the end of the decade in reference to temporary protection.[61]

Some experts considered that in certain regions, mass influx had changed the nature of protection that could be granted, even though the principle of *non-refoulement* had, of course, to be maintained. The question was, however, whether a new concept was necessary, or whether the problems arising in mass influx situations could not be resolved by the application and amplification of existing concepts. The solution settled upon was that of temporary protection. The emphasis was placed on the right to admission rather than the obligation of the State of reception to grant a permanent solution. Temporary protection was presented in the context of an impossibility to confer refugee status on such a large number of people, and as a means to observe the principle of *non-refoulement* in such a context. The scope and content of those international obligations required by IRL were increasingly diluted into vague commitments to make 'best efforts,' to work in 'international solidarity,' and to 'burden-share.'[62] This rather dramatic shift in the global understanding of protection and its requirements only eroded it further as a legal concept, replaced instead by protracted encampment and cyclical international aid.

At the same time, the UNHCR shifted from a law- and policy-centric organisation to a broadly based humanitarian agency.[63] This had multiple flow-on

60 UN General Assembly, *Resolution 2956 (XXVII): Report of the United Nations High Commissioner for Refugees* (12 December 1972) (GA/RES/2956(XXVII)).

61 ExCom Conclusion No. 19 (XXXI) on 'Temporary Refuge' referred to temporary protection as a 'durable solution.' See: Executive Committee of the High Commissioner's Programme, *Conclusion No. 19 (XXXI): Temporary Refuge* (16 October 1980); Executive Committee Conclusion 15 (XXX) on 'Refugees without an Asylum Country' adopted in 1979, stated that "In cases of large-scale influx, persons seeking asylum should always receive at least temporary refuge," providing that States should ensure beneficiaries are "fully protected, are given emergency assistance, and that durable solutions are sought." See: Executive Committee of the High Commissioner's Programme, *Conclusion No. 15 (XXX) on Refugees without an Asylum Country* (16 October 1979).

62 Multiple General Assembly Resolutions called for increased financial contributions, durable solutions, and burden-sharing in respect of refugees and displaced persons in South-East Asia and Africa. See, for example: UN General Assembly, *Report of the Secretary-General on the Meeting on Refugees and Displaced Persons in South-East Asia* (29 November 1979) A/RES/34/62; UN General Assembly, *Situation of African Refugees* (29 November 1979) A/RES/34/61; UN General Assembly, *Report of the United Nations High Commissioner for Refugees* (29 November 1979) A/RES/34/60; UN General Assembly, *Report of the United Nations High Commissioner for Refugees* (29 November 1978) A/RES/33/26.

63 Jeff Crisp, 'Working Paper No. 43: Mind the gap! UNHCR, humanitarian assistance and the development process' (2001) New Issues in Refugee Research 7; Laura Barnett,

effects for the relationships between State and refugee, State and organisation, and organisation and refugee. The maintenance of local settlements became the primary focus of the UNHCR's work. Concurrently, the organisation increasingly relied on private organisations to assume various 'protection' obligations, previously the charge of UNHCR or the State of reception. This dispersion of obligations was in part due to the dilution of the term 'protection' to encompass expansive interpretations of human rights. As Stevens warned decades later, "[i]f, for example, an expansive, human-rights oriented notion of protection is promoted by the UNHCR or humanitarian organisations, some States might become increasingly resistant to receiving and accepting refugees."[64] This is precisely what transpired across the continent of Africa in the 1960s and 1970s. The UNHCR and private actors increasingly began to interpret the organisation's mandate as one to protect and guarantee a broad array of human rights which complemented the provision of humanitarian aid to asylum seekers. In response, States retreated from previously well-accepted State obligations in respect of refugees, which in turn broadened the 'protection gap' that then needed to be filled by further humanitarian actions and initiatives.

Temporary protection and the provision of aid in fulfilment of 'burden-sharing' obligations had not always been the approach to situations of mass influx. As a result of events occurring in Hungary in late 1956, over 100,000 refugees entered Austria in November of that year. The solution was not to flood the country with aid in the form of emergency funds and technical support. Rather, within days of an appeal by the Austrian State Secretary to the UN and Western States for "quick action to provide a solution," a total of 25,000 refugees were resettled in the United States, Canada, Switzerland, Argentina, Australia, Western Germany, France, the United Kingdom, Italy, the Netherlands, Norway, Sweden, and New Zealand.[65] In the succeeding months, the vast majority of those remaining refugees were also resettled.[66]

'Working Paper No. 54: Global Governance and the Evolution of the International Refugee Regime' (2002) New Issues in Refugee Research 11; S. Alex Cunliffe, Michael Pugh, 'UNHCR as Leader in Humanitarian Assistance: A Triumph of Politics over Law?' in Frances Nicholson and Patrick Twomey (eds), *Refugee Rights and Realities: Evolving International Concepts and Regimes* (CUP 1999) 176.

64 Dallal Stevens, 'What Do We Mean by Protection?' (2013) 20(2) International Journal on Minority and Group Rights 233, 234.

65 UN High Commissioner for Refugees, *Report of the Meeting of the Expert Group on Temporary Refuge in Situations of Large-Scale Influx (Geneva 21–24 April 1981)* (17 July 1981) (EC/SCP/16/Add.1).

66 *Id.*

This approach began to waver in the early 1970s. As a result of events occurring in 1971 in what was then Eastern Pakistan, some ten million refugees entered India within the space of several months.[67] The Indian Government insisted that refugees could not remain as permanent residents in India, and that the "evacuees" had sought only temporary refuge in India. They would be returned as soon as the conditions in their homeland would permit.[68] At an ECOSOC meeting on 16 July 1971, the Indian representative stressed that plans for accelerated economic and social development in India had been severely jeopardised by the massive influx of refugees, and that relief efforts could, at best, be only a temporary matter. The real humanitarian solution lay in stopping the flow of refugees and in expediting their return.[69] The temporary nature of the admission placed the international community under pressure to resolve the crisis created by the mass influx of refugees into India by working to obtain the conditions necessary for voluntary repatriation.

On 6 December 1971, the General Assembly passed a resolution which recognised that voluntary repatriation would be the only satisfactory solution to the refugee problem, and urged all Member States to intensify their efforts to bring about conditions necessary for speedy and voluntary repatriation. Following 11 days of hostilities between India and Pakistan in the same month, which led to India's recognition of the independent State of Bangladesh, the UN Security Council called for "international assistance in the relief of suffering and the rehabilitation of refugees and their return in safety and dignity to their homes."[70] The repatriation of 10 million refugees began on 1 January 1972 and was completed two and a half months later.[71]

The problems with temporary protection were evident from the outset:

> Since the late 1980s, there has been a marked shift in refugee policy in Africa, which became particularly pronounced in the 1990s. While the refugee problem has on the whole increased, African states have been

67 UN High Commissioner for Refugees, *The State of The World's Refugees 2000: Fifty Years of Humanitarian Action* (1 January 2000) chap 3.

68 Louise W. Holborn, *Refugees, a Problem of Our Time: The Work of the United Nations High Commissioner for Refugees, 1951–1972, Volume 1* (Scarecrow Press 1975) 758–780.

69 UN High Commissioner for Refugees, *Report of the Meeting of the Expert Group on Temporary Refuge in Situations of Large-Scale Influx (Geneva 21–24 April 1981)* 17 July 1981) (EC/SCP/16/Add.1).

70 UN Security Council, *Resolution 307(1971): The India/Pakistan Subcontinent* (21 December 1971) S/RES/307.

71 UN High Commissioner for Refugees, *The State of The World's Refugees 2000: Fifty Years of Humanitarian Action* (1 January 2000) 68 *et seq.*

> less committed to asylum. Instead of opening their doors to persons fearing harm in their own states, African countries now prefer refugees to receive protection in "safe zones" or similar areas within their countries of origin. African states now routinely reject refugees at the frontier or return them to their countries of origin even if the conditions from which have fled still persist. Refugees who manage to enter and remain in host countries receive "pseudoasylum."[72]

Furthermore, the restriction of movement through encampment meant that "[M]embers of the same family are separated in different parts of the same country of temporary asylum. This often occurs when refugees are confined in camps in situations of mass influx."[73] In addition to the practical impediments, temporary protection allowed refugee protection to be watering down to a series of 'minimum standards' which in effect treated the international obligations of the 1951 Convention as principles of good practice against which a State could apply a margin of appreciation. This was particularly detrimental to the integrity of protection in the context of mass influx, as the speed at which refugee crises unfolded, and the sheer scale of the numbers, legitimised the securitisation and militarisation of refugee movement, which in turn necessitated the limitation of civil and economic entitlements that were fundamental to the realisation of protection per the 1951 Convention. Furthermore, the ongoing maintenance of encampments meant that those States of reception hosting large numbers of refugees in specially designated zones were in a position of reliance on donor States. The imbalanced nature of this relationship permitted donor States to exert significant power over States of reception, and to utilise the provision of aid as a means to enforce compliance with a variety of other interests.

3 Countermeasures and the Conditionality of Aid

The use of countermeasures in the aid and development era were not only prevalent, but were implemented with the clear objective to enforce compliance with the bartering system established and reinforced by the multilateral development of IRP. Countermeasures were invariably premised on the con-

72 Bonaventure Rutinwa, 'The End of Asylum? The Changing Nature of Refugee Policies in Africa' (2002) 21(1/2) Refugee Survey Quarterly 12–13.

73 UN High Commissioner for Refugees, *Note on Family Reunification* (18 July 1983) pt. 5.

ditionality of humanitarian aid, material or technical assistance, cooperation in resettlement, and unrelated military and development aid. In the context of the refugee crises that emerged during the 1960s, 1970s, and 1980s, the conditionality of aid was frequently utilised by donor States to exercise substantial influence over sovereign matters of refugee management under municipal law and policy, occasionally with the assistance of international organisations. The conditionality of aid typically required a number of mechanisms, including not only the establishment of containment policies, the prevention of secondary movement, and cooperation with resettlement programmes, but assurances by the host State of political alignment with the donor State or States. As Loescher noted:

> Humanitarian work is generally perceived to be somehow separated from politics. This perception has persisted to some extent in the field of refugee protection and assistance. Yet workers in the field, especially those who assist refugees, are keenly aware that their activities are deeply intertwined with politics. Refugees are, in fact, an intensely political issue, and their existence affects both foreign and domestic policy, exacerbates interstate conflicts, and influences international attitudes.[74]

Perhaps most notably, in response to the Indochinese refugee crisis, Western States, including the US, Canada, and Australia, imposed conditions on South-East Asian States to prevent secondary movement, relying in turn on the conditionality of aid as a means to enforce compliance. These and other similar actions should be considered as what they were in the context of a burgeoning system of IRP – the threat of countermeasures in the event of a 'violation' of novel international obligations.

From the mid-1970s, multiple conflicts in the Indochinese region caused a massive outflow of refugees from Vietnam, Laos, Cambodia (then Kampuchea), and to a lesser extent, China. The international war in Vietnam, the bombardment of Laos, the Vietnamese invasion of Kampuchea, and the brief Sino-Vietnamese war displaced over 2 million people across the region. While the Indochinese refugee crisis created many 'land refugees,' it also precipitated a mass exodus by sea:

74 Gil Loescher, 'Humanitarianism and Politics in Central America' (1988) 103(2) Political Science Quarterly 295.

> A terrifying spectre emerged, of small, ramshackle boats containing thousands of desperate refugees roaming the seas of South-East Asia, before they either drowned or starved.[75]

On 31 May 1979, the British Prime Minister proposed to the UN Secretary-General that an international conference be convened to deal with the problem.[76] Sixty-five States attended the conference in July of the same year. The Secretary-General emphasised the need for all States to realise the interrelationship of obligations and responsibilities on the part of States of origin, States of asylum, and States of final settlement. States of origin had an obligation to respect the right of emigration and family reunification. They also had an obligation to avoid any action leading to the departure of their nationals under dangerous conditions, and to cooperate with the UNHCR to ensure 'an orderly outflow.'[77] Vietnam agreed to enforce a moratorium on 'illegal' departures for the purposes of creating 'orderly and safe' channels. As the Secretary-General announced at the conference:

> As a result of my consultations, the government of the Socialist Republic of Vietnam has authorized me to inform you that for a reasonable period of time it will make every effort to *stop illegal departures*. In the meantime, the government of Vietnam will cooperate with the UNHCR in expanding the present seven-point program designed *to bring departures into orderly and safe channels*.[78]

As Stein noted, the moratorium gave Vietnam "U.N. approval to apply draconian measures to citizens forced into life-periling flight by other draconian

---

75 Arthur C. Helton, 'Asylum and Refugee Protection in Thailand' (1989) 1(1) IJRL 21, 23–24. See also, comments of the UN Secretary General: UN General Assembly, *Meeting on Refugees and Displaced Persons in South-East Asia, convened by the Secretary-General of the United Nations at Geneva, on 20 and 21 July 1979, and Subsequent Developments: Report of the Secretary-General* (7 November 1979) A/34/627.

76 UN General Assembly, *Meeting on Refugees and Displaced Persons in South-East Asia, convened by the Secretary-General of the United Nations at Geneva, on 20 and 21 July 1979, and subsequent developments: Report of the Secretary-General – Corrigendum* (19 November 1979) (A/34/627/Corr.1), 6.

77 UN General Assembly, *Meeting on Refugees and Displaced Persons in South-East Asia, convened by the Secretary-General of the United Nations at Geneva, on 20 and 21 July 1979, and Subsequent Developments: Report of the Secretary-General* (7 November 1979) A/34/627, 5.

78 *Id.*, 6; Barry Wain, *The Refused: The Agony of the Indochina Refugees* (Simon and Schuster 1981) 225. Emphasis added.

measures and to curtail fundamental U.N. recognized rights to travel freely and to choose one's place of residence."[79] It also permitted States to deem as 'illegal' those refugees that did not follow the 'safe and orderly' routes established by UNHCR and Vietnam – those that set out on overcrowded and unseaworthy vessels and were intercepted on the high seas.

Malaysia and Thailand had refused to accept any more refugees,[80] and certain States in the region were unwilling to allow disembarkation of rescued vessels without guaranteed resettlement in third States, despite UNHCR's undertaking to meet the expenses incurred. In some cases, vessels in need of rescue on the high seas had already reached land only to be turned away or towed back to sea.[81] In one instance, Thai Navy and marine police vessels were deployed along the east coast to intercept Vietnamese on 16 January 1988, and on 28 January, Deputy Permanent Secretary Somphorn of the Ministry of the Interior presided over a push-off of refugees at Khlong Yai port, deputising local fishermen to join the blockade.[82] Thai officials maintained that Vietnamese refugees were to be considered 'illegal immigrants.'[83] The ban on boat people was extended to cover the entire south coast from Bangkok to the Malaysian border.[84]

In 1989, the UN Secretary-General convened the *International Conference on Indochinese Refugees*,[85] which produced a *Declaration and Comprehensive Plan of Action*. During prior consultations, a draft *Declaration and Comprehensive Plan of Action* was drawn up for submission to the Conference as the basis of a new international consensus on the approach to be adopted in seeking a comprehensive and durable solution to the continuing problem of Indo-

79 Barry Stein, 'The Geneva Conferences and the Indochinese Refugee Crisis' (1979) 13(4) The International Migration Review 716, 722.

80 *Id.*, 717. 'Conferences' refers to the three conferences on Indochinese refugees that occurred in Geneva in July 1979: the International Council of Voluntary Agencies Consultation on the Indo-China Refugee Problem on the 18th and 19th; the United Nations Meeting on Refugees and Displaced Persons in South-East Asia on the 20th and 21st; and the World Council of Churches Consultation on Indochinese Refugees on the 24th and 25th.

81 UN General Assembly, *Meeting on Refugees and Displaced Persons in South-East Asia, convened by the Secretary-General of the United Nations at Geneva, on 20 and 21 July 1979, and Subsequent Developments: Report of the Secretary-General* (7 November 1979) A/34/627, Annex I, 5.

82 Arthur C. Helton, 'Asylum and Refugee Protection in Thailand' (1989) 1(1) IJRL 21.

83 *Id.*

84 *Id.*

85 UN General Assembly, *Resolution 43/119: International Conference on Indo-Chinese Refugees* (8 December 1988) (A/RES/43/119).

Chinese asylum-seekers and refugees, including the question of clandestine departures, and regular departure programmes.[86]

It was "imperative that humane measures be implemented to deter such departures" that had caused loss of life at sea,[87] and that refugees be offered a "preferable solution" through "emigration from Viet Nam through regular departure procedures and migration programmes, such as the current Orderly Departure Programme."[88]

As geographically proximate States, Malaysia, China, Vietnam, Japan, the Philippines, Indonesia, Singapore, and Thailand bore the brunt of the Indo-Chinese refugee crisis. In the four years preceding the 1979 *Meeting on Refugees and Displaced Persons in South-East Asia*,[89] over a million refugees left their States of origin in Indo-China, often arriving at the border of other Indo-Chinese States. At the time of the conference, nearly a million refugees had left their States of origin, half of whom has been received by others in the region.[90] Yet only 200,000 people had been processed for resettlement outside the region.[91] The UN Secretary-General characterised displacement from Indo-China as a "humanitarian problem,"[92] expressing the opinion that "[s]ince the countries of first asylum were developing countries confronted with serious economic and social constraints, it was essential that countries outside the area assumed the principal responsibility for resettlement."[93] The President of the Conference also considered that in relation to the continuing influx of asylum seekers, the Conference needed to address three basic issues: the early removal of the burden placed on the States of first asylum; the full commitment of the State of origin to take effective measures to prevent clandestine departures, to expand orderly departures, and to accept the return of those determined not to be refugees; and the continuing commitment of third

86 UN General Assembly, *Declaration and Comprehensive Plan of Action of the International Conference on Indo-Chinese Refugees, Report of the Secretary-General* (22 September 1989) A/44/523, 2.

87 *Id.*, 11.

88 *Id.*, 12.

89 UN General Assembly, *Meeting on Refugees and Displaced Persons in South-East Asia, convened by the Secretary-General of the United Nations at Geneva, on 20 and 21 July 1979, and Subsequent Developments: Report of the Secretary-General* (7 November 1979) A/34/627. Several other governments attended as observers and interested intergovernmental organisations and groupings of non-governmental organisations were also represented.

90 *Id.*

91 *Id.*

92 *Id.*

93 *Id.*, II (12).

States to resettle readily and quickly all refugees.[94] All those seeking asylum would be granted temporary protection pending an individual status determination, to be carried out by a national authority with UNHCR participating in an observer and advisor capacity. A Resettlement Programme for Newly-Determined Refugees would accommodate all those who arrive after the introduction of status-determination procedures and are determined to be refugees.[95]

> Wherever possible, a pledge shall be sought from the resettlement countries to place all those determined to be refugees, except those expressing the wish to return to Viet Nam, within a prescribed period. It shall be the responsibility of UNHCR, with the full support of all the resettlement countries and countries of asylum, to co-ordinate efforts to ensure that departures are effected within that time.[96]

Prior to the meeting, the Secretary General had appealed to States in the Asian region to accept greater numbers of refugees from Indo-China and to increase their financial contributions to the UNHCR so that the High Commissioner could pursue resettlement solutions in third states.[97] As it transpired, Western States would go on to provide the majority share of financial assistance necessary to establish refugee camps within Asia, while accepting comparatively few cases for resettlement. States that had positioned themselves as those of resettlement utilised limited quota systems and the assignment of obligations to parties other than the State as methods to limit the scope and content of their own international obligations. In July 1979, the government of Canada issued a new policy which raised the quota of Indochinese refugees to 50,000 and introduced the one-to-one matching formula between government- and privately-sponsored refugees, making use of a provision in *The New Immigration Act* of 1978 which made it possible for local groups of at least five Cana-

94 UN General Assembly, *Declaration and Comprehensive Plan of Action of the International Conference on Indo-Chinese Refugees, Report of the Secretary-General* (22 September 1989) A/44/523, pg 7, para 21.

95 *Id.*, pg 15, paras. 10–11.

96 *Id.*, pg 15, para. 11.

97 This proposition was taken up very seriously by Japan, who contributed half the funds required that year for the High Commissioner's Assistance Programme for Indo-Chinese Refugees. See: UN General Assembly, *Record of meeting held on 25 Sept. 1979* (25 September 1979) (A/34/PV.8), Mr Sonado of Japan at [137].

dian citizens (or permanent residents) and local legally incorporated organisations to sponsor refugees.[98] US Congress passed the *Indochina Migration and Refugee Assistance Act* of 1975, which authorised a temporary programme of relief and resettlement and the establishment of the *Indochinese Refugee Assistance Program* (IRAP). As originally envisioned, IRAP was to expire in 1977, but events intervened, and IRAP continued until it was essentially superseded by the standardised US Refugee Admissions Program (USRAP) in the *Refugee Act* of 1980.

From late 1979, the US began processing so-called 'Category IV entrants.' According to the American admissions criterion for Indochinese refugees, that category accommodated persons who do not have close relatives in the US, are not former employees of the US, and were not associated with American programmes in Indochina during the war. The residual Category IV ('other') was added for humanitarian reasons, and to assure first-asylum States that they would not be left with unskilled and uneducated refugees – a modern day 'hardcore.'[99] Programmes such as these exacerbated the already disproportionate division of the refugee 'burden' between States in the 'Global South' and those in the 'Global North.' This was noted in the 1989 report of the High Commissioner for Refugees to the UN Secretary-General, where he wrote that increased accession to the 1951 Convention was:

> [O]ffset by the increase in unilateral measures by States that not only deteriorated the plight of asylum-seekers and refugees, but even posed a threat to the humanitarian institution of asylum.
>
> These included new or revamped legal or administrative measures relating to admission, immigration, detention and screening procedures intended to, or resulting in, deterring the movements of asylum-seekers, whether they were arriving at their first, or had crossed several other, borders. Measures which may have been taken in light of valid political, economic or security needs in the context of more general migratory flows occurring for economic reasons have, nevertheless, adversely affected the plight of asylum-seekers and refugees and threat-

98 Gertrud Neuwirth, Lynn Clark, 'Indochinese Refugees in Canada: Sponsorship and Adjustment' (1981) 15(1/2) The International Migration Review 131.

99 Astri Suhrke, 'Indochinese Refugees and American Policy' (1981) 37(2) The World Today 54, 55.

> ened the humanitarian principles and practices universally recognized as essential for their protection.[100]

In addition to the pressure on Vietnam to cooperate with the terms of the moratorium and orderly departure programme, ASEAN were under pressure to cooperate with international resettlement programmes, restricting the movement of refugees to camp environments in exchange for aid, leading to severe overcrowding, with refugees facing prolonged periods of confinement and limited access to livelihoods. In a report by the US Joint Economic Committee, it was noted:

> The general disposition of the ASEAN governments to leave policy initiatives in matters of Indochinese refugees to the UNHCR and the United States, and to accept – however reluctantly – their role as providing first asylum, will probably continue as long as (i) the direct economic costs of maintaining camps and the Khmer relief operation are covered by foreign sources, (ii) third countries maintain a sufficiently high resettlement rate to visibly draw down the camp population, (iii) the refugees do not arrive en masse in big vessels (as happened in early 1979), and (iv) the ASEAN governments are confident that their policy is rewarded by a generally supportive relationship with the United States, as manifested in American assistance on a wide range of issues not directly related to refugees.[101]

This model was replicated across multiple refugee crises and multiple regions. In Africa, during the 1980s, international aid for refugee camps in States such as Sudan, Somalia, and Ethiopia was at times tied to agreements that refugees would not be permitted to settle permanently or move freely outside designated areas. In Sudan at the end of 1981, approximately 425,000 out of a total of 520,000 refugees were Ethiopian or Eritrean, with the much larger number being Eritrean.[102] The Sudanese Government organised a donors' conference in Khartoum in June 1980, and though only about half of the funds sought were pledged, even those limited funds would only be paid once detailed proj-

100 UN High Commissioner for Refugees, *Report of the United Nations High Commissioner for Refugees* (9 May 1989) (E/1989/64), 2.

101 USA: Joint Economic Committee, *Indochinese Refugees: The Impact on First Asylum Countries and Implications for American Policy* (25 November 1980) (69–826 O) 9–10.

102 David R. Smock, 'Eritrean Refugees in the Sudan' (1982) 20(3) The Journal of Modern African Studies 451.

ects were formulated. Donors contended that they would have been more generous in their response if the planning of projects had progressed further.[103] Civil wars in El Salvador, Guatemala, and Nicaragua led to large-scale displacement, with refugees fleeing to neighbouring States, including Honduras, Mexico, and Costa Rica. US aid to these States of reception was often tied to their cooperation with containment policies and opposition to leftist political movements. In Honduras, the refugee situation was "intimately tied to the geopolitics of the region" and included "not only the Honduran government and military, but also the Honduran Refugee Commission (CONARE), the US government, the UNHCR, the Honduran Catholic church, voluntary agencies, the Nicaraguan contras, international human rights and religious groups, and the refugees themselves."[104] Accordingly, "the treatment and protection accorded to refugees [was] determined largely by geopolitical and strategic considerations, in particular by Honduran relations with the U.S. and Salvadoran governments."[105] In response to the mass influx of Afghan refugees to Pakistan and Iran during the Soviet–Afghan War, Western States – in particular the US – implemented 'Operation Cyclone' – a covert programme supporting the Afghan mujahideen, which included the provision of substantial aid. Concurrently, Pakistan hosted millions of Afghan refugees fleeing the conflict for which the State also received substantial humanitarian aid. As Loescher wrote of the political conditionality of aid:

> Today, pressures to politicize refugee crises are increasing everywhere in the world. Humanitarianism has become a political tool used to justify arming refugee camps in Pakistan, Thailand, and Honduras; aiding insurgencies in Nicaragua, Ethiopia, and Angola; and suppressing insurgencies in El Salvador and elsewhere. The practice of using refugees in the service of foreign policy or military objectives is by no means limited to the United States, as indicated by the activities of the Palestine Liberation Organization (PLO), Algerian support of Polisario guerrillas claiming the West Sahara, use by Libya of the northern Chadians in operations against Chad, the activities of South West African People's Organisation (SWAPO) in southern Africa, the sanctuary offered to anti-government Ethiopian groups by Sudan and to Sudanese secessionists by Ethiopia, and numerous other cases. Through such developments,

103 Id., 462–463.

104 Gil Loescher, 'Humanitarianism and Politics in Central America' (1988) 103(2) Political Science Quarterly 295, 306.

105 *Id.*

> any independence of the humanitarian space on the landscape of politics among nations has evaporated.[106]

The consequences of the conditionality of aid were predictable, as were its criticisms. Conditionality prioritised the political and security objectives of Western States asserting control over sovereign matters of refugee management, with little regard to the entitlements of refugee status beneficiaries required by the 1951 Convention. The restriction of movement and access to livelihoods led to overcrowded camps, poor living conditions, and prolonged dependency on aid. The sovereignty of States of reception was undermined not only by conditionality, but by the imposition of countermeasures in the case of non-compliance. The politicisation of aid and its consequences for compliance with the political, ideological, and economic objectives of Western States, contributed in no small part to the politicisation of refugee crises. As conditionality ultimately required long-term containment of refugees by States of Reception, the language of durable solutions replaced permanent solutions to include not only such measures as temporary protection, cessation, and ostensibly voluntary return, but also the widespread use of cessation.

4 State Responsibility at the International Conferences on Refugee Questions

The scale of the global refugee crisis during the era in question led to the revival of the conference on refugee questions, and like its predecessors, conferences in the aid and development era were concerned primarily with the financial obligations assumed by Western States, and the maintenance of geographically proximate States as primary States of reception. The financial incentivisation of the 'Global South' in this era revolved around the provision of humanitarian aid in exchange for the containment and encampment of refugee populations. Among the most notable during this period were the two ICARA conferences on African refugees. Held in Arusha, Tanzania, in May 1979, the *Pan-African Conference on the Situation of Refugees in Africa* brought together African States in an attempt to resolve some fundamental questions of the continental refugee crisis.[107] The following year, the *International Conference on Assistance to Refugees in Africa* (ICARA I) was convened

106 *Id.*, 296.

107 *Recommendations from the Pan-African Conference on the Situation of Refugees in Africa, Arusha (Tanzania)* (17 May 1979)

with 199 countries and over 120 non-governmental organisations participating to resolve the crisis.[108] The objectives of ICARA I were threefold:

(a) To focus public attention on the plight of refugees in Africa;
(b) To mobilize additional resources for refugee programmes in Africa; and
(c) To assist countries of asylum adversely affected by the large-scale presence of refugees to obtain international assistance for projects aimed at strengthening the ability of those countries to carry the extra burden placed on their services and facilities.[109]

In organising the Conference, African States were certainly aware of the model of refugee protection that Western States wished to impose on them. This was clear at ICARA I, when then-President of Sierra Leone and Chairman of OAU, Siaka Stevens, commented:

> Refugees should not be assisted in ways which would create conditions of overdependence [...]. Rather, they should be guided and enabled to become self-supporting as quickly as possible.[110]

The outcome of the conference was as foreseeable as those conferences of the inter-war period. The conference recognised "the need of the countries of asylum for adequate human, technical and financial assistance to enable them properly to shoulder their increased responsibilities and assume the additional burden which the presence of refugees represents for their economies,"[111] and "the need to assist similarly the countries of origin in the voluntary repatriation and resettlement of returnees,"[112] but referred only once to resettlement programmes. In their assumed role as benefactors of refugee containment, Western States were unable to provide the funds necessary for the aid and development model to function. A document entitled 'The Refugee Situation in Africa: Assistance Measures Proposed,' containing all proposals made by Governments for additional humanitarian and infrastructure assistance, was assembled by the Conference secretariat and served as the

108 UN General Assembly, *International Conference on Assistance to Refugees in Africa* (14 December 1981) A/RES/36/124.

109 UN General Assembly, *International Conference on Assistance to Refugees in Africa (ICARA I): Report of the Secretary-General* (11 June 1981) A/36/316.

110 See: Statement by the Chairman of the Organization of African Unity, UN General Assembly, *Second International Conference on Assistance to Refugees in Africa* (14 December 1984) A/RES/39/139, 6.

111 *Id.*

112 UN General Assembly, *International Conference on Assistance to Refugees in Africa* (14 December 1981) A/RES/36/124.

principal document for the Conference. These proposals called for assistance totalling $893,126,792. In the end, contributions totalled only $566,649,472.[113]

At the Second International Conference on Assistance to Refugees in Africa (ICARA II), held in 1984, 128 different refugee aid and development project proposals in Africa were presented to the donor community. Significantly less financial aid was requested at ICARA II, amounting to some US$362 million – "an average of just under US$3 million per project and almost as much as UNHCR's total global expenditure the previous year, which had amounted to $397 million."[114] Stevens noted that of the projects submitted to UNHCR, those that had not been funded were mainly ones "where large numbers of refugees are to be found in some of the least developed countries of the world, and where the presence of a large concentration of refugees in care and maintenance situations is regarded as an important impediment to development."[115] As Gorman noted at the time:

> No matter how well-coordinated the UN agencies are, the ultimate success of ICARA II will depend on the availability of resources and in this regard it is the donor governments rather than the international agencies that exercise ultimate control.

The final document of ICARA II emphasised:

> [T]he vital importance of the *complementarity of refugee aid and development assistance* and of achieving durable solutions to the problems of refugees in Africa *through the voluntary repatriation or local integration of refugees* and the necessity of providing assistance for the strengthening of the social and economic infrastructures of African countries receiving refugees and returnees.[116]

In turn, the General Assembly continued to urge all Member States and all intergovernmental and non-governmental organisations to "assist the coun-

113 UN General Assembly, *International Conference on Assistance to Refugees in Africa (ICARA I): Report of the Secretary-General* (11 June 1981) A/36/316.

114 Jeff Crisp, 'Mind the Gap! UNHCR, Humanitarian Assistance and the Development Process' (2001) 35(1) The International Migration Review 168, 171.

115 See: Statement by the Chairman of the Organization of African Unity, UN General Assembly, *Second International Conference on Assistance to Refugees in Africa* (14 December 1984) A/RES/39/139, 6.

116 UN General Assembly, *Second International Conference on Assistance to Refugees in Africa* (14 December 1984) A/RES/39/139. Emphasis added.

tries of asylum materially and otherwise to enable them to continue to discharge their humanitarian obligations towards refugees."[117] The firm entrenchment of the aid and development model continued to be replicated again and again in respect of other evolving refugee crisis across the globe. As Richter noted, the 1988 *International Conference on the Plight of Refugees, Returnees and Displaced Persons in Southern Africa* (SARRED) "continued to link humanitarian and rehabilitation assistance for refugees, returnees, and displaced persons with recovery and development assistance to the SADC-States,"[118] requesting that "additional financial resources should be channelled in the framework of the *United Nations Programme of Action for African Economic Recovery and Development 1986–1990* (UN-PAAERD) and the *African Priority Programme for its Economic Recovery 1986–1990* (APPER) of the OAU."[119]

Much like the international conferences of the inter-war period, and indeed, much like the international conferences that would eventually transpire in the 21st century, those of the aid and development era would inevitably achieve only what was permitted by those parties that drove them. The imbalance of power relations between States and regions permitted law and policy to evolve in a direction that was consistent with the foreign interests of those States that provided the terms of conference agreements and the undertaking of individual parties. It is unsurprising in that context, that the outcome of aid and development era conferences largely accommodated the reinforcement of the aid and development agenda.

---

117 UN General Assembly, *Resolution on assistance to student refugees in southern Africa* (13 December 1985) A/RES/40/138; UN General Assembly, *Resolution on assistance to refugees in Somalia* (13 December 1985) A/RES/40/132; UN General Assembly, *Resolution on assistance to student refugees in southern Africa* (4 December 1986) A/RES/41/136; UN General Assembly, *Resolution on assistance to refugees in Somalia* (4 December 1986) A/RES/41/138; UN General Assembly, *Assistance to refugees and displaced persons in Malawi* (7 December 1987) A/RES/42/132; UN General Assembly, *Assistance to student refugees in southern Africa* (7 December 1987) A/RES/42/138.

118 Roland Richter, 'International Conference on the Plight of Refugees, Returnees and Displaced Persons in Southern Africa (SARRED), Oslo, 22–24 August 1988' (1989) 2(2) Journal of Refugee Studies 284, 290.

119 *Id.* The SADOC States comprised Angola, Botswana, Comoros, Democratic Republic of Congo, Eswatini, Lesotho, Madagascar, Malawi, Mauritius, Mozambique, Namibia, Seychelles, South Africa, United Republic of Tanzania, Zambia, and Zimbabwe.

5 Conclusion

In the decades following WWII, the architecture of IRL that had until that time maintained a relatively stable presence in IL, began to unravel and in its place, a multitude of regional multilateral initiatives solidified novel concepts of IRL and the international obligations now required of States. In particular, the common understanding of refugee protection and its scope and content shifted quite dramatically from the provision of clear legal entitlements to refugee status beneficiaries, to the provision of humanitarian aid to States of reception, in turn required to maintain refugees in a suspended legal state of ostensibly 'temporary' protection with severely limited entitlements. The enduring impact of this era cannot be underestimated. As Aleinikoff noted in 1992:

> The international preference for voluntary repatriation and concern with root causes, coupled with deterrent measures adopted by states, [...] produced a dramatic shift in the focus of refugee law and policy. As resettlement possibilities become more remote and "temporary" arrangements become depressingly long-term, primary attention is now being directed to the countries of origin of refugee flows.[120]

The 'aid and development' era, characterised by the proliferation of zonal developments, the restriction of refugee movement, the implementation of limited protection regimes, and the imposition of novel international obligations on 'first States,' not only marked a significant departure from IRL as it was widely understood until that time, but enabled as a consequence the exertion of extreme political power in the management of refugee crises by those States that established the bartering system of aid and development. The financial countermeasures imposed on States of reception, and in some cases, States of origin, were utilised as tools to enforce compliance with the new multilateral order of IRP. Donor States (as they were able to position themselves) leveraged financial contributions to exert political authority over the municipal law and policy of States of reception and States of origin, commonly requiring containment and the restriction of secondary movement.

The inherent inequalities that existed between States and regions permitted the development of IRP in a manner that was consistent with the foreign

---

120 T. Alexander Aleinikoff, 'State-Centered Refugee Law: From Resettlement to Containment' (1992) 14(1) Mich J Int'l L 120, 130.

policy objectives of Western States. The international conferences of the aid and development era are a testament to that, as were their predecessors. As forums for the division, retention, and assignment of international obligations, conferences allowed concepts such as 'first State of asylum' obligations to contain refugees in encampments, and to confer temporary protection status, and State of origin obligations to restrict 'illegal' departure to become legitimate international policies of IRL, despite inconsistencies with the 1951 Convention.

These measures were, of course, ultimately concerned with the limitation of international obligations and the circumstances in which SR could be attributed. By positioning themselves, once again, as donor States and benefactors of refugee crises, Western States maintained a remoteness that did not interact sufficiently with any discernible international obligation so as to create a causal nexus necessary for the attribution of wrongfulness. This trajectory of inventing and later reinforcing remoteness would continue into the proceeding decades, and would form the basis of the IRP of the first decades of the 21st century.

PART 3

Application

CHAPTER 6

Jurisdiction and Attribution in International Refugee Law

1 Introduction

Though it is a sovereign right, and the "constant companion" of law, both municipal and international,[1] the precise content and scope of jurisdiction as a legal concept remains elusive. It is "a word of many, too many, meanings."[2] It is "normative, not empirical, primarily concerning the competence to control and alter the legal relations of those subject to that competence through the creation and application of legal norms."[3] Its normative value makes it "an abstract concept that is in constant need of application and elaboration in particular areas of substantive and procedural law."[4] Despite the absence of a "general principle or a general theory of jurisdiction" that would provide "a meaningful insight into what 'jurisdiction' really is,"[5] there are elements of jurisdiction that are persistent in municipal and international law, and that are fundamental to its exercise. These are territoriality and nationality, and together, these elements of jurisdiction establish, in the majority of cases, the lawfulness or unlawfulness of State conduct. They are expressed, variously, through certain jurisdictional competencies, namely, legislative, judicial, and executive jurisdiction, also known as prescriptive, adjudicative, and enforcement competences, respectively. In law generally, a State exer-

1 Stephen Allen and others, 'Introduction: Defining State Jurisdiction and Jurisdiction in International Law' in Stephen Allen and others (eds), *The Oxford Handbook of Jurisdiction in International Law* (OUP 2019) 4.

2 *United Phosphorus, Ltd v Angus Chemical Co.* [2003] 322 F 3d 942, 948 (7th Cir) cited in Allen et al, *id.*, 4.

3 Allen et al, *id.*, citing Patrick Capps, Malcolm Evans, Stratos Konstadinidis, 'Introduction' in Patrick Capps, Malcolm Evans and Stratos Konstadinidis (eds), *Asserting Jurisdiction: International and European Legal Perspectives* (Hart Publishing 2003) xix fn 1, and xix–xx; Wesley Hohfeld, 'Some Fundamental Legal Conceptions as Applies in Judicial Reasoning' (1913–1914) 23 Yale LJ 16, 49. See also: Robert Alexy, *A Theory of Constitutional Rights* (Oxford University Press 2002) 132–138 and 149–159.

4 Cedric Ryngaert, *Jurisdiction in International Law* (OUP 2015).

5 Stephen Allen and others, 'Introduction: Defining State Jurisdiction and Jurisdiction in International Law' in Allen and others (eds), *The Oxford Handbook of Jurisdiction in International Law* (OUP 2019) 5.

 | DOI:10.1163/9789004722835_008

cises jurisdiction by establishing rules (also called the exercise of legislative jurisdiction or prescriptive competence), by establishing procedures thereof (judicial jurisdiction or adjudicative competence), and by forcibly imposing consequences such as loss of liberty or property for breaches or, pending adjudication, alleged breaches of the rules (enforcement jurisdiction or enforcement competence).[6] Internationally, a State may perform acts in the territory of another State outside the bounds of its territorial jurisdiction (executive jurisdiction); its judiciary may try cases involving a foreign element (judicial jurisdiction); and a State may apply its laws to cases involving a foreign element (legislative jurisdiction).[7]

As with any international convention that relies on complementary municipal law to give it expression, there is increasingly a disassociation between the scope and content of the international obligations of the 1951 Convention, and the municipal legal systems that purport to implement them. Among instruments of IL, this disjuncture is perhaps most acute in IRL as the 1951 Convention relies *primarily* on municipal law for its implementation, in the absence of robust international jurisprudence. As previous chapters have demonstrated, the implementation of IRL in municipal law, policy, and practice has been at best discordant, and at worst irreconcilable. The result has been the limitation and qualification of circumstances capable of engaging SR. This has relied significantly on interpretations of jurisdiction.

Though States have a long history of redefining the limits of jurisdiction in the context of IRL to diminish or circumvent obligations arising therefrom (in particular, Article 33 (prohibition of expulsion or return (*non-refoulement*) but increasingly, Article 31 (refugees unlawfully in the country of refuge) and Article 32 (expulsion) this has never been more pervasive than over the course of the past four decades, during which time, the limits of jurisdiction have arguably been the primary preoccupation of the interpretation and application of IRL globally. For that reason, the question of jurisdiction is a particularly fraught one in IRL. The exercise of extraterritorial jurisdiction is now commonplace in immigration law, policy, and practice, and while in general IL, questions of jurisdiction are "particularly prone to conflicts and overlaps,"[8] in

6 Bernard H Oxman, 'Jurisdiction of States' in *Max Planck Encyclopedias of Public International Law* (North-Holland, 1987) 277.

7 *Id.*; Maarten Den Heijer, *Europe and Extraterritorial Asylum* (Hart Publishing 2012) 20 citing: Michael Akehurst, 'Jurisdiction in International Law' (1972–1973) 46 BYBIL 179.

8 Stephen Allen and others, 'Introduction: Defining State Jurisdiction and Jurisdiction in International Law' in Allen and others (eds), *The Oxford Handbook of Jurisdiction in International Law* (OUP 2019) 7.

IRL, conflicts and overlaps do not tend to arise from State assertions of jurisdiction over the same matter, claiming that the exercise of jurisdiction by one encroaches on the sovereign rights of the other, as they do in general IL. Instead, jurisdictional overlaps arise in IRL from the municipal regimes that implement primary rules of IL – commonly the legislative or normative IHRL regime that derives from IRL – through which the individual asserts his *locus standi* as a subject of IL. By extension, all jurisdictional conflicts that arise in IRL do so from these overlaps. The question of jurisdiction in IRL is therefore one of both general IL and municipal law, commonly manifesting in an assertion of the latter in conflict with the former.

Those conflicts and overlaps are complicated further by the absence of clear rules of jurisdiction in IL, and of circumstances arising in general IL with comparable jurisdictional conflicts and overlaps in IRL, from which applicable norms can be inferred. Scholars often point to the positive test of jurisdiction provided in the *Lotus* case to resolve questions of jurisdictional conflicts and overlaps, in which the PCIJ held that a State may not "overstep the limits which international law places upon its jurisdiction," as a jurisdictional norm of general IL:

> [T]he first and foremost restriction imposed by international law upon a State is that – *failing the existence of a permissive rule to the contrary* – it may not exercise its power in any form in the territory of another State.[9]

There is, however, some resistance to the notion that the positive test remains applicable in contemporary IL. That debate aside, the question of jurisdiction in IRL does not commonly arise from disputes between States, nor from the violation of an explicit delimitation of jurisdiction in the 1951 Convention, per the *Lotus* test (though there is much case law on the exercise of extraterritorial jurisdiction in relation to its positive statement in IHRL). The jurisdictional conflicts that arise in IRL are rather the result of a consensual bilateral or multilateral exercise of concurrent jurisdictional or a division of jurisdictional competencies. In much the same way that jurisdictional conflicts and overlaps were resolved in early responses to refugee crises (see chapters 2 and 3) through the division, retention, and assignment of jurisdictional competencies with a view to the minimisation of circumstances engaging SR, so too are contemporary multilateral and bilateral laws and policies engaging IRL.

---

9 *SS 'Lotus' (France v Turkey)* [7 September 1927] PCIJ Series A No 10, [19]. Emphasis added.

Of course, the consensual division of jurisdictional competencies among States is not *per se* internationally wrongful. Where it relates to jurisdiction, the question of SR in IRL is rather that the division of jurisdictional competencies is done with the *intention* of minimising circumstances in which a violation of either the municipal or regional regimes that implement IRL could be attributed to a State. As jurisdiction turns on territoriality as one of its fundamental bases, the exercise of State authority that would otherwise be extraterritorial and potentially wrongful, is instead exercised by the State on whose territory the conduct occurs, bringing it within the territorial jurisdiction of that State, and creating sufficient distance between the first State and the conduct in question. The conflict that arises is therefore not the exercise of jurisdiction by a State outside its territory, but rather, "the limitations derived from international law concepts which restrict the intraterritorial exercise of jurisdiction by a state over persons and activities outside its territory."[10] That is, "the assertion of jurisdiction against persons *regardless of their presence within the state*."[11] As the conflicts and overlaps that arise in contemporary IRL concern specifically the exercise of jurisdiction over persons regardless of their presence within the State, the question of jurisdiction in IRL is not one of disputes over primacy, but one of attribution.

There is one further consideration that is particularly relevant to the specific jurisdictional conflicts and overlaps that arise in IRL. That is the question of political and economic inequality between States that cooperate on matters of immigration control. As Chimni has noted, "[i]n examining and analysing these different bases of exercising jurisdiction [territoriality and nationality] what is not sufficiently appreciated by [mainstream international law scholarship] is that while jurisdiction is a legal doctrine it also has critical social and political dimensions."[12] Through these secondary dimensions, a State may "sustain the institution of patriarchy through the promulgation of jurisdictional rules."[13] This is most certainly the case in the division of jurisdictional competencies as they exist today between the US and Mexico, the US and Central American States, the EU and North Africa, and within the EU, where Southern Border States commonly exercise jurisdiction over immigration control on behalf of the entire EU bloc. This system of 'bartering' jurisdictional

10 Arthur Lenhof, 'International Law and Rules on International Jurisdiction' (1964) 50(1) Cornell LR 5.

11 *Id.* Emphasis added.

12 B.S. Chimni, *International Law and World Order: A Critique of Contemporary Approaches* (CUP 2017) 33.

13 *Id.*

competencies should be viewed as a continuation of the 'aid and development' model of immigration control, as it continues to permit Western States to position themselves as States of limited resettlement, while providing financial assistance to the so-called 'Global South' for the containment of the 'refugee problem.'

The evasion of jurisdictional competences in general, have a direct effect on the attribution of conduct to a State, and as unilateral measures affecting various jurisdictional competencies (commonly through the limitation and qualification of territoriality and nationality) are particularly prevalent in the interpretation and application of IRL, it is fundamental that the question of jurisdiction form part of any investigation of SR in IRL. This chapter is limited in that endeavour however, to a study of the contemporary exercise and function of legislative, judicial, and enforcement jurisdiction, not of theoretical questions of a doctrine of jurisdiction in municipal or international law. Similarly, though much has been written about externalisation and extraterritoriality, this chapter does not wrestle with the finer points of legality regarding the effect such policies have had on the right of refugees to seek, claim, and be granted international protection. It is instead concerned with the implications for attribution in the broader context of SR.

Chapter 5 considers the contemporary division, retention, and assignment of jurisdictional competencies between States in the implementation of municipal immigration regimes, and the evasion of SR through the interpretation and application of limited jurisdiction. It argues that developments in contemporary IRL have occurred in three iterations and that collectively, they have created a receding line of jurisdiction, minimised the circumstances capable of engaging the international obligations of the 1951 Convention, and that those developments have responded to judicial decisions affecting attribution.

Section 2 considers the characterisation of jurisdiction in IRL, in particular, the conceptualisation of jurisdictional competencies as they relate to a number of specific elements including physical presence and territoriality. It examines also the political and economic factors impacting jurisdictional conflicts and overlaps that result in the division, retention, and assignment of jurisdictional competencies between States, and posits that IRL continues to be particularly susceptible to the realpolitik of bilateral and multilateral bartering systems.

Section 3 examines those legal measures that form part of the first iteration of jurisdiction-based laws, policies, and practices, specifically, those measures that proliferated in response to the Indochinese refugee crisis of the 1970s, when States began to enact 'pushback' policies, intercepting vessels on the high seas and redirecting them back into international waters, and which have continued through the US response to the Haitian and Cuban refugee crises, and became a cornerstone of both Australian immigration law and policy in its efforts to halt 'maritime arrivals,' and the EU response to refugee crises in the Mediterranean.

Section 4 examines the second iteration of legal measures, including on the 'first country of asylum' concept, carrier sanctions, and the stationing of State agents abroad in relation to the exercise of executive (enforcement) jurisdiction. Much like the settlement of African refugees, the recommendations of expert groups were grounded in a humanitarian rationale that favoured resettling refugees in what were deemed 'appropriate cultural environments.' In contemporary IRL, the 'first country of asylum' principle has become a central feature of European immigration law and policy in particular. In recent decades, European institutions have repeatedly sought to establish common EU regulations based on this principle. This has permitted the introduction of complementary regional law and policy rooted in the principle of territorial jurisdiction, including carrier sanctions, which ushered in an era of privatisation in migration management. Common features of these laws included the imposition of fines or other penalties on carriers for transporting undocumented individuals and requiring carriers to remove such persons from the destination country.

Section 5 considers the third iteration of legal measures affecting the exclusion of refugees from the jurisdiction of the State. This is exemplified by Australia's bilateralism in Papua New Guinea, Cambodia, Malaysia, and Nauru where the State has claimed at all times that it does not exercise any jurisdiction over refugees, despite the findings and implications of several courts. The EU has also engaged in a similar model of bilateralism with Turkey, Morocco, and Libya, claiming that it exercises no jurisdiction over immigration control. In recent years, the US, in its bilateral relations with Central American States, has enacted a number of migration agreements that essentially deputise southern States with judicial jurisdiction over asylum and immigration matters.

Chapter 5 concludes that the interpretation of jurisdiction as it pertains to IRL has further exacerbated the division of international obligations between Western States and the Global South. While the US, the UK, central and northern EU States, and Australia continue to style themselves as exclusively States of resettlement, States across Africa, Central and South America, and South Asia bear the disproportionate burden of refugee reception. It argues that by examining the significance of territoriality and nationality as foundational elements of jurisdiction – and thus central to the division of jurisdictional competencies – the need for divergent terminology and legal theories is diminished. Rather, the legal innovations of the past four decades can be reframed as fundamental 'aspects of sovereignty,' providing a clearer rationale for the underlying causes and effects of these dynamics. Chapter 5 concludes that the measures analysed in this chapter reflect a broader legal trajectory that prioritised obligations over rights. The consequences of these measures on the rights of individuals are profound and far-reaching, underscoring the serious implications of jurisdictional practices in IRL.

2 Characterising Jurisdiction in International Refugee Law

From the 1980s onwards, a number of individual States and blocs began to institute increasingly restrictive municipal laws and policies, intended to exclude refugees from entering their respective jurisdictions, in response to a sharp increase in the number of asylum applications made globally.[14] Collectively, the legal measures that proliferated in the 1980s, and have continued well into the 21st century, are "largely understood as an attempt to minimise state obligations to refugees."[15] They create ever more remote interactions between States and refugees by instituting "step-by-step successive operations taking place in zones that are incrementally further away from the intercepting State's territory."[16]

Not only have these developments been instituted incrementally, but they have been built upon the interpretative innovations and irregularities of the preceding decades, and though they vary in content, common to each successive innovation is a reliance on wide-ranging interpretations of jurisdiction and the circumstances in which it is (and is not) engaged. Such legal measures have "test[ed] the minimum threshold of obligations required of States by the

14 Maarten Vink, Frits Meijerink, 'Asylum Applications and Recognition Rates in EU Member States 1982–2001: A Quantitative Analysis' (2003) 16(3) JRS 298, 299; Council of Europe: Parliamentary Assembly, *Arrival of asylum seekers at European airports* (2000) *Report, Committee on Migration, Refugees and Demography, Rapporteur: Mr. Gross, Switzerland, Socialist Group* (8 June 2000) (Doc. 8761).

15 Michelle Foster, 'Protection Elsewhere: The Legal Implications of Requiring Refugees to Seek Protection in Another State' (2007) 28 MichJIntlL 223, 225.

16 Anja Klug, Tim Howe, 'The Concept of State Jurisdiction and the Applicability of the Non-refoulement Principle to Extraterritorial Interception Measures' in Bernard Ryan and Valsamis Mitsilegas (eds), *Extraterritorial Immigration Control* (Martinus Nijhoff 2010) 91.

1951 Convention,"[17] and regional instruments incorporating norms of IRL through the adoption of conflicting municipal laws and practices, and their subsequent 'testing' in judicial fora. Notably, some States have made concerted effort to exclude certain elements of border control from the purview of judicial oversight through the inclusion of privative clauses. In many cases, the inherent jurisdictional limits of the 1951 Convention and general rules pertaining to application and interpretation of jurisdiction in international and municipal law have permitted the fragmentation of IRL into multiple State regimes. The overall effect has been the limitation and qualification of international obligations and consequently, of SR arising therefrom.

These global trends in refugee law and policy have been conceptualised in myriad ways, largely depending on the effect of the law, policy, or practice on refugees. Much like the language of 'protection,' such laws and policies have been described using various terminologies. They are commonly classified as externalisation, extraterritoriality, push-backs, or *non-entrée* policies, but are better understood in terms of their legal cause rather than their practical effect. Much like the early attempts to resolve refugee crises, they rely on the division, assignment, and retention of legal competencies, in this case, jurisdictional competencies. Collectively, these trends affect jurisdiction as a means to disrupt the causal nexus that establishes a legal relationship between the State and the refugee, and can be classified in three distinct iterations relative to their utilisation of jurisdiction as a tool to limit SR, and that, taken together, have created a receding line of jurisdiction that has incrementally minimised the circumstances capable of engaging the international obligations of the 1951 Convention.

In the first instance, State A has exercised enforcement jurisdiction on the high seas, outside the ordinary boundaries of its territorial jurisdiction. This has relied on the primarily territorial nature of jurisdiction, and on the construction of the 1951 Convention as engaging the State's obligations only where the refugee has entered its territory. In these circumstances, States have maintained that they did not exercise jurisdiction over persons outside their territorial jurisdiction for the purposes of IRL or municipal immigration law.

In the second iteration, State A has exercised executive jurisdiction in the territory of State B, authorised by consent of State B. State A has engaged State B and private actors to operate within the jurisdiction of State B in the administration of State B's own municipal law and policy, in line with the foreign policy objectives of State A, relative to immigration control. This has relied in

17 Rosemary Byrne, Andrew Shacknove, 'The Safe Country Notion in European Asylum Law' (1996) 9 Harv Hum Rts J 185.

large part on the concept of first country of asylum and its reinforcement in bilateral and multilateral law and policy.

In the third iteration, State B has exercised legislative jurisdiction ordinarily within its own territory in a manner consistent with the execution of State A's foreign policy objectives relative to refugees. This is a new form of the aid and development model of IRL, in which State A 'barters' cooperation on immigration control from State B. Large aid packages and other *quid pro quo* measures including limited 'safe, orderly, and legal' migration pathways permit State A to exercise some influence over the immigration control practices of State B, while maintaining a remoteness from legal obligations by circumventing norms of attribution. State A commonly continues to assert enforcement jurisdiction in respect of detention and removal but maintains that the concurrent legislative and enforcement jurisdiction of State B takes precedence on the basis of territoriality, rendering it the authority to exercise judicial jurisdiction only.

In practice, the latter two iterations have relied on the exercise of concurrent legislative jurisdiction. As Mann explains, this is not an anomaly:

> [j]urisdiction is by no means concerned only with the problem of ascertaining the State, which, in a given case, has the sole right of regulation. There are many sets of circumstances which, by their nature, more than one State may be entitled to regulate. To a large extent legislative jurisdiction is concurrent rather than exclusive.[18]

Nonetheless, the effect (and the apparent purpose) of iterations two and three has been to divide and assign legislative competencies. This has relied heavily on the conflation of refugees and migrants as classes of person subject to undifferentiated legal processes, and in that sense, the application of indistinct immigration processes to both groups, aided significantly by the focus on 'safe and orderly' pathways. Facilitated by multiple inter-governmental processes such as The Global Compact for Safe, Orderly and Regular Migration,[19] the Quito Process,[20] and the Los Angeles Summit on Migration,[21] the era of 'safe and orderly' movement has permitted the treatment of refugees

18 Fritz Alexander Mann, 'The Doctrine of Jurisdiction in International Law' (1964) 111 RCADI 10.

19 UN, *The Global Compact for Safe, Orderly and Regular Migration* (11 July 2018).

20 Argentina and others, *Declaración de Quito* (4 Septiembre 2018).

21 USA: Department of Homeland Security, *Los Angeles Declaration on Migration and Protection* (10 June 2022).

and migrants to become increasingly harmonised. As with many events described in this book, this is not a new phenomenon. In reference to the Indochinese refugee crises, Suhrke noted that "[t]he mode of departure, rather than reasons for departure, [became] a principal criterion for bestowing refugee status, thus turning the process into a human obstacle course where those willing to risk the perilous flight to first-asylum areas were rewarded with refugee status."[22]

Despite it being commonplace in contemporary IRL for States to attempt to preclude judicial oversight, municipal and regional judicial bodies have in many instances forced States to align municipal refugee law and policy with principles of IRL. At other times, courts have found that the legal measures in question were lawful exercises of jurisdiction. Incidentally, in both scenarios, it has been this judicial oversight that has served as the principal impetus for the furtherance of normative developments intended to keep refugee populations technically and legally unadmitted. In the case of the former, States have been incentivised to invent new and creative ways to exclude refugees from their jurisdiction. In the case of the latter, States have continued to apply the relevant policy in the knowledge that it has judicial approval. This interaction between legislature and judiciary has created a receding line of jurisdiction in which conflicts and overlaps have proliferated, in turn frustrating norms of attribution.

2.1 *Jurisdictional Overlaps and Conflicts*

Critical to all exercises of jurisdictional competencies is the matter of territoriality. Den Heijer distinguishes between legislative and enforcement jurisdiction in the following terms, referring to the importance of territoriality to legislative jurisdiction in particular:

> One of the differences between [legislative and executive] jurisdiction is that it is well established in international law that legislative jurisdiction may be based on other grounds than territorial considerations.[23]

Each of these jurisdictional competencies has been exercised in municipal and regional law and policy relative to IRL. In particular, much of the interpretation and application of jurisdiction in IRL has relied on a distinction

---

22 Astri Suhrke, 'Indochinese refugees: The Law and Policy of First Asylum' (1983) 467 Annals Am Acad Pol & Soc Sci 102.

23 Maarten Den Heijer, *Europe and Extraterritorial Asylum* (Hart Publishing 2012) 20 citing: Michael Akehurst, 'Jurisdiction in International Law' (1972–1973) 46 BYBIL 179.

between legislative jurisdiction and executive jurisdiction on the one hand (or prescriptive competence and enforcement competence) and judicial jurisdiction on the other (or adjudicative competence). In legal scholarship, this has led to the classification of the nexus between jurisdiction and asylum in numerous ways, depending on the characteristics or content of the actions or omissions described, and the broader purpose in describing them. These incidentally classify the jurisdictional conflicts and overlaps in IRL variously as externalisation, extraterritorialisation, *non-entrée* or non-admission policies, deterrence policies, and pushbacks, to name some of the more common terms. Gammeltoft-Hansen and Feith Tan have categorised such measures in terms describing the desired outcome, as 'non-admission policies limiting access to asylum procedures, non-arrival measures preventing access to the territory of asylum States through migration control, offshore asylum processing and relocation of refugees to third countries, criminalisation of irregular migration and human smuggling, and indirect deterrence measures intended to make the asylum country less attractive.'[24] Guiraudon, Loescher, and Den Heijer each describe such measures with reference to intention, as aiming at "short-circuiting judicial constraints on migration control,"[25] effectively "limit [ing] the number of asylum-seekers in a country to stop them arriving in the first place,"[26] and as a means to foster migration through 'regular' channels on the one hand, and to prevent the inflow of 'unauthorised' arrivals on the other.[27]

The use of divergent terminology to diagnose the nexus between jurisdiction and asylum, or between State and refugee, is itself in a constant State of evolution, due in large part to the constant innovation in law and policy intended to disrupt that nexus, but common among terms is their reliance – either predominantly or entirely – on territoriality or physical presence as the primary factor in determining the scope of inclusion or exclusion of refugees, and as a consequence, the limits of lawful and unlawful conduct of States. The constant revision and rephrasing of the asylum–jurisdiction nexus on the basis of territoriality in particular, prioritises the spatial element of jurisdiction, to the exclusion of others. It also focuses on the effect of the law, policy,

24 Thomas Gammeltoft-Hansen, Nikolas F. Tan, 'The End of the Deterrence Paradigm – Future Directions for Global Refugee Policy' (2017) 5 J on Migration & Hum Sec 28, 34.

25 Virginie Guiraudon, 'Before the EU Border: Remote Control of the 'Huddled Masses'" in Kees Groenendijk, Elspeth Guild and Paul Minderhoud (eds), *In Search of Europe's Borders* (Kluwer 2003) 194.

26 Gil Loescher, 'The European Community and Refugees' (1989) 65(4) International Affairs 617, 624.

27 Maarten Den Heijer, *Europe and Extraterritorial Asylum* (Hart Publishing 2012) 5.

or practice on the refugee, rather than on the interpretation or application of legal modalities as the cause of the measure in question. In that sense, it tends to negate the need to engage with jurisdictional conflicts and overlaps in competencies as central to the exercise of jurisdiction in IRL. As Szigeti has observed, "[T]erritoriality never solves jurisdictional conflicts, but only rephrases them."[28]

> Territoriality is an unreliable guide to distributing jurisdictional competences not only because of the impossibility of determining the boundaries of events and actions but also because territoriality itself is a shifting concept that is easy to manipulate legally.[29]

Excessive reliance on territoriality as the decisive factor in the asylum–jurisdiction nexus may rephrase jurisdictional matters, and frequently resolves questions of lawfulness of specific conduct, but it does little to provide a comprehensive account of the underlying jurisdictional conflict. The same may be said of excessive reliance on physical aspects; either the physical presence of the refugee within the jurisdiction of the State, or the fact of physical control exercised by the State over the refugee. Much is made of the physical aspects of the asylum–jurisdiction nexus, and with good reason. They have formed the basis of much jurisprudence establishing the jurisdiction of States, bringing municipal systems of law in line with fundamental principles of IRL. However, increasingly, the assertion by States and blocs that they do not exercise jurisdiction over refugees is not in essence based on territoriality or physical aspects, but on the absence of jurisdictional competence.

Throughout the relative period, and in particular during the past decade, the delegation by States of their own jurisdictional competence to third States has permitted a wealth of legal developments that are commonly categorised as externalisation, extraterritorialisation, *non-entrée* policies, etc. These terms are useful to describe the relationship between conduct and effect (or rather between obligation and responsibility) but they do not adequately define the fundamental elements of jurisdiction that have been subject to constant revision. That devolution of authority has alternately concerned executive jurisdiction or legislative jurisdiction; the former being a common feature of earlier laws and policies and the latter increasingly the basis for new jurisdictional conflicts. This has in turn affected the assumption or rejection of judi-

28 Péter D. Szigeti, 'The Illusion of Territorial Jurisdiction' (2017) 52(3) Texas Int L J 369, 372.
29 *Id.*, 371.

cial jurisdiction, which has then influenced either the continuation or the revision of refugee law and policy.

2.2 *Jurisdictional Competence and State Responsibility*

The authority to exercise legislative jurisdiction in certain limited circumstances, and deputise third States to exercise it in others, has become a common underlying feature of contemporary bilateral and multilateral 'migration management' policy. The US, Australia, the UK, and the EU have all actively pursued foreign relations with this fragmentation of jurisdiction as a central focus of their immigration agenda. The same may be said of executive jurisdiction. It is increasingly common practice for States to exercise executive jurisdiction for the purposes of detention and removal, but assert a lack of legislative jurisdiction for the purposes of refugee status determination. This "test[ing] the minimum threshold of obligations required of States by the 1951 Convention"[30] has required judicial determinations on attribution in order to develop further – whether it be to continue or to recalibrate.

There are a number of conditions that have fostered this era of law and policy. First, and despite assertions by some that there is "a strong norm of responsibility sharing inherent in the international refugee protection regime" that "requires States to cooperate in dealing with the global refugee problem,"[31] fundamentally, "there is no strategy – comprehensive or otherwise – to ensure that the responsibility for providing protection to the world's refugees is shared."[32] As Wall notes, the best known reference to this supposed 'norm' is in the preamble to the 1951 Convention, which recognises that the grant of asylum may place "unduly heavy burdens on certain countries," and that a satisfactory solution "cannot therefore be achieved without international co-operation[.]"[33] However the exact nature of the 'responsibility-

30 Rosemary Byrne, Andrew Shacknove, 'The Safe Country Notion in European Asylum Law' (1996) 9 Harv Hum Rts J 185.

31 B.S. Chimni, *International Refugee Law: A Reader* (Sage Publications 2000) 146; Benjamin Cook, 'Method in Its Madness: The Endowment Effect in an Analysis of Refugee Burden-Sharing and a Proposed Refugee Market' (2004) 19 GeoImmLJ 333, 337–338; Agnes Hurwitz, *The Collective Responsibility of States to Protect Refugees* (OUP 2009) 139–146, cited in: Patrick Wall, 'A New Link in the Chain: Could a Framework Convention for Refugee Responsibility Sharing Fulfil the Promise of the 1967 Protocol?' (2017) 29(2) IJRL 201, 205–206.

32 Wall, *id.*, 208.

33 *Id.*, 206.

sharing norm' is not clear.[34] The legal basis of burden- or responsibility-sharing is in fact "subject to a very weak legal and normative framework,"[35] and its proponents tend to rely on the existence of moral foundations as the basis to assert its status as a norm of IRL.[36]

The second and third conditions are creations of States in the interpretation and application of IRL, rather than conditions of the 1951 Convention. The second is the long-standing proposition that the first State of reception should be considered *de facto* the State of asylum, subject to its objective safety, and that the 'burden-sharing' obligation of third States is to provide humanitarian aid and limited resettlement. This was first raised seriously at the *International Conference on the Indo-Chinese Refugee Question* by those regional States most affected by the crisis.

At the time, the proposition was met with staunch resistance from the West. Though clearly not at risk of becoming first countries of asylum, Western States considered the proposition to pose an imminent risk to their status as States of resettlement, as it would create the expectation that States outside those of first asylum would increase their national resettlement quotas. This concern was amplified by the historically colonial relationships between South-East Asian States and the US and France, in particular. The counter-proposal from the West – driven in large part by the US and France – was that of humanitarian aid. ASEAN States would accept refugees on a temporary basis, with the expectation that they would eventually return to their States of origin, and in exchange, Western States would make available substantial humanitarian aid packages. This relationship of 'responsibility-sharing' was less cooperative than it was exploitative. Western States provided extensive humanitarian aid but did little to affect resettlement quotas, and the obligation to provide protection fell disproportionately on South-East Asian States. This model of burden-sharing has continued since then across global regions,

34 *Id.*, 207.

35 Alexander Betts, *Protection by Persuasion: International Cooperation in the Refugee Regime* (Cornell University Press 2009) 3.

36 See, for example: B.S. Chimni, *International Refugee Law: A Reader* (Sage Publications 2000) 146; J.P.L. Fonteyne, 'Burden-Sharing: An Analysis of the Nature and Function of International Solidarity in Cases of Mass Influx of Refugees' (1978) 8 AusYBIL 162, 175, 177, 178–184 ("the moral and legal foundations of burden sharing"); James C. Hathaway, R. Alexander Neve, 'Making International Refugee Law Relevant Again: A Proposal for Collectivized and Solution-Oriented Protection' (1997) 10 HarvHRJ 115, 117–118 ("The critical right of at-risk people to seek asylum will survive only if the mechanisms of international refugee protection can be reconceived ... dependably and equitably to share responsibilities and burdens") 169–171.

redirecting the disproportionate burden of refugee reception onto developing and least-developed States.[37]

A third condition is the qualification of entry based on the mode of arrival, in particular, the creation of 'safe and orderly' pathways and the invention of an obligation of refugees to arrive at designated ports of entry in order for their applications for refugee status to be accepted as 'valid' or 'lawful.' Despite the concept having no basis in the 1951 Convention, and indeed in contravention of non-penalisation for unlawful entry, it has increasingly become a cornerstone of municipal and regional refugee law and policy. Richmond refers to this 'assault on freedom of movement' and the closure of borders by the more advanced States of the world as a form of 'global apartheid,' "designed to preserve the wealth and power of Western societies and to segregate their people from the crises in the Third World."[38] Perhaps the most effective means of achieving such aims has been the concentration or delegation of obligations to third States, frequently through the imposition of inter-State obligations based on novel conceptions of jurisdiction. Increasingly, asylum frameworks are designed to minimise international obligations of Western States in general, and to concentrate what remains of 'collective responsibility' in a limited number of States, geographically proximate to the State of origin. This is exemplified by the Common European Asylum System (CEAS), which, under the guise of 'responsibility-sharing,' has operationalised a number of oppressive measures that concentrate obligations associated with the reception and protection of refugees southward to Border States, aided by novel constructions of national and regional jurisdiction, and legitimised through the mechanism of the Dublin Convention.[39]

37 Patrick Wall, 'A New Link in the Chain: Could a Framework Convention for Refugee Responsibility Sharing Fulfil the Promise of the 1967 Protocol?' (2017) 29(2) IJRL 201, 209; Alexander Betts, *Protection by Persuasion: International Cooperation in the Refugee Regime* (Cornell University Press 2009) 3; James C. Hathaway, R. Alexander Neve, 'Making International Refugee Law Relevant Again: A Proposal for Collectivized and Solution-Oriented Protection' (1997) 10 HarvHRJ 115, 141; J.P.L. Fonteyne, 'Burden-Sharing: An Analysis of the Nature and Function of International Solidarity in Cases of Mass Influx of Refugees' (1978) 8 AusYBIL 162, 166–167; Benjamin Cook, 'Method in Its Madness: The Endowment Effect in an Analysis of Refugee Burden-Sharing and a Proposed Refugee Market' (2004) 19 GeoImmLJ 333, 344–345; Jack I. Garvey, 'Toward a Reformulation of International Refugee Law' (1985) 26(2) HarvIntlLJ 483; Khalid Khoser, *Australia and the 1951 Refugee Convention* (Lowy Institute Analyses 2015) 7.

38 Anthony H. Richmond, 'Refugees and Racism: Canada and Global Apartheid' *The Refugee Crisis: British and Canadian Responses* (1989) University of Oxford 32.

39 European Union: Council of the European Union, *Convention Determining the State Responsible for Examining Applications for Asylum lodged in one of the Member States*

Collectively, these conditions have contributed to an environment in which States have retreated from the international obligations of IRL. That retreat has precipitated a receding line of jurisdiction, and while much of the relative conduct is categorised with reference to territoriality and physical aspects as effects of law and policy, such conduct has been based primarily on novel conceptions of jurisdiction. It should thus be analysed with reference to such, as it has permitted States (predominantly Western States) to limit their international obligations and ultimately redefine the terms of attribution in SR.

2.2.1 Physical Presence and Jurisdiction

In IL, it is understood that legal obligations are generally determined by the limits of jurisdiction provided in the relevant treaty, and although the territorial scope of Article 33 of the 1951 Convention is not explicitly defined, the phrase "in any manner whatsoever" is widely considered to refer to subject-matter jurisdiction, and therefore to include extraterritorial activity.[40] This has been the basis for much jurisprudence establishing the jurisdiction of a State where it has exercised a degree of control over a refugee, and where his or her physical presence is in question. As Goodwin-Gill notes, "[T]he fact of interception – the taking of control and custody – establishes the necessary juridical link between the state and the consequence."[41] Lawson has proposed that 'the scope of a State's obligations depend on the degree of control and

of the European Communities (Dublin Convention) (15 June 1990); European Union: Council of the European Union, *Regulation (EU) No 604/2013 of the European Parliament and of the Council of 26 June 2013 establishing the criteria and mechanisms for determining the Member State responsible for examining an application for international protection lodged in one of the Member States by a third-country national or a stateless person (recast)* (29 June 2013).

40 Elihu Lauterpacht, Daniel Bethlehem, *The Scope and Content of the Principle of Non-Refoulement (Opinion)* (20 June 2001) UNHCR 30: "[...] there is nothing in Article 33(1) of the 1951 Convention to suggest that it must be construed subject to any territorial limitation [...]."; Cathryn Costello, Yulia Ioffe, Teresa Büchsel, *Article 31 of the 1951 Convention Relating to the Status of Refugees* (July 2017) UNHCR Legal and Protection Policy Research Series 24: "It should be recalled that Article 33 has no territorial qualification whatsoever, referring to the expulsion or return of a refugee 'in any manner whatsoever.'"; Michelle Foster, 'Protection Elsewhere: The Legal Implications of Requiring Refugees to Seek Protection in Another State' (2007) 28 MichJIntlL 223, 251: "Article 33 is not conditioned on a refugee being within the territory of state parties."

41 Guy S. Goodwin-Gill, 'The Extraterritorial Processing of Claims to Asylum or Protection: The Legal Responsibilities of States and International Organisations' (2007) 9 UTS L Rev 26, 33.

authority that they exercise,'[42] and Wilde and Kamchibekova have both proposed a variant of this theory, whereby there is a differentiation between State control over 'spatial objects' – being particular swaths of territory – and State control over persons.[43] Milanović argues that, while the power to exercise jurisdiction primarily pertains to acts occurring within the territory of a State, extraterritorial jurisdiction is established where a strong connection to the State exists.[44] Cerone considers the degree of control to be a determining factor, and while negative obligations apply in situations of extraterritoriality, "the degree of positive obligations will be dependent upon the type and degree of control."[45] On the connection between territoriality and physical presence, Szigeti writes:

> Territorial jurisdiction is a chimera; there are only two instances in which it "works." One is when the physical presence of an object or person, in and of itself, is enough to ground exclusive jurisdiction. This is quite rare: Only immigration law, customs law, and trespass focus on authorisation for the presence of persons or objects in a place. The second is a negative test, where we disqualify some assertions of jurisdiction through the lack of (any) physical links.[46]

Though classified here as subject to the 'positive' test of exclusive jurisdiction, recent developments in immigration law have brought it increasingly in line with the negative test, whereby the State itself will seek to disqualify its own jurisdiction (and any assertion that it exercises it) on the basis of an absence of physical presence. Consequently, reliance on physical presence or physical control as the main determinate of jurisdiction may rephrase a jurisdictional

42 Rick Lawson, 'Life After Banković: On the Extraterritorial Application of the European Convention on Human Rights' in F. Coomans and M.T. Kamminga (eds), *Extraterritorial Application of Human Rights Treaties* (2004) 84.

43 Ralph Wilde, 'Legal "Black Hole"? Extraterritorial State Action and International Treaty Law on Civil and Political Rights' (2005) 26 MichJIntlL 739, 770; Damira Kamchibekova, 'State Responsibility for Extraterritorial Human Rights Violations' (2007) 13 Buff Hum Rts L Rev 87.

44 See generally: Marko Milanović, *Extraterritorial Application of Human Rights Treaties: Law, Principles, and Policy* (OUP 2011).

45 John Cerone, 'Out Of Bounds? Considering The Reach Of International Human Rights Law (Working Paper No 5)' (2006) Center For Human Rights And Global Justice, New York University School of Law 1, 32.

46 Péter D. Szigeti, 'The Illusion of Territorial Jurisdiction' (2017) 52(3) Texas Int L J 369, 372.

conflict, and has certainly resolved questions of attribution relative to specific conduct, but like territoriality, it does not provide a comprehensive account of the constant cycle of revisionism that occurs in relation to jurisdiction in municipal and regional immigration law and policy. In that sense, it also 'rephrases' but does not resolve the jurisdictional conflicts and overlaps that arise.

2.2.2 Territoriality and Jurisdiction

As a foundation for the lawful exercise of jurisdiction, territoriality is subject to certain rules where municipal law interacts with international law. As the PCIJ provided in the *Lotus* case, jurisdiction "cannot be exercised by a State outside its territory except by virtue of a permissive rule derived from international custom or from a convention."[47] In the case of IRL, the 1951 Convention and 1967 Protocol "lay down rules and standards of treatment which are primarily, though not exclusively, territorial in nature."[48]

The territorial scope of the 1951 Convention is neither explicit in providing that a refugee must be within the territory of a State party, but nor does it limit the engagement of a State party's jurisdiction in territorial terms. Article 1A provides only that a refugee is "outside the country of his nationality" or in the case of a stateless person, is "outside the country of his former habitual residence," not that he or she must be *within* the territory of the State party. Article 33 does not premise *refoulement* on the presence of the refugee within the territory of the State party, but provides only that *refoulement* "in any manner whatsoever" is strictly prohibited, though the same qualification applies here regarding implicitness. The purpose of drawing attention to those limitations is not to advocate for their limited interpretation, but rather to identify why and how precisely they have been subject to such narrow interpretation.

Predictably, the absence of explicit territorial parameters in the 1951 Convention has not produced a harmonised body of jurisprudence. Interpretations of the territorial scope of Article 33 have in particular varied greatly depending on the applicable rules governing jurisdictional conflicts between municipal and international law. The long-standing view of the US, reflected in the *Restatement (Third) of the Foreign Relations Law of the United States*, is that IL allows a State to regulate "conduct outside its territory that has or is

---

47 *SS 'Lotus' (France v Turkey)* [7 September 1927] PCIJ Series A No 10, 18–19.

48 Guy S. Goodwin-Gill, 'The Extraterritorial Processing of Claims to Asylum or Protection: The Legal Responsibilities of States and International Organisations' (2007) 9 UTS L Rev 26, 27.

intended to have substantial effect within its territory";[49] however, US courts have consistently interpreted the jurisdictional scope of the *Immigration and Nationality Act* (INA) as strictly territorial in nature, excluding those actions of State agents that occur outside the territorial jurisdiction of the State. As Knox asserts:

> If the United States has no basis under international law for extending its law to a situation, courts should presume that Congress did not intend the law to extend so far. The presumption should be strict, able to be overcome only with a clear statement of congressional intent.[50]

Such a presumption is evident in the State's jurisprudence pertaining to encounters between State agents and refugees, and is premised on the absence of explicit jurisdictional parameters in the 1951 Convention and 1967 Protocol. By contrast, the scope of jurisdiction in Article 1 of the *European Convention on Human Rights* (ECHR) has been consistently interpreted by the European Court of Human Rights (ECtHR) as not strictly limited by territoriality, but engaged where a Member State has exercised a requisite level of control over any person then deemed to be within its jurisdiction.[51] This jurisprudence has developed alongside a marked increase in European *non-entrée* policies that can be noted from the 1980s, following a series of judicial decisions by the European Commission on Human Rights on the centrality of territoriality to the doctrine of jurisdiction.[52]

Judicial responses to interdiction on the high seas have varied greatly depending on the State or region involved, but in the US and Australia, the highest federal courts have provided strong judicial support for the application of jurisdiction on strictly territorial grounds. With the aid of these decisions, both States have continued to develop asylum systems that built upon a

---

49 American Law Institute, *Restatement (Third) of the Foreign Relations Law of the United States* (American Law Institute Publishers 1987) §402(1)(c).

50 John H. Knox, 'A Presumption against Extrajurisdictionality' (2010) 104(3) AJIL 351, 358.

51 See, for example: *N.D. and N.T. V Spain* [13 February 2020] ECtHR (App Nos 8675/15 and 8697/15); *Hirsi Jamaa and Others v Italy* [23 February 2012] ECtHR (App No 27765/09).

52 *Cyprus v Turkey* [26 May 1975] EComHR (App Nos 6780/74 and 6950/75) DR 2, p 125, 125; *Cyprus v Turkey* [10 July 1978] EComHR (App No 8007/77) DR 13, p 85, 85; *X. and Y. v Switzerland* [3 October 1978] EComHR (App No 8166/78) DR 13, p 241; See also: James Hathaway, Thomas Gammeltoft-Hansen, 'Non-Refoulement in a World of Cooperative Deterrence' (2015) 53(2) Colum J Transnat'l L 244, 245; Elspeth Guild, 'The Border Abroad – Visas and Border Controls' in Kees Groenendijk, Elspeth Guild and Paul Minderhound (eds), *In Search Of Europe's Borders* (Kluwer Law International 2002).

territorial application of jurisdiction. By contrast, while repeatedly reiterating the primarily territorial nature of jurisdiction, the ECtHR has not absolved Member States of their international obligations in respect of refugees, maintaining that certain interactions between State agents and refugees engage the jurisdiction of the State and accordingly the primary obligations of the ECHR. Those decisions have in turn spurred even more creative interpretations and applications of jurisdiction. In both cases, an obvious procedural consequence of judicial decisions is that the exercise of control over the 'unauthorised' arrival of a refugee cannot be affected by jurisdictional error.

For its part, the position of UNHCR on extraterritorial measures has not always been clear. Though it has since clarified and consistently maintained that the 1951 Convention does not place jurisdictional limits on a State party's capacity to engage with refugees on the basis of territoriality, UNHCR's 1979 *Handbook on Procedures and Criteria for Determining Refugee Status* stated that the "basic requirements" of the High Commissioner's office imposed an exclusively territorial burden, and that any alien protected by the Convention (and by its promise of *non-refoulement*) will be found either "at the border or in the territory of a Contracting State."[53] The Handbook referred to the 1977 report of the Executive Committee of the High Commissioner's Programme (ExCom), which provided:

> The competent official (e.g., immigration officer or border police officer) to whom the applicant addresses himself *at the border or in the territory of a Contracting State* should have clear instructions for dealing with cases which might come within the purview of the relevant international instruments. He should be required to act in accordance with the principle of *non-refoulement* and to refer such cases to a higher authority.[54]

The 1977 Conclusion No. 6 of the ExCom on *non-refoulement* also reaffirmed "the fundamental importance of the observance of the principle of *non-refoulement* – both at the border and within the territory of a State" irrespective of a person's status as an asylum seeker or recognised refugee. It did not

53 UN High Commissioner for Refugees, *Handbook on procedures and criteria for determining refugee status under the 1951 Convention and the 1967 Protocol relating to the Status of Refugees* (September 1979) (ST/HCR(092.1)/H26), 46.

54 UN High Commissioner for Refugees, *Addendum to the Report of the United Nations High Commissioner for Refugees* (6 November 1979) A/34/12/Add.1, para 53(6)(e)(i). Emphasis added.

account for circumstances arising outside the territorial jurisdiction of the State in which a State agent would be required to conduct a refugee status determination or at a minimum, receive a claim for international protection.

The UN General Assembly previously referred to territoriality as the basis for the admission of refugees. In Resolution 428(V) of 16 December 1950, to which the Statute of UNHCR was annexed, the General Assembly specifically called upon governments to co-operate with UNHCR in the performance of its functions "especially by admitting refugees to their territories." The Final Act of the Conference of Plenipotentiaries that adopted the Convention also recommended that governments "continue to receive refugees in their territories."[55] Though they referred to territoriality as the basis for admission, there is little to suggest that they did so in order to preclude the reception of refugee claims at places outside the territory of the State by stressing that such events could *only* occur within the territory of the State. However, the Institute of International Law made this distinction between territorial and exterritorial refugee protection as early as 1950, when it provided that: "[A]sylum is the protection which a State grants *on its territory or in some other place* under the control of certain of its organs, to a person who comes to seek it."[56]

Nonetheless, a strong global push to reiterate the importance of *non-refoulement* began in the late 1960s, and at the same time, the territorial nature of refugee protection was also reiterated. The UN *Declaration on Territorial Asylum* of 1967 provided that no asylum seeker shall be "subjected to measures such as rejection *at the frontier* or, *if he has already entered the territory* in which he seeks asylum, expulsion or compulsory return to any State where he may be subjected to persecution."[57] The Council of Europe's 1967 *Resolution on Asylum to Persons in Danger of Persecution* provided that Member Governments "should act in a particularly liberal and humanitarian spirit in relation to persons *who seek asylum on their territory*."[58] The previous year, the Asian-African Legal Consultative Committee had adopted the *Principles con-*

---

55 UN General Assembly, *Addendum to the Report of the United Nations High Commissioner for Refugees* (31 October 1977) (A/32/12/Add.1), para 53(6)(e)(i).

56 Institut de Droit International, *Projet de Résolutions* (1950) 43 I Bath, pg. 167, Art. 1. Emphasis added. "Tout Etat, dans l'exercice de la faculté que lui laisse le droit international de recevoir sur son territoire tout individu étranger et de lui permettre d 'y séjourner, doit remplir les devoirs d'humanité envers les individus qui cherchent asile sur son territoire."

57 UN General Assembly, *Declaration on Territorial Asylum* (14 December 1967) A/RES/2312 (XXII) Article 3.

58 Council of Europe: Committee of Ministers, *Resolution (67)14: Asylum to Persons in Danger of Persecution* (29 June 1967) 14. Emphasis added.

cerning the Treatment of Refugees, providing that "[a] State has the sovereign right to grant or to refuse asylum *in its territory* to a refugee in accordance with its international obligations and national legislation."[59] In 1977, the Committee of Ministers of the Council of Europe also adopted a *Declaration on Territorial Asylum* reaffirming "their liberal attitude with regard to persons seeking asylum on their territory."[60]

There are, however, some notable exceptions to the strict imposition of territorial limitations, though much like several of the aforementioned instruments, this recognition is not explicit. The 1969 OAU *Convention Governing the Specific Aspects of Refugee Problems in Africa* provides that no person shall be subjected by a Member State to measures "*such as* rejection at the frontier, return or expulsion."[61] Similarly, the 1984 *Cartagena Declaration on Refugees* provides that the principle of *non-refoulement* included the prohibition of rejection at the frontier,[62] and that States in the region should established a minimum standard of treatment for refugees, in accordance with ExCom Conclusion No. 22 on the *Protection of Asylum Seekers in Situations of Large-Scale Influx*, which also did not limit *refoulement* to territorial cases, providing only that the principle *included* non-rejection at the frontier.[63]

Predictably, the lack of explicitness in these instruments has permitted their misuse as legal tools for the exclusion of refugees, based on technicalities regarding the limits of jurisdiction. Certain State practices that have relied on creative interpretations of jurisdiction have frequently been tested in courts, and, depending on the acceptance or rejection of those constructions by the judiciary, have then gone on to be either reinforced through continued State practice, or altered in order to circumvent the technicalities of the relevant decisions in furtherance of a new, often more creative application of jurisdiction. The following three sections demonstrate the extent to which this has occurred across jurisdictions over the past four decades in particular, affecting a receding line of jurisdiction, relative to refugee protection.

---

59 Asian-African Legal Consultative Organization, *Bangkok Principles on the Status and Treatment of Refugees* (31 December 1966) Article II(2).

60 Council of Europe: Committee of Ministers, *Declaration on Territorial Asylum* (18 November 1977).

61 Article II(3).

62 *Cartagena Declaration on Refugees, Colloquium on the International Protection of Refugees in Central America, Mexico and Panama* (19–22 November 1984) Article III(5).

63 Executive Committee of the High Commissioner's Programme, *Conclusion No. 22 (XXXII): Protection of Asylum-Seekers in Situations of Large-Scale Influx* (21 October 1981) Article II(2).

3 First iteration: Operations outside Territorial Jurisdiction

The implementation of law and policy affecting interdiction on the high seas has been a common response from numerous States to the maritime arrival of refugees and migrants. Its practical effect has been "to shut out refugees from full and fair refugee status determination procedures. The consequence is the loss of adequate protection, not only from *refoulement*, but also from orbit, prolonged detention, and other deprivations."[64] In numerous instances, interdiction on the high seas has required the cooperation of two or more States, or the exercise of concurrent jurisdiction. In each of the following examples, one State has permitted another to carry out migration control within the ordinary bounds of its jurisdiction; an act of jurisdictional deferral entitling the State carrying out measures of migration control to "exercise all or some of the public powers normally to be exercised by that Government."[65] Though the following three examples occurred at different times and in different regions, there are a number of commonalities among them when considered with reference to jurisdictional competencies. Namely, that State A exercised legislative jurisdiction that extended to the territory of State B, and concurrent enforcement jurisdiction with effects on State B (both with the consent of State B), with the intended purpose of evading judicial jurisdiction, thus avoiding questions of attribution for the purposes of determining lawfulness of conduct.

3.1 *'Wet Foot/Dry Foot': The US Haitian and Cuban Interdiction Programmes*

In US law and policy, interference with the application of IRL through the limited application of jurisdiction began seriously in the early 1990s with the interdiction of Haitian and Cuban refugees and migrants under Operations Able Manner and Able Vigil respectively. The US Naval Institute's *Proceedings* describes the operations in the following terms:

> [M]any of the operational details were planned essentially at the last minute [...]. Able Manner and Able Vigil were largely plan-as-you-

64 Stephen H. Legomsky, 'The USA and the Caribbean Interdiction Program' (2006) 18 IJRL 677, 686.

65 Anja Klug, Tim Howe, 'The Concept of State Jurisdiction and the Applicability of the Non-refoulement Principle to Extraterritorial Interception Measures' in Ryan and Mitsilegas (eds), *Extraterritorial Immigration Control* (Martinus Nijhoff 2010) 94.

> go [...] with operational orders written literally the night before they were needed.[66]

Despite their *ad-hoc* implementation, these operations, and the judicial decisions that arose therefrom, set US asylum law on a particular trajectory of restrictive application of jurisdiction on a territorial basis, accounting for its current substantive, procedural, and operational status. This would in turn act as a model for other States and regions.[67] The jurisdictional basis for Able Manner and Able Vigil was strictly territorial, in that even in US territorial waters, the *Immigration and Nationality Act* 1952 (INA) was not applied. As Ryan explains:

> The practical limitations to extraterritorial processing are significant in part because a feature of United States approach is that the Coast Guard is permitted to interdict even within United States territorial waters. The reason for allowing this form of interdiction is that, under the so-called 'wet foot/dry foot' theory, it is only upon reaching shore that the protections of the Immigration and Nationality Act 1952 apply.[68]

The formal effort to interdict Haitian migrant vessels, Operation Able Manner, began on 15 January 1993, five days before President Clinton took office, and formally concluded on 26 November 1994 but repatriations continued until early 1995. In the time Able Manner was active, the US Coast Guard interdicted 25,177 Haitian nationals, many of whom were taken to the American naval base at Guantanamo Bay, Cuba for processing.[69] President Clinton finally ended the no-screening policy in May 1994, entering into agreements with Jamaica and the Turks and Caicos Islands (the latter through the UK) to

66 Ivan T. Luke, *Shooting from the Hip* (1997) U.S. Naval Institute 53.

67 See, for example: Daniel Ghezelbash, *Refuge Lost: Asylum Law in an Interdependent World* (CUP 2018).

68 Bernard Ryan, 'Extraterritorial Immigration Control: What Role for Legal Guarantees?' in Bernard Ryan and Valsamis Mitsilegas (eds), *Extraterritorial Immigration Control* (Martinus Nijhoff 2010) 27; citing USA: Department of Justice, *Immigration Consequences of Undocumented Aliens' Arrival in United States Territorial Waters* (13 October 1993).

69 *Records on Operation Able Manner* Clinton Presidential Library (2011-1040-F). Guantanamo Bay migrant camp soon reached near capacity. While waiting for it to re-open, the Navy and Marine Corps had constructed a camp for 2,500 migrants on Grand Turk Island in Turks and Caicos, at a cost of $18 million. But construction delays and poor environmental conditions had prevented even a single migrant from being housed there. See: Ivan T. Luke, *Shooting from the Hip* Proceedings (1997) U.S. Naval Institute 53.

conduct full RSDs in the territories of those States. UNHCR was permitted to monitor the hearings, and private agencies were allowed to assist.[70]

Operation Able Vigil began on 19 August 1994, in response to a wave of migration from Cuba, interdicting a total of 30,224 Cuban refugees and migrants, who were transferred to Latin American States, or held at Guantanamo Bay migrant camp. In negotiations with Cuba the US agreed to allow 20,000 Cubans to immigrate each year in return for a Vietnam-style moratorium on unauthorised departures. Cuba pledged to stop any further exodus of Cubans aboard makeshift rafts and small boats trying to reach the shores of Florida. All others who attempted to illegally migrate and were picked up at sea would be taken back to Cuba. Those who reached US soil would be allowed to stay. On 25 April 1995, the remaining 21,000 refugees remaining at Guantanamo Bay were allowed to resettle in the US.[71] Those Cubans who had managed to reach US shores had generally been admitted (or 'paroled') into the State, and were eventually granted lawful permanent resident status, under the *Cuban Adjustment Act* of 1966.[72]

The legality of 'Operation Able Manner' came before the US Supreme Court in 1993. Though it was subject to extensive litigation resulting in the renowned case, *Sale v Haitian Council Inc.*,[73] the course of events leading to that case, and to the application of a strictly territorial interpretation of jurisdiction is worth noting. In 1965, the US Congress abandoned the national quota system of immigration and added a provision to the INA prohibiting discrimination in the granting of visas on the basis of "race, sex, nationality, place of birth, or place of residence." This provision was deemed to have been violated in the 1980 case of *Haitian Refugee Center v Civiletti*,[74] in which Haitian plaintiffs alleged their interception and deportation from US territory had been motivated by discrimination.[75] A District Court concluded:

> The Haitians allege that the actions of INS constitute impermissible discrimination on the basis of national origin. They have proven their claim. This court cannot close its eyes, however, to a possible underlying

70 Stephen H. Legomsky, 'The USA and the Caribbean Interdiction Program' (2006) 18 IJRL 677, 681.

71 USA: United States Coast Guard, *1994 – Alien Interdiction: The Flow Becomes a Flood* United States Coast Guard Aviation History.

72 USA, *Cuban Adjustment Act* (1966) 80 Stat. 1161.

73 *Chris Sale, Acting Commissioner, Immigration and Naturalization Service, et al. v Haitian Centers Council, Inc., et al.* [21 June 1993] 509 US 155.

74 *Haitian Refugee Center v Civiletti* [2 July 1980] 503 F Supp 442.

75 *Id.*, affirmed by *Haitian Refugee Center v Smith* [14 May 1982] 676 F2d 1023.

> reason why these plaintiffs have been subjected to intentional "national origin" discrimination.[76]

That litigation led directly to the proposal for the introduction of a maritime interdiction programme with the express purpose of limiting access to judicial recourse through the exclusion of asylum applicants from US jurisdiction. In the July 1981 report of a presidential task force on immigration and asylum, it was stated that:

> The purpose of an interdiction program would be both to deter directly further unlawful migration by expeditiously returning migrants to Haiti, and *incidentally, to curtail the flow of aliens into administrative and judicial proceedings in the United States.*[77]

The report explicitly acknowledged that such a programme would limit and qualify the international obligations of the State under IRL, which it recognised as applicable in the very circumstances it now sought to avoid:

> Although required by the UN Protocol and Convention to adjudicate refugee claims prior to returning a claimant to his homeland, if interdiction occurs outside of US territorial waters, *the determination would not be governed by the Immigration Act.*[78]

As discussed in Chapter 4, by agreement with Haitian authorities, and by Executive Order No. 12324, President Reagan authorised the interdiction of Haitian flag vessels and US flag vessels outbound from Haiti to prevent "the entry of undocumented aliens from the high seas."[79] Per the agreement, US authorities were permitted to board Haitian flag vessels, examine documents, and "undertake such measures as are necessary to establish the […] destination of the vessel and the status of those on board the vessel […]."[80] Where an offence again US law was suspected, authorities were empowered to detain

76 *Id.*

77 Bernard Ryan, 'Extraterritorial Immigration Control: What Role for Legal Guarantees?' in Ryan and Mitsilegas (eds), *Extraterritorial Immigration Control* (Martinus Nijhoff 2010) citing: Naomi Flink Zucker, 'The Haitians versus the United States: The Courts as Last Resort' (1983) 467 Annals Am Acad Pol & Soc Sci 151, 159. Emphasis added.

78 *Id.*

79 USA, Haiti, *Agreement of 23 September 1981* (23 September 1981) 33 UST 3559, TIAS 10241; USA, *Executive Order 12324: Interdiction of Illegal Aliens* (29 September 1981) 46 FR 48109.

80 *Id.*

the vessel and persons on board on the high seas. Haiti undertook to permit the return of detained vessels and persons to Haitian ports, or into the custody of Haitian authorities on the high seas. The US–Haiti Agreement included the qualification:

> It is understood that under these arrangements the United States Government does not intend to return to Haiti any Haitian migrants whom the United States authorities determine to qualify for refugee status.

Six days after the Agreement was signed, President Reagan issued Presidential Proclamation No. 4865, characterising "the continuing illegal migration by sea of large numbers of undocumented aliens into the southeastern United States" as "a serious national problem detrimental to the interests of the United States,"[81] and suspended the entry of undocumented aliens from the high seas, authorising the prevention of such entries by interdiction.[82] The careful choice of the word '*intend*' in the US–Haiti Agreement qualified the prohibition of *refoulement* by providing that the State did not undertake *not* to return refugees to Haiti, merely that if such returns were to occur, they would be unintentional. However, the depth of inquiries made into the status of persons on board interdicted vessels (revealed in *Sale*) made it clear that the US had made few operational provisions to ensure the fulfilment of its protection obligations. Of the 905 Haitians intercepted by US Coast Guard cutters, not a single one was deemed to have a credible fear of return, and US officials provided no advice about the right to seek protection.[83] Those on board were not interviewed, but were instead transported to the US Naval Base at Guantanamo Bay, Cuba, for preliminary screening of their refugee claims. In a 1990 report, the former Lawyers Committee for Human Rights (now Human Rights First) found that of the 364 Haitian vessels interdicted between 1981 and 1990, the US returned more than 21,000 Haitians, and had found only six persons to have claims that warranted a full asylum hearing.[84] Of the 905

81 USA, *Proclamation 4865: High Seas Interdiction of Illegal Aliens* (29 September 1981) 46 FR 48107 cited in: Lory Diana Rosenberg, 'International Association of Refugee Law Judges Conference – The Courts and Interception: The United States' Interdiction Experience and Its Impact on Refugees and Asylum Seekers' (2003) 17 Geo Immigr LJ 199, 201.

82 USA, *Proclamation 4865: High Seas Interdiction of Illegal Aliens* (29 September 1981) 46 FR 48107.

83 Bill Frelick, 'Abundantly Clear: Refoulement' (2004) 19 Geo Immigr LJ 245.

84 Stephen H. Legomsky, 'The USA and the Caribbean Interdiction Program' (2006) 18 IJRL 677, 679 citing: Lawyers Committee for Human Rights, *Refugee Refoulement: The Forced Return of Haitians under the US-Haitian Interdiction Agreement* (February 1990).

Haitians intercepted by US Coast Guard cutters, not a single person was deemed to have a credible fear of return. Those intercepted by US officials were not provided information about the right to seek protection.[85]

Respondents in the case of *Sale* sought a temporary injunction, contending that Executive Order No. 12807 directed the Coast Guard to return persons to Haiti "without first determining whether they qualify as refugees" and authorised repatriations "to be undertaken only beyond the territorial sea of the United States" in violation of §243(h)(1) of the INA ("the Attorney General shall not deport or return any alien [...] to a country if the Attorney General determines that such alien's life or freedom would be threatened in such country [...]"), and Article 33 of the 1951 Convention.

Previously, a District Court had denied relief, concluding that §243(h)(1) did not protect aliens in international waters and that the 1951 Convention's provisions were not self-executing.[86] Later, in reversing that decision, the Court of Appeals held that the same section was not limited in its application to aliens within the US, and that Article 33, like the INA, was applicable to all refugees, regardless of location.[87] The Supreme Court reversed the decision of the Court of Appeals, holding that §243(h)(1) "applies only in the context of the domestic procedures" and that "[N]either §243(h) nor Article 33 limits the President's power to order the Coast Guard to repatriate undocumented aliens intercepted on the high seas."[88]

> Since the INA nowhere provides for the conduct of such proceedings outside the United States, since Part V of the Act, in which §243 is located, obviously contemplates that they be held in this country, and *since it is presumed that Acts of Congress do not ordinarily apply outside the borders* [...] §243(h)(1) must be construed to apply only within United States territory.[89]

In reaching its conclusion that the 1951 Convention was not intended to have extraterritorial effect, the majority referred to Article 33(2) of the 1951 Convention, which provides:

---

85 Bill Frelick, 'Abundantly Clear: Refoulement' (2004) 19 Geo Immigr LJ 245.

86 *Haitian Refugee Center, Inc. v Baker* [24 February 1992] 953 F2d 1498.

87 *Haitian Centers Council, Inc. v McNary* [29 July 1992] 969 F2d 1350.

88 *McNary v Haitian Refugee Ctr., Inc.* [20 February 1991] 498 US 479.

89 *Chris Sale, Acting Commissioner, Immigration and Naturalization Service, et al. v Haitian Centers Council, Inc., et al.* [21 June 1993] 509 US 155. Emphasis added.

> The benefit of the present provision may not, however, be claimed by a refugee whom there are reasonable grounds for regarding as a danger to the security of the country in which he is, or who, having been convicted by a final judgment of a particularly serious crime, constitutes a danger to the community of that country.

The majority held that Article 33(2) "affirmatively indicate[d] that it was not intended to have extraterritorial effect." This was, according to the majority, a matter of sequential logic:

> Under the second paragraph of Article 33 an alien may not claim the benefit of the first paragraph if he poses a danger to the country in which he is located. If the first paragraph did apply on the high seas, no nation could invoke the second paragraph's exception with respect to an alien there: an alien intercepted on the high seas is in no country at all. If Article 33(1) applied extraterritorially, therefore, Article 33(2) would create an absurd anomaly: Dangerous aliens on the high seas would be entitled to the benefit of 33(1) while those residing in the country that sought to expel them would not.[90]

Though *Sale* related to the implementation of Executive Order No. 12324 (1981), it must be noted that during the course of the extensive litigation that resulted in the 1993 decision, a far more explicit limitation of the *non-refoulement* obligation was included in another Executive Order, issued by President George HW Bush in May 1992. Executive Order No. 12807 revoked and replaced Executive Order No. 12324, and provided that:

> The international legal obligations of the United States under the United Nations Protocol Relating to the Status of Refugees [...] to apply Article 33 of the United Nations Convention Relating to the Status of Refugees *do not extend to persons located outside the territory of the United States.*[91]

90 *Id.* Though the court acknowledged that the parallel provision in para 243(h)(2)(D), 8 U.S.C. that was added to the INA in 1980 did not contain the phrase "country in which he is," it concluded that the "general understanding that it was intended to conform the statute to the Protocol leads us to give it that reading [...]."

91 USA, *Executive Order 12807: Interdiction of Illegal Aliens* (24 May 1992) 57 FR 23133. Emphasis added.

The Order further stipulated that any entitlement to an RSD or a review of any decision pertaining thereto could not be claimed of any entity of the State:

> Neither this order nor any agency guidelines, procedures, instructions, directives, rules or regulations implementing this order shall create, or shall be construed to create, any right or benefit, substantive or procedural [...]. *Nor shall this order be construed to require any procedures to determine whether a person is a refugee.*[92]

The Order not only instructed the Coast Guard, under the same terms of Executive Order No. 12324 to "return the vessel and its passengers to the country from which it came, or to another country, when there is reason to believe that an offense is being committed against the United States immigration laws" but also included a privative clause, providing that the Attorney General, "in his unreviewable discretion" may decide that a person who is a refugee "will not be returned without his consent."[93]

In the wake of the *Sale* litigation, the US continued to limit the application of the INA. Between 1 April 1995 and 1 October 1997, the US Coast Guard conducted 'Operation Able Response,' with enhanced operations dedicated to the interdiction of Dominican migrants that sought to enter the US via Puerto Rico through the Mona Passage.[94] Over 9,500 migrants were interdicted and subjected to *refoulement*. Several years later, Executive Order No. 13276 of 2002 authorised the Attorney General to maintain custody of migrants interdicted or intercepted in the Caribbean region, and to transfer them to any location he deems appropriate, including Guantanamo Bay.[95] It provided that "[T]his order shall not be construed to require any procedure to determine whether a person is a refugee or otherwise in need of protection," and that "[T]his order is not intended to, and does not, create any right or benefit, substantive or procedural, enforceable at law or equity or otherwise against the United States, its departments, agencies, entities, instrumentalities, offi-

---

92 *Id.*

93 *Chris Sale, Acting Commissioner, Immigration and Naturalization Service, et al. v Haitian Centers Council, Inc., et al.* [21 June 1993] 509 US 155; Lory Diana Rosenberg, 'International Association of Refugee Law Judges Conference – The Courts and Interception: The United States' Interdiction Experience and Its Impact on Refugees and Asylum Seekers' (2003) 17 Geo Immigr LJ 199, 202.

94 USA, *Executive Order 13276: Delegation of Responsibilities Concerning Undocumented Aliens Interdicted or Intercepted in the Caribbean Region* (15 November 2002) 67 FR 69983.

95 *Id.*

cers, employees, or any other person." It also deemed "any action, omission, or matter that otherwise would not be reviewable" to not be reviewable in any judicial or administrative proceeding.[96]

The intention of this Order was laid out when, in a statement on 25 February 2004, President George W. Bush declared, "I have made it abundantly clear to the Coast Guard that we will turn back *any refugee that attempts to reach our shore*."[97] As Frenick noted, President Bush's use of the term "refugee" did not appear to have been a misstatement, as "neither the White House nor the State Department issued a correction or clarification of his quote" and that several months later, following the return of another 651 Haitian boat people, the State Department's web page repeated the President's quote as a statement of US policy, termed "Operation Able Sentry"; an interdiction operation that essentially replicated Operation Able Manner.[98]

> Without an ambitious and workable program for thorough and otherwise adequate refugee determinations somewhere – in the countries of origin, in the destination states, or in third countries – a key question remains unanswered: What, exactly, is a Haitian (or other foreign national) who genuinely fears persecution on one of the five Convention grounds expected to do?[99]

This model of maritime interdiction provided a template for other States and regions pursuing the limitation of jurisdiction over refugees, and has been replicated often enough to become something of a consistent feature in the refugee law and policy of Western States in particular. Among them, Border States of the EU have notably employed the interdiction model in an attempt to disrupt the asylum–jurisdiction nexus, repeatedly asserting the lack of jurisdiction over maritime arrivals as the basis for the legitimacy of State actions. However, unlike the political support provided to the 'orderly departures' programme, or the judicial support provided to the 'wet foot/dry foot' policy, the ECtHR has repeatedly rejected the argument as manifestly unsubstantiated, on the basis of certain jurisdictional realities. This has inadvertently led to the implementation of further restrictive policies, straining the conception of jurisdiction to keep asylum seekers technically and legally unadmitted.

---

96 *Id.*

97 Emphasis added.

98 Bill Frelick, 'Abundantly Clear: Refoulement' (2004) 19 Geo Immigr LJ 245, 247.

99 Stephen H. Legomsky, 'The USA and the Caribbean Interdiction Program' (2006) 18 IJRL 677, 695.

3.2 De Facto *and Functional Control: Interdiction in Europe*

Maritime interdiction has been a long-standing practice of European States in operations across the southern border of the continent. It has been extensively litigated at the municipal level, and at the ECtHR, which has developed in response a vast body of consistent jurisprudence based primarily on a test of functional jurisdictional control, complemented by the application of the formula 'knew or ought to have known' to establish the objective knowledge of State agents that persons interdicted were asylum seekers. As Giuffrè notes:

> [A] state engaged in joint patrolling within the territorial waters of another state may be responsible for the breach of the principle of *non-refoulement* on three accounts: (i) 'as a co-author of *refoulement*' under Article 47 of ARSIWA; (ii) for providing 'aid or assistance in the commission of an internationally wrongful act' under Article 16; and (iii) for a breach of a principle of international law, i.e., 'positive due diligence obligations.'[100]

The ECHR requires the High Contracting Parties to "secure to everyone within their jurisdiction the rights and freedoms defined in Section I of this Convention,"[101] which includes the prohibition of torture, from which the ECtHR has habitually attributed the negative obligation to refrain from *refoulement* in asylum cases. The issue of control and authority in extraterritorial situations has been a recurring theme before the ECtHR, and while it has long been the jurisprudence of the court that "whenever the State, through its agents, exercises control and authority over an individual, and thus jurisdiction, the State is under an obligation under Article 1 to secure to that individual the rights and freedoms under Section I of the Convention that are relevant to the situation of that individual,"[102] the court has been repeatedly confronted with new scenarios in which Contracting States have sought to establish the outer limits of the applicable rules on the scope of jurisdiction.

---

100 Mariagiulia Giuffrè, 'State Responsibility Beyond Borders: What Legal Basis for Italy's Push-backs to Libya?' (2012) 24 IJRL 692, 693.

101 Council of Europe, *European Convention for the Protection of Human Rights and Fundamental Freedoms, as amended by Protocols Nos. 11 and 14* (4 November 1950) ETS 5, Article 1.

102 *Al-Skeini and Others v the United Kingdom* [7 July 2011] ECtHR (App No 55721/07) paras 137.

The scope of conduct capable of constituting an exercise of jurisdiction outside the territory of a Member State has proven to be quite extensive according to the jurisprudence of the ECtHR. The application of the 'functional control test' to establish the function of jurisdiction of Member States for the purposes of Article 1 has developed in response to an array of conduct intended to exclude asylum seekers from the purview of Member States' jurisdiction.[103] It follows from the formula consistently applied by the predecessor European Commission of Human Rights in cases where State activity produced 'incidental' effects in foreign territories. In such cases, the Commission found that 'authorised agents of a State bring other persons or property within the jurisdiction of that State, to the extent that they exercise authority over such persons or property'; and that '[i]n so far as they affect such persons or property by their acts or omissions, the responsibility of the State is engaged.'[104]

In determining that a State "ought to have known," the ECtHR has used quite an expansive interpretation, by providing that the burden of proof extends beyond information given directly to the State to encompass information that should reasonably be considered available to the State.[105] Interestingly, the threshold applied in contemporary asylum cases to establish the extraterritorial jurisdiction of Member States developed from the law of diplomatic protection. Though many were declared inadmissible for various reasons, a number of key cases on diplomatic protection and the extraterritorial jurisdiction of Member States included *obiter* that would form the basis of the ECtHR's jurisprudence on extraterritorial jurisdiction in other cases, including in asylum cases.

In the 1965 case of *X. v the Federal Republic of Germany*,[106] the Commission noted that:

> [I]n certain respects, the nationals of a Contracting State are within its "jurisdiction" even when domiciled or resident abroad; whereas, in par-

103 See: *Al-Skeini and Others v the United Kingdom* [7 July 2011] ECtHR (App No 55721/07); Samantha Besson, 'The Extraterritoriality of the European Convention on Human Rights: Why Human Rights Depend on Jurisdiction and What Jurisdiction Amounts to' (2012) 25(4) Leiden JIntlL 857.

104 *X v Federal Republic of Germany* [25 September 1965] EComHR (App No 1611/62); *X v UK* [15 December 1977] EComHR (App No 7547/76); *Stocké v Germany* [12 October 1989] EComHR (App No 11755/85) para 166; *Vearncombe v UK and Germany* [18 January 1989] EComHR (App No 12816/87).

105 *Hirsi Jamaa and Others v Italy* [23 February 2012] ECtHR (App No 27765/09) para 171.

106 *X v Federal Republic of Germany* [25 September 1965] EComHR (App No 1611/62).

> ticular, the diplomatic and consular representatives of their country of origin perform certain duties with regard to them which may, in certain circumstances, make that country liable in respect of the Convention.[107]

This decision was cited in *Hess v the United Kingdom*,[108] in which the Commission reiterated that:

> As the Commission has already decided, a State is under certain circumstances responsible under the Convention for the actions of its authorities outside its territory. The Commission is of the opinion that there is in principle, from a legal point of view, no reason why acts of the British authorities in Berlin should not entail the liability of the United Kingdom under the Convention.[109]

In *X v United Kingdom*,[110] the Commission noted that:

> [A]uthorised agents of a State, including diplomatic or consular agents bring other persons or property within the jurisdiction of that State to the extent that they *exercise authority over such persons or property*. Insofar as they affect such persons or property by their acts or omissions, *the responsibility of the State is engaged*.[111]

Each of these cases was cited in the jurisprudence of the ECtHR to define the parameters of jurisdiction of Contracting Parties in situations concerning asylum seekers, where State agents had exercised a degree of control and authority over persons who the Court considered to be subject to Article 1 jurisdiction.[112] The jurisprudence of the Court relative to extraterritorial jurisdiction was applied in the 1991 expulsion case of *Cruz Varas and his Family v Sweden*, in which the ECtHR held that expulsion by a Contracting Party of an asylum

107 *Id.*, 168. *X v the Federal Republic of Germany* was declared inadmissible on various grounds.

108 *Hess v the United Kingdom* [28 May 1975] EComHR (App No 6231/73).

109 *Id.*, 73, citing: *X v Federal Republic of Germany* [25 September 1965] EComHR (App No 1611/62). *Hess v the United Kingdom* was also declared inadmissible on the grounds that the UK acted only as a partner in the joint responsibility with other Allied Powers.

110 *X v UK* [15 December 1977] EComHR (App No 7547/76) 158.

111 *Id.*, 168. *X v UK* was dismissed as manifestly unfounded. Emphasis added.

112 See also: *M v Denmark* [14 October 1992] EComHR (App No 17392/90) cited numerous times in subsequent extraterritorial jurisdiction cases.

seeker may give rise to an issue under Article 3 (prohibition of torture and of inhuman or degrading treatment or punishment), and hence engage the responsibility of that State under the ECHR, where substantial grounds had been shown for believing that the person concerned faced a real risk of being subjected to torture or to inhuman or degrading treatment or punishment in the country to which he was returned.[113]

Later that same year, citing *Cruz Varas*, the ECtHR expanded the scope of evidence that it could examine in determining the well-foundedness of an applicant's fear in expulsion cases:

> [S]ince the nature of the Contracting States' responsibility under Article 3 (art. 3) in cases of this kind lies in the act of exposing an individual to the risk of ill-treatment, the existence of the risk must be assessed primarily with reference to those facts which were known or ought to have been known to the Contracting State at the time of the expulsion; the Court is not precluded, however, from having regard to information which comes to light subsequent to the expulsion. This may be of value in confirming or refuting the appreciation that has been made by the Contracting Party or the well-foundedness or otherwise of an applicant's fears.[114]

In the 2000 case of *T.I. v. United Kingdom*,[115] the ECtHR found that the indirect removal to an intermediary country which is also a Contracting Party did not affect the responsibility of Contracting States to ensure that an applicant was not, as a result of its decision to expel, exposed to treatment contrary to the ECHR, nor could Contracting States rely automatically on the arrangements made in the Dublin Convention. The circumstances capable of engaging the obligations of Contracting Parties continued to expand when, that same year, the ECtHR delivered its judgment in the case of *Al-Saadoon and Mufdhi v United Kingdom*[116] concerning the detention and transfer of two Iraqi nationals to Iraqi custody by the Contracting Party. Citing *Hess* and *X v United Kingdom*, The ECtHR considered that:

---

113 *Cruz Varas and Others v Sweden* [20 March 1991] ECtHR (App No 46/1990/237/307) [69], [70].

114 *Case of Vilvarajah and Others v The United Kingdom* [30 October 1991] ECtHR (Application no 13163/87; 13164/87; 13165/87; 13447/87; 13448/87) [107].

115 *T.I. v UK* [7 March 2000] ECtHR (App No 43844/98).

116 *Al-Saadoon and Mufdhi v UK* [30 June 2009] ECtHR (App No 61498/08).

> [G]iven the total and exclusive *de facto*, and subsequently also *de jure*, control exercised by the United Kingdom authorities over the premises in question, the individuals detained there, including the applicants, were within the United Kingdom's jurisdiction.[117]

Though it had repeatedly emphasised the preponderance of territoriality in the application of the ECHR, and that the concept of jurisdiction within the meaning of Article 1 of the ECHR was not necessarily restricted to the national territory of Contracting Parties,[118] the ECtHR eventually confirmed that Article 1 jurisdiction extended to the activities of Contracting Parties on the high seas. In the 2010 case of *Medvedyev and Others v France*[119] in which crew members of a merchant ship were intercepted on the high seas by agents of the Member State, the ECtHR found that while "Article 1 sets a limit, notably territorial, on the reach of the Convention,"[120] France had exercised full and exclusive control over the merchant ship and its crew, "at least *de facto*, from the time of its interception, in a continuous and uninterrupted manner" meaning the applicants were effectively within France's jurisdiction for the purposes of Article 1 of the Convention.[121] Two years after *Medvedyev*, the ECtHR found that its jurisprudence on extraterritorial activity of Contracting Parties applied also to maritime interceptions in the context of immigration control. The 2012 case of *Hirsi Jamaa and Others v Italy*[122] was the first instance in which the ECtHR found that actions taken by a Contracting Party established its extraterritorial jurisdiction in relation to Article 4 of Protocol No. 4 (prohibition of collective expulsion). While much of the decision simply reaffirmed existing jurisprudence (the court reaffirmed that there was no distinction between *de facto* and *de jure* jurisdiction where the actions of a Contracting Parties met the threshold requirement for functional control), its application to the specific circumstances of the case was critical.

The applicants were part of a group of about 200 individuals who left Libya in 2009 aboard three vessels with the aim of reaching the Italian coast. They

117 At [88], citing *Hess v the United Kingdom* [28 May 1975] EComHR (App No 6231/73).

118 See: *Loizidou v Turkey* [23 February 1995] ECtHR (App No 40/1993/435/514) [52]; *Ilaşcu and Others v Moldova and Russia* [8 July 2004] ECtHR (App No 48787/99) [314].

119 *Medvedyev and Others v France* [29 March 2010] ECtHR (App No 3394/03).

120 *Id.*, [63] citing: *Banković and Others v Belgium and Others* [12 December 2001] ECtHR (App No 52207/99), *Ilaşcu and Others v Moldova and Russia* [8 July 2004] ECtHR (App No 48787/99), and *Loizidou v Turkey* [23 February 1995] ECtHR (App No 40/1993/435/514).

121 *Medvedyev and Others v France* [29 March 2010] ECtHR (App No 3394/03) [65].

122 *Hirsi Jamaa and Others v Italy* [23 February 2012] ECtHR (App No 27765/09).

were intercepted by the Italian authorities while in the Maltese Search and Rescue Region, transferred onto Italian military ships, and returned to Tripoli. The applicants submitted that during that voyage the Italian authorities did not inform them of their destination and took no steps to identify them. Italy acknowledged that the ships onto which the applicants had been embarked were fully within Italian jurisdiction, but characterised the events as "rescue operations on the high seas" and submitted that State agents exercised *only a minimal level of control* over the applicants, therefore not establishing full and exclusive control per the standard applied in *Medvedyev*.[123] The ECtHR rejected this submission:

> Italy cannot circumvent its "jurisdiction" under the Convention by describing the events in issue as rescue operations on the high seas. In particular, the Court cannot subscribe to the Government's argument that Italy was not responsible for the fate of the applicants on account of the allegedly minimal control exercised by the authorities over the parties concerned at the material time.[124]

Following the decision in *Hirsi*, the approach to border policy of Contracting Parties evolved to take account of the circumstances in which jurisdiction was engaged. This included the characterisation of interception and expulsion as non-admission, in conjunction with a minimal level of control incapable of establishing Article 1 jurisdiction. Notably, in Spain, the *Guardia Civil Operations Protocol of 26 February 2014 on Border Surveillance*, introduced the term "operational border," which described the demarcation of the frontier between Morocco and the Spanish enclaves of Melilla and Ceuta by a system of fences. Spain had enacted *Institutional Law 4/2000 of 11 January 2000 on the rights and freedoms of aliens in Spain and their social integration*, but had amended it by *Law 4/2015 on the protection of citizens' safety* in the wake of Hirsi. *Law 4/2015* provided for special rules for Ceuta and Melilla:

> Aliens attempting to penetrate the border containment structures in order to cross the border unlawfully, and whose presence is detected within the territorial demarcation lines of Ceuta or Melilla, may be returned in order to prevent their unlawful entry into Spain.

123 *Id.*, [66].
124 *Id.*, [79].

These measures were the subject of the 2020 case, *N.D. and N.T. v Spain* before the ECtHR,[125] which also concerned the alleged violation of Article 4 of Protocol No. 4 (prohibition of collective expulsion). While the ECtHR again applied and restated existing jurisprudence, it had not, until that point, ruled on the distinction between the non-admission and expulsion of aliens, and in particular of migrants or asylum seekers, who are within the jurisdiction of a State that is forcibly removing them from its territory.[126]

The events took place on the border between the Spanish enclave of Melilla and surrounding Morocco, where Spanish authorities had constructed a series of fences for the purposes of immigration control. Applicants had attempted to scale the fences but were apprehended by Spanish authorities and handed over to Moroccan authorities. Applicants alleged that they had not undergone any identification procedure and had had no opportunity to explain their personal circumstances or to be assisted by lawyers or interpreters. Two of the applicants successfully scaled the fence system a second time, entering Melilla. Eventually, expulsion orders were issued against them.

The respondent State acknowledged the existence of a systematic practice of collective summary expulsions at the Melilla border fence,[127] but maintained that it did not exercise jurisdiction, invoking an exception to territorial jurisdiction which not only encompassed any land between the Moroccan–Spanish border and the outer fence of the Melilla border-protection system, but extended up to the point of descent from the 'inner' (third) fence (on the Spanish side) and the area between that fence and the police line, up to the point where the latter had been passed.[128]

The State submitted that the three fences at the Melilla border constituted an "operational border" designed to prevent unauthorised entry by non-nationals and that after the introduction of the system of border controls, Spain had limited its jurisdiction, which began beyond the police line forming part of "measures against persons who [had] crossed the border illegally" within the meaning of Article 13 of the Schengen Borders Code.[129] In the Government's assertion, it was only after that point that Spain was bound by the

125 *N.D.* and *N.T. v Spain* [13 February 2020] ECtHR (App Nos 8675/15 and 8697/15).

126 *Id.*, [184].

127 *Id.*, [81].

128 *Id.*, [104].

129 European Union, *Regulation (EU) 2016/399 of the European Parliament and of the Council of 9 March 2016 on a Union Code on the rules governing the movement of persons across borders (Schengen Borders Code)* (2016) L 77/1.

procedural safeguards applicable to expulsion procedures, and by the Convention obligation to identify the persons concerned.[130]

The Chamber did not consider it necessary to determine whether the fences scaled by the applicants were located on Spanish or Moroccan territory. It took the view that from the point in time at which the applicants climbed down from the fences they had been under the continuous and exclusive control – at least *de facto* – of the Spanish authorities, and that there were "no considerations regarding the powers, functions and actions of the Spanish security forces capable of leading to any other conclusion."[131]

As the State argued that the applicants' case concerned a refusal of admission to Spanish territory rather than an expulsion, the court was called upon to ascertain whether the concept of 'expulsion' as used in Article 4 of Protocol No. 4 also covered the non-admission of aliens at a State border. The Grand Chamber observed that the prohibition of *refoulement* included the protection of asylum-seekers in cases of *both* non-admission and rejection at the border.[132] It held that the protections of the ECHR could not be dependent on formal considerations such as whether the persons to be protected were admitted to the territory of a Contracting State in conformity with a particular provision of national or European law applicable to the situation in question.

> The opposite approach would entail serious risks of arbitrariness, in so far as persons entitled to protection under the Convention could be deprived of such protection on the basis of purely formal considerations, for instance on the grounds that, not having crossed the State's border lawfully, they could not make a valid claim for protection under the Convention. States' legitimate concern to foil the increasingly frequent attempts to circumvent immigration restrictions cannot go so far as to render ineffective the protection afforded by the Convention, and in particular by Article 3 […].[133]

The fact that such measures were largely unsuccessful does not exclude them as relevant to ongoing policy development. On the contrary. The lack of success of States enacting these measures is precisely what led to a recalibration of law and policy in order to affect a receding line of jurisdiction, as the following section demonstrates.

---

130 *N.D. and N.T. v Spain* [13 February 2020] ECtHR (App Nos 8675/15 and 8697/15) [91].

131 *Id.*, [90].

132 *Id.*, [178].

133 *Id.*, [184].

4 Second Iteration: Operations within Third States

The second iteration forming part of the receding line of jurisdiction concerns prescriptive jurisdiction, authorised by consent of another State. Goodwin-Gill has described this construction in the following terms:

> In this version of [extra-territorial processing], one state uses another's territory, with or without the assistance of an international organisation, in order to decide claims to asylum which either have already been lodged on its own territory, or might have been lodged there if the claimant had not been intercepted en route.[134]

A critical (if not *the* critical) element of refugee policy that has affected and supported the implementation of those measures described in this section has been the 'first country of asylum' principle. Much of the actions taken in this second iteration of border control (and indeed in the third) are premised on the first country of asylum principle. Though not its creation, the EU (or rather, the EC as it was at the time) played a significant role in the popularisation of the concept; sometimes referred to as 'protection elsewhere.'

4.1 *First Country of Asylum Principle*

Though first utilised in the 1970s, as described in previous chapters, the 'first country of asylum' principle was refined and significantly reinforced during the 1980s. Between 1983 and 1989, the annual number of asylum applications made in Europe more than trebled, and the backlog of cases rose from 100,000 to approximately 250,000.[135] By the time the Yugoslavian war was at its peak, several million people were internationally displaced. Within that context, "Primary consideration should be given to the possibility of finding suitable solutions *within the regional context*."[136] Action with a view to burden-sharing "should be directed towards facilitating voluntary repatriation, promoting local settlement in the receiving country, providing resettlement possibilities in third countries, as appropriate."

---

134 Guy S. Goodwin-Gill, 'The Extraterritorial Processing of Claims to Asylum or Protection: The Legal Responsibilities of States and International Organisations' (2007) 9 UTS L Rev 26.

135 Gil Loescher, 'The European Community and Refugees' (1989) 65(4) International Affairs 617, 622.

136 Emphasis added.

In October 1980, the ExCom requested the High Commissioner to convene a group of experts to examine temporary refuge in all its aspects within the framework of the problem raised by large-scale influx. As the group of experts acknowledged, although according to the classical doctrine, the granting of asylum was a prerogative of States, an individual right to asylum had already taken on specific form in a number of States.[727] As one expert commented:

> If solutions could be envisaged that took clearly into account the need for new asylum-seekers to be resettled, preferably within the region or at least in a cultural environment appropriate for their well-being as had been done in Africa, the global commitment might be more readily forthcoming.[137]

Much like the settlement of African refugees, recommendations of the group of experts were based on the same humanitarian premise that preferred the resettlement of refugees in 'appropriate cultural environment.' Consequently, measures of burden-sharing should include, as necessary, emergency financial and technical assistance, assistance in kind and advance pledging of further financial or other assistance beyond the emergency phase until durable solutions are found, and where voluntary repatriation or local settlement cannot be envisaged, the provision for asylum-seekers of resettlement possibilities in "a cultural environment appropriate for their well-being."[138]

The group of experts agreed that there was a need to give a more concrete content to the operation of 'international solidarity,' and to formalise cooperation in order to permit the High Commissioner's Office or any other appropriate institution, "to obtain more effectively the assistance needed to cope with situations of mass influx."[139] The solution remained of a political nature. Other speakers felt, however, that the technique of using an "emergency fund" should be further developed. In support of the notion of temporary protection, one expert mentioned that the 1951 Convention already made a distinction between those rights to be accorded to persons whose presence was 'lawful' (Article 32) and those who had illegally entered a coun-

137 UN High Commissioner for Refugees, *Report of the Meeting of the Expert Group on Temporary Refuge in Situations of Large-Scale Influx, Geneva, 21–24 April 1981* (3 June 1981) (EC/SCP/16), 26.

138 *Id.*, 41–43.

139 *Id.*, 29.

try of asylum (Article 31). Persons in the former category were entitled to a more comprehensive range of rights involving the exercise of a State's sovereignty than those whose presence in a country of asylum was deemed to be illegal.

In contemporary IRL, the 'first country of asylum' principle has been a particularly prevalent cornerstone of European immigration law and policy. In recent decades, various European institutions have made multiple attempts to develop common regulations in the EU, based on the 'first country of asylum' principle.[140] This eventually became the central tenet of the *Convention determining the State responsible for examining Applications for Asylum lodged in one of the Member States of the European Communities* ("Dublin Convention") that has concentrated the obligations of refugee reception, processing, and settlement southward to Border States. In response, several Border States have concluded largely secretive treaties with north African States that provide for the exchange of generous development packages for certain collaborative operations preventing refugee departure and intercepting vessels on the high seas, resulting in the death and disappearance of an unknown number of people. But as with previous examples, regional law and policy has fomented around developments of the 1970s and 1980s, in particular.

Throughout that period, attempts were made in the Council of Europe (CoE) and between the twelve countries of the EC to develop common regulation of the zone.[141] In 1977, Western European States successfully lobbied for the UN to convene a Conference of Plenipotentiaries to draw up a Convention on Territorial Asylum; the draft of which was principally written by the 'Western Group.' The conference was a complete failure and no convention was ever adopted, but its failure immediately led to several attempts to reinforce European regionalism in respect of refugee law and policy. Shortly after the conference, the CoE established the Ad-Hoc Committee of Experts on the Legal Aspects of Territorial Asylum, Refugees and Stateless Persons, which promptly drew up a *European Convention on Territorial Asylum*, later watered down to a *Declaration on Territorial Asylum*.[142]

Several years later, the 1980 *European Agreement on Transfer of Responsibility for Refugees* was adopted, but remained largely impractical as only five States acceded to it. The broad objectives of the Western Group in pushing

---

140 Morten Kjærum, 'The Concept of Country of First Asylum' (1992) 4(4) IJRL 514.

141 *Id.*

142 Göran Melander, 'Basic Differences in Refugee Policy in Western Europe and North America' (1989) In Defense of the Alien 97, 98–99.

for a UN *Convention on Territorial Asylum*, in pursuing a *European Convention on Territorial Asylum*, and later in adopting the *European Agreement on Transfer of Responsibility for Refugees* was to provide an international legal basis for the restriction of refugee movement to so-called 'first countries of asylum.' Part of its history involves the exclusion of key parties from involvement in its development, in large part due to it being instituted in a very indirect way. The first country of asylum principle became the central tenet of the *Convention determining the State responsible for examining Applications for Asylum lodged in one of the Member States of the European Communities* (Dublin Convention),[143] and arguably the principle cornerstone of Western European asylum policy.[144]

Following consultations in a number of regional *fora*, such as the Council of Europe, the European Communities and the Schengen Group (the three Benelux countries, France and the Federal Republic of Germany), a convergence began to emerge on the principle that the country which first admitted an asylum-seeker on its territory would be the country responsible for examining the asylum request. This question is of particular importance in relation to the stated aim of the 12 Member States of the European Community to abolish internal frontier controls by 1992.[145]

In furtherance of a unified policy on immigration and asylum, the founding Member States created the Trevi Group; a consultative network of immigration and justice ministers from the EC, originally established to examine terrorism, but in reality devoting the vast majority of its efforts to asylum procedures in the EU.[146] The activities of the Trevi Group were largely kept secret, though the Group attributed this fact to a lack of interest on the part of other actors. Negotiations initially did not include the UNHCR, which the Trevi Group ascribed to "no formal request for participation [being] submitted by the UNHCR to the Schengen Secretariat."[147] The Group eventually drafted

143 European Union, *Convention determining the State responsible for examining applications for asylum lodged in one of the Member States of the European Communities – Dublin Convention* (1997) C 254.

144 Alberto Achermann, Mario Gattiker, 'Safe Third Countries: European Developments' (1995) 7(1) IJRL 19.

145 UN High Commissioner for Refugees, *Report of the United Nations High Commissioner for Refugees*9 May 1989) (E/1989/64) 5.

146 Gil Loescher, 'The European Community and Refugees' (1989) 65(4) International Affairs 617, 629.

147 Schengen Group, *ad hoc Immigration Group and other European intergovernmental bodies in view of a Europe without internal borders*, 4.

what would become the Dublin Convention, and though it noted that "the various drafts of the Convention were kept secret" it attributed the lack of public awareness to "[p]ersistent incompetence on the part of those who ought to have monitored the activities of the Schengen Group."[148]

In June 1990, the Dublin Convention was signed without the participation of the European Parliament.[149] In September that year, at the *European Consultation on Refugees and Exiles,* participants were highly critical of both the content of the Dublin Convention, a Convention on the crossing of external borders, and the Schengen Agreement harmonising refugee procedures, citing specifically "the non-consultative and even secretive process in which [they] were developed."[150] The Dublin Convention prescribed a hierarchy of circumstances that would determine the State responsible for the assessment of an applicant's claim for refugee status, among them, family reunification was of primary consideration, possession of valid residence permits of a Member State was secondary, and the first country of asylum was tertiary. In the case of family reunification, the State responsible for the RSD was the State in which a family member of the applicant resided, but was limited to the spouse of the applicant, the unmarried minor child of the applicant, or in the case that the applicant themselves was an unmarried minor child, the State where their parent(s) resided.[151] Where an applicant for asylum had irregularly crossed the border from a non-Member State into a Member State by land, sea or air, the latter was responsible for examining the application for asylum.[152] The third priority concerned the first country of asylum principle. It also prescribed that where an applicant for asylum had irregularly crossed the border into a Member State by land, sea or air, having come from a non-Member State, that Member State was responsible for examining the application for asylum.[153] Article 7 assigned the obligation to examine an asylum application to the Member State that was responsible for controlling the entry of the alien into EEC territory.

---

148 *Id.*

149 European Union, *Convention determining the State responsible for examining applications for asylum lodged in one of the Member States of the European Communities – Dublin Convention* (1997) C 254.

150 Helga Kutz-Hadm, 'Report on European Consultation on Refugees and Exiles (ECRE) Meeting September 22–23,1990, Geneva, Switzerland' (1990) 10(1) Refuge.

151 Article 4.

152 Articles 6 – 7.

153 Article 6.

Despite its tertiary status, the first country of asylum principle was the most operatively significant principle of the Dublin Convention. Family reunification was subordinate to the first country of asylum principle in a very practical sense: the vast majority of applicants for asylum entered without a visa, via sea crossings, arriving in a first country of asylum, and therefore requiring that country to consider any subsequent claims from family members. In that way, the first and second principles of 'burden-sharing' were in reality subservient to the third. The Dublin Convention was, as one NGO put it, "the first attempt by the Member States' immigration ministers to bring order to asylum by restricting asylum seekers' rights."[154]

The pressure that the Dublin Convention placed on southern Border States of the EU was immense. As the first countries of asylum, Border States were responsible for all maritime arrivals by virtue of geography. That pressure led to certain Border States enacting their own bilateral treaties with North African States in an effort to relieve some of the burden imposed by those so-called 'burden-sharing' measures of the Dublin Convention. In 2008, both Spain and Italy concluded separate treaties with African States that provided for generous development packages in exchange for certain collaborative operations to prevent migration.[155] On 21 February 2008, Spain and Cape Verde concluded the *Agreement between the Kingdom of Spain and the Republic of Cape Verde on Monitoring Joint Maritime Areas Under the Sovereignty and Jurisdiction of Cape Verde*. Later, in 2012, Spain and Morocco entered into the *Agreement between the Kingdom of Spain and the Kingdom of Morocco on the movement of people, the transit and the readmission of foreigners who have entered illegally*. The previous year, Italy and Libya had signed a protocol allowing join maritime patrols of Libya's territorial waters and the provision of Italian coastguard cutters to Libya, manned by a mixed crew.[156] This last Agreement was the subject of litigation before the ECtHR in the case of *Hirsi Jamaa and Others v Italy*.[157]

---

154 State Watch, *Key texts on justice and home affairs in the European Union, Volume 1 (1976–1993) From Trevi to Maastricht* (1997) 49.

155 Spain, Cape Verde, *Agreement between the Kingdom of Spain and the Republic of Cape Verde on Monitoring Joint Maritime Areas Under the Sovereignty and Jurisdiction of Cape Verde* (21 February 2008); Italy, Libya, *Treaty on Friendship, Partnership and Cooperation* (30 August 2008); *Khlaifia and Others v Italy* [15 December 2016] ECtHR (App No 16483/12); See also: Maarten Den Heijer, *Europe and Extraterritorial Asylum* (Hart Publishing 2012) 213.

156 Maarten Den Heijer, *Europe and Extraterritorial Asylum* (Hart Publishing 2012) 213.

157 *Hirsi Jamaa and Others v Italy* [23 February 2013] ECtHR (App No 27765/09).

Though the conception of jurisdiction in those treaties has been subject to litigation before the ECtHR, and has been broadly rejected by the court as not precluding the jurisdiction competence of the Contracting State, those latter measures were intended to place the refugee outside the scope of the State's jurisdiction by effectively delegating immigration control from State A to State B. The remoteness of the interaction between State A and the refugee, in those cases, attempted to evade implications of jurisdictional control, as provided in the submissions of States before the ECtHR.

4.2 *Carrier Sanctions*

In the 1980s, the global number of applications for asylum increased exponentially, including across EU Member States.[158] The increased availability of air travel allowed many asylum seekers to arrive via airports at the frontiers of High Contracting Parties.[159] This shift in global migratory patterns popularised the dormant practice of carrier sanctions on airline carriers, their personnel, and private citizens.[160] Carrier sanctions were founded on the principle of territorial jurisdiction, as asylum requests could only be made validly from inside the territory of the prospective State of reception.[161] Though carrier sanctions existed for a long time prior to the 1980s, in that decade, immigration laws pertaining to carrier sanctions were extensively amended to impose far more severe restrictions. By 1989, legislative provisions for sanctions against transport carriers were already in force in several countries, including

158 The number of asylum applications lodged in the Netherlands, for example, increased from approximately 7,500 in 1994 to 52,500 in 1998; See: Sophie Scholten, *The Privatisation of Immigration Control through Carrier Sanctions: The Role of Private Transport Companies in Dutch and British Immigration Control* (Brill 2015) 2.

159 Council of Europe: Parliamentary Assembly, *Arrival of asylum seekers at European airports* (2000) *Report, Committee on Migration, Refugees and Demography, Rapporteur: Mr. Gross, Switzerland, Socialist Group* 8 June 2000) (Doc. 8761) 1.

160 Early examples of carrier sanctions can be found in legislation of the United Kingdom passed in 1793 concerning aliens. This law required masters of vessels arriving in the United Kingdom to declare the numbers, names and occupations of foreigners on board or face a fine of £10; See: Frances Nicholson, 'Implementation of the Immigration (Carriers' Liability) Act of 1987: Privatising Immigration Functions at the Expense of International Obligations' (1997) 46(3) ICLQ 586, 588.

161 Lydia Morris, 'Governing at a Distance: The Elaboration of Controls in British Immigration' (1998) 32(4) International Migration Review 952. See generally: Erika Feller, 'Carrier Sanctions and International Law' (1989) 1 Int'l J Refugee L (1) IJRL 48.

Australia,[162] Belgium,[163] Brazil,[164] Canada,[165] Denmark,[166] the Federal Republic of Germany,[167] New Zealand,[168] the UK,[169] and the US.[170]

Against this backdrop, in 1990, Germany, France, and the Benelux Economic Union entered into the *Convention implementing the Schengen Agreement*,[171] pursuant to which carriers that brought aliens to the external border of a Contracting Party were, in the case that their entry was denied, obliged to assume the cost of returning the alien to the third State from which they were transported.[172] With this, privatisation became a crucial element of immigration control. As Ryan noted:

> The consequence of this 'privatisation' [was] to further distance states from the prospect of legal action based on an individual's entitlement to travel and from claims to international protection.[173]

Between 1988 and 1989, the number of asylum applications filed in the UK increased by 191% and increased again in 1990 by 125%.[174] In response to the unprecedented numbers of asylum applications, the UK introduced the *Asylum and Immigration Appeals Act* in 1993, which increased the scope of the *Carriers' Liability Act* so that airline companies had to demand transit visas to ensure that transit passengers did not disembark in the UK and claim asylum. The *Immigration and Asylum Act*, 1999, further extended carrier sanctions, or 'pre-entry controls,' to include trucking companies and train passenger serv-

---

162 Australia, *Migration Legislation Amendment Act* (1989).

163 Belgium, *Loi du 15 décembre 1980 sur l'accès au territoire, le séjour, l'établissement et l'éloignement des étrangers* (5 December 1980) Article 52bis, Article 52ter.

164 Brazil, *Law No. 6,815: The Foreigner's Statute* (*Estatuto do Estrangeiro*) (19 August 1980).

165 Canada, *Immigration Act* (1976) section 94.

166 Denmark, *Aliens Act* (*Udlændingeloven*) (9 June 1983) section 59.

167 Germany, *Aliens Act* (*Ausländergesetz*) (1965) section 63.

168 New Zealand, *Immigration Act* (1987) section 142.

169 United Kingdom, *Immigration* (*Carriers' Liability*) *Act* (1987) section 40.

170 USA, *Immigration Reform and Control Act* (1986) section 273.

171 *Convention Implementing the Schengen Agreement of 14 June 1985 between the Governments of the States of the Benelux Economic Union, the Federal Republic of Germany and the French Republic, on the Gradual Abolition of Checks at their Common Borders* (19 June 1990). The Convention came into force in September 1993.

172 *Id.*, Article 26(1)(a).

173 Bernard Ryan, 'Extraterritorial Immigration Control: What Role for Legal Guarantees?' in Ryan and Mitsilegas (eds), *Extraterritorial Immigration Control* (Martinus Nijhoff 2010) 22.

174 Alice Bloch, 'A New Era or More of the Same? Asylum Policy in the UK' (2000) 13(1) Journal of Refugee Studies 29–42.

ices. In 1998, as a direct result of the UK's carrier sanctions, British Airways incurred approximately £2.5 million in fines.[175] Carrier sanctions in Greece included truck drivers and taxi drivers who carried passengers into Greek territory who did not have the right to enter. The Greek legislation criminalised both the act of carrying an undocumented passenger and the act of being transported into Greek territory without a visa, thus penalising both the carrier and the asylum seeker. The penalty included both a fine and a one-year term of imprisonment.[176] Similarly, in 1994, the Netherlands introduced carrier sanctions into domestic law which provided that a 6-month term of imprisonment may be imposed on carriers for failing to photocopy the essential pages of the passports of passengers boarding in or coming from countries from which so called 'risk flights' departed.[177]

In 2001, *Council Directive 2001/51/EC supplementing the provisions of Article 26 of the Convention implementing the Schengen Agreement of 14 June 1985* formalised carrier sanctions in the EU and extended carrier liability to third-country nationals in transit.[178] *Council Directive 2001/51/EC* provided that EU Member States should take necessary measures to:

> [O]blige carriers which are unable to effect the return of a third-country national whose entry is refused to find means of onward transportation immediately and to bear the cost thereof, or, if immediate onward transportation is not possible, to assume responsibility for the costs of the stay and return of the third-country national in question.[179]

Common to the laws were the imposition of fines or other penalties on a carrier for bringing in an undocumented non-national, and an obligation to remove said person from the country of destination. This in turn meant that the obligation to check visas and passports was now that of private corporations. Also common was that "[n]one of the legislation in the countries reviewed makes any distinction between refugees and asylum-seekers,"[180] though some provided discretionary powers to waive fines for the carriage of

---

175 *Id.*

176 *Id.*

177 *Id.*, 6.

178 Council of the European Union, *Council Directive 2001/51/EC of 28 June 2001 Supplementing the Provisions of Article 26 of the Convention Implementing the Schengen Agreement of 14 June 1985* (2001) preambular para 1.

179 *Id.*, Article 3.

180 Erika Feller, 'Carrier Sanctions and International Law' (1989) 1 Int'l J Refugee L (1) IJRL 48, 55.

refugees later recognised as such.[181] Where carrier sanctions were not sufficient to stem the flow of asylum seekers, some States reclassified disembarkation areas in airports as 'international zones' outside the State's ordinary jurisdiction.[182] Other States declared airports, harbours, coastlines, and islands to be non-territory.[183] In France, the practice of holding asylum seekers in the international zone, or 'transit zone,' was the subject of the 1996 case of *Amuur v. France*,[184] for instance, where the applicants were held within the international zone of Paris-Orly airport, the Court noted that:

> [e]ven though the applicants were not in France within the meaning of the Ordinance of 2 November 1945, holding them in the international zone of Paris-Orly Airport made them subject to French law. Despite its name, the international zone does not have extra-territorial status.[185]

By contrast, the UK implemented similar laws, but with a very different corresponding judicial opinion. In the 2004 case of *R* (*European Roma Rights Centre and others*) *v Immigration Officer at Prague Airport and another*,[186] the House of Lords held that the 1951 Convention did not apply in international zones.[187] It found (citing *Sale*) that in refusing the applicants and others leave to enter the UK without first examining the merits of their asylum claim, the actions of the UK immigration authorities operating at Prague Airport "could [not] possibly be said to be an exercise of jurisdiction in any relevant sense [...]."[188]

> There would appear to be general acceptance of the principle that a person who leaves the state of his nationality and applies to the authorities of another state for asylum, whether at the frontier of the second state or from within it, should not be rejected or returned to the first state without appropriate enquiry into the persecution of which he claims to have a well-founded fear. But that principle, even if one of

181 *Id.*, 56–57.

182 *Amuur v France* [25 June 1996] ECtHR (App No 17/1995/523/609) [20].

183 James Hathaway, Thomas Gammeltoft-Hansen, 'Non-Refoulement in a World of Cooperative Deterrence' (2015) 53(2) Colum J Transnat'l L 244.

184 *Id.*

185 *Id.*

186 *European Roma Rights Centre and Others v the Immigration Officer at Prague Airport and the Secretary of State for the Home Department* [20 May 2003] EWCA Civ 666.

187 *Id.*

188 *Id.*, [21].

> customary international law, cannot avail the appellants, *who have not left the Czech Republic nor presented themselves, save in a highly metaphorical sense, at the frontier of the United Kingdom.*[189]

In that case, the State's actions were deemed lawful by the judiciary, in that asylum seekers could not fulfil the jurisdictional fact of engaging the UK's 1951 Convention obligations, having not crossed an international border. The effectiveness of carrier sanctions has in turn contributed significantly to perpetuating the receding line of jurisdiction. Those jurisdictions in which is has been successfully implemented has allowed the policy to be widely utilised as a central tenet of immigration control, affecting refugees and migrants alike.

4.3 *State Agents Stationed Abroad*

After the September 11 terror attacks, the Homeland Security Act 2002 established the Department of Homeland Security and consolidated numerous agencies and bureaux under its department, including Customs and Border Patrol (CBP), United States Citizenship and Immigration Service (USCIS), and the United States Immigration and Custom Enforcement (ICE).

In 1999 and 2000, Coast Guard cutters on counter-drug patrol in the Eastern Pacific encountered increasing numbers of migrants being smuggled from Ecuador to points in Central America and Mexico. In most cases these people cross the southern border and enter the United States by land route. Eventually, the government introduced Operation streamline; a zero tolerance policy in certain border patrol sectors prosecuting everyone that crossed the border. Created in 2005 as a joint initiative of the Department of Homeland Security (DHS) and the Department of Justice (DOJ), the programme fast-tracked resolution of these immigration offenses, providing for mass proceedings in which as many as 80 unlawful border crossers were tried together in a single hearing. Under federal law, those caught making a first illegal entry could be prosecuted for a misdemeanour (under 8 U.S.C. §1325) punishable by up to six months in prison, and those who re-entered after deportation could be prosecuted for a felony (under 8 U.S.C. §1326) punishable by up to 20 years in prison.

A total of 171 immigrants' rights, criminal justice reform, faith-based, and human rights and civil rights organisations wrote to then-Attorney General, Loretta Lynch expressing "profound concern" with the ongoing criminal pros-

189 *Id.*, [26]. Emphasis added.

ecution of asylum seekers and opposing federal criminal prosecution as the response to immigration at the southern border.[190] The UN Committee on the Elimination of Racial Discrimination called on the US government to abolish Operation Streamline and deal with any breaches of immigration law through the civil, rather than criminal immigration system,[191] and the Vatican called for its suspension.[192]

Starting in 2013, US Southern Command (SOUTHCOM) built bases, delivered vehicles and equipment, and provided training to Inter-Agency Task Forces (IATFs): combined military-police-prosecutorial units stationed in Guatemala's border zones.[193] SOUTHCOM's *Operation Hornet* and *Operation Together Forward* established collaboration between US soldiers and counterparts in Guatemala, Honduras, and El Salvador to improve cross-border collaboration against threat networks.[194]

In January of 2020, then-DHS Undersecretary Chad Wolf met privately with newly elected President of Guatemala, Alejandro Giammattei, just days prior to his inauguration. Wolf subsequently expressed his expectations that the two countries would continue their "already strong partnership to reduce illegal immigration to the United States."[195]

Upon returning to Washington, Wolf expressed confidence in a Fox Radio interview that the Trump administration had established enough obstacles to prevent members of the migrant caravan from reaching the US border or pursuing asylum claims in the United States, despite US laws guaranteeing

190 American Civil Liberties Union et al., 'Letter to Attorney General Loretta Lynch Re: Prosecutions for Illegal Entry (8 U.S.C. § 1325) and Illegal Re-entry (8 U.S.C. § 1326)' (28 July 2015).

191 UN Committee on the Elimination of Racial Discrimination, *Concluding observations on the combined seventh to ninth periodic reports of the United States of America* (25 September 2014) (CERD/C/USA/CO/7-9).

192 UN Human Rights Council Working Group on the Universal Periodic Review, *Report of the Working Group on the Universal Periodic Review: United States of America* (4 January 2011) A/HRC/16/11, para 68.

193 Adam Isacson, *80 Homeland Security Agents to Guatemala? We've Seen This Before. It Doesn't Work* (5 June 2019) Washington Office on Latin America.

194 USA: United States Congress, *Posture Statement of Admiral Kurt W. Tidd Commander, United States Southern Command Before the 115th Congress Senate Armed Services Committee* (15 February 2018).

195 USA: Department of Commerce, *Secretary of Commerce Leads U.S. Delegation to Guatemala* (15 January 2020); Sofia Menchu, Frank Jack Daniel, 'Turbulent Inauguration Day in Guatemala, Outgoing President Hit by Eggs' (14 January 2020) Reuters, cited in: USA: Committee on Foreign Relations, *A Democratic Staff Report Prepared for the use of the Committee on Foreign Relations, United States Senate, DHS Run Amok? A Reckless Overseas Operation, Violations, and Lies* (12 October 2020) 5.

the right to seek asylum. Wolf asserted in his interview, "[w]hat has changed from 2018 or even from last year are the number of agreements that we have in place with Honduras, Guatemala, as well as Mexico."[196] To reinforce the Trump administration's aggressive stance, he stated, "[w]e have CBP agents – tactical agents – in Guatemala."[197]

The Bureau of International Narcotics and Law Enforcement Affairs (INL) and the DHS frequently joined in inter-agency agreements. An INL–DHS agreement with Guatemala explicitly stated: "U.S. personnel under this agreement will not conduct immigration or law enforcement operations; they are in country for mentoring, advising and capacity-building purposes only." In 2020, Democratic staff on the Senate Foreign Relations Committee uncovered DHS misuse of State Department funding for an unauthorised operation in which CBP personnel stationed in Guatemala transported an unidentified number of Honduran migrants in unmarked vans to the Guatemala–Honduras border, without protocols in place to ensure family separation did not occur, nor to ensure the personal safety and human rights of migrants, nor to take any measures to ensure screening for individuals seeking asylum.[198]

5 Third Iteration: Operations by Third States within Territorial Jurisdiction

As described in the introduction to this chapter, the third iteration of novel constructions of jurisdiction involves the exercise of legislative jurisdiction by State B within the bounds of its ordinary jurisdiction in a manner that is consistent with the execution of State A's foreign policy objectives relative to refugees. In this model, State A will commonly continue to assert enforcement jurisdiction in respect of detention and removal but maintain that the concurrent legislative and enforcement jurisdiction of State B takes precedence on the basis of territoriality, rendering it the authority to exercise judicial jurisdiction.

Almost invariably, such scenarios involve either the exchange of aid and development funds, or direct funding of the immigration operations that are

196 Chad Wolf (Acting Secretary of Department of Homeland Security), interview with Brian Kilmeade 'The Brian Kilmeade Show' *Fox News* (16 January 2020).

197 *Id.*

198 USA: Committee on Foreign Relations, *A Democratic Staff Report Prepared for the use of the Committee on Foreign Relations, United States Senate, DHS Run Amok? A Reckless Overseas Operation, Violations, and Lies*12 October 2020) 2–3.

implemented by State B in service of the immigration agenda of State A. In that sense, this model of inter-State cooperation is not dissimilar to the aid and development model, in which States of first arrival were incentivised to maintain large refugee populations in encampment settings, while States outside the region positioned themselves as States of resettlement.

The bartering system in which concurrent legislative jurisdiction and a majority share of enforcement jurisdiction is exchanged for increased development aid or funding of 'migration management' operations is integral to this third construction of jurisdiction. As the scenarios presented in this section demonstrate, this model has formed the basis of a vast number of bilateral and multilateral 'processes' concerning migration control, which have in turn aided significantly in the homogenisation of legal and policy responses to 'mixed migration,' raising dire protection concerns. In particular, the need to provide 'safe and orderly' pathways to migrants has increasingly been applied to refugees despite there being no such requirement in IRL. In a similar fashion, the desire to address 'root causes' of migration has had the predictable consequence of permitting States to advance the claim that conditions in States of origin are such that irregular movement – including that of refugees – is no longer justified as political and economic stability have neutralised any real imperative to cross an international border without prior permission.

Bilateral and multilateral processes have typically included actions stemming the flow of migrants and refugees, purportedly motivated by the imperative to disrupt smuggling and trafficking groups. Processes have also been utilised as forums to reinforce the concept of 'State of origin responsibility' and to indirectly affirm the parameters of 'burden-sharing' as involving the immediate and practical involvement of States in the immediate geographical vicinity to the mixed movement – almost invariably States of the 'Global South' – substituted by 'humanitarian' (financial) support of Western States.

The measures described in this section have permitted State A to exercise some influence over the immigration control practices of State B, while maintaining a remoteness from legal obligations by circumventing norms of attribution, shielded by the exercise of concurrent legislative jurisdiction where State B legislates within its territorial jurisdiction, by the remoteness created by financial support, and by the absence of a clear legal relationship between States and the refugee. However, as this section demonstrates, judiciaries have not in all instances accepted those facts as sufficient to evade attribution of conduct to State A.

5.1 *Excision of Territory: An Australian Solution*

The trajectory of Australian asylum law points clearly to a methodical degradation of norms of jurisdiction, achieved through outsourcing the State's primary functions to third States and private actors, aided in part by conservative judicial interpretation of the scope and content of the *non-refoulement* principle as it relates to, and interacts with, Australian law and international obligations.[199] This has been affected in two ways. First, through the excision of territory formerly within the 'Australian Migration Zone'; excluding swathes of territory from the legislative jurisdiction of the State. Secondly, by excluding certain applications for protection as illegitimate. This began in 2001, when the federal parliament enacted seven pieces of legislation, six of which amended the *Migration Act* 1958 and one of which provided increased border protection powers to Australian authorities. Among them was the *Migration Amendment (Excision from Migration Zone) Act* 2001 which effected the excision of certain external territories from the Australian Migration Zone (AMZ), and inserted a provision to the effect that an application for a visa was not a valid application if it was made by an offshore entry person who was in Australia.[200]

Australian efforts to exclude certain asylum seekers from the effects of its legislative jurisdiction began in earnest on 1 September 2001, when the then Prime Minister John Howard announced that agreements had been reached between the Australian government and the governments of New Zealand and the Pacific island of Nauru that all those aboard a vessel that had previously been rescued by the Norwegian container ship MV *Tampa* would be processed in those third countries rather than in Australia or Australian territories. The Australian government assumed all financial obligations associated with the operation in Nauru "so that in no way will Nauru be disadvantaged by what has been offered and accepted by Australia."[201] Australia would establish and operate a processing centre on Nauru in exchange for increased development aid to the Pacific island nation.[202]

---

199 Sophie Capicchiano Young, 'The Responsibility of Australia for Internationally Wrongful Acts: The Offshore Detention Regime, the Principle of non-refoulement, and a Case for Litigation' (2018) 32(4) JIANL 331, 332.

200 Australia, *Migration Amendment (Excision from Migration Zone) Act* (2001) s 46A(1)(a).

201 John Howard, *Joint Press Conference with the Minister for Immigration the Hon Philip Ruddock MP* (1 September 2001).

202 Australia, Nauru, *Memorandum of Understanding between the Republic of Nauru and the Commonwealth of Australia for Cooperation in the Administration of Asylum Seekers and Related Issues* (11 December 2001); See: Australia: Federal Parliament, *Report of the Select Committee for an inquiry into a certain maritime incident, Chapter 10, Pacific Solution:*

A separate piece of legislation, the *Migration Amendment (Excision from Migration Zone) (Consequential Provisions) Act* 2001, inserted s198A, providing that an 'offshore entry person may be taken to a declared country'; that the Minister for Immigration was empowered to declare that a specified country provides access to effective asylum procedures; and that an authorised officer may take an 'offshore entry person' from Australia to a 'declared' country. After Papua New Guinea (PNG) was made a declared country, the governments of Australia and PNG announced they had reached an agreement on the establishment of the Manus Island Processing Centre (MIPC), the cost of which would be absorbed entirely by Australia.[203]

In August 2012, the Australian government enacted the *Migration Legislation Amendment (Regional Processing and Other Measures) Act* 2012, which repealed section 198A and substituted it with a section that was semantically, though not materially different. The Minister was still under no obligation to consider the international obligations or domestic law of a country before designating it a 'regional processing country' – the new term for 'declared country.'[204] The impetus for this change was the decision by the High Court of Australia in *M70/2011 v Minister for Immigration and Citizenship*.[205] In that case, the court found that the Minister had erred in his decision to deem Malaysia a declared country, as he had disregarded relevant information in the exercise of his statutory power and that the decision of the Minister was not informed by the criteria prescribed in section 198A(3)(a), which were indicative of 'enduring legal frameworks.' Accordingly, the Minister "did not look to, and did not find, any basis for his declaration in Malaysia's international obligations or relevant domestic laws."[206]

A critical element of section 198A, and later section 198AD(11), concerned the State's conception of what constituted a jurisdictional fact in the wake of *M70/2011*, Section 198AD(11) providing that '[a]n unauthorised maritime arrival who is being dealt with under subs (3) is taken not to be in immigration detention.' The *Migration Act* defined 'immigration detention' as being:

Negotiations and Agreements (2002) Senate Printing Unit, Parliament House (10.33–10.34).

203 John Howard, *Arrangement with Papua New Guinea to Process Unauthorised Arrivals* (10 October 2001).

204 Australia, *Migration Act* (1958) section 198AB(4).

205 *Plaintiff M70/2011 v Minister for Immigration and Citizenship; Plaintiff M106 of 2011 v Minister for Immigration and Citizenship* [2011] HCA 32; 244 CLR 144.

206 *Id.*, [66].

> [I]n the company and restrained by an officer or a person directed by the Australian Border Force Commissioner, or; being held by, or on behalf of, an officer in a detention centre established under the Migration Act; in a prison or remand centre of the Commonwealth, a State or a Territory; in a police station or watch house; on a vessel; or in another place approved by the Minister in writing.

The effect of this section was that at no point in time, even during the chain of custody where an officer of the State was exercising control over an unauthorised maritime arrival, was that person being dealt with under the *Migration Act* 1958. Put another way, section 198AD(11) provided that the exercise of custody over an 'offshore entry person' by an agent of the State did not constitute a jurisdictional fact – a requirement conditioning the exercise of statutory power – sufficient to trigger the application of the *Migration Act* 1958 specifically, or Australian law generally. An obvious procedural consequence of this was that the exercise of control over an 'unauthorised maritime arrival' could not be affected by jurisdictional error.[207]

Further legislative changes were made in 2014, when the government passed amending legislation removing all references to the 1951 Convention from the *Migration Act* 1958, instead referring to Australia having protection obligations in respect of a person because they are a refugee.[208] The explanatory memorandum accompanying the amending legislation provided that references to the 1951 Convention and 1967 Protocol had been omitted "in order to give effect to the new statutory framework relating to refugees [...] which articulates Australia's interpretation of its protection obligations under the Refugee Convention."[209]

Various elements of the offshore detention regime have been litigated extensively throughout the years, but several proceedings are critical to the question of the 'bartering' system that permits the exercise of concurrent legislative and executive jurisdiction over elements of immigration law and policy in exchange for development aid. The first is the 2016 case of *Plaintiff S99/2016 v Minister for Immigration and Border Protection.*[210] Plaintiff was a female

207 Sophie Capicchiano Young, 'The Responsibility of Australia for Internationally Wrongful Acts: The Offshore Detention Regime, the Principle of non-refoulement, and a Case for Litigation' (2018) 32(4) JIANL 331, 341.

208 Australia, *The Migration and Maritime Powers Legislation Amendment (Resolving the Asylum Caseload Legacy) Act* (2014) amended section 36(2)(a) of the *Migration Act.*

209 *Id.*

210 *Plaintiff S99/2016 v Minister for Immigration and Border Protection* [2016] FCA 483.

detainee on Nauru who, after falling unconscious following an epileptic seizure, was raped and subsequently fell pregnant. She sought an abortion and the privately contracted health provider, IHMS, which administered medical care to immigration detainees on the island, recommended that she be transferred to Australia to undergo the procedure. The Minister for Immigration and Border Protection instead arranged for her to be taken to Papua New Guinea (PNG) for the procedure. Plaintiff commenced legal proceedings in the Australian courts, arguing that it would be neither safe nor legal to undergo a termination in PNG. Relying on the legal relationship that arose between herself and the Minister subject to the jurisdiction that he exercised over her as an immigration detainee, Plaintiff submitted that the Minister had a duty of care to procure for her a safe and legal abortion.

On the basis of extensive expert medical evidence adduced by the applicant about her particular medical conditions, and the lack of necessary resources available in PNG, Bromberg J accepted that there was a "heightened risk of very serious physical and/or psychological harm to the applicant" if she were to terminate her pregnancy in PNG.[211] Importantly, his Honour held that the applicant *had* established a duty of care owed to her by the Minister and the Australian Government that they would "exercise reasonable care in the discharge of the responsibility that they assumed to procure for her a safe and lawful abortion."[212]

The question of the legal relationship that arose between the Minister and offshore immigration detainees would again be considered in the 2017 case of *Kamasee v Minister*, however the government was able to avoid raising questions of jurisdiction in federal court by settling the case. The matter of jurisdiction was nonetheless addressed indirectly in the settlement approval. On 19 December 2014, a class action proceeding was issued in the Supreme Court of Victoria. The class comprised 1,905 individuals and included a 'Negligence Group' and a 'False Imprisonment Group' whose claims related to the conditions of their detention by or on behalf of the Commonwealth pursuant to the *Migration Act*.[213] On 17 July 2017, the parties reached a settlement in the amount of AUD $70 million. In approving the settlement, Justice Macaulay observed that the settlement avoided a number of risks to liability, including the assertion by the Australian government that it did not control the MIPC.[214]

211 *Id.*, [382].

212 *Id.*, [276].

213 *Kamasee v Commonwealth of Australia & Ors (No 8) (Class closure ruling)* [2017] VSC 167.

214 Approved in: *Kamasee v Commonwealth of Australia & Ors (Approval of Settlement)* [2017] VSC 537.

Despite these decisions, the High Court of Australia has made clear that, in domestic law, Australia's international obligations under the 1951 Convention are limited by the terms of the *Migration Act* 1958, which provides clearly for the application of the State's jurisdiction solely on a territorial basis. In *CPCF v Minister for Immigration and Border Protection*,[215] the High Court found, citing *inter alia*, *Sale* and *Prague Airports* that:

> Judicial authority in Australia, the United Kingdom and the United States of America suggests that a state's obligations under the Convention arise *only with respect to persons who are within that state's territory*. The plaintiff does not accept that this body of authority is correct, but it is unnecessary to come to a conclusion on that point. Whatever the true affect of the Convention may be, the terms of the Migration Act are clear.[216]

Those 'terms' referred to the power conferred by s72(4) of the *Maritime Powers Act* 2013, which authorised maritime officers to detain persons for the purpose of taking them to places outside Australia. This, the High Court concluded, was "not subject to observance of Article 33(1) of the Convention."[217] In that sense (and much like the interactions between the executive the judiciary on the subject of carrier sanctions), the successful implementation of laws affecting the limitation of jurisdiction in Australia has depended in large part on interpretations of such by the judiciary. The excision of territory from the AMZ, recognised as lawful by the judiciary, has sanctioned actions affecting the receding line of jurisdiction that has all but made Australia a State of resettlement exclusively.

5.2 *Bilateral and Multilateral 'Migration Management'*

A particularly effective means to solidify cooperation in the division of jurisdictional competencies has been through bilateral and multilateral agreements on immigration control, ostensibly to devise solutions to address the 'root causes' of large-scale mixed movement. This has been critical to the development of regional refugee law and policy in recent years. The fact of mixed migration has allowed immigration control to focus primarily on management of irregular migratory movement through 'safe and orderly pathways'

215 *CPCF v Minister for Immigration and Border Protection & Anor* [2015] HCA 1.
216 *Id.*, [461]. Emphasis added.
217 *Id.*, [461], [463].

with few measures in place to differentiate legal processes for refugees and migrants. International obligations for the protection of refugees and the provision of minimum standards of reception and status determination are obfuscated within migration management arrangements or are otherwise subject to a bartering system of separating and delegating jurisdictional competencies.

A particularly stark example of this is the contemporary bilateralism between the US and Central American States. This includes the conclusion of the Migrant Protection Protocols (commonly known as 'Remain in Mexico'),[218] the failed Asylum Cooperative Agreements,[219] the use of Title 42 during the COVID pandemic,[220] and the Final Rule on Circumvention of Lawful Pathways.[221] Collectively, these measures signal a significant recalibration in regional refugee law and policy which has, at its core, the minimisation of refugees as a legal category and their absorption into the broader, unprotected class of unlawful migrants.

5.2.1 The Migration Protection Protocols

The Migrant Protection Protocols (MPP) were implemented subject to Section 235(b)(2)(C) of the INA, which provides that "[I]n the case of [an alien seeking admission is not clearly and beyond a doubt entitled to be admitted] who is arriving on land (whether or not at a designated port of arrival) from a foreign territory contiguous to the United States, the Attorney General may return the alien to that territory pending a proceeding under section 1229a of this title." The MPP permitted nationals of States other than Mexico that arrived in the US by land from Mexico "illegally or without proper documentation"[222] to be returned to Mexico for the duration of their removal proceedings.

---

218 USA: Department of Homeland Security, *Policy Guidance for Implementation of the Migrant Protection Protocols* (25 January 2019).

219 USA, El Salvador, *Agreement between the Government of the United States and the Government of the Republic of El Salvador for Cooperation in the Examination of Protection Claims* (20 September 2019); USA, Honduras, *Agreement between the Government of the United States and the Government of the Republic of Honduras for Cooperation in the Examination of Protection Claims* (25 September 2019); USA, Guatemala, *Agreement between the Government of the United States and the Government of the Republic of Guatemala on Cooperation in the Examination of Protection Claims* (26 July 2019).

220 USA: Department of Health and Human Services, *Order Suspending Introduction of Persons from a Country Where a Communicable Disease Exists* (26 March 2020) 85 FR 17060.

221 USA: Department of Homeland Security & Department of Justice, *Final Rule: Circumvention of Lawful Pathways* (16 May 2023) 8 CFR Part 208/8 CFR Parts 1003 and 1208.

222 USA: Department of Homeland Security, *Policy Guidance for Implementation of the Migrant Protection Protocols* (25 January 2019).

On 2 February 2021, US President Biden issued Executive Order 14010 directing the Secretary of Homeland Security "to promptly review and determine whether to terminate or modify" the MPP, and on 1 June 2021, the Secretary issued a memorandum concluding that the MPP should be terminated. The following month, the District Court for the Northern District of Texas determined that the June 1 memo was not issued in compliance with the *Administrative Procedure Act* (APA) because it failed to address all the relevant considerations, and remanded the matter to the Department for further consideration.[223] Plaintiffs sought a preliminary injunction partly on the basis that DHS was required to "consult with Texas and consider its views before taking any action, adopting or modifying a policy or procedure, or making any decision."

The court found that in terminating the MPP, Defendants had failed to consider a number of factors, including the advice of DHS personnel, resulting in a violation of the APA. As the APA requires federal administrative agencies to engage in reasoned decision-making, the failure of which may result in actions that are "arbitrary, capricious, an abuse of discretion, or otherwise not in accordance with law,"[224] the failure of DHS to consult with Texas meant that the decision to terminate the MPP was in fact 'arbitrary and capricious.' The government sought to stay the injunction in an application to the Supreme Court, but was denied on the basis that the applicants had failed to show a likelihood of success on the claim that the July 1 memorandum terminating the MPP was not arbitrary and capricious. Though the administration presented this decision as a result of a conservative judiciary, the court had itself provided a roadmap to rectify the violation of the APA:

> To be sure, DHS could have determined, in the particular context before it, that other interests and policy concerns outweigh[ed] any [benefits MPP had]. Making that difficult decision was the agency's job, but the agency failed to do it.[225]

That is, DHS could have fulfilled the requirements of its agreement with Texas, considered the issued identified by the state, considered the advice of DHS personnel, included these considerations in a reasoned opinion, and demonstrated that it had examined the relevant data and articulate a satisfactory explanation for its action including a rational connection between the facts

223 See: *Texas v Biden* [13 August 2021] No 2:21-cv-067, 2, 2021 WL 3603341.
224 USA, *Administrative Procedure Act* 5 U.S.C. § 706(2)(A).
225 [77].

found and the choice made, *and then determined that other interests and policy concerns outweighed any benefit of the MPP*. In other words, DHS could have rectified this issue in a matter of days. It should be noted that the District Court identified other issues that hindered DHS from properly terminating the MPP, including that the MPP "is also substantively unlawful because, in these circumstances, termination of MPP causes Defendants to systemically violate Section 1225. It will continue to be unlawful to terminate MPP until DHS has the capacity and willingness to detain immigrants claiming asylum under Section 1225."[226] However, it remains the case that as far as reasoned decision-making is concerned, it was open to the government to fulfil those requirements.

In addition to not rectifying the matter of the APA, the Biden administration later extended the use of the MPP. At the time the case was filed, the MPP had only been implemented at the San Ysidro port of entry on the California–Mexico border – the first US town north of Tijuana. However, it was very quickly extended to the Calexico port of entry, also on the California–Mexico border, north of Mexicali, and then to the notorious border crossing at El Paso, Texas, the first US town north of Ciudad Juarez.

5.2.2 The Asylum Cooperative Agreements

Following the increase in aid to central America under the Obama administration's US Strategy for Engagement in Central America, the Trump administration subsequently withheld assistance appropriated for the Northern Triangle in FY2017, reprogrammed nearly all assistance appropriated for the Northern Triangle in FY2018, and in March 2019, suspended over $400 million in US foreign assistance aimed at addressing the 'root causes' of irregular migration due to the continued northward flow of migrants and asylum-seekers from the region.[227]

Following this action, the Trump administration concluded a series of Asylum Cooperative Agreements (ACAs) with Guatemala,[228] Honduras,[229] and El

226 para 121.

227 USA: Congressional Research Service, *U.S. Strategy for Engagement in Central America: Policy Issues for Congress* (12 November 2019) 2.

228 USA, Guatemala, *Agreement between the Government of the United States and the Government of the Republic of Guatemala on Cooperation in the Examination of Protection Claims* (26 July 2019).

229 USA, Honduras, *Agreement between the Government of the United States and the Government of the Republic of Honduras for Cooperation in the Examination of Protection Claims* (25 September 2019).

Salvador.[230] The ACAs permitted the US to transfer asylum seekers already within US territory or under control of US authorities to those States for asylum processing.[231] The ACAs reaffirmed the obligation of the Parties to provide protection to refugees who meet the requirements of the 1951 Convention and 1967 Protocol and who are *physically in their respective territories*, in accordance with their obligations under those instruments and subject to the respective laws, treaties, and declarations of the Parties, however their conclusion subject to the 'safe third country' provision of US immigration law permitted the administration to claim that the ACAs did not violate the INA.[232] This permitted the US to transfer asylum seekers to third States where those States met certain statutory requirements concerning asylum processing availability and general country conditions. Consequently, asylum seekers already within the territory of the US were unable to rely on territoriality to establish the jurisdictional link required for the application of the INA. Instead, those persons would be subject to transfer to Guatemala, Honduras, or El Salvador (provided they were not of that nationality), regardless of whether they transited through that State, as part of the 'burden-sharing' objectives of the ACAs.[233]

In November 2019, the Executive Office for Immigration Review (Department of Justice) and the US Citizenship and Immigration Services (Department of Homeland Security) adopted an Interim Final Rule (IFR) on 'Implementing Bilateral and Multilateral Asylum Cooperative Agreements under the Immigration and Nationality Act.'[234] The IFR adopted a "modified approach to the expedited removal (ER) and section 240 processes in the form of a threshold screening as to which country will consider the alien's claim" to apply to all ACAs concluded with Central American States. At the same time, the US expanded legal pathways to migrants to enter the US as temporary and non-

230 USA, El Salvador, *Agreement between the Government of the United States and the Government of the Republic of El Salvador for Cooperation in the Examination of Protection Claims* (20 September 2019).

231 Yael Schacher, Rachel Schmidtke, Ari Sawyer, 'Deportation with a Layover: Failure of Protection Under the US-Guatemala Asylum Cooperative Agreement' (19 May 2020) Refugees International.

232 USA, *Immigration and Nationality Act* 8 U.S.C. § 208(a)(2)(A).

233 The ACA s with Honduras and El Salvador provided that States were "committed to the notion that cooperation and burden-sharing with respect to refugee status claimants can be enhanced," though the US–Guatemala ACA did not mention burden-sharing, but referred instead to "the distribution of responsibility."

234 *Implementing Bilateral and Multilateral Asylum Cooperative Agreements under the Immigration and Nationality Act* (19 November 2019) 84 FR 64,008.

temporary agricultural workers,[235] in an attempt to appear as if it were providing 'legal pathways' to those same persons that were affected by the ACAs.

The 'safe third country' provision of the INA provides that the an alien "physically present in the United States or who arrives in the United States (whether or not at a designated port of arrival and including an alien who is brought to the United States after having been interdicted in international or United States waters" may be transferred to another State with whom the US has a bilateral or multilateral agreement "where the alien would have access to a full and fair procedure for determining a claim to asylum or equivalent temporary protection."[236]

Despite Guatemala, Honduras, and El Salvador each joining the *Marco Integral Regional para la Protección y Soluciones*,[237] a regional initiative intended to implement the Global Compact on Refugees, the asylum systems of all States were demonstrably weak. As noted in a US Congressional report on the ACAs, the leaders of each State expressed concern about their ability to fulfil the 'safe third country' requirements of the ACA:

> As Guatemala's then president-elect, Alejandro Giammattei said in August 2019, just after the outgoing government signed the ACA, "I do not think Guatemala fulfils the requirements to be a third safe country. That definition doesn't fit us. If we do not have the capacity for our own people, just imagine other people." Honduras' autonomous National Human Rights Commissioner asserted that Honduras lacks the capacity and resources necessary to provide "dignified treatment" to individuals transferred under the ACA. In response to the question of whether El Salvador was ready to receive asylum seekers through the ACA, President Bukele said in December 2019, "[w]ell, not right now. We don't have asylum capacities, but we can build them."[238]

235 USA, Guatemala, *Agreement between the United States of America and the Republic of Guatemala concerning a Temporary Agricultural Workers Program* (30 June 2019); USA, Honduras, *Agreement Concerning the Temporary Agricultural and non-Agricultural Workers Programs* (27 September 2019).

236 USA, *Immigration and Nationality Act* 8 U.S.C. § 208(a)(1)–(2)(A).

237 Belize and others, *Marco Integral Regional para la Protección y Soluciones* (2017) (EN: *Comprehensive Regional Protection and Solutions Framework*).

238 Sonia Pérez, 'President-elect Says Guatemala Can't do Migrant Deal with US' (13 August 2019) AP; '"Acuerdo con EEUU debe ser Aprobado por el Congreso": Roberto Herrera Cáceres' (12 November 2019) La Prensa (Honduras); Sharon Alfonsi, '"Our Whole Economy is in Shatters:" El Salvador's President Nayib Bukele on the Problems Facing his Country' (15 December 2019) 60 Minutes.

The exceptions to the presumption in favour of transfer were severely limited under the ACAs. Article 4 common provided that the obligation to determine and conclude requests for international protection within its territory would rest with the US, only in cases when it was established that the applicant was an unaccompanied minor; or had arrived in the territory of the US with a validly issued visa or other valid admission document, other than a transit visa, issued by the US; or without the US requiring him to obtain a visa. Under the ACA with Guatemala (the only ACA that was implemented), the US transferred 939 Honduran and Salvadoran asylum seekers between 21 November 2019 and 16 March 2020, the vast majority of them women and children. Of those 939 transferees, only 20 applied for asylum in Guatemala.[239] At the end of March 2020, there was a backlog of 713 asylum cases in Guatemala, including every one of the few asylum applicants among ACA transferees.[240] Guatemalan authorities also imposed a 72 hours limit for transferees to decide to either remain in Guatemala, return to their State of origin, or try to find refuge elsewhere.[241] A US Congressional report from January 2021 noted:

> Since implementation of the U.S.–Guatemala ACA began over one year ago, not one of the 945 asylum seekers transferred from the United States to Guatemala has been granted asylum.[242]

The legality of the ACAs was also immediately litigated. Plaintiffs in the US case of U.T. *v Barr* asserted that Guatemala did not fulfil the requirements of

239 Asylum Cooperative Agreement (ACA) Transfers from November 2019 through 16 March 2020, reported by instituto guatemalteco de migración, cited in: Yael Schacher, Rachel Schmidtke, Ari Sawyer, 'Deportation with a Layover: Failure of Protection Under the U.S.-Guatemala Asylum Cooperative Agreement' (19 May 2020) Refugees International, 6.

240 Human Rights Watch and Refugees International phone call with a UN official, 17 April 2020, cited in: Schacher et al, *id.*, 4.

241 According to interviews Refugees International conducted with *El Refugio de la Niñez*, the *Office of the Human Rights Ombudsman*, and *Casa del Migrante*. February 5, 6, and 7 of 2020, cited in: Yael Schacher, Rachel Schmidtke, Ari Sawyer, 'Deportation with a Layover: Failure of Protection Under the U.S.-Guatemala Asylum Cooperative Agreement' (19 May 2020) Refugees International, 5.

242 USA: United States Congress, *Cruelty, Coercion, and Legal Contortions: The Trump Administrations Unsafe Asylum Cooperative Agreements with Guatemala, Honduras, and El Salvador, A Majority Staff Report Prepared for the Use of The Committee on Foreign Relations United States Senate, 117th Congress 1st Session* (18 January 2021) 3, citing: UN High Commissioner for Refugees, *Guatemala office meeting with SFRC Democratic Staff* (21 October 2020).

the INA to provide effective access to protection, and that the US Department of Justice and Department of Homeland Security had violated the requirement of the APA to provide reasoned decision-making in their categorical designations of Guatemala as a safe third country.[243] The National Citizenship and Immigration Services Council, a union of the US Citizenship and Immigration Services filed an amicus brief on behalf of its members, asserting that the ACA with Guatemala compelled members "to follow departmental directives that conflict with their oath to uphold the laws of the United States."[244]

Upon assuming office, President Biden issued an Executive Order suspending the effect of all the ACAs and announced that the administration would "implement a multi-pronged approach toward managing migration throughout North and Central America [...]."[245] As the following subsections demonstrate, that approach has not differed in any material sense from those programmes that were implemented by previous administrations.

5.2.3 Title 42

Under the policy commonly known as 'Title 42,' after the relevant title of the US Code, the US government rapidly expelled migrants and refugees alike under the guise of public health considerations. In particular, Title 42 applied to refugees without sufficient safeguards in place to allow people to apply for asylum or withholding of removal before expulsion. This occurred largely because of the way Title 42 expulsions were characterised. In August 2021, the Department of Homeland Security (DHS) defended the use of Title 42 as a public health authority, as opposed to an immigration authority.[246] This attempt by the government to carve out expulsions of noncitizens from ordinary immigration law and reclassify those actions as public health measures served a very specific purpose – it denied those noncitizens the right to relief under ordinary immigration laws, that is (at least in the opinion of the government) a noncitizen that was subject to expulsion under Title 42, *could not have recourse to relief under the INA*.

243 U.T. *et al. v Barr et al., Complaint for Declarative and Injunctive Relief* [15 January 2020] 1:20-cv-00116.

244 *Brief of Amicus Curiae Council 119 In Support Of Plaintiffs' Motion for Summary Judgment And Permanent Injunction,* U.T. *v Barr* [30 June 2020] 1:20-cv-00116, 10.

245 USA, *Executive Order 14010: Creating a Comprehensive Regional Framework to Address the Causes of Migration to Manage Migration Throughout North and Central America, and to Provide Safe and Orderly Processing of Asylum Seekers at the United States Border* (2 February 2021) 86 FR 8267.

246 USA: Department of Homeland Security, *DHS Statement on Updated CDC Order* (2 August 2021).

The introduction of Title 42 as a means to ostensibly halt cross-border contagion of COVID-19 is worth noting. On 20 March 2020, as the COVID-19 virus spread globally, the Department of Health and Human Services issued an Interim Final Rule (IFR) pursuant to the relevant section of Title 42, suspending the introduction of 'covered aliens,' for a period of 30 days. The term 'covered aliens' was defined as:

> [p]ersons traveling from Canada or Mexico (regardless of their country of origin) who would otherwise be introduced into a congregate setting in a land Port of Entry [("POE")] or Border Patrol station at or near the United States borders with Canada and Mexico.[247]

The 1944 *Public Health Service Act* is codified in Title 42 of the US Code, Section 265 of which provides:

> Whenever the Surgeon General determines that by reason of the existence of any communicable disease in a foreign country there is serious danger of the introduction of such disease into the United States, and that this danger is so increased by the introduction of persons or property from such country that a suspension of the right to introduce such persons and property is required in the interest of the public health, the Surgeon General [...] shall have the power to prohibit, in whole or in part, the introduction of persons and property from such countries or places as he shall designate in order to avert such danger, and for such period of time as he may deem necessary for such purpose.[248]

On 11 September 2020, the CDC published its Final Rule (FR) (superseding the IFR) defining the phrase 'prohibit, in whole or in part, the introduction into the United States of persons' in section 265 of Title 42 to mean:

> [t]o prevent the introduction of persons into the United States by suspending any right to introduce into the United States, physically stopping

247 USA: Department of Health and Human Services, *Order Suspending Introduction of Persons from a Country Where a Communicable Disease Exists* (26 March 2020) 85 FR 17060.

248 USA, *Public Health Service Act* (1944).

> or restricting movement into the United States, or physically expelling from the United States some or all of the persons.[249]

The CDC extended the application of the FR on 2 August 2021, when it issued another Order continuing the suspension of the right to introduce 'covered noncitizens' into the US. While the IFR and the FR were issued during the Trump administration, the Biden administration maintained the policy, continued Title 42 expulsions, and defended it forcefully in the Court of Appeals for the D.C. Circuit.

In January 2021, Plaintiffs filed an action against the Secretary of State for Homeland Security, Alejandro Mayorkas, asserting that prior to Title 42, and pursuant to long-standing immigration statutes protecting asylum seekers, they were entitled to assert claims for asylum and related forms of humanitarian protection, and to procedures Congress established to ensure the fair determination of their right to remain in the US, and that if they and others like them are expelled pursuant to the CDC Order, they would face grave danger in their States of origin.[250]

An emergency stay was granted, and on 16 September 2021, the Federal District Court of D.C. granted a preliminary injunction on the basis that Plaintiffs were likely to succeed on the merits, and that Title 42 expulsions were likely unlawful. The Court found that although Congress provided for specific penalties in Title 42 for those persons or vessels that violated public health regulations, "[r]emoval from the United States [...] is not included as a penalty." While the relevant section of Title 42 authorised the Secretary to use various public health measures to "prevent the introduction, transmission, or spread of communicable diseases," the provision only mentioned regulations that provided for the "apprehension, detention, examination, or conditional release of individuals" and makes no mention of the authority to remove. As the Court noted:

> [i]n a section where one would expect the term to appear – where Congress has delineated the government's power to prevent the spread of contagious disease from individuals coming into the United States from a foreign country – it does not.

249 USA: Department of Health and Human Services, *Control of Communicable Diseases; Foreign Quarantine: Suspension of the Right to Introduce and Prohibition of Introduction of Persons into United States from Designated Foreign Countries or Places for Public Health Purposes* (11 September 2020) 85 FR 56424.

250 *Huisha-Huisha v Mayorkas* [*4 March 2022*] *No 21–5200*.

Furthermore, the statute as a whole "does not contain a word about the power of the [CDC] to expel anyone who has come into the country." The Secretary of State for Homeland Security appealed the decision. In presenting oral arguments, the court turned its attention to the compatibility of Title 42 with the protection of refugees, noting that at the time that Title 42 was enacted (1944), there were not the Title 8 humanitarian provisions that exist now. Counsel responded that in enacting the Convention against Torture and the Refugee Protocol, Congress did set out generally applicable rules for immigrants, but that the relevant section of Title 42 nevertheless constitutes the more specific rule of decision. Here counsel made an astonishing claim – the government contended that relief under Title 8 was not at issue as Title 42 related to public health matters. In the government's view, it did not need to, as expulsions under Title 42 did not engage relief measures under Title 8. These were, in the government's view, separate and distinct legal matters that do not engage one another.

The court asked counsel if the government distinguished between the three forms of Title 8 relief – asylum, withholding of removal, and withholding of removal under the Convention Against Torture – or took them as one package of humanitarian relief measures, to which counsel responded, "we have not distinguished between the three forms of relief. *We think that in these circumstances where section 265 has been invoked, all of them are displaced.*"[251] That is, in the government's view, an Order made pursuant to the relevant section of Title 42 validly displaced all forms of relief under the ordinary immigration laws, including in the case of persecution and torture. Persons with asylum claims on the basis of persecution or torture are not able to validly seek withholding of removal.

5.2.4 Circumvention of Lawful Pathways

On 8 May 2023, DHS and the Department of Justice issued a Notice of Proposed Rule Making (NPRM) on 'Circumvention of Lawful Pathways' in anticipation of "a potential surge of migration at the southwest border" following the eventual termination of the Title 42 Order.[252] The NPRM is intended to "encourage migrants to avail themselves of lawful, safe, and orderly pathways into the United States, or otherwise to seek asylum or other protection in countries through which they travel" by introducing "a rebuttable presumption of asylum ineligibility for certain noncitizens who neither avail them-

251 Emphasis added.

252 USA: Department of Homeland Security & Department of Justice, *Proposed Rule: Circumvention of Lawful Pathways* (23 February 2023) 8 CFR Part 208/8 CFR Part 1208.

selves of a lawful, safe, and orderly pathway to the United States nor seek asylum or other protection in a country through which they travel."[253]

The NPRM would require all applicants for refugee status to arrive at the US border at a regular port of entry, without having passed through another State that is signatory to the 1951 Convention or the 1967 Protocol, and to then "schedule a time and place to present at a port of entry and thus seek asylum or other forms of protection in a lawful, safe, and orderly manner, or to seek asylum or other protection in one of the countries through which they travel on their way to the United States."[254]

The NPRM would also establish a rebuttable presumption on asylum eligibility; a "presumptive condition on asylum eligibility for certain noncitizens who fail to take advantage of the existing and expanded lawful pathways, being those that do not comply with the conditions of arrival, and who cannot establish the requisite exceptions." But the circumstances in which the presumption of asylum ineligibility could be rebutted were extremely limited in scope and arbitrarily apply to persons that satisfy the criterion of facing an 'imminent' threat. Those were persons or family members of persons who, at the time of entry, "had an acute medical emergency; faced an imminent and extreme threat to life or safety, such as an imminent threat of rape, kidnapping, torture, or murder; or satisfied the definition of 'victim of a severe form of trafficking in persons.'"[255]

At the same time, DHS has introduced a number of processes intended to allow 'safe and orderly' passage to the US for persons of specific nationalities; again, appearing to provide regular pathways as a kind of substitute for those 'unlawful' pathways that have been blocked. These are the processes for Cubans,[256] Haitians,[257] Nicaraguans,[258] and Venezuelans[259] also known collectively as 'CHNV.' Under the processes, nationals of those States, and their immediate family members, may request admission to the US "in a safe and orderly way" and would be considered "on a case-by-case basis" for travel to the

253 *Id.*, 1.

254 *Id.*, 8.

255 *Id.*, 12.

256 USA: Citizenship and Immigration Services, *The Cuban Family Reunification Parole Program* (1 September 2022).

257 USA: Citizenship and Immigration Services, *Haitian Family Reunification Parole* (HFRP) *Program* (22 June 2022).

258 USA: Citizenship and Immigration Services, *Processes for Cubans, Haitians, Nicaraguans, and Venezuelans* (18 May 2023).

259 USA: Department of Homeland Security, *Implementation of a Parole Process for Venezuelans* (19 October 2022) 87 FR 63507.

US on a temporary period of parole for up to two years "for urgent humanitarian reasons or significant public benefit."[260] That is, they were intended to provide pathways to persons who may otherwise apply for asylum, by requiring them to stay within their State of origin and apply to the parole programme, or travel to a third State that is a signatory to the 1951 Convention or 1967 Protocol. These alternative pathways were presented in the NPRM as viable alternatives for asylum seekers to arrival at the border. Due to the geography of the relevant States, all nationals of those States would have to pass through Central American States (as well as Colombia in the case of Venezuelans) that are parties to the 1951 Convention and 1967 Protocol, despite non-functional asylum systems, and would therefore be subject to the rebuttable presumption of asylum ineligibility at the US Southwest border, unless they could satisfy the requirements of the narrow exceptions.

Each of the legal measures described in this section were instituted by the US in response to ostensibly unsustainable circumstances of migration, which in turn required severe restriction of entry through 'alternative pathways' of migration control. The compliance of such measures with the international obligations of the 1951 Convention and the 1967 Protocol are quite clearly deficient, however they are wholly reflective of the State's region efforts in relation to migration management.

Collectively, these actions are consistent with attempts by the US to position itself as exclusively a State of limited and selective resettlement, consistent with its multilateral diplomatic endeavours of recent years, including the Los Angeles Declaration on Migration and Protection 2022, the Collaborative Migration Management Strategy,[261] and the US Strategy for Addressing the Root Causes of Migration in Central America.[262] The Los Angeles Declaration in particular lays out the goal of collectively "expand[ing] access to regular pathways for migrants and refugees" and includes a commitment from the US to resettle 20,000 refugees from the Americas during Fiscal Years 2023 and 2024; an undertaking the NPRM explicitly states that it fulfils.[263]

---

260 USA: Citizenship and Immigration Services, *Processes for Cubans, Haitians, Nicaraguans, and Venezuelans* (18 May 2023).

261 USA: The White House, *Fact Sheet: The Collaborative Migration Management Strategy* (29 July 2021).

262 USA: The White House, *Fact Sheet: Strategy to Address the Root Causes of Migration in Central America* (29 July 2021).

263 USA: Department of Homeland Security & Department of Justice, *Proposed Rule: Circumvention of Lawful Pathways* (23 February 2023) 8 CFR Part 208/8 CFR Part 1208, 46–47.

6 Conclusion

As territoriality and nationality are fundamental elements of IRL and its IHRL and municipal derivatives, and in light of the particular conflicts and overlaps that arise in IRL, jurisdiction is fundamental to the relationship between States and between State and refugee in a way that it is not in other systems of IL. A consideration of the import of territoriality and nationality as fundamental elements of jurisdiction, and therefore integral to the division of jurisdictional competencies, negates the need for divergent terminology and legal theories, and restores the legal developments of the last four decades to a discussion of fundamental 'aspects of sovereignty'[264] as a means of rationalising underlying causes and effects.

The exercise of jurisdiction in new and ever-more-inventive ways, specifically in the context of IRL, may be attributable to the legal environment in which IRL exists; with no international authority to make pronouncements on its proper application and interpretation, and with the UNHCR only mandated to exercise supervisory powers. Intended to be executed primarily under municipal immigration regimes, it does no prescribe nor proscribe the conduct of States extensively, but rather implores States to 'use their best efforts,' 'where possible' and permits extensive reservation. While it is particularly the case in IRL, that "[T]oday, jurisdiction on the international plane must [...] be thought of as a combination of state rights and obligations in relation to individual rights, which reflects the more complex reality of contemporary international law,"[265] this is complicated further by the conflicts and overlaps that arise in IRL due to the relationship between municipal, regional, and international legal regimes.

The limits of jurisdiction in IRL are a clear example of the frailties of the *Lotus* principle, that 'whatever is not explicitly prohibited by international law is permitted.'

---

264 B.S. Chimni, 'The international law of jurisdiction: A TWAIL perspective' (2022) 35 Leiden JIL 29, 31, citing: L. Oppenheim, *Oppenheim's International Law: Parts 1–4* (OUP 1992) 456; Ian Brownlie, *Principles of Public International Law* (7th edn, OUP 2008); Fritz Alexander Mann, 'The Doctrine of International Jurisdiction Revisited after Twenty Years' (1984) 186 RCADI 9, 20; A.V. Lowe, 'The Problems of Extraterritorial Jurisdiction: Economic Sovereignty and the Search for a Solution' (1985) 34 ICLQ 724, at 724.

265 Stephen Allen and others, 'Introduction: Defining State Jurisdiction and Jurisdiction in International Law' in Allen and others (eds), *The Oxford Handbook of Jurisdiction in International Law* (OUP 2019) 9.

> [J]urisdiction is *permissive*, since, within its territory, a state may freely exercise its jurisdiction subject only to certain rules of international law; and, second, jurisdiction is *prohibitive*, because outside of its territory a state may exercise its jurisdiction unless international law prohibits it from doing so.[266]

But this accounts only for jurisdictional conflicts that arise from disputes between States that simultaneously assert jurisdictional primacy. In IRL, competing assertions of jurisdictional competencies (where for example, a state exercises extraterritorial jurisdiction in a manner that creates conflict with another State) do not arise. Rather, they are a product of the consensual, concurrent exercise of jurisdictional competencies. Much like the division of international obligations in early refugee responses, the continued evasion of attribution of wrongful conduct in IRL has created a widespread and consistent practice of division of jurisdictional competencies in immigration control and refugee processing, which is complicated further by the *realpolitik* of inter-State relations. While "[a] State cannot use coercive power to enforce its rules outside its territory,"[267] the power to enforce goes beyond the legal and must include the economic and political, in particular where the exercise of concurrent jurisdiction is tied to aid and development:

> If deference to foreign governmental protests were considered to be a norm of international law, one may conflate an external legal norm with an internal realist norm. States do not defer to foreign governmental protests because they are required to do so by some legal norm 'out there' which they comply with in spite of their perception that not complying with it will advance their interests (external legal norm). On the contrary, States defer to such protests precisely because they have no other choice than deferring: foreign retaliation may directly cause them political or economic harm (internal realist norm). Accordingly, it appears that the restraints on the exercise of extraterritorial jurisdiction are not necessarily governed by law, but rather spontaneously by the intricate workings of the balance of power. This obviously hampers the construction of a legal framework of jurisdictional restraint.[268]

266 *Id.*, 7.

267 Cedric Ryngaert, *Jurisdiction in International Law* (OUP 2015) 33.

268 *Id.*

This dynamic is clearly observable in the actions of Western States at each of the three iterations of jurisdiction in IRL described in this chapter, which together create the receding line of jurisdiction. Despite the Biden administration's assertions that it has attempted to rectify the policies it inherited from the previous administration,[269] it has actively pursued and expanded several immigration control strategies that expose refugees to human rights abuses by dividing jurisdictional competencies. On the one-year anniversary of President Biden's inauguration, government lawyers were in fact in court *defending* the continued application of Title 42.[270] At the same time, and despite its insistence that it had no choice but to continue the policy after the relevant Federal Court decision, the Biden administration not only actively continued the MPP, but expanded it.

The measures described in this chapter each contribute to an overarching trend that is, legally speaking, far more closely aligned with obligations than with rights. The impact of these measures on the rights of individuals is unequivocally serious. It is beyond question that each of these measures has had, or is likely to have, life-threatening consequences. That said (and to borrow the language of the ECtHR), that which has been 'divided and tailored' is not limited to the rights of individuals, but extends to include (as a catalyst and point of origin) the jurisdictional competencies of States in the discharge of their international obligations under IRL. These have been, and continue to be, divided, tailored, assigned, and bartered in much the same way as they have been in early international responses to refugee crises, in order to minimise the circumstances engaging the legal responsibility of the State.

This fact has been rejected by some scholars as an unsustainable model of international protection, but as with certain responses to the proposition that SR does not broadly apply to IRL, those arguments are rooted in moral and ethical objections, not legal ones. According to Ryan:

> If all extraterritorial action by states gives rise to legal responsibility, states will have an incentive not to engage in safety-oriented surveil-

269 See for example: USA: The White House, *Statement by Press Secretary Jen Psaki on the Emergency Presidential Determination on Refugee Admissions for Fiscal Year 2021* (16 April 2019).

270 On 19 January 2022, oral arguments were heard in the case of *Huisha-Huisha v Mayorkas* [4 March 2022] No 21–5200.

> lance, or in rescue operations – particularly where several states are potentially responsible for surveillance and rescue.[271]

Similarly, Ryan concludes:

> It is clear that the rejection of any responsibility by states acting extraterritorially is normatively unsustainable. This is for the obvious reason that that position would give states an incentive to manufacture a vacuum in international protection. In other words, they would be free to create a situation in which an individual in principle qualified for international protection, but no state was responsible for its provision.[272]

However, far from being unsustainable, it is precisely those circumstances that have permitted States to manufacture a vacuum in international protection. This has been a very deliberate development in the trajectory of migration control, and has guided the creation of the international consensus that now sustains it. In that sense, it is unsustainable only insofar as it is subject to judicial oversight that considers the international obligations of the 1951 Convention to have a binding effect on the State, in both its legislative and enforcement jurisdiction. Where international protection is not considered to have such effect by a State's judiciary, it is clear that the evolving legal framework is indeed sustainable and will continue to be reinforced further through the favourable interaction between the legislative and judicial branches of State. Questions of moral sustainability notwithstanding, there is no basis then for the suggestion that such systems of law and policy cannot continue, and we are, once again, faced with the question of what is the practical value of an obligation where there is no attribution and no enforcement of SR.

While there are of course fundamental distinctions between jurisdictional competencies, their application and interpretation specifically to matters of municipal and regional law relative to IRL often reveals a number of inconsistencies, relative to other systems of law. A clear example of this is the US case of *Boumediene v Bush*,[273] in which the Supreme Court held that alien detainees at Guantanamo Bay are constitutionally entitled to petition for the

---

271 Bernard Ryan, 'Extraterritorial Immigration Control: What Role for Legal Guarantees?' in Ryan and Mitsilegas (eds), *Extraterritorial Immigration Control* (Martinus Nijhoff 2010) 37.

272 *Id.*

273 *Boumediene v Bush* [2008] 553 US 723.

writ of *habeas corpus*. The court's reliance on functional control to determine the reach of the Constitution suggested that the rights of detainees held overseas would expand,[274] however as recent developments in the region as well as within the State has demonstrated, even the act of holding a person in detention is not taken to establish the jurisdiction of the State for immigration purposes, even where that purpose is the provision of international protection.[275] As Knox has noted:

> [The Supreme Court's] decisions have treated foreign ships within U.S. territory as subject to a presumption against extraterritoriality, a presumption against interference with their "internal affairs," a presumption against interference with their maritime operations, a balancing test to determine whether U.S. law should apply, and no presumption at all. The Court has said that the presumption may be overcome only by a clear statement of congressional intent, that the statutory structure, legislative history, and agency interpretations are relevant, and that some circumstances may justify extending law extraterritorially without any direct evidence of legislative intent at all.[276]

Arguably, the intention behind the development and application of those measures described in this chapter has been their effect on rules of attribution – both municipally and internationally. Overwhelmingly, they have received judicial and political support, the effect of which has been to reconstruct not only norms of jurisdiction, based on those fundamental elements of territoriality and nationality, but also to obstruct the attribution of conduct. What remains is a system of individual municipal bodies of jurisprudence relative to activities of States that share some fundamental substantive and procedural commonalities. It is from those commonalities that we might be able to construct some cohesive system of principles of due diligence relative to IRL and the responsibility of States *vis-à-vis* their international obligations, irrespective of the absence of an international judicial forum.

274 Harvard Law Review, 'Extraterritoriality' (2011) 124(5) Harv L Rev 1226, 1230.
275 John H. Knox, 'A Presumption against Extrajurisdictionality' (2010) 104(3) AJIL 351, 352.
276 *Id.*

CHAPTER 7

State Responsibility and Due Diligence Standards in International Refugee Law

1 Introduction

With the exception of those countermeasures detailed in Chapter 4 (which in any case have no basis in IL) there is little to suggest that norms of SR apply also to IRL. There is instead a long history of evasive and exploitative conduct that has aimed specifically to minimise the scope and content of international obligations and in turn the circumstances capable of engaging SR. This is not to say, however, that there is no unifying body of legal norms that are *comparable* to the attribution of SR across municipal systems. There is instead a body of jurisprudence from which one can deduce clear rules applicable to the performance of those international obligations established in the 1951 Convention. These are established by the development of applicable rules of due diligence. As due diligence standards are integral to the attribution of conduct to a State, they are in turn integral to SR. Just as the law of aliens formed the basis of SR, and later informed the development of IRL, so too were due diligence standards a prominent part of the law of aliens across multiple municipal jurisdictions. They were applied and advanced by the many Claims Commissions of the early 20th century,[1] and though the duty to prevent, punish, and repair had been that of the sovereign *vis-à-vis* the protection of aliens for centuries prior,[2] the protection of aliens was thus the first area of IL in which due diligence obligations were broadly acknowledged.[3] Just as IRL and SR are intrinsically linked through the law of aliens, so too is due diligence. As such, any examination of SR in IRL must consider its relevance.

1 See generally: John Bassett Moore, *A Digest of International Law, Volume iii* (Government Printing Office 1906); Marjorie M. Whiteman, *Damages in International Law* (Government Printing Office 1937); Joanna Bourke-Martignoni, 'The History and Development of the Due Diligence Standard in International Law and Its Role in the Protection of Women Against Violence' in Carin Benninger-Budel (ed), *Due Diligence and Its Application to Protect Women from Violence* (2008) 47, 48.

2 *Id.*; Jan Arno Hessbruegge, 'The Historical Development of the Doctrines of Attribution and Due Diligence in International Law' (2004) 36 NYUJIntlL&Pol 265.

3 Maria Monnheimer, *Due Diligence Obligations in International Human Rights Law* (CUP 2021) 83.

 | DOI:10.1163/9789004722835_009

Unlike most other international conventions, the 1951 Convention does not designate an authority to make pronouncements on matters of interpretation, nor does it establish any special judicial mechanism to determine its proper application. It charged the High Commissioner only with "the task of supervising international conventions providing for the protection of refugees"[4] and later, the *Executive Committee of the High Commissioner's Programme* (ExCom) to serve as the advisory committee foreseen in the UNHCR Statute.[5] While the ExCom and the UNHCR provide some interpretative authority, neither can adequately fill this international juridical void, and their pronouncements are, in any case, frequently treated by States as subordinate to municipal statute and jurisprudence.

The absence of an enforcement mechanism has frequently been lamented by scholars of IRL as its implicit frailty; a *lacuna* from which a wealth of legal complications have arisen.[6] It has led some to quite overstate the role of IHRL as a kind of remedial system of IL that substitutes these implicit failures and all but renders IRL defunct.[7] Whether or not it is quite the problem that some believe it to be, the deficiency itself is worthy of some attention. Those consequences that ordinarily arise in general IL from the imposition of international obligations do not arise in IRL. This is particularly significant where States have not only failed collectively to respect the most fundamental tenets

4 UN General Assembly, *Convention Relating to the Status of Refugees* (28 July 1951) UNTS 189, preambular para 6.

5 UN General Assembly, *Resolution 1166(XII): International Assistance to Refugees within the Mandate of the United Nations High Commissioner for Refugees* (26 November 1957) A/RES/1166(XII); UN Economic and Social Council, *Resolution 672(XXV): Establishment of an Executive Committee of the Programme of the United Nations High Commissioner for Refugees* (30 April 1958) E/RES/672(XXV).

6 James C. Hathaway, Hugo Storey, 'What Is the Meaning of State Protection in Refugee Law – A Debate' (2016) 28(3) International Journal of Refugee Law 480, 482; James C. Hathaway, 'The Architecture of the UN Refugee Convention and Protocol' in Costello, Foster and McAdam (eds), *The Oxford Handbook of International Refugee Law* (OUP 2021) 171, 172; Ruvi Ziegler, 'International Humanitarian Law and Refugee Protection' in Costello, Foster and McAdam (eds), *The Oxford Handbook of International Refugee Law* (OUP 2021) 221, 222.

7 See in particular: Vincent Chetail, 'Are Refugee Rights Human Rights? An Unorthodox Questioning of the Relations between Refugee Law and Human Rights Law' in Rubio-Marín (ed), *Human Rights and Immigration* (OUP 2014) 19; Vincent Chetail, 'Moving Towards an Integrated Approach of Refugee Law and Human Rights Law' in Costello, Foster and McAdam (eds), *The Oxford Handbook of International Refugee Law* (OUP 2021) 202, 212–213; See also: James C. Hathaway, Michelle Foster, *The Law of Refugee Status* (2 edn, CUP 2014) 1: Refugee law is an "international human rights mechanism."; A more nuanced position is advanced by Goodwin-Gill. See: Guy S. Goodwin-Gill, 'The Language of Protection' (1989) 1(1) IJRL 6, 16.

of IRL, but have made concerted, collective efforts to contravene them, and to reinforce the legitimacy of those contraventions through the adoption of municipal and regional law and policy.

But the supposed implicit 'deficiencies' of the 1951 Convention in not providing a designated authority for the adjudication of IRL are not accidental. Municipal legal regimes were always intended to be the principal means of implementing IRL. In that sense, the question of how to adjudicate the lawfulness of State conduct in IRL is not quite the problem it appears to be. The question of an inherent 'deficiency' is less a matter of compliance than it is one of harmonising standards of conduct. In that respect, harmonising standards of conduct are provided quite clearly in those rules of due diligence that have developed in response to the litigation of IRL matters, predominantly under IHRL.

Questions then arise in relation to those standards and their scope and content in IL. Specifically, the question of due diligence in IL as a discrete field of scholarly inquiry has yielded quite a diverging body of literature. This is the case not only in relation to due diligence in general IL, but in the application of concepts of due diligence to IRL, where a particularly fractious body of literature has emerged. That said, much like those question of the 'frailties' and 'deficiencies of IRL,' questions of due diligence in IRL raise a number of issues that are not quite as problematic as they might appear. The question of due diligence in IRL has been the subject of some academic inquiry that in almost all cases stumbles on the question of SR and its import to both due diligence and IRL.[8] Most of the relevant literature bases its analysis on misconceptions about how SR and IRL interact, and how due diligence standards may then be applied to the latter.[9] These misconceptions create their own self-fulfilling prophesies that due diligence has no place in IRL.[10]

8 Joanna Bourke-Martignoni, 'The History and Development of the Due Diligence Standard in International Law and Its Role in the Protection of Women Against Violence' in Benninger-Budel (ed), *Due Diligence and Its Application to Protect Women from Violence* (2008) 47, 48.

9 Jan Arno Hessbruegge, 'The Historical Development of the Doctrines of Attribution and Due Diligence in International Law' (2004) 36 NYUJIntlL&Pol 265; Joanna Bourke-Martignoni, 'The History and Development of the Due Diligence Standard in International Law and Its Role in the Protection of Women Against Violence' in Benninger-Budel (ed), *Due Diligence and Its Application to Protect Women from Violence* (2008) 47, 48.

10 Maria Monnheimer, *Due Diligence Obligations in International Human Rights Law* (CUP 2021) 83.

As is often repeated in international legal theory, there are broadly two categories of legal obligation: obligations of result, and obligations of conduct.[11] The former requires that a result follow from particular conduct; the obligation attaching to the result itself having achieved a certain outcome, as opposed to the conduct alone. Violation then arises from the non-fulfilment of the promised result. By contrast, the latter requires the performance of certain conduct irrespective of outcome; the obligation attaching to the conduct alone without the requirement of a particular outcome. Violation then arises from the fact that the 'debtor did not use the diligence required by the circumstances.'[12] Similarly, there are broadly two conceptions of due diligence in law generally: due diligence as an integral part of a primary obligation, and due diligence as a corollary duty of a primary obligation.[13] In the case of the former, the relevant due diligence standard is an essential feature of attribution. The fact of its exercise must be demonstrable in order to rebut any claim of violation, and its absence will necessarily inform the determination of conduct as unlawful. In the case of the latter, the content of the relevant due diligence standard varies and does not necessarily form part of the adjudication of conduct.[14] This binary conception of due diligence is the point of departure for any examination of its applicable standards, as in either case, its scope changes quite dramatically.

At its most fundamental, the principle of due diligence is the obligation to take appropriate measures to prevent resultant harm, where that harm con-

11 *Case Concerning Application of the Convention on the Prevention and Punishment of the Crime of Genocide* (*Bosnia and Herzegovina v Serbia and Montenegro*) [2007] ICJ Rep 47, at [221].

12 Riccardo Pisillo-Mazzeschi, 'Due Diligence and the International Responsibility of States' (1992) 35 German Yearbook of International Law 9, 48.

13 *Certain Activities carried out by Nicaragua in the Border Area* (*Separate opinion of Judge Dugard*) [2015] ICJ Rep 842, at [845]; *Island of Palmas* (*or Miangas*) (*The Netherlands v The United States of America*) [4 April 1928] II RIAA 829, at [839]; *Corfu Channel* (*United Kingdom of Great Britain and Northern Ireland v Albania*) [1949] ICJ Rep 244 at [22]; *Pulp Mills on the River Uruguay* (*Argentina v Uruguay*) [2010] ICJ Rep 58; *Armed Activities on the Territory of the Congo* (*Democratic Republic of the Congo v Uganda*) [2015] ICJ Rep 23, at [171]–[268]; See also: Robert Kolb, 'Reflections on Due Diligence Duties and Cyberspace' (2016) 58 German Yearbook of International Law 113.

14 *Island of Palmas* (*or Miangas*) (*The Netherlands v The United States of America*) [4 April 1928] II RIAA 829, at [839]: "Territorial sovereignty, as has already been said, involves the exclusive right to display the activities of a State. This right has as corollary a duty: the obligation to protect within the territory the rights of other States, in particular their right to integrity and inviolability in peace and in war, together with the rights which each State may claim for its nationals in foreign territory."

stitutes a violation of a primary obligation.[15] The observance of due diligence standards is therefore as much an obligation as any other element of a primary rule, where it does in fact form part of that primary rule. As Eagleton noted in his seminal work on SR:

> The members of the community of nations have, in practice, agreed to respect certain principles for their mutual guidance; and, in so doing, it has been understood that they were thereby accepting obligations to observe the conduct prescribed.[16]

While variation exists within jurisprudence relative to IRL, a clear preference emerges for the integral nature of due diligence standards to primary obligations. This is revealed in tests of attribution – again, both between and within systems of law that interpret and apply the rules of IRL – which tend to regard both obligations of conduct and obligations of result as requiring certain standards of due diligence. In general, jurisprudence relative to IRL considers a want of due diligence to equate with an objective failure to fulfil an international obligation. In other words, it rejects the notion that due diligence is a corollary duty, and instead requires the objective fulfilment of the standard as an integral part of the primary rule.

There may be a relatively simple explanation for this. IRL does not impose international obligations requiring measures of *prevention* in respect of refugee status. As a system of law, IRL proscribes as wrongful both actions and omissions that occur *post-facto*. This is a reflection of the temporal environment in which IRL is activated: When the State encounters the refugee. It is concerned with the responsive conduct of States of reception, not with the conduct of States of origin, and as such, due diligence requirements ascribe standards of conduct adapted to a reactive temporal environment. But this in itself does not make IRL exceptional among systems of IL, many of which are concerned with reactive rather than proactive conduct. A second explanation may be that the standards of conduct required by IRL are less concerned with what is reasonably expected, than with what is legally required in light of the heightened risk of harm.

---

15 A.V. Freeman, 'Responsibility of States for Unlawful Acts of their Armed Forces' (1955) 88 RCADI 263, 277–278; Riccardo Pisillo-Mazzeschi, 'Due Diligence and the International Responsibility of States' (1992) 35 German Yearbook of International Law 9, 44; Joanna Kulesza, *Due Diligence in International Law* (Brill 2016) 264.

16 Clyde Eagleton, *The Responsibility of States in International Law* (New York University Press 1928) 3.

This chapter argues that while general IL tends to favour the conception of due diligence as a corollary duty attached to a primary obligation and not necessarily relevant to responsibility,[17] within IRL, judicial opinion and State practice appear to favour a conception of due diligence as indivisible from a primary rule. It demonstrates that there are a number of reasons for this, some evolutionary, some contextual, but the effect is that in its assessment of risk, fault, and attribution, IRL is quite exceptional among systems of PIL. Part 2 considers the critical importance of due diligence in general IL. It argues that much like SR and IRL, due diligence standards emerged from laws relative to the treatment of aliens and functioned as an essential element in the enforcement of SR as it related to the protection of the alien. Part 3 argues that several overarching assumptions underpin the current conception of due diligence in general IL and in IRL. It posits that due diligence standards that apply to IRL are conditioned by a number of distinct factors that in large part turn on the perception of risk. It analyses three critiques of common scholarly constructions of due diligence in IRL and responds to each in turn.

Part 4 posits that due diligence standards are present within the primary instruments of IRL and comprise two corresponding modes of SR that include obligations of result and obligations of conduct, conditioned by different levels of risk, and requiring different regimes of proof. It demonstrates that, with reference to the assessment of risk, the conception of fault, and the process of attribution, judicial opinion and State practice favour the conception of due diligence as indivisible from the primary obligation itself. Part 5 argues that due diligence standards do not derive principally from IHRL but are established in the 1951 Convention and regional instruments of IRL. Rather, human rights conceptions of international protection – such as effective protection, sufficiency of protection, and implementation – are in many instances coterminous with due diligence standards applicable to primary obligations of IRL, merely redefining due diligence standards by using divergent terminology.

This chapter concludes that in the absence of a robust system of SR at the inter-State level, due diligence standards across municipal and regional jurisdictions exact a standard of conduct of States that is consistent with the due diligence standards of the 1951 Convention, in turn strengthening adherence to its primary obligations by affirming the integral nature of due diligence

17 Neil McDonald, 'The Role of Due Diligence in International Law' (2019) 68(4) ICLQ 1041, 1049; Carla Ferstman, 'Human Rights Due Diligence Policies Applied to Extraterritorial Cooperation to Prevent "Irregular" Migration: European Union and United Kingdom Support to Libya' (2020) 21 German Law Journal 459, 470.

standards. It concludes that internationally, due diligence standards provide a unifying system of international standards of conduct, relative to the protection of the refugee, and in that sense, provide a means of enforcement.

2 Due Diligence in General International Law

Due diligence first appeared in contemporary PIL by way of compensation claims arising from the American Civil War. The UK and the US agreed to the settlement of an international dispute concerning the sale of a ship by a private British company to the Confederate Army by way of arbitration; the so-called Alabama Arbitration. In 1871, the parties concluded the *Treaty of Washington* on certain rules that the Tribunal should use in deciding the claims. The treaty provided that neutral States were bound to apply due diligence standards in the prevention of certain types of conduct that threatened another State with which it was at peace.[18] In this context, SR arose from a failure to fulfil the due diligence standards required by the obligations of neutrality. The 1907 *Hague Convention concerning the Rights and Duties of Neutral Powers in Naval War* largely reproduced the wording of the so-called 'Washington Rules' in establishing primary rules of neutrality, though it used the phrases "employ the means at its disposal" and "vigilance to prevent" in place of "due diligence."[19]

As with other aspects of SR, the US–Mexico General Claims Commission was instrumental in establishing due diligence principles in respect of aliens. In *Neer (U.S.) v. United Mexican States*,[20] the Commission established a standard of due diligence applicable to the investigation of private actors for injurious acts to aliens, though it was an exceedingly high standard, which ultimately precluded attribution of wrongful conduct to Mexico. The standard prescribed that:

> [T]he treatment of an alien, in order to constitute an international delinquency, should amount to an outrage, to bad faith, to wilful neglect

18 *Alabama Claims Arbitration (United States of America v United Kingdom)* [1872] II RIAA 713; *Frederick Wipperman Arbitration (United States of America v Venezuela)* [1890] III RIAA 3041; *William E. Chapman Arbitration (United States of America v United Mexican States)* [1930] IV RIAA 632; Horst Blomeyer-Bartenstein, 'Due Diligence' in *Max Planck Institute, Encyclopedia of Public International Law* 1987) 138, 139.

19 *Convention (XIII) concerning the Rights and Duties of Neutral Powers in Naval War* (1907) Article 8.

20 *L.F.H. Neer and Pauline Neer* [1926] 4 RIAA 73, at [60].

> of duty, or to an insufficiency of governmental action so far short of international standards that every reasonable and impartial man would readily recognize its insufficiency.[21]

The *Neer* standard became the minimum standard of treatment to be applied to the protection of aliens,[22] and continues to be cited,[23] though some tribunals consider that a broader interpretation may be warranted.[24] At the same time, the *Neer* standard considered fault (negligence) as part of the determination of SR. This construction became quite entrenched in the conception of due diligence within IL. Blomeyer-Bartenstein and Brownlie noted that in the wake of the Alabama Arbitration, it became increasingly common to view the State as liable only for the faulty conduct of its organs in cases where the breach of an international obligation was due to the actions of private individuals.[25] Though in international arbitration, evidence of bad faith or malicious intention on the part of the State is not a requirement of attribution, it may be sufficient to establish a violation of the customary international law of the minimum standard of conduct.[26]

As due diligence in IL continues to function primarily as a standard of conduct that defines the obligations of States to prevent and repress the commission of internationally wrongful acts by private individuals,[27] it is easy to see how it emerged from laws relative to the treatment of aliens. States were required to demonstrate a level of conduct, established by precedent, in

---

21 *Id.*, at [61]–[62].

22 See for example: *Harry Roberts (USA) v United Mexican States* [1926] IV RIAA 80; *George W. Hopkins (USA) v United Mexican States* [1926] IV RIAA 16.

23 See for example: *Cargill, Incorporated v United Mexican States* [2009] NAFTA (ICSID) at [286]; *Glamis Gold, Ltd. v The United States of America* [2009] NAFTA (UNCITRAL) at [614]–[616].

24 See for example: Windstream Energy LLC v Government of Canada [2016] NAFTA (UNCITRAL) at [352].

25 *Horst Blomeyer-Bartenstein, 'Due Diligence'* in Max Planck Institute, Encyclopedia of Public International Law 1987); Ian Brownlie, *System of the Law of Nations: State Responsibility, Part I* (1 edn, OUP 1983) 161.

26 *Merrill & Ring v Canada* [2010] NAFTA (ICSID) at [208]; *Cargill, Incorporated v United Mexican States* [2009] NAFTA (ICSID) at [286].

27 Jonathan Bonnitcha, Robert McCorquodale, 'The Concept of "Due Diligence" in the UN Guiding Principles on Business and Human Rights' 28(3) EJIL 899, 903; Antal Berkes, 'The Standard of 'Due Diligence' as a Result of Interchange between the Law of Armed Conflict and General International Law' (2018) 23(3) Journal of Conflict and Security Law 433; Holly Cullen, 'The Irresistible Rise of Human Rights Due Diligence: Conflict Minerals and Beyond' (2016) 48 Geo Wash Int'l L Rev 743, 745.

response to threatened or actual injury by private persons against foreign nationals. The failure to exercise due diligence in the prevention, investigation, or punishment of private actors resulted in a denial of justice where the State failed to discharge that duty. In that sense, the development of due diligence in IL is a direct consequence of SR for injuries to aliens. The law of neutrality and the law of aliens might appear to be strange bedfellows, but for the fact that fundamentally, each was quite exceptional within public IL at the time of their development: Both concerned the conduct of States in relation to the activities of private persons resulting in an injury to another State.

In the era of codification, consensus could not be reached even on the most fundamental questions of due diligence. Prominent IL institutions could not resolve the question of the primary or secondary nature of due diligence, and thus its inclusion as a secondary rule of SR. In preparation for the codification conference on the international responsibility of States for injuries to aliens, the *Institut de Droit International* defined due diligence very generally as "the measures to which under the circumstances, it was proper normally to resort in order to prevent or check such actions."[28] The following year, Harvard Law School's draft articles defined due diligence with specific reference to the law of aliens:

> A state is responsible if an injury to an alien results from its failure to exercise due diligence to prevent the injury, if local remedies have been exhausted without adequate redress for such failure. The diligence required may vary with the private or public character of the alien and the circumstances of the case.[29]

This conception, which reflected the *Neer* standard, was the formulation preferred by the LoN, which concluded at the Conference for the Codification of International Law:

> The state is only responsible where the damage sustained by the foreigner results from the fact that the state has failed to take such meas-

28 'International Responsibility of States for Injuries on their Territory to the Person or Property of Foreigners' (1928) 22 (Supp.) AJIL, 330.

29 'The Law of Responsibility of States for Damage Done in Their Territory to the Person or Property of Foreigners' (1929) 23 AJIL 131, 133.

> ures as in the circumstances should normally have been taken to prevent, redress or inflict punishment for the acts causing the damage.[30]

Several decades later, the ILC re-examined due diligence when it considered the codification of SR and the question of injuries to aliens.[31] Much like the role of the individual in the codification of the SR, the concept of a due diligence standard relevant to secondary rules of SR was considered, rejected, and finally omitted from the final draft. Much like injuries to aliens, the inclusion of due diligence was opposed in the numerous codification processes because it was considered relative to primary, rather than secondary rules of SR. It is interesting to note that the perceived proximity of the two issues (due diligence and the protection of aliens) contributed in large part to the ultimate exclusion of due diligence from the codification process. As Blomeyer-Bartenstein noted, "[t]he reason for the ultimate failure to attain agreement was controversy over the special protection of aliens."[32] Indeed, the second Special Rapporteur for SR, Roberto Ago, referred repeatedly to the failure of the 1930 codification conference, in part due to the association between SR and controversial primary rules, namely, the protection of aliens – an association that was unavoidable in view of the purpose of the conference.[33]

To this day, the question of whether due diligence forms part of primary or secondary rules of IL is far from settled.[34] Monnheimer argues that due diligence standards form part of the objective content of primary obligations, rather than a secondary or corollary duty; the primary obligation incorporating a requirement to act in an overall diligent manner.[35] She concludes that due diligence standards are in principle primary obligations imposing duties

30 League of Nations, 'Conference for the Codification of International Law' (28 January 1929).

31 International Law Commission, *Second report of the Special Rapporteur, Mr. F.V. García Amador*1957) (A/CN.4/106) 104.

32 *Horst Blomeyer-Bartenstein, 'Due Diligence*' in Max Planck Institute, Encyclopedia of Public International Law 1987) 141.

33 *Id.*, 142. Though Crawford cautioned that too much should not be read into this position. See: James Crawford, *State Responsibility: The General Part* (CUP 2013) 38; Tarcisio Gattini, 'Smoking/No Smoking: Some Remarks on the Current Place of Fault in the ILC Draft Articles on State Responsibility' (1999) 10 EJIL 397.

34 Samantha Besson, *Due Diligence in International Law* (Brill 2023) 28: "[O]ne may wonder whether the regime of due diligence should not also be that of a standard or even an obligation of so-called general international law."

35 Maria Monnheimer, *Due Diligence Obligations in International Human Rights Law* (CUP 2021) 97.

of a material content.[36] The precise content of that duty is "objectively derived" from the international obligation itself, and there is thus "no need for installing a separate regime of state responsibility for due diligence obligations."[37] In a similar sense, Cassella and Longobardo consider that while due diligence is not technically a component of SR,[38] due diligence obligations require a State to constantly monitor the implementation of international obligations of conduct.[39]

There is jurisprudential support for both conceptions of due diligence. In the *Island of Palmas* arbitration, Huber noted that there was a corollary duty of territorial sovereignty that required "the obligation to protect within the territory the rights of other States, in particular their right to integrity and inviolability."[40] But rather than providing a definitive answer, the relative jurisprudence seems to demonstrate that the integral or corollary nature of due diligence standards varies within general IL – both between and within systems, and depends quite specifically on the content and application of the primary rule.

2.1 *Some Conceptual Errors*

The question of due diligence in general IL has unfortunately suffered from being falsely 'problemised,' both in its scope and content, and in its relevance to SR in general. Regarding its scope and content, questions seem to arise that want for a clear definition of due diligence standards, or at least some clear parameters that provide some certainty as to their scope and content in IL.[41] Bourke-Martignoni asserts that "both the content and scope of due diligence obligations remain vague."[42] Krieger, Peters, and Kreuzer have claimed that "[T]he lack of clarity about the status of due diligence as a primary or secondary norm, or both, is matched by a confusing variety of terms used to describe

---

36 *Id.*

37 *Id.*, 97–98.

38 Sarah Cassella, 'Les travaux de la Commission du droit international sur la responsabilite internationale et le standard de due diligence' in SFDI (ed), *Le Standard de Due Diligence et la Responsabilité Internationale* (2018) 11; Marco Longobardo, 'The Relevance of the Concept of Due Diligence for International Humanitarian Law' (2019) 37(1) Wis Int'l LJ 44.

39 *Id.*, 48.

40 *Island of Palmas (or Miangas) (The Netherlands v The United States of America)* [4 April 1928] II RIAA 829, 839.

41 See generally discussion in: Alice Ollino, *Due Diligence Obligations in International Law* (CUP 2022) 131–186.

42 *Id.*, 47.

the normative quality of due diligence. [...] A further challenge for the analysis of due diligence in international law is the difficulty of comprehensively identifying all due diligence norms."[43] This concern for the apparent 'vagueness' of due diligence presents itself also in IRL scholarship. Hathaway and Foster claim that it is still not possible to describe with precision the meaning of due diligence.

> "[B]oth the content and scope of due diligence obligations remain vague," and the Horvath standard in particular has been recognized as not constituting "the clearest of tests."[44]

And yet, in citing this apparent deficiency, Hathaway and Foster acknowledge that, "[t]his lack of a uniform and clearly articulated due diligence standard is likely inevitable because, as recognized by the International Law Commission, the due diligence standard varies 'from one context to another for reasons which essentially relate to the object and purpose of the treaty provision or other rule giving rise to the primary obligation.'"[45] The task of identifying all due diligence norms is not only a Sisyphean one, but one that lacks a clear objective. It resolves no complication. Within IL generally, the content of due diligence lacks a succinct definition and universal application for the simple reason that there is no broad rule of due diligence in IL. It is consequential only as a component of a primary rule, and as such, its standards are as broad

43 Heike Krieger, Anne Peters, Leonhard Kreuzer, 'Introduction' in Heike Krieger, Anne Peters and Leonhard Kreuzer (eds), *Due Diligence in the International Legal Order* (OUP 2020) 3, 8–9.

44 James C. Hathaway, Michelle Foster, *The Law of Refugee Status* (2 edn, CUP 2014) 315, citing *inter alia*: Joanna Bourke-Martignoni, 'The History and Development of the Due Diligence Standard in International Law and Its Role in the Protection of Women Against Violence' in Benninger-Budel (ed), *Due Diligence and Its Application to Protect Women from Violence* (2008) 47. The 'Horvath standard' refers to the British case: *Horvath v Secretary of State for the Home Department* [2000] Imm AR 205, in which Hale L.J. noted that: "It is common ground, and generally understood, that the Geneva Convention provides for a system of surrogate state protection" at [242].

45 James C. Hathaway, Michelle Foster, *The Law of Refugee Status* (2 edn, CUP 2014) 315, citing: James Crawford, 'The International Law Commission's Articles on State Responsibility: Introduction, Text and Commentaries' (2002) 82; See also: Joanna Bourke-Martignoni, 'The History and Development of the Due Diligence Standard in International Law and Its Role in the Protection of Women Against Violence' in Benninger-Budel (ed), *Due Diligence and Its Application to Protect Women from Violence* (2008) 47, 49.

and varied as primary rules themselves. As a legal standard of conduct, the content of due diligence must be determined on a case-by-case basis, with reference to a specific obligation,[46] and as a result, standards of due diligence relative to particular systems of IL are revealed in the various tests of attribution applied across those systems.

This leads to the second false 'problemisation' of due diligence; that of attribution. The relevance of due diligence to SR, in particular the history of due diligence as part of SR, has led to some misconceptions regarding the application of due diligence standards to primary rules of international law on the one hand, and to SR on the other. Krieger, Peters, and Kreuzer have questioned:

> Generally, how can due diligence be simultaneously relevant on the levels of both primary and secondary norms? One stumbles against the apparent doctrinal inconsistency. Does this dual relevance show that the concept is in itself conceptually flawed and confused? Or does the dual relevance, quite to the contrary, indicate that the concept has a potential to enhance accountability irrespective of doctrinal categories?[47]

Similarly Kulesza has concluded:

> Due diligence remains [...] one of the criteria for attributing state responsibility. The duty to show due diligence is to be viewed as part of a given international obligation, violated when a state fails to manifest due diligence. Therefore not always does an internationally unlawful omission of a state follow its failure to show due diligence, yet whenever a state fails to act with due diligence in performing its international obligation to do so, its responsibility for internationally wrongful omission may be attributed.[48]

46 Neil McDonald, 'The Role of Due Diligence in International Law' (2019) 68(4) ICLQ 1041, 1044; Holly Cullen, 'The Irresistible Rise of Human Rights Due Diligence: Conflict Minerals and Beyond' (2016) 48 Geo Wash Int'l L Rev 743, 748; *Certain Activities carried out by Nicaragua in the Border Area* (*Separate opinion of Judge Donoghue*) [2015] ICJ Rep 782 at 785.

47 Heike Krieger, Anne Peters, Leonhard Kreuzer, 'Introduction' in Krieger, Peters and Kreuzer (eds), *Due Diligence in the International Legal Order* (OUP 2020) 8.

48 Joanna Kulesza, *Due Diligence in International Law* (Brill 2016) 266, citing: Riccardo Pisillo-Mazzeschi, 'Due Diligence and the International Responsibility of States' (1992)

Again, there is no doctrinal inconsistency to be analysed and resolved. Due diligence in general IL is not only relevant to secondary rules of attribution. As it relates to primary rules of IL, due diligence may be understood as relevant to the administration of law. This is of course the basis of any subsequent question of attribution. The integral or corollary nature of a given due diligence standard vis-à-vis a primary obligation is revealed in tests of attribution. Incidentally, tests of attribution also clarify the scope of content of a due diligence standard. But, as latter sections of this chapter demonstrate, over-reliance of strict interpretations of attribution has led many to divorce due diligence and IRL completely.

3 Due Diligence in International Refugee Law

Though variation exists in the conception of due diligence in general IL, collectively, the jurisprudence of international courts and tribunals makes clear that due diligence standards are not only applied to achieve a minimum standard of conduct, but to avoid arbitrary and discriminatory application of the rules and principles of IL.[49] This is also a critical function of due diligence in IRL, in particular in the application of the standard of constructive knowledge in the evaluation of fault. Where States have sought to create distance between asylum seekers and State agents to affect plausible deniability, courts and tribunals have responded by applying a standard of constructive knowledge – commonly formulated as 'knew or ought to have known' – in order to establish the breach of the primary obligation of *non-refoulement*. This is perhaps the most critical standard of due diligence relative to IRL. It establishes fault as a necessary component of attribution, despite the fact that as a system of law, IRL favours a construction of due diligence as imposing obligations of result, rather than of conduct. That is, while fault is not *required* in order to attribute SR, it is nonetheless uniformly assessed.

The standard was principally developed in the *Corfu Channel* case where the ICJ established that "[T]he obligations incumbent upon the Albanian authorities consisted in notifying [...] the existence of a minefield in Albanian territorial waters and in warning the approaching British warships of the

35 German Yearbook of International Law 9, 46; Ian Brownlie, *System of the Law of Nations: State Responsibility, Part I* (1 edn, OUP 1983) 440.

49 See: *Elettronica Sicula S.p.A. (ELSI) (USA v Italy)* [1989] ICJ Rep 15, Memorial of the United States of America (15 May 1987) 93, citing *L.F.H. Neer and Pauline Neer* [1926] 4 RIAA 73.

imminent danger to which the minefield exposed them."[50] This was based, *inter alia*, on "every state's obligation not to allow knowingly its territory to be used for acts contrary to the rights of other states."[51] Though the court concluded that the laying of the minefield "could not have been accomplished without the knowledge of the Albanian Government," it definitively excluded any fault requirement from the determination of conduct as wrongful, providing that the task of the court was to determine the fact of Albania's prior knowledge of mine-laying in its territorial waters "independently of any connivance on her part in this operation."[52]

The standard developed in *Corfu Channel*, and applicable in general IL, differs from its IRL iterations in several ways. The assessment of evidence to establish prior knowledge (the standard 'to know or ought to have known') is undertaken with reference to the fault of the State – whether it acted with negligence or recklessness. While the ICJ did not infer prior knowledge from jurisdiction alone,[53] by contrast, in IRL-related jurisprudence, courts and tribunals have more frequently applied tests to establish jurisdiction first, as a necessary precondition to constructive knowledge. Secondary rules of IL are engaged not at the point of establishing that a breach has occurred, but where it is determined that the State knew or ought to have known of the breach; the exercise of jurisdiction being the necessary corollary of prior knowledge. In that sense, it appears as an obligation of conduct, rather than one of result, however the broad application of the standard of constructive knowledge – encompassing even situations in which courts or tribunals have acknowledged that the State could not have known – suggests that the standard is no longer an obligations of conduct, but has instead become one of result. That is, the assessment of fault has become an integral part of the formal attribution of conduct though it is not necessary for the determination of SR. This is due in large part to the fact that, as a standard of due diligence, it is applied to the most serious of IRL violations – that of *non-refoulement* – and has by virtue of that association, become a standard applicable to an obligation of result due to the heightened risk of harm associated with the violation.

It is perhaps useful here to delineate certain terminology. Due diligence obligations within IRL are often addressed under the misnomers of 'implementation,' 'effective protection,' and 'sufficiency of protection.' Specifically,

50 *Corfu Channel* (*United Kingdom of Great Britain and Northern Ireland v Albania*) [1949] ICJ Rep 244, 22.

51 *Id.* See also: *Pulp Mills on the River Uruguay* (*Argentina v Uruguay*) [2010] ICJ Rep 58, 14.

52 *Id.*, at 18.

53 *Id.*

the terms are frequently used to describe what is essentially the proper administration of primary obligations through the observance of due diligence standards. The obligation of implementation and the due diligence requirements attached to primary obligations can be delineated by the practical function of the terms. As concepts, 'implementation,' 'effective protection,' and 'sufficiency of protection' lack a legal quality. Rather, they describe the administrative duties required by the primary obligations of IRL whose scope and content are defined by such. At its most fundamental, 'implementation' requires the establishment of a legal or administrative framework to support the proper function of a primary obligation, and the enactment of a law, policy, or regulation could hardly be considered as the fulfilment of a due diligence requirement. The lack of proper supervision or administration of the law, policy, or regulation may represent a failure of due diligence, but this is separate and distinct from implementation *per se*. By comparison, the requirements of due diligence are associated with the legal function of the primary rule, whether those requirements are of conduct or of result. Due diligence may *form* part of implementation, in that the realisation of a legal framework might require conduct or result, but the inverse cannot be true. Due diligence does not *include* implementation, as the latter is a requirement separate and distinct from the former.

The 1951 Convention is an example of the convergence and divergence in these concepts of protection and its scope and content. It requires faithful implementation of its provisions, even where States are permitted a margin of appreciation through reservation or adaptation to municipal legal regimes, however a number of provisions also require the observance of due diligence standards, both of conduct and result. This is not simply a matter of semantics. The language of 'respect' and 'consideration' does not strictly denote obligations of conduct, and the language of 'shall' and 'will' does not necessarily denote result. Article 12 (personal status) provides that rights acquired by a refugee and dependent on personal status, more particularly attaching to marriage, "shall be respected by a Contracting State." This is clearly an obligation of result requiring non-interference with existing rights. By comparison, Article 17 (wage-earning employment) uses the language of 'shall,' but requires only that the State "give sympathetic consideration to assimilating the rights of all refugees with regard to wage-earning employment [...]." This is an obligation of conduct. While these examples may seem relatively simple, the concept of due diligent in IRL has been particularly fraught with misconceptions of both the due diligence in IL generally, and its application to IRL. As the following section shows, much of the scholarship on due diligence in IRL mischaracterises some of the fundamental premises of both.

3.1 *Three Critiques of Due Diligence in International Refugee Law*

Contemporary scholarship on IRL reveals several overarching assumptions that underpin the conception of due diligence within general IL and its application to IRL specifically. While the literature on due diligence within general IL is relatively wide, if not divergent, much of its conventional wisdom proves either too reductive or inapplicable to IRL. This appears to be the source of several presumptions within the literature, which overwhelmingly attempts to apply due diligence standards derived from general IL to IRL, and unsurprisingly concludes that the exercise produces an irreconcilable result.

There are broadly three critiques of due diligence in IRL that emerge from the literature, each asserting that due diligence standards are inapplicable to IRL.[54] The first critique is definitional in nature, though it hinges partly on the refugee definition, and partly on the nature of the 1951 Convention as an instrument of IHRL. It considers that, as due diligence derives from the adjudication of SR, it is inconsistent with the nature of IRL as requiring surrogate protection. As due diligence is relevant in IL only insofar as it informs the determination of SR in certain circumstances, it could only be relevant to the determination of wrongfulness (in the case of IRL, 'persecution') on the part of the State of origin. As IRL solely imposes international obligations on the State of reception, it is an inapplicable standard.

The second critique is temporal in nature, though it derives also from the refugee definition and the conception of the 1951 Convention as providing surrogate protection. It considers due diligence to be "a duty of process, not of result"[55] and accordingly, inappropriate to accommodate the particular challenges of IRL; due diligence being largely retrospective, and IRL being palliative in nature. It is not designed to equip adjudicators with the tools necessary to undertake the injunctive function of assessing prospectively whether State protection is likely to be available – an evaluation of what is likely to be the result on return.[56]

The third critique is conceptual. It posits that irrespective of other considerations, due diligence in any case lacks precision as a legal concept,[57] and that the lack of uniformity of due diligence standards is inevitable because

54 James C. Hathaway, Michelle Foster, *The Law of Refugee Status* (2 edn, CUP 2014) 310.

55 *Id.*, 314.

56 *Id.*, 314–315.

57 *Id.*, 314; Joanna Bourke-Martignoni, 'The History and Development of the Due Diligence Standard in International Law and Its Role in the Protection of Women Against Violence' in Benninger-Budel (ed), *Due Diligence and Its Application to Protect Women from Violence* (2008) 47.

the due diligence standard varies "from one context to another for reasons which essentially relate to the object and purpose of the treaty provision or other rule giving rise to the primary obligation."[58] As a result of this inconsistency, due diligence cannot provide a 'workable standard' in IRL, nor should it in its current form be 'domesticated' in legislation implementing the Convention.[59] The due diligence standard "provides a starting point but it by no means delivers an authoritative response" to questions of SR, due to the number of unsettled aspects of the doctrine,[60] and it is thus inappropriate to "[rely] on a standard designed in the context of state responsibility [...]."[61]

Each of these critiques is predicated on one or more suppositions that are theoretical in nature, or rely on a misattribution or misinterpretation of due diligence and its scope and content in IRL. The following three subsections address each critique in turn.

3.1.1 Due Diligence and the Refugee Definition

The first critique – that due diligence is inapplicable to IRL – is predicated on both a theoretical conception of IRL as providing surrogate protection, and on a narrow interpretation of the scope and content of due diligence in SR. It considers that SR relates only to the assessment of wrongfulness – being in the case of IRL, 'persecution' on the part of the State of origin – which does not form part of the refugee definition. But due diligence in SR is more than the assessment of wrongfulness on the part of a State, and IRL is more than the refugee definition of Article 1(A). The definitional theory of due diligence in IRL is, at its most fundamental, predicated on the surrogacy theory of protection; that the meaning of protection in the 1951 Convention requires the State of reception to provide 'surrogate' protection for the failures of the State of origin in fulfilling its obligations to 'protect' its national.[62]

Hathaway and Foster argue that while due diligence (as it is understood in IHRL) can provide a rich source of guidance in IRL, is not an appropriate standard for assessing the failure of State protection in the refugee definition

58 James Crawford, 'The International Law Commission's Articles on State Responsibility: Introduction, Text and Commentaries' (2002) 82.

59 James C. Hathaway, Michelle Foster, *The Law of Refugee Status* (2 edn, CUP 2014) 315; Michael G. Heyman, 'Protecting Foreign Victims of Domestic Violence: An Analysis of Asylum Regulations' (2008) 12 New York University Journal of Legislation & Public Policy 115, 147.

60 Anne Gallagher, *The International Law of Human Trafficking* (CUP 2010) 247.

61 James C. Hathaway, Michelle Foster, *The Law of Refugee Status* (2 edn, CUP 2014) 315.

62 See generally: James C. Hathaway, Hugo Storey, 'What Is the Meaning of State Protection in Refugee Law – A Debate' (2016) 28(3) International Journal of Refugee Law 480.

for three key reasons, among them that "it is a standard derived from various subsets of international law concerned with ascertaining state responsibility, and for this reason is at odds with the conceptual basis of a palliative regime designed to protect individuals prospectively from a well-founded risk of harm."[63] Similarly, Goodwin-Gill and McAdam presume that the question of due diligence is relevant only to the responsibility of the State of origin and therefore to persecution as it relates to Article 1A of the 1951 Convention. They argue that "the issue of state responsibility for persecution, relevant though it may be in other circumstances, is not part of the refugee definition" and accordingly, SR is not applicable to any assessment of persecution.[64]

> Likewise, where the state is either unable or unwilling to satisfy the standard of due diligence in the provision of protection, the circumstances may equally found an international claim, as provide a basis for fear of persecution within the meaning of the Convention. The correlation is coincidental, however, not normative. The central issue remains that of risk of harm amounting to persecution; the principles and practice of state responsibility can contribute to that assessment, for example, by confirming the level of protection and judicial or other guarantees that may be due under responsibility intent, so be in other may arise, protection. As responsibility not part of considering putative persecution, the refugee definition the availability and/or responsibility provides private groups universal and regional human rights instruments.[65]

Crawley also conflates the surrogacy theory with SR and due diligence, and finds them irreconcilable:

> "[t]here is a difference between a failure of state protection under international refugee law and the notion of state responsibility in human rights law. This is important because the aim of the Refugee Convention is not to hold states responsible but to ensure that effective surrogate protection is available."[66]

---

63 James C. Hathaway, Michelle Foster, *The Law of Refugee Status* (2 edn, CUP 2014) 314.

64 Guy S. Goodwin-Gill, Jane McAdam, *The Refugee in International Law* (3rd edn, OUP 2007) 100. But note that this passage is absent from the 2021 edition.

65 *Id.*, 195.

66 Heaven Crawley, *Refugees and Gender: Law and Process* (Jordan Publishing Limited 2001) 48; See also: Julie Goldscheid, Debra Liebowitz, 'Due Diligence and Gender Violence: Parsing its Power and its Perils' (2015) 48 Cornell Int'l LJ 301, 303.

Though she advocates for the application of due diligence in IRL, Mullally also considers its relevance of due diligence in IRL only in reference to the State of origin:

> [T]he robust approach taken by international and regional bodies, in assessing the adequacy of state protection and the state's positive obligations of due diligence, could usefully inform the practice of refugee law on the availability of state protection and the risks of *refoulement* facing survivors of domestic violence if returned to their countries of origin. If applied in the context of asylum adjudication, the due diligence standard would require much greater scrutiny of states' legislative and policy frameworks on domestic violence and of law enforcement practices on the ground, than has occurred to date. The reasonableness of relocation alternatives would also be open to much greater question.[67]

Though the surrogacy theory enjoys quite substantial support, it suffers from several fundamental deficiencies. Primarily, it is premised on the classification of IRL as inherently of an IHRL character, which in turn relies on the notion that IRL is constructed principally from Articles 1A (definition of the term "refugee") and 33 (prohibition of expulsion or return ("*refoulement*")) of the 1951 Convention, to the exclusion of the 44 remaining articles, and the instruments of IRL that preceded 1951. Although Articles 1A and 33 are indeed the cornerstones of contemporary IRL, the surrogacy theory removes the law of aliens and the law of SR from the sphere of relevance, and hence, disregards the due diligence standards within these systems of law as extraneous to IRL proper.

This presumption is at the core of the perceived 'inappropriateness' of due diligence. This conception of IRL is deficient in one other very fundamental way: in considering that due diligence derives only from the adjudication of SR, it presumes that it is inconsistent with IRL, and therefore does not exist within the 1951 Convention, which requires surrogate protection, and is not concerned with SR. In doing so, it limits the scope of due diligence to the assessment of SR on the part of the *State of origin*, though there is no logical reason to do so. This is an unnecessarily narrow conception of due diligence and it is not supported by law. Due diligence standards may, however, attach

67 Siobhán Mullally, 'Domestic Violence Asylum Claims and Recent Developments in International Human Rights Law: A Progress Narrative?' (2011) 60 International & Comparative Law Quarterly 459, 483.

to any primary obligation of law, being necessary to its proper administration, and as IRL establishes primary obligations *only* of the State of reception, so too do the relevant due diligence standards attach to the conduct of the State of reception in the fulfilment of those obligations.

There is an irony in this. Due diligence as it relates to SR has its origins in the law of aliens, of diplomatic protection, and therefore of those foundations of IRL. The obligation of a State to investigate, prosecute, and punish derived from 'traditional' SR, being relative to the treatment of aliens. Traditional SR obliged the State to demonstrate the exercise of due diligence in the protection of aliens against the injurious acts of nationals; the failure to do so resulting in a denial of justice.[68] Apart from the fact that due diligence standards have developed significantly since that time, and are in no way limited to investigation, prosecution, and punishment, their origins cannot be disregarded. The notion that due diligence derives only from modern SR as a series of secondary rules of IL, and therefore only relevant to the State of origin, is based on both a narrow construction of SR and on the notion that due diligence could only be relevant to Article 1A of the 1951 Convention. By extension, it is based on a conception of due diligence as relative only to SR as the consequences of violations of PIL, that is, relative to secondary rules of IL only. Again, there is no logical reason to draw this conclusion. Due diligence obligations have been incorporated into primary instruments of IL, including the 1951 Convention, as corollary duties of primary obligations. That said, even within IRL-derived instruments, there are variations between essentially parallel primary obligations.

Consider the due diligence standards that attach to the primary rules of the *Convention Governing the Specific Aspects of Refugee Problems in Africa* ("OAU Convention").[69] Despite the fact that the OAU Convention is "the effective regional complement in Africa of the 1951 United Nations Convention on the Status of Refugees,"[70] and though widely considered to be a more inclusive instrument than the 1951 Convention for reasons of its comparatively broader definition of the term 'refugee,' it is the only IRL-derived instrument that makes the reception and settlement of refugees an obligation of conduct, not of result. Despite *non-refoulement* being an obligation of result (Article 2 (3)), Article 2 of the OAU Convention ('asylum') provides that Member States

---

68 See generally: Alfred Verdross, 'Règles internationales concernant le traitement des étrangers' (1931) 37 RCADI.

69 Organization of African Unity, *Convention Governing the Specific Aspects of Refugee Problems in Africa* (10 September 1969) UNTS Vol. 1001, No. 14691.

70 *Id.*, Article VIII(2).

of the OAU "shall use their best endeavours" consistent with their respective legislations to receive refugees and secure their settlement. As an obligation, it exacts as a result the reception and settlement of refugees, but requires only that certain conduct be observed, in stark contrast with the requirements of the 1951 Convention.

Consider also that within the Americas, very few international legal obligations are established by regional instruments, though adherence to principles of regional refugee law is extraordinarily high. The *Cartagena Declaration on Refugees*[71] has no legally binding effect, and yet a vast number of States have incorporated the Cartagena definition of 'refugee' into municipal law, providing refugee status to a great number of people beyond the scope of Article 1(A) of the 1951 Convention.[72]

These examples illustrate that the limitation of the scope and content of due diligence to the assessment of State of origin responsibility is an illogical exercise, as due diligence standards may attach to any primary obligation of law, being necessary to its proper administration.

3.1.2 The Temporal Scope of Due Diligence in IRL

In respect of the second critique – that due diligence is a duty of conduct, not of result, and accordingly, is inappropriate to accommodate the palliative system of IRL – this again limits the relevance and application of due diligence standards based on the conception of IRL as surrogate in nature. While it is true that in general IL, due diligence is relevant to obligations of conduct, and not to obligations of result, this is not the case in IRL. IHRL courts and tribunals have imposed due diligence obligations on States in relation to the administration of obligations of result, as well as obligations of conduct. Contrary to the notion that due diligence is of little use to adjudicators in assessing the likely result of return, the scope of due diligence is far broader in its relevance to IRL than the *non-refoulement* obligation.

Hathaway and Foster claim that, "the due diligence test is simply not designed to accommodate the particular challenges of refugee law both because it is ultimately a duty of process, not of result, and because it is largely

71 *Cartagena Declaration on Refugees, Colloquium on the International Protection of Refugees in Central America, Mexico and Panama* (19–22 November 1984).

72 Brazil, Chile, Colombia, Ecuador, and Peru are among those Latin American States that define 'refugee' in the same terms as the Cartagena Declaration. See: Sophie Capicchiano Young, *Programas de regularización y facilidades administrativas para las personas refugiadas y migrantes de Venezuela Análisis comparativo de ordenamientos jurídicos y buenas prácticas en América Latina y el Caribe* (2022) R4V.

retrospective."[73] For this reason, it is not designed to equip decision-makers with "the tools necessary to undertake the injunctive function of assessing prospectively whether state protection is likely to be available – an evaluation of what is likely to be the result on return."[74]

The 1951 Convention does establish minimum standards of treatment applicable to refugee populations in relation to a number of State obligations. Though commonly referred to collectively as 'minimum standards,' these are in essence obligations of *comparable* treatment, recommending or requiring the Contracting State to guarantee treatment of refugees either *equal to* that of nationals or to aliens generally. If these guarantees are collectively considered to constitute the scope of refugee 'protection,' then protection has the general effect of ensuring non-discrimination. As the principle of non-discrimination is itself an obligation of result, the vast majority of Convention provisions recommend or require a standard of due diligence as a corollary of obligations of result.

Though there are differences in the language used to denote equality of treatment,[75] in their effect, all such provisions require the same level of adherence to the principle of non-discrimination. This is true even where equal treatment provisions permit reservation. Concessions such as these may be interpreted as allowing obligations to apply subjectively, but this is not the case. Though the application of certain provisions might be subjectively *applied* according to the stipulations of the reservation, this would not alter the fact that, in its application, the provision *exacted* an obligation of result, not of conduct. The obligation remains one of result and therefore one of objective SR.

The 'exemption' clauses in the 1951 Convention are examples of this. These include the exemption from reciprocity (Article 7), the exemption from exceptional measures (Article 8), the exemption from paying bond (*cautio judicatum solvi*) (Article 16), and the exemption from certain restrictive employment measures (Article 17). Several states entered reservations relative to the exemption provisions, in particular in respect of exemption from reciprocity

73 *Id.*

74 James C. Hathaway, Michelle Foster, *The Law of Refugee Status* (2 edn, CUP 2014) 314–315

75 Article 4 requires 'treatment at least as favourable' as nationals'; Article 7 requires 'the same treatment'; Article 13 requires 'treatment as favourable as possible and, in any event, not less favourable than that accorded to aliens generally in the same circumstances'; Article 13 requires 'the most favourable treatment accorded to nationals of a foreign country, in the same circumstances.'

(Article 7)[76] and wage-earning employment (Article 17).[77] Though the obligations of exemption are constructed as both positive and negative obligations, they are uniformly obligations of result that require the state to ensure the specific outcome of non-discrimination. While in some cases the effect of reservations was the subjective application of the provision, this did not alter the character of the obligation as one of result. In other words, Contracting States were free to stipulate that the implementation of the rule would take account of economic, social, democratic and security needs, existing or future conventions or agreements with third countries, or existing or future internal laws and regulations, but the obligation continued to require the result of exemption. Similarly, a number of States entered reservations to Article 17 (wage-earning employment), to the effect that the states parties did not consider themselves bound to grant certain refugees automatic exemption for the obligation to obtain a work permit, though the effect of those reservations was not necessarily one of restriction or exclusion from the labour market.

The 1951 Convention also contains several obligations of conduct that do not exact a result, but are binding on States only insofar as they require due regard to be given to the position of refugees in relation to nationals or aliens generally. These are collectively the obligations of 'sympathetic consideration.' There are six such obligations in the 1951 Convention, and of them, three relate to the admission of refugees and the issuance of travel documents, and two concern the participation of the refugee in the labour market.[78]

Article 11 (refugee seamen) requires the State to give sympathetic consideration to the establishment, temporary admission, and issuance of travel documents to refugees serving as crew members. Paragraph 6(3) of Schedule 1 requires Contracting States to give sympathetic consideration to renewing or extending the validity of travel documents or issuing new documents to refugees no longer lawfully resident in their territory who are unable to obtain a travel document from the country of their lawful residence. While Article 28 (travel documents) requires the State to issue travel documents to 'refugees

76 Honduras, Madagascar, Uganda, Finland, Malta, Korea (though Malta and Korea later withdrew reservations to Article 7).

77 Angola, Austria, Chile, Denmark (later partially withdrawn), France, Greece (later withdrawn), Honduras, Ireland, Jamaica, Latvia, Lichtenstein (later withdrawn), Madagascar, Malawi, Mexico, Norway, Moldova, Sierra Leone, Sweden (later withdrawn), Switzerland (later withdrawn) Uganda, the UK, Zambia, and Zimbabwe.

78 The remaining obligation of 'sympathetic consideration' is article 30 (transfer of assets). The Convention does not oblige States parties to allow the transfer of assets, but only to give sympathetic consideration to refugees applying to transfer assets "which are necessary for their resettlement."

lawfully staying in their territory' for the purpose of travel outside their territory, it requires only that the State give 'sympathetic consideration' to the issue of travel documents to refugees in their territory who are unable to obtain a travel document from the country of their lawful residence. Though the language of Article 28 places emphasis on this latter point (that States "shall in particular give sympathetic consideration") this remains an obligation of conduct.

Of the remaining obligations of conduct, two provisions of the Convention permit the limitation or restriction of the refugee's full participation in the labour market. Article 17 (wage-earning employment) requires that sympathetic consideration be given to assimilating the rights of all refugees with regard to wage-earning employment to those of nationals. In particular, this is extended to explicitly include those refugees that entered the territory of the State "pursuant to programmes of labour recruitment or under immigration schemes." Indirectly, Article 24 (labour legislation and social security) is also intended to apply to programmes of labour recruitment and immigration schemes, by requiring the State only to give sympathetic consideration to the extension of labour agreements concluded between States to refugees "so far as possible."

Though these provisions are in striking contrast to the multitude of labour exchanges and labour settlement schemes of the inter-war period which persisted well into the post-war era, they remain obligations of conduct and are subject to corresponding standards of due diligence.

3.1.3 The Perceived Imprecision of Due Diligence

In respect of the third critique – that due diligence lacks precision as a legal concept – this is something of a false problem. It too relies on a misconception of due diligence, both as relevant principally to IHRL, taking a very narrow definition of the term, and as irrelevant to SR because of its imprecise definition. The lack of clarity would indeed complicate matters if there were a single due diligence standard,[79] which formed part of secondary rules of IL, but this is not the case. As Brownlie noted, "[O]bviously no very dogmatic definition would be appropriate, since what is involved is a standard which will vary according to the circumstances."[80] Due diligence forms part of a primary obligation and thus its relevance to secondary rules is much the same as any other

79 Hathaway and Foster refer to 'the due diligence test' in the singular. See: James C. Hathaway, Michelle Foster, *The Law of Refugee Status* (2 edn, CUP 2014) 315.

80 Ian Brownlie, System of the Law of Nations: State Responsibility, Part I (1 edn, OUP 1983); Ian Brownlie, Principles of Public International Law (7th edn, OUP 2008) 438.

element of a primary rule. The assessment of a violation of a primary rule is not altered by the incorporation of due diligence standards. That is, due diligence is as circumstantial to SR as it is to any primary rule of IL.

Though the theory that IRL is *lex specialis* of IHRL has already been mentioned, it is worthy of a short reprise here for one particular reason: this theory is perhaps most starkly undermined by the import of due diligence standards to the predecessor of modern IRL, in that within the law of aliens, one can note the precedents to due diligence applied in modern IHRL in respect of the actions and omissions of the State *vis-à-vis* refugees.[81] Due diligence has played a vital role in the development of IRL from its inception. The imposition of due diligence standards on the State in respect of the protection of aliens has a long and well-established history, and its impact on modern IRL remains critical. This included cases concerning the improper use of weapons against aliens by soldiers, military reserves, or police; cases concerning the consequence of arbitrary arrest of aliens, mistreatment during arrest, custody, prison, or detention for an unreasonable period by administrative authorities; and cases involving the violation, by administrative organs, of contracts, property rights, or of other economic interests covered by the State duty towards aliens.

Hathaway and Foster also warn that due diligence standards are varyingly expressed as 'effective,' 'meaningful,' or 'adequate' protection, adding to the imprecision of the definition. Again, this is to create a problem where there is none. Though the literature certainly tends to differentiate breaches of primary obligations as resulting from "indifference, inefficiency, or outright tolerance"[82] and maintains that breaches may occur variously where the State "facilitates, conditions, accommodates, tolerates, justifies, or excuses"[83] breaches in its obligations (arising either through its own conduct or the conduct of private actors), these distinctions are conceptual rather than legal. They are immaterial to any assessment of due diligence in IRL as the scope of SR is far narrower and more precise.

There is one notable exception. Pisillo-Mazzeschi argues that arbitrators distinguished between the due diligence requirements attached to the State

81 Riccardo Pisillo-Mazzeschi, 'Due Diligence and the International Responsibility of States' (1992) 35 German Yearbook of International Law 9, 23.

82 Michael G. Heyman, 'Protecting Foreign Victims of Domestic Violence: An Analysis of Asylum Regulations' (2008) 12 New York University Journal of Legislation & Public Policy 115, 137; *Minister for Immigration and Multicultural Affairs v. Khawar* [2002] 210 CLR 1, 114.

83 Cecilia Bailliet, 'Persecution in the Home: Applying the Due Diligence Standard to Harmful Traditional Practices within Human Rights and Refugee Law' (2012) 30(1) Nordic Journal of Human Rights 36, 41.

for the failure to protect aliens against the injurious acts of individuals, and its responsibility for injurious acts inflicted by its own organs.[84] In principle, States were not responsible for the damage caused by private citizens in the case of riot, insurrection, or civil war, but this did not extend to cases where States had not sought to *prevent* the injurious acts with the due diligence required by the circumstances.[85] In the case of injury caused by its own organs, the State was responsible as it was in the case of a failure to prevent the injurious acts of private persons. That said, there is little to distinguish the two forms of responsibility when one considers that the principle that underlies both is the failure of due diligence. In the case of private actors, it is a breach of the obligation of conduct in the context of prevention.[86] In the case of a State's organs, it is a breach of the obligation of result in the context of investigation, prosecution, and punishment.[87] In both cases, due diligence was required and a failure to demonstrate it resulted in a denial of justice, resulting in the attribution of the responsibility of the State.

Pisillo-Mazzeschi also asserts that the law of aliens did not accommodate the wrongful acts of States directly, either *intra vires* or *ultra vires*. In relation to the law of aliens, due diligence did not play any role in early cases involving 'direct' injuries against aliens on the part of a State.[88] The reality is not quite so absolute. Numerous claims commissions of the late 19th and early 20th centuries established principles of direct responsibility of States for the acts of soldiers involving the reckless use of arms against aliens.[89] In the case of responsibility arising from the failure to prevent injury, there are many examples of States being held responsible for the acts of revolutionaries.[90] The French-Venezuelan Mixed Commission recognised the principle of responsibility in respect of the local government for damages caused to French subjects by

84 Riccardo Pisillo-Mazzeschi, 'Due Diligence and the International Responsibility of States' (1992) 35 German Yearbook of International Law 9, 23–24.

85 'Résolutions votes par l'institut au cours de sa XXXIVème session: Responsabilité internationale des états a raison des dommages causés sur leur territoire a la personne et aux biens des étrangers' (1927) 33(3) AnnIDI 330, Article 7.

86 See for example: *Sambiaggio case* [1 January 1903] X UNRIAA 499, at [524]; *Thomas H. Youmans (USA) v United States of Mexico* [23 November 1926] IV UNRIAA 110, at [114]; Edwin M. Borchard, 'Important Decisions of the Mixed Claims Commission, United States and Mexico' (1927) 21 AJIL 516, at [521].

87 *Id., Youmans.*

88 *Id.*

89 *Lillie S. Kling (U.S.A.) v United Mexican States* [8 October 1930] IV RIAA 575.

90 John Bassett Moore, *A Digest of International Law, Volume VI* (Government Printing Office 1906) 1723, 1724.

revolutionists.[91] In a similar vein, the Italian-Venezuelan Mixed Commission found that:

> The protection and security of person and property which the Venezuelan Government explicitly guarantees [...] to Italians residing in Venezuela would be a mockery did it not include indemnity for injuries inflicted on Italian subjects by the frequent revolutions, against the abuses of which so far no adequate steps have been taken, either preventive or repressive. From the sole fact that Venezuela does not sufficiently and for long periods protect the persons and property of Italians resident in her territory, and has failed of fulfilling the obligations imposed on her [...], there arises the right to claim compensation for damages.[92]

In the case of injuries arising from the acts of State agents and organs, the US–Mexico Claims Commission provided that:

> Soldiers inflicting injuries or committing wanton destruction or looting always act in disobedience of some rules laid down by superior authority. There could be no liability whatever for such misdeeds if the view were taken that any acts committed by soldiers in contravention of instructions must always be considered as personal acts.[93]

The US–Venezuela Claims Commission also found that requisitions and forced loans exacted from foreigners by the military or administrative authority were not merely abuses, but constituted "crimes which the Government of Venezuela is of its own motion and by the requirements of its internal laws bound to visit upon the offenders without awaiting report or denunciation from the injured parties."[94] The legal rationale for this vicarious responsibility was summarised by Fiore:

> Let us assume that a government has failed to take proper steps to obviate certain disturbances. [...] In these and similar cases justice and equity require that the State be held to an account and compelled to pay the damages.[95]

91 *Sambiaggio case* [1 January 1903] X UNRIAA 499.

92 *Id.*

93 *Thomas H. Youmans (USA) v United States of Mexico* [23 November 1926] IV UNRIAA 110.

94 *Id.*

95 *Sambiaggio case* [1 January 1903] X UNRIAA 499.

Though the attribution of conduct to a State is no longer limited to the acts of agents *ultra vires*, in observing due diligence standards associated with the duty to abstain, the conduct of the State may still be wrongful where the State exercises authority *intra vires* but did not observe the applicable due diligence standard. As these critiques of due diligence in IRL collectively demonstrate, these fundamental elements of due diligence appear to be overlooked. This necessarily leads to the development of theories that are based on erroneous conceptions of due diligence in terms of its origins in general IL, and its application to IRL. As the following section further demonstrates, much of the conditions that underpin the conception of IRL as a system of IHRL overlook fundamental feature of IRL as it incorporates due diligence.

4 Due Diligence in International Human Rights Law: A Harmonising Standard

Though it may be possible to talk in general terms of a singular 'due diligence standard' as an international legal norm – being an obligation to use one's best efforts to prevent harm – this is a theoretical exercise that is largely redundant in reference to the precise work of law or practice, being that the specific content of due diligence obligations varies so widely, to talk of 'a' or 'the' due diligence standard not only simplifies questions of due diligence, but invents a field of international law where there is none – one called 'due diligence in international law.' It divorces due diligence standards from the primary obligations to which they correlate or form part, and amalgamates them into one generalised standard of practice, only to then lament the varied, diverse, unspecific and undefinable field that is 'due diligence in international law.' This is an unnecessary and fruitless exercise.

This appears to be a feature of the resurgence in references to due diligence in IL, both in practice and in scholarship. In Besson's opinion:

> This revival of due diligence may be attributed, to start with, to an increase in the risks of harms, to the diversification of both the sources of these harms and the entities causing them and to the addition of new institutional duty-bearers capable of anticipating or preventing such harms.[96]

96 Samantha Besson, *Due Diligence in International Law* (Brill 2023) 48–49.

By comparison, "earlier publications on due diligence tended to focus on its negative dimension, that is, negligence, and therefore on the issue of fault in the law of international responsibility."[97] This is certainly the case in scholarly critiques of due diligence in IRL, which have focused excessively (and unnecessarily) on questions of fault, negligence, State of origin responsibility, and an international legal norm called 'due diligence in international law.' Many of the questions that arise in critiques of due diligence in IRL are fomented in the conceptualisation of the 1951 Convention as essentially an instrument of IHRL.[98] Though it is undeniable that much of the content of *modern* IRL – the evolving definition of 'refugee,' the content of 'protection,' and the concept of persecution – is attributable in large part to IHRL as a system of enforcement, there is a distinction between IHRL surpassing IRL proper as the primary source of refugee protection, and relying on IHRL to *elaborate* IRL. That said, there is a third possibility that turns on due diligence. Much of the development of due diligence standards in IRL is closely related to IHRL in that it is either misattributed to IHRL where it in fact forms part of the primary obligations of the 1951 Convention, or it is *not* attributed to IHRL at all, where it *is* in fact attributable.

---

97 *Id.*, 50, citing: P.A. Zannas, *La responsabilité internationale des États pour des actes de negligence* (1952); Riccardo Pisillo Mazzeschi, 'Le chemin étrange de la due diligence: d'un concept mystérieux à un concept surévalué' in SFDI (ed), *Le standard de due diligence et la responsabilité internationale: Journée d'études franco-italienne du Mans* (2018) 323, 323–324, 326.

98 James C. Hathaway, *The Rights of Refugees under International Law* (CUP 2010) 5; Alice Edwards, 'Human Rights, Refugees and the Right "to Enjoy" Asylum' (2005) 17 IJRL 306; Brian Gorlick, 'Human Rights and Refugees: Enhancing Protection through International Human Rights Law' (2000) 69 Nordic Journal of International Law 122; Frances Nicholson, Patrick Twomey, 'Introduction' in Frances Nicholson and Patrick Twomey (eds), *Refugee Rights and Realities: Evolving International Concepts and Regimes* (1999) 2; Tom Clark, François Crépeau, 'Mainstreaming Refugee Rights. The 1951 Refugee Convention and International Human Rights Law' (1999) 17(4) Netherlands Quarterly of Human Rights 391; A.C. Helton, 'Refugees and Human Rights' (1993) 15 In Defense of the Alien 142, 146–147; Ivor C. Jackson, 'The 1951 Convention Relating to the Status of Refugees: A Universal Basis for Protection' (1991) 3(3) IJRL 403, 404. Others have argued for a more nuanced conception of that relationship. See, for example: Vincent Chetail, 'Are Refugee Rights Human Rights? An Unorthodox Questioning of the Relations between Refugee Law and Human Rights Law' in Rubio-Marín (ed), *Human Rights and Immigration* (OUP 2014) 19; Emma Haddad, 'Refugee Protection: A Clash of Values' (2003) 7(3) International Journal of Human Rights 1; Patricia Tuitt, 'Human Rights and Refugees' (1997) 1(2) International Journal of Human Rights 66; Kate Jastram, 'Economic Harm as a Basis for Refugee Status and the Application of Human Rights Law to the Interpretation of Economic Persecution' in James C. Simeon (ed), *Critical Issues in International Refugee Law: Strategies Toward Interpretative Harmony* (2010) 143.

Irrespective of the scope or content of obligations established by primary instruments of IRL, the vast majority of adjudication occurs internationally through IHRL courts and tribunals, and domestically through special immigration courts and tribunals. Within the international sphere, this is perhaps the single greatest contribution of IHRL to IRL. As the 1951 Convention did not establish any judicial mechanism, and endowed the High Commissioner only with supervisory authority over the application of the Convention, the adjudicators of refugee matters within IL are limited to IHRL bodies that give judicial expression to rules of IRL where they coincide with a relative IHRL instrument. This is perhaps most apparent in the assessment of prior knowledge.

4.1 *Risk, Fault, and the Establishment of Prior Knowledge*

The jurisprudence of IHRL has contributed in two significant ways to the development of due diligence standards applicable to IRL matters. First, by imposing on States primary responsibility for the construction of both objective and subjective international standard of conduct through specific due diligence standards. Second (and perhaps more critically to this article) by developing the conception of fault that is particular in its application to IRL matters. That is, fault did not form any part of the adjudication of IRL until the application of IHRL as the primary legal means of adjudication of SR. This is perhaps most notable in the collective IHRL jurisprudence on matters of detention, externalisation, non-entrée policies, and *non-refoulement*. However, subjective responsibility is not an invention of IHRL.

In Grotian theory, subjective responsibility required that a psychological element form part of the attribution of wrongfulness. Liability then arose from fault. By comparison, objective responsibility arises from a wrongful action or omission alone, without regard to fault as a precondition. Both theories of responsibility have attracted prominent adherents, but as Brownlie and Barnidge both argued, irrespective of whether a responsibility regime is defined by subjective and objective theory, both regimes are concerned with "the extent to which a party can be held accountable for its acts or omissions."[99] Barnidge considered that in fact, theories of subjective and objective responsibility describe a common phenomenon,[100] and that Article 2 of the ARSIWA (elements of an internationally wrongful act of a State) seems to support the conclusion that the legal consequences of a State's actions and omis-

99 Robert Barnidge, 'The Due Diligence Principle under International Law' (2006) 8(1) ICLR 81, 84–85.

100 *Id.*, 83.

sions are, or at least should be, the same.[101] Similarly, Tzevelekos considers the distinct points and classifications between directly attributable wrongfulness and fault on the part of the State are in fact complementary, operating circuitously, and opening the door for concurrent responsibility for States involved in the same commission of wrongfulness.[102] Elaborating on these premises, Olleson posits that the type of conduct required by the primary obligation may reliably indicate the responsibility regime; affirmative State action tends to attract objective responsibility, while a State's failure to act, or an omission, in most cases triggers subjective responsibility.[103] The distinction, as Longobordo notes, is that different primary obligations require different standards of care.[104]

Much of the differentiation in the due diligence standards applicable in IL turns on the conception of fault-based responsibility within the particular field. There is some divergence within scholarship on the meaning of fault in IL. Pisillo Mazzeschi considers that fault focuses on the underlying rules within a regime of responsibility for breach of due diligence obligations.[105] He observes that the role of fault is not certain, in that it is not clear "whether State responsibility in principle is contingent upon the existence of fault or, vice versa, upon the sole existence of conduct attributable to the State and contrary to an international obligation."[106] The answer would have a profound impact on regimes of international responsibility, as "[i]n the first case we would have in general international law a unitary regime of fault responsibility, and in the second case a unitary regime of objective responsibility."[107] Cassese described fault in the same binary terms with reference to intent or recklessness.[108]

101 *Id.*, 90.

102 Vassilis Tzevelekos, 'Reconstructing the Effective Control Criterion in Extraterrestrial Human Rights Breaches: Direct attribution of Wrongfulness, Due Diligence, and Concurrent Responsibility' (2014) 36 Mich J Int'l L 129, 132.

103 James Crawford, Simon Olleson, 'The Nature and Forms of International Responsibility' in Malcolm D. Evans (ed), *International Law* (OUP 2003) 443.

104 Marco Longobardo, 'The Relevance of the Concept of Due Diligence for International Humanitarian Law' (2019) 37(1) Wis Int'l LJ 44, 52.

105 Riccardo Pisillo-Mazzeschi, 'Forms of International Responsibility for Environmental Harm' in Francesco Francioni and Tullio Scovazzi (eds), *International Responsibility for Environmental Harm* (1991) 15, 16.

106 Riccardo Pisillo-Mazzeschi, 'Due Diligence and the International Responsibility of States' (1992) 35 German Yearbook of International Law 9.

107 *Id.*

108 Antonio Cassese, *International Law* (2nd edn, OUP 2005) 250–251.

Due diligence in IRL does not sit comfortably within the classic subjective/objective conception of a responsibility regime. In IRL, due diligence standards do not require any specific determination of intent, or for that matter, of recklessness or negligence. Rather, the primary due diligence standard – the establishment of constructive knowledge – is formulated as if it denoted fault-based responsibility, and yet it requires objective fulfilment. Again, this is not simply a theoretical exercise. The consequence of this regime of SR is that the corresponding regime of proof shifts from the individual to the State, or from plaintiff to defendant. In a regime of subjective responsibility, the victim of the presumed wrongful act must prove the fault of the offending actor. In a regime of objective responsibility, responsibility arises as a sole consequence of conduct contrary to an obligation.[109] This is a critical distinction in the responsibility regime that has developed principally in IHRL as it relates to IRL.

The rationale for this complex regime of SR may lie in the applicable liability. As IRL as it is incorporated into IHRL does not require a determination of knowledge in fact – that is, a specific determination of recklessness or negligence – but rather a determination of constructive knowledge, the responsibility regime establishes strict liability. As the obligation is one of result, not of conduct, the failure to fulfil the requirements results in objective responsibility; that is, strict liability. Strict liability, or liability without fault, has thus been applied in reference to two forms of causal liability: objective responsibility in customary law and liability for injurious consequences. This has led to a critical development in municipal law and practice. As strict liability precludes defences, States are forced to exert more control over the organs of their apparatus than under a fault-based responsibility regime.[110] But the exertion of control over elements of States' refugee systems improved by the imposition of strict liability where the State's capacity to execute its due diligence requirements is hindered.[111] In that sense, capacity in the due diligence standards applicable to IRL is the equivalent of reasonableness in the due diligence standards of general IL. That said, far from implying a discretionary standard, variation of due diligence standards on account of capacity is in effect non-existent in IRL. A further complication of due diligence in IRL is that it relies on an assessment of risk.

Ollino has referred to questions of risk and their relevance to due diligence in international law in the following terms: "The first condition for triggering a

109 Riccardo Pisillo-Mazzeschi, 'Due Diligence and the International Responsibility of States' (1992) 35 German Yearbook of International Law 9.

110 Malcolm N. Shaw, *International Law* (5th edn, CUP 2003) 700.

111 *M.S.S. v Belgium and Greece* [21 January 2011] ECtHR (App No 30696/09).

duty to act with diligence is that the State holds power over the source of risk (PSR) linked to the due diligence primary rule,"[112] being a "capacity or ability to produce some effects over this source."[113] By extension:

> If a State has no PSR, the State lacks the capacity to affect the situation that the primary rule of due diligence intends to change or manage. Hence, PSR informs States' capacity to affect a certain outcome. Capacity to affect creates possibility for the State to act.[114]

In the case of IRL, the risk over which a State holds power is *refoulement.* However, the State is not adjudged on its power over the source of risk. Instead, the process of attribution requires an evaluation of knowledge. This is bifurcated into an assessment of actual knowledge or an obligation to have acquired such knowledge. In both cases, a due diligence standard attaches to the primary obligation. In the case of the former, where the State has actual knowledge of a risk to the individual upon his or her *refoulement*, the State is required to refrain from both *refoulement* to the State or origin, and from removing the individual to a third State where there is a risk of *refoulement.* In the case of the latter, the State is required to have exercised due diligence in the acquisition of knowledge regarding the conditions in the State of origin that would put the asylum seekers at risk in violation of the applicable law. Capacity does not form any part of evaluation in either case. The tests of attribution in IRL do not rely on a State's capacity to prevent or manage risk *per se*, but in the possession of knowledge necessary to prevent and manage the risk. Attribution relies solely on control, and for that reason, jurisdiction. That is, there is no *requirement* to establish fault, and yet, in all cases, it is uniformly assessed.

4.2 *State Responsibility, Attribution, and Differing Regimes of Proof*

Properly understood, the doctrine of attribution in international law serves the purpose of allocating responsibility to the State for the consequences of certain wrongful acts or omissions of its organs and officials. It also defines the sphere of private or non-State conduct for which the State bears no responsi-

112 Alice Ollino, *Due Diligence Obligations in International Law* (CUP 2022) 133.

113 *Id.*, 134.

114 *Id.*

bility.[115] As discussed, in general IL, it is relatively common for integral due diligence to be equated with objective responsibility, and corollary due diligence with subjective responsibility. Where fault is considered a constituent element of attribution, the nature of SR is widely regarded to be necessarily subjective. This is not the case in IRL. As case law and State practice demonstrate, fault commonly forms part of the attribution of wrongfulness, and yet, due diligence in IRL remains integral – not corollary – to a primary obligation. The failure to fulfil a primary obligation of IRL is treated simultaneously as engaging subjective responsibility and requiring due diligence.

The distinction between these two conceptions is not simply theoretical, where one is an obligation to succeed, and the other is an obligation to make every effort. It also results in two distinct regimes of proof, which has very practical implications. As the regime of proof required to demonstrate the fulfilment of an outcome is distinct from that necessary to prove a sufficient effort, the distinction turns mainly on the fact that the two categories of obligation are conditioned by different risks.[116] Where the primary rule anticipates a high degree of risk (risk meaning 'probability' rather than 'danger') it will in most cases establish an obligation of result, and in turn require a regime of proof conditioned by an elevated risk. IRL is no exception to this. It comprises obligations of result and obligations of conduct, and requires different regimes of proof that are conditioned by varied levels of risk. The result is that there are broadly two corresponding responsibility regimes within IRL – one that flows from obligations of low-risk conduct, and one that flows from obligations of high-risk result. Within those regimes of responsibility, the role of due diligence serves two different purposes, depending on the category of legal obligation. This is expressed in varying tests of attribution, conceptions of fault, and levels of liability, but these features are not static. They have been, and continue to be subject to fluctuation, affected by State practice and judicial opinion, often advocating opposing standards. Variations to the content of primary rules have often depended on the re-categorisation of obligation – whether the rule is in fact one of conduct or one of result. In turn, this has depended in large part on the perception of risk. Where standards have shifted, so too has the applicable regime of proof. This might be understood

115 Gordon Christenson, 'The Doctrine of Attribution on State Responsibility' in Richard B. Lillich (ed), *International Law of State Responsibility for Injuries to Aliens* (Virginia 1983) 321.

116 Riccardo Pisillo-Mazzeschi, 'Due Diligence and the International Responsibility of States' (1992) 35 German Yearbook of International Law 9, 48; Maria Monnheimer, *Due Diligence Obligations in International Human Rights Law* (CUP 2021) 205.

as an application of diligence ('dis-ligentia') in the literal sense, requiring first an assessment of fault to determine negligence ('neg-ligentia').[117]

The role of fault within the law of SR has been just as controversial as that of the law of aliens. Just as the ILC excluded injuries to aliens and due diligence from the scope of the ARSIWA, so too did it exclude the concept of fault (*culpa*) from the final text.[118] It was perceived to restrict the effect of the ARSIWA to require a psychological element, which would preclude wrongfulness where a breach had occurred but no *culpa* could be established.[119] Although SR in general IL remains predicated on objective responsibility,[120] and while fault is not ordinarily required on the part of the State, States are free in the establishment of primary rules to introduce such a requirement.[121] As García Amador wrote, the rule of 'due diligence' is the expression *par excellence* of the theory of fault.[122] As a result, "different forms of secondary obligations requiring fault in some cases but not in others do not exist."[123]

It has been argued that in cases of obligations of conduct, SR may entail subjective elements in the form of negligence on behalf of State officials.[124] The international crime of genocide is an illustrative example – a State must have had "the capacity to influence effectively the action of persons likely to

117 Samantha Besson, *Due Diligence in International Law* (Brill 2023) 21; Giulio Bartolini, 'The Historical Roots of the Due Diligence Standard' in Heike Krieger, Anne Peters and Leonhard Kreuzer (eds), *Due Diligence in the International Legal Order* (OUP 2020) 23.

118 International Law Commission, *Second report on State responsibility, by Mr. Gaetano Arangio-Ruiz, Special Rapporteur* (22 July 1989) (A/CN.4/425 and Add. 1) 162–188.

119 As Crawford noted, throughout the period in which the Draft Articles were before the ILC, no government argued in favour of the specification of a general requirement of fault as a prerequisite to state responsibility. See: James Crawford, *State Responsibility: The General Part* (CUP 2013) 60; International Law Commission, *First report on State responsibility, by Mr. James Crawford, Special Rapporteur* (12 August 1998) (A/CN.4/490) 28.

120 *Id.*, Crawford, *State Responsibility*, 61.

121 *Id.*, at 38; International Law Commission, *Report of the International Law Commission to the General Assembly* (10 August 2001) (A/56/10); Jan Arno Hessbruegge, 'The Historical Development of the Doctrines of Attribution and Due Diligence in International Law' (2004) 36 NYUJIntlL&Pol 265, 270.

122 ILC, *supra* note 29, at 122.

123 *Id.*, 98.

124 *Id.*, 96, citing Charles de Visscher, *La responsabilité des États* (Bibliotheca Visseriana 1924) 92; Manuel R. García-Mora, *International Responsibility for Hostile Acts of Private Persons against Foreign States* (Martinus Nijhoff 1962); International Law Commission, *Draft articles on Responsibility of States for Internationally Wrongful Acts, with Commentaries*2001) II (PART II) Yearbook of the International Law Commission, 34.

commit, or already committing, genocide."[125] This is also the case with the principle of *non-refoulement*. Though generally, fault plays a very marginal role in IL, and then only in the State's breach of certain obligations to prevent,[126] as due diligence standards vary from one context to another,[127] there is no reason why the failure to observe a due diligence standard as part of an obligation of result (such as the due diligence standard 'to know or ought to have known') should not culminate in the subjective responsibility of a State. The ARWISA lays down no general rule in that regard, and as Barnidge noted, the legal consequences may be the same.[128]

Courts have imposed due diligence standards beyond those provided in legislation, and created a number of further obligations, beyond those to which the State has explicitly consented to be bound. For example, the due diligence requirement to consider credible information in the public domain regarding States of origin is a due diligence standard developed in response to the selective evidence compiled by certain States in the designation of another as a 'safe country of origin.'

As described, the development of due diligence standards is often attributed to IHRL due to the deliberation of IRL matters by IHRL courts and tribunals. While the interpretative value of international (and in many cases, municipal) human rights law in the administration of the 1951 Convention cannot be overstated, much of the development of due diligence standards in IRL is misattributed to IHRL where it in fact forms part of the primary obligations of the 1951 Convention, other primary instruments of IRL, and the law of aliens in early SR.

---

125 *Case Concerning Application of the Convention on the Prevention and Punishment of the Crime of Genocide* (*Bosnia and Herzegovina v Serbia and Montenegro*) [2007] ICJ Rep 47, at [430]. Though the court issued the proviso that "[t]he decision of the Court does not, in this case, purport to establish a general jurisprudence applicable to all cases where a treaty instrument, or other binding legal norm, includes an obligation for States to prevent certain acts." At [429].

126 Ian Brownlie, *System of the Law of Nations: State Responsibility, Part I* (1 edn, OUP 1983); Ian Brownlie, *Principles of Public International Law* (7th edn, OUP 2008) 37–49. See also: Ian Brownlie, *Principles of Public International Law* (4th edn, OUP 1990) 436 *et seq.*

127 International Law Commission, *Draft articles on Responsibility of States for Internationally Wrongful Acts, with Commentaries*2001) II (part II) Yearbook of the International Law Commission, 34.

128 Robert Barnidge, 'The Due Diligence Principle under International Law' (2006) 8(1) ICLR 81.

5 Conclusion

In international law, the concept of due diligence often hinges on whether it is understood as a standard of conduct required to fulfil an obligation or as a process for managing risk. This distinction can be framed as the difference between the expected standards of State conduct and the tests of attribution applied in litigation. In the execution of all international obligations, States are required to meet certain standards of conduct, while judicial bodies evaluate these actions in relation to specific risks. As noted in the introduction, the principles of responsibility in IL are as varied as they are fundamental, with each system of IL developing its own regime of responsibility tailored to its specific context. These regimes are differentiated by the scope and content of due diligence requirements, which vary in terms of objectivity, subjectivity, flexibility, and limitation. At their core, these differences reflect the tension between fault-based and risk-based responsibility, and the standards they impose on States.

In IRL, due diligence standards are often conceptualised in terms of protection and implementation, rather than as strict legal standards. This has led to critiques of due diligence in IRL, many of which are based on misconceptions. A recurring theme in these critiques is the tendency to compare due diligence in IRL to its application in other areas of international law, without fully accounting for the unique features of IRL.

The first critique argues that due diligence is inapplicable to IRL, based on the view of IRL as a system of surrogate protection. This critique assumes that due diligence standards are absent from the 1951 Convention and other primary sources of IRL, attributing them instead to other legal systems. The second critique claims that due diligence is inappropriate for IRL's palliative system, viewing IRL as providing surrogate protection and due diligence standards as relating only to duties of conduct, not duties of result. While this may hold true in general IL, due diligence standards in IRL often impose obligations of result, particularly in relation to the principle of non-discrimination, which is central to the 1951 Convention. The third critique asserts that due diligence lacks precision as a legal concept. However, this critique conflates due diligence with broader notions of effective protection or implementation, rather than recognising it as a distinct legal standard. In reality, due diligence in IRL is an integral part of its primary obligations, shaping the relationship between primary and secondary rules.

The notion that due diligence sits on the boundaries between law, morality, and politics can be addressed by understanding it as a concept fundamentally concerned with the administration of law. It is not a vague or moralistic notion but a clear and objective element of fulfilling a primary obligation. Challenges arise when attempts are made to impose a uniform standard of due diligence across all areas of international law, an exercise that is both illogical and unproductive. As the International Law Association's Study Group on Due Diligence has noted, the separation of procedural and substantive obligations complicates the application of due diligence, but in the context of IRL, these distinctions have minimal practical impact.

These common theses on due diligence in IRL often stem from a conflation of IRL with IHRL. While IHRL has undoubtedly contributed to the development of due diligence standards in IRL, it is incorrect to attribute these standards solely to IHRL. Many due diligence obligations are rooted in the primary obligations of the 1951 Convention. That said, in the absence of inter-State attribution of SR, the scope and content of IRL's primary rules are often adjudicated internationally under IHRL and domestically under immigration, constitutional, and human rights laws. This interplay highlights the significant contribution of IHRL to IRL, particularly in enforcing due diligence standards.

Despite a history of minimisation, limitation, and qualification of international obligations, due diligence standards nonetheless continue to provide a unifying framework of legal norms across jurisdictions. These standards clarify the scope and content of international obligations established by the 1951 Convention. While IHRL has played a crucial role in shaping modern IRL, it has not superseded IRL in relevance or utility. The role of IHRL has been to reinforce existing legal requirements of IRL, and to provide a complementary system of enforcement. IHRL has inherited a strong tradition of due diligence, particularly in relation to the treatment of foreign nationals, but it does not follow that due diligence standards in IRL are entirely attributable to IHRL. Rather, IHRL has provided a judicial framework for expressing these standards, enhancing their application in refugee matters.

This chapter demonstrates that due diligence standards in IRL are integral to its primary obligations, providing a unifying system of international conduct. These standards are essential not only for protecting refugees but also for countering State efforts to erode the minimum thresholds of acceptable conduct. In the absence of a robust inter-State system of SR, due diligence standards across municipal and regional jurisdictions ensure that States meet their obligations under the 1951 Convention, thereby strengthening the foundation of IRL.

The content of due diligence standards must be determined on a case-by-case basis, with reference to a specific obligation, and this variability is reflected in the tests of attribution applied across legal systems. Broadly, legal obligations fall into two categories: obligations of result, which require a specific outcome, and obligations of conduct, which require a specific action regardless of outcome. Similarly, due diligence can be understood as either an integral part of a primary obligation or a corollary duty. In IRL, jurisprudence and State practice tend to favour the former, treating due diligence as inseparable from primary obligations.

This preference can be explained by the reactive nature of IRL, concerned as it is with State conduct after the fact, rather than on preventive measures. The reactive context in which IRL is engaged necessitates a higher standard of due diligence, tailored to the specific challenges of refugee protection. While general IL often treats due diligence as a corollary duty, IRL treats it as indivisible from primary obligations. This distinction reflects the unique nature of IRL, which operates in a reactive environment and requires States to meet specific standards of conduct.

Due diligence in IRL is not a vague or moralistic concept but a clear and objective legal standard. It is essential for ensuring non-discrimination, effective protection, and the fulfilment of State obligations under the 1951 Convention. While IHRL has influenced the development of due diligence standards, they remain rooted in the primary obligations of IRL. By affirming the integral role of due diligence, this chapter underscores its importance in safeguarding refugee rights and strengthening the international legal order.

Conclusion: The Legal Nature of What Remains

The intention of this book was to provide a legal rationale for the absence of clear instances of SR in IRL. Being premised on that absence, it did not require the location of law that was overlooked or omitted but inquired into the circumstances that permitted such an absence to exist. That inquiry produced a rationale that is as political as it is legal. This was perhaps a foreseeable conclusion. In the development of IL, those terms are less binary than they are complementary, and have proven to be so in the inter-State enforcement of IRL. As Jessup noted, "[t]he history of the development of international law on the responsibility of States for injuries to aliens is thus an aspect of the history of 'imperialism,' or 'dollar diplomacy.'"[1] Concurring with Dunn, Jessup wrote, "[t]he function of the law of responsibility of States for injuries to aliens, in terms of the modernization of international law, is to provide, in the general world interest, adequate protection for the stranger, to the end that travel, trade, and intercourse may be facilitated."[2] As this book has demonstrated, the protection of the stranger has been the subject of a complex, controversial, and highly politicised history, concerned principally with travel, trade, and intercourse. This has been made all the more fraught by the introduction of the refugee as an anomalous actor in early IL, and by the resolution of the 'refugee problem' subject to the existing legal framework and competing political ambitions.

As this book was primarily concerned with an analysis of the factors that resulted in such an absence, as a consequence, the conclusion to that analysis must present a response to those questions posed in the introduction on the legal nature of what remains; that is, whether the international legal obligations of IRL can be said to exist in the absence of a 'necessary corollary' in SR,[3] or whether the 1951 Convention is of legal relevance only insofar as it provides principles of IL that are applied in domestic immigration law and regional human rights law. The continued relevance of SR in contemporary IL was the question posed by former Special Rapporteur, García Amador, in 1958:

1 Philip C. Jessup, *A Modern Law of Nations* (Archon Books 1968) 95–96, 105.

2 *Id.*, citing: F.S. Dunn, *The Protection of Nationals: A Study in The Application of International Law* (The Johns Hopkins Press 1932).

3 Charles de Visscher, *La responsabilité des États* (Bibliotheca Visseriana 1924); Alain Pellet, 'The Definition of Responsibility in International Law' in Crawford and others (eds), *The Law of International Responsibility* (OUP 2010) 3.

 | DOI:10.1163/9789004722835_010

> Perhaps because of the existence and influence of extraneous factors which are not always compatible with the law, artificial legal concepts and principles have been evolved which often appear markedly incongruent. [...] [T]he question to be considered now is what validity can continue to be attached to some of those concepts and principles in contemporary international law.[4]

Of course, the most significant development in post-war IL is the abandonment of a strict doctrine that conceived of IL as a system that existed only between States and the recognition of the individual as a subject of IL. Jessup was among the first to address it when he wrote of SR for injuries to aliens in light of two weaknesses in traditional international legal doctrine: the conception of the individual as merely an object, rather than a subject of IL, and the notion that IL was concluded on a bilateral basis, to the exclusion of a "community interest."[5] This question was addressed in the introduction and though it was outside the scope of this book to inquire into the enforcement of individual rights and interests arising from IRL, it must of course be acknowledged that (in most cases) the refugee has legal recourse against the State for violations of rights and interests arising from IRL, though these are overwhelmingly litigated with reference to municipal and regional law, rather than IL proper. This book was limited to an inquiry into IL as it exists between States, as an original contribution to the literature. In furtherance of that original contribution, Chapter 1 analysed the development and application of the law of SR, from its inception to its codification, and its evolving relevance to the individual alien as an object of IL. It examined the conflicting development of IL governing SR for injuries to aliens and SR as general secondary rules of IL. It argued that the latter was not only subject to political interests, but that it developed in a manner akin to what the ILC Rapporteur of the Committee on the Progressive Development of International Law and its Codification described in his final report:

> [F]or the codification of international law, the Committee recognized that no clear-cut distinction between the formulation of the law as it is and the law as it *ought to be* could be rigidly maintained in practice. [...] It was pointed out that in any work of codification, the codifier inevita-

4 F.V. García Amador, 'State Responsibility: Some New Problems' (1958) 94 RDCADI 367, 370.

5 Phillip Jessup, 'Responsibility of States for Injuries to Individuals' (1946) 46(6) Colum L Rev 903.

> bly has to fill in gaps, and amend the law in the light of new developments.[6]

It concluded that despite the law of aliens being "one of the most highly developed branches of that law,"[7] the codification of SR not only drew from sources extraneous to the clear and consistent existing law and practice relating to injuries to aliens, but that it did so in order to exclude the law of aliens in the interests of what 'ought to be,' and that those same interests that steered the codification of SR also played a significant role in the eventual development of SR as it applied to the refugee in burgeoning IRL.

Chapter 2 analysed the first international responses to refugee crises under the auspices of the LoN. It considered the unique circumstances that made the refugee an exception in IL, requiring a novel understanding of the law of refugee protection. It argued that these circumstances engendered concern among States regarding the assumption of international obligations, and that consequently, a cautious approach was taken in the theorisation and application of SR in early IRL, resulting in the division of obligations assigned to different actors, including refugees themselves. Chapter 2 concluded that the evolving priorities of States in resolving refugee crises led to the development of critical solutions including employment, repatriation, and colonisation, and that these legal foundations informed subsequent developments in refugee protection.

Chapter 3 explored the significance of the 'Jewish refugee problem' in solidifying key principles in the treatment of refugee protection within IRL. It contended that, similar to previous crises, the response to the Jewish refugee crisis was largely driven by Anglo-American interests in the minimisation of the scope and content of international obligations. It argued that both the US and the UK were able to maintain control over the continuing development of IRL by retaining administrative and legal obligations and delegating financial obligations to private charitable organisations and refugees themselves. Concurrently, Western States continued implementing strict and inflexible immigration laws domestically, while insisting on the assumption of international obligations by States of the 'New World,' and to a lesser extent, Africa, setting the stage for the ongoing friction between the Global North and the

6 UN Secretary-General, *Survey of International Law in Relation to the Work of Codification of the International Law Commission: Preparatory work within the purview of article 18, paragraph 1, of the of the International Law Commission – Memorandum submitted by the Secretary-General* (1949) (A/CN.4/1/Rev.1). Emphasis added 4.

7 *Id.*, 904.

Global South in what would eventually become known as 'burden-sharing.' Chapter 3 concluded that, akin to previous refugee crises, Western States favoured repatriation and resettlement in third States as solutions to the Jewish refugee 'problem,' and considered the assumption of international obligations for refugee resettlement in terms of labour markets and economic stability. The financial benefits derived from refugees contributing to national economies were weighed against the costs of resettlement and the potential burden on public resources. Consequently, preference was given to single men, resulting in the emergence of a 'hard core' of refugees who could not be resettled or repatriated.

Chapter 4 considered the contributions and innovations of the 1951 Convention. It argued that, though the 1951 Convention did not depart substantially from previous Arrangements and pre-1951 Conventions, the innovations of the Convention were remarkable, among them, the rejection of the presumption that the relationship between State and subject had been definitively severed, in favour of the presumption that the nationality of the refugee endured, irrespective of his status as such. This approach recognised that the State of reception's assumption of diplomatic protection did not sever the refugee's ties to their State of origin, thereby linking the two States in a manner similar to the law of aliens, where nationality and alienage created a relationship between the State of origin and the host State. This innovation was foundational to the development of modern IRL and the theorisation of SR within it, marking a significant shift in the legal framework for refugee protection. Its conclusions were twofold: that Articles 7 and 8 support a reading of the 1951 Convention as extending a modified form of diplomatic protection to refugees, which obliged States of reception to assume the role of provider of diplomatic protection, but distinguished norms of traditional diplomatic protection from any question of nationality, in contrast to all preceding instruments; and that the unintended consequence of this has been the inclusion of refugees in measures used by States against others in the enforcement of immigration control, despite those measures being overwhelmingly abusive exercises of power and unlawful in IL.

Chapter 5 considered the enduring legacy of the 'aid and development' era of international refugee policy. It argued that, as the immediate post-war era of multilateralism drew to a close, the developments of IRL were relatively few and were in any case, quite inconsequential. This changed rapidly with the destabilisation of multiple regions across Africa, and later Indo-China. In response, the international conference was revived as a forum for the coordination of responses to emerging refugee questions, and much like the international conferences of previous decades, the policies that emerged from the conferences of the aid and development era supported the objectives of Western States in further dividing and assigning novel international obligations for the management of refugee crises. In particular, the era permitted the reinforcement of temporary protection in encampment settings, the limitation of Convention entitlements that would accompany the recognition of refugee status, and the invention of first State and State of origin obligations. These all permitted Western States to position themselves as donor States, financing the containment of refugee populations through the bartering system enabled by the aid and development agenda.

Chapter 6 considered the extraterritorial actions of States in terms of their underlying legal rationale rather than their practical consequences. In particular, the chapter analysed the utilisation of jurisdiction as a means to disrupt the legal relationship between a State and a refugee, and proposed that certain legal trends relative to immigration control can be classified in three iterations based on their use of jurisdiction to limit SR. It concluded that collectively, these iterations have in turn created a 'receding line of jurisdiction;' progressively minimising the circumstances that trigger the international obligations of the 1951 Convention. It argued that the interpretation of jurisdiction in municipal and regional law relative to refugees has further deepened the division of international obligations between wealthy Western States and developing Southern States, allowing the former to position themselves as exclusively States of resettlement, while the latter bear the disproportionate burden of refugee reception and maintenance.

Chapter 7 argued that the application of due diligence standards to municipal and regional laws derived from IRL do not require fault on the part of State authorities to form any part of the evaluation of liability, but rather support a legal framework imposing strict liability, in accordance with fundamental principles of SR. It argued that municipal and regional laws relative to refugees reflect early international legal doctrine, which recognised the extraneous nature of fault as a criterion for the attribution of wrongfulness. Chapter 7 concluded that although fault (and to a lesser extent, risk) were inferred at various points throughout history where discussion turned to SR for injuries to aliens and later, in relation to IRL, these suggestions did not materialise in law. Rather, the applicable standards of due diligence clearly demonstrate a preference for intent, and reject fault as the basis of SR as it applies to individuals as subjects of IL.

In summarising these chapters, there are a number of critical observations to make. First, the theory that in constructing IRL, the 'international community' (however the term might be defined) essentially built a *lex specialis* from the foundations up could not be further from the truth. The international response to the refugee crises of the 20th century – from the denationalisation of Russians and Armenians, to the breakup of former Yugoslavia – were formed from existing legal precepts, and from political and economic priorities of States. As it was then, so it continues to be: The protection of refugees seldom drives the development and implementation of IRL. This is not a recent deviation from a previous commitment or conviction of the 'international community' to respect and uphold the primacy of refugee protection. Rather, the theorisation and application of IRL has commonly been the reflexive expression of competing State priorities, and as such, does not frequently respond to refugee crises by prioritising the protection of refugees.

Goodwin-Gill notes that the drafting history of the 1951 Convention reveals:

> The two specific objectives of protection were to prevent forcible repatriation and to facilitate repatriation when it was both possible and desired. For if the right to seek asylum was a human right, its corollary was that no refugee could be deprived of the right to return to his or her own country.[8]

Hathaway also considers that the first generation of refugee accords were "designed by European States for the protection of European refugees" and that "the relative conceptual and administrative generosity of these arrangements was possible because they codified a cultural compact of long standing [...]." In his opinion, these instruments were intended "to regularise and coordinate a moral duty of reciprocal protection already recognised by [European states]."[9] In reality, the international instruments that preceded the 1951 Convention served the same national self-interests and accounted for the same national concerns as those that later informed the drafting of the 1951 Convention. As Chapters 2 and 3 in particular demonstrate, these assertions beg a number of questions and rest on a number of presumptions. The objectives of 'protection' were not to 'prevent' forcible repatriation and to 'facilitate' safe and voluntary repatriation. The 1951 Convention, much like previous instruments of IRL, was not based on individual rights or on any burgeoning recognition of human rights, but on the immediate need to resolve an international crisis. This conception of protection is also based on the erroneous presumption that individual rights arose from early IRL as a meaningful and deliberate consequence of the assumption of international obligations. There is little

8 Guy S. Goodwin-Gill, 'The Language of Protection' (1989) 1(1) IJRL 6, 9.

9 James C. Hathaway, 'A Reconsideration of the Underlying Premise of Refugee Law' (1990) 31(1) Harv Int'l LJ 129, 175.

evidence to suggest that the rights of individuals were considered in any respect to have any import to the resolution of refugee crises, and much evidence to the contrary.

Second, while there certainly continues to be an invocation of inter-State responsibility in contemporary bilateral and multilateral relations, as examined in Chapter 6, these discussions are relegated to questions of ethics and morality that now dominate the legal parlance of IRL relative to 'international co-operation,' 'burden-sharing,' and addressing the 'root causes' of displacement. Türk and Garlick cite a general obligation of States to "act in solidarity," pointing to the OAU Convention, the Cartagena Declaration, and Article 80 of the Treaty on the Functioning of the European Union.[10] Milner similarly considers 'burden-sharing' to be "the mechanism through which the diverse costs to a State of granting asylum to refugees are more equitably divided among states."[11] Goodwin-Gill and McAdam note that "a significant level of practical cooperation exists, even if contributions and political and moral support for the displaced waver and formal obligations are elusive."[12] These are not representative of legal standards. Questions of morality, solidarity, and equity are not substitutes for discernible enforcement of SR, and should not be mistaken as such. To do so is to lend a degree of legitimacy to the long-standing and ever-evolving political agenda of Western States in dividing and assigning international obligations for the resolution of refugee crises onto the developing world, while retaining control over the trajectory of global refugee policy.

Furthermore, discussions of 'root causes' have only aided and abetted the conflation of 'migrant' and 'refugee' as forming part of the same legal class of person in IL, subject to undifferentiated legal processes. As discussed in Chapter 6, Western States have taken a particular interest in the resolution of 'root causes' of migration and the provision of 'safe and orderly' pathways, and have included in that assessment the movement of refugees. This has permitted a more unified legal response at the point of arrival that has had a detrimental effect on refugee protection. Consider for example, the UK's *Illegal Migration Act* 2023, which would remove persons from the UK that did not utilise 'lawful pathways,' irrespective of any protection considerations. Consider the US rule

10 Volker Turk, Madeline Garlick, 'From Burdens and Responsibilities to Opportunities: The Comprehensive Refugee Response Framework and a Global Compact on Refugees' (2016) 28 IJRL 656, 661–663.

11 James Milner, 'Burden-Sharing' in Matthew Gibney & Randall Hansen (ed), *Immigration and Asylum: From 1900 to the Present* (ABC-CLIO 2005) 56, 57.

12 Guy S. Goodwin-Gill, Jane McAdam, *The Refugee in International Law* (3rd edn, OUP 2007) 504.

on Circumvention of Lawful Pathways, which required asylum seekers to avail themselves of 'lawful pathways' or otherwise satisfy one of the extremely narrow exceptions to the presumption against asylum eligibility. Consider the US introduction and expansion of the CBP One mobile phone app, forcing asylum seekers to wait months in northern Mexico to receive an appointment to assert their right to asylum, or the introduction of 'alternative pathways' for nationals of Cuba, Haiti, Nicaragua, and Venezuela, requiring nationals of those countries to fulfil certain stringent conditions incompatible with the 1951 Convention, in order to migrate 'lawfully' to the US. Consider the EU's Migration Pact, which does not provide anything approaching adequate refugee protection per the 1951 Convention. This shift towards the creation of responses to 'refugees and migrants' under one unified policy necessarily results in significant protection gaps, as refugee definitions become divorced from the social and political realities that bring about the condition of refugeehood in the first instance.[13] The greatest risk that creates protection gaps today is this incremental incorporation of refugees as a class of person within the ambit of ordinary immigration law. The effect of this is also the incremental shift away from IRL towards domestic legal frameworks, which are increasingly divorced from the norms of IRL on which they are (or ought to be) based. As Hathaway notes:

> The thoughtful compromises built into the architecture of the Refugee Convention and Protocol are important, but clearly insufficient to withstand the pressures of continuous large-scale refugee flows in the absence of significantly enhanced oversight and coordination.[14]

Once again, this leads to the conclusion that SR serves no practical purpose if it only exists theoretically, and its theoretical existence will remain irrelevant unless it is consequential. As Eagleton noted, "[t]he study of the responsibility of States in international law involves an examination of the theory upon which reparation may be demanded by one State of another, and of the processes by which it may be obtained."[15]

13 *Id.*, 17.

14 James C. Hathaway, 'The Architecture of the UN Refugee Convention and Protocol' in Costello, Foster and McAdam (eds), *The Oxford Handbook of International Refugee Law* (OUP 2021) 171, 185.

15 Clyde Eagleton, *The Responsibility of States in International Law* (New York University Press 1928).

SR was once regarded as the consequence of a breach or non-performance of an international obligation, the State being then under a "duty to make reparation" for the injury caused. Traditional doctrine and practice saw in SR only a duty to make reparation for the injury sustained; a duty incumbent upon the State that violated an international obligation.[16] Similarly, traditional SR did not consider that an injury to one State might be an injury to the whole comity of nations.[17]

Of course, Eagleton's observations can no longer be construed as applying only to the State as a subject of IL, as noted earlier. Notwithstanding that fact, as this book was confined to an examination of SR as it arises between States, it must conclude that the unilateral reprisals and countermeasures levelled by one State against another for purported 'injuries' associated with refugee movement cannot, and should not, be considered legitimate exercises of SR. Certainly, they do not correspond with the violation of any identifiable international obligation, and certainly not one arising from IRL, and they must therefore be excluded from any legitimate assessment of wrongfulness and its lawful attribution.

In concluding, this book must return to the question raised in the introduction; that is, whether IRL may be said to exist as a system of IL in the absence of corollary SR, and if answered in the affirmative, in what circumstances can international legal obligations exist without corollary responsibility. To argue that it can, would be to argue that an international obligation neither loses authority through the absence of demonstrable enforcement, nor that it gains authority through demonstrable enforcement, but that it remains somehow static and continues to hold its full authoritative force in the face of violations that do not result in any international action. This is not a sustainable proposition. A principle may be widely considered an international obligation, but without the recognition of a corollary responsibility, its value is undeniably diminished. As IRL is expressed through municipal and regional law, relative to the individual, at the inter-State level, it is akin to a foundational principle that informs the development of municipal and regional law and policy.

Eustathiades argued that in post-war legal doctrine, the effects of an international wrong were no longer limited to the reaction of the State, which is directly injured, but impinge on the whole community as well. In his opinion,

16 Constantin Eustathiades, 'Les sujets du droit international et la responsabilité internationale. Nouvelles tendances' (1953) 84 RCADI 399, 405.

17 Clyde Eagleton, 'International Organization and the Law of Responsibility' (1950, I) 76 RCADI 323, 423.

WWII demonstrated that international offences could no longer be considered merely in terms of the reparation due to the injured State, but should rather be treated as a general question.[18] This is perhaps best characterised in IRL as the rights and interests that accumulate to the individual and are enforceable in law, and the less-defined, but often-discussed *erga omnes* obligations of States to act in 'solidarity,' or as was the favoured phrase in early SR, 'with a thought for humanity.'

It is in the implementation of the 1951 Convention in municipal and regional law that rights and interests accumulate to the refugee. As described in this book, the enforcement of those interests and rights transpires – in the great majority of cases – under municipal immigration law and regional human rights law and consequently, it is in these *fora* that SR for injuries to those interests or rights are determined. Herein lies the critical importance of due diligence: it creates a general interest out of private interests in the imposition of uniform standards of conduct associated with the performance of international obligations. That said, these standards remain within the realm of SR relative to individual rights, and though critical to the creation and maintenance of uniform, international standards, they cannot be properly characterised as arising from SR as it is enforced *inter-se*.

This is perhaps not a satisfactory conclusion for those who wish IL to be aspirational in its objectives. The development of law may indeed be aspirational, as should be the enforcement of law, but any analysis of *existing* law for the purposes of deciphering its scope, content, and above all its vulnerabilities, must be faithful to what is clear and demonstrable. It must not be tempted by what might be deemed a favourable outcome. This book was intended to provide such an analysis and in its conclusions must resist any temptation to provide aspirational interpretations of law. Instead, it has provided a clear-eyed account of the existing state of SR in IRL, with all its frailties, in the hope that it might form the basis of serious and candid discourse on the future development and enforcement of IRL.

---

18 Constantin Eustathiades, 'Les sujets du droit international et la responsabilité internationale. Nouvelles tendances' (1953) 84 RCADI 399, 433.

Bibliography

Secondary Sources

Abella, I. & Tropper, H., *None Is Too Many: Canada and the Jews of Europe, 1933–1948* (University of Toronto Press 2012).

Achermann, A. & Gattiker, M., 'Safe Third Countries: European Developments' (1995) 7(1) *IJRL 19*.

'"*Acuerdo con EEUU debe ser Aprobado por el Congreso": Roberto Herrera Cáceres*' (12 November 2019) La Prensa (Honduras).

Adams, W., 'Extent and Nature of the World Refugee Problem' (1939) 203 *Annals Am Acad Pol & Soc Sci* 26.

Ahmad, N., 'Refugees: State Responsibility, Country of Origin and Human Rights' (2009) 10(2) *Asia-Pac JHRL 1*.

Akehurst, M., 'Jurisdiction in International Law' (1972–1973) 46 *BYBIL*.

Akhavan, P. & Bergsmo, M., 'The Application of the Doctrine of State Responsibility of Refugee Creating States' (1989) 58(3–4) *Nordic J Int* L 243.

Aleinikoff, T. A., 'State-Centered Refugee Law: From Resettlement to Containment' (1992) 14(1) *Mich J Int'l L* 120.

Alexy, R., *A Theory of Constitutional Rights* (Oxford University Press 2002).

Alfonsi, S., '*"Our Whole Economy is in Shatters:" El Salvador's President Nayib Bukele on the Problems Facing His Country*' (15 December 2019) 60 Minutes.

Allen, S., Costelloe, D., Fitzmaurice, M., Gragl, P. & Guntrip, E., 'Introduction: Defining State Jurisdiction and Jurisdiction in International Law' in Allen S, Costelloe D, Fitzmaurice M., Gragl P., and Guntrip E. (eds), *The Oxford Handbook of Jurisdiction in International Law* (OUP 2019).

Allott, P., 'State Responsibility and the Unmaking of International Law' (1988) 29(1) *Harv Int'l LJ*.

Amerasinghe, C. F., *State Responsibility for Injuries to Aliens* (Clarendon Press 1967).

American Law Institute, *Restatement (Third) of the Foreign Relations Law of the United States* (American Law Institute Publishers 1987).

'American Institute of International Law: Texts of Projects' (1926) 20(4) *AJIL 328*.

Anzilotti, D., 'La Responsibilité Internationale des États à raison des dommages soufferts par des étrangers' (1906) 13 *RGDIP*.

Anzilotti, D., *Teoria generale della responsibilità dello Stato nel diritto internazionale* (F. Lumachi Libraio-Editore 1902).

'Appointment of Committees and Distribution of Work' (1924) 21 LNOJ Special Supplement 7.

Arangio-Ruiz, G., 'State Responsibility Revisited. The Factual Nature of the Attribution of Conduct to the State' (2017) *C Quaderni della rivista di diritto internazionale*.

Armstrong, A., 'Aspects of Refugee Wellbeing in Settlement Schemes: An Examination of the Tanzanian Case' (1988) 1(1) *Journal of Refugee Studies* 57.

Arsanjani, M. H. & Carbonneau, T. E., 'The Codification of the Law of State Responsibility' (1989) 83 *ASILPROC*.

Associated Press, '*New Orleans to apologise for worst mass lynching in America's history*' (1 April 2019) *The Guardian*.

Aust, H. P., *Complicity and the Law of State Responsibility* (CUP 2011).

Bailliet, C., 'Persecution in the Home: Applying the Due Diligence Standard to Harmful Traditional Practices within Human Rights and Refugee Law' (2012) 30(1) *Nordic Journal of Human Rights* 36.

Bakhet, O., '*UNHCR Experience in Implementing Rural Settlements for Refugees*' (1985) Conference Box RSC Archives, Refugee Studies Programme, Oxford.

von Bar, L., 'De la responsabilité des États à raison des dommages soufferts par des étrangers en cas de troubles, d'émeute ou de guerre civil' (1899) *Revue de droit international et de législation comparée* 464.

Barnett, L., 'Working Paper No. 54: Global Governance and the Evolution of the International Refugee Regime' (2002) *New Issues in Refugee Research*.

Barnidge, R., 'The Due Diligence Principle under International Law' (2006) 8(1) *ICLR* 81.

Bartolini, G., 'The Historical Roots of the Due Diligence Standard' in Krieger H., Peters A., and Kreuzer L. (eds), *Due Diligence in the International Legal Order* (OUP 2020).

Bass, G. J., *Freedom's Battle: The Origins of Humanitarian Intervention* (Vintage Books 2008).

Baudry-Lacantinerie, G., *Précis de Droit Civil Contenant des Principes et dans Une Deuxième les Questions de Détail et les Controverses* (*Tome II*) (Libraires de la Société du Recueil Sirey 1913).

Bederman, D. J., *International Law in Antiquity* (CUP 2004).

Bellamy, A. J., 'Whither the Responsibility to Protect? Humanitarian Intervention and the 2005 World Summit' (2006) 20(2) *Ethics & International Affairs* 143.

Benhabib, S. & Nathwani, N., 'The Ethics of International Refugee Protection' in Costello C., Foster M., and McAdam J. (eds), *The Oxford Handbook of International Refugee Law* (OUP 2021).

Bentwich, N., 'The Evian Conference and After' (1928) *Fortnightly Rev* 291.

Berkes, A., 'The Standard of 'Due Diligence' as a Result of Interchange between the Law of Armed Conflict and General International Law' (2018) 23(3) *Journal of Conflict and Security Law* 433.

Bertrand, P., 'An Operational Approach to International Refugee Protection' (1993) 26 *Cornell Int'l LJ* 495.

Besson, S., *Due Diligence in International Law* (Brill 2023).

Besson, S., 'The Extraterritoriality of the European Convention on Human Rights: Why Human Rights Depend on Jurisdiction and What Jurisdiction Amounts to' (2012) 25(4) *Leiden JIntlL* 857.

Betts, A., *Protection by Persuasion: International Cooperation in the Refugee Regime* (Cornell University Press 2009).

Betts, A., *Survival Migration: Failed Governance and the Crisis of Displacement* (Cornell University Press 2013).

Black, E., *The Transfer Agreement: The Dramatic Story of the Pact between Nazi Germany and Jewish Palestine* (Carroll & Graf Publishers 2001).

Blakemore, H., 'Chilean Revolutionary Agents in Europe, 1891' (1964) 33(4) *Pacific Historical Review*.

Blakeney, M., 'Proposals for a Jewish Colony in Australia: 1938-1948' (1984) 46(3/4) *Jewish Social Studies* 277.

Blanchard, R., 'The Exchange of Populations between Greece and Turkey' (1925) 15(3) *GeogrRev* 449.

Bloch, A., 'A New Era or More of the Same? Asylum Policy in the UK' (2000) 13(1) *Journal of Refugee Studies* 29.

Blomeyer-Bartenstein, H., 'Due Diligence' in *Max Planck Institute, Encyclopedia of Public International Law* 1987).

Bodansky, D. & Crook, J. R., 'Symposium: The ILC's State Responsibility Articles: Introduction and Overview' (2002) 96 *AJIL* 773.

'The Bolivian Option' (2007) 40(4) *The Shekel* 9.

Bonnitcha, J. & McCorquodale, R., 'The Concept of "Due Diligence" in the UN Guiding Principles on Business and Human Rights' (1997) 28(3) *EJIL* 899.

Borchard, E. M., *The Diplomatic Protection of Citizens Abroad* (The Banks Law Pub. Co. 1915).

Borchard, E. M., 'Important Decisions of the Mixed Claims Commission, United States and Mexico' (1927) 21 *AJIL* 516.

Borchard, E. M., '"Responsibility of States" at the Hague Codification Conference' (1930) 24(4) *AJIL* 517.

Bourke-Martignoni, J., 'The History and Development of the Due Diligence Standard in International Law and Its Role in the Protection of Women against Violence' in Benninger-Budel C (ed), *Due Diligence and Its Application to Protect Women from Violence* (2008).

Bray, H., 'Venezuelan Claims Commissions' in *Max Planck Encyclopedias of International Law* (OUP, 2018).

Brown, J. R., 'The Chilean Nitrate Railways Controversy' (1958) 43 *The Hispanic American Historical Review*.

Brownlie, I., *Principles of Public International Law* (4th edn, OUP 1990).

Brownlie, I., *Principles of Public International Law* (7th edn, OUP 2008).

Brownlie, I., 'State Responsibility and the International Court of Justice' in Fitzmaurice M. and Sarooshi D. (eds), *Issues of State Responsibility before International Judicial Institutions* (Bloomsbury 2004).

Brownlie, I., *System of the Law of Nations: State Responsibility, Part 1* (1 edn, OUP 1983).

Brusa, E., 'Responsabilité des États à raison des dommages soufferts par des étrangers en cas d'émeute ou de guerre civile' (1898) 17 *AnnIDI* 96.

Brusa, E. & von Bar, L., 'Responsibilité des États à raison des dommages soufferts par des étrangers en cas d'émeute ou de guerre civile' (1900) 18 *AnnIDI* 47.

Bubb, R., Kremer, M. & Levine, D. I., 'The Economics of International Refugee Law' (2011) 40(2) *J Leg Stud* 367.

Byrne, R. & Shacknove, A., 'The Safe Country Notion in European Asylum Law' (1996) 9 *Harv Hum Rts J* 185.

Calvo, C., *Le droit international théorique et pratique, Volume 2* (4 edn, Guillaumin 1888).

Capicchiano Young, S., Programas de regularización y facilidades administrativas para las personas refugiadas y migrantes de Venezuela Análisis comparativo de ordenamientos jurídicos y buenas prácticas en América Latina y el Caribe (2022) R4V.

Capicchiano Young, S., 'The Responsibility of Australia for Internationally Wrongful Acts: The Offshore Detention Regime, the Principle of Non-refoulement, and a Case for Litigation' (2018) 32(4) *JIANL* 331.

Capicchano Young, S., 'State Responsibility for COVID-19: Does International Contagion Constitute Transboundary Harm?' (2021) 11(2) *AsianJIL*372.

Capps, P., Evans, M. & Konstadinidis, S., 'Introduction' in Capps P., Evans M. and Konstadinidis S. (eds), *Asserting Jurisdiction: International and European Legal Perspectives* (Hart Publishing 2003).

Caron, D., 'The ILC Articles on State Responsibility: The Paradoxical Relationship between Form and Authority' (2002) 96(4) AJIL 857.

Cassella, S., 'Les travaux de la Commission du droit international sur la responsabilite internationale et le standard de due diligence' in SFDI (ed), *Le Standard de Due Diligence et la Responsabilité Internationale* (2018).

Cassese, A., *International Law* (2nd edn, OUP 2005).

Cerone, J., 'Out Of Bounds? Considering The Reach Of International Human Rights Law (Working Paper No 5)' (2006) Center For Human Rights And Global Justice, New York University School of Law.

'The Cerruti Arbitrations' (1912) 6(4) *AJIL* 965.

Wolf Chad (Acting Secretary of Department of Homeland Security), interview with Kilmeade B 'The Brian Kilmeade Show' *Fox News* (16 January 2020).

Chetail, V., 'Are Refugee Rights Human Rights? An Unorthodox Questioning of the Relations between Refugee Law and Human Rights Law' in Rubio-Marín R. (ed), *Human Rights and Immigration* (OUP 2014).

Chetail, V., 'Moving Towards an Integrated Approach of Refugee Law and Human Rights Law' in Costello C., Foster M., and McAdam J. (eds), *The Oxford Handbook of International Refugee Law* (OUP 2021).

Chimni, B. S., *International Law and World Order: A Critique of Contemporary Approaches* (CUP 2017).

Chimni, B. S., 'The international law of jurisdiction: A TWAIL perspective' (2022) 35 *Leiden JIL* 29.

Chimni, B. S., *International Refugee Law: A Reader* (Sage Publications 2000).

Chinkin, C. and Baetens, F. (eds), *Sovereignty, Statehood and State Responsibility: Essays in Honour of James Crawford* (CUP 2015).

Christenson, G., 'The Doctrine of Attribution on State Responsibility' in Lillich R. B. (ed), *International Law of State Responsibility for Injuries to Aliens* (Virginia 1983).

'Christie Affair' in Kinsbruner J (ed) *Encyclopedia of Latin American History and Culture* (2 edn) (Gale Cengage, 2008).

'Chronique des faits internationales' (1894) RGDIP.

Clark, T. & Crépeau, F., 'Mainstreaming Refugee Rights. The 1951 Refugee Convention and International Human Rights Law' (1999) 17(4) *Netherlands Quarterly of Human Rights* 391.

Cohen, R., *The Responsibility to Protect: Human Rights and Humanitarian Dimensions* (Brookings Institute 2009).

Cole, S. D., 'Draft Code of International Law Adopted by the Japanese Branch of the International Law Association, and the Kokusaiho Gakkwai (International Law Association of Japan)' (1926) 34 *International Law Association Reports of Conferences* 378.

Coles, G. J. L., *State Responsibility in Relation to the Refugee Problem, with Particular Reference to the State of Origin: A Study* (1993).

Inter-American Judicial Committee, *Contributions of the American Continent to the Principles of International Law that Govern the Responsibility of the State* (Organization of American States 1962).

Conrad, R., *The Destruction of Brazilian Slavery 1850–1888* (University of California Press 1972).

Cook, B., 'Method in Its Madness: The Endowment Effect in an Analysis of Refugee Burden-Sharing and a Proposed Refugee Market' (2004) 19 *GeoImmLJ* 333.

Crawford, J., *Brownlie's Principles of Public International Law* (9 edn, OUP 2012).

Crawford, J., 'The International Law Commission's Articles on State Responsibility: Introduction, Text and Commentaries' (2002).

Crawford, J., 'On Re-reading the Draft Articles on State Responsibility' (1998) 92 *ASIL-PROC* 295.

Crawford, J., *State Responsibility: The General Part* (CUP 2013).

Crawford, J. & Olleson, S., 'The Nature and Forms of International Responsibility' in Evans MD (ed), *International Law* (OUP 2003).

Crawford, J., Peel, J. & Olleson, S., 'The ILC s Articles on Responsibility of States for Internationally Wrongful Acts: Completion of the Second Reading' (2001) 12(5) *EJIL* 963.

Crawley, H., *Refugees and Gender: Law and Process* (Jordan Publishing Limited 2001).

Creutz, K., *State Responsibility in the International Legal Order: A Critical Appraisal* (CUP 2020).

Crisp, J., 'Mind the Gap! UNHCR, Humanitarian Assistance and the Development Process' (2001) 35(1) *The International Migration Review* 168.

Crisp, J., 'Working Paper No. 43: Mind the gap! UNHCR, humanitarian assistance and the development process' (2001) New Issues in Refugee Research.

Cullen, H., 'The Irresistible Rise of Human Rights Due Diligence: Conflict Minerals and Beyond' (2016) 48 *Geo Wash Int'l L Rev* 743.

Cunliffe, S. A. & Pugh, M., ' UNHCR as Leader in Humanitarian Assistance: A Triumph of Politics over Law?' in Nicholson F. and Twomey P. (eds), *Refugee Rights and Realities: Evolving International Concepts and Regimes* (CUP 1999).

Czapliński, W., 'UN Codification of Law of State Responsibility' (2003) 41(1) *Archiv Des Völkerrechts* 62.

'Evian Conference on Political Refugees' (1938) 12(3) *Social Service Review* 514.

'The Evian Conference on Refugees (2)' (1938) 15 *Bulletin of International News* 8.

Dawson, F. G., Head, I. L. & Herzog, P. E., *International Law, National Tribunals and the Rights of Aliens* (Syracuse University Press 1971).

Dean, V. M., 'European Power Politics and the Refugee Problem' (1939) 203 *Annals Am Acad Pol & Soc Sci* 18.

Delbez, L., 'Responsabilité internationale d'un Etat pour des crimes commis sur le territoire d'un Etat' (1930) *RGDIP*.

Dietz, B., Lebok, U. & Polian, P., 'The Jewish Emigration from the Former Soviet Union to Germany' (2002) 40(2) *International Migration* 29.

Dinnerstein, L., *America and the Survivors of the Holocaust* (Columbia University Press 1982).

Distefano, G., *Fundamentals of Public International Law: A Sketch of the International Legal Order* (Brill 2019).

Ditchburn, R. W., 'The Refugee Problem' (1939) 28(110) *Studies: An Irish Quarterly Review* 275.

Dumas, J., 'Du déni de justice considéré comme condition de la responsabilité internationale des États en matière criminelle' (1929) *RDILC*.

Dunn, F. S., *The Protection of Nationals: A Study in The Application of International Law* (The Johns Hopkins Press 1932).

Eagleton, C., 'International Organization and the Law of Responsibility' (1950, I) 76 RCADI 323.

Eagleton, C., *The Responsibility of States in International Law* (New York University Press 1928).

Edwards, A., 'Human Rights, Refugees and the Right "to Enjoy" Asylum' (2005) 17 *IJRL*.

Edwards, A., 'Tampering with Refugee Protection: The Case of Australia' (2003) 15 *IJRL* 192.

Einarsen, T., 'Part One Background, Drafting History of the 1951 Convention and the 1967 Protocol' in Zimmermann A., Machts F., and Dörschner J. (eds), *The 1951 Convention Relating to the Status of Refugees and its 1967 Protocol: A Commentary* (OUP 2011).

Eriksson, L.-G., Melander, G., and Nobel, P. (eds), *An Analysing Account of the Conference on the African Refugee Problem, Arusha, May 1979* (Scandinavian Institute of African Studies 1981).

Eustathiades, C., 'Les sujets du droit international et la responsabilité internationale. Nouvelles tendances' (1953) 84 RCADI 399.

Evans, G., *The Responsibility to Protect: Ending Mass Atrocity Crimes Once and For All* (Brookings Institution Press 2008).

Feller, E., 'Carrier Sanctions and International Law' (1989) 1(1) IJRL 48.

Ferstman, C., 'Human Rights Due Diligence Policies Applied to Extraterritorial Cooperation to Prevent "Irregular" Migration: European Union and United Kingdom Support to Libya' (2020) 21 *German Law Journal* 459.

Field, H., *"M" Project for F.D.R.: Studies on Migration and Settlement* (Ann Arbor 1962).

Fink, C., 'The League of Nations and the Minorities Question' (1995) 157(4) *World Affairs* 9.

Foighel, I., *Nationalization: A Study in the Protection of Alien Property in International Law* (Stevens & Sons 1957).

Fonteyne, J. P. L., 'Burden-Sharing: An Analysis of the Nature and Function of International Solidarity in Cases of Mass Influx of Refugees' (1978) 8 *AusYBIL* 162.

Fortín, A., 'The Meaning of Protection in the Refugee Definition' (2000) 12(4) IJRL 548.

Foster, M., 'Protection Elsewhere: The Legal Implications of Requiring Refugees to Seek Protection in Another State' (2007) 28 *MichJIntlL* 223.

Foster, M. & Lambert, H., *International Refugee Law and the Protection of Stateless Persons* (OUP 2019).

'Fourth Meeting (Private, Then Public)' (1935) 16(6) *LNOJ* 628.

François, J. P. A., 'Régles générales du droit de la paix' (1938-IV) 66 *RCADI*.

Frank, M., *Expelling the Germans: British Opinion and Post-1945 Population Transfer in Context* (OUP 2008).

Frank, M. & Reinisch, J., 'Introduction: Refugees and the Nation-State in Europe, 1919–59' (2014) 49(3) *JContempHist* 477.

Freeman, A. V., *The International Responsibility of States for Denial of Justice* (Longmans, Green and Company 1938).

Freeman, A. V., 'Responsibility of States for Unlawful Acts of their Armed Forces' (1955) 88 *RCADI* 263.

Frelick, B., 'Abundantly Clear: Refoulement' (2004) 19 *Geo Immigr LJ* 245.

Frenzen, N., 'Extraterritorial Refugee Protection' in *Nollkaemper and Plakokefalos'* in Nollkaemper A. and Plakokefalos I. (eds), (CUP 2017).

G.A.I., 'Sic Utere Tuo Ut Alienum Non Laedas' (1907) 5 *MichLRev.*

Gallagher, A., *The International Law of Human Trafficking* (CUP 2010).

Gallagher, D., 'The Evolution of the International Refugee System' (1989) 23(3) *Int Migr Rev.*

Gammeltoft-Hansen, T. & Tan, N. F., 'The End of the Deterrence Paradigm – Future Directions for Global Refugee Policy' (2017) 5 *J on Migration & Hum Sec*28.

García Amador, F. V., 'State Responsibility in the Light of the New Trends of International Law' (1955) 49(3) *AJIL 339*.

García Amador, F. V., 'State Responsibility: Some New Problems' (1958) 94 *RDCADI* 367.

García Amador, F. V., Sohn, L. B. & Baxter, R. R., *Recent Codification of the Law of State Responsibility for Injuries to Aliens* (Oceana Publications Inc. 1974).

García Mora, M. R., *International Responsibility for Hostile Acts of Private Persons against Foreign States* (Martinus Nijhoff 1962).

Garvey, J. I., 'Toward a Reformulation of International Refugee Law' (1985) 26(2) *HarvIntlLJ* 483.

Gatrell, P., *The Making of the Modern Refugee* (OUP 2013).

Gattini, T., 'Smoking/No Smoking: Some Remarks on the Current Place of Fault in the ILC Draft Articles on State Responsibility' (1999) 10 *EJIL*.

Ghezelbash, D., *Refuge Lost: Asylum Law in an Interdependent World* (CUP 2018).

Giuffrè, M., 'State Responsibility Beyond Borders: What Legal Basis for Italy's Push-Backs to Libya?' (2012) 24 *IJRL* 692.

Goldenziel, J., 'The Curse of the Nation-State: Refugees, Migration, and Security in International Law' (2016) 48(3) *Ariz St LJ*.

Goldie, L. F. E., 'State Responsibility and the Expropriation of Property' (1978) 12(1) *The International Lawyer*.

Goldscheid, J. & Liebowitz, D., 'Due Diligence and Gender Violence: Parsing its Power and its Perils' (2015) 48 *Cornell Int'l LJ* 301.

Goodwin-Gill, G. S., 'Asylum: The Law and Politics of Change' (1995) 7(1) *IJRL* 1.

Goodwin-Gill, G. S., 'The Extraterritorial Processing of Claims to Asylum or Protection: The Legal Responsibilities of States and International Organisations' (2007) 9 *UTS L Rev* 26.

Goodwin-Gill, G. S., 'The Language of Protection' (1989) 1(1) *IJRL* 6.

Goodwin-Gill, G. S., *The Refugee in International Law* (Clarendon Press 1983).

Goodwin-Gill, G. S., 'Refugees: The Functions and Limits of the Existing Protection System' in Nash A. E., (ed), *Human Rights and the Protection of Refugees Under International Law* (Canadian Human Rights Foundation 1988).

Goodwin-Gill, G. S. & McAdam, J., *The Refugee in International Law* (3rd edn, OUP 2007).

Gorlick, B., 'Human Rights and Refugees: Enhancing Protection through International Human Rights Law' (2000) 69 *Nordic Journal of International Law.*

Gorman, R. F., 'Beyond ICARA II: Implementing Refugee-Related Development Assistance' (1986) 20(2) *The International Migration Review* 283.

Graham, R., *Britain and the Onset of Moderization in Brazil 1850–1914* (CUP 1968).

Grahl-Madsen, A., *Commentary on the Refugee Convention 1951* (1963 UNHCR).

Grahl-Madsen, A., 'International Refugee Law Today and Tomorrow' (1982) 20(4) *Archiv des Völkerrechts* 411.

Grahl-Madsen, A., *The Status of Refugees in International Law, Volume I (Sijthoff* 1966).

Grotius, H., *De iure belli et pacis* (first published 1625, Thomas Basset 1682).

Guild, E., 'The Border Abroad – Visas and Border Controls' in Groenendijk K., Guild E., and Minderhound P. (eds), *In Search Of Europe's Borders* (Kluwer Law International 2002).

Guiraudon, V., 'Before the EU Border: Remote Control of the 'Huddled Masses'' in Groenendijk K., Guild E., and Minderhoud P. (eds), *In Search of Europe's Borders* (Kluwer 2003).

Haddad, E., *The Refugee in International Society: Between Sovereigns* (CUP 2008).

Haddad, E., 'Refugee Protection: A Clash of Values' (2003) 7(3) *International Journal of Human Rights* 1.

Hanotaux, M., 'The General and Professional Education and the Employment of Russian Refugees' (1924) 5 *LNOJ* 373.

Harrell-Bond, B., *Imposing Aid: Emergency Assistance to Refugees* (OUP 1986).

Harris, C., 'Edwin F. Atkins and the Evolution of United States Cuba Policy, 1894–1902' (2005) 78(2) *The New England Quarterly.*

Harvard Law Review, 'Extraterritoriality' (2011) 124(5) *Harv L Rev* 1226.

Hathaway, J. & Gammeltoft-Hansen, T., 'Non-refoulement in a World of Cooperative Deterrence' (2015) 53(2) *Colum J Transnat'l L* 244.

Hathaway, J. C., 'The Architecture of the UN Refugee Convention and Protocol' in Costello C., Foster M., and McAdam J. (eds), *The Oxford Handbook of International Refugee Law* (OUP 2021).

Hathaway, J. C., 'The Emerging Politics of Non-Entrée' (1992) 91 Refugees 40.

Hathaway, J. C., 'The Evolution of Refugee Status in International Law: 1920–1950' (1984) 334 *Int'l & Comp LQ* 348.

Hathaway, J. C., 'Reconceiving Refugee Law as Human Rights Protection' (1991) 4(2) *Journal of Refugee Studies* 113.

Hathaway, J. C., 'A Reconsideration of the Underlying Premise of Refugee Law' (1990) 31(1) *Harv Int'l LJ* 129.

Hathaway, J. C., *The Rights of Refugees under International Law* (CUP 2010).

Hathaway, J. C. & Foster, M., 'Internal Protection/Relocation/Flight Alternative as an Aspect of Refugee Status Determination' in Feller E., Türk V., and Nicholson F. (eds), *Refugee Protection in International Law: UNHCR's Global Consultations on International Protection* (CUP 2003).

Hathaway, J. C. & Foster, M., *The Law of Refugee Status* (2 edn, CUP 2014).

Hathaway, J. C. & Neve, R. A., 'Making International Refugee Law Relevant Again: A Proposal for Collectivized and Solution-Oriented Protection' (1997) 10 *HarvHRJ* 115.

Hathaway, J. C. & Storey, H., 'What Is the Meaning of State Protection in Refugee Law–A Debate' (2016) 28(3) *International Journal of Refugee Law* 480.

Heijer, M. D., *Europe and Extraterritorial Asylum* (Hart Publishing 2012).

Heijer, M. D., 'Refoulement' in Plakokefalos ANaI (ed), *The Practice of Shared Responsibility in International Law* (CUP 2017).

Helton, A. C., 'Asylum and Refugee Protection in Thailand' (1989) 1(1) *IJRL* 21.

Helton, A. C., 'Refugees and Human Rights' (1993) 15 *In Defense of the Alien* 142.

Hessbruegge, J. A., 'The Historical Development of the Doctrines of Attribution and Due Diligence in International Law' (2004) 36 *NYUJIntlL&Pol* 265.

Heyman, M. G., 'Protecting Foreign Victims of Domestic Violence: An Analysis of Asylum Regulations' (2008) 12 *New York University Journal of Legislation & Public Policy* 115.

Hofmann, R., 'Refugee-Generating Policies and the Law of State Responsibility' (1985) 45 *ZaöRV* 694.

Hohfeld, W., 'Some Fundamental Legal Conceptions as Applies in Judicial Reasoning' (1913–14) 23 *Yale LJ* 16.

Holborn, L. W., 'The League of Nations and the Refugee Problem' (1939) 203 *Annals Am Acad Pol & Soc Sci* 124.

Holborn, L. W., *Refugees, a Problem of Our Time: The Work of the United Nations High Commissioner for Refugees, 1951-1972, Volume 1* (Scarecrow Press 1975).

Holzer, V., *Refugees from Armed Conflict: The 1951 Refugee Convention and International Humanitarian Law* (CUP 2015).

Housden, M., 'White Russians Crossing the Black Sea: Fridtjof Nansen, Constantinople and the First Modern Repatriation of Refugees Displaced by Civil Conflict, 1922–1923' (2010) 88(3) *Slavon East Eur Rev* 495.

L'Huillier, J., *Elements de Droit International Public* (Editions Rousseau et Cie. 1950).

Hurwitz, A., *The Collective Responsibility of States to Protect Refugees* (OUP 2009).

Hutchinson, T. & Duncan, N., 'Defining and Describing what we do: Doctrinal Legal Methods' (2012) 17(1) *Deakin Law Review* 83.

Hyndman, P., 'The 1951 Convention Definition of Refugee: An Appraisal with Particular Reference to the Case of Sri Lankan Tamil Applicants' (1987) 9 *HumRightsQ* 49.

Islam, R., 'The Origin and Evolution of International Refuge Law' in Islam R. and Bhuiyan J. H. (eds), *Refugee Law* (Brill 2013).

'International Responsibility of States for Injuries on their Territory to the Person or Property of Foreigners' (1928) 22 (Supp.) *AJIL*.

Jackson, I. C., 'The 1951 Convention Relating to the Status of Refugees: A Universal Basis for Protection' (1991) 3(3) *IJRL* 403.

Jastram, K., 'Economic Harm as a Basis for Refugee Status and the Application of Human Rights Law to the Interpretation of Economic Persecution' in Simeon J. C. (ed), *Critical Issues in International Refugee Law: Strategies Toward Interpretative Harmony* (2010).

Jennings, R. Y., 'Some International Law Aspects of the Refugee Question' (1939) 20 *BYIL* 98.

Jessup, P., 'Responsibility of States for Injuries to Individuals' (1946) 46(6) *Colum L Rev* 903.

Jessup, P. C., *A Modern Law of Nations* (Archon Books 1968).

Jewish Telegraphic Agency, '*Schacht Plan to Form Basis of Rublee Talks, Opening in Berlin Today*' (11 January 1939).

Joanis, J. P., 'A Pyrrhic Victory: Applying the Trail Smelter Principle to State Creation of Refugees' in Miller R.A. & Bratspies R.M. (ed), *Transboundary Harm in International Law: Lessons from the Trail Smelter Arbitration* (CUP 2006).

Jouannet, E., *Emer de Vattel et l'émergence doctrinale du droit international classique* (Pedone 1998).

Kamchibekova, D., 'State Responsibility for Extraterritorial Human Rights Violations' (2007) 13 *Buff Hum Rts L Rev* 87.

Kamminga, M. T., *Inter-State Accountability for Violations of Human Rights* (University of Pennsylvania Press 1992).

Kellogg, V., 'The Russian Famine Region' (1922) 100 Annals Am Acad Pol & Soc Sci 105.

Kellor, F. & Hatvany, A., *Security against War* (The MacMillan Co. 1924).

Kelsen, H., 'Theorie Generale du Droit International' (1932) 42 RCADI.

Kenny, J. T., 'Manley O. Hudson and the Harvard Research in International Law 1927–1940' (1977) 11(2) *The International Lawyer* 319.

Khoser, K., *Australia and the 1951 Refugee Convention* (Lowy Institute Analyses 2015).

Kingston, L. N. & Datta, S., 'Strengthening the Norms of Global Responsibility: Structural Violence in Relation to Internal Displacement and Statelessness' (2012) 4(4) *Global Responsibility to Protect.*

Kjærum, M., 'The Concept of Country of First Asylum' (1992) 4(4) *IJRL* 514.

Klug, A. & Howe, T., 'The Concept of State Jurisdiction and the Applicability of the Non-refoulement Principle to Extraterritorial Interception Measures' in Ryan B. and Mitsilegas V. (eds), *Extraterritorial Immigration Control* (Martinus Nijhoff 2010).

Knox, J. H., 'A Presumption against Extrajurisdictionality' (2010) 104(3) *AJIL* 351.

Kolb, R., *The International Law of State Responsibility* (Edward Elgar 2018).

Kolb, R., *'Reflections on Due Diligence Duties and Cyberspace'* (2016) 58 German Yearbook of International Law 113.

Koskenniemi, M., *International Legal Theory and Doctrine* (Max Planck Encyclopedia of Public International Law, Max Planck Institute and OUP 2012).

Krieger, H., Peters, A. & Kreuzer, L., 'Introduction' in Krieger H., Peters A., and Kreuzer L. (eds), *Due Diligence in the International Legal Order* (OUP 2020).

Kulesza, J., *Due Diligence in International Law* (Brill 2016).

Kutz-Hadm, H., 'Report on European Consultation on Refugees and Exiles (ECRE) Meeting September 22-23, 1990, Geneva, Switzerland' (1990) 10(1) *Refuge.*

Ladas, S. P. & Bureau of International Research of Harvard University and Radcliffe College, *The Exchange of Minorities: Bulgaria, Greece and Turkey* (Macmillan Co 1932).

Lauterpacht, H., *Annual Digest and Reports of Public International Law Cases: 1933–1934* (Butterworth & Company 1933).

'The Law of Responsibility of States for Damage Done in Their Territory to the Person or Property of Foreigners' (1929) 23 *AJIL* 131.

Lawson, R., 'Life After Banković: On the Extraterritorial Application of the European Convention on Human Rights' in Coomans F. and Kamminga M. T. (eds), *Extraterritorial Application of Human Rights Treaties* (2004).

League of Nations, '17th Session of the Council, Annex 321' (1922) 3 *LNOJ*.

League of Nations, '18th Session of the Council, Annex 344' (1922) 5 *LNOJ*.

League of Nations, 'Armenian Refugees in Greece: Memorandum' (1924) 5 *LNOJ* 933.

League of Nations, 'Conference on the Question of the Russian Refugees' (1921) 2(8) *LNOJ* 899.

League of Nations, 'Convention Concluded at Geneva between the Hellenic Government and the Refugee Settlement Commission on January 24th, 1930' (1930) 11 *LNOJ* 555.

League of Nations, 'Eighth Meeting (Public, Then Private) Sixty-First Session of the Council' (1930) 11(11) *LNOJ* 1527.

League of Nations, 'Evacuation of the Russian Refugees from Constantinople' (1922) 3(7) *LNOJ* 725.

League of Nations, 'Extract from the Letter from the Secretary of the Armenian Refugees (Lord Mayor's Fund to Mr. Morgenthau)' (1924) 5 *LNOJ* 973.

League of Nations, 'Fifth Meeting (Private, Then Public)' (1935) 16(11) *LNOJ* 1159.

League of Nations, 'Fifth Meeting (Public, Then Private)' (1927) 8(7) *LNOJ* 152.

League of Nations, 'Fifth Meeting (Public) Eighteenth Session of the Council' (1922) 3 *LNOJ* 530.

League of Nations, 'Fourth Meeting (Public) Forty-Fifth Session of the Council' (1927) 8 *LNOJ* 773.

League of Nations, 'Plan for the Issue of a Certificate of Identity to Armenian Refugees, 31st May 1924. Submitted for the consideration of interested governments by Dr. Nansen, High Commissioner for Russian Refugees in execution of the Resolution of the Council of the League' (1924) 5(7) *LNOJ*.

League of Nations, 'The Question of the Russian Refugees' (1921) 2(2) *LNOJ* 225.

League of Nations, 'Refugee Questions' (1929) 10(2) *LNOJ* 323.

League of Nations, 'Refugee Questions' (1928) 9(6) *LNOJ* 838.

League of Nations, 'Relief Work in Russia and the Question of the Russian Refugee' (1922) 3(4) *LNOJ* 338.

League of Nations, 'Reply from the Greek Prime Minister to the Settlement Commission' (1924) 5 *LNOJ*.

League of Nations, 'Report of the High Commissioner for Russian Refugees (Annex 321b)' (17 March 1922) 3(5) *LNOJ*.

League of Nations, 'Russian Refugees in Annexes' (1922) 3(6) *LNOJ* 556.

League of Nations, 'Russian Refugees: Report by Dr. Fridtjof Nansen, High Commissioner for Refugees, presented to the Council on June 12th, 1924' (1924) 5 *LNOJ* 958.

League of Nations, 'Russian Refugees: Report by the High Commissioner Submitted to the Council on March 15th, 1924' (1924) 5 *LNOJ* 551.

League of Nations, 'Russian, Armenian, Assyrian, Assyro-Chaldean and Turkish Refugees' (1930) 11(11) *LNOJ* 1324.

League of Nations, 'Second Meeting (Private) Seventeenth Session of the Council' (1922) 3(5) *LNOJ* 375.

League of Nations, 'Settlement of the Assyrians of Iraq' (1935) 16(9) *LNOJ* 989.

League of Nations, 'Sixth Meeting (Public, Then Private) Forty-Fifth Session of the Council' (1927) 8 *LNOJ* 791.

League of Nations, 'Third Meeting (Public) Twenty-Seventh Session of the Council' (1924) 5(2) *LNOJ* 330.

League of Nations, 'Work of the Armenian Refugee Settlement Commission' (1926) 7(7) *LNOJ* 896.

Lee, L. T., 'The Right to Compensation: Refugees and Countries of Asylum' (1986) 80(3) *AJIL* 532.

Léger, J. N., *Haiti, her History and her Detractors* (The Neale Publishing Company 1907).

Legomsky, S. H., 'The USA and the Caribbean Interdiction Program' (2006) 18 *IJRL* 677.

Lenhof, A., 'International Law and Rules on International Jurisdiction' (1964) 50(1) *Cornell LR* 5.

Levmore, B. W., 'A Stimulus for American Industry: Nonprofessional Refugees' (1939) 203 *Annals Am Acad Pol & Soc Sci* 162.

Lillich, R. B., 'The Current Status of the Law of State Responsibility for Injuries to Aliens' (1979) 73 *ASILPROC* 244.

Loescher, G., 'The European Community and Refugees' (1989) 65(4) *International Affairs* 617.

Loescher, G., 'Humanitarianism and Politics in Central America' (1988) 103(2) *Political Science Quarterly* 295.

Loescher, G., 'The International Refugee Regime: Stretched to the Limit?' (1994) 47(2) *JIntAff* 351.

Loescher, G. & Scanlan, J. A., *Calculated Kindness: Refugees and America's Half-Open Door, 1945 to the Present* (Free Press 1986).

Long, K., 'Early Repatriation Policy: Russian Refuge Return 1922-1924' (2009) 22 *JRS* 133.

Longobardo, M., 'The Relevance of the Concept of Due Diligence for International Humanitarian Law' (2019) 37(1) *Wis Int'l LJ* 44.

Lowe, A. V., 'The Problems of Extraterritorial Jurisdiction: Economic Sovereignty and the Search for a Solution' (1985) 34 *ICLQ* 724.

Lubbers, R., 'Asylum for All: Refugee Protection in the 21st Century' (2002) 24(1) *HarvIntLJ* 60.

Lugusha, E., 'Socio-economic Survey of Burundi Refugees in Kigoma Region, *Economic Research Bureau'* (1981) University of Dar es Salaam.

Mann, F. A., 'The Doctrine of International Jurisdiction Revisited after Twenty Years' (1984) 186 *RCADI* 9.

Mann, F. A., 'The Doctrine of Jurisdiction in International Law' (1964) 111 *RCADI*.

Mann, T. (ed), *Australian Law Dictionary* (OUP 2010).

Martin, S. F., 'The Global Refugee Crisis' (2016) 17(1) *GJIA*.

Matte, A. & Ross, A., *Memoria presentada a la excelentísima junta del gobierno* (Imprimerie et Libraire Administrative et Classique, Paul Dupont 1892).

Mazzeschi, R. P., 'Le chemin étrange de la due diligence: d'un concept mystérieux à un concept surévalué' in SFDI (ed), *Le standard de due diligence et la responsabilité internationale: Journée d'études franco-italienne du Mans* (2018).

Mazzeschi, R. P., 'The Marginal Role of the Individual in the ILC's Articles on State Responsibility' (2004) 14 *ItYBIL* 39.

McDonald, N., 'The Role of Due Diligence in International Law' (2019) 68(4) *ICLQ* 1041.

Melander, G., 'Basic Differences in Refugee Policy in Western Europe and North America' (1989) *In Defense of the Alien* 97.

Menchu, S. & Daniel, F. J., '*Turbulent Inauguration Day in Guatemala, Outgoing President Hit by Eggs*' (14 January 2020) Reuters.

Ménos, S., *L'Affaire Lüders* (Imprimerie J. Verrollot 1898).

Meron, T., *Human Rights and Humanitarian Norms as Customary Law* (Clarendon 1989).

Milanović, M., *Extraterritorial Application of Human Rights Treaties: Law, Principles, and Policy* (OUP 2011).

Milner, J., 'Burden-Sharing' in Hansen MGR (ed), *Immigration and Asylum: From 1900 to the Present* (ABC-CLIO 2005).

Monnheimer, M., *Due Diligence Obligations in International Human Rights Law* (CUP 2021).

Moore, J. B., *A Digest of International Law, Volume III* (Government Printing Office 1906).

Moore, J. B., *A Digest of International Law, Volume VI* (Government Printing Office 1906).

Moret, S., 'Italy V. Colombia (The Cerruti Case)' (1912) 6(4) *AJIL* 1003.

Morin, A., *Les Lois Relatives a la Guerre Selon le Droit des Gens Moderne, le Droit Public et le Droit Criminel des Pays Civilisés (Tome II)* (Imprimerie et Libraire Générale de Jurisprudence Cosse, Marchal et Billard 1872).

Morris, L., 'Governing at a Distance: The Elaboration of Controls in British Immigration' (1998) 32(4) *International Migration Review* 952.

Mosler, H., 'The International Society as a Legal Community' (1974-IV) 140 *RCADI*.

Mullally, S., 'Domestic Violence Asylum Claims and Recent Developments in International Human Rights Law: A Progress Narrative?' (2011) 60 *International & Comparative Law Quarterly* 459.

Nahon, G., 'Bombardements, dommages de guerre et réquisitions' (March 2019) Archives de Paris.

Nansen, F., *Armenia and the Near East* (George Allen & Unwin Ltd 1928).

Neuwirth, G. & Clark, L., 'Indochinese Refugees in Canada: Sponsorship and Adjustment' (1981) 15(1/2) *The International Migration Review* 131.

Nicholson, F., 'Implementation of the Immigration (Carriers' Liability) Act of 1987: Privatising Immigration Functions at the Expense of International Obligations' (1997) 46(3) *ICLQ* 586.

Nicholson, F. & Twomey, P., 'Introduction' in Nicholson F. and Twomey P. (eds), *Refugee Rights and Realities: Evolving International Concepts and Regimes* (1999).

Nissel, A., 'The Duality of State Responsibility' (2013) 44 *Colum Hum Rts L Rev.*

Ollino, A., *Due Diligence Obligations in International Law* (CUP 2022).

Oppenheim, L., *Oppenheim's International Law: Parts 1-4* (OUP 1992).

Ormsby, E. A., 'The Refugee Crisis as Civil Liberties Crisis' (2017) 117(5) *ColumLRev* 1191.

Oxman, B. H., *'Jurisdiction of States' in Max Planck Encyclopedias of Public International Law* (North-Holland, 1987).

Pellet, A., 'The Definition of Responsibility in International Law' in Crawford J., Pellet A., Olleson S., and Parlett K. (eds), *The Law of International Responsibility* (OUP 2010).

Penkower, M. N., *Decision on Palestine Deferred: America, Britain and Wartime Diplomacy, 1939–1945* (Routledge 2013).

Pérez, S., *'President-Elect Says Guatemala Can't do Migrant Deal with US'* (13 August 2019) *AP*.

Pisillo-Mazzeschi, R., 'Due Diligence and the International Responsibility of States' (1992) 35 *German Yearbook of International Law* 9.

Pisillo-Mazzeschi, R., 'Forms of International Responsibility for Environmental Harm' in Francioni F. and Scovazzi T. (eds), *International Responsibility for Environmental Harm* (1991).

Pobjoy, J. M., *The Child in International Refugee Law* (CUP 2017).

Pons, L., *La responsabilité de l'état à raison de dommages causés sur son territoire aux étrangers* (Imprimerie F. Boisseau 1936).

Pradier-Fodére, P., *Traité de droit international public Européen et Américain suivant les progrès de la science et de la pratique contemporaine* (G. Pedone-Lauriel 1885).

Price, D. H., *Anthropological Intelligence* (Duke University Press 2008).

'Questions Concerning Russian and Armenian Refugees' (1926) 7(12) LNOJ 1667.

Ramsey, S. D., 'State Responsibility Under the Restatement' (1989) 83 *ASILPROC* 232.

Richmond, A. H., 'Refugees and Racism: Canada and Global Apartheid' *The Refugee Crisis: British and Canadian Responses* (1989) University of Oxford.

Richter, R., 'International Conference on the Plight of Refugees, Returnees and Displaced Persons in Southern Africa (SARRED), Oslo, 22–24 August 1988' (1989) 2(2) *Journal of Refugee Studies* 284.

Rizvi, H.-A., 'United Nations and the Refugee Problem' (1985) 38(1) *Pakistan Horizon.*

Robinson, N., *Convention Relating to the Status of Refugees: Its History, Significance and Contents* (Institute of Jewish Affairs 1952).

Root, E., 'The Basis of Protection to Citizens Residing Abroad, Proceedings' (1910) 4 *ASIL*.

Rosenberg, L. D., 'International Association of Refugee Law Judges Conference – The Courts and Interception: The United States' Interdiction Experience and Its Impact on Refugees and Asylum Seekers' (2003) 17 *Geo Immigr LJ* 199.

Rosenstock, R., 'The ILC and State Responsibility' (2002) 96(4) *AJIL*.

Roth, A., *Das völkerrechtliche Delikt vor und in der Verhandlungen auf der Haager Kodifications Konferenz 1930* (Universitatsverlag von Robert Noske 1932).

Roucek, J. S., 'Minorities – A Basis of the Refugee Problem' (1939) 203 *Annals Am Acad Pol & Soc Sci* 1.

Roucek, J. S., *The Working of the Minorities System Under the League of Nations* (Orbis Publishing Co. 1929).

Rutinwa, B., 'The End of Asylum? The Changing Nature of Refugee Policies in Africa' (2002) 21(1/2) *Refugee Survey Quarterly* 12.

Ryan, B., 'Extraterritorial Immigration Control: What Role for Legal Guarantees?' in Ryan B. and Mitsilegas V. (eds), *Extraterritorial Immigration Control* (Martinus Nijhoff 2010).

Ryngaert, C., *Jurisdiction in International Law* (OUP 2015).

Schacher, Y., Schmidtke, R. & Sawyer, A., 'Deportation with a Layover: Failure of Protection Under the U.S.-Guatemala Asylum Cooperative Agreement' (19 May 2020) *Refugees International.*

Schacht, H., *Confessions of 'The Old Wizard': The Autobiogrphy of Hjalmar Horace Greeley Schacht* (1956).

Scholten, S., *The Privatisation of Immigration Control through Carrier Sanctions: The Role of Private Transport Companies in Dutch and British Immigration Control* (Brill 2015).

Schwartzenberger, G., *A Manual of International Law* (Stevens and Sons 1967).

Shacknove, A., 'From Asylum to Containment' (1993) 5 *IJRL* 516.

Shacknove, A., 'Who Is a Refugee?' (1985) 95 *Ethics* 274.

Shaw, M. N., *International Law* (5th edn, CUP 2003).

Shields, S., 'The Greek-Turkish Population Exchange: Internationally Administered Ethnic Cleansing' (2013) 267 *Middle East Report.*

Sieghart, P., *The International Law of Human Rights* (Clarendon Press 1983).

Simma, B. & Pulkowski, D., 'Of Planets and the Universe: Self-Contained Regimes in International Law' (2006) 17(3) *Eur J Int'l L* 483.

Simpson, J. H., *The Refugee Problem: Report of a Survey* (OUP 1939).

Simpson, J. H., 'The Work of the Greek Refugee Settlement Commission' (1929) 8(6) *Journal of the Royal Institute of International Affairs* 583.

Sjöberg, T., *The Powers and the Persecuted: The Refugee Problem and the Intergovernmental Committee on Refugees (IGCR), 1938-1947* (Lund University Press 1991).

Skordas, A., 'Article 7: (Exemption from Reciprocity/Dispense de Réciprocité)' in Zimmermann A., Machts F., and Dörschner J. (eds), *The 1951 Convention Relating to the Status of Refugees and its 1967 Protocol: A Commentary* (OUP 2011).

Skran, C., *Refugees in Inter-war Europe* (OUP 1995).

Smock, D. R., 'Eritrean Refugees in the Sudan' (1982) 20(3) *The Journal of Modern African Studies* 451.

Sohn, L. B. & Baxter, R. R., 'Responsibility of States for Injuries to the Economic Interests of Aliens: I. Introduction' (1961) 55(3) *AJIL*.

Souter, J., 'Towards a Theory of Asylum as Reparation for Past Injustice' (2014) 62(2) *Political Studies* 326.

Spanish Treaty Claims Commission, *Final Report of the Spanish Treaty Claims Commission* (Government Printing Office 1910).

Stahn, C., 'Responsibility to Protect: Political Rhetoric or Emerging Legal Norm?' (2007) 101(1) *AJIL* 99.

Stein, B., 'The Geneva Conferences and the Indochinese Refugee Crisis' (1979) 13(4) *The International Migration Review* 716.

Steinberg, J., 'A Jewish Settlement in the Kimberleys' (1940) 12(1) *The Australian Quarterly* 24.

Stevens, D., 'What Do We Mean by Protection?' (2013) 20(2) *International Journal on Minority and Group Rights* 233.

Stoessinger, J., *The Refugee and the World Community* (University of Minnesota Press 1956).

Strisower, M. L., 'Responsabilité internationale des États à raison des dommages causés sur leur territoire à la personne ou aux biens des étrangers' (1927) 33(1) *AnnIDI* 455.

Strupp, K., *Die völkerrechtliche Haftung des Staates insbesondere bei Hanshagen Privater, Abhandlung zur fortschreitenden Kodification des internationalen Rechts, Heft 1 (Kiel* 1927).

Suhrke, A., 'Indochinese Refugees and American Policy' (1981) 37(2) *The World Today* 54.

Suhrke, A., 'Indochinese refugees: The Law and Policy of First Asylum' (1983) 467 *Annals Am Acad Pol & Soc Sci* 102.

Szigeti, P. D., 'The Illusion of Territorial Jurisdiction' (2017) 52(3) *Texas Int L J* 369.

Tams, C. J., 'All's Well That Ends Well: Comments on the ILC s Articles on State Responsibility' (2002) 62 *ZaöRV* 759.

Tams, C. J., 'Law-Making in Complex Processes: The World Court and the Modern Law of State Responsibility' in Chinkin C. and Baetens F. (eds), *Sovereignty, Statehood and State Responsibility* (CUP 2015).

Tomuschat, C., 'State Responsibility and the Country of Origin' in Gowlland-Debbas V (ed), *The Problem of Refugees in the Light of Contemporary International Law Issues* (Brill Nijhoff 1995).

Triepel, H., *Droit International et Droit Interne* (OUP 1920).

Triepel, H., 'Les Rapport entre le Droit International et le Droite Interne' (1923) 1 *RdC*.

Tuitt, P., 'Human Rights and Refugees' (1997) 1(2) *International Journal of Human Rights* 66.

Tunkin, G., *Theory of International Law* (Harvard University Press 1974).

Türk, V. & Garlick, M., 'From Burdens and Responsibilities to Opportunities: The Comprehensive Refugee Response Framework and a Global Compact on Refugees' (2016) 28(4) *IJRL* 656.

Tzevelekos, V., 'Reconstructing the Effective Control Criterion in Extraterrestrial Human Rights Breaches: Direct attribution of Wrongfulness, Due Diligence, and Concurrent Responsibility' (2014) 36 *Mich J Int'l L* 129.

UN High Commissioner for Refugees, *The State of The World's Refugees 2000: Fifty Years of Humanitarian Action* (1 January 2000).

UN High Commissioner for Refugees, *The State of the World's Refugees: In Search of Solidarity* (UNHCR 2012).

de Vattel, E., *Droit des gens ou principes de la loi naturelle appliqués à la conduite & aux affaires des Nations et des Souverains, Tome II* (London 1758).

Verdross, A., 'Règles internationales concernant le traitement des étrangers' (1931) 37 *RCADI*.

Vink, M. & Meijerink, F., 'Asylum Applications and Recognition Rates in EU Member States 1982–2001: A Quantitative Analysis' (2003) 16(3) *JRS* 298.

de Visscher, C., *La responsabilité des États* (Bibliotheca Visseriana 1924).

de Visscher, C., 'Notes sur la responsabilité internationale des états et la protection diplomatique d'après quelques documents récents' (1927) *RDILC*.

de Visscher, C., 'Responsabilité Internationale des États à raison des dommages causes sur leur Territoire a la Personne ou aux biens des Étrangers' (1927) 33 III (III) AnnIDI 81.

de Vitoria, F., *De Indis et De Iure Belli, Relectiones* (first published 1557, Carnegie Institution of Washington 1917).

Wain, B., *The Refused: The Agony of the Indochina Refugees* (Simon and Schuster 1981).

Walker, K., 'Defending the 1951 Convention Definition of Refugee' (2003) 17 *GeoImmigrLJ* 583.

Wall, P., 'A New Link in the Chain: Could a Framework Convention for Refugee Responsibility Sharing Fulfil the Promise of the 1967 Protocol?' (2017) 29(2) *IJRL* 201.

Watenpaugh, K. D., 'Between Communal Survival and National Aspiration: Armenian Genocide Refugees, the League of Nations, and the Practices of Interwar Humanitarianism' (2014) 5(2) *Humanity: An International Journal of Human Rights, Humanitarianism, and Development* 159.

Weil, S., *The Need for Roots: Prelude to a Declaration of Duties towards Mankind* (Routledge 1952).

Weis, P., 'The Development of Refugee Law' (1982) 3(1) *Mich J Int'l L* 27.

Weis, P., 'The International Protection of Refugees' (1954) 48(2) *AJIL* 193.

Weis, P., 'Legal Aspects of the Convention of 21 July 1951 Relating to the Status of Refugees' (1953) 30 *BYBIL* 478.

Weis, P., *The Refugee Convention, 1951: The Travaux Preparatoires Analysed with a Commentary by Dr Paul Weis* (UNHCR 1990).

Weiss, E. B., 'Invoking State Responsibility in the Twenty-First Century' (2002) 96(4) *AJIL* 798.

Wells, A., *Tropical Zion: General Trujillo, FDR, and the Jews of Sosúa* (Duke University Press 2009).

Whiteman, M. M., 'The Codification of the Responsibility of States' (1930) 8(2) *New York University Law Quarterly Review* 185.

Whiteman, M. M., *Damages in International Law* (Government Printing Office 1937).

Wilde, R., 'Legal "Black Hole"? Extraterritorial State Action and International Treaty Law on Civil and Political Rights' (2005) 26 *MichJIntlL* 739.

Williams, J. F., *Chapters on Current International Law and the League of Nations* (Longmans, Green and Co. 1929).

Wyman, D. S., *The Abandonment of the Jews: America and the Holocaust, 1941-1945* (Pantheon Books 1984).

Wyman, D. S., *Paper Walls: America and the Refugee Crisis 1938–1941* (Pantheon Books 1985).

Zannas, P. A., *La responsabilité internationale des États pour des actes de negligence* (1952).

Ziegler, R., 'International Humanitarian Law and Refugee Protection' in Costello C., Foster M., and McAdam J. (eds), *The Oxford Handbook of International Refugee Law* (OUP 2021).

Zimmermann, A., 'Article 8: (Exemption from Exceptional Measures/Dispense de Mesures Exceptionnelles)' in Zimmermann A., Machts F., and Dörschner J. (eds), *The 1951 Convention Relating to the Status of Refugees and Its 1967 Protocol: A Commentary* (OUP 2011).

Zucker, N. F., 'The Haitians versus the United States: The Courts as Last Resort' (1983) 467 *Annals Am Acad Pol & Soc Sci* 151.

'Tuesday, 19 June 1956, at 9:30 a.m.' (1956) 1 UNYBILC 226.

(No title) (24 February 1891) The London Gazette.

Official Documents

'The Acting Secretary of State to the Commission to Negotiate Peace' (Washington, 8 September 1919) Papers Relating to the Foreign Relations of the United States, Volume I 1920).

Ad Hoc Committee on Refugees and Stateless Persons, Ad Hoc Committee on Statelessness and Related Problems, Status of Refugees and Stateless Persons – Memorandum by the Secretary-General (3 January 1950) E/AC.32/2Ad Hoc Committee on Statelessness and Related Problems, Summary Record of the Fourth Meeting E/AC.32/SR.4.

American Civil Liberties Union et al., 'Letter to Attorney General Loretta Lynch Re: Prosecutions for Illegal Entry (8 U.S.C. § 1325) and Illegal Re-entry (8 U.S.C. § 1326)' (28 July 2015).

Asian-African Legal Consultative Committee, Principles concerning Treatment of Refugees (1966).

Asian-African Legal Consultative Committee, Report of the 7th Annual Session, Baghdad: 1965 (1965).

Asian-African Legal Consultative Committee, Report of the Fourth Session, Tokyo: 1961 (1961).

Asian-African Legal Consultative Committee, Report of the Second Session, Cairo: 1–13 October 1958 (1958).

Asian-African Legal Consultative Committee, Report of the Tenth Session, Karachi, 1969 (1969).

Asian-African Legal Consultative Committee, Report of the Third Session, Colombo: 1960 (1960).

Asian-African Legal Consultative Committee, Report: First Session, New Delhi: India, April 18 to 27, 1957 (1957).

Australia: Federal Parliament, Report of the Select Committee for an inquiry into a certain maritime incident, Chapter 10, Pacific Solution: Negotiations and Agreements (2002) 10.33–10.34 Senate Printing Unit, Parliament House.

'Baron Fava to Mr. Blaine' (Washington, 15 March 1891) Papers Relating to the Foreign Relations of The United States, Transmitted to Congress, with the Annual Message of the President (United States Government Printing Office, 9 December 1891).

Bennouna, M., Preliminary report on diplomatic protection, by Mr. Mohamed Bennouna, Special Rapporteur (4 February 1998) A/CN.4/484.

Borchard, E. M., Draft Convention on the Law of Responsibility of States (February 1929).

'The Brazil correspondence in the cases of the "Prince of Wales" and officers of the "Forte" (Reprinted from the Papers laid before Parliament)' (1863) W. Ridgeway.

'The British Appointed Ambassador on Special Mission (Grey) to the Secretary of State' (Washington, 13 November 1919) Papers Relating to the Foreign Relations of the United States, Volume I 1920).

'Chen Lan Pin to Mr. Evarts' (Washington, 10 November 1880) Papers Relating to the Foreign Relations of the United States, Transmitted to Congress, with the Annual Message of The President (Department of State, 5 December 1881).

Christensen, H., Refugees and Pioneers, Report 85–4 (1985) UNHCR Research Institute for Social Development.

Cleveland, G., *Papers Relating to the Foreign Relations of the United States, with The Annual Message of the President Transmitted to Congress December 7, 1896, and the Annual Report of the Secretary of State* (United States Government Printing Office 1897).

Cleveland, G., *United States Department of State, Papers Relating to Foreign Affairs* (United States Department of State 1896).

International Law Commission, Report by Mr. R. Ago, Chairman of the Sub-Committee on State Responsibility (1963) A/CN.4/152.

The Commission to Negotiate Peace to the Secretary of State (Paris, 9 October 1919) (1935) Papers Relating to the Foreign Relations of the United States, 1920, Volume I: United States Government Printing Office.

'Confidential Communication from the Director to the Chairman and Vice-Chairman of the Intergovernmental Committee' (July-August 1938) Myron C. Taylor Papers – Evian Intergovernmental Committee Conference (folder 2) F.D.R. Library.

'Confidential Memorandum for the American Delegate' (undated) box 3, Myron C. Taylor Papers.

'Consul Corte to Baron Fava' (New Orleans, 14 March 1891) Papers Relating to the Foreign Relations of the United States, Transmitted to Congress, with the Annual Message of The President (Department of State, 9 December 1891).

'Consul Corte to Baron Fava (New Orleans, 14 March 1891)' (9 December 1891) United States Government Printing Office.

Costello, C., Ioffe, Y. & Büchsel, T., Article 31 of the 1951 Convention Relating to the Status of Refugees (July 2017) UNHCR Legal and Protection Policy Research Series.

Council of Europe, Protocol to the European Convention on Consular Functions concerning the Protection of Refugees (1967) ETS 61A.

Council of Europe: Parliamentary Assembly, Arrival of asylum seekers at European airports (2000) Report, Committee on Migration, Refugees and Demography, Rapporteur: Mr. Gross, Switzerland, Socialist Group (8 June 2000) Doc. 8761.

Department of State Instruction, to the United States Delegation to the Fifth Regular Session of the General Assembly (Washington, 5 September 1950) Foreign Relations of the United States, 1950, The United Nations; The Western Hemisphere, Volume II.

'Deputy Foreign Minister von Weizsaecker to the British Ambassador in Berlin: Memorandum AA 83/29 8/7' (8 July 1938).

García Amador, F. V., 'First Report on State Responsibility' (1956) 2 UNYBILC 173.

Gasarasi, C., The Life of a Refugee Settlement: the Case of Muyenzi in Ngara District (1976) UNHCR Research Project, Dar es Salaam.

Harvard Law School, Research in International Law, II. Responsibility of States (1929).

Harvard Research in International Law Group, Draft Convention on 'Responsibility of States for Damage Done in their Territory to the Person or Property of Foreigners' (1929) 23.

Howard, J., *Arrangement with Papua New Guinea to Process Unauthorised Arrivals* (10 October 2001).

Howard, J., *Joint Press Conference with the Minister for Immigration the Hon Philip Ruddock MP* (1 September 2001).

'Hull to Taylor' (8 July 1938) Myron C. Taylor Papers.

Institut de Droit International, The National Character of an International Claim Presented by a State for Injury Suffered by an Individual (1965).

Institut de Droit International, Projet de Résolutions (1950) 43 I Bath.

Institut de Droit International, The Rule of the Exhaustion of Local Remedies (1956).

Intergovernmental Committee, 'Agenda of the Committee, Communicated by the Government of the United States of America to the Governments invited' (5 July 1938) Myron C. Taylor Papers – Evian Intergovernmental Committee Conference, F.D.R. Library.

Intergovernmental Committee, Decision taken at the Evian Conference on Jewish Refugees (14 July 1938).

Intergovernmental Committee, 'Intergovernmental Committee to Continue and Develop the Work of the Evian Meeting: Copy of a letter dated 19 August, 1938, to the Chairman of the Committee from the Chairman of the United States of American Delegation' (19 August 1938) Myron C. Taylor Papers – Evian Intergovernmental Committee Conference (folder 2), July-August 1938.

Intergovernmental Committee, 'Memorandum' (3 June 1947) Myron C. Taylor Papers – Intergovernmental Committee on Political Refugees Correspondence, 1947–1954.

Intergovernmental Committee, 'Memorandum by George L. Warren' (4 June 1947) Myron C. Taylor Papers–Intergovernmental Committee on Political Refugees Correspondence, 1947–1954.

Intergovernmental Committee, The Refugee Problem After the War (no date recorded) Myron C. Taylor Papers–Intergovernmental Committee on Political Refugees Correspondence, 1942-1943.

Intergovernmental Committee, 'Revised List of Delegates' (July 1938) Myron C. Taylor Papers – Evian Intergovernmental Committee Conference, F.D.R. Library.

Intergovernmental Committee, 'Verbatim Report of the First Meeting (Public)' (6 July 1938) Myron C. Taylor Papers – Evian Intergovernmental Committee Conference, F.D.R. Library.

Intergovernmental Committee, Verbatim Report of the Fourth Meeting (Public) (11 July 1938) Myron C. Taylor Papers – Evian Intergovernmental Committee Conference, F.D.R. Library.

Intergovernmental Committee, 'Verbatim Report of the Second Meeting' (7 July 1938) Myron C. Taylor Papers – Evian Intergovernmental Committee Conference, F.D.R. Library.

Intergovernmental Committee, 'Verbatim Report of the Third Meeting (Public)' (9 July 1938) Myron C. Taylor Papers – Evian Intergovernmental Committee Conference, F.D.R. Library.

Intergovernmental Committee, Technical Sub-Committee, Declaration by the Norwegian Delegation on the Immigration Laws and their Application in Norway (8 July 1938) Myron C. Taylor Papers – Evian Intergovernmental Committee Conference, F.D.R. Library.

Intergovernmental Committee: Technical Sub-Committee, Memorandum on Australian Immigration Laws and Practices and the Present Policy of his Majesty's Government in the Commonwealth of Australia (8 July 1938) Myron C. Taylor Papers – Evian Intergovernmental Committee Conference, F.D.R. Library.

Intergovernmental Committee: Technical Sub-Committee, Statement of Details Regarding the Number and the Type of Immigrants which the Government of the United States in Prepared to Receive Under its Existing Laws and Practices (8 July 1938) Myron C. Taylor Papers – Evian Intergovernmental Committee Conference, F.D.R. Library.

Intergovernmental Committee: Technical Sub-Committee, Statement of the Immigration Laws and Practices of the United States of America Governing the Reception of Immigrants (8 July 1938) Myron C. Taylor Papers – Evian Intergovernmental Committee Conference, F.D.R. Library.

International Law Commission, Digest of the decisions of international tribunals relating to State responsibility, prepared by the Secretariat (1964) A/CN.4/169.

International Law Commission, Draft articles on Responsibility of States for Internationally Wrongful Acts, with Commentaries (2001) II (Part II) Yearbook of the International Law Commission.

International Law Commission, First report on State responsibility by Mr. Roberto Ago, Special Rapporteur – Review of previous work on codification of the topic of the international responsibility of States (1969) A/CN.4/217 and Corr.1 and Add.1.

International Law Commission, First report on State responsibility, by Mr. James Crawford, Special Rapporteur (12 August 1998) A/CN.4/490.

International Law Commission, "Force majeure" and "fortuitous event" as circumstances precluding wrongfulness: survey of State practice, international judicial decisions and doctrine – Study prepared by the Secretariat (1978) A/CN.4/315.

International Law Commission, Proposals submitted to, and decisions of, various United Nations organs relating to the question of State Responsibility: supplement prepared by the Secretariat to document A/CN.4/165 (1969) A/CN.4/209.

International Law Commission, Report by Mr. R. Ago, Chairman of the Sub-Committee on State Responsibility (16 January 1963) A/CN.4/152.

International Law Commission, Report of the International Law Commission covering the work of its 14th session, 24 April–29 June 1962 (1962) A/5209.

International Law Commission, Report of the International Law Commission on the work of its Fifteenth Session, 6 July 1963, Official Records of the General Assembly, Eighteenth Session, Supplement (A/5509) (1963) A/CN.4/163.

International Law Commission, Report of the International Law Commission on the work of its fifty-third session, 23 April–1 June and 2 July–10 August 2001, Official Records of the General Assembly, Fifty-sixth session, Supplement No. 10 (2001) A/56/10.

International Law Commission, Report of the International Law Commission to the General Assembly (10 August 2001) A/56/10.

International Law Commission, Report on International Responsibility by Mr. F. V. García Amador, Special Rapporteur (1956) A/CN.4/96.

International Law Commission, Responsibility of States for Internationally Wrongful Acts (2001) II (Part II) Yearbook of the International Law Commission.

International Law Commission, Second report of the Special Rapporteur, Mr. F. V. García Amador (1957) A/CN.4/106.

International Law Commission, Second report on State responsibility, by Mr. Gaetano Arangio-Ruiz, Special Rapporteur (22 July 1989) A/CN.4/425 and Add. 1.

International Law Commission, Second report on State responsibility, by Mr. Roberto Ago, Special Rapporteur: The origin of international responsibility (20 April 1970) A/CN.4/233.

International Law Commission, Second report on State responsibility, by Mr. Roberto Ago, Special Rapporteur: The origin of international responsibility (20 April 1970) A/CN.4/233.

International Law Commission, State Responsibility – Summary of the discussions in various United Nations organs and resulting decisions – Working paper prepared by the Secretariat (1964) A/CN.4/165 and Corr.1.

International Law Commission, Summary record of the 415th meeting (1957) A/CN.4/SR.415.

International Law Commission, Summary record of the 416th meeting (1957) A/CN.4/SR.416.

International Law Commission, Supplement, prepared by the Secretariat, to the "Digest of the decisions of international tribunals relating to State responsibility" (1969) A/CN.4/208.

Isacson, A., 80 Homeland Security Agents to Guatemala? We've Seen This Before. It Doesn't Work (5 June 2019) Washington Office on Latin America.

'Johnson to Rublee to Hull: Telegram' (16 December 1938) Documents on German Foreign Policy 1918–1945.

Lauterpacht, E. & Bethlehem, D., The Scope and Content of the Principle of Non-Refoulement (Opinion) (20 June 2001) UNHCR.

Lawyers Committee for Human Rights, Refugee Refoulement: The Forced Return of Haitians under the US-Haitian Interdiction Agreement (February 1990).

'Le Vicomte de Lavaur de Sainte-Fortunade, Chargé d'affaires de France près le Gouvernement italien à M. Develle, Ministre des Affaires étrangères' (Rome, 21 August 1893) Ministère des affaires étrangères, Documents Diplomatique: Indemnités franco-italiennes ("Indemnités franco-italiennes") (imprimerie national, 1894).

'Le Vicomte de Lavaur de Sainte-Fortunade, Chargé d'affaires de France près le Gouvernement italien, à M. Develle, Ministre des Affaires étrangères' (Rome, 30 August 1893) Ministère des affaires étrangères, Documents Diplomatique: Indemnités franco-italiennes ("Indemnités franco-italiennes") (imprimerie national, 1894).

'Le Vicomte de Mouy, gérant le Consulat général de France à Naples, à M. Develle, Ministre des Affaires étrangères' (Naples, 21 August 1893) Ministère des affaires étrangères, Documents Diplomatique: Indemnités franco-italiennes ("Indemnités franco-italiennes") (imprimerie national, 1894).

League of Nations, 'Conference for the Codification of International Law' (28 January 1929).

League of Nations, 'Conference for the Control of the International Trade in Arms, Munitions and Implements of War' (Geneva 1925).

League of Nations, Conference on Russian and Armenian Refugee Questions: Report by the High Commissioner (5 June 1926) C.327.1926.

League of Nations: Committee on International Assistance to Refugees, Report by the Committee Submitted to the Council of the League of Nations (1936).

League of Nations, 'The Question of the Russian Refugees' (1921) 2(6) LNOJ 485.

League of Nations, 'Refugee Questions' (1928) 9(5) LNOJ 2008.

League of Nations, 'Refugee Questions' (1928) 9(9) LNOJ 1408.

League of Nations, 'Relief Work in Russia and the Question of the Russian Refugee' (1922) 3(3) LNOJ 274.

'Letter from Antonio C. Gonzalez to Franklin D. Roosevelt' (Caracas, 15 September 1938) Myron C. Taylor Papers.

'Letter from Antonio C. Gonzalez to Secretary of State, 'Interview with General López Contreras, President of Venezuela'' (Caracas, 16 December 1938) Franklin D. Roosevelt Presidential Library & Museum, series 3, box 53 'Venezuela'.

'Letter from Franklin D. Roosevelt to Isaiah Bowman' (2 November 1938) 'President's Personal File 5575 – Bowman, Isaiah, 1938-1939' Franklin D. Roosevelt Presidential Library & Museum.

'Letter From President Franklin D. Roosevelt to Myron C. Taylor' (23 November 1938) Myron C. Taylor Papers.

Luke, I. T., Shooting from the Hip (1997) U.S. Naval Institute.

'M. Barthélemy-Saint-Hilaire, Ministre des Affaires étrangères, à Paris à S. Exe. M. le Duc De Fernan Nunez, Ambassadeur d'Espagne' (Paris, 19 September 1881) Ministère des affaires étrangères, Documents Diplomatique: Affaires de Saïda: 1881–1882 ("Affaires de Saïda") (imprimerie nationale, 1882).

'M. Barthélemy-Saint-Hilaire, Ministre des Affaires étrangères, à S. Exe. M. le Duc De Fernan-Nunez, Ambassadeur d'Espagne à Paris' (Paris, 23 July 1881) Ministère des affaires étrangères, Documents Diplomatique: Affaires de Saïda: 1881-1882 ("Affaires de Saïda") (imprimerie nationale, 1882).

'M. Casimir-Périer, Président du Conseil, Ministre des Affaires étrangères, à S. Exe. M. Ressman, Ambassadeur d'Italie à Paris' (Paris, 9 December 1893) Ministère des affaires étrangères, Documents Diplomatique: Indemnités franco-italiennes ("Indemnités franco-italiennes") (imprimerie national, 1894).

'M. Meyer, Consul général de France à Gênes, à M. Develle, Ministre des Affaires étrangères' (Genoa, 21 August 1893) Ministère des affaires étrangères, Documents Diplomatique: Indemnités franco-italiennes ("Indemnités franco-italiennes") (imprimerie national, 1894).

'Marquis Rudini to Baron Fava' (Rome, 15 March 1891) Papers Relating to the Foreign Relations of The United States, Transmitted to Congress, with the Annual Message of the President (United States Government Printing Office, 9 December 1891).

'Marquis Rudini to Baron Fava' (Rome, 14 March 1891) Papers Relating to the Foreign Relations of The United States, Transmitted to Congress, with the Annual Message of the President (United States Government Printing Office, 9 December 1891).

'Memorandum' (3 June 1947) Myron C. Taylor Papers – Confidential memorandum regarding Refugees by Myron C. Taylor, 1938–1947.

'Memorandum' (9 August 1938) 'August 1938' folder, Myron C. Taylor Papers.

'Memorandum to Secretary of State' (undated) box 3, Myron C. Taylor Papers.

'Mr. Blaine to Marquis Imperiali' (Washington, 12 April 1892) Papers Relating to the Foreign Relations of the United States, Transmitted to Congress, with the Annual Message of The President (Department of State, 9 December 1891).

'Mr. Blaine to Marquis Imperiali' (Washington, 14 April 1891) Papers Relating to the Foreign Relations of the United States, Transmitted to Congress, with the Annual Message of The President (Department of State, 9 December 1891).

'Mr. Evarts to Chen Dan Pin' (Washington, 30 December 1880) Papers Relating to the Foreign Relations of the United States, Transmitted to Congress, with the Annual Message of The President (Department of State, 5 December 1881).

Mr. Tsuroaka's "Working Document" for the International Law Commission (1963) 2.

Ocbru, B., Tanzanian Refugee Caseload Survey (1983) UNHCR, Dar es Salaam.

Organization of American States: Inter-American Juridical Committee, Contributions of the American Continent to the Principles of International Law that Govern the Responsibility of the State (1965).

Organization of American States: Inter-American Juridical Committee, Contributions of the American Continent to the Principles of International Law that Govern the Responsibility of the State (1962).

Pan American Union, Contributions of the American Continent to the Principles Governing the Responsibility of the State (1961).

Position Paper Prepared in the Department of State (Washington, 9 September 1950) Foreign Relations of the United States, 1950, The United Nations; The Western Hemisphere, Volume II.

'President's Personal File 5575 – Bowman, Isaiah, 1938-1939' (undated) Franklin D. Roosevelt Presidential Library & Museum.

Recommendations from the Pan-African Conference on the Situation of Refugees in Africa, Arusha (Tanzania) (17 May 1979) Records on Operation Able Manner 2011-1040-F Clinton Presidential Library.

'Resolutions of the Institute of International Law Adopted at Lausanne' (1928) 22(1) AJIL 330.

'Résolutions votes par l'institut au cours de sa XXXIVème session: Responsabilité internationale des états a raison des dommages causés sur leur territoire a la personne et aux biens des étrangers' (1927) 33(3) AnnIDI 330.

'S. Exe. M. le Duc De Fernan Nunez, Ambassadeur d'Espagne, à M. Barthélemy-Saint-Hilaire, Ministre des Affaires étrangères, à Paris' (Paris, 19 September 1881) Ministère des affaires étrangères, Documents Diplomatique: Affaires de Saïda: 1881–1882 ("Affaires de Saïda") (imprimerie nationale, 1882).

'S. Exe. M. le Duc De Fernan-Nunez, Ambassadeur d'Espagne, à M. Barthélemy-Saint-Hilaire, Ministre des Affaires étrangères, à Paris' (Paris, 30 June 1881) Ministère des affaires étrangères, Documents Diplomatique: Affaires de Saïda: 1881–1882 ("Affaires de Saïda") (imprimerie nationale, 1882).

'Second Session of the Committee of Experts for the Progressive Codification of International Law' (1926) 20 AJIL Supplement 18.

'The Secretary of State to the Ambassador in the United Kingdom (Kennedy)' (23 March 1938) Foreign Relations Of The United States Diplomatic Papers, 1938, General, Volume I.

'The Secretary of State to the British Chargé (Lindsay)' (Washington, 6 January 1920) Papers Relating to the Foreign Relations of the United States, Volume I 1920).

'Special Supplement No. 53; reproduced in AJIL Special Supplement 22 (1928)' (October 1927) LNOJ.

'Speech by Myron C. Taylor (USA) Intergovernmental Committee to Continue and Develop the Work of the Evian Meeting' (3 August 1938) box 3, Myron C. Taylor

Papers – Evian Intergovernmental Committee Conference (folder 2), July-August 1938.

State Watch, Key texts on justice and home affairs in the European Union, Volume 1 (1976-1993) From Trevi to Maastricht (1997).

'Strictly Confidential Memorandum: The Emigration of Jews from Germany' (February 1939) Myron C. Taylor Papers – Confidential memorandum regarding Refugees by Myron C. Taylor, 1938–1947.

Stein, B., Returnee Aid and Development (1 May 1994) EVAL/RAD/15.

'Supplement: Official Documents' (1920) 14(4) AJIL 356.

Taylor, M. C., 'Confidential Memorandum for the President Regarding Refugees 1938 – 1947' (30 July 1947) Myron C. Taylor Papers – Intergovernmental Committee on Political Refugees Correspondence, 1947-1954.

'Taylor to Hull' (20 July 1938) Myron C. Taylor Papers.

'Taylor to Secretary of State' (July 7 1938) Myron C. Taylor Papers.

'Transfer of Jewish and Non-Aryan Property from Germany Including Austria. Part A.: Jewish Emigration and Transfer of Jewish Property since 1933' (15 August 1938) Myron C. Taylor Papers – Evian Intergovernmental Committee Conference (folder 2).

UN Committee on the Elimination of Racial Discrimination, Concluding observations on the combined seventh to ninth periodic reports of the United States of America (25 September 2014) CERD/C/USA/CO/7-9.

UN Economic and Social Council, Report of the Commission on Human Rights (25 July 1960) E/RES/772(XXX).

UN Economic and Social Council, Special Committee on Refugees and Displaced Persons: Suggested draft of broad definition, for the purposes of the work of the Committee, of the terms "refugee" and "displaced person". Note by the Director of the Intergovernmental Committee on refugees (10 April 1946) E/REF/12.

UN General Assembly, Addendum to the Report of the United Nations High Commissioner for Refugees (31 October 1977) A/32/12/Add.1.

UN General Assembly, Meeting on Refugees and Displaced Persons in South-East Asia, convened by the Secretary-General of the United Nations at Geneva, on 20 and 21 July 1979, and subsequent developments: Report of the Secretary-General – Corrigendum (19 November 1979) A/34/627/Corr.1.

UN General Assembly, Official Record of the Twentieth Session, 3rd Committee, 1361st Meeting (1 December 1965) A/C.3/SR.1361.

UN General Assembly, Official Record of the Twenty-First Session, 3rd Committee, 1449th Meeting (6 December 1966) A/C.3/SR.1449.

UN General Assembly, Record of meeting held on 25 Sept. 1979 (25 September 1979) A/34/PV.8.

UN General Assembly, Report of the United Nations Conference on Territorial Asylum (21 April 1977) A/CONF.78/12.

UN General Assembly, Resolution 43/119: International Conference on Indo-Chinese Refugees (8 December 1988) A/RES/43/119.

UN General Assembly, Resolution 2956 (XXVII): Report of the United Nations High Commissioner for Refugees (12 December 1972) GA/RES/2956(XXVII).

UN High Commissioner for Refugees, Guatemala office meeting with SFRC Democratic Staff (21 October 2020).

UN High Commissioner for Refugees, Handbook on procedures and criteria for determining refugee status under the 1951 Convention and the 1967 Protocol relating to the Status of Refugees (September 1979) ST/HCR(092.1)/H26.

UN High Commissioner for Refugees, Handbook on procedures and criteria for determining refugee status under the 1951 Convention and the 1967 Protocol relating to the Status of Refugees (September 1979) ST/HCR(092.1)/H26.

UN High Commissioner for Refugees, Note on Family Reunification (18 July 1983).

UN High Commissioner for Refugees, Note on International Protection (1986) A/AC.96/680.

UN High Commissioner for Refugees, Note on International Protection (1990) A/AC.96/750.

UN High Commissioner for Refugees, Note on International Protection (10 July 2020) A/AC.96/1200.

UN High Commissioner for Refugees, Practical Recommendations and Good Practice to Address Protection Concerns in the Context of the COVID-19 (9 April 2020).

UN High Commissioner for Refugees, Report of the Meeting of the Expert Group on Temporary Refuge in Situations of Large-Scale Influx (Geneva 21–24 April 1981) (17 July 1981) EC/SCP/16/Add.1.

UN High Commissioner for Refugees, Report of the Meeting of the Expert Group on Temporary Refuge in Situations of Large-Scale Influx, Geneva, 21–24 April 1981 (3 June 1981) EC/SCP/16.

UN High Commissioner for Refugees, Report of the United Nations High Commissioner for Refugees (9 May 1989) E/1989/64.

UN High Commissioner for Refugees, Self-Study Module 1: An Introduction to International Protection. Protecting Persons of Concern to UNHCR (1 August 2005).

UN High Commissioner for Refugees, UNHCR Submission for the Universal Periodic Review – Colombia – UPR 30th Session (2018).

UN High Commissioner for Refugees, UNHCR Submission for the Universal Periodic Review – Bolivia – UPR 34th Session (2019).

UN Secretary-General, Survey of International Law in Relation to the Work of Codification of the International Law Commission: Preparatory work within the purview of article 18, paragraph 1, of the of the International Law Commission– Memorandum submitted by the Secretary-General (1949) A/CN.4/1/Rev.1.

USA: Committee on Foreign Relations, A Democratic Staff Report Prepared for the use of the Committee on Foreign Relations, United States Senate, DHS Run Amok? A Reckless Overseas Operation, Violations, and Lies (12 October 2020).

USA: Congress Committee on Foreign Affairs, Displaced Persons and the International Refugee Organization. Report of a Special Subcommittee on the Committee on Foreign Affairs (1947) Government Printing Office.

USA: Congressional Research Service, U.S. Strategy for Engagement in Central America: Policy Issues for Congress (12 November 2019).

USA: Department of Commerce, *Secretary of Commerce Leads U.S. Delegation to Guatemala* (15 January 2020).

USA: Department of Homeland Security, *DHS Statement on Updated CDC Order* (2 August 2021).

USA: Department of Homeland Security, Policy Guidance for Implementation of the Migrant Protection Protocols (25 January 2019).

USA: Department of Justice, Immigration Consequences of Undocumented Aliens' Arrival in United States Territorial Waters (13 October 1993).

USA: Department of State, Memorandum: Acting Under-Secretary of State for External Affairs, with attached letter to the Deputy Minister of Citizenship and Immigration and draft telegram (4 July 1951) T-2367 Library and Archives Canada.

USA: Department of State, Soviet Refugees: Processing and Admittance to the United States (1990) GAO/NSIAD-90-158.

USA: Department of State, 'Statement by Lieutenant-Colonel Jerry M. Sage, United States Army, Headquarters of European Command, Frankfurt, Germany, Before the House Subcommittee on Immigration and Naturalization' (2 July 1947) Myron C. Taylor Papers – Intergovernmental Committee on Political Refugees.

USA: Federal Congress, Committee on Foreign Affairs, Displaced Persons and the International Refugee Organization. Report of a Special Subcommittee on the Committee on Foreign Affairs (1947) Government Printing Office.

USA: Joint Economic Committee, Indochinese Refugees: The Impact on First Asylum Countries and Implications for American Policy (25 November 1980) 69-826 O.

USA: The White House, *Fact Sheet: Strategy to Address the Root Causes of Migration in Central America* (29 July 2021).

USA: The White House, *Fact Sheet: The Collaborative Migration Management Strategy* (29 July 2021).

USA: The White House, Memorandum for the Secretary of State Hon. Norman H. Davis for the Necessary Action, F.D.R. (8 November 1941) Myron C. Taylor Papers, Official File 3865, F.D.R. Library.

USA: The White House, *Statement by Press Secretary Jen Psaki on the Emergency Presidential Determination on Refugee Admissions for Fiscal Year 2021* (16 April 2019) USA: United States Coast Guard, 1994 – Alien Interdiction: The Flow Becomes a Flood United States Coast Guard Aviation History.

USA: United States Congress, Cruelty, Coercion, and Legal Contortions: The Trump Administrations Unsafe Asylum Cooperative Agreements with Guatemala, Honduras, and El Salvador, A Majority Staff Report Prepared for the Use of The Committee on Foreign Relations United States Senate, 117th Congress 1st Session (18 January 2021).

USA: United States Congress, Posture Statement of Admiral Kurt W. Tidd Commander, United States Southern Command Before the 115th Congress Senate Armed Services Committee (15 February 2018).

Verbatim Report of the Sixth Meeting (Public) (15 July 1938) Myron C. Taylor Papers – Evian Intergovernmental Committee Conference, F.D.R. Library.

Index

www.ingramcontent.com/pod-product-compliance
Lightning Source LLC
Chambersburg PA
CBHW051356240926
51852CB00001B/46
9789004722828